P9-DXS-518

The New World History

A Teacher's Companion

Edited by

Ross E. Dunn

San Diego State University

BEDFORD/ST. MARTIN'S   BOSTON ♦ NEW YORK

WINGATE UNIVERSITY LIBRARY

For Bedford/St. Martin's

History Editor: Katherine E. Kurzman
Developmental Editor: Katherine E. Kurzman
Production Editor: Ara Salibian
Production Supervisor: Joe Ford
Marketing Manager: Charles Cavaliere
Editorial Assistant: Chip Turner
Production Assistant: Helaine Denenberg
Copyeditor: Linda Leet Howe
Text Design: Geri Davis, The Davis Group, Inc.
Cover Design: Donna Lee Dennison
Composition: Pine Tree Composition
Printing and Binding: Haddon Craftsmen, Inc.

President: Charles H. Christensen
Editorial Director: Joan E. Feinberg
Director of Editing, Design, and Production: Marcia Cohen
Managing Editor: Elizabeth M. Schaaf

Library of Congress Catalog Card Number: 99–65255

Copyright © 2000 by Bedford/St. Martin's

All rights reserved. No part of this book may be reproduced, stored in a retrieval system, or transmitted in any form or by any means, electronic, mechanical, photocopying, recording, or otherwise, except as may be expressly permitted by the applicable copyright statutes or in writing by the Publisher.

Manufactured in the United States of America.

4   3   2   1   0   9
f   e   d   c   b   a

For information, write: Bedford/St. Martin's, 75 Arlington Street, Boston, MA 02116 (617-399-4000)

ISBN: 0–312–18327–5

Acknowledgments

Michael Adas, *Islamic and European Expansion.* Excerpted and reprinted from the introduction to *Islamic & European Expansion: The Forging of a Global Order,* edited by Michael Adas for the American Historical Association, by permission of Temple University Press. © 1993 by Temple University. All Rights Reserved.

Acknowledgments and copyrights are continued at the back of the book on pages 595—96, which constitute an extension of the copyright page. It is a violation of the law to reproduce these selections by any means whatsoever without the written permission of the copyright holder.

WINGATE UNIVERSITY LIBRARY

PREFACE

For me this book is a sort of silver anniversary celebration. In the fall of 1974 I joined with William Phillips and Ray Smith, two colleagues at San Diego State University, to team-teach a new course in world history to A.D. 1500. The following spring I taught 1500 to the present with Neil Heyman and Frank Stites. Our textbook was L. S. Stavrianos, *A Global History*. In both semesters all three of us attended every class regardless of which one of us was lecturing, and we met frequently to plan strategy, grade essays, and assess our performance. We agreed to type out and file our lectures so that department members who wished to offer the course in subsequent years might, if they were so inclined, consult a set of exemplary resources. Student evaluations of the course were good, and no faculty member opposed the experiment. It took several years and two attempts, however, to persuade the department to add world history as an alternative to Western Civ to the university's General Education program. Eventually the team-teaching stopped, and individuals offered the two courses on their own. Today, a quarter century later, the San Diego State class schedule lists nearly two dozen sections of introductory world history. The department is also developing upper-division courses aimed at students who plan careers teaching history and social studies in California schools.

In developing my own introductory courses at SDSU, I have had no success at settling on a set of definitive lectures, readings, or classroom strategies. The field has not stood still for a moment, and every month brings some new breakthrough in scholarship, a clever teaching idea, or a good book to assign students. Under pressure from the steadily accumulating corpus of research on comparative, cross-cultural, and global history, as well from as publications on innovative teaching practice, I have felt obliged to rethink, revise, and otherwise tinker with my courses each year.

In 1997 Katherine Kurzman, Executive Editor for History at Bedford/St. Martin's, phoned me for advice about a project she was exploring to compile an anthology on world history teaching. The more I pondered Katherine's proposal, the more it appealed to me. World history has been gaining momentum in colleges and universities for about twenty-five years, and the World History Association is nearing two decades of service to the profession. Perhaps the moment is ripe, I thought, to take stock of the body of writing that over the years has contributed so profoundly to my world history education and that has given me and many colleagues a reasonable degree of confidence in teaching world-scale history to college students.

Plunging forward, I took on the editorship of the anthology with assurances from Bedford/St. Martin's that the scope of selections could be fairly broad and that I could include my own reflections on the development and present condition of the "new world history" as both a scholarly and a pedagogical movement. Compiling the selections and writing the introductions turned out, naturally enough, to be a more ambitious undertaking than I originally envisioned. But I persuaded myself and my publisher that the book must be comprehensive enough to signify how rich and inventive the world history field has become and to explore several different dimensions of its development. The fifty-six selections included in the book span a period of scholarship from 1874, when William Swinton defined world history as the story of the Caucasian race, to 1999, when Patrick Manning reported on the progress of the new world history Ph.D. program at Northeastern University. The book includes many of what I would regard as seminal or classic writings in the field, notably Marshall Hodgson's proposal in 1954 for "hemispheric interregional history" and L. S. Stavrianos's appeal in 1959 for global history education. The great majority of the essays, however, were written within the past two decades.

The general introduction has more to say about the aims of the book, its intended audience, and the criteria used for making selections. Readers should be forewarned, however, that my primary criterion has been the relevance of each selection to the practical challenge of thinking through a world history course — not only the design of its syllabus, but also its intellectual premises, conceptual structure, and historiographical genealogy. I hope, in other words, that this book will encourage both new and veteran world history teachers to be more self-conscious about the assumptions and precommitments that influence their classroom choices.

During my own pedagogical journey through world history, I have relied continuously on the intelligence and insight of numerous colleagues and scholars, from the field's intellectual pioneers — William McNeill, Philip Curtin, Marshall Hodgson, and Leften Stavrianos — to the many middle- and high-school teachers who have shared their classroom tactics with me and proven that globe-girdling history is eminently teachable to America's youth. A few of the contributors to this volume are no longer with us, but most are active in the profession today. I thank them or, as the case may be, their publishers for permission to reprint their work. I would also like to thank several comrades-in-world-history for critiquing all or some of my introductory statements and for advising me on the selections: Jerry Bentley, Edmund Burke III, Julia Clancy-Smith, Ralph Croizier, Thomas Davis, David Fahey, Marc Gilbert, Farid Mahdavi, Patrick Manning, Howard Mehlinger, Mark Newman, John Patrick, Kevin Reilly, Warren Solomon, Robert Tignor, and Helen Wheatley. I take full responsibility for instances where I failed to understand what they were getting at or to include selections that they recommended. I had steadfast research assistance from Darren Bardell, Jennifer Honigman, and Katherine Pierce, all San Diego State University graduate students.

CONTENTS

INTRODUCTION

Colleges and universities in the United States have taught world history, defined one way or another, since the nineteenth century. Out of the curriculum of the early Republic, which was centered on Holy Scripture and the classics, emerged "general history," a course of study designed for the multitude of both native-born and immigrant Americans entering post-primary education after the Civil War. The general history one-year "short course," taught in either high school or college, was the story of humankind defined unabashedly as the progressive evolution of peoples of Aryan race and Christian faith to world dominion. As an approach to teaching, it encouraged students to exercise interpretive judgment but also demanded a good deal of fact-drilling. In the 1890s two scholarly commissions denounced it for stifling the historical imagination of young Americans.[1] Endorsing the recommendations of the commissions, the secondary schools largely abandoned general history after 1900, replacing it with a solid four-year block of courses in classical, medieval/modern, English, and American history.

History's reign over the humanities curriculum was glorious but brief. After World War I, the one-year world history survey reappeared in secondary schools in response to new educational ideologies promoting social control, acculturation, vocational training, and civic responsibility. At the same time, the burgeoning social science disciplines were also demanding a place in the curriculum. In public schools, "social studies," a phrase added to the American lexicon in the 1920s, largely replaced the four-year history block. The new pedagogy assigned world history to the tenth grade, where it served as a social mechanism for delivering geography, government, sociology, citizenship, and a kind of resurrected general history in one efficient nine-month package.

Paralleling this development, Columbia College (later Columbia University) introduced in 1919 a general survey course, Contemporary Civilization. This program, which had its origin in the War Issues Course taught at many colleges during the war as part of the Student Army Training Corps program, aimed to further America's cultural unification in a time of massive immigration, to imbue the rising educated class with shared standards of civic action, and to train young citizens "to meet honest and serious criticism of the present order not by blind prejudice and blustering talk but by carefully reasoned argument."[2] The Columbia experiment was a smashing success, and the course spread rapidly to colleges and universities across the land as the required freshman survey in "Western Civ."

Under the leadership of world-minded professors and educationists, both tenth-grade history and college Western Civ paid attention to the big international issues of the times. This practice reflected public interest in European and world affairs, which had been growing since before the war. Nevertheless, the prewar cultural assumption that one part of humankind was historical but another part was not, endured throughout the interwar period — a time when most European colonial empires grew larger than they were before 1914 and when Western science, medicine, and engineering appeared to be transforming the material world. Non-American history studies therefore excluded all but the very contemporary or very ancient experience of the peoples of Africa, Asia, and Latin America. College Western Civ was concerned explicitly with Europe and its cultural outliers, but its practitioners recognized no possible alternative model for studying world history.

WORLD HISTORY AFTER WORLD WAR II

As the "American century" reached its zenith in the two decades after the war, the Western Civ course maintained its preeminence as a framework for explaining what seemed to matter most. Many citizens recognized, however, that the second global war made the world at once smaller as a social sphere and much larger as a cultural construct in the collective consciousness not only of Americans and Europeans but of peoples virtually everywhere. A bigger world required a bigger world history.

The critical challenge to the Western habit of discerning causation and meaning in the human past through what James Blaut calls the "European tunnel of time" came slowly but from several directions.[3] One was the twin postwar phenomena of nationalism in European colonies and the Cold War as a global struggle for the allegiance of the "nonaligned." These trends prompted the "area studies" movement in American colleges and a new call, notably from education specialists, to internationalize the secondary and collegiate curricula. In the universities the refutation of raced-based theories of culture, the explosion of historical and social scientific knowledge, the social broadening of faculties, and, in the late 1970s, the rise of multiculturalist ideology all contributed to serious reevaluation of the postulate that world history was largely equivalent to the experience of people inhabiting Eurasia's westerly peninsula. Moreover, the long-running debate over the question of what constituted a culturally literate and humanely educated American gave strength to the view that the histories and cultural traditions of Africans, Asians, and indigenous Americans should be assigned at least *some* space in the liberal curriculum.

By the 1970s a movement was under way among a significant minority of college and secondary teachers to expand the cultural scope of textbooks and syllabi. Few, however, seemed to know how to make non-American history more inclusive without producing tenth-grade and college history courses even more unwieldy and content-stuffed than they already were. Fortunately, a few learned pioneers had been working since the 1950s to discover approaches to the human experience that did not start at the portals of nation-states or pass along the "European tunnel of time." These scholars drew ideas from the metahistorians Oswald Spengler and Arnold Toynbee and from the increasingly nuanced disciplines of historical sociology and cultural anthropology. But they also aimed to stay true to the methodological rules of the historical discipline.

William H. McNeill had the greatest influence, his *The Rise of the West* (1963) climbing the best-seller lists and "propelling world history to public consciousness and professional legitimacy."[4] Leften Stavrianos published the first survey textbooks for colleges and high schools that offered a persuasive unifying structure. He also directed much of his energy toward improving school curricula, championing social studies programs responsive to postwar internationalism, and persistently denouncing the hoary tenth-grade course, which by the 1960s had managed to become slightly less Eurocentric but also hopelessly incoherent.[5] Marshall Hodgson, who died in 1968, had much less influence than either McNeill or Stavrianos in jump-starting world history as an academic field, yet both acknowledge a serious intellectual debt to him. In the past decade world historians have been paying more attention to Hodgson's remarkably visionary articles, the earliest published in 1944, on interregional and comparative history.[6] Finally, Fernand Braudel and the methodological school associated with the French journal *Annales* put forward conceptions of "total history" and the *longue durée* that opened whole new realms of subject matter just made for world-scale investigation.

By the mid 1970s, introductory world history was beginning to gain acceptance in collegiate education as a distinct curricular alternative to Western Civ. At the same time, hundreds of young scholars, the intellectual heirs of the earlier generation of social historians and cultural anthropologists, were enthusiastically turning to economic, social, technological, popular cultural, and other spheres of inquiry where nation- and culture-bound categories of analysis were a methodological hindrance. One of the most interesting features of the world history movement is that the teaching project nourished research more abundantly than research nourished teaching. American social history, for example, grew steadily as a scholarly enterprise from the early part of the century, when the New Historians began writing, until the 1960s and 1970s, when the field exploded in all directions. With only a few exceptions, college and high school textbooks lagged well behind advances in scholarship, and in the 1980s they were still catching up. By contrast, the pressure on curriculum makers and textbook publishers to broaden the scope of world history beyond the Western mega-narrative has until recently exceeded scholarly energy to produce new studies on comparative, cross-cultural, or interregional themes. Much of the exciting new work in world history has come from the pens of scholars who either taught the subject already or were intellectually affiliated with a network of teachers who did.

Philip Curtin, for example, has made several important contributions to the literature of comparative world history, but these began to appear only after he started teaching "The Expansion of Europe," later called "The World and the West," at the University of Wisconsin.[7] Moreover, as each new book offering fresh ideas on world history has appeared — Crosby's *The Columbian Exchange*, Wallerstein's *The Modern World System*, Curtin's *Cross-Cultural Trade in World*

History, and Bentley's *Old World Encounters* among others — hungry teachers have immediately seized on it as a potential source of innovative concepts for the world history courses they have already been teaching. In the public schools, where majority sentiment has over two decades favored, at least in principle, a more inclusive world history, the eagerness of teachers to develop livelier courses has consistently outpaced the labors of academic scholars to offer fresh conceptual and organizational solutions. Except in some independent schools and advanced placement history courses, the old-style Western Civ textbook has vanished from the high school classroom. Even so, the "global history" texts now in use throughout the fifty states tend to lack conceptual or thematic coherence beyond chronologically organized factual and interpretive surveys of various civilizations.

SEARCH FOR ALTERNATIVES TO THE WESTERN CIV MODEL

Although college-level world history courses have flourished since the 1980s, the traditional freshman Western Civ course has by no means withered away. Why has it remained strong, handily surviving the movement of the 1960s and 1970s to terminate college core requirements? It is certainly not because its proponents have carefully reexamined its ideological presumptions and declared them valid for the classrooms of the twenty-first century. Indeed, the organizational structure of the typical Western Civ book, which continues to embrace the idea of a northwestward drift of history from Hominid Ethiopia to industrial England, has never been systematically subjected by its practitioners to the sort of self-conscious critique that they claim is a core trait of the Western intellectual tradition. Typical Western Civ textbooks and course outlines continue to include East Africa in the paleolithic era but not the modern, the Greek past up to the Byzantine age but not later, Muslim civilization in its first three hundred years but not after the tenth century, and Western Hemispheric history only when Cortez and John Smith appear on the scene. Advocates of this approach typically justify it by asserting that young Americans should understand the "origins" of Western civilization, even though much of the historical profession now regards scholarly exercises that explain the present by selectively tracing the roots of things back in time as methodologically suspect and more often than not in the service of nationalist ideology. Western Civ has endured, rather, owing to simple academic inertia, the lucrative textbook market, and the course's continuing allure as a structuring of the past that, as J. H. Hexter has argued (see Part Two), simply "works" better than any other introductory teaching program. Moreover, the Western Civ tradition received considerable moral and in some measure funding support in the 1980s and early 1990s from educators holding federal office, notably William Bennett and Lynne Cheney.

    J. H. Hexter, it must be admitted, did have a point about Western Civ "working." World history teachers have had little success devising a conceptual plan of their own that commands anything like general allegiance or that might readily replace Western Civ's story-oriented but historically cramped framework. In the 1990s world history courses sprang up in two- and four-year colleges all across the country. Nevertheless, the current situation is ironic: syllabi and textbooks are proliferating as if college faculties actually agree on a definition of their subject and on the epistemological objectives of their programs, when they most emphatically do not. In 1999, for example, H-World, the electronic discussion list on world history, hosted a lively and contentious debate on the problem of defining world history. (Of course, Western Civ has had its own aggravations. Columbia's elegant construct of the West's cavalcade of freedom has since the 1950s sunk progressively deeper beneath layers of new subject matter, especially social and cultural history. Western Civ textbooks can boast no more claim to thematic coherence than can the best world history texts.)

A world history course is indeed hard to design and harder to teach, though not because anyone thinks that such a course must strive to cover "everything" (as if a full-year history even of, say, a small town in Missouri could hope to attain such a goal). Archimedes is reported to have remarked, "Give me a place to stand on, and I will move the earth." Like him, global history instructors have agonized over how to build and then properly position a platform from which to expostulate human history in all its variety and confusion. The presumed platform of Western Civ is a unitary cultural tradition exhibiting a set of distinctive and enduring traits on which a well-anchored linear narrative may be erected. World history, as opposed to European, Japanese, or Iroquois history, cannot be told from within a frame of "culture" that remains stationary and may be taken for granted (however mythical such cultural constants really are). Moreover, the notion of *human* culture is analytically useful only at levels of generalization higher than most global history teachers wish to pitch their courses (though see the argument for "big history" in Part Eleven).

The teaching project has often sought a relatively easy solution to the problem of standpoint by setting up four or more different platforms, that is, civilizations or conventionally defined regions such as "Africa," from which to present information and ideas. This solution has not proved satisfactory to many teachers and students because the large-scale, interregional patterning of the human venture is usually neglected in order to "cover" several civilizational story lines, none of them analytically connected to any of the others. Teaching world history civilization by civilization (China, India, Europe) or region by region (Africa, the Middle East, South America) offers no more convincing a path to world-scale understanding than would teaching the eighteenth-century history of North America British colony by British colony be a sensible way to give students a lucid view of the most important changes in colonial America. Not to criticize the culturalist approach too harshly, it must be recognized that many teachers who stress the serial study of civilizations — and investigation of changes within them is a perfectly valid undertaking — also pay close attention to the causes and effects of various types of interaction among civilizations.

As world history teachers grope for footing, skeptics of the project fire questions: How can one reasonably expect to survey human history from paleolithic times to the present in a single academic year? How can world history be anything but superficial? What principles of selection and theoretical postulates guide inclusion and omission of subject matter? How is one to determine which themes are important and which are not? Since Western civilization is *our* civilization, why spend so much time on the others? Why should students learn about crop diffusion, cross-cultural trade, or the Bantu migrations rather than meditate on the timeless insights of Plato, Aquinas, and Locke? The questions go on and on, and committed world history teachers fret over them even more anxiously than the critics. These teachers also believe, however, that students who must live and work in an ever more complicated world should not be told that the human experience as a whole is far too tangled and confusing to explore profitably or that what David Hollinger called "species-centered discourse" is too much trouble to bother with when courses on civilizations, countries, and ethnic groups are so much easier to organize.[8]

World history teachers who wish to persist in making the human experience intelligible should almost certainly give up the quest for a convincing master narrative to replace Western Civ, that is, a general heuristic formula that will make everything conveniently fall into place. They should also abandon the goal, which is perennially attractive to school-reforming politicians, to identify a precise body of "facts" about the global past that every young American ought to know. World history is not so much a matter of deciding what data should be learned as it is a way of addressing historical problems that resists their being caged behind civilizational, national, or ethnic bars. Patrick Manning suggests that world history may, at this early date in the development of the field, be characterized as a project to examine "the interaction of the pieces (be they community, societal, or continental) in human history" and "to assess the experience of the whole of humanity through study of those interactions."[9] Carrying this line of thought further, world history is the search for answers to questions about the past in which the inquiry embraces whatever geographical, social, or cultural field is appropriate and in which conventionally defined entities such as nation-states are not allowed to limit the scope of investigation arbitrarily.

When novice world history teachers accept as their initial task the posing of historical questions, the ensemble of human ancestors they and their students will find themselves studying may sometimes coincide with the population of a particular nation, empire, or civilization. On the other hand, the appropriate space in which to locate a historical problem may also, as Philip Curtin argues (see Part Three), be some other "relevant aggregate" of human interrelationships, such as the northerly region spanning the Bering Strait, the rim lands of the Sahara Desert, the Atlantic basin, the belt of land running from the Mediterranean to north India, or even the globe as a whole.

Toward a New World History

Except for the work of the earliest world history pioneers, serious thinking about the subject as a teaching field has taken place only in the past quarter century. Hundreds of first-year courses have sprung up in two- and four-year colleges, usually as part of general education programs. Some of these courses are offered as alternatives to Western Civ or area studies, and some have replaced Western Civ altogether. Though comprehensive survey data are lacking (partly owing to the problem of determining what a course in "world history" might actually include), the greatest expansion of world history curricula has almost certainly occurred in state universities and community colleges.[10] This pattern is probably a consequence of opportunities and demands for large-enrollment introductory courses on a greater scale than in either liberal arts colleges or major research universities. Also, faculty, especially tenured faculty, may be under less pressure than they would be in Ph.D.-granting institutions to focus exclusively on specialized research. Another factor is that state colleges and universities train large numbers of teachers who will be expected to teach world history in K–12 schools.[11] To cite just one example of growth, world history was introduced at San Diego State University in 1974 as a two-semester sequence of courses. It was an experimental team-taught elective for a single classroom of freshmen, and it drew heavily on the conceptual thinking of McNeill, Hodgson, and Curtin. Today freshman-sophomore world history at SDSU is a pillar of the general education program: the class schedule for spring 1999 semester lists twenty-four sections of the two courses.

Another promising trend is world history for juniors and seniors. Such courses are less likely to be surveys than to focus on specific comparative, cross-cultural, interregional, or historiographical topics in the field. One area in need of further development is teacher-training curricula, that is, courses in either history departments or schools of education that expose prospective teachers not only to knowledge about various societies but to the overarching problems of conceptualizing and organizing world history education for younger learners. Ironically, thousands of middle and high school teachers go into classrooms every day to teach world history courses of sweeping dimension in time and space. Yet college training for future social studies teachers seldom offers much help in thinking through the organization of an entire course, contextualizing the histories of nations and civilizations, or making sense of big patterns of change.

In the last several years undergraduate world history has come to more of the major research universities, and indeed, graduate education in the field has begun to blossom. The history department at Northeastern University now offers a Ph.D. exclusively in world history. At other institutions students may choose world history as one of their academic fields. More students have become aware that even M.A. or minor-field training in comparative or interregional history may improve their chances in the job market owing to the growing demand for instructors ready and willing to teach freshman world history. Graduate education is discussed further in Part Ten.

In addition to the proliferation of world history courses, the professionalization of the field has moved apace. The World History Association (WHA), founded in the early 1980s, has continued to build sturdy bridges between college and K–12 teachers, publish its award-winning journal, and expand internationally. Several regional affiliates of the WHA do grassroots work in colleges and schools. Conferences, institutes, and in-service workshops have multiplied around the country. The College Board is developing a new Advanced Placement program in world history for university-bound students. One of the liveliest forums for debating and sharing information about world history is the H-World electronic mail list, which is part of the H-Net network of scholarly discussion groups based at Michigan State University.[12]

Academic textbook writers have produced a wide range of approaches to the problem of attaining world-inclusive history that makes sense. A few of these books express the vision of a single scholar. Perhaps half a dozen team-produced texts display a clear conceptual design and succeed in some measure in unifying the subject matter. Others are deliberately structured to capture a share of both the world history and Western Civ student market. Books in this category claim global coverage, but the organizational strategy, which allows teachers to lop off entire regions of the world they prefer not to deal with, militates against more integrated understanding. Whatever the approach adopted, textbook authors rarely take the trouble (or get assent from their publishers) to explain systematically the intellectual precommitments that informed their decisions to choose and fashion the contents of their volume in one way or another. The organizational scheme of a textbook may have great influence on the selection, arrangement, or omission of course subject matter. The intellectual premises guiding authors, however, usually remain implicit, and teachers who do not want the assigned book to drive the classroom experience must devise their own system for ordering content in a comprehensive and engaging way.

Fortunately, help other than textbook tables of contents is at hand. In the past few decades an impressive corpus of literature has been accumulating that addresses many of the problems faced by teacher-conceptualizers of world history. These writings, which began to appear as early as the 1950s, are scattered here and there in books, scholarly journals, and professional bulletins. Much of this writing is concentrated in four or five periodicals, but not all of the most helpful contributions have appeared in obvious places. A few particularly thoughtful statements included in this volume have not previously been published.

Because world history has now firmly established itself within the discipline and the profession, it seems a good time to pause and take stock of some of the best thinking in the field over the past few decades. This reader aims to encourage history professionals to consider the directions the discipline has taken and to contemplate where it might go from here. The book is offered to new and veteran educators, graduate students considering the possibilities of the field, and all scholars interested in the historiography and pedagogy of a new branch of learning. First-time world history teachers often find themselves leaping into their course without much guidance from peers, graduate school advisers, or department chairs. Consider, for example, the thousands of instructors who enjoy only part-time employment. They may be partially isolated from professional networks, but they also staff freshman surveys in community colleges and public universities. These teachers often carry a large part of an institution's growing world history load, and they look wherever they can for help in designing their course. Instructors who have been teaching world history for many years will find both the "classic" articles and the more up-to-date contributions in this book helpful as they strive to make their courses more lucid and engaging. Finally, the emergence of world history as a legitimate teaching and research field is itself a significant development in the context of debates over cultural identity, educational progress, and international relations, especially since globally minded economic, cultural, and environmental approaches to the past seem more appropriate to contemporary life than ever before.

This volume is aimed primarily at college teachers, but thousands of middle and high school educators are struggling with the same basic conceptual and organizational problems. Many teachers and school districts are claiming creative responsibility for their world history programs even when they might conveniently fall back on textbooks and guidelines assigned by boards of education and state agencies. Between 1991 and 1993, for example, the Woodrow Wilson National Fellowship Foundation sponsored three summer institutes on world history for a total of 150 high school social studies teachers. An unforeseen consequence of this program was the emergence of a spirited cadre of secondary educators (some of them formerly dyed-in-the-wool Advanced Placement European history teachers!) who have gone on to assume positions of leadership in the world history movement.

In addition to K–12 teachers, this book should also be of use to social studies specialists in schools of education, who need to know how world history teaching has grown and changed. Education agencies in most of the fifty states have been writing and implementing new academic standards that will require far larger numbers of middle and high school students to study genuinely globe-encircling history. In the coming years thousands of new teachers will be needed whose college training has included more than bits of African, Asian, and Native American history, who have thought systematically about the organization and objectives of world history education, and who wish to offer American teens something more substantive than presentist culture studies or fragmented civilization-of-the-month surveys.

The selections in this reader are organized in eleven parts, beginning with writings that describe and interpret the emergence of academic world history and concluding with a section on those innovations and challenges in the field that are likely to be prominent in the coming century. The choices made in assigning selections to one part of the book or another were in some measure arbitrary since some essays might justifiably be placed in two or more categories. Since the focus here is on the problems of world history teaching, the book largely excludes discussion of writings in the philosophical, universalist tradition of Spengler, Toynbee, Quigley, and other metahistorians. The book also steers clear of interpretive debates among scholars over particular world-historical problems, though such a volume would be a good idea. Nor does this reader include course outlines, lesson plans, and day-to-day classroom strategies except where these are incorporated into a narrative description of a teaching innovation. I have made selections with an eye to their length, sometimes choosing one essay over another because it was more concise. Some selections are excerpts from articles or books. Page numbers in the source note on the opening page of each selection correspond to the portion(s) of the essay included in the present volume. The annotated bibliography at the end of each part is not meant to be exhaustive but to suggest other useful works that may be pertinent to teaching. For a comprehensive annotated list of works in the field, readers should consult the "world history" section developed by Kevin Reilly and Lynda Shaffer in *The American Historical Association's Guide to Historical Literature*, 3rd ed., vol. 1, ed. Mary Beth Norton (New York: Oxford University Press, 1995).

Notes

1. National Education Association, Committee of Ten on Secondary School Studies, *Report of the Committee on Secondary School Studies* (U.S. Government Printing Office, 1893); and American Historical Association, Committee of Seven, *The Study of History in Schools* (New York: Macmillan, 1903).

2. Harry J. Carman, "The Columbia Course in Contemporary Civilization," *Columbia Alumni News* 17 (1925): 143.

3. J. M. Blaut, *The Colonizer's Model of the World: Geographical Diffusionism and Eurocentric History* (New York: Guilford Press, 1993), 5.

4. *The American Historical Association's Guide to Historical Literature*, 3rd ed., vol. 1, ed. Mary Beth Norton (New York: Oxford University Press, 1995), 48. William H. McNeill, *The Rise of the West: A History of the Human Community* (Chicago: University of Chicago Press, 1963).

5. The textbooks of L. S. Stavrianos have appeared in numerous editions. See *A Global History: From Prehistory to the Present*, 5th ed. (Englewood Cliffs, N.J.: Prentice-Hall, 1991). The textbooks of T. Walter Wallbank, first published during World War II, also displayed a broader internationalist sensibility than most texts. His two-volume *Civilizations Past and Present* (Glencoe, Ill.: Scott, Foresman, 1942) included sympathetic coverage of Asia and North Africa in ancient and medieval times. Of a total of thirty-three chapters, eight dealt exclusively or in part with those regions; the other twenty-five focused on the classical world and Europe.

6. See Marshall G. S. Hodgson, *Rethinking World History: Essays on Europe, Islam, and World History*, ed. Edmund Burke III (Cambridge: Cambridge University Press, 1993). Burke's introduction and conclusion are insightful complements to Hodgson's writings.

7. Curtin acknowledges that "I have already raided my lectures for [The World and the West] to publish two books, one on cross-cultural trade and one on plantations." Philip D. Curtin, "Graduate Teaching in World History," *Journal of World History* 2 (Spring 1991): 83.

8. David A. Hollinger, *Postethnic America* (New York: Basic Books, 1995), 109.

9. Patrick Manning, "The Problems of Interactions in World History," *American Historical Review* 101 (June 1996): 772.

10. Both the College Board and textbook publishers have periodically canvassed college history departments to determine where and how world history is taught. In 1997, the World History Association conducted a modest survey that indicated growth in

course offerings at the introductory, upper division, and graduate levels. See Heidi Roupp, "Results of the WHA Survey of World History Courses," *World History Bulletin* 14 (Spring 1998): 18–19. Also see the table in the essay by Michael F. Doyle in Part Ten.

11. Kevin Reilly argues that world history was more popular in two-year colleges than four-year institutions for many years, beginning in the 1960s when the community college movement took off. One reason was the Vietnam War, which exposed the smug cultural parochialism of American decision-makers. Another was the pragmatic mission of the community colleges to create from scratch what the public wanted, unencumbered by curricular conventions. Personal communication from Kevin Reilly, 8 November 1997.

12. For information about H-Net and H-World see <http://www.h-net.msu.edu>.

PART ONE

WORLD HISTORY TEACHING OVER TIME

Educators exploring the potentials of world history will do well to consider how the field has been defined and redefined since the late nineteenth century, when history emerged as a modern discipline. Representations of the human past have drastically changed since the first textbooks on "general history" appeared. The first selection in Part One is an excerpt from the introduction to William Swinton's *Outlines of the World's History*, published in 1874. The statement is typical of school texts in the era of the Second Industrial Revolution and the New Imperialism, when assumptions of racial hierarchy and progressive cultural evolution, as well as the analytical blurring of race, culture, and language, informed virtually all historical scholarship in the United States and Europe. Swinton's book, which was designed for use in both high schools and colleges, plots history backward from "the present civilization of the advanced nations" along "a direct and unbroken line" to Rome and Greece. The author puts forth the nineteenth-century Western truism that some races and subraces are "historical" and some are not. This "scientific fact" allowed Swinton and other textbook writers of his era to define world history and its narrative of moral and political progress without any of the serious struggles late twentieth-century teachers face over principles of inclusion, selection, and coverage. After World War I, the racial and cultural triumphalism that flavored general history texts became less overt as new social scientific theory began to influence Western views of human development. Even so, the axiom that history halted in Asia sometime in the first millennium B.C.E. and that it never took any intelligible form among human groups inhabiting sub-Saharan Africa or the Americas, at least until Europeans introduced progressive change to those places, continued for another three decades to govern what young Americans learned about civilization and the world's past.

In his book *The Opening of the American Mind*, Lawrence Levine describes how academics at Columbia and other prestigious colleges urged humanistic studies that would exercise the critical faculties and transform students into loyal but politically alert citizens. In reforming the curriculum to meet perceived postwar social needs, these teacher-scholars invented Western Civ. Levine shows that the course originated in the national wartime policy to strengthen moral and emotional bonds between Americans (who were traditionally wary of the hypercivilized Old World) and their military allies in democratic Europe. The first Western Civ courses served the postwar strategy to assimilate new immigrants by teaching the "common and deeply rooted heritage that bound them together." Thus, Western Civ was not the traditional and normative way of teaching non-American history but an artifact of the special social conditions that prevailed during and immediately following the war. It consequently "came into being with a significant amount of political and ideological content," including a North Atlantic-centered definition of world history compatible with education in democratic citizenship and Euro-American internationalism.

Harry Carman, a young lecturer at Columbia, describes the Contemporary Civilization course that he and his colleagues introduced in the college in 1919. The very idea of an introductory, cross-disciplinary survey required for all freshmen was a radical departure in American higher education. Carman defends the innovation, arguing that dispassionate critical examination of modern civilization's values fortifies democracy. Like all his fellows at Columbia, he assumed synonymy between "civilization" abstractly defined and the collective cultural traditions of the European and North American nation-states. The course syllabus gathers the rest of the human community into the residual category of "backward peoples." Indeed, the intellectual continuity from race-based general history to the Western Civ of the 1920s is unmistakable. Nevertheless, Contemporary Civilization demanded attentive, critical study of broad trends at the international level, and it established a new standard for core education in the liberal arts. However narrow its cultural lens may seem to us now, Western Civ of the interwar era was the direct ancestor of the reconceptualized world history courses that colleges began to offer more than forty years later.

In the spring 1990 inaugural issue of the *Journal of World History*, Gilbert Allardyce aptly reviewed the growth of world history as a teaching field from early in the century to the 1980s. In "Toward World History" he traces the movement by examining the intersecting careers of three important pioneers: Louis Gottschalk, Leften Stavrianos, and William McNeill, all of whom helped release world history from the European tunnel of time. The excerpt reprinted here omits the account of Gottschalk's leadership in writing one of the six volumes of the UNESCO *History of Mankind: Cultural and Scientific Development*. Allardyce links this colossal project, which ran from 1951 to 1976, to postwar yearnings for international understanding and peace education. The *History of Mankind* stands as a learned and monumental reference work. Allardyce demonstrates, however, that precisely because of its commitment to "equal time" for all peoples and cultures, it failed as conceptually coherent world history. Gottschalk was a specialist on early modern Europe, but in the process of writing volume 4 of the series he became an eager convert to universal history suitable for a round world. Allardyce acknowledges, nevertheless, that Stavrianos and McNeill have had much greater influence on world history as an "art of classroom teaching." He shows just how persistent these two men have been in their efforts to persuade the historical profession, whose direction in the 1960s was toward ever more exquisite specialization, to take world history seriously as an academic subject.

Craig Lockard explores the singular contributions of Philip Curtin and other scholars at the University of Wisconsin, who in the early 1960s built what must be regarded as the first successful graduate program to train future college teachers in comparative world history. Out of the Wisconsin program marched a cadre of junior instructors, including Lockard himself, who earnestly preached the world history gospel, helped found the World History Association, and produced several of the selections included in this book. Despite McNeill's special achievement in legitimizing world history, the University of Chicago remained wedded to its venerable tradition of advancing humanistic study of the West. Wisconsin, by contrast, trained Asianists, Africanists, and Latin Americanists who were eager not only to show just how *historical* those regions were but to compare developments in different regions and situate the peoples of each of them in the stream of long-term global change.

WILLIAM O. SWINTON

Outlines of General History

Viewing history as confined to the series of leading civilized nations, we observe that it has to do with but one grand division of the human family, namely, with the Caucasian, or white race. To this division belonged the people of all the elder nations, — the Egyptians, Assyr′ians and Babylo′nians, the Hebrews and the Phœni′cians, the Hin′doos, the Persians, the Greeks, and the Romans. Of course, the modern European nations, as also the states founded by European *colonists*, all belong to this ethnological division. Thus we see that history proper concerns itself with but one highly developed type of mankind; for though the great bulk of the population of the globe has, during the whole recorded period, belonged, and does still belong, to other types of mankind, yet the Caucasians form the only truly *historical* race. Hence we may say that civilization is the product of the brain of this race.

Of the peoples outside of the Caucasian race that have made some figure in civilization, the Chinese, Mexicans, and Peruvians stand alone. But though those races rose considerably above the savage state, their civilization was stationary, and they had no marked influence on the general current of the world's progress.

Modern scholars divide this historical stock — the Caucasian race — into three main branches: I. The A′ryan, or Indo-European branch; II. The Semit′ic branch; III. The Hamit′ic branch. This classification is a *linguistic* one, — that is to say, it is a division based on the nature of the languages spoken by the three families of nations, — but at the same time it represents three distinct civilizations.

The Aryan branch is that division to which we ourselves belong: it includes nearly all the present and past nations of Europe, — the Greeks, Latins, Germans or Teu′tons, Celts, and Slavo′nians, — together with two ancient Asiatic peoples, namely, the Hindoos and the Persians.

The evidence of language shows that the Celtic, German, Slavonian, Greek, and Latin tongues all bear a remarkable family likeness, and that they share this likeness with the Sanscrit, which was the ancient language of India,

William O. Swinton, "Outlines of General History," in *Outlines of the World's History, Ancient, Mediaeval, and Modern, with Special Relation to the History of Civilization and the Progress of Mankind* (New York: Ivison, Blakeman, Taylor, 1874), 2–4.

and with the Zend, the ancient language of Persia. It is quite certain that the forefathers of the Persians and of the Hindoos and the forefathers of all the European nations were once one people, and lived together somewhere in Western Asia. This was at a time long before the beginning of recorded history (for we know nothing of the Greeks, Latins, Germans, Celts, etc., *as such,* until we find them in *Europe*); but still it is proved by the evidence of language that their original home and native seat was Asia.

The Semitic branch includes the ancient inhabitants of Syria, Arabia, and the Tigris and Euphrates countries. The leading historical representatives of the Semitic branch are the Hebrews, Phœnicians, Assyrians, and Arabs.

The Hamitic branch has but one prominent representative, — the Egyptians. It is probable, however, that the ancient Chaldæ'ans also belonged to this race.

The history of the civilized world is the history of the Aryan, Semitic, and Hamitic races. It is of interest to know that the race to which we belong, the Aryan, has always played the leading part in the great drama of the world's progress. The Hamitic nations, the Egyptians and Chaldæans, though they developed a peculiar type of civilization, yet grew up and remained in a great degree *apart* from the rest of the world, having no considerable influence on the main current of history. As to the Semites, there is one respect in which they have the greatest place in the story of mankind, namely, in religious development; for the three religions that have taught men that there is but one God — namely, the Jewish, the Christian, and the Mahom'etan — have all come from among them. But, aside from this, the Semites do not make nearly so important or so conspicuous a figure in history as do the Aryans, or Indo-Europeans. They have never been greatly progressive. They have generally shown a conservative disposition that has, in the main, kept them fixed to their native seat, in the small tract of country between the Tigris, the Mediterranean, and the Red Sea. Thus they have not, like the Aryans, been the planters of new nations; and they have never attained a high intellectual development, or that progress in political freedom, in science, art, and literature, which is the glory of the Aryan nations.

If we trace back the present civilization of the advanced nations of the world, — our own civilization, and that of England, Germany, France, Italy, etc., — we shall find that much of it is connected by direct and unbroken line with the Roman. The Romans, in turn, were heirs of the Greeks. Now, all this is *Aryan;* and when we go back to the primitive age of the undivided Aryans in Asia, we see that this race must even then have been placed far above the condition of mere savages, and that they had made good beginnings in government, and social life, and religion, and the simple mechanical arts. Thus we are fully authorized to say that the Aryans are peculiarly the race of *progress;* and a very large part of the history of the world must be taken up with an account of the contributions which the Aryan nations have made to the common stock of civilization.

LAWRENCE W. LEVINE

Looking Eastward
The Career of Western Civ

It was not the neoclassicists who filled the vacuum many perceived after the demise of the classical curriculum. That distinction went to a group of educators during World War I who, with the encouragement of a federal government anxious to help Americans understand why after almost two centuries they were turning once again to Europe, devised new general education courses soon to bear the name Western Civilization, or in the college vernacular, Western Civ.

The historian Daniel Boorstin has depicted the First World War as a watershed for American conceptions of Europe. Prior to the war Americans tended to see their country as "a kind of non-Europe." The designations "American" and "European," he maintains, were used less as geographical terms than as "logical antitheses." Europe "was a handy mirror in which to see what we were not, and hence to help us discover what we were." Certainly European history courses existed before 1914 — in Berkeley, University of California freshmen could take History 1 which covered "the progress of western European civilization from prehistoric times to the completion of the Panama Canal" — but the war brought such courses new meaning. Irwin Edman, a sophomore at Columbia College in 1914, remembered how the European conflict made Professor Carlton Hayes's course on Europe since 1815 increasingly popular with undergraduates: "Up to the autumn of 1914 Europe seemed to most American college students a solar system away." The war changed all of this. "European history ceased to be the anthropology and archaeology of distant peoples who spoke remote languages. It became as alive as yesterday's events; it was what explained today's news."

Indeed, in a sense Western Civilization courses did grow out of this desire to explain "today's news." After the United States entered the war, the federal government's Committee on Education and Special Training established the Student Army Training Corps (SATC) on campuses throughout the nation and requested the host colleges to create an interdisciplinary War Issues Course ex-

Lawrence W. Levine, "Looking Eastward: The Career of Western Civ," in *The Opening of the American Mind: Canons, Culture, and History* (Boston: Beacon Press, 1996), 54–60, 63–68.

plaining the underlying and immediate causes of the war. Although propagandistic motives were denied by everyone concerned, the courses inevitably reflected the Wilsonian notion that the war was a struggle between Enlightenment and Barbarism, between the principles and practices of democracy and those of autocracy, with the future of civilization hanging in the balance. At the University of Michigan, for example, Professor Claude Van Tyne gave a series of lectures on Germany with such titles as, "How Autocracy Drills Its Subjects," "Dreams of World Power," "Superman," and "A State Without Moral Obligations," while Professor Edward R. Turner taught his students that "the English, more than any other people in the world, except the French and ourselves . . . have the humanitarian spirit, a desire for fair play and to do what is right, to help people who are weaker than themselves, not to take advantage of weaker people, in other words to do to others as they would be done by." The Germans, on the other hand, "carry on war as they have in France and Belgium because the German people do not have the humanitarian spirit of fair play, which the English, American and French do have." Albert Kerr Heckel, Dean of Lafayette College, wrote that "we were advised not to make the course one of propaganda, and yet it could not escape being propaganda." The purpose of the course, he felt, should be to "tell the ugly truth about Germany" by explaining how the "dominant democratic ideal among European peoples in general" had "failed with the Teuton," and exploring "what is wrong with Germany . . . the defects of German character . . . the falsity of her political creed and her philosophy of might." Never before, he concluded, "have we felt more definitely that there are moral forces at work in history making. And as a result it may be that the teacher of history will, for at least a time, be also something of an advocate." The Committee on Education and Special Training made it clear that the purpose of the course was "to enhance the morale of the members of the corps by giving them an understanding of what the war is about and of the supreme importance to civilization of the cause for which we are fighting."

The course was so successful at Columbia College that its director, Dean F. J. E. Woodbridge, began to consider it a potential foundation for a course "which will give the generations to come a common background of ideas and commonly understood standards of judgment." Thus at Columbia the War Issues Course became not an end but a beginning. It was followed by a Peace Issues Course and ultimately in the fall of 1919 by a required freshman course, Contemporary Civilization, which surveyed the development of Western Civilization and familiarized students with contemporary world problems. Ten years later, a second year of Contemporary Civilization was prescribed for sophomores. As Carol Gruber has shown, CC, as it quickly became known, manifested its wartime origins and continued to serve patriotic purposes. One of its founders, Dean Herbert E. Hawkes, maintained that it was intended to thwart the "destructive element in our society" by equipping students to "meet the arguments of the opponents of decency and sound government" and make the college student a "citizen who shall be safe for democracy." Since this course was so instrumental in the establishment of Western Civ as the norm across the nation, it is worth noting that it came into being with a significant amount of political and ideological content both during and after World War I.

The urges that established Western Civ as the core liberal arts course included more than the patriotism of the moment. For a decade or more before the war, Columbia and many other American colleges were perplexed: what would, what should replace classics as the core of undergraduate education? "The college," declared President Jacob Gould Schurman of Cornell in 1907, "is without clear-cut notions of what a liberal education is and how it is to be secured." This "paralysis," Schurman insisted, affected "every college of arts in America."

The happy discovery professors made on a number of campuses during the war was that the immediate needs of the federal government coincided with several long-term educational demands. Even before World War I a few U.S. historians had been looking for ways to place American history in greater perspective. The Committee of Seven, appointed by the American Historical Association to study the teaching of history in the secondary schools, argued in its 1899 report that the history of the United States taught by itself was, in the words of Professor Lucy M. Salmon, "insufficient. It gives but a warped, narrow, circumscribed view of history, — it is history detached from its natural foundation — European history, it is history suspended in mid-air." This conviction won a wider audience with the advent of global wars on either side of a worldwide depression, shared experiences which certainly nurtured feelings of connection with Europe that had not been characteristic of nineteenth-century Americans. These events prompted Americans to look eastward, back toward Europe, with an intensity they had not experienced for most of their national history and promoted a feeling of belonging to a "Western" civilization.

It would be a mistake to attribute the attraction of Western Civ primarily to international factors. There were important domestic forces at work as well. At a time when ethnic diversity bore heavily on American consciousness because of the massive immigration from Southern and Eastern Europe, the migrations of African Americans from the South to the cities of the North, and the European war which exacerbated tensions between ethnic groups in the United States and gave rise to President Wilson's warnings about "hyphenated" Americans, the advent of Western Civ promised to be a unifying and assimilative force which taught the separate groups that they had a common and deeply rooted heritage that bound them together. Columbia University's president, Nicholas Murray Butler, who complained that the elective system had destroyed "that common body of knowledge which held educated men together in understanding and in sympathy" for more than a thousand years, hailed the advent of the Contemporary Civilization course as a worthy substitute which would serve as "a unifying force of common understanding, common appreciation and common sentiment." As the historian Carolyn Lougee has put it, "In cultural terms, the Western Civ ideal was homogenizing and normative: it socialized the young from whatever particularist background traditions to a uniform standard of thinking and behaving that ought to characterize America's expanding educated class.

It performed the same function *within* the colleges themselves. The elimination first of Greek and then of Latin as entrance requirements increased the number of public high school graduates at elite schools like Columbia which meant, as Lionel Trilling later observed, a considerable increase in the number of students who "came from ethnic and social groups not formerly represented in the College." Dean Herbert Hawkes complained in 1918 that too many students now lived at home, attended college from nine to five, and regarded it primarily as a means to further their careers: "They have no use for college affairs and regard Columbia less as an Alma Mater than as an Efficiens Pater." Dean Frederick Keppel broached the issue more frankly, noting in 1914, "One of the commonest references that one hears with regard to Columbia is that its position at the gateway of European immigration makes it socially uninviting to students who come from homes of refinement. The form which the inquiry takes in these days of slowly-dying race prejudice is, 'Isn't Columbia overrun with European Jews who are most unpleasant persons socially?'" Lionel Trilling surmised that the problem of diminishing social homogeneity and unity was behind Columbia's restoration of football in 1915, after a decade of banishment, in "an effort to create the sense of collegiate solidarity among the students." From the point of view of Trilling and many of his colleagues, the introduction of Western Civ was a more satisfactory means to the same end. Clearly, the shaping of the college curriculum in response to an increasingly diverse population has not been confined to our own time.

The Western Civ courses that evolved on campus after campus in these years went beyond the immediate, practical connections to Europe and envisioned the United States and Europe tied together in a cultural embrace that had its historical origins in the classical world and its development in medieval, Renaissance, and modern Europe. It was a Whiggish view of history that pictured "Western Civilization" as the end product of all of world history, or at least all of world history that *mattered,* since entire continents, whole peoples, and complete historical epochs were ignored as if they had not existed, and for the purposes of the new Western Civ ethos, they hadn't. Justus Buchler, a professor of philosophy at Columbia University, made — and defended — the point that as taught at Columbia, one must always qualify the term "Contemporary Civilization" with the phrase "in the West." This limitation, Buchler explained, stemmed "not from dim awareness of the Orient . . . nor from perversity and false cultural pride, but because Western society is the society of Western students, and because the number of available men versed in Eastern culture has always been lamentably small." It is not inappropriate to note that such scholars were "lamentably" few largely *because* "civilization" as understood and taught in twentieth-century American colleges invariably carried the adjective "Western," whether it was articulated or not. It is also instructive to recognize that Buchler viewed the world as a simple polarity between the "Orient" and the "Occident," and felt no need to mention Africa, in spite of America's substantial demographic and cultural connections to that continent. James Harvey Robinson, whose European history textbooks were deeply influential in shaping the nature of Western Civ courses, was similarly open about the process of inclusion. In *The Ordeal of Civilization* (1926), he revealed that in making "a fresh selection from the records of the past," he decided that "only those considerations would properly find a place which clearly served to forward the main purpose of seeing more and more distinctly how this, our present Western civilization . . . has come about." . . .

Although Western Civ remained dominant in the years immediately following the Second World War, and even penetrated such new territory as the University of Chicago, its momentum soon ebbed. As Gilbert Allardyce has argued persuasively, postwar developments were simply not conducive to its continued primacy. The struggle with the Soviet Union for technological superiority heightened America's awareness of the increased need for specialized knowledge. The decline of colonialism and the growing recognition of the existence and importance of the Third World taught Americans that the world they lived in consisted of diverse cultures and peoples who could neither be understood nor explained through the concepts at the center of the Western Civ course. Domestic developments which saw the emergence of minority peoples and power in the United States and the increased presence on campuses of students and faculty from minority groups, including those from Eastern and Southern European immigrant cultures, reminded the nation of the diversity at the center of our own history which could not be comprehended solely through tracing the development of Western and Northern European civilization.

A more anthropological and comprehensive way of perceiving culture also undermined the Western Civ curriculum with its evolutionary and hierarchical predispositions. During a 1976 American Historical Association session on the Western Civ survey, Frederic L. Cheyette of Amherst College articulated the growing skepticism when he argued that despite its claims to universality, the Western Civ curriculum was "truncated and provincial: its culture was essentially political and philosophical, nodding occasionally towards science, less often towards poetry. It dismissed the visual arts with a slide show and ignored music completely, as though on some absolute ontological scale Mozart had been weighed against Voltaire and found wanting. Popular culture, of course, was beneath notice."

Although it declined, Western Civ did not die in those years after World War II; it lived — and lives — on in a bewildering array of forms. I took and later taught a two-semester Western Civ course first as a freshman and then as a young instructor at the City College of New York in the 1950s, just as students throughout the country were — and still are — taking such courses. What died, or at least began a precipitous decline, was a certain set of assumptions that had surrounded Western Civ from its inception and had given it, for a short time, an unparalleled position of privilege in the humanities and the university. What died, or at least suffered an inexorable blow, was a certain arrogance, an unquestioned assurance that Western Civilization embodied *all* the culture and history and literature we needed to know to live our lives and comprehend our past and present.

It is important to recognize that the Western Civilization survey course, which many critics of the contemporary university imply has long constituted the heart and soul of the humanities curriculum and therefore must be defended to the death, did not come into being until somewhere around the First World War and remained in the ascendancy for less than fifty years before fading from prominence in the decades after the Second World War. The complexity of knowledge, the complexity of culture, the complexity of the world, and the complexity of the United States itself became more difficult and more dangerous to deny and more imperative to confront and comprehend. All of these developments created an atmosphere less supportive to ideas of a unified core curriculum devoted to promulgating the dominance of a single cultural stream that would explain the United States to its people, whether that curriculum was dominated by classics or by Western Civ. The appealingly simple syllogistic universe and solutions of Robert Hutchins and his colleagues appeared less and less credible.

Almost everywhere in the post–World War II university world, colleges took a second and far more critical look at their general education programs and core courses. Although Harvard issued its famous 1945 report, *General Education in a Free Society*, which recommended that all students be required to take a course in "Great Texts of Literature" and another course in "Western Thought and Institutions," the objective of which would be "an examination of the institutional and theoretical aspects of the Western heritage," the faculty adopted so many options to the report's recommended core curriculum that it began to resemble the very elective system it was meant to modify. During the 1949 debate on the report's proposed Western Civ course, which was modeled on Columbia's Contemporary Civilization course, faculty critics insisted that the stress on *Western* thought and institutions embodied a myopic and limited view of the modern world, perpetuated the myth of civilization as a monopoly of those countries bordering the Atlantic Ocean, and ignored the virtues of comparing the values and institutions of Western societies with those of other cultures.

In 1968, the year before Stanford University's History of Western Civilization course, which had been initiated as a prescribed course for all freshmen in 1935, was dropped as a requirement, its director, Paul S. Seaver, admitted that "many of us as faculty are no longer convinced that there is a standard or specifiable body of knowledge or information necessary for a liberal education." The crucial function "of introducing historical concepts, modes of analysis, etc.," he concluded, "is common to all history courses and does not, therefore, require the setting of a Western Civ survey." The authors of the multivolume report, *The Study of Education at Stanford* (1968), agreed. "General education, as epitomized by the Chicago curriculum of the Hutchins era and the Columbia two-year sequences in Humanities and Contemporary Civilization," they observed, "is dead or dying." Why, they asked, "is it more important for a student to learn some calculus than some economics? Are we really sure that mastery of a foreign language is more important than mastery of one of the fine arts?" Rather than a series of inflexible, prescribed requirements, representing "a set of political compromises among interest groups in the faculty," they called for "a new kind of general education" based upon the understanding that "the University cannot in any event impress upon its students the total content of present knowledge, and [that] it is impossible to choose what exactly it is that every student should know without imposing arbitrary constraints on the range of free inquiry." Thus instead of teaching overviews of their field as a whole, professors should be permitted to cover those aspects about which they knew and cared most deeply: "the Intellectual History of Europe in the Nineteenth Century rather than the History of Western Civilization, ... Organizational Behavior rather than Introduction to Sociology." Students should be given the freedom "to discover new interests ... and to explore the many fields and endeavors" open to them. "From this common freedom," the report concluded, "may emerge a form of general education far better suited to the characteristics of a university than that to which we pay lip service now."

Four years later, the Carnegie Commission on Higher Education criticized Western Civilization programs for covering too much and exploring too little in depth and recommended dropping the term *general education* "because it carries with it connotations of past efforts at a general coverage of all essential knowledge. Such coverage has proved impossible, despite repeated experiments over the past 70 years. 'Essential knowledge' no longer has the intellectual (classical) and/or theological core that once allowed a student to cover it all in one college career." Instead of the "preselected content" of general education programs, the commission stressed both process — emphasis should be placed "on cultivation of curiosity, on development of critical ability, on wider perspectives on self and on cultures, on ways to approach knowledge" — and relevance: the curriculum should have a direct relationship to the students for whom it is intended and the times in which it is taught. There was certainly nothing particularly new or revolutionary about these proposals; Charles William Eliot might have been heard whispering "Amen!"

At Columbia University itself, the famous CC course, which had served as a model for so many Western Civ courses, was severely diluted. In 1959 the second year of the CC requirement was discontinued, and in 1968 its common source book — which had constituted the very heart of the course for over two decades and had been regarded "by staff and students alike, as one of the most valuable features of the course" — was abandoned for paperbacks chosen by faculty. When the Columbia College faculty met to consider Daniel Bell's report on reforming general education in 1964, they opted to do absolutely nothing. "From my long experience of the College," Lionel Trilling reported, "I can recall no meetings on an educational topic that were so poorly attended and so lacking in vivacity. . . . Through some persuasion of the *Zeitgeist*, the majority of the faculty were no longer concerned with general education."

Trilling was entirely correct. The diminution of Western Civ courses and general education programs, like their adoption earlier in this century, were caused not by willful groups of malcontents and philistines, who somehow seized power, but by deep societal changes and developments — by alterations in the *Zeitgeist*. College curricula do not exist apart from the culture in which they develop; they are products of that culture and both reflect and influence it.

Thus, significant curricular changes are invariably and inextricably linked to significant changes in the general society and culture. The reasons behind the transformation of the classical college curriculum into the modern system of electives at the end of the last century and the rapid decline of Western Civ more recently illustrate this truth.

HARRY J. CARMAN

The Columbia Course in Contemporary Civilization

In introducing the general survey course Columbia has operated on the assumption that it is not the fundamental business of the College to turn out specialists in a narrow field, and that an individual is, after all, not well educated unless he or she has at least some conception of the broad field of intellectual endeavor. By this we do not mean to infer that Columbia College does not fully realize that the day has apparently long since passed when a person could be a profound scholar in a wide field, or that the specialist is not a very useful human being in our present complex civilization. Such an inference would be sheerest nonsense. It simply means that Columbia College is primarily concerned with liberalization rather than with specialization, and that in addition to feeling responsible for guiding its students into particular channels it considers it even more important to help them see life broadly. It is with this in mind that such general survey courses as the History of Science, Fine Arts, Religion, and Contemporary Civilization have been added to its curriculum.

INTRODUCTION AT COLUMBIA

The course in Contemporary Civilization, which was introduced in September, 1919, in place of the required courses in History and Philosophy, aims (1) to inform the student of the more outstanding and influential factors of his physical and social environment; (2) to survey the historical background of contemporary civilization; (3) to raise for consideration the insistent problems of the present; (4) to enable the student to understand the civilization of his own day and to participate more effectively in it; and (5) finally to give the student early in his college course objective material on which to base his own further studies.

Harry J. Carman, "The Columbia Course in Contemporary Civilization" (address delivered before the Association of History Teachers of the Middle States and Maryland at Bryn Mawr, 2 May 1925). *Columbia Alumni News* 17 (1925): 143–44.

These aims become doubly significant when we consider that in our present complex society the vast majority, as far as we can ascertain, for various reasons never critically examine our existing social standards; neither the historical origins nor the social significance of these standards are known, and yet by many they are criticised and oftentimes denounced. To label these critics as radicals, to heap vituperation upon their heads, to confine them within prison walls, or even to harry them out of the land will lead nowhere. Only through a careful examination of the existing order can their challenge be met or sane changes in our institutions be made. Force and repression at best are only temporary expedients and lend nothing to the inculcation of that spirit of cooperation so necessary if men are to live and work together happily. Nowhere is there more urgent need for an intelligent understanding of the insistent problems of today than among college youth. As citizens who should participate in affairs with clear judgment and intelligence, and as the leaders of tomorrow it is vitally important that they understand the civilization of their day. More important still, they should be trained to meet honest and serious criticism of the present order not by blind prejudice and blustering talk but by carefully reasoned argument.

THE THREE DIVISIONS

The course is divided into three main divisions: *The Basis of Civilization, A Survey of the Characteristics of the Present Age*, and *The Insistent Problems of Today*. Part of the first division deals with the physical world in its relation to the activities of man. Here the aim is to present as vividly as possible the intimate interdependence of man and nature. This section is treated topically and requires about a week. Following this, six weeks are devoted to a discussion of The World of Human Nature. The chief purposes of this part of the course are (1) to state and illustrate the interdependence of "man" and "society"; (2) to present a working picture of the different kinds of activity natural to human beings; (3) to present the fact of individual differences; and (4) to show how man has created different types of institutions and thought structures in order to express and satisfy his needs.

The second main division traces the history of our present-day institutions, while the third presents in considerable detail the chief problems arising in attempts to find satisfactory solutions of the difficulties incident to the major relationships which men sustain. Five problems in particular are considered, namely (1) Imperialism and Backward Peoples; (2) Nationalism and Internationalism; (3) Industrialism and Raising the Standards of Living; (4) Political Control and (5) Education.

DEPARTMENTS REPRESENTED

The first syllabus for the course was prepared by a group of instructors from the departments of History, Philosophy, Economics and Government. At the beginning they determined not to be restricted by consideration of available text books, but to be guided by a desire to present in simple nontechnical fashion such information and discussion as they thought desirable for the average college freshman. The syllabus, therefore, was not built around a particular text book nor was it the product of one man. When completed it represented the combined efforts of men with somewhat diverse training and frequently of opposing points of view.

The course, which runs through the year, meets five times a week for periods of fifty minutes each. Students meet in sections of thirty, sections being determined on the basis of psychological tests. In all, there are twenty sections, each being taught by the same instructor throughout the year. The course therefore is not made up of a series of lectures given by specialists in various fields. These instructors are drawn from the departments of Economics, Government, History, Philosophy and Psychology, and great care is exercised in selecting them. In fact only those who are willing or eager to do a great deal of painstaking and diligent study in order to acquaint themselves with such a diversified field, and who have shown marked ability to cooperate are taken. The classroom work is devoted almost exclusively to discussion based upon the syllabus and outside reading. . . .

CRITICISMS AGAINST THE COURSE

Four main criticisms have been directed against the course. In the first place, criticism has been made of its location in the freshman year. It has been found after half a dozen years' experience that the freshmen are more interested in the material of the course than in anything else they are studying, that there are disproportionately fewer failures as compared with a number of other courses, and that section representatives have frequently expressed the opinion that the course is the best thing in the freshman year. The senior class for the past two years has voted it the most helpful of all courses taken. In the judgment of certain of the older instructors who have taught either freshman Philosophy or History, the course is no more difficult than the older required courses. There are three good pedagogical reasons for putting the course in the freshman year:

1. It is an initiation into college study, marking a break from the work of the secondary schools and recognizing the ability of the freshman to take up the serious discussion of the problems of the world in which he lives.

2. It brings together and shows the interrelations of a variety of disciplines ordinarily thought of by the student as distinct departments. Within the course the relationships of Psychology, Anthropology, Ethics, History, Economics, Government, Sociology, and Education are brought out and the artificial distinctions eliminated. In other words, it is a step in the direction of abolishing the "pigeon-hole" type of education.

3. In the third place, students at the very outset of their course are given an introduction to a variety of subjects in which opportunity for advanced study is

offered by the University. Their early acquaintance may sufficiently arouse their interest to lead them to make elections which would be impossible if the first contact with the subjects came in the last year of college.

A second criticism is that the instructors may be incompetent to meet the heavy demands laid upon them. In other words, it is asserted that the course touches so many different departmental fields that it must be impossible to find instructors capable of conducting the entire course. Fortunately this has not been the case. True, we have never had an instructor who was able to handle the entire course without hard work on some part of it. Most of our staff, however, who have worked primarily in one field have had a considerable amount of undergraduate or graduate training in one or more of the allied fields. The men who have been drawn to the course have been willing to work hard not only to be in a position to handle the course but to advance their own knowledge and to gain a broader perspective for the work in their particular fields. Furthermore, it should be noted that the course by no means requires a searching acquaintance with the technical detail of every field.

Some believe, in the third place, that it is impossible to cover such a wide field without being superficial. It is obvious that such a survey course as Contemporary Civilization cannot enter deeply into the detailed content of any one field. But the description of the surface of a broad field need not be superficial either in its intellectual aims or its intellectual results.

Lastly, the criticism has been made that a survey course such as Contemporary Civilization fails to teach the student how to think. Whether this be true or not depends largely upon what is meant by the term "to think." Contemporary Civilization is not primarily intended as a survey of the thought process as it manifests itself throughout the entire range of intellectual enterprise. Such a course is given under the Department of Philosophy. In this required course it has seemed wiser to give particular emphasis to the formation of well supported opinion in the fields of the social sciences. Certainly we have every reason to believe that the course broadens the student's intellectual horizon perhaps more than would a course devoted primarily to thought processes.

GILBERT ALLARDYCE

Toward World History
American Historians and the Coming of the World History Course

Historians have been death on world history. Most believe that the subject is simply too vast and visionary for academic study and too alien to the modern temper of their profession. In fact, however, Andrew D. White, first president of the American Historical Association (AHA), called upon his members at their first public meeting in 1884 to make the new organization a place for both specialized work and the higher endeavor that he described as "the summing up of history," the study of the past on a world scale. "We may indeed consider it as the trunk on which special histories and biographies are the living branches," he said of world history, "giving to them and receiving from them growth and symmetry, drawing life from them, sending life into them." The branches spread, but historians in the AHA sawed off the trunk. Not synthesis but empiricism became house style — history in fine grain, layered, textured, nuanced, footnoted. To criticize this style, one historian commented recently, is to criticize the practice of academic history in the United States. "This is the work we are good at," he concluded; "it is the essence of professional history."[1]

If so, world history plainly does not come naturally to historians. Some say the fault is in ourselves and the narrowness of our discipline. Others say it is in the sheer impossibility of the subject itself. Is world history possible? Those who say it is begin from a simple premise: all the history in the world is not world history. Bishop Bossuet in the seventeenth century commented that just as world maps could be projected to appropriate detail, so world history could be scaled to proper size. This same idea, that world history was not more boundless than other histories but merely different in focus, became common to the literature that most influenced American historians on the subject. Thus Lord Acton in 1898 defined world history as "distinct from the combined history of all nations" and concentrated only upon "the common fortunes of mankind." To H. G. Wells in 1920, it was "something more and something less than the aggregate of the national histories," just as European history was something more and

Gilbert Allardyce, "Toward World History: American Historians and the Coming of the World History Course," *Journal of World History* 1 (Spring 1990): 23–26, 40–76.

something less than the aggregate of all national histories, "just as European history was something more and something less than the aggregate of all national histories on the continent. Others have explained that, to have a place in world history, events must be large, comprehensive, and compelling enough to affect whole segments of humanity. In sum, because humankind is so vast, its common history probably is fairly limited.[2] Indeed, someone said that world history can be written on a single page.

But what is world history? Here, on this question of the content of world history, some historians believe that this old subject simply has too much bad history to live down. They look on it in the way that astronomers look on astrology, that is, as an early and immature form of their discipline, a form all bound up in religion, metaphysics, and prophecy. Through twelve centuries, major church historians from Augustine to Bossuet infused world history with concepts of the sacred and profane. They identified it as the unfolding of the divine idea, as a revelation of the truth of Christianity, as the story of God's people in Europe and the Middle East. Thereafter, in the secular, universal histories of the Enlightenment, these religious ideas merely gave way to moral philosophy and metaphysical abstractions. However, with the rise of "scientific" history, the whole enterprise came under a cloud. As the practice of history became professional, the practice of world history became identified with amateurism. The new history defined itself against the old, and apprentices in the vocation, reared on specialized research, learned to hold world history in suspicion as something outmoded, overblown, and metahistorical. Whoever said world history, said amateurism.

In our century, Oswald Spengler and Arnold Toynbee formed new versions of world history out of the cultural pessimism of western society. They opened the subject to a new civilizational approach and, at the same time, turned it back upon itself, returning to ultimate questions about God and humanity that had aroused historians against the old universal history in the first place. Their work seemed to set university historians on edge, to challenge something fundamental in the contemporary practice of history. This response revealed, on the one hand, the considerable solidarity of the history profession in opposition to world history; on the other, it revealed the isolation of the profession from the reading public. Spengler and Toynbee made world history popular in the twentieth century, and their success with the book-buying populace, particularly in the United States, indicated the public appeal of histories with a claim to global scale and cosmic significance. In most academic literature, however, the writings of Spengler and Toynbee generally were dismissed as works of imagination, as philosophy, prophecy, pap. British historian Hugh Trevor-Roper, in reaction to the commercial success of Toynbee's work in America, quipped: "As a dollar earner . . . it ranks second only to whiskey."[3] Indeed the influence of these modern masters of world history, rather than inspiring historians to return to the subject, caused them instead to harden against it. The result was to make universities hostile ground for world history in the United States.

This article concerns three historians who fought against this opposition in the profession and the universities. Louis Gottschalk and William H. McNeill of the University of Chicago and Leften S. Stavrianos of Northwestern University in the Evanston suburbs made Chicago the capital of world history in the United States. This is not a study of the works and ideas of these three men. Rather the purpose here is to draw from the lessons of their experiences in preparing the coming of world history in American education. The work of McNeill and Stavrianos in particular inspired the rise of the World History Association (WHA), formed by young historians in 1982 to take over the cause of world history from these men of the older generation. This organization wants historians to turn the leading scholarship of the men studied here into effective world history courses through the art of classroom teaching. Their message, in short, is this: the way to make world history possible is to teach it. The late Warren I. Susman, vice president of the AHA Teaching Division in 1982, remarked that good scholarship becomes good history when it is forced to teach, when it is made to communicate knowledge in clear and systematic form. "The fact remains," he concluded, "that an effective course demands to be informed by effective scholarship and effective scholarship to have its impact fully felt needs to be *taught*." This, in effect, is what McNeill told world historians as well. "So my injunction to you is this," he declared: "Try to teach world history and you will find that it can be done."[4] . . .

TOWARD GLOBAL PERSPECTIVE: LEFTEN STAVRIANOS AND THE HIGH SCHOOL COURSE IN WORLD HISTORY

Gottschalk described a coming revolt against Eurocentrism in the study of world history. The future of the subject, he believed, lay in a more pluralist and universal approach. Europe had been the world for too long; now the earth was round. Today this perception of a need to "de-Europeanize" world history has become gospel in the world history movement. This section of the present article concerns the work of Leften Stavrianos (b. Vancouver, 1913) in bringing this idea to teachers of world history in American high schools. Stavrianos called for "a view from the moon," a higher, unifying vision of the whole human past. To him, world history in American education had never been about world history: it had been about Europe. The subject was always the west and the westernization of other continents, with Europeans at the center, Americans on the side, and everyone else on the planet in limbo.[5]

It seems, however, that western historians have always resisted larger histories. Eurocentrism is us. Even though the history of ancient China, for example, was known to Europeans from the writings of Jesuit missionaries nearly a generation before Bossuet wrote his universal history in 1681, it took another century to break through the old western limits of sacred history. And even after the discovery of other peoples on the planet, the world beyond Europe often still remained as nonhistorical as before. In the nineteenth century, as the study of European states became the subject matter of history, the study of peoples without states became the subject matter of anthropology. Nonwestern peoples became "societies" and "cultures." Some, like the Egyptians and Chinese, were perceived as exhausted civilizations left behind by history. Others, supposedly more isolated, were conceived as primitives and "exotics" who had never been part of history in the first place. Europeans had a history; others had customs, which were timeless and unchanging. "The history of European peoples could be found in the archives," a historian comments, "the customs of . . . peoples overseas were to be found in the field."[6]

Scholars have described how western thinkers consistently invented categories to define this duality of the west and "the people without history": civilization and primitivism, modernism and traditional society, development and underdevelopment, core and periphery. "Many of us," explained Eric R. Wolf, "even grew up believing that this West has a genealogy, according to which ancient Greece begat Rome, Rome begat Christian Europe, Christian Europe begat the Renaissance, the Renaissance the Enlightenment, the Enlightenment political democracy and the industrial revolution."[7] This was not only the history that most westerners knew, it was their perception of the nature of history itself as well — its oneness, linear direction, and progressive movement. Incapable of transcending European experience, they were also incapable of so-called global perspective. For this reason, Toynbee compared the west to Sleeping Beauty: fair, alluring, but dead to the world. However, there is a kind of allure and romance in the idea of global perspective as well. British historian Geoffrey Barraclough, for example, claimed that such a universal vision could bring a revolution in consciousness, a breakout from the parochialism of histories limited to particular regions and peoples. "The change," he asserted, "can be compared with that from the Ptolemaic to the Copernican picture of the universe; and its results, in opening new dimensions and changing our perspective, may well be no less revolutionary." Such leaps of imagination perhaps suggest why the writing of world histories has been as persistent in western culture as the writing of utopian literature.[8] In taking a different angle of vision, utopian literature attempts to transcend old limits to perception. There is something of this as well in Stavrianos's attempt to transcend the limits of Eurocentrism in the teaching of world history.

What gives Stavrianos's thought significance here as a study in the reaction against Eurocentrism is his radical separation of western and world history. To him, neither western civilization courses, European imperialism courses, nor courses of "the west in world history" type were offerings in world history. Instead, they were western histories, versions in which dynamic Europeans did their stuff to the passive populations that made up the rest of humankind. "It needs to be recognized," Stavrianos explained, "that world history and Western Civilization are inherently and fundamentally different, that they cannot be combined in any fashion, and each teacher must make the basic policy decision as to whether he will offer either the one or the other."[9]

To him, this decision had important consequences in the education of American youth. For world history, Stavrianos argued, had one message for them and western history had another. His is a brave new world, with nuclear annihilation lying in one direction and a more vibrant interaction of cultures in the other. "We have the privilege," he wants students to know, "of living in what is without a doubt the most exciting and significant era in history." But this, he laments, is not what students learn from western history. Instead, as Europe and the United States lose mastery in the world, western history becomes like a dirge for the human race. Innocently, students project this dark present into a vision of a dark future. To Stavrianos, the answer to this western gloom is global perspective. It offers students not only a different past but also a different future to go with it.[10] Someone said the future is not what it used to be. That, to Stavrianos, was the good news of world history in global perspective.

Originally a Europeanist specializing in Greek history, Stavrianos was long conscious of the influence of boundaries between peoples. (Significantly, the two foremost world history academics in the United States, Stavrianos and Mc-Neill, were born in Canada and published their early work in Greek history.) As early as the 1940s, he turned to world history in reaction to what he perceived to be the limitations of the traditional western civilization survey as education for Americans involved after the Second World War in larger international commitments. "I felt the need at the time for another course with a global perspective," he recalled of his first thoughts about world history, "and this feeling was strengthened during the Korean War when so many of our students left our campuses for the Far East with negligible knowledge or understanding of what they were about to face."[11] After Sputnik in 1957, this perception of a national need for education in nonwestern cultures became more widely shared in the United States, and with the National Defense Education Act in the next year, government, universities, and private foundations in the field of education came together in the idea that instruction in foreign languages, area studies, and international education was in the national defense interests of the United States. In this way, Stavrianos's ideas were part of a larger cultural expression, with origins in a period when Americans were more at home in the world, when students looked on nonwestern peoples with a kind of peace corps idealism, and when international education was identified with American political interests.

In particular, Stavrianos's ideas connected him with those advocating the "global approach" to international education, and the work of his Global History Project at Northwestern University largely coincided with the rise and decline of the globalism idea in American learning between 1957 and 1975. Partly, the term global history was simply a modish, space age name for world history. Partly, it was a term intended to contrast a world overview, transcending cultures and states, with the older, limited focus of area studies on particular nonwestern regions and languages. Area studies stressed the need to understand nonwestern cultures in their own context. This, to Stavrianos, was as parochial as Eurocentrism. Even before Sputnik, however, area studies methods, first developed for national strategic reasons during the Second World War, were already losing influence. After Sputnik, the work to supersede them with a new global approach took off with the first voyages into space.

Before Sputnik, Stavrianos in 1952 had modest plans for a single course in world history at Northwestern. After Sputnik, he designed a whole new world

history program from freshman survey to graduate studies. By 1961, he thought —
wrongly, as it turned out — that he had convinced the entire faculty to convert
most introductory courses in the liberal arts to the global approach. Writing to
departments in that year, he stressed that changing the perspective of courses depended first on changing the perspective of teachers:

> The potentiality can be realized only if each course is genuinely global and
> meaningfully integrated. . . . In the case of the World History course, for
> example, it would not suffice to have the specialist on Asia, followed by the spe-
> cialists on Europe, Africa, Latin America, etc., and thus cover the globe and as-
> sume that the course is global. This would be a superficial and worthless
> hodgepodge of fragments of existing courses. Rather it is essential that one per-
> son invest the time and thought required to really integrate the course and to
> master the interrelationships and inner dynamism that inevitably would be
> overlooked in a vaudeville-style course.[12]

Gathering faculty resistance indicated, however, that the hold of traditional
approaches was too strong. So was the hold of traditional histories. "Stavrianos
knows full well that all of his own colleagues do not share his convictions," the
history department chairman reported; "Perhaps he is engaged in a controversy
which will make the quarrels of the ancients and the moderns . . . seem like
mere skirmishes."[13]

"You can not globalize courses," Stavrianos concluded, "without globalizing the instructors." This was the lesson that he carried into the work of his
World History Project on the world history course in high schools. Supported by
the Carnegie Foundation, this project was part of the response to the crisis of
confidence in American education that followed the Sputnik surprise, when an
infusion of federal and foundation grants opened opportunities for reform in the
teaching of high school subjects. None needed it more than the world history
course. This was a lady with a past. World history was at once the oldest history
course in public high schools and the most despised by teachers and students
alike. To Stavrianos, this failing was the result of what he described as "the
sheepskin curtain" — the communications barrier between universities and secondary schools that kept the influence of professional historians out of the social
studies. Therefore, to understand Stavrianos's place in the story of the world history course in high schools, it is necessary to review the history of this relationship between historians and secondary teachers in the making of the world history class and fixing it on the European past.

The original high school world history course, called "General History," can be
traced back to the beginning of the high school itself in Boston in 1821. It
evolved from a second-year course, "Ancient and Modern History and Chronology," given at Boston English High School in that year, a course itself developed from older Latin school instruction designed to provide historical background to the study of classical languages. As it spread to other locations, the
course continued to focus on the ancient past, and only gradually did it expand

to include later centuries. Covering a history beginning with Adam and Eve, the course mixed biblical history and classical mythology; but the line of development toward European history was clear. For, despite a reputation for dreariness and dry facts, the course had a clear organizing idea: history was the story of the "true religion" of Christianity. "Civilization," affirmed Samuel G. Goodrich in his course textbook in 1828, "has followed in the train of Christianity." When, with the decline of religious thinking in the nineteenth century, this principle of organization lost influence in textbook writing, other authors turned to secular themes of race and "progress," thus continuing in the same way to make Europe the equivalent of civilization. If, today, world history is represented as a way to overcome ethnocentrism, General History at this time was more a way to teach it. "The history of the civilized world is the history of the Aryan, Semitic, and Hametic races," explained William Swinton in his *Outlines of the World's History*, one of the most popular texts of the 1870s. "We are fully authorized to say that the Aryans are peculiarly the race of *progress*; and a very large part of the history of the world must be taken up with an account of the contributions which the Aryan nations have made to the common stock of civilization."[14]

At the end of the nineteenth century, as amateur historians gave way to professionals, Philip V. N. Myers virtually cornered the textbook market in General History. Where earlier texts fixed on politics and wars, Myers' *A General History for Colleges and High School* gave coverage to economic and social developments and added brief sections on nonwestern areas. Whereas Swinton in 1874, for example, failed even to list either India or China in his index, Myers in 1889 gave five pages of coverage to each of these areas (compared with 373 on ancient civilization and 328 on Europe) and ten to the expansion of Islam. Other authors followed the leader, but plainly no one knew what to do with the rest of the world. Bare descriptions of nonwestern peoples were added as supplements, chapters standing in isolation — usually at the end of the book — from the European story. Thus General History grew, but it did not change. Myers in 1889 continued the racial theme that gave justification to the old preoccupation with European history. "Of all the races," he explained, "the White, or Caucasian, exhibits by far the most perfect type, physically, intellectually, and morally."[15] However, by the time his text appeared in the 1906 edition, Myers had removed these racial references, and Eurocentrism was simply left on its own, without a legitimizing myth or clear principle of organization.

In a survey of teachers and students of General History in 1887, Albert Bushnell Hart of Harvard reported that the class — like most high school history at the time — was taken up with recitation drills and the textbook method. "It was mostly conglomerate, scrap-book history," an educator recalled some time later, "and merely tied together dynastic and ecclesiastical occurrences. . . . It was predominantly political, with a few comments on cultural developments and religious clashes. It stressed wars and schisms; pictured kings and queens, feudal lords and bishops, popes and emperors; emphasized dates and names . . . and made the study of history largely an exercise of the memory. Geographically it was confined to the Mediterranean basin, and to Western Europe, with brief allusions to the New World, Asia, and Africa."[16]

To enliven student interest, Wellesley College historian Mary D. Sheldon tried unsuccessfully in 1885 to introduce the source method to General History, but the course resisted everything new — except more names and dates. In these years, therefore, just as historians began to organize their profession in the United States, General History was a sitting duck for critics of history in the schools. Observers described it as a course in disorder: overstuffed, meaningless, and plain boring. Meeting in 1892, members of the Conference on History, Civil Government, and Political Economy, a subcommittee of the famous Committee of Ten on Secondary School Subjects, recorded their fears that the class was turning students away from the study of history altogether. "The opinion of the Conference is decidedly against single courses in general history," they reported, "because it is almost impossible to carry them on without the study degenerating into a mere assemblage of dates and names."[17]

On came the American Historical Association. From the beginning of their organized existence as a profession, historians in the AHA wanted to get rid of General History. In 1899, the report of the organization's Committee of Seven, the first group of college historians to review systematically the condition of history in high schools, made the course anathema. The committee found General History offered in about half of the over two hundred schools it surveyed in 1897; by 1915, reports to the United States Commissioner of Education from over seven thousand schools indicated that only 5% were still teaching the course. Instead, the new order in schools across the country was the four-block curriculum recommended by the Committee of Seven: (1) ancient history, (2) European history, (3) English history, and (4) American history. These were the good old days. "Those in charge of these schools had so much confidence and faith in the leadership of the American Historical Association," recalled Rolla M. Tryon in 1935, "that they almost ceased merely *offering* history, but *required* it instead." Scholars have described a period of cooperation between colleges and schools in curriculum making that began in 1884. For historians, this defeat of General History was evidence of their own breakthrough of influence in high schools. The course, it seemed, was gone with the wind. "It was eliminated root and branch," a midwestern professor commented in 1919, "and the space which it once occupied has since been so covered that few, if any, of the later generation of school pupils know of its former existence."[18]

However, this was not the final solution to the General History problem. After America's crusade for democracy in the First World War, some educators called for a return to world history — the term "world" history was now used in part to distinguish the subject from the old, discredited General History — in order to prepare citizens for the nation's new international involvements. In 1919, the National Education Association (NEA) asked the AHA for recommendations to adjust school work to this wider conception of citizenship education. What followed was an important episode in AHA history in which historians renounced all association with the world history idea and school teachers took it up in their place.

What was involved was the report of the AHA Committee on History and Education for Citizenship in Schools. During 1919–20, committee members debated two ideas of world history, both a response — in different ways — to the war experience. One, which set the new direction for the subject in schools, was the idea of world history as the story of democracy, a progressive version of the Whig interpretation of history in which the human past became, as someone has described it, "American history pushed back through time." This approach, in effect, gave Eurocentrism a new lease on life in world history, with the theme of democratic development in the west taking the place of the old themes of religion and race. Conversely, the other idea, a reflection of the crisis of confidence caused by the Great War, was an expression of the loss of faith in western values. Here began the reaction against Eurocentrism in world history. Influential, in this connection, was the work of H. G. Wells, *The Outline of History*, calling in 1920 for world history in schools as a basis for a world community of understanding and belief. The AHA committee, however, wanted no part of this world "religion," recommending instead a tenth-grade world survey based on a "growth of democracy" theme. But the AHA wanted no part of this either. Members opposed anything resembling the old General History, and, with widespread resistance to the committee recommendation, the organization decided to stick to the friendly old Committee of Seven curriculum.[19]

However, these good old days of AHA influence in the schools were numbered. The early grip of history on the curriculum can be explained in part by the fact that the history profession got into the schools first, establishing a virtual monopoly in humane studies long before the social science disciplines organized their own efforts to crack the curriculum. What broke this monopoly was not only the crush of these new competitors, but the influence as well of the so-called New History, developed by historians of the progressive movement to make the study of the past useful to public life in the present. Historian of education Hazel W. Hertzberg has explained how educators during the period of the First World War brought this New History together with ideas of citizenship education to form the social studies movement. In the work of the Committee on Social Studies of the Commission on the Reorganization of Secondary Education (in which secondary teachers outnumbered college professors), established by the National Education Association in 1913, the father of the New History, James Harvey Robinson, stole the show with his ideas on recent history as instruction for democratic citizenship. Members complained of the Committee of Seven curriculum as being too academic for this kind of practical teaching, too remote from problems of contemporary life, and too much an instrument of "college domination" over the schools. "The customary four units," asserted the committee report in 1916, "which have been largely fixed in character by the traditions of the historian and the requirements of the college, are more or less discredited as ill adapted to the requirements of secondary education."[20] Over the following years, this committee's proposals for a new social studies curriculum did battle with the old Committee of Seven subjects. The result was a "terrific overhauling" of the secondary curriculum, which broke the influence of the history profession in schools and brought on the reign of the social studies.

The social studies, a term used originally to describe offerings in history, civics, and political economy, became more broadly defined after the turn of the century as "the social sciences simplified for pedagogical purposes." From this conception came the professional mythology of the "education men" of the schools and teachers colleges as specialists in course-making and curricula in the field. If history and the social sciences were the subject matter of university scholars, they asserted, social studies was the subject matter of teachers and educators. In this way, the struggle of education reformers for the social studies was a struggle against the influence of historians in the schools. In 1921, reform leaders established the National Council for the Social Studies (NCSS) as the professional organization of social studies teachers. From now on, remarked a reformer, the curriculum was the business of educators.[21] One result, as described below, was the return of the once and future course in world history. Swept from the schools during the rise of history professionals, the course returned with the rise of professional educators. If, therefore, the passing of General History marked the rise of AHA influence in secondary education, this second coming of world history was a sign of its decline.

Visiting high schools during 1923–24, Columbia University Teachers College historian J. Montgomery Gambrill found principals caught up everywhere in curriculum making. The squeeze was on. With subjects old and new clamoring for space, these educators worked to compress subject matter into new social studies offerings. In this, the discipline of history, still dominant, served them as the integrating subject for social studies material — but Gambrill did not like the form of history that some were using. His complaint: General History was coming back. This new tenth-grade course, he lamented, was too much like the old one, "overwhelmingly European in content and point of view," with none of the sweep and spirit that H. G. Wells tried to bring to the subject:

> Any one who has the opportunity of visiting schools and making inquiries will soon learn that very often the new course is introduced simply to cover as much ground as possible in the one year of history other than American which is offered, and that the . . . conflicting demands of other social studies are the real explanation, rather than any recognition of a World Community or of the need for a new world history. Such a practice is simply a reversion to the old "general history" so vigorously attacked a generation ago and for many years so completely discredited.

Historians objected that the course had no recommendation from any of their organizations. To some educators, however, it was "the answer to the curriculum-maker's prayers." The subject and the social studies just seemed to go together. "The world story naturally brings in world geography," a school principal told Gambrill; "the world-wide race contacts permit a natural introduction of all required sociology; the historical development of governmental and economic problems furnishes more concrete material for elementary study of political science and economics than the textbook presentation based almost entirely on recent or present-day government and economic questions."[22] Further, this world story made room not only for other subjects but also for other histories. "Here was a one-year course into which could be compressed all that was worthwhile which had formerly been taught in ancient, medieval and modern, and English history," remarked another educator. "A three-year course in one to be taught on the sophomore level in high school seemed almost too good to be true." Thus in 1924 the History Curricula Inquiry, organized by the AHA to examine the crumbling of the Committee of Seven curriculum, reported that world history was feeding on other history offerings, and that, as a result, separate courses in ancient, medieval, and English history were dwindling in number. The Inquiry found American history — as much a fixture in the classroom as Old Glory — taught in all of the 504 high schools that it surveyed; in contrast world history, as yet, was taught in only eighty. But even this slow advance of the subject contrasted significantly with what appeared to be a larger retreat of history subjects in general. "It does seem to be true," concluded Inquiry chairman Edgar Dawson, "that as leadership in the making of curricula passes from the Committee of Seven to the NEA Committee on Social Studies, the amount of history other than that of the United States tends to decrease."[23]

Professors complained of a power grab by educators and lamented the passing of a history of cooperation between academic scholars and secondary teachers in forming history programs. Hazel Hertzberg, however, in her study of the social studies movement, identified these complaints as part of a mythology among historians of a golden age of history in public schools, which, as they perceive it, was suddenly ended by the barbarian invasions of educationists and administrators. In fact, this parting between historians and social studies teachers, Hertzberg explains, was more civilized, with cooperation between the AHA and NCSS continuing across the growing distance between universities and high schools. Over time, however, unfamiliarity bred contempt. Hertzberg notes that historians lost interest in pedagogy and made "education" and "social studies" terms of opprobrium. Educators, in turn, belittled historians in ivory towers. "These specialists," one remarked in 1934, "have been viewed, perhaps justly, in education circles as remote from classroom activities and experimental and progressive activity, as conservative or even reactionary, and as uncooperative or even hostile to schoolmen."[24] So descended the sheepskin curtain.

As this curtain came down, however, world history course enrollment went up, and up. Observers traced the steady rise of enrollments in the class. In 1934 student numbers reached a half million (12% of all pupils in grades nine to twelve), marking the breakthrough of world history as the leading course in "foreign" (read non-American) history. The drawing power of this one-year survey, authorities concluded, was not in the appeal of its subject matter but in the opportunity that it offered students to avoid two years of work in other foreign history areas. Thus the success of world history was both preserving instruction in non-American history and reducing the amount of time that pupils were devoting to the study of history in general. The United States Office of Education reported in 1934 that enrollment gains in world history, in fact, were making up for losses in all other foreign histories:

> Within the history groups of subjects the evidence indicates . . . that American
> history has been largely holding its own, English history has almost been elimi-
> nated, and two-year sequences in foreign history are gradually giving way to
> one-year courses in world history. . . . While the percentages of pupils studying
> foreign history might at first sight suggest a falling off in number of pupils
> reached, more careful examination of the data does not justify such a conclu-
> sion. Pupils are now much more often than some years ago giving only one
> year to study of the history of foreign nations, but, owing to the rapid rise of
> world history, the proportion of the pupils who are exposed to foreign history at
> some place in their high school courses appears not to have diminished.[25]

By 1949 the numbers in world history, over 870,000 students (16%), were much
greater than those in all other foreign history courses combined (4%) — and rising. From nearly 59% of all tenth graders in 1949, world history enrollments
reached over 69%, a million and a half students, by 1961. "The one-year course
in world history," reported an educator, "has emerged as the model offering next
in popularity to American history."[26] Thus, at the beginning of the 1960s, history
in high schools was standing on two legs. One was the eleventh-grade course in
American history, a national institution, made compulsory by law in many
states, and safeguarded everywhere by civic and patriotic organizations. The
other was world history. This course, in terms of enrollment, was one of the
great success stories in the history of American education; in terms of everything
else, it was a running failure. Students declared it to be too aimless; teachers,
too boundless; educators, too stale. In 1949, NCSS president Dorothy McClure
identified the course as the sick man of the social studies curriculum. "Random
surveys of opinion among teachers and students alike," she remarked, "indicate
that perhaps no other part of the social studies program is more criticized than
the one-year, elective world history course." Making his rounds of high schools,
James Bryant Conant in 1958 reported "widespread disappointment" with the
class. Education critic Martin Mayer, after his own survey in 1961, described it
as the course "everyone hates."[27] So fared world history when, in the same year,
Stavrianos called teachers to a new global approach to the subject.

These criticisms of the world history class were part of a larger and more powerful attack at this period on the condition of secondary education in America.
Critics spoke of a "failure by comparison," an incapacity of schools to match the
rigor of Soviet education in teaching fundamental skills. After Sputnik in 1957,
this criticism widened into a wholesale condemnation of the "progressive" curriculum in the United States. This was the background to a "decade of experiment" during which, as indicated earlier, various funded "projects," based
mainly in universities, worked on methods to bring new toughness and stimulation to school subjects. One result was the development of the "new social studies," designed to involve students in critical thinking and the celebrated "discovery method." Another was the effort to give relevance to the curriculum by
opening it to the "issues" of the 1960s. Involved in this was the effort of Stavri-

anos's World History Project at Northwestern to bring "globalism" to the world history course. This course, since its rebirth in the movement for citizenship education after the First World War, had little internal development. Instruction concentrated on the evolution of western democracy, with more and more "ground covering" of other world areas added on over the years. Against this, the small band of critics calling for a more international approach made little progress.[28] Now, however, in a period of popular fascination with the new space age, the course appeared more vulnerable to change.

Future historians are likely to make much of this impact of space on American education. As if conjured up by the magic of the first photographs from space of the blue planet, movements appeared to advocate the education of youth in global consciousness. Most wanted to bring a global perspective to the whole curriculum, and, in this connection, Stavrianos's work with the world history course was but a small part of a larger design. All global studies movements were together, however, in using the woeful reputation of this course to beat their opponents over the head and to explain why Americans were ignorant of world affairs. The quaint little Eurocentric world that boys and girls learned about in schools, argued one of these global educators, was no longer the world they lived in:

> For over one hundred years there has been some form of teaching about people outside America's geographical borders in both elementary and secondary schools. All of us have traced the storied Nile to its source while learning that Egypt is her gracious gift. We have memorized the Plantagent kings and sung about the Alps. Events of the 1960s, however, changed all that. The Soviet launching of Sputnik had set the USA on her ear. . . . When most of us try to recall what we were taught about human cultures from kindergarten through grade 12, we remember only United States history, the history of our own home state, and what was lumped into a bag known as "world" history, namely European, emphatically Western culture, commencing in Mesopotamia and the Nile Valley. Suddenly out of the 1960s, sprang Africa, Asia, Latin America, and Canada.[29]

Through the work of global studies movements, this idea of a wider world made inroads into the social studies. For a time, globalism was the word. In some schools, old world history offerings, once bound to western perspectives, were converted to surveys of "World Cultures." More importantly, attacks on the old Eurocentric approach now became the most familiar criticism of world history teaching. Thus the larger influence of global studies movements carried along the effort of Stavrianos to bring the ideal of "global perspective" in world history to intellectual fashion. The ideal endured, but the movements did not.

Oil crisis, pollution crisis, population crisis — these were some of the concepts that spread the idea after 1973 that an era of affluence and growth was over. "Spaceship Earth" became part of the new imagery of the global studies movements to educate pupils in the notion of global interdependence on a small and endangered planet. "We humans are all in this together," affirmed one movement leader. "The fate of some of us is quickly becoming the fate of all of us." After the Vietnam war, however, Americans were coming in from the cold of international involvements and looking to themselves. Popular writers spoke of the "big chill"; educators called it "back to basics." A poll by the National School Board Association found that public school officials ranked high the need for more instruction in basic skills, consumerism, and parenting; they ranked low the needs of global studies and world history. To them, the most important issues for the nation were domestic problems of crime, violence, and family breakdown; the least important were global problems of conflict and poverty. Spaceship Earth would not fly. By 1979, global studies movements lamented the decline of funding and the hard reality that their cause was dead at the roots.[30]

With the sharp decline of history enrollments in colleges and schools after 1970, some educators feared that the same fate was overtaking the subject of history itself. At fault, some believed, were antihistorical currents within global studies and the "new social studies." True, certain elements in global studies movements always doubted the value of history to international education. Understanding the historical causes of global problems, they believed, was less useful — and potentially more divisive — than understanding the need for world cooperation in the present. The global village was no place to dig up the past. In addition, some in the new social studies questioned the value of history in developing individual powers of analysis and conceptualization useful to problem solving in the present. To them, history instead was associated with older methods of recitation and drill, intended to compel students to memorize a body of accumulated knowledge about the past. In 1975, the Committee on the Status of History, appointed by the Organization of American Historians (OAH), reported that it found a troubling opinion in the land. "This is the widely held assumption," explained chairman Richard S. Kirkendall, "that history is not a useful subject, not useful for an individual eager to find a job and not useful for a society eager to solve its problems."[31] This report on history's time of troubles in the 1970s revived old fears among historians that the social studies were undoing history in the schools. In reality, history teachers were undoing the new social studies.

Surveys in the 1970s confirmed that the vogue of the new social studies was passing with little influence on instruction. "The decade of change and innovation in the schools," concluded a Kettering Foundation report in 1973, "had little or no lasting effect on the content of school programs or the quality of teaching and learning." The great chain of teaching was strong. As part of this triumph of teacher conservatism over the innovations of the new social studies, history continued to dominate the social studies. But lack of student interest in the subject, critics noted, appeared to have become a generational phenomenon. Americans, one remarked, were never much interested in history in the first place; now, among the young, the subject seemed to be ready for the waxworks.[32]

"Something must be done," warned an educator, "and done shortly, or world history, as well as history in general, will no longer be a part of the school curriculum." A perception that the universities were failing the schools, and that the subject of history was paying the price, was gaining strength. Responding, the AHA, OAH, and NCSS became active in programs to encourage contacts between history educators at both levels. Writing in 1978, AHA Teaching Division vice-president Warren Susman lamented the difference between the good old days, now "almost legendary," when historians involved themselves in high school matters, and the current separation between professors and teachers. "It is still *them* and *us*," he complained, "still two separate worlds, with a few tentative bridges thrown across the gap."[33]

In one way, the bridge thrown across by Stavrianos helped to open the road toward global perspective in world history. In another, it was a bridge to nowhere. As indicated, Stavrianos believed that breaking the hold of Eurocentrism over world history depended on breaking the barrier between universities and schools. In truth, however, world history in universities was as dead a language as Latin. Historians, in fact, were probably more distant from the subject than school teachers. "I liked teaching high school world history, and I wanted to be the best high school world history teacher I could be," remarked one educator, for example, in recalling his return to university to better prepare himself in the subject. "I asked for all their courses in world history. They did not have any. I suggested pasting some courses together from the catalog. They said I first had to choose a speciality." What such students did not learn in universities they could not pass on as teachers in the schools. "Thus," Stavrianos observed, "there has been a vicious circle of inadequate training at both levels, interacting back and forth between high school and college, and preventing substantial progress all along the line." Teachers taught the world history they knew. In sum, they taught European history.[34] By 1965, Stavrianos, in response, was planning a graduate program at Northwestern to produce future teachers in world history. However, events within the university (not discussed here) caused him to put these plans on hold and, eventually, to take up opportunities at another institution. When, in 1973, he ended his teaching at Northwestern, America's fascination with globalism was ending as well.

Stavrianos believes today, however, that the intellectual transition from European to global perspective in world history largely has been achieved — "at least in theory." A survey in 1985 by Douglas D. Alder of current high school textbooks on the subject confirmed that, while most works continued to give priority to western history, a gradual trend was underway toward broader world coverage. However, the result, Alder observed, was much diversity in new approaches and little agreement on new content. "There seems to be no clear ideas about what to include," he remarked, "and what to leave out."[35] Thus the effect of the global approach was to discredit the old Eurocentrism, which once provided easy and familiar themes for the world history course, without replacing it with an integrating concept that historians could agree on. Having gained the whole world, the course lost its bearings. In this sense, the idea of global perspective was a form of negativism, powerful in overturning the old approach but powerless to produce a new one. Figuratively, Stavrianos spoke of global perspective as "a view from the moon"; in fact, however, a view from the moon reveals only the globe itself, with nothing human or historical in sight. Rather than solving the problem of the world history course, global perspective made it more difficult. There was nothing wrong with the Eurocentric approach to world history — except that it was not world history. Now, however, with the intellectual conversion to the global approach, teachers faced a question made more terrible by this loss of western orientation: what is world history?

Finding an answer, Stavrianos agrees, is the next task for world historians. When he wrote his high school textbook, *A Global History of Man*, in 1962, Stavrianos was involved in an "equal time" philosophy designed to counter the prevailing western approach. "At all times," he told teachers of the period, "one basic rule must be kept in mind: that no European movement or institution be treated unless non-European movements or institutions of similar magnitude and world significance also be taught." Beginning with a unified survey of the human past, his text mostly was taken up with separate chapters on different cultural regions, each approached through a "flashback technique" in which — in pursuit of "relevance" — present conditions were traced back to origins in the past. Critics objected to Stavrianos's present-mindedness, his treatment of the west as one civilization among equals, and his separate, area-studies approach to world cultures. Now, however, observers note that of all the world history textbooks produced in the era of the new social studies, only this one continues to be used widely in schools.[36] Today, Stavrianos affirms, he would write a different book. Global perspective was a first step toward global history; but most writers, he explains, simply piled global history upon western history, the new social history upon the old political history, history from below upon history from above. Thus the new approach added to the old problem: too much material and too few principles of selection. The need, Stavrianos concludes, is for historians to take the second step toward global history: the design of an integrating framework, an overarching idea of organization, which can raise up the value of the course and cut down the size. "Dare to be relevant," he urges. "Dare to omit."[37]

In 1973, at the end of the "decade of experiment" in schools, members of the Kettering Foundation commission mentioned above concluded that dissatisfaction with the world history course probably was greater than before. After this, the rising influence of the global approach made the subject still more difficult to handle for teachers and students alike. Researchers Douglas D. Alder and Matthew T. Downey, in a 1985 study on the condition of history in schools, reported: "From many quarters comes the message that the course is not well taught, is not received well by students, and is confined to the unimaginative presentation of far too much detail." Courses on ancient, European, and English history once made up a large part of the history curriculum in high schools; now this beleaguered one-year course on world history was about all that remained on the human past outside the United States.

Saving this course, Alder and Downey concluded, was the major task for teachers of history. "What the world history course needs," they affirmed, "is an adequate conceptual base."[38] After turning away from a long and hard course toward the west, the ship of world history was lost at sea. To the rescue came the World History Association. For this organization, saving world history was part of an even greater task in American education: saving the study of history itself.

IN SEARCH OF WORLD HISTORY: WILLIAM H. MCNEILL AND THE WORLD HISTORY ASSOCIATION

For the good of history, the AHA in the last century wanted to banish world history from American education. For the same reason, the World History Association (WHA) now wants to bring it back. Thus the subject once accused of deadening student interest in history is presently acclaimed as the one needed to restore it to life. In so identifying world history with the larger needs of history in the curriculum, WHA members, now numbering around 700, were taking up the cause of one of their idols in the older generation of historians. "No one would have any difficulty in explaining the rise of world history as a movement and as a field of study," remarked WHA President Kevin Reilly in 1986. "It is due to William McNeill."[39]

McNeill's book, *The Rise of the West*, winner of the National Book Award in History and Biography in 1960, gave him a place among modern masters of world history.[40] In the history profession, however, he was long a voice in the wilderness. But just as this lonely warrior came to retire from his teaching career at the University of Chicago in 1983, he was joined by the small army of the WHA. Established in the previous year, this organization represented the coming of a new generation to what had been a long and losing battle waged by McNeill (b. Vancouver, 1917), Stavrianos, and a few other isolated figures in the history profession. Importantly, the WHA was a response as well to the crisis in history enrollments, which, as indicated, had come to consciousness in the 1970s. In McNeill these young historians found someone whose prescription for world history was, at the same time, a prescription for this crisis in their discipline.

For years, McNeill had been crying world history or ruin. "Without such a course to teach the students of any and every specialism," he contended during the enrollments crunch in 1976, "the place of history in our colleges and universities is going to continue to shrink, almost for sure." Students, he asserted, simply were not listening to historians any more. Without something important and useful to teach, history professors, McNeill warned, were fated to follow classics professors down the road to irrelevance and antiquarianism. "Who besides ourselves really cares for the details that fill our learned journals and monographs?" he asked. "Why should we expect to be paid for doing things no one cares much about? Why should students listen to us? Why should anyone?"[41] So in the thought of McNeill, the continuing influence of history — and the career interests of historians — were identified with the cause of world history. Therefore, to the global ideas that the WHA inherited from Stavrianos and the international education movements of the previous period, members added a critique of things in the profession that McNeill held responsible for the crisis of history teaching in the first place: the reign of specialization, the primacy of empirical research over historical synthesis, the breakdown of the introductory course, the failure to educate youth for public duties of citizenship, and the irrelevance of much of the old Eurocentric subject matter.

The WHA, in terms of organization, came out of the effort of the AHA to turn historians and high school teachers to thoughts of cooperation. Appropriately, it was founded at the AHA annual meeting at Washington in December 1982, a meeting marking the high point of anguish over the state of university — high school relations. In spirit, however, the organization was born earlier at a Teaching Division regional conference on world history instruction at the Air Force Academy (May 12–14, 1982). There, reported an organizer, participants experienced "a definite sense of movement on behalf of the world history course which includes secondary, college, and university teachers." World historians were off to the crusades. During his own difficult struggle against an unyielding profession, McNeill had come to represent this fight for world history as a moral imperative for historians, a professional duty, "a great and holy calling." There was, he believed, a real hunger for world history out there. "Human minds," he affirmed, "yearn to understand things in the largest possible way." The present generation of historians was the first, McNeill believed, able to respond to this yearning in a serious way. Events had shaken them loose from western ethnocentrism. At the same time, these young historians were the first to be active at a period when study and description of nonwestern societies had achieved global coverage.[42] For WHA members, therefore, real world history now was possible in the classroom.

In America, however, it was not the crusading season. Gottschalk and Stavrianos began their work when universities were at ease with the federal government and Americans were at ease with their place in the world. Now, after Vietnam, universities were more wary and citizens more insular. In Washington, a new administration reflected a new mood in the nation. "The college curriculum must take the non-Western world into account," acknowledged the chairman of the National Endowment for the Humanities in 1984. "But the core of the American college curriculum — its heart and soul — should be the civilization of the West, source of the most powerful and pervasive influences on America and all of its people."[43] Internationalism runs warm and cold in the life of the country, and interest in international education runs with it. In the 1980s, advocates of world history found a cold climate in America. Within the history profession, as always, they faced a virtual nuclear winter.

As described, world history in high schools was a course that never worked. In colleges, it was a course never really tried. When, for example, an international mood in the nation after the First World War caused some voices to call on universities for world history instruction, historians instead developed the western civilization course, giving the European past a world dimension of its own. After the Second World War, educators called again for world history and international subjects to educate Americans for world leadership. "Modern man," a commission on education advised President Harry S. Truman in 1947, "needs to sense the sweep of world history in order to see his own civilization in the context of other cultures." Instead, historians and social scientists turned this time to the study of other cultures in their own context. Not the sweep of world history but the closed theaters of area studies increased in universities, adding to the proliferation of electives that expanded the curriculum in the 1960s. To Mc-Neill, this era of area studies, like the era of Eurocentric history before it, post-poned and complicated the development of a unified world approach. Indeed the increased funding for international education in this period following Sput-nik, he concluded, provided historians with the means to do what they wanted to do. They wanted to specialize. In his presidential address to the AHA in 1983, Philip D. Curtin summed up the result: "Where the field of history grew broader and richer, the training of historians grew narrower."[44]

McNeill believes that this aversion of the historical profession to world his-tory has something to do with the immensity of the subject itself. Trained to value accuracy of fact above conceptual synthesis, historians, he contends, shrink before the scale of world history. It appears, however, that some historians find the subject not so much awesome as simply too amateur. Revealing, in this connection, is a practice on some campuses where history departments provide a solitary world history course open to nonhistory majors only and offer the sub-ject in the way that colonists once offered beads to natives. Not taking the course seriously themselves, these departments make it light and breezy for stu-dents as well. Evident here is a state of mind, a presumption that world history is good enough for science majors and the football team, but not for historians in training.

Thus, to establish the subject in the curriculum, WHA members, McNeill observes, must first make world history intellectually compelling. Second, they must convince deans and administrators that — with university budgets strained — it can be taught inexpensively to large survey classes. This, he told his following in 1982, was the way in which the western civilization course swept the country during the interwar period. At this particular time, however, these young world historians were more concerned with still another possibility: namely, that western civilization was about to sweep the country again. The re-turn of Harvard University to a core curriculum in 1978 marked the coming of a chill to college campuses — the end of a period of lively curricular change and a return to the general education philosophy of a common learning and core courses. Among historians, discussions focused particularly on the old western civilization survey, a course battered and sometimes blown away by the storms of the sixties. Critics dismissed the course as something for an earlier day, a form of citizenship education intended to teach sons and daughters of old world im-migrants to identify with a common culture: one heritage, one history, one course. American values and the practice of history itself, they argued, were now too different and diverse to be contained in such a course. So was the planet we live on. "Emerging," the present writer remarked in a study of the western civi-lization course in 1982, "were other peoples, other histories, a globe of historic

diversity beyond the imagination of earlier Westerners, a cosmos where pluralism replaced the oneness of history and where human experience could not be
ordered into a unilineal pattern of development."[45] No matter. As educators revived the idea of core courses, some history departments revived the teaching of
western civilization. Who says you can't go home again?

However, the western civilization course has a special place in the imagination of WHA members. Although they want to see world history implanted at
every level of education from high school to graduate training, their time and
energy is devoted in particular to the project of replacing western civilization as
the freshman survey. In part, they are inspired by the old western civilization
success story; in part, they are troubled by the continuing hold of the course
upon the history profession. McNeill recalled that his own student encounter
with western civilization was one of the most "dazzling experiences of my life";
now, however, he believes that the whole idea of "civilization" is time-bound.
From the eighteenth century, he explains, came the idea of the west as civilization itself, the one and only, a high, singular, and unique unit in history. In the
early twentieth century, masters of world history described in turn a multiplicity
of civilizations, each different in style but alike in historical development. Now,
McNeill speculates, as modern communications transcend all boundaries, the
prospect arises that the era of civilizations is a passing phase in world history.
Thus, he concludes, the concept of civilizational units needs to be rethought;
and so does the concept of civilizational history based upon it.[46]

The civilizational approach, McNeill observes, by concentrating study on a
defined geographic area rather than the larger space over which cross-cultural
and global developments occur, divides historical experience. In contrast, world
history unites it. Therefore, world history is the proper subject for the introductory survey; equally, the survey is the proper course for world history. Specialized work in the field at advanced and graduate levels generally must focus on
specific topics and time periods. The survey, however, provides the sweep for
world history to do what only world history can do: unite the whole human past
and be total, global, and universal in time and space. In consequence, however,
the survey, more than any other course in world history, poses the old, awful
question: What is world history? So far, a compelling response has eluded the
WHA. What the organization needs, a member remarked, is "a simple, all-
encompassing, elegant idea" with the power to order all human experience.

In fact, just such an elegant idea explained the appeal of the original western civilization course. The course was based on what McNeill described as "a
great idea about the whole human past," the idea of history as the evolution of
freedom. The most compelling interpretations of the past, he observed, are
those that people want to believe in. This one, in which a flattering view of English history was elevated into a Eurocentric perception of the whole human adventure, "set the mold within which the English-speaking world has tended to
view modern times ever since."[47] To become effective classroom history, however, a great idea requires a good teacher to make it clear and simple. At Columbia University early in this century, James Harvey Robinson, father of western

civilization, formed this idea, generally known as the Whig interpretation of history, into a course that became the model for the most successful class in the history of higher education in America. However, McNeill has explained how, with time, this original vision faded, how new subject matter clouded over the old liberal theme of the progress of freedom, and how historians in the 1960s, having lost faith in western civilization ideas, gave up this grand old survey and the mass enrollments that went with it. Says McNeill, "We cut our own throats." With the waning of Whig history, he comments, historians returned to confusion about the larger shape of the past. Such was the background to the search of the WHA for another idea and another teacher.

It seems what members want is an idea of history at once global and American, something that reacts against the Eurocentrism of western civilization and yet remains "our history," a history with the kind of spirit and values that American youth want to believe in. For this reason, the two most common approaches to global analysis, modernization theory and world system methods, appear unbefitting, the first being too western, the second too much the other way around. When Cyril E. Black in 1982 advocated modernization theory as a conceptual theme for the world history survey, he was careful to explain that, contrary to received opinion, this theory was neither conditioned by western bias nor constructed on European experience. Critics, however, objected that this approach made world history appear too much the son of western civilization, a global version of western "progress," drawing again on ancient perceptions of a core civilization bringing light to a periphery in darkness. In contrast, world system theory provided quite a different analysis of core and periphery in which the west's werewolf accumulation of wealth was used to explain the poverty of almost everyone else on the planet.[48] Here critics objected that this approach would make the world history survey not an extension of the western civilization idea but a revolt against it: an antiwestern civilization course and a judgment on the west, its imperialism, its economic hegemony, and its hold over the lives of other peoples. Educators were aware that the focus of global studies on world hunger, pollution, resource exploitation, and other issues that could implicate the economic behavior of rich and developed nations made this subject matter delicate for Americans; the focus of world system theory on a historical explanation of how the world got this way would likely make the world history course more disturbing still. Stavrianos believed that a view of world history from the moon would challenge American consciousness; no doubt, a view from the Third World would challenge it even more. Western civilization, originating in friendly Whiggish ideals, and subject to little public controversy as a result, was good, consensus history for educating American youth. Compared to this, world history in world-system style is likely to appear, to some taxpayers at least, as downright subversive.

Gottschalk and UNESCO historians believed that such core–periphery theories of world history were too often theories of cultural superiority or economic exploitation. Their desire, instead, was not to take sides but to perceive, beyond human conflicts and systems of exploitation, a unified and constructive direction to the human enterprise. Where humankind is one, there is no side to take. In assuming this same attitude, WHA historians reveal themselves as heirs not only of this international education tradition, but also of the western civilization outlook; that is, of a liberal, optimistic, and progressive interpretation of the past that affirms the good American belief in human potential, cultural contacts, and open societies. To them, no one has done more than McNeill to bring world history out of European metaphysics and into the positive and practical spirit of this form of American historiography. "William H. McNeill," asserted WHA president Kevin Reilly, "has turned the study of the human past from a philosophical meditation into an empirical, historical account."[49] McNeill himself describes all histories as "mythistories," rival versions of the past, which, for those who accept them, provide collective identities and respond to human needs for belief and belonging. In this sense, his own version of world history probably can be described as the mythistory of most WHA members.

McNeill himself came to world history after "delving into the earth" of material history (his Ph.D. dissertation was on the potato). Importantly, this old history lived on in the new. His journey began in a revolt in 1939 against his graduate supervisor at Cornell, Carl Becker, and against the kind of Eurocentric history that Becker represented. On his own, he discovered first the contrasting history of eastern Europe, which aroused his interest in the diversity of cultures, and thereafter Toynbee's larger history of the world, which instilled the idea of a unity behind the whole human experience. McNeill recalled that he was "transported" by the global sweep of Toynbee's vision — but only so far. "The aspect of human life on which my attention fastened — the technological, material and ecological — was the polar opposite," he explains, "from what had come to interest Toynbee."[50] Toynbee looked to God and McNeill to the good earth.

His own world history, therefore, combined an enchantment with the sweep of the human adventure with a secular and materialist approach to subject matter. On the one hand, McNeill loved the task of high synthesis (he confides that, during ten years of research for *The Rise of the West*, he never took a note!). On the other, his works were solid and down to earth, with ideas and concepts borrowed from the same familiar sources used by most other working historians in the United States — from the social sciences, the Annales school, and the tradition of history as social process. The result was at once academic and American. Thus McNeill comments that he learned from *Annales* historians to recognize the power of geography and climate over life and mind, yet tempered this determinism by holding to his American faith in the influence of the human will in history as well. His native attitudes can be recognized too in his account of world history as the human ascent through know-how, skills, and inventions, to a position of power over the natural world. Here, in McNeill's celebration of global intercourse and enterprise, in liberal notions of a human impulse to truck and barter, in assumption of an invisible hand turning cultural contacts to larger human ends, was a world history in American dress. McNeill reports, in this connection, that he had never been at home with Toynbee's perception of civilizations as separate organisms, each alone, self-absorbed, and little affected by other peoples. Influenced by the work of American anthropologists on cultural borrowings among Native Americans, he fixed instead on the opposing thesis that cultural interaction was "the main drivewheel" of world history. Encounters with outsiders possessing superior skills, McNeill concluded, set cultures into motion to imitate or resist the stranger. So evolved the organizing idea of *The Rise of the West* in 1963: "I simply set out to identify in any given age where the center of highest skills was located," he explained. "By describing them and then asking how neighboring peoples reacted to such achievements, a comprehensive structure for successive periods of world history emerges." The result, therefore, was an approach that featured the diversity of cultures and, at the same time, ordered world history into one story.

It was also an approach with a moral dimension, a people-to-people history, concerned with cultural exchanges and the ties that bind. To Stavrianos, the world before 1500 was a lonely place of separate civilizations. To McNeill, cultural encounters broke through this separation much earlier. In *The Rise of the West,* he described how "the stimulus of contacts" was inseparable from the development of civilized life in the ancient Middle East. Rejecting the UNESCO "equal time" approach to the history of world cultures, McNeill, in this work in 1963, portrayed the ascendancy of the west as the predominant development in modern history. More recently, however, he has drawn earlier civilizations more closely together. He describes now an "ecumenical cosmopolitanism" emerging in ancient times along the cord of agrarian lands running from China into Africa and Mediterranean Europe — the so-called Eurasian ecumene. By A.D. 1000, trade routes here developed into a "sophisticated world market" where east and west came together.[51] In this perspective, the European voyages of discovery in 1500, for example, mark not the origins of world history but a further extension to the Americas of this vast Eurasian network of communications and commerce. Thus, to WHA members in search of an authentic and integral world history with particular relevance to American students, McNeill offers a version that, in settling accounts with the old Eurocentrism, provides these students at the same time with a sense of the place of their own western civilization within the longer and larger history of an ecumenical global community.

What attracts WHA members to McNeill as well is his easy gift for making the transition to this history in American education appear to be a matter of simple logic and public interest. "Surely it takes only a little common sense," he explains, "to see that some sort of world history is the only way a college can do justice to students who live in a world where events in Asia, Africa, and Latin America are as likely to involve the United States in critical actions as anything happening in Europe and North America." Indeed McNeill makes historians and their craft seem important to life. Versions of history, he observes, provide peoples with ideals and inspirations, with motivation to bond together and act in common. When believed in and acted upon, histories thus can condition and direct collective behavior. In this sense, histories are to humans what instincts are to animals. World history alone, McNeill acknowledges, is too pale and pluralistic to satisfy the depth of human needs for identity and belonging. Separate peoples need separate histories, strident histories, histories of "us" against "them," myths that unite fellow citizens against enemies. But in a nuclear age, he insists, something is needed to make up for these separate mythistories; something is needed to balance them and to nurture the sense that all peoples are world citizens as well. If historians do not take up their duty to develop this ecumenical history, he warns, the profession will have nothing important to teach, and other mythmakers will lead opinion in more dangerous directions.[52]

This summary reveals McNeill's faith in world history as something involving larger human interests and appealing to the better part of ourselves. His version of it, as described here, is compelling, ethical, American — and problematic. Scholars have noted that the process of cultural diffusion, the process on which McNeill has constructed his whole interpretation of the past, is the most difficult and debated issue in the field of world history. Indeed the great philosophers of the subject have disagreed most on the very questions of whether cultural borrowing or cultural isolation was the way of the past, and whether, as a result, unity or pluralism was the nature of human history. But one of McNeill's achievements, we have observed, was to lead the subject of world history out of such abstract quarrels in the philosophy of history. As a result, the impulse of his WHA admirers is not so much to theorize about world history as to think about how to teach it. However, if they have taken McNeill's diffusion theory as their own, some have found less satisfaction in the general theme of his work; that is, the human struggle for control over the environment, the natural world — and other humans. Certainly the pursuit of power is less "elegant" as a structuring concept than the old western civilization idea of the pursuit of liberty. Thus Ross E. Dunn, first president of the WHA, concluded in 1985 that most members still sought a more appealing vision of the world past.[53]

Neither Stavrianos nor McNeill left disciples at Northwestern and the University of Chicago to continue the development of the world history courses that they taught there. And although these two pioneers of world history in American education remain active in retirement, the further elaboration of their design for the subject probably depends now on their WHA offspring who continue to work the classroom. Thus the question, "What is world history?" passes to the next generation. Important here is the fact that this new interest in world history came on the heels of a vast expansion of history fields in the 1960s and 1970s. The WHA, as a result, is an ingathering of historians of all kinds, with many engaged, in their own way, in shaping the world history course in the image of their own fields. Therefore, the struggle to define world history is also a struggle for turf. One WHA member, for example, dismissed another's textbook on international history as "too political" for use in world history instruction. The proper subject of world history, this social historian explained, was social contacts, not political affairs; it was the everyday life of common people, not the military power of nations. The international historian disagreed — by half. Wrote he: "Let our students be exposed to both perspectives — world history from the bottom up, international history from the top down, if you will — through a multiplicity of texts and assigned readings."[54] The more the better. Thus, in the new organization, world historians find themselves in the same old double bind: they have too much history to put into one course and not enough agreement on what history to take out of it.

During a tour of campuses in 1985, however, AHA president Carl H. Degler noted the spreading influence of the new organization. "I was surprised," he reported, "by the rising interest in courses in world history." Degler found most departments were recovering on their own from the decline in student numbers; most were still leaning heavily on the western civilization course; and most still had the same old doubts about world history. But most also believed that the subject was coming nevertheless. "Even the most conservative departments," he concluded, "including those with a limited number of faculty, display a growing sense of the need to look beyond Europe and its offspring in North America." In the same year, after debate at a national conference on the question of the introductory course in history — western civilization or world history? — Professor Richard E. Sullivan reported the same verdict. "I predict that one of the prime messages conveyed to our colleges across the country," he remarked, "is the necessity — perhaps even the urgent necessity — to consider developing a world history course as a substitute for a western civilization course."[55]

"World history," McNeill observed, "was once taken for granted as the only sensible basis for understanding the past." It seems some historians now think so again. Dr. Johnson said that second marriages represent the triumph of hope over experience. Hope for this second time around between historians and world history depends in large part on a realistic assessment of the problems and limitations of world history as a course of study. As indicated in comments here on Gottschalk and the UNESCO project, the subject has always promised more than it can deliver. Others have warned historians of a high price to pay. Richard Sullivan, for example, commented that a conversion to freshman world history would require teachers to acquire a whole new knowledge base and "survey wisdom." It would mean more abstraction, more synthesis, more "teaching by generalization," more techniques borrowed from the social sciences. It would mean, in Sullivan's terms, a focus on history of a different kind: "long term processes in place of accretive events, commonalities in place of lineality, collectivities in place of individuals, structure in place of conscious choices, problems in place of shared values." All this, Sullivan concludes, will mean "revolutionary changes" for a history profession raised on inductive methods.[56] As the previous section on Stavrianos indicates, however, revolutionary changes are not academic style. Probably, given the conservatism of educators, the WHA must somehow make world history come easy to American teachers and students, or it will not come at all.

Thus, in effect, the question, "What is world history?" can be reduced to another: What is world history in the United States? Gottschalk learned two things from his UNESCO experience: first, that future world history must focus more on the nonwestern world; and, second, that each nation, at the same time, must work out a version of this history appropriate to its own people.[57] These are the directions in which Stavrianos and McNeill have led the world history survey. In conception, the general advance is toward a course that is neither global history in pure form nor western civilization in world dimension. It is something in between. Beyond this, it seems that the search for an elegant and meaningful idea behind the human experience on earth, a search probably as old as human thought, is likely to continue as long as the subject of world history itself. Finally, then, what is world history in the United States? It is not everything that some historians claim it to be, but it is something that more historians should try to teach.

Notes

1. Eric H. Monkkenen, "The Dangers of Synthesis," *American Historical Review* (hereafter cited as *AHR*) 91 (1986): 1149. Andrew D. White, "On Studies in General History and the History of Civilizations," *Papers of the American Historical Association* 1 (1885): 8.

2. Marshall Hodgson, "Interregional History as an Approach to World History," *Cahiers d'histoire mondiale (Journal of World History*, published by UNESCO, hereafter cited as *CHM*) 1 (1954): 716. H. G. Wells, *The Outline of History*, 2 vols. (London, 1920), 2: v. Lord Acton, "Letter to Contributors to the *Cambridge Modern History*," in *Lord Acton: Essays in the Liberal Interpretation of History: Selected Papers*, ed. William H. McNeill (Chicago, 1967), 398. Jacques Benigne Bossuet, *Discourse on Universal History*, ed. Orest Ranum (Chicago, 1976), 4.

3. Hugh Trevor-Roper, "Arnold Toynbee's Millennium," *Encounter* 8 (1957): 14.

4. William H. McNeill, "The World History Survey Course," in 1982 *World History Teaching Conference*, ed. Joe C. Dixon and Neil D. Martin (Colorado Springs, 1983), 5. Warren I. Susman, "Annapolis Conference on the Introductory Course," *AHA Perspectives* 20 (1982): 23.

5. L. S. Stavrianos, "A Global Perspective in the Organization of World History," in *New Perspectives in World History: 34th Yearbook of the National Council for the Social Studies*, ed. Shirley H. Engle (Washington, D.C., 1964), 616.

6. Bernard S. Cohn, "Anthropology and History in the 1980s," *Journal of Interdisciplinary History* 12 (1981): 231. Edwin J. Van Kley, "Europe's 'Discovery' of China and the Writing of World History," *AHR* 76 (1971): 385.

7. Eric R. Wolf, *Europe and the People without History* (Berkeley, 1982), 5.

8. On the idea of world history as utopian literature, see W. Warren Wagar, *The City of Man: Prophecies of a World Civilization in Twentieth Century Thought* (Boston, 1963). Geoffrey Barraclough, "Universal History," in *Approaches to History*, ed. H. R. Finberg (London, 1962), 88, 101.

9. L. S. Stavrianos, "The Teaching of World History," *HT* 3 (1969): 24.

10. L. S. Stavrianos, "From 'Why World History' to 'What World History'?" *Social Education* (hereafter cited as *SE*) 39 (1975): 362. Stavrianos's world optimism is best expressed in his *The Promise of the Coming Dark Age* (San Francisco, 1976); it is more tempered in *Global Rift: The Third World Comes of Age* (New York, 1981).

11. L. S. Stavrianos, "Project for Research and Teaching in World History" (grant application, 1957), in the papers of Dean of Faculties Payton S. Wild, Northwestern University Archives.

12. L. S. Stavrianos to Northwestern University Faculty, memorandum, April 14, 1961, Wild Papers, Northwestern University Archives. Stavrianos's plans for global studies at Northwestern are outlined in his "Memorandum to the History Department: World History Project" (1958), and "Project for the Introduction of Globally-Oriented Introductory Courses" (1961), in the papers of the Dean of the College of Liberal Arts, Simeon E. Leland, Northwestern University Archives.

13. Gray C. Boyce, "Department of History: Annual Report, 1958–59," Leland Papers, Northwestern University Archives.

14. William Swinton, *Outlines of the World's History: Ancient, Medieval and Modern* (New York, 1874), 3, 4. Samuel G. Goodrich, *Outlines of Chronology: Ancient and Modern* (Boston, 1828), 201. On the origins and spread of General History, see John E. Stout, *The Development of High School Curricula in the North Central States from 1860 to 1918* (Chicago, 1921), 174–79; William F. Russell, "The Entrance of History into the Curriculum of the Secondary School," *History Teachers' Magazine* 5 (1914): 311–18; and Calvin O. Davis, "Public Secondary Education in Michigan: Its History and Contemporary Tendencies" (Ph.D. dissertation, Harvard University, 1914), 59–66, 262.

15. Philip V. N. Myers, *A General History for Colleges and High Schools* (Boston, 1889), 2.

16. Alexander C. Flick, "Content of World History Courses in Schools and Colleges," *Proceedings of the Association of History Teachers of the Middle States and Maryland*, no. 25 (1927), 60–61. Albert Bushnell Hart, *History in High and Preparatory Schools* (Syracuse, 1887), 5–6.

17. National Education Association, *Report of the Committee on Secondary School Subjects* (Washington, 1893), 174. Albert Bushnell Hart, "Conference on History, Civil Government and Political Economy: Preliminary Report, January 13, 1893" (typescript), Charles W. Eliot papers, Harvard University Archives. Mary D. Sheldon, *Studies in General History* (Boston, 1895). For a description of daily instruction in a General History class at this period, see Stuart MacKibbin, "Outline Course of Study in History," *Education* 10 (1889): 164–66.

18. Calvin O. Davis, "A Course in World History," *The Historical Outlook* (hereafter cited as *HO*) 10 (1919): 453. Rolla M. Tryon, *The Social Sciences as School Subjects: Report of the Commission on the Social Studies* (New York, 1935), 177. American Historical Association, *The Study of History in Schools: Report to the American Historical Association by the Committee of Seven* (New York, 1899). For a rearguard defense of General History as a course preserving the unity of history, see Lucy M. Salmon, "Unity in College Entrance History," *Educational Review* 12 (1896): 165–68; and Edward Van Dyke Robinson, "An Ideal Course in History for Secondary Schools," *The School Review* 6 (1898): 672–78. On college-school cooperation in this period, see Edward A. Krug, *The Shaping of the American High School* (Madison, 1969).

19. Daniel C. Knowlton, "Report of the Committee on History and Education for Citizenship: Syllabus for Modern History in the Tenth Grade," *HO* 12 (1921): 165–84.

20. National Education Association, *The Social Studies in Secondary Education: Report of the Committee on Social Studies of the Commission on the Reorganization of Secondary Education* (Washington, 1916), 40. Hazel W. Hertzberg, *Social Studies Reform, 1880–1980* (Boulder, n.d.), 27.

21. Harold O. Rugg, letter published in *HO* 12 (1921): 184–89.

22. J. Montgomery Gambrill, "Some Tendencies and Issues in the Making of Social Studies Curricula," *HO* 15 (1924): 54; and "The New World History," *HO* 18 (1927):

267. Observers first noted the return of the General History survey in 1919. Arley B. Show, "One or Two Years of European History in High Schools?" *HO* 10 (1919): 283.

23. Edgar Dawson, "The History Inquiry," *HO* 15 (1924): 269. A. K. King, "Is World History as Successful as We Thought It Would Be?" *High School Journal* 20 (1937): 185.

24. E. M. Hunt, "The Conclusions and Recommendations of the Commission on the Social Studies of the American Historical Association," *The Social Studies* (hereafter cited as *SS*) 25 (1934): 282. Hertzberg, 65–92 (n. 43 above). Arthur E. Bestor, *Educational Wastelands: The Retreat from Learning in Our Public Schools* (Urbana, 1953), 44, 103.

25. U.S. Office of Education, *Offerings and Registrations in High School Subjects: 1933–1934*, Bulletin no. 6 (Washington, 1938), 6. Arthur Dillman Gray, "The One Year Course in World History," *HO* 23 (1932): 407–9.

26. Edgar B. Wesley, "The Potentialities of World History in a World Society," in *Improving the Teaching of World History*, ed. Edith West (Washington, 1949), 1. William E. Pulliam, *The Status of World History Instruction in American Secondary Schools* (Washington, 1972), 8, 15–16, 20. In 1961, according to Pulliam, world history was taught in 87% of all four-year high schools, American history in 93%, modern Europe in 4%, and ancient and medieval Europe in 3%.

27. Martin Mayer, *Where, When, and Why? Social Studies in American Schools* (New York, 1962), 22. James Bryant Conant, *The American High School Today* (New York, 1959), 42. Dorothy McClure, "Needed Revisions in World History Programs," in West, ed. (n. 49 above), 25.

28. For a remarkable example of this criticism, anticipating present arguments for the "global" approach, see Marshall Hodgson, "World History and a World Outlook," *SS* 35 (1944): 297–301. Elmer Ellis, "The Permanence of Learning in World History," *SS* 25 (1934): 133–36.

29. Betty Bullard, "Personal Statement to the President's Commission on Foreign Language and International Studies," *President's Commission on Foreign Language and International Studies: Background Papers and Studies* (Washington, D.C., 1979), 2. On global education movements, see James M. Becker, ed. *Schooling for a Global Age* (New York, 1979), 245–336.

30. *Strength through Wisdom: A Critique of United States Capability. A Report to the President from the President's Commission on Foreign Language and International Studies* (Washington, 1979), 1, 9, 16–17. James H. Mecklenburger, *What Priority for Global Education: A National School Board Association Survey of School Board Members and School Superintendents* (Washington, 1979), 1–12. James M. Becker and Gerald Marker, *A Final Report on the Mid-America Program for Global Perspectives in Education* (Bloomington, 1979), 1.

31. Richard S. Kirkendall, "The Status of History in the Schools," *Journal of American History* 62 (1975): 563; and "More History, Better History," *SE* 40 (1976): 449. On the new social studies, see John D. Haas, *The Era of the New Social Studies* (ERIC, 1977).

32. Fred M. Hechinger, "Waxworks History," *Saturday Review* (May 29, 1976). *The Reform of Secondary Education: A Report to the Public and the Profession: The National Commission on the Reform of Secondary Education, Established by the Charles F. Kettering Foundation* (New York, 1973), 7. For surveys on the decline of the new social studies, see James P. Shaver, G. L. Davis, and Suzanne W. Helburn, "The Status of Social Studies Education," *SE* 43 (1979): 150–53, and Richard E. Gross, "The Status of the Social Studies in the Public Schools of the United States," *SE* 41 (1977): 194–200.

33. Warren Susman, "Report of the Vice-President, Teaching Division," *AHA Annual Report: 1978* (Washington, 1979), 58. Pulliam (n. 49 above), 79.

34. L. S. Stavrianos, "New Viewpoints in Teaching World History" (paper presented to the NCSS, November 25, 1961), 6–7; "World History Program: Northwestern University" (grant report, 1959), Wild Papers, Northwestern University Archives. Howard Mehlinger, "World History in Secondary Education," *1982 World History Teaching Conference* (Colorado Springs, 1983), 8–9.

35. Douglas D. Alder, "World History Textbooks for the Secondary Schools," (typescript, 1986), 11.

36. Howard Mehlinger (n. 57 above), 10. L. S. Stavrianos, Loretta Kreider Andrews, John R. McLane, Frank R. Safford, and James E. Sheridan, *A Global History of Man* (Boston, 1962). Stavrianos's original ideas on the structure of world history were outlined in the introduction to this text. They are elaborated in his "Technology as a Central Theme for World History," in *Proceedings: The Conference on Technology in World History, Aspen, June 14–15, 1985*, ed. John P. Mueller (Greeley, Colo., 1986), 1–6.

37. L. S. Stavrianos to the author, March 5, 1987.

38. Douglas D. Adler and Matthew T. Downey, "Problem Areas in the History Curriculum," in *History in the Schools*, ed. Matthew T. Downey (Washington, D.C., 1985), 14, 16. On recent trends in world history enrollments, see Douglas D. Alder, "Is World History Disappearing?" (typescript).

39. Kevin Reilly, *World History Bulletin* 4 (1987): 1 (this newsletter of the WHA is cited hereafter as *WHB*).

40. William H. McNeill, *The Rise of the West: A History of the Human Community* (Chicago, 1963).

41. William H. McNeill, "A Defense of World History," and "Beyond Western Civilization: Rebuilding the Survey," in *Mythistory and Other Essays* (Chicago, 1986), 94, 105.

42. William H. McNeill, "A Defense of World History," 93, and "The Rise of the West as a Long-Term Process," 43, in *Mythistory*. The Teaching Division conference proceedings were published by the Air Force Academy, *1982 World History Teaching Conference*. Kevin Reilly describes the founding meeting in Washington in "World History Association Established," *AHA Perspectives* 21 (1983): 7. Four sessions at the 1982 AHA meeting were devoted to teaching issues. The gloom at these proceedings over university–high school relations is reported by David Felix in *Network News Exchange* 8 (1983): 2.

43. William J. Bennett, *To Reclaim a Legacy: A Report on the Humanities in Higher Education* (Washington, D.C., 1984), 39.

44. Philip D. Curtin, "Depth, Span, and Relevance," *AHR* 80 (1984): 1. McNeill, "The World History Survey Course," *1982 World History Teaching Conference*, 3. *Higher Education for American Democracy: A Report of the President's Commission on Higher Education* (New York, 1947), 17.

45. Gilbert Allardyce, "The Rise and Fall of the Western Civilization Course," *AHR* 87 (1982): 717. McNeill, "The World History Survey Course" (n. 4 above), 4.

46. William H. McNeill, "The Era of Civilizations in World History," *WHB* 4 (1986–87): 1–4. On world history as graduate study, see the paper of Jerry H. Bentley on the new Ph.D. field in world history (inspired by the comparative approach of Philip Curtin) at the University of Hawaii, "Graduate Education and Research in World History," *WHB* 5 (1988): 3–7.

47. William H. McNeill, "Introduction" to *Lord Acton* (n. 2 above), xviii. McNeill, "Beyond Western Civilization: Rebuilding the Survey," 101–2.

48. Craig A. Lockard, "Global History, Modernization, and World System Approach: A Critique," and Cyril E Black, "Modernization as an Organizing Principle for

World History," in 1982 *World History Teaching Conference*, 55–67, 69–83. On modernization theory, see Black's *The Dynamics of Modernization: A Study in Comparative History* (New York, 1966). On world system analysis, see Immanuel Wallerstein, *The Modern World System: Capitalist Agriculture and the Origins of the European World-Economy in the Sixteenth Century* (New York, 1974).

49. Kevin Reilly (n. 62 above), 1.

50. William H. McNeill, "Arnold J. Toynbee," in *Mythistory*, 197. McNeill recounts his intellectual development in the essays republished in *Mythistory*.

51. William H. McNeill, "The Rise of the West as a Long-Term Process," in *Mythistory*, 64. The concept of an Eurasian ecumene was first proposed by anthropologist A. L. Kroeber and developed by Marshall Hodgson. See Hodgson, "Hemispheric Interregional History as an Approach to World History," *CHM* 1 (1954): 715–23.

52. William H. McNeill, "Mythistory, or Truth, Myth, History, and Historians," in *Mythistory*, 13–17.

53. Ross E. Dunn, "The Challenge of Hemispheric History," *HT* 18 (1985): 329–38. For a good discussion on the problems of diffusion theories in world history, see Matthew Melko, "The Interaction of Civilizations: An Essay," *CHM* 11 (1969): 559–77. Critics have cited McNeill's spare coverage of isolated pre-Columbian America as evidence of the limits of his diffusion theory. He defends this approach to the world history course in "World History in the Schools," *New Movements in the Study and Teaching of History*, ed. Martin Ballard (London, 1970), 16–25.

54. See the reply of William R. Keylor, "World History and International History," *WHB* 3 (1985): 3, to the review by Joe Gowaskie of Keylor's *The Twentieth-Century World: An International History* (New York, 1984), in *WHB* 2 (1984): 8.

55. Richard E. Sullivan, "Summary Statement," in *What Americans Should Know: Western Civilization or World History?: Proceedings of a Conference at Michigan State University, April 21–23, 1985*, ed. Josef W. Konvitz (East Lansing, 1985), 260. Carl H. Degler, "How Fares History: A Personal and Impressionistic Report, Part II," *AHA Perspectives* 25 (1987): 4–6.

56. Richard E. Sullivan (n. 78 above), 262–63.

57. Louis Gottschalk, "Projects and Concepts of World History in the Twentieth Century" (n. 16 above), 14–15.

CRAIG A. LOCKARD

The Contributions of Philip Curtin and the "Wisconsin School" to the Study and Promotion of Comparative World History

America's new position in the world after 1945 called for a new perspective. . . . Our earlier view of world history was . . . distorted . . . Instead of trying to explain the modern world in terms of its past, or even tracing the rise of human civilizations, the older history began with the United States. It then searched for the roots of American civilization. It was, in effect, "history taught backward" — back to the colonial period on this continent, then back to Europe, and still further back to the western Middle Ages, Rome, Greece, and the ancient civilizations of the Near East. This pattern of "world history" not only moved through time, it moved through space as well, hopping a quarter of the way around the earth from Mesopotamia to America. It was not even the history of our own ancestors. . . . This "world history" was really the history of those peoples from whom we borrowed most of our technology and culture that later developed into American civilization. By any objective standard, it was a very distorted view of world history, but it served a purpose. It *did* help to explain the origins of the modern American way of life. It was therefore distorted for a sufficient reason. The danger of misunderstanding enters only when we forget that it *was* distorted and come to believe that it is really the history of the modern world. . . . We were not even trying to teach world history — only American history pushed back through time.[1]

Amidst the retrospective in the recent quincentennial year it seems appropriate to assess the contributions of one of America's most distinguished and catholic historians,[2] pioneer in the study of both Atlantic history, a field only made possible by the voyages of 1492 and after, and comparative world history. Philip Curtin's teaching career was divided between African and Caribbean history, his first loves and initial specializations, and a variety of broader transatlantic, global and comparative courses at the graduate and undergraduate level. Hence he inspired in many of his students, and the readers of his many books and articles, not only an enthusiasm for, and understanding of, the history of

Craig A. Lockard, "The Contributions of Philip Curtin and the 'Wisconsin School' to the Study and Promotion of Comparative World History," *Journal of Third World Studies* 11, no. 1 (1994): 180–82, 199–211, 219–23.

Africa and the African diaspora, but the larger interregional picture of historical change, in the Atlantic realm and in the wider world. Curtin's commitment to a comparative global perspective constituted an early and sustained thrust in what has become an ongoing and often bitter conflict about what historians and history departments ought to emphasize as their core offerings to students, many of whom suffer from historical illiteracy, as well as the most appropriate framework for scholarly analysis.

During the 1980s in particular a debate raged between two broad camps vying for influence on American college and university campuses. On one side are the proponents of teaching Western Civilization, often with a stress on the "Great Books" of the Western heritage. The rationale of these scholars (and the political leaders and media pundits who support them) is that American students must comprehend the dominant Europe-derived cultural and intellectual underpinnings of this country before they can begin to grasp those of others. On the other side are those arguing for a broader global perspective; they contend that not only do Americans live in a multicultural and increasingly interdependent world, they live in a multicultural nation whose inhabitants derive from many parts of the globe. Hence they believe that a grounding in Western civilization, however valuable, is insufficient for an understanding of this country, much less the entire world. Some historians, Curtin among them, have argued that a Eurocentric or Westerncentric perspective promotes a narrow and misleading view of historical change and hence of the wider world. This debate has been fought in curriculum committees, on the pages of scholarly journals, on panels at academic conferences, and even in the national and state political arenas. . . .

There are, of course, some serious methodological problems in conceptualizing world history and selecting an appropriate analytical framework. As one globalist puts it: "we concede that world history is conceptually difficult but we insist that it is teachable."[3] The subject is immensely broad. Hence there is the danger, as Curtin warns, that a world history course will become little more than a brief overview at a very high level of generalization without coherence.[4] This provides a serious challenge, since it is indeed hard to master all of the knowledge required. The solution is to find the threads and patterns of global or semiglobal or long-term significance to serve as focal points; this renders world history more than the sum of its parts. This historian must focus on certain relevant aspects of reality and pass others by, identifying common patterns and neglecting exceptions. In other words, world history must be more about the forest than the individual trees, no matter how fascinating.[5] But there are no agreed upon criteria among global historians; what to consider and what to omit remain matters for debate.[6]

But some consensus does exist among global historians that the story of human beings over the broad sweep of history does have some basic unity; most would also concur with McNeill that interaction between peoples and civilizations has been a major force for change. Most would agree that this interaction was considerably less substantial, although by no means negligible, before the overseas expansion of Western Europeans beginning in the fifteenth century, a development that led eventually to direct contacts between nearly all the societies in the world. As Curtin has argued, "European voyages around the Cape of Good Hope and across the Atlantic brought revolutionary changes in world history," although the consequences were only slowly apparent.[7] But even before 1500, few societies were completely isolated and there were important interactions between regions, for example, the trade between China and Europe and around the Indian Ocean realm, as well as between North and South America, that has been analyzed in detail by Curtin.[8] It seems clear that 1450–1500 C.E. or thereabouts is a watershed, after which the interaction between societies, regions, and continents increased dramatically, leading up to the present universal and interdependent human society. While historians differ greatly on how developments in recent centuries should be identified and interpreted, it is clear to many that some sort of global or broadbased perspective on human history is necessary.[9]

The growth of the world history field, if it is to continue, requires an increasing commitment to graduate-level preparation of world history oriented teachers and scholars. Unfortunately, world history has been virtually nonexistent as a graduate history field in the United States. It is not hard to identify some of the reasons for this state of affairs. Graduate programs in history mirror undergraduate ones, in that Eurocentrism and Americocentrism, not to mention increasing emphasis on the narrow specialization bemoaned by Curtin, have long been fashionable. For some decades, the history discipline has been increasingly compartmentalized into regional specializations, of which U.S. and West European history receive far and away the most attention. Normally, 75% to 90% of historians in a department specialize in one of these two regional areas. Only four other regional specializations enjoy even modest "respectability:" East Asian, Latin American, South Asian, and Russian/Soviet history. Other regional fields such as African, Middle Eastern, Southeast Asian, Canadian, and East European history are much less widely taught.[10]

The 1960s and early 1970s was an era hospitable to program innovation in which the U.S. enjoyed a remarkable intellectual renaissance in history. Some nontraditional specializations of history grew rapidly, among them ethnic and women's history and several Third World areas, including Africa, Latin America, and Southeast Asia. Many schools launched freshmen-level world history or Western Civilizations courses. The writings of globalists like Marshall Hodgson, McNeill, and L. S. Stavrianos began reaching a wider audience. But the tide of interest in many of these specializations as teaching fields soon subsided and many a world history or Western Civilizations requirement was dropped. World history was a victim of the return of more conventional concerns.[11]

World history began to take a significant comeback as a teaching field in the 1980s, due in part to the efforts of the World History Association.[12] But world history never became established at the graduate level, largely because history departments were not structured for inter-regional scholarship or training. Until recently, only one major university had made a serious attempt to mount a coherent doctoral program in world history. That program was conceived at the

University of Wisconsin-Madison in the late 1950s, flourished in the 1960s, but was disbanded by the late 1970s. An M.A.-level program in comparative world history partly inspired by the Madison model was developed at the University of California-Santa Cruz in the early 1980s; it ultimately failed to thrive and has since been heavily modified and somewhat "deglobalized." Hence the track record for graduate programs in world history has not been encouraging.

Nonetheless, the Wisconsin Comparative World History Program (CWHP), of which Curtin was the moving force, was a model for a global approach that merits more attention, an approach that might be termed the "Wisconsin School";[13] it also contributed in many ways to the rise of world history teaching and scholarship in the past decade and a half. For that reason it requires analysis in any serious discussion of the teaching and writing of world history in the U.S. Madison's program began life as the Comparative Tropical History Program and frankly pronounced the comparability of regions as diverse as Africa, Latin America, and Southeast Asia. Curtin, the Program's founding Director, characterized the aims of the program thusly:

> The program itself was founded in 1959 as a way of helping Ph.D. candidates in various fields of non-Western history to avoid the problem of fragmented historical knowledge. In addition to the interdisciplinary training of the typical area-studies program, it insisted on cross-area training within the discipline of history as a counterweight to excessive area specialization.[14]

The program did not appear in an intellectual vacuum, of course, since a number of scholars in the U.S. and abroad were becoming more interested in the possibilities of comparative history as well as in blending social science and historical approaches.[15]

The Madison program emphasized the study of modern "Third World" societies within a global context, and grew out of a complex intellectual interaction between several specialists on African, Latin American, South Asian, and Southeast Asian history. But the guiding force was Curtin, trained at Harvard as a specialist on Europe who meanwhile taught himself African and the Caribbean history since graduate specialization in these fields was then virtually nonexistent in the U.S.; he was later instrumental in establishing the African Studies Program at Madison (the program included such other major Africanists as historian Jan Vansina and political scientist M. Crawford Young). But even his earliest scholarship had a strongly comparative focus, particularly in viewing slavery and related issues in a much broader context than had hitherto been common.[16] Hence his first book, on Jamaica, suggested that breadth of his interests and first introduced the notion of the "South Atlantic System," placing Jamaican slavery in a broader perspective of African origins, European capitalism, and West Indian socioeconomic patterns, not to mention making references to U.S. experiences.[17] His second book continued the intellectual odyssey, exploring aspects of the relationship between Europe and Africa, in this case the way British misunderstanding of African realities resulted in ethnocentric and racist perspectives.[18] Patrick Manning contends that this was also essentially a study in world history since Britain constituted the leading world power; consequently British ideas and actions necessarily both caused and — reflected major world developments of the time. Furthermore, Curtin always viewed African history as part of world history rather than in parochial terms.[19]

Increasingly interested in even wider connections between tropical societies, Curtin managed to attract Carnegie Foundation funding for the project and helped organize and teach the cross-regional thematic seminars that formed the heart of the comparative program. He and Southeast Asianist John Smail, the two key senior figures of the "Wisconsin School," also taught the two semester sequence that surveyed the relationship between Western and non-western societies in modern history, especially the history of the European impact on the "Third World."[20] Curtin later utilized some of the ideas from that course in several important books and articles that constitute the "core" of his comparative world history scholarship.[21]

Later the Comparative Tropical History Program would be expanded into a Comparative World History Program (CWHP) that also encompassed East Asia (a move designed mostly to give the orphaned East Asianists a "home" in the tripart departmental division between American, European, and Tropical History). From the early 1960s through the early 1970s around one hundred graduate students went through the program at the Ph.D. level, many of whom have gone on to teach or write about world and/or comparative history.[22] Some of the students gained enough familiarity with several regions of the world to publish on societies outside their original area of specialization.[23] Graduates of the program were also prominent among the founding leaders of the World History Association.[24] In most conventional Ph.D. programs a student in, for example, Southeast Asian history would have combined that field with one or two other regional specializations such as East Asian, European or U.S. diplomatic history. But students in the CWHP selected another "Third World" field (e.g., Africa) as well as a mandatory minor in Comparative World history. This minor field included familiarity with the content of two undergraduate comparative history courses, the "Expansion of Europe" to 1800 and "The World and the West" since 1800,[25] as well as a graduate research seminar on a particular comparative topic such as contract labor, plural societies or peasant rebellion. Furthermore, the preliminary exams for the Ph.D. required the doctoral candidate to prepare a paper demonstrating knowledge of comparative material relevant to the dissertation topic.

Curtin's interests were always oriented more to a particular kind of world history, one in which thematic comparison holds a central place. He continues to promote this approach:

> What we need is a new kind of course that will have the perspective of world history, and will ask and try to answer the question, how did the world come to be as it is?, by treating topics selectively, with examples detailed enough to be comprehensive, rather than by surveying the entire panorama too superficially to be worth remembering.[26]

Hence the intellectual essence of the "Wisconsin School" as developed by Curtin, Smail and the others was essentially comparative, in which case studies were utilized to elucidate certain patterns or themes of historical development and socioeconomic change. Curtin describes the basic premise:

> Comparative history is a difficult concept because it has so many different meanings to different people. The kind of comparative history I have in mind crosses the boundaries of the major culture areas to pick out similarities or differences and to make comparisons in the perspective of world history.[27]

Curtin is the first to admit that this approach sacrifices coverage for breadth, and is necessarily idiosyncratic since no two historians will approach a topic in precisely the same way.[28]

Fredrickson has outlined several types of comparative history undertaken in the United States over the past several decades. The first is the close examination of a particular community or social action utilizing conceptual categories or schemes with wider ramifications, what he terms "microcosmic" studies.[29] The second, or "macrocosmic" framework, explores international or transregional developments broadly conceived without explicit attention to the variables within particular societies; some kinds of global history might fall into this category. The third type, in Fredrickson's view the model, has the main objective of the systematic comparison of a particular system or institution in two or more societies in different geographical regions. The goal is not primarily the understanding of a global or transregional pattern but rather the peculiarities of the societies under study.[30] Curtin's work, and that of the "Wisconsin School" generally, tends to blend the macrocosmic framework (hence its compatibility with global history) with attention to case studies; hence it incorporates many elements of Fredrickson's concept of comparative history. The scholarship also generally eschews (or downplays) the theoretical or ideological thrusts of comparative social scientists like Jack Goldstone, Barrington Moore, Theda Skocpol, Immanuel Wallerstein or Eric Wolf.

The "Wisconsin School" stood in contrast to other popular global history approaches that have developed, such as the comprehensive chronological survey of major cultural areas, and the interactions between them, pioneered by historians like McNeill and Stavrianos (what Curtin labels, somewhat dismissively, the "World History Survey" idea), or the history as topical inquiry model promoted most notably by Kevin Reilly.[31] All of these approaches can be defended with vigor and have advantages; the world history field is enriched by the diversity of views. Although the "World History Survey" is probably the most utilized model in college-level world history courses, Curtin fears it is necessarily superficial in its treatment, and in that sense perhaps even inferior to the old Western Civilizations survey.[32] Curtin's work explicitly rejects what Manning terms the "master narrative" (an analysis of the main line of world history) although it does make broad cross-cultural generalizations albeit soundly grounded in a documentary base. His assertions tend to be modestly presented.[33]

It was the comparison across geographical regions and the chiefly Third World emphasis that distinguished the Wisconsin program from the Comparative History program at Michigan, which specialized on Europe. The scholarly fruits of the "Wisconsin School" can be seen in the published work not only of Curtin, but of some of the program graduates and former Curtin students such as Michael Adas, Ross Dunn, Richard Eaton, Franklin Knight, Patrick Manning, and Joseph Miller. A few examples convey the breadth of this work. For example, Adas has explored millennial rebellions against colonial rule in societies as far afield as Indonesia, New Zealand, and Tanganyika, as well as the interrelationship of science, technology and ideology in Western imperialism. Dunn uses the expansive travels of the intrepid fourteenth century Moroccan, Ibn Battuta, as a vehicle to paint a vivid picture of a cohesive, interlinked Islamic realm stretching from western Africa to Southeast Asia. Manning provides the most comprehensive survey of the vast scope of the African slave trade to both Asia and the Americas, and the demographic impact on Africa and the world.[34]

Curtin's own scholarship was gradually altered by his participation in the CWH program, transforming him into a major figure in the writing of comparative world history as he increasingly sought to comprehend major patterns of history.[35] During the 1960s he pursued research on the larger transatlantic slave trade, in the process producing a demographic analysis of the trade over four centuries that still stands as the standard, but by no means unchallenged, work in the field. These studies helped to make possible the comparative study of slavery and certainly qualify as monographs in world history.[36] The larger slave trade of what he initially called the "South Atlantic System" spurred him to turn his attention to a major source of slaves, the Senegambia region, producing a comprehensive study of the economic parameters of both legitimate and slave trading in that region of West Africa. Curtin's work has always transcended the conventional disciplinary boundaries, and he was an especially assiduous reader of anthropology; hence, he was one of the first historians to appropriate social science concepts such as "trade diasporas," a theme that played a major role in his study of Senegambia.[37]

More recently Curtin has concentrated on broader themes of comparative history, utilizing his African-Caribbean data and lecture notes from his World and the West courses as an initial base to produce three important books. The first examines the patterns of commerce in the world prior to the Industrial Revolution, emphasizing the various "trade diasporas" that existed prior to or in the early stages of Western expansion but mostly disappeared with industrialization; based on exhaustive source materials, Curtin's study reveals a rich economic heritage in which many peoples crossed cultural boundaries in their pursuit of trade goods of profit in the centuries before true capitalism became dominant.[38] As Jerry Bentley has recently argued, Curtin's work on trade along with McNeill's studies on technology and diseases are crucial to an understanding of crosscultural contacts in the premodern era.[39] Curtin's long interest in epidemiological themes, particularly in his pioneering studies of Africa and the slave trade, led to a larger analysis of European soldiers sent to the tropics between 1815 and 1914, during the era of colonial scrambling; the study documents the advent of scientific medicine and the relationship of that to the colonial enterprise.[40]

His most recent study constitutes a summary of his sustained fascination with the comparative evolution of plantation societies in the Mediterranean, Atlantic Islands, and Caribbean zone, and provides a stimulating overview of the triangular trade linking Africa and the Americas with the wider world, including Asia, from which many post-slavery laborers were recruited. Curtin's analysis of what he now terms the "plantation complex," a distinctive form of cultural encounter between non-Western societies and Europeans, contributes a landmark study to Atlantic history, a field in which he has long established a preeminent position. In many respects it constitutes a core summary of many of the themes long central to his teaching at both Wisconsin and Hopkins, and draws as well on the work of some of his students in those courses.[41] It has been suggested that Curtin's writings, grounded in case studies, have a symbiotic relationship with the more speculative global studies oriented toward the "master narrative" which gives his work a particular strength.[42]

Unfortunately, by the mid-1970s the CWHP which had so stimulated both Curtin and his students was in decline, and it was essentially dissolved by the end of the 1970s. The reasons for the decline are varied. Because the CWHP was rooted and "housed" in the Third World "caucus" of the History department, it never attracted the interest or support of most Americanists or Europeanists. Occasionally a specialist on French colonial or British Commonwealth history would participate in the program, but for all practical purposes students in the program were concentrating on Third World areas. This reflected the realities of faculty politics and was probably unavoidable. Nor did all the faculty in the Third World caucus participate in the program; indeed, some ostensibly affiliated with the program either ignored it openly or expressed skepticism about the possibilities and value of comparative history. Four or five of the faculty carried the burden of teaching the requisite courses and seminars.[43]

While a student in Southeast Asian history was required to take Comparative World as a minor field, students could finish doctorates in African, East Asian or Latin American history without ever coming into contact with it, especially if they specialized on the premodern period. Probably only about half of those students elected to join the program. Later the program lost three of its major faculty participants through death or resignation.[44] Most damaging was Curtin's decision to leave Wisconsin in 1975 for the intellectually exciting challenge of a new Atlantic Studies program at Johns Hopkins, a challenge that the pioneer in the field of Atlantic Studies as a coherent area of analysis could not resist, particularly given the presence at Hopkins of other major Atlanticists such as anthropologist Sidney Mintz and historians A. J. R. Russell-Wood and Franklin Knight. The Carnegie money was also used up by the mid-1970s, by which time few students selected the program, a trend that accelerated with retrenchment and an uncertain academic job market in the late 1970s.

The Madison experience would seem to suggest that the establishment of a world or comparative world history emphasis in graduate study apparently has several requirements. An initial prerequisite would seem to be a cooperative faculty with reasonably diverse regional interests, embracing North American and European as well as Asian, African, and Latin American history. In other words, a department must be well-balanced in regional specializations. It would also seem crucial to have a visionary sparkplug or two to provide inspiration and leadership, the sort of role that Curtin played at Wisconsin. The program must also have some intellectual coherence; at Madison this was grounded in a set of undergraduate and graduate courses centered around themes and concepts of comparative history. At Madison graduate students were expected to familiarize themselves with several general studies on comparative and global history including Cyril Black's *Dynamics of Modernization* (often held up as a negative example), and, more importantly, McNeill's *Rise of the West*. But the courses emphasized content and analysis more than theory, and they did not attempt the sort of comprehensive coverage suggested by the McNeill model.

A program can also not survive without students. There is little point in pursuing a Ph.D. with a world history emphasis if few academic positions exist in the field, especially since the history profession tends to mistrust or devalue generalists. While some small liberal arts colleges may find broadly trained historians attractive, most of the larger universities with graduate programs seem to prefer to hire the narrow specialists bemoaned by Curtin, who can fit into a particular and recognizable niche. Indeed, with a few exceptions,[45] these universities on the whole have yet to demonstrate much interest in even offering undergraduate courses in world history. Still, the growth of undergraduate courses in recent years, a development concentrated in the mid-size state colleges and regional universities, has the possibility of expanding the job market for global historians.

Indeed, this development, along with the increasing interest in world history in the secondary schools, prompted the University of Hawaii to establish a Ph.D. program in world history in 1987;[46] Hawaii also launched a *Journal of World History* in 1989 (published under the auspices of the World History Association). In addition to launching an important series with Cambridge University Press on comparative world history in 1983, Curtin presided over a small Ph.D. program in Comparative World History at Hopkins, with several students electing this as a second field along with their regional specialization on the Madison model. Several other programs have also been developed elsewhere.[47] In many respects these programs, like the earlier Santa Cruz project, are descendants of the CWHP at Madison; but they have been careful to integrate Western and Third World history together as well as orienting the programs around a core seminar.

Global history is indeed a growth field, due in part to the intellectual stimulation provided by, and the historians associated with, Wisconsin's pioneering program. World history, whether of the comparative sort associated with the "Wisconsin School," the more conventional McNeillesque global survey, or Reilly's topical inquiry, will continue to constitute a challenge to the Western Civilizations approach. Curtin pioneered in, and articulately promoted, the teaching and writing of an unusual variety of historical fields: African, Caribbean, Atlantic, world, and comparative. In the process he has provided a model for the integration of depth and span, combining scholarly rigor with personal virtuosity.

Notes

1. Philip D. Curtin, *African History* (Washington, D.C.: Service Center for Teachers of History, American Historical Association, 1964), 1–2.

2. Curtin has been president of both the American Historical Association and the African Studies Association, as well as patron, along with William McNeill, of the World History Association.

3. Joe Gowaskie, "Continuing the Revolution: World History in the Liberal Arts Curriculum," paper read to American Historical Association, December 27–30, 1983, 10.

4. See Philip D. Curtin, "Depth, Span, and Relevance," *American Historical Review* 89 (February 1984): 3–4.

5. See William H. McNeill, "Surveying the Sweep of the Human Adventure," *Chronicle of Higher Education*, 30 January 1978, 32; and Craig Lockard, "Global History, Modernization, and the World-System Approach: A Critique," *The History Teacher* 14 (August 1981): 489–508.

6. For some of the major approaches, see Lockard, "Global History;" Symposium on "What Is an Attainable Global Perspective for Undergraduates in History?," *The History Teacher* 18 (August 1985), 501–35; Lawrence Chase, "Teaching All There Is to Know: The Annales 'Paradigm' and the World History Survey Course," *The History Teacher* 18 (May 1985): 409–21.

7. *Cross-Cultural Trade in World History* (Cambridge: Cambridge University, 1984), 126.

8. *Cross-Cultural Trade in World History.*

9. See Lockard, "Global History," 489–516.

10. Many universities offer parochial curricula. For example, one large branch of the University of Texas employs 30 historians: 20 Americanists (7 on Texas history), 8 Europeanists, and 2 Latin Americanists. That department offers no courses on the world south of Sicily or east of the Bosporus. A university is unlikely to view world history as very important if it does not even offer a course on China or India.

11. Charts in the *1980–1981 AHA Guide to Departments of History* showed 70 fields of history and where they were offered. Included were such specializations in U.S. history as labor, urban, and business history. World and comparative history failed to make the list.

12. See Gilbert Allardyce, "Towards World History: American Historians and the Coming of the World History Course," *Journal of World History* 1 (Spring 1990): 23–76.

13. I use this term with some trepidation, since several other "Wisconsin Schools" of history have been identified, including the "frontier" scholars founded by Frederick Jackson Turner and the critical approach to American foreign relations inaugurated at Madison by William Appleman Williams.

14. "Foreword," in Michael Adas, *Prophets of Rebellion: Millenarian Protest Movements against the European Colonial Order* (Cambridge: Cambridge University Press, 1979), xiii.

15. This interest helped generate the foundation in 1958 of an important new journal, *Comparative Studies in Society and History,* based at the University of Michigan.

16. This approach is suggested by Paul E. Lovejoy, "Introduction," in Paul E. Lovejoy, ed., *Africans in Bondage: Studies in Slavery and the Slave Trade* (Madison: African Studies Program, University of Wisconsin, 1986), 1–2.

17. *Two Jamaicas: The Role of Ideas in a Tropical Colony,* 1830–1865 (Cambridge: Harvard University Press, 1955).

18. *The Image of Africa: British Ideas and Action,* 1780–1850 (Madison: University of Wisconsin, 1964).

19. Patrick Manning, "The Monograph in World History: Philip Curtin's Comparative Approach" (unpublished paper, 1992), 5–6.

20. See "Program in Comparative Tropical History-Information Sheet 1968–1969 (Department of History, University of Wisconsin-Madison). For an overview of that course, see Curtin, "Graduate Teaching in World History," *Journal of World History* 2 (Spring 1991): 81–89; and "The Comparative World History Approach," *The History Teacher* 18 (August 1985): 520–27.

21. *Cross-Cultural Trade in World History* (Cambridge: Cambridge University Press, 1984); *The Rise and Fall of Plantation Complex* (Cambridge: Cambridge University Press, 1990); *Death by Migration: Europe's Encounter with the Tropical World in the Nineteenth Century* (Cambridge: Cambridge University, 1989). See also "The Environment Beyond Europe and the European Theory of Empire," *Journal of World History* 1 (Fall 1990): 131–50.

22. Curtin, "Foreword," xiii.

23. For example, Southeast Asianist Guy Gran has published on Zaire and Latin Americanist David Sweet on the Philippines, while Michael Adas, originally a South Asianist, has written more voluminously on Southeast Asia. See also the author's essay on Surinam, in addition to his writings on Southeast Asian and comparative history.

24. CWHP graduate Ross Dunn was the first President of the Association, and the author was the founding Secretary.

25. The titles of the two interlinked courses changed several times between 1959 although the basic content and approach remained the same. Personal communication from Curtin.

26. "Depth, Span and Relevance," 4. For a more detailed discussion of Curtin's approach, see Curtin, "Comparative World History Approach," 520–27.

27. "Graduate Teaching in World History," 82.

28. Curtin, "Comparative World History Approach," 527.

29. Fredrickson believes this type of study has been the norm in *Comparative Studies in Society and History.* But it should be emphasized that this journal also published several seminal articles in world history such as Marshall Hogsden's "The Interrelations of Society and History," 5 (January 1963): 227–50.

30. "Comparative History," 457–59. Fredrickson's own work comparing the U.S. and South Africa constitutes an example of this approach. See *White Supremacy.*

31. On some of these approaches see the essays by Reilly, McNeill, Stavrianos, Curtin, and Immanuel Wallerstein in *The History Teacher* 18 (August 1985): 501–36. See also Reilly, *The West and the World: A History of Civilization,* 2nd ed. (New York: Harper and Row, 1989), 2 vols.; Kevin Reilly, "Introductory History as Topical Inquiry" (unpublished paper, 1982).

32. "Comparative World History Approach," 520–21; "Depth, Span, and Relevance," 3–4.

33. Manning, "The Monograph in World History," 10–12.

34. See Adas, *Prophets of Rebellion*; Adas, *Machines as the Measure of Men: Science, Technology, and Ideologies of Western Dominance* (Ithaca, N.Y.: Cornell University, 1989); Peter N. Stearns, Michael Adas, and Stuart B. Schwartz, *World Civilizations: The Global Experience* (New York: HarperCollins, 1992); Dunn, *The Adventures of Ibn Battuta* (Berkeley: University of California, 1986); Eaton, *Islamic History as Global History* (Washington, D.C.: American Historical Association, 1992); Knight, *The African Dimension in Latin American Societies* (New York: Macmillan, 1974); Manning, *Slavery and African Life: Occidental, Oriental, and African Slave Trades* (Cambridge: Cambridge University, 1990); Miller, *Way of Death: Merchant Capitalism and the Angolan Slave Trade, 1730–1830* (Madison: University of Wisconsin Press, 1988). See also Craig Lockard, "The Javanese as Emigrant: Observations on the Development of Javanese Settlements Overseas," *Indonesia* 11 (April 1971): 41–62; Craig Lockard, "Repatriation Movements Among the Javanese in Surinam," *Caribbean Studies*, 18 (April 1978): 85–113; Craig A. Lockard, "Meeting Yesterday Head-On: The Vietnam War in Vietnamese, American, and World History," *Journal of World History* 5 (Fall 1994): 227–70.

35. For a general overview of his scholarly career and a bibliography of his work, see Lovejoy, "Introduction," 1–10.

36. *The Atlantic Slave Trade: A Census* (Madison: University of Wisconsin, 1969). See also Manning, "The Monograph in World History," 8–9.

37. *Economic Change in Precolonial Africa: Senegambia in the Era of the Slave Trade* (Madison: University of Wisconsin, 1975).

38. *Cross-Cultural Trade in World History*. Already this book has stimulated work by other scholars verifying or challenging or elaborating on aspects of this argument. See, e.g., Sanjay Subrahmanyam, "Iranians Abroad: Intra-Asian Elite Migration and Early Modern State Formation," *Journal of Asian Studies* 51 (May 1992): 340–63.

39. *Old World Encounters: Cross-Cultural Contacts and Exchanges in Pre-Modern Times* (New York: Oxford University, 1993), 5, 185.

40. *Death by Migration*.

41. *The Rise and Fall of the Plantation Complex*.

42. Manning, "The Monograph in World History," 13–14.

43. Curtin and Smail were the most central figures but Robert Frykenberg, John Phelan, and John Richards were also closely identified with the program.

44. Phelan died unexpectedly in 1976 and Richards left Madison in 1978 for a position at Duke University; the latter was a critical loss since he had taught the lower-level introductory course on Afro-Asian history.

45. Among them Rutgers, Ohio State, Hawaii, and Indiana.

46. For a critique and discussion of that program, see *World History Bulletin*, 5 (Spring–Summer 1988): 2–10.

47. The University of Denver established an M.A. program in world history in 1989, and several other universities are reported to be considering graduate programs in global or comparative history as well. It is also possible for graduate students at schools like Ohio State and Rutgers to gain some training in world history. Several Canadian universities, including Victoria and Manitoba, have also recently established world history courses of study at the undergraduate and graduate levels. On the Manitoba program, see T. E. Vadney, "World History as an Advanced Academic Field," *Journal of World History* 1 (Fall 1990): 209–23.

SELECTED BIBLIOGRAPHY

Allardyce, Gilbert. "The Rise and Fall of the Western Civilization Course." *American Historical Review* 87 (1982): 695–725. A cogent history of the Western Civ course and its ideology. The author concludes that "the world has outgrown the old Western Civ ideas." Commentaries by Carolyn Lougee, Morris Rossabi, and William Woehrlin follow (pp. 726–43).

Bentley, Jerry H. *Shapes of World History in Twentieth-Century Scholarship.* Essays on Global and Comparative History, edited by Michael Adas. Washington, D.C.: American Historical Association, 1996. A concise historiography of the scholarly field by the editor of the *Journal of World History.* The essay considers in turn "the philosophers of history," "the social scientists," and "the professional historians." (An excerpt from Bentley's pamphlet is included in Part Eleven of this book.)

Burke, Edmund III. "Marshall G. S. Hodgson and the Hemispheric Interregional Approach to World History." *Journal of World History* 6 (Fall 1995): 237–50. This essay not only explains Hodgson's approach to world history but also elucidates the particular time and place that shaped his ideas. (This article is reprinted in Part Four.)

Costello, Paul. *World Historians and Their Goals: Twentieth-Century Answers to Modernism.* DeKalb, Ill.: Northern Illinois University Press, 1993. A critical investigation of metahistorical paradigms of the twentieth century, focusing on the work of H. G. Wells, Oswald Spengler, Arnold Toynbee, Pitirim Sorokin, Christopher Dawson, Lewis Mumford, and William H. McNeill.

Ledbetter, Rosanna. "Some Thoughts on the Historiography of World History." *World History Bulletin* 9 (Fall/Winter 1992–93): 12–17. The author surveys world history writing since the seventeenth century, arguing that only in recent decades has enough knowledge accumulated to write genuine global history.

Lockard, Craig A. "World History." In *Encyclopedia of Historians and Historical Writing.* Edited by Kelly Boyd, 1330–35. London and Chicago: Fitzroy Dearborn, 1999. A concise, expert summary of the historiography of world history, emphasizing developments in scholarship since the 1950s.

McNeill, William H. *Arnold J. Toynbee: A Life.* New York: Oxford University Press, 1989. McNeill demonstrates that Toynbee's reputation as a metahistorical systems builder and, in the end, religious mystic has overshadowed his brilliance at formulating important world-historical questions.

Moore, R. L. "World History." In *Companion to Historiography*, edited by Michael Bentley, 941–59. New York: Routledge, 1997. A British historian's astute observations on the development and future prospects of world history as "a distinctive mode of inquiry."

Nash, Gary B., Charlotte Crabtree, and Ross E. Dunn. *History on Trial: Culture Wars and the Teaching of the Past*. New York: Alfred A. Knopf, 1997. Public controversy over both United States and world history curriculum in K–12 education is the subject of this study by three scholars involved in the development of the National Standards for History, which were first published in 1994 (revised edition 1996). Transformations in world history education are related to the changing American political and cultural scene.

Reilly, Kevin, and Lynda Norene Shaffer, "World History." In *The American Historical Association's Guide to Historical Literature*, 3d ed., vol. 1, edited by Mary Beth Norton, 42–45. New York: Oxford University Press, 1995. In their introduction to the extensive world history section of this volume, Reilly and Shaffer identify eight distinct approaches to world history that scholars have worked out over the past few decades.

PART TWO

THREE ARGUMENTS FOR TEACHING WORLD HISTORY – AND TWO REMONSTRATIONS

Following World War I, a handful of scholars were prepared to argue that the geopolitical scene across the Northern Hemisphere had been transformed and that the new conditions of international life demanded serious reconsideration of the traditional scope of the history curriculum. Writing in 1919, K. S. Latourette wondered why students should continue learning as little as they were about the history of Asia:

> The world is becoming a unit, and in the future our half can ignore the other only at its peril. . . . There is open to historians a great opportunity to aid in furthering world-wide understanding between great and divergent peoples, and to prepare the way for intelligent action. If we persist in our provincialism, in our neglect of half of the human race, the nation may well accuse us of blindness to our task and faithlessness to our trust.[1]

Such pleas were heard only sporadically in the 1920s and 1930s, decades when the college Western Civilization course spread widely and when tenth-grade "world history" encompassed the non-European world largely in connection with study of contemporary issues.

World War II and its aftermath altered human affairs once again, but no sustained challenge to the customary and inherited framework of world history appeared for another two decades or so. Educators knew in theory that any large disturbance of world relationships must inevitably disrupt and in some measure revolutionize prevailing understandings of the past. But they took a long time, as they usually do, to grasp the fact that the content of textbooks and course outlines was running too far behind the growth of knowledge and innovative shifts in interpretation.

A vigorous, persevering argument for a new kind of world history was launched in the early writings of L. S. Stavrianos. In the published version of a paper he presented at the 1958 meeting of the American Historical Association, he declared that educators can no longer afford to pretend that European history and world history are the same thing. World history cannot be created by renaming, expanding, or otherwise fiddling with European history. The globe must be accepted as the primary field of investigation, and topics of study must be defined and chosen from within that field. Students must learn not only about all the major civilizations but also about "those forces and movements that had a world-wide impact." In making his case, Stavrianos points to the postwar explosion of historical knowledge and to the new realities of international conflict and symbiosis, both exemplified by *Sputnik* I "circling the globe every ninety-five minutes." In this early article more often than he would later in his career, Stavrianos invokes Europe in explaining what he means by "global" history. More remarkable, however, is his identification of conceptual and pedagogical challenges that world history educators still wrestle with today. Over the ensuing forty-plus years, he continued to reiterate and refine his case for world history in numerous essays and textbooks.

Like Stavrianos, William McNeill has persistently exhorted educators to teach world history as a foundational course. He published "Beyond Western Civilization: Rebuilding the Survey" in 1977, when the movement to eliminate breadth requirements for college freshmen and sophomores had reached its peak. Moreover, history majors were getting scarcer, and the doors leading to university posts for young Ph.D.s were barely ajar. In this essay McNeill does not press the issue of global interdependence and transformation as a justification for world history, finding the power of that argument "self-evident." He worries rather that if professors gather into ever more localized circles of specialization and intellectual self-reference, they will one day find their classrooms empty. They must therefore rouse themselves to discover "something of general importance to teach all students." McNeill wants the required freshman survey back, but as globe-girdling world history, not Western Civ. Against the objection that introductory world history is sure to be shapeless and superficial, he counters that large-scale history, like any other, is a "verbal construct" requiring proper calibration of the scale of generalization and detail to fit the learning objective. The influence of McNeill's particular line of argument is hard to measure, but since he wrote this article college world history has made large gains, and teachers of the course command, on the whole, more respect.

The late Marilyn Robinson Waldman, a former student of Marshall Hodgson and a scholarly collaborator of William McNeill, anchors her argument for world history in a passionate universalism. Writing in a characteristically disarming way, she puts her case in terms of the ever-controversial issues of cultural relativism, perspective, and linearity. Her viewpoint is multicultural in its dedication to social and cultural inclusiveness in the curriculum. However, she eschews world history as a scheme for balancing the histories and literary canons of various ethno-racial groups. "What I want," she writes, "is a movement toward a set of questions that all human data are theoretically needed to answer. I think we need to stop arguing over which books to read or which cultures to study and start talking about which questions to ask."

World history education of course has its detractors. Some critics of the introductory course have drawn attention to the purely pragmatic problems of getting the material covered or training instructors to do a proper job. Others, often political commentators, have lumped world history indiscriminately with presumed multiculturalist agendas to disunite America. The most thoughtful skeptics have made their protest out of deeply held conviction that the values, institutions, and great turning points of Western civilization must be imparted to young Americans ahead of any other humanistic subject matter. None of these skeptics dismisses the study of societies outside the West. However, because they believe that shared ideals and systems of cultural communication are what hold nations together, they also contend that schools and universities have a public obligation to explore, analyze, and indeed critique the dominant cultural heritage. In the United States, this means focusing general history studies on the political, philosophical, and aesthetic truths expounded in the classic texts that issued from ancient Athens, Renaissance Italy, seventeenth-century England, and other centers of intellectual ferment and political experimentation in Europe.

J. H. Hexter, the late professor of history at Washington University and an acerbic prose stylist, argues that the best way to combat ignorance, cynicism, and moral aimlessness among college freshmen is to immerse them in the Western canon from Plato to Martin Luther King. No matter where young Americans or their ancestors were born, they possess a Western inheritance "institutionally embedded in the habituations and institutions of our civilization." Students might reasonably take on world history, which Hexter understands to be study of "the differences among the many cultures the world has known and knows," only when they are "solidly planted" in their own civilization.

Even more emphatically than Hexter, Jacob Neusner contends that school and college curriculum should emphasize Europe "because the West has in fact made the world we know." Stavrianos, McNeill, and Waldman would argue that the rise of Western nations to temporary world domination was an anomalous phenomenon in the long run of history and can therefore be explained only within the wider frame of interrelated changes occurring all around the world. Neusner, on the other hand, envisions the globe as a terrain of "disparate cultures" and the study of world history as a matter of sizing one culture up against another. Both he and Hexter accept the premise that particular cultural traits may be understood as belonging inherently to one group but not to another. From this premise Neusner poses questions about non-Western cultures in terms of what constituent qualities they are missing and he insists that "the indicative traits of Western civilization demand close study" in schools and colleges.

Note

1. K. S. Latourette, "The Study of the Far East," *The Historical Outlook* 10 (March 1919): 131–32.

L. S. STAVRIANOS

The Teaching of World History

The Carnegie Corporation of New York has made two grants to Northwestern University to study problems in the teaching of world history and to develop specific courses in that field. The work completed thus far indicates that this is a field that is perhaps unequaled in the problems it presents and the opportunities it offers.

At least there can be little disagreement about the scope and the urgency of the problems. They are only too evident at all levels of our educational system, from the high school to the graduate school. At the high school level, for example, Dr. Dorothy McClure of the United States office of education has concluded: "Random surveys of opinion among teachers and students alike indicate that perhaps no other part of the typical social studies program is more criticized than is the one year, elective world history course."[1] This is an unfortunate, even tragic, situation, because world history is being offered more and more widely in our high schools in response to the pressure of world events, and yet it is the course that seems to be the least satisfactory.

Nor do we in the colleges have any reason to be complacent. All the evidence suggests that the teaching of world history is in as melancholy a state in the colleges as in the high schools. Dr. Jennings B. Sanders, of the United States office of education, conducted in 1951 a survey of catalogue announcements in 272 colleges and universities. His conclusions are sobering:

> Not infrequently the title of a course suggests a wider or a more restricted coverage of a subject matter than the content description that follows. For instance, a course . . . titled "World Civilization" is described as dealing with the "cultural and social history of western civilization from Ancient Greece to the contemporary world." Similarly, the first half of a course titled "History of Europe" is concerned with "world events from the Middle Ages to 1800." The over-all impression gathered from descriptions of Western civilization and World-civilization courses is that the hard core of these courses is European history.[2]

This is a damning indictment. What Sanders is saying, in effect, is that course titles frequently do not mean what they say, and that whatever the title

L. S. Stavrianos, "The Teaching of World History," (paper presented at the annual meeting of the American Historical Association, Washington, D.C., 29 December 1958). *Journal of Modern History* (University of Chicago) 31 (June 1959): 110–12, 113–16.

might be, the course in almost all cases is European history, either naked or with a fig-leaf.

What is the reason for this extraordinary confusion and anarchy in what is, after all, our basic introductory history course? The answer is to be found in the historical evolution of the introductory European history course. Prior to 1900 this course was restricted to political and diplomatic matters. These were commonly treated in a narrative, non-interpretative fashion. The first protest against this procedure was voiced by James Harvey Robinson in his address to the American Historical Association in 1896 on "The teaching of European history in college." On that occasion Robinson expounded his concept of the "New History." This, he urged, should incorporate the economic, social, and cultural manifestations of human endeavor as well as the traditional political and diplomatic ones.

The "New History" came into its own after World War I. The shock of that catastrophe led historians to conclude that what they had hitherto taught had failed to prepare their students for the four years' holocaust and for the infinitely more troubled and more complex world that followed. Accordingly, historians drew upon the rapidly growing stock of research materials to broaden their courses and to expand their textbooks. Thus the interwar period witnessed the appearance of the thousand-page, closely packed textbook, spanning the entire period from the Stone Ages to the present, and dealing with Beethoven and Marx and Darwin, as well as with Napoleon and Metternich and Bismarck.

Since World War II our introductory college courses and textbooks have been undergoing another reappraisal. The stimulating factor this time appears to be a combination of World War II and of the fantastic technological progress of our time. World War II accelerated the awakening of colonial peoples, with the result that Cairo, Delhi, and Peking today are crowding Washington, London, and Paris in the daily headlines. And the technological advances had, in effect, made all peoples neighbors even before Sputnik I began circling the globe every ninety-five minutes. These epochal developments have caused many to question whether the traditional Western civilization course, *by itself,* is adequately preparing students for the one world in which they are destined to live. At the 1948 meeting of the American Historical Association, Professor George L. Mosse, now of the University of Wisconsin, asserted: "Surely a student, in order to make intelligent political choices in our society, must know more about Russia and more about the Far East than such a [Western civilization] course can give him."[3] Two years later Professor Sydney H. Zebel of Rutgers University stated before the same body: "We must re-evaluate our course, reorganize our syllabi and, if necessary, rewrite our textbooks so that we deal with all the great peoples of the world, rather than with those of western Europe alone."[4]

This advice has not been ignored. Various attempts have been made to "re-evaluate," "reorganize," and "rewrite." This is reflected in the titles of the introductory textbooks and courses, many of which now include the term "world," or at least exclude the terms "European" and "Western." Furthermore, chapters have been added dealing with Africa, India, China, and the Middle East. Yet these modifications have proven unsatisfactory for two reasons.

First, and most important, the end product of these modifications is a strange hybrid that is neither fish nor fowl, neither European history nor world history. I cannot emphasize too strongly that world history is *not* European history, with China tacked on whenever Europe impinges on China, or with Africa tacked on whenever Europe impinges on Africa. This sort of thing perhaps may be correctly defined as "Europe and its world relationships." But no matter how much the "world relationships" are stressed, such a course is not world history, in the same manner that a "History of France and its European relationships," even in the periods of Louis XIV or the French Revolution, is not European history.

The modifications in our European history courses and textbooks have proved unsatisfactory for a second reason, namely, that both courses and textbooks have been bloated to the point of obsolescence. Indeed they remind one of our automobile mastodons in the fashion in which they have been broadened and lengthened and loaded down with accessories. Consider what we have done to our textbooks during the past half-century. First, we added chapters on economic and social and cultural developments for the sake of broader coverage. Then we added more chapters on the interwar years and on World War II and on postwar developments in order to bring the textbooks up to date. And now we are adding still more chapters on Africa, the Middle East, India, and China in an effort to attain global perspective. It is scarcely surprising that both courses and textbooks have become virtually unmanageable. Professor Lacey Baldwin Smith of Northwestern University, following a study of the evolution of the European history textbook, has concluded: "No matter how much telescoping the author attempts, no matter how ingeniously it is done, the fact remains that in most cases it is still insufficient."[5] . . .

The first need, in my opinion, is to end the existing confusion and blurring of lines between European and world history. We must differentiate definitely and unequivocally between what are, after all, quite different topics — European history or civilization, and world history or civilization. Where we decide for the latter, then our courses and textbooks should be organized clearly and consistently on a global basis.

The second need in the field of world history is to determine the place of this subject in the high school and college curricula. Frequently it is asked whether world history should be offered in the high school or in the freshman college year or in the graduate school. The posing of these alternatives is, in my opinion, misleading. World history should not be viewed as a subject to be taught in a single course and then forgotten. Rather world history should be regarded as a field of study comparable to European history or American history. The latter two subjects are taught at all levels, beginning with the high school and progressing through the undergraduate college to the graduate school. Precisely the same variety and gradation of courses should be offered in world history. At the high school and freshman college levels the subject should be surveyed in comprehensive fashion, though the survey in these two cases must, and can, be based on different principles in order to take into account the varying degrees of maturity of high school and college students. Advanced undergraduate and graduate courses should then concentrate on selected limited phases of world history.

Implicit in the above statements is the assumption that world history is a feasible subject for instruction. Since this assumption is not universally accepted, the remainder of this paper will be devoted to the problem of precisely how world history might be taught.

We might begin at the graduate level, where presumably there is the least difference of opinion. Graduate courses in world history normally would be highly specialized, either chronologically or topically. The purpose of these courses should be to familiarize the students with the sources and with the opportunities for research in the particular topic or period selected. The possibilities here are virtually limitless, apart from the usual restrictions imposed by the resources of the library and the equipment of the instructor and his students. . . .

Considering next the advanced undergraduate world history courses, one might define them on a chronological or topical basis like their counterparts in the American and European fields. In European history, for example, it is customary to devote a full year of an advanced course to the classical, the medieval, the early modern, modern, or the contemporary period. Precisely the same pattern may be followed with world history, the extent depending naturally on the faculty available and the student demand.

Finally, the freshman world history course should be comprehensive in scope, corresponding to the American and European history courses at the same level. This introductory world history course should have two objectives. First, it should give to the average student, who will take no further work in history, some understanding of the story of mankind — and I mean all of mankind and not merely the European and American segments thereof. Secondly, the introductory course should provide those students who take further work in history with a global perspective that will enable them later better to understand and appreciate regional and national developments.

At this point we come to the crucial question of the practicability of a comprehensive freshman world history course. Frequently it is stated that it is difficult enough to deal with the history of Western civilization in one year without attempting to include also the Chinese, Indian, Middle Eastern, and other civilizations. This observation cannot be denied. Of course it is true that in a one-year world history course one cannot deal with the histories of all the world's civilizations, just as in a one-year European history course one cannot deal with the histories of England, France, Germany, Italy, Spain, Russia, the Balkan countries, the Scandinavian countries, etc. In other words, the essential point here is that a world history survey course should not consist of the sum of the histories of the various world civilizations, in the same manner that a European history survey course does not consist of the sum of the histories of the various European states.

Turning from the negative to the positive, how should the introductory world history course be organized? Here again our experience in the teaching of European history provides a clue. The European history course is organized with at least two main objectives in mind. The first is to make clear the essential internal developments and characteristics of the outstanding empires and states. The second, and equally important, objective is to trace those forces or movements that had a continent-wide impact — for example, Christianity, Islam, the Crusades, the Renaissance, the Reformation, the French Revolution, the Industrial Revolution, nationalism, imperialism, communism, etc.

The objectives of the introductory world history course are of a corresponding nature. The essential characteristics and experiences of the major world civilizations should be made clear. But equally important are those forces or movements that had a world-wide impact — for example, the spread of agriculture and of civilization, the interregional trade in silk and spices, the invasions of the central Eurasian nomads, the diffusion and effect of the great religions, and the world-wide expansion of Europe. This means that the focus of the course no longer will be on Europe. It will, of necessity, shift from region to region, depending on the period under consideration. And at all times, one basic rule must be kept in mind: that no European movement or institution be treated unless non-European movements or institutions of similar magnitude and world significance also be treated. Or, to put it in another way, the whole rather than the parts, the globe rather than the regions, should be kept in mind at all times.

As an illustration we might take the early modern period between the voyages of Columbus and the outbreak of the French Revolution. In the Western civilization course the principal topics usually considered for this period include: for the sixteenth century, dynastic conflicts, Protestant revolt, overseas expansion; for the seventeenth century, Thirty Years' War, rise of absolute monarchies, English Revolution; for the eighteenth century, dynastic and colonial wars, Enlightenment, enlightened despots.

If, in a world history course, these traditional topics are retained, and others are added in order to take into account the developments in non-European regions, then the burden becomes impossible and the end product is in no sense world history. It is essential, therefore, to start afresh and to organize the course on a new and genuinely global basis. When this is done it becomes apparent at once that the outstanding development of world-wide significance during this early modern period was the emergence of Europe. At the end of the fifteenth century Europe was only one of four Eurasian centers of civilization, and by no means the most prominent. By the end of the eighteenth century Europe had gained control of the ocean routes, had organized an immensely profitable world-wide commerce, and had conquered vast territories in the Americas and in Siberia. Thus this period stands out in the perspective of world history as a period of transition from the regional isolationism of the pre-1492 era to the European global hegemony of the nineteenth century.

If the early modern period is appraised from this viewpoint, then it becomes apparent immediately that the traditional topics of European history are irrelevant for world history and must be discarded. In their place might be substituted the following three general topics:

1. The roots of European expansion (why Europe expanded rather than one of the other Eurasian centers of civilization).
2. The Confucian, Moslem, and non-Eurasian worlds on the eve of Europe's expansion (their basic conditions and institutions, and the manner in which they affected the nature and course of European expansion).
3. The stages of European expansion (Iberian stage 1500–1600; Dutch, French, British stage 1600–1789; Russian stage in Siberia).

I believe an arrangement of this type makes clear the main trends in world history during these centuries, and it does so in a manner no more difficult to teach or to comprehend than the material usually presented for this period in the Western civilization course. Perhaps it should be repeated that the role of Europe in the early modern period is emphasized, not because of any implicit Western orientation, but because from a global viewpoint Europe in fact was the region of innovation and decision during those centuries, just as the Near East was during the millennia before Christ.

Notes

1. Dorothy McClure, "Needed Revisions in World History Programs," in Edith West, ed., *Improving the Teaching of World History* (Washington, D.C.: National Council for the Social Studies, Twentieth Yearbook, 1949), 25.

2. Jennings B. Sanders, "College Introductory Courses on the History of Europe, the Western World, or World Civilization," Department of Health, Education, and Welfare, Office of Education, *Circular No. 327* (Sept. 25, 1951), 2.

3. George L. Mosse, "Freshman History: Reality or Metaphysics?" *The Social Studies* 40 (March 1949): 102.

4. Sydney H. Zebel, "Basic Issues and Problems of the Freshman History Course," *Social Education* 15 (December 1951): 383.

5. Lacey Baldwin Smith, "A Study of Textbooks on European History During the Last Fifty Years," *Journal of Modern History* 23 (September 1951): 254.

William H. McNeill

Beyond Western Civilization
Rebuilding the Survey

I come before this meeting not because I have anything new to say, but because what I have to say seems to me sufficiently important to bear repetition. In the *A.H.A. Newsletter* for March, 1976, I wrote a little essay entitled, "History for Citizens," and what I wish to say here and now is no more than a reaffirmation and repetition of what I said there.

I am not really apologetic, since if I am right in the diagnosis of our professional condition that I made in that essay, our discipline is in danger of slipping away from the privileged position it has hitherto occupied in high school and college curricula. Indeed, if we cannot turn the tide, we and any successors who undertake study of peoples beyond the national borders may find ourselves relegated to the margins where a few oddly curious students will seek us out in the way we have been accustomed to seeing classicists sought out by a tiny handful of unusually motivated individuals whose fewness keeps classics departments small. I must say that it takes more imagination than I possess to think of a time when the study of history would become as marginal as the study of Greek and Latin language and literature is in our institutions of higher learning today; but if we persist in offering undergraduate students a rich diet consisting largely of the fine fruit of our private researches and expect them to be interested in demographic reconstitution of old parishes, the metal trades of Nuremberg, or the latest nuances of interwar diplomacy as revealed by newly declassified foreign office files, then I think the historical profession in America will deserve to be relegated to the fringes of higher education, and those of us not yet on tenure had better abandon history and seek another career at once and without further ado.

The only thing that can rescue us from such a fate is to find something worth teaching to undergraduates en masse: something all educated persons should know; something every active citizen ought to be familiar with in order to conduct his life well and perform his public duties effectively.

National history was invented for this purpose and still continues to fulfill a useful function, protected often by state laws requiring high schools to teach

William H. McNeill, "Beyond Western Civilization: Rebuilding the Survey," *The History Teacher* 10 (1977): 509–15.

United States history to all students. National history may sometimes be badly taught, sanitized so that anything offensive to any pressure group that can get to textbook publishers is carefully excised from the record. But there is little chance that the patriotic tradition that sustains compulsory courses in U.S. history will not continue to give history instruction a privileged place at the high school level. This is a strategic advantage, no doubt, as against other disciplines seeking entry into high school classrooms. But there is a risk as well. For if such courses are poorly taught, students in college, given a chance to choose courses freely, will stay away from history like the plague. This may, in fact, have happened in the 1960s. In the course of that decade college and university historians surrendered their privileged position as teachers of compulsory courses — and did so without a fight, for the most part. College students became free to avoid history — and did so in such numbers as to exacerbate the job crisis our junior colleagues face so cruelly. Nothing I have heard in the 1970s convinces me that this rebound effect is not still working against us, and powerfully, too.

The reasons our profession did not defend the privileged position for history in the curriculum we had inherited from an older generation's empire building was that most historians had lost interest in teaching an introductory survey course. Young scholars wanted to escape the stigma of indentured labor; professors wanted to teach something of their own. No one was very happy with the intellectual presuppositions behind the existing surveys, whether in United States history or Western Civilization. Above all, no one thought it his or her responsibility to think of something better to do instead.

That is the central failure of our profession in the last two decades. So busy with research and exploration of new forms of history, often on a more and more minute scale because refined techniques required narrowing of vision, historians in this country seem to have been unable or unwilling to devote much effort to thinking about how to improve existing survey courses for freshmen and sophomores, or invent new ones that might be capable both of speaking to the concerns of the rising generation and of commanding the enthusiasm of those asked to teach such courses.

Doubtless any such sweeping indictment overlooks worthy and admirable efforts scores or perhaps hundreds of isolated historians have made to invent a new basic course. But in a more important sense I think the indictment still will stand: for whatever private personal efforts there may have been, the new courses that resulted have not been able to achieve a normative standing so as to spread from campus to campus with suitable modification and variation to fit local needs. Yet that is what happened in the 1930s and 1940s, when Western Civilization was rising to prominence so triumphantly. Whatever efforts individuals may have made to respond constructively to the need for finding a valid general introductory course in history for undergraduates at large, the profession as a whole as well as deans, chairmen and other academic authorities, did not recognize the validity of whatever may have been proffered. New courses died a-borning, or became one of a thousand flowers allowed to bloom in departmental course listings by indulgent chairmen and generous budgetary officers.

The profession, in short, did not recognize any obligation to find something of general importance to teach all students. Each historian's course was presumed to be as good as everyone else's. It seemed professionally insulting to deny the right of any holder of the Ph.D. union card to do his thing with any and every undergraduate who might drift in, attracted by the course title, the professor's reputation — whether for easy grades or scholarly distinction — and the way the class hour fitted his schedule of other classes.

So, we cut our own throats, acting on the implausible proposition that intensive exposure to the chapters of a Ph.D. dissertation, slightly glossed, was as good for students as any mere survey course. After all, the instructor teaching his own dissertation could really know what he was talking about, and thus avoid all errors, hateful oversimplification, and unfounded generalization. Besides, by keeping his teaching close to his research, the scholar could reasonably expect to publish early and often, and thus advance his career, if need be, at the expense of his students. For surely it is self-evident that according to these principles, history became intellectually precise — only by becoming trivial as far as the interests of ordinary undergraduates and future citizens were concerned.

I need not say that this microscopic view of what makes histories true seems to me a sad misunderstanding of what historians do in making the past intelligible. Rather, I claim that each scale of history has an appropriate conceptualization and amount of detail, just as each scale of map has an appropriate projection and amount of detail. And just as a map is not a replica of reality, but a schematic representation of selected features from the relevant landscapes, so a history, too, is not a replica of what really happened, but a verbal construct that makes intelligible what is otherwise a confused jumble of potentially infinite and thoroughly unmanageable information.

If this is what historians do, the level of accuracy attainable does not increase automatically as the scope in space and time diminishes. Adequate schematizations of tiny themes may be easier, especially when a model of how someone else handled data for a similar topic or time span is available and commands respect. (I remember how, when I was a graduate student, one of my professors always invited his students to take on another railroad, and write a thesis by simply transferring the professor's own vocabulary worked out in his own history of the Illinois Central Railroad to the data provided by another railroad's files. Yet he attracted few students to a task which called for minimal inventiveness and maximal industry. Ever since, this has stood in my mind's eye as an example of how not to do Ph.D. theses and how not to study history. But this is beside the point.)

What matters, it seems to me, is the adequacy of the organizing concepts, the key terms, the point of view brought to bear upon the subject matter of study. An adequate organizing principle can make a world history or a national history just as accurate and far more exciting than any Ph.D. thesis is likely to be. In the not-so-far distant past, our forerunners did invent a great idea about the whole human past. They saw all history as moving towards the realization of human freedom, and were able to direct attention in the light of this idea to the critical episodes and periods, places and transactions that constituted the principal turning points in that story. The late-lamented survey of western civilization was a curricular embodiment of that idea, though the clear focus of Lord Acton's generation had already been lost when the Western Civilization course was invented, and other matter soon so overlaid the original organizing structure that most who taught and, I suppose, nearly everyone who took such courses, remained unaware of the principle that had once governed the distribution of attention — what was put in and what left out. And just because the original idea had been forgotten, these courses ceased to have any obvious justification, and were surrendered gladly by almost all who had been teaching them when some bold spirits challenged the right of historians to inflict what had become a hodge-podge of oddly assorted facts and opinions on innocent undergraduates.

What our profession ought to have done, surely, was to think again and see whether there was not some other way of organizing a course of general significance for undergraduates, or whether the old idea, if refurbished and suitably criticized, might not again sustain a meaningful course. So far as I know, we did nothing of the sort, and have not even responded to the fairly widespread student withdrawal from our classrooms by doing much more than complain. Indeed, the profession seems far readier to try to set up an effective lobby with state legislatures so as to assure legal protection against encroaching "social studies" than we are to undertake the intellectual work of trying for a new course which we could defend with conviction against any and all critics as a suitable and proper building-block in every young person's education.

If it is really true that we cannot agree upon some kind of general course, then it seems to me that historians are saying to the rest of academia that we have nothing to teach young people that they ought to know. To say, "Take any of a score of different courses, differing in content, point of view, emotional color and intellectual rigor," is simply not an answer that anyone outside the profession will take seriously — nor should they. If all we have to say to the young is what individual scholars and idiosyncratic teachers care to put into their courses, then history as a key element in everyone's education does not exist. No one can take all such courses; if each is as good as the others, and all but one or two are dispensable, then in logic all are dispensable! And it takes no more than an average level of critical acumen to arrive at that conclusion.

As I stand here today, I must confess that it seems to me self-evident, as it did fifteen years ago when I started work on *The Rise of the West*, that the only frame suitable for introducing students to the world in which they live is world history. It seems to me obvious that beyond the national frame we must have a genuinely global history to offer the young — or else fall short of the imperatives of our time, when affairs of Africa, China, Viet Nam or any other part of the globe may acquire critical importance for public life and demand an informed judgment of ordinary citizens.

I have no doubt, for instance, that the ill-fated adventures of the American government on the continent of Asia since 1950 have been facilitated by the massive ignorance of those countries that prevailed in the upper echelons of government and society, not to mention the innocence of the American rank-and-file for whom Asia was as unknown as Darkest Africa had been for the early Victorians.

Yet what have historians done to move into this gap? Mighty little, I regret to say; and those efforts that have been made were the work of isolated, idiosyncratic individuals, who have not given birth to contagious course structures that could sweep the country as Western Civ once did. No such sweep will occur unless and until the historians of this land agree that a world history course is possible, desirable and important. I think that most historians today do not believe any of these things and have not thought seriously at all of what it is we ought to be teaching students who do not intend to become professional historians, and who in all probability, will never take another history course or even read a book of history once they escape from our hands. Can anyone really doubt that such persons need to know something about the way the heirs of the great cultures of the past differ from us and among themselves? And how can historians teach students something about these things except on a world scale?

As I say, these propositions seem self-evident to me, and I am surprised that so few have done anything to try to meet the need. I find the apathy truly amazing; suicidal; absurd. Maybe I should be less surprised than I am at the folly of the historical profession: after all, historians are human and the past bears ample testimony to humanity's capacity for folly. But when professional self-interest is so clearly at stake, when intellectual imperatives point so clearly in the same direction; and when the difficulty and delights of the effort are both so challenging, it does seem surprising to me that so very few historians of this country have tried to teach world history, argued for it, interested themselves in it, or done anything at all to move outside their chosen specialisms.

Well, my Jeremiad is now at an end. I could offer suggestions for models of world history in addition to that which I have myself worked out; but this is not what I think most important. What is needed is a multiplex effort on many different campuses to do something intellectually serious and practically effective to invent a new basic course that will be meaningful in itself and useful to all students, capable of commanding the loyalty of those who teach it, and important enough that historians can argue once more for a greater share of student time.

Without such a course to teach to students of any and every specialism, the place of history in our colleges and universities is going to continue to shrink, almost for sure. What have you done to make that dismal future less likely? That is the question each of us ought to ask, those here and those far more numerous outside of this room. Doctors, perhaps, can afford to become narrow specialists, for at least they can still sometimes cure a patient through their specialized skills; yet even they have been much criticized for the loss of contact with ordinary human beings and their concerns that narrow specialism involves. How much more vulnerable is our profession to that reproach? Why should the American public be conned into paying our salaries if we have nothing to say to them? Why indeed? Specialists talking only to specialists have a place in the profession as we all know and recognize; but the ultimate justification for such behavior is that specialists' ideas and data filter down to others, who can use them for testing and correcting broadly interpretative history useful to the general public. A pyramid without a base is a *lusus naturae*; that, it seems to me, is what the historical profession has tried to become. Small wonder that we see the edifice tumbling down.

MARILYN ROBINSON WALDMAN

The Meandering Mainstream
Reimagining World History

For me the study of history is ultimately important as part of a larger attempt to understand what it means to be human; for an important part of what it means to be human is what it *has* meant to be human, during that long, long stretch of time when humans did without writing as well as during that relatively brief moment in which some of them have come to depend on it to preserve their memories. And I, in a rather old-fashioned way, assume that my own struggle to become fully human will benefit from that broad historical knowledge.

The human animal has many unusual traits as animals go. It communicates through symbols, uses technology, and can act according to a sense of value and meaning. But for the historically inclined, and there are "historians," in this sense, in many disciplines, it is the human animal's being situated in time and space, subject to change and influenced by the past in complex ways, that takes pride of place. I think of history, then, as part of human studies, what the French call "les sciences humaines," which for me should involve a cooperative effort by the biological sciences, social sciences, and humanities, and even such non-human studies, like geology, as can place human history in the larger scheme of things.

Ironically, of all the human studies, the humanities have often been the most selective in their choice of data and the most restrictive in their "anthropology," that is, in their definition of what it means to be fully human. Focused as they have been on human excellence and achievement, on the exceptional rather than the typical, they have often decided a priori that certain human phenomena, certain cultures, certain individuals within them, and certain types of

Marilyn Robinson Waldman, "The Meandering Mainstream: Reimagining World History" (inaugural address, College of Humanities, Ohio State University, 2 March 1988).

expression, are more able to tell us something profoundly important about the human condition than others. Of late, however, these principles of selectivity and the authority to establish them have been challenged from all sides — by approaches to texts that deny a special status to what has conventionally been viewed as "literature," and by approaches to history that try to give voice to the voiceless — women's history, history from the bottom, "la longue durée" of the Annales school, and my own particular focus tonight, world history, whether it means simply the comparative study of civilizations or the adding together of regional histories, or it refers to the more ambitious attempt to take the world as a unit of analysis.

Because it challenges the allocation of resources, material and nonmaterial, the effort to give voice to all the cultures of the world has a political dimension, just as the failure or refusal to do so involves a political position. The politics of multicultural studies, or of world history, is a politics not unlike the one of which Leila Rupp spoke so effectively some months ago, the politics of women's history. For in this country, those who study human phenomena from cultures outside the United States and Europe, or from certain sub-cultures within the United States, study another silent majority, one whose members are all without voice regardless of gender.

Anyone who doubts that politics are involved need only witness the recent flurry of responses to Saul Bellow's plaintive and profoundly contemptuous cry, "Who is the Tolstoy of the Zulus? The Proust of the Papuans?" The reply that best reflected the challenges I have just delineated said,

> In fact the Zulus and Papuans do have their Tolstoys and Prousts; they just aren't novelists. Rather, they are reflective individuals who have used ritual, art, song and myth to convey their meditations on the world. It seems silly to ask who is more profound, for if a Papuan cosmology seems pointless in Hyde Park, so Tolstoy and Proust make little sense in the bush.[1]

When I identify with the respondent, it is not out of lack of sympathy with Bellow's end, to discover profound statements about the human condition, but with his means. In fact, I share his goal; I just don't believe that we can any longer pretend to be able to reach it better without taking these newer openings seriously.

ISLAM AND THE MAINSTREAM OF HISTORY

In the study of world history, what would that mean? In this culture, as in most others throughout history, the history of the world has generally been imagined in such a way as to promote a positive self-image. In so doing we have promoted our own cultural identity in sometimes productive ways, but have kept the study of history from teaching us as much as it can about the human condition as a whole.

As my own mentor Marshall Hodgson wrote in the early 1960s,

> We know how the traditional story runs: history began in the "East" — in
> Mesopotamia and Egypt (but not in Paradise, still further east, as the medieval
> Westerners had said); the torch was then passed successively to Greece and
> Rome and finally to the Christians of northwestern Europe, where medieval
> and modern life developed. During the Middle Ages, Islam temporarily was
> permitted to hold the torch of science, which properly belonged to the West,
> until the West was ready to take it over and carry it forward. India, China, and
> Japan also had "ancient" civilizations but were isolated from the mainstream of
> history and "contributed" still less to it (that is, to Western Europe). In modern
> times Western Europe expanded over the rest of the world, so that Islam and
> India and China ceased to be isolated, and have entered the orbit of the ongo-
> ing Western civilization, now becoming a world civilization.
>
> In this story, there are two key notions. There is a "mainstream" of history,
> which consists of our own direct antecedents. This includes all West-European
> periods from areas to the southeast: Greek history till the time of the Roman
> empire (but not since — the Byzantines do not count as mainstream); and the
> Near East till the rise of the Greeks, but not since. Note that this conception of
> "mainstream" is not identifiable with the history of lands of cultural creativity,
> or times of intensity of historical change. The "mainstream" of history, in the
> traditional image, runs through northwestern Europe in the Dark Ages of the
> Merovingians — although everyone knows that the Byzantines and the Mus-
> lims (and the Indians and the Chinese) were far more civilized then. The
> "mainstream" of history is simply our own closest historical antecedents. . . .[2]

It is ironic in the extreme that since World War II and the passage of the
National Defense Education Act, this country has invested more resources than
any society in human history to study the cultures of the *whole* world, but we
have not yet collectively committed ourselves to construct a new historical vision that can make responsible use of our new knowledge. The burden of proof
is still on those who, taken together, study most of the world. Whatever change
has occurred in scholarly circles is offset by the continuing power of the mainstream concept in popular culture. This country's single most popular world history lesson is taught at Epcot Center in Walt Disney World in Orlando, Florida.
Each year millions of Americans, many of them very young, ride through the
world's history in the Spaceship Earth to see Hodgson's mainstream translated
into life-size animated tableaus. The only non-European, non-U.S. people to
appear are the Arabs, who are credited with holding on to Greek science until
the West was ready to make something of it.

To be fair, elsewhere in the park, in the World Showcase, an effort is being
made to display all the cultures of the world, but they are presented as current
realities capable of being absorbed into and participating in our marketplace,
not as past realities that have shared the history of the world with us; in short,
they appear as providers of novel things to buy. After a brief multi-media encounter with selected aspects of the individual cultures, the visitor is invariably
led out into an emporium of imported wares. As in the scholarly world, so too at

Epcot Center growing awareness of the world's living cultural diversity has not yet effected a fundamental change in our vision of its history, or generated a desire to redefine "our" heritage as the history of humanity. True, there is a World History Association in this country, kept alive largely by faculty from less prestigious schools, and a growing literature of world historical writing; but few colleges and universities offer world history courses (the University of Chicago abandoned its world history course after William McNeill retired) or even an adequate array of regional courses, and one still can't be sure that a book called *A History of Civilization* or *Introduction to World Literature* is global in scope.[3]

By now you will have begun to wonder about my title. It emerged, of course, from the foregoing critique but also from several years of helping five of my colleagues in the Department of History teach an unusual course entitled Asian civilizations, which theoretically covers everything from Mediterranean to Pacific and from the Arctic to the Indian Ocean, but in fact focuses "only" on three major civilizational areas, West Asia, South Asia, and East Asia. When I teach the course I usually talk to students about the mainstream concept much the way I have talked with you; and if you think it isn't powerful, you should see how easy it is for most of them to get it right without doing the reading. Not long into the first half of the course, which runs from late Neolithic times to 1500, one is often tempted to remark that if there *was* a mainstream of history, it has been in Asia for most of the time, and may some day soon return there, I might add. One day after making such a remark in class, I went on to quip to my teammate, Chang Hao, that if there was a mainstream of history, it certainly did meander. Let's allow ourselves to meander with it for a little while tonight.

If you identify with my larger project, it is easy for you to understand how important a world civilization like Islam is. But even if you merely want to explain what the mainstream explains, how *we* came to be as we are, you need world history, and you especially need Islamic civilization. Most Muslims grow up assuming that Judaism, Christianity, and Islam have been intertwined from the day of creation; their book of revelations, the Qur'an, tells them so. In that, they have an advantage over Jews and Christians, who have to learn it the hard way. So let me pose a breathless series of questions that will give you some idea of the scope of the problem, and the need to begin to focus on the *interrelations* of societies that we tend to study in isolation from each other.

Do we really understand the rise of Christianity if we don't know that a position it rejected — the humanness of Jesus — became normative in Islam, where he is revered as a major prophet. Were the arguments over Jesus as uncreated or created Logos really over until the Muslims solved the problem of the created or uncreated Qur'an in the tenth century? Do we need to know the life of Muhammad to know just how far Greco-Semitic traditions of divine intermediation could be taken? Does it matter that when some Christians pray, they call God "Allah"? Is the significance of the Greco-Semitic synthesis that came to dominate the West clearer when compared with the Irano-Semitic synthesis that dominated the lands of Islam? Do we really appreciate the significance of the Greek heritage in world history by studying only the part that went west and not the part that went east? Is it significant that al-Biruni, a Muslim scientist, al-most correctly measured the circumference of the earth in the eleventh century, or that a Mamluk physician in Egypt accurately described secondary pulmonary circulation 400 years before Harvey? Could we understand the rise of the university in Italy better if we knew more about Fatimid madrasahs on the island of Sicily? Does it matter that St. Thomas Aquinas was influenced by Avicenna and Averroes, whose mothers called them by their Persian and Arabic names? Should we know that Judaism entered a renaissance under medieval Islam but not under medieval Christianity, such that the great scholar S. D. Goitein once remarked that Islam saved Judaism from decline? Is it important that West Asian wind-tower technology still heats and cools some Spanish village homes? Should we be impressed with the fact that the Ottomans admired the Roman Empire so much they spent hundreds of years trying to conquer it and when they did named their favored territories "Rum" (Rome)? Does it matter that living Muslim societies feel themselves heirs to some of the same ancient civilizations we claim as "ours"? Should I be troubled when a student tells me I can't teach ancient Mesopotamia in my Asian civilizations course because it belongs to the West, not to the people who have lived there since it ceased to be on the mainstream? Does Bossuet's defense of divine monarchy look the same after it is set against the millennia's worth of similar theory coming out of West Asia? Is it significant that Columbus bumped into North America because he was trying to compete with Muslim economic power in the Indian Ocean? Should we know that fifteen to twenty per cent of the slaves brought to the New World may have been Muslim, or take seriously Islam's indigenous Afro-American form? Is it meaningful that the following diverse words are among the many Arabic cognates in English: apricot, lemon, checkmate, damask, cotton, sherbet, arsenal, algebra, algorithm, sofa, zero, lilac, magazine, taffeta, admiral?

But to me the ultimate example of the interrelatedness of things occurred in the early sixteenth century, when a new imperial power, the Spanish Christians, sailing across the Pacific from the New World, met an old imperial power, the Muslims, in Manila, and called them what they had been calling them at home for 700 years, Moros, Moors. Or will we wait until the combination of anti-Americanism and the Moros rebellion in the Philippines hurts us directly enough to convince us of the value of knowing world history?

NONLINEAR IMAGING

One of the biggest obstacles to achieving a new vision will be our lack of facility with nonlinear images and metaphors and with multidimensional models. . . . Adequate historical and cultural explanation will not be achieved by substituting new linear metaphors for old ones. To explain how the world got to be the way it is will need curves and spirals, not just lines and angles; it will demand models that can capture simultaneity and exchange, not just sequence and effect, that can trace the delicate filigree and articulation of boundaries and borders, that can fit

things together in such a way as to allow overlapping of pieces and subtle continuous change in their sizes and shapes, that generate complexities adequate to the
messiness of human phenomena distributed over time and space.

No, "meandering mainstream" probably won't do; it is an oxymoron that in
its perpetual act of self-destruction reminds us of our need and goads us to meet
it. Yet words like meandering that make us so uneasy as scholars may in fact capture the historical process better, just as they may technically capture the movement of actual streams better. More than fifty years ago Ralph Linton penned a
classic little piece on the sources of American material culture that really does
celebrate meandering. Coming at the end of a brilliant and amusing description
of an average morning in the life of an average American male, Linton's last
paragraph is still a ringing challenge to our capacity to grasp the nonlinearity of
historical realities:

> When our friend has finished eating he settles back to smoke, an Ameri-
> can Indian habit, consuming a plant domesticated in Brazil in either a pipe,
> derived from the Indians of Virginia, or a cigarette, derived from Mexico. If he
> is hardy enough he may even attempt a cigar, transmitted to us from the An-
> tilles by way of Spain. While smoking he reads the news of the day, imprinted
> in characters invented by the ancient Semites upon a material invented in
> China [and passed westward by Muslims, I might add] by a process invented in
> Germany. As he absorbs the accounts of foreign troubles, he will, if he is a
> good conservative citizen, thank a Hebrew deity in an Indo-European language
> that he is 100 percent American.[4]

PLURAL PERSPECTIVES AND PERSPECTIVELESS PERSPECTIVES

My critique of the mainstream approach to historical and cultural studies is not
a critique of the concept as *a* perspective but as *the perspective*. It is the same
critique I would make of any perspective — culture, field, discipline, subdiscipline — that is never self-consciously evaluated for both what line of vision
it makes possible and what ones it closes off, never informed by or related to any
other perspective. I believe that the value of a perspective must be judged in regard to the viewer's articulation of what she wants to see and what she wants to
relegate to someone else's line of vision.

The matter of perspective is so intriguing and important to me that I have a
special collection of stories that help me convey my sense of wonder and surprise at its richness. One of my favorites is told by Umberto Eco in *A Theory of
Semiotics*:

> There is an old joke according to which two dogs meet in Moscow, one of
> them very fat and wealthy, the other pathetically emaciated. The latter asks the
> former: "How can you find food?" The former zoosemiotically replies: "That's
> easy. Every day, at noon, I enter the Pavlov Institute and I begin to salivate: im-
> mediately afterward a conditioned scientist arrives, rings a bell and gives me
> food."[5]

Such radically surprising perspectives abound in historical and cultural studies, too. Victor Turner, the late great Africanist and anthropologist of religion, once said he had become a Catholic because it was the closest thing he could find to Ndembu religion in Western culture. And then there is the classic line from Charles Kuralt's 1972 television documentary, "Misunderstanding China": An Asian was once asked what he thought of Western civilization. He said he thought it would be a good idea. When you consider that the Great Wall of China is the only manmade object that can be seen from the moon, that remark makes a special kind of sense.

Disciplines, like all perspectives, are necessary precisely because there is always a radically different way of looking at things. Disciplines, like definitions, are necessary ways of holding the world still long enough to look at it and think about it. Like all forms of perspective, disciplines free us to see some things and keep us from seeing others. They do not have to be abandoned or destroyed in order to be juxtaposed and combined with each other. There are many ways to think about the word "field," after all:

for the farmer, it may be a fixed piece of territory marked by a permanent fence,

for the painter, the eye's range of vision when located at a particular point,

or, for the migratory peoples of the world, wherever they or their animals happen to be (and don't think I haven't been accused of identifying with the nomads).

As fields or disciplines actually operate, of course, they are themselves multiperspectival, more like the painter's or nomad's field than the farmer's.

For me the question is, should we celebrate that fact, should we celebrate our ability unique among the animals to adopt more than one perspective, or should we try to restrict it? Should we recognize it as scholars and minimize it in our teaching, or vice versa? In pleading with our mutual students for eclecticism in perspectives, our late and valued colleague Dan Hughes used to employ a very homely example. If you want to understand the tomato, he used to say, you can slice it as many ways as you like and you will never grasp the whole all at once, *as an entity*, but you will learn more from making many cuts than from making just one.

So why are persons who want to make more than one cut often accused of not wanting to make any? Is their attitude to disciplines really summed up in the Mae West one-liner: "Whenever I'm confronted by a choice between two evils, I choose the one I haven't tried before." Or is it really the case that without disciplines, there is no cross-discipline, no multi-discipline, no inter-discipline, no supra-discipline, words which in fact just refer to perspectives designed to remind us that disciplines are perspectives, too?

I see the academy as locked in an unresolved, in fact not yet fully engaged conflict between two positions I like to pose as competing alliterations: the pursuit of the perspectiveless perspective and the pursuit of plural perspectives. The attempt to go beyond perspective to an absolute truth is hardly new. Even though the children of the Enlightenment see themselves as finally capable of transcending the parochialism and localism of religious worldviews, the attempt to transcend time-bound and space-bound perspective has often been the product of religious faith itself, especially of mystical insight, which often viewed the transcending of perspective as the attainment of an altered state of consciousness. Listen to the verses of the Persian poet Rumi, to whose music the Mevlevi dervishes still turn, more than 700 years later:

> What is to be done, O Moslems? I do not recognize myself.
> I am neither Christian, nor Jew, nor Gabr [Zoroastrian], nor Muslim.
> I am not of the East, nor of the West, nor of the land, nor of the sea;
> I am not of Nature's mint, nor of the circling heavens,
> I am not of the earth, nor of water, nor of air, nor of fire;
> I am not of the empyrean, nor of the dust, nor of existence, nor of entity.
> I am not of India, nor of China, nor of Bulgaria [Bulghar on the Volga]
> nor of Saqsin,
> I am not of the kingdom of 'Iraqain [the two Iraqs], nor of the country of
> Khorasan.
> I am not of this world, nor of the next, nor of Paradise, nor of Hell;
> I am not of Adam, nor of Eve, nor of Eden and Rizwan.
> My place is the Placeless, my trace is the Traceless;
> 'Tis neither body nor soul, for I belong to the soul of the Beloved.[6]

What seems new to me about the modern age is that there are now people who hold that the achievement of a perspectiveless perspective is possible without the "Soul of the Beloved," and that there are so many others who believe that it is not possible at all. And among those who hold it possible, some hold that it requires the a priori avoidance of plural perspectives, others still, that plural perspectives must be explored on the way to the perspectiveless perspective. Disciplines argue this way within themselves, as well as with each other.

CULTURAL RELATIVISM AND MORAL RELATIVISM

It is in this context that I wish to address the unavoidable issues of cultural relativism, whether by "cultural" we mean societies or disciplines. How can we allow everything to be studied equally and in many different ways and maintain the ability to judge and evaluate and discriminate that has been so vital to the humanities? Are relativism and morality mutually exclusive? Is relativism necessarily easy? I don't believe so, but if we are to overcome that assumption, which does seem to be easy, we must take seriously a distinction made recently by George Marcus and Michael Fischer in their thought-provoking book, *Anthropology as Cultural Critique*.

I am speaking of the distinction between relativism as a methodology and relativism as an ideology. As they remind us, cultural relativism emerged as part of a larger project — it was to be the systematic empathetic description of cultural diversity across the world that could make possible a generalized science of humankind. As the latter objective fell out of favor, the former came to be "portrayed as a doctrine rather than as a method and reflection on the process of interpretation itself. This has made it especially vulnerable to critics who charge that relativism asserts the equal validity of all value systems, thus making moral judgments impossible."[7]

Thus it has in fact never been demonstrated that the method of relativism will lead inevitably to the celebration of moral relativism, rather than of cultural and moral universalism. Until we allow ourselves fully to describe and appreciate cultural diversity, how can we possibly be able to assess its value implications? What if the discovery of the other, the exotic, the strange, really is a vehicle to the deeper understanding of ourselves and to a discovery of the universal, of our common or at least shared humanity?

The only way I can convey what I mean is to quote a passage from the fictional diary of Daphne Manners, an important early character in Paul Scott's "Raj Quartet":

> I hate the impression we automatically get of things and places and people that make us say, for instance, "This is Indian. This is British." When I first saw the Bibighar I thought: How Indian! Not Indian as I'd have thought of a place as Indian before I came out, but Indian as it struck me then. But when you say something like that, in circumstances like that, I think you're responding to the attraction of a place which you see as alien on the surface but underneath as proof of something general and universal. I wish I could get hold of the right words to say just what I mean. The Taj Mahal is "typically Indian," isn't it? Picture-book Moghul stuff. But what makes you give out to it emotionally is the feeling of a man's worship of his wife, which is neither Indian nor un-Indian, but a general human emotion, expressed in this case in an "Indian" way. This is what I got from the Bibighar. . . . I said, "How Indian," because it was the first place in Mayapore that hit me in this way, and the surprise of being hit made me think I'd come across something typical when all the time it was typical of no place, but only of human acts and desires that leave their mark in the most unexpected and sometimes chilling way.[8]

Isn't the university . . . still supposed to be a forum for the clash of ideas? Isn't the educated person one who knows that it is all right, indeed even desireable or necessary, to understand things you do not like or think you care about? Why do we feel we can dismiss or ignore things we don't know? Are we afraid that understanding will make it harder to dislike or dismiss or judge? Or that the effort to understand attributes an importance to things they shouldn't have?

For now what is needed is a position I describe as located between canon and cacophony — a framework that allows us to hear each other's voices engaged in a debate over questions we all care to learn the answers to. Without any ordering at all our voices will be noise, cacophony. With too much, most of them won't be heard at all, which is what canon is all about. What I want is a movement toward a set of questions that all human data are theoretically needed to answer. I think we need to stop arguing over which books to read or which cultures to study and start talking about which questions to ask.

The problem is as much social as intellectual. Canons of any sort come into being because an interpretive community exists. Hirsch and Bloom can make all the lists they like, but unless there is a community of human beings willing to commit themselves to chew on something together over an extended period of time, no book in the world can inherently produce norms.[9] Canonized books work, seem to be inherently capable of greater wisdom, partly because living communities have put their faith in them and expect them to be special.

Perhaps when we're through, or even partially through, with the monumental task I've described, we will after all discover together that some books do it better than others, or that forms of expression other than books do it better than books, or that given our abilities we can *make* some do it better than others; but for now I would be willing to make the radical proposal that we start with whatever we can commit ourselves to as communities, and that's more likely to be a set of questions than a list of books. Once we have the questions, let's see how the answers can best be discovered.

I myself feel some urgency about the need to reimagine world history, just as Arnold Toynbee already did more than thirty years ago when he wrote

> In order to save [hu]mankind we have to learn to live together in concord in spite of traditional differences of religion, civilization, nationality, class, and race. In order to live together in concord successfully, we have to know each other, and knowing each other includes knowing each other's past. . . . "All of human history is relevant to present and future human needs." "The knowledge of the history of [hu]mankind should be one of [hu]mankind's common possessions."[10]

For me, though, it's not just a question of *whether* we survive, but *how* we survive, and what human possibilities we open up for ourselves in the process. That sense of urgency, like many things, is best captured for me by a story about my favorite folk-hero, known variously among the peoples I study as the Mulla, Mulla Nasruddin, the Hoca, Juha, or Goha. It seems that

> Nasrudin sometimes took people for trips in his boat. One day a fussy pedagogue hired him to ferry him across a very wide river. As soon as they were afloat the scholar asked whether it was going to be rough. "Don't ask me nothing about it," said Nasrudin. "Have you never studied grammar?" "No," said the Mulla. "In that case, half your life has been wasted." The Mulla said nothing. Soon a terrible storm blew up. The Mulla's crazy cockleshell was filling with water. He leaned over toward his companion. "Have you ever learned to swim?" "No," said the pedant. "In that case, schoolmaster, *all* your life is lost, for we are sinking."[11]

Not long ago, William McNeill delivered a public lecture at Ohio State in which he reflected upon his experiences on the national Quincentenary commission. Having noted the triumphalist tone that pervaded the 1892 celebration, he wondered aloud how our nation could in 1992 mark responsibly an event that sensitive souls can no longer wholeheartedly *celebrate*. What better response than a national commitment to reimagine "our" heritage as the history of all of humanity, and to try to draw maximum benefit from the unprecedented effort our nation has made to support the study of all the world's peoples and cultures? What more fitting opportunity to leave the security of the mainstream for a voyage on the open seas, where risk and uncertainty are still the price of discovery?

Notes

1. Steven M. Albert, letter to the editor, *New York Times*, January 24, 1988, section 6, p. 8.

2. Marshall G. S. Hodgson, "The Interrelations of Societies in History," *Comparative Studies in Society and History* 5 (1963): 229–30.

3. See for example the new 1988, seventh edition of Robin Winks et al., *A History of Civilization*. According to Prentice Hall's own advertising brochure, "this all-encompassing, basic survey text probes the . . . history of the West."

4. Ralph Linton, *A Study of Man* (London: Appleton, 1936), 326–27.

5. Umberto Eco, *A Theory of Semiotics* (Bloomington: Indiana University Press, 1976), 20.

6. Jalaluddin Rumi, *Selected Poems from the Divani Shamsi Tabriz*, trans. Reynold A. Nicholson (London: Cambridge University Press, 1898), 17.

7. George E. Marcus and Michael M. J. Fischer, *Anthropology as Cultural Critique: An Experimental Moment in Human Sciences* (Chicago: University of Chicago Press, 1986), 32.

8. Paul Scott, *Jewel in the Crown* (New York: Avon Books, 1979), 403–4.

9. E. D. Hirsch, *Cultural Literacy: What Every American Needs to Know* (Boston: Houghton Mifflin, 1987); and Allan Bloom, *The Closing of the American Mind* (New York: Simon and Schuster, 1987).

10. Arnold Toynbee, *A Study of History* (New York: Oxford University Press, 1961), 12:138.

11. Idries Shah, *The Exploits of the Incomparable Mulla Nasrudin* (New York: Simon and Schuster, 1966), 17.

J. H. Hexter

Introductory College Course in Non-American History
An Ethnocentric View

Many years ago I conned a committee of five educationists and two heathens, of whom I was one, to direct a meeting of New York City teachers of education to address itself to the problems of teaching gifted students. The cornucopian gifts of educationists for obfuscation and idiocy defeated whatever malign purpose tempted me at the time to propose such a subject for discussion. When the educationists gathered they spent two hours listing the characteristics desirable in a teacher of gifted children. Somewhere in the first half hour I caught wise to where the discussion was heading. At the end of two hours it would be manifest that the only teacher adequately equipped to teach gifted students had died about two millennia ago on the cross. The exercise seemed to produce a blurry but amiable glow in the participants without incurring any of the risks inherent in actually coming to grips with the problem. The experience just described is usefully monitory. It warns us who are considering proposals about the introductory college course in non-American history, the hereafter acronymed ICCINAH, to keep our aspirations somewhere within range of the possibility of execution. That means that ICCINAH must be within the capacity of the students to understand it and of the instructional staff to deal with its requirements, given the constraints imposed by their respective abilities and attention spans and by the curriculum time we can reasonably hope to snatch away from the hogs on the other side in return for a tolerable compensatory input into their swill box.

To avoid the tendency of discussions like the present one to vanish into effluctions of hot air let us optimistically suppose that by heroic feats of academic imperialism and fraud we were able to establish for ICCINAH control over a territory of five credit hours in each of two semesters. (This I promise you is the last time I will indulge in such utopian fantasies.) We now have a concrete measured foundation. We can start building our conception of ICCINAH on the basis of a precise question: How to the greatest profit of college freshmen do we spend ten credit hours of their entering college year on their introduction to his-

J. H. Hexter, "Introductory College Course in Non-American History: An Ethnocentric View," *Proceedings of a Conference at Michigan State University, April 21–23, 1985*, ed. Josef W. Kronitz (East Lansing: Michigan State University, 1985), 179–181, 192–97.

tory that is not American history? There are two ways we can take toward answering this question, and it is important that we pick the right one — important, because if we do not, we will all spend more pages than the constraints of fee warrant on arriving at an ill-founded answer.

The first way is to start *tabula rasa*. We make believe that we know nothing about ICCINAH, that past experience in teaching and administering such a course is wholly irrelevant. Having burned the books of experience, we then ask: What is the best possible historical instruction not in American history that we could offer entering students? The answer is not difficult; ideally we could offer them instruction that would open to their understanding the whole panorama of mankind's sufferings, actions and reflections in the past: What people did and thought, believed and built and destroyed in the past hundred thousand years. And here a question shows the virtue of imposing an initial realistic time constraint on our course: *In ten credit hours?* You've got to be kidding! Making the contrafactual assumption of teachers capable of presenting such a panorama and students capable of absorbing it, doing so at any but the most trivial level calls not for ten hours but the whole 120 of the four-year undergraduate curriculum, and several years of graduate study. One fears that the departments of physics, chemistry, biology, English and all the rest may stubbornly and unanimously dissent. That would leave us with the intractable, indeed impossible task of deciding — on what principle or principles, God only knows — where to apply the thousands of ax strokes needed to cut our overblown aspirations down to manageable size, each stroke requiring justification wholly in terms of ideal desiderata.

The alternative way of answering the question turns away from the ridiculous assumption that in the matter of ICCINAH we are *tabulae rasae*. On the contrary we are slates well scribbled over, in my particular case for fifty-six years since in the spring semester of 1929, as a freshman I enrolled in the one-semester modern European history survey, starting about 1517 and using the text of Professor Ferdinand Schevill. Beginning a decade later, for eighteen years, minus a war and a fellowship or so, I taught in the basic required history course at Queens. That course underwent a series of catastrophic remodellings during the first nine lean years. It settled down into being the most effective course in the curriculum of a superb undergraduate college in the latter nine, fat years. I continued to teach in a fundamentally similar course when I moved to a Midwestern university in 1957, and did so again when I moved back there in 1978. In the latter year, however, I taught in a version of the course which, though excellent in some respects, had had a vital member amputated from it — its assigned source readings.

The course, in which from my ninth year at Queens College I always taught with a success ascribable not to the teacher but to what he was teaching, has for four decades been the basic required history course at two of the best undergraduate university colleges in the country, Chicago and Columbia. It was so for two decades in another, Harvard. There in the sixties the faculty abandoned the undergraduates in a rush to be the greatest university in the world, transforming Harvard College to a place where the best college students in the country are given a second rate undergraduate education. And what is this course which has worked so long so well in the schools where the faculty has given it the attention that is due it? It is Western Civilization.

To leave it at that without further specification, however, is to leave so much to chance that the course so named might be the standard educational disaster: a straight lecture course, with assignments out of a survey textbook, which the students sensibly do not read. They need not because the ultimate testing at exam time requires them only to dish back cold to the lecturer the by then stiff porridge that during the past several months has been dished out to them tepid in lectures. On the basis of experience the right Western Civilization course requires of the students close reading of selections from texts beginning with Plato and the Bible and coming up perhaps to Solzhynitzen and Martin Luther King. It requires of them that they be prepared — each one, each class — to talk about the assigned selection in a discussion session. It requires each faculty member guiding a discussion to help his students toward finding some of the crucial human issues raised in or by the assigned text. For the provision of continuity the course director assigns reading in a recent textbook as little immersed in minutia as he can find and delivers lectures that provide some further element of continuity for the whole class. . . .

That a Western Civilization course is in a sense ethnocentric is beyond dispute. Its ethnocentricity is branded on the contents of every collection of sources ever made for assignment in the course. Nowadays such collections always start with source readings from the Bible and from the Greeks. Then they move on to a small patch of the earth's surface, about one percent of it, a band 400 or 500 miles wide, east to west, and a bit more than twice that distance north and south between Rome and London. For about 1800 years it sticks there. Almost everyone who during that time span shows up in any of the Western Civ source books was born on that small fragment of the earth's surface and spent his whole life there. During that span no source in the books is the work of anyone born more than 400 miles from the bounds of that patch. If one wanted to run a competition for ethnocentricity, surely an inquiry into the development of culture so constrained over about two-thirds of its span would be a plausible candidate for the prize. Americans live 3,500 miles to 7,000 miles from that patch of the earth's surface. They live in a land seven times as big. Half of them are not even ancestrally linked to the patch. Why in the United States should we subject the large cohort of our people doomed to higher education to a historical inquiry about two-thirds of which concerns only the chin wagging and pen scratching that went on in that patch 200 to 2000 years ago?

To that at least we know the past answer: that is where we came from. Not just those of us whose ancestors migrated from there to here, but all of us, those who fled here from the potato blight in Ireland, from the Czar's pogroms in Russia, from the reprisals of mad zealots in Cambodia and Iran. We all come from there because it is from there that we have taken our religions, our family structure, our economic ideas, our literary, artistic, and architectural forms, our modes of moral judgment, our sciences, our laws and our language. Most of the things we do or the ways we do them, we do as we do because it is the way people living in the territory of Western civilization decided to or came to do them between the beginning of our era and 1800 or after. For better or worse Western civilization is our civilization; we belong to it and it to us.

That would seem to settle the issue — but of course it does not. It does not because it leaves open the hard question — so what? I gather from my usual inattentive reading of the bits of science which show up in the daily press that we human beings are probably all descendants of a rather unprepossessing small mammal like a rat from the Age of the Dinosaurs. Still we do not insist that all college freshmen spend even an hour much less a quarter of an academic year on an inquiry into nature and destiny of that ancestral rodent.

Our civilization, our cultural inheritance, however, is different from our generic inheritance. We are stuck with the latter. Only over very long time spans is it likely to change in any major way or by our conscious action. It is otherwise with the cultural inheritance institutionally imbedded in the habituations and institutions of our civilization. In two millennia we have rejected parts of that inheritance — religious persecution, surbordination of women, and the theory of humors for example. Nevertheless, we are what we are, will be what we will be, because of what we have been. About that we need to know, or we will not be at home even with ourselves.

The consequence of the temporary — one longs to believe — collapse of parts of our curricula in high school and college has been that in terms of formal education we have effectively lobotomized a generation or so of our society. The operation has deeply impaired in that generation some of the important sensors by which men systematically orient themselves. Americans go about with a most ill-structured notion of where they are in time and space. They do not know where they are in space because primary and secondary schools have taken human geography out of the center of their curricula. A young American adult today does not know where he is in time because over a decade ago by insouciantly whisking the Western Civ courses out of his curriculum so many colleges obliterated his view of the historic mass on which he actually stands.

One must not overdo this, or make too much of the gravity of the loss, or one will expose oneself to ridicule. After all the Western Civilization course is not more than a half-century old. Before that the small portion of the population that went to college learned whatever they learned about the civilization of which they were the most recent flowering fragmentarily and casually, by accident rather than design. And still people managed to stumble through the days of their lives without having to think systematically about Calvin on original sin or Descartes on the mind-matter problem or most of the other things one meets up with in a Western Civ sequence. Of course. Anyone who has managed to survive to college age out of custody or an asylum has had to acquire an encyclopaedic if unself-conscious experiential grasp of the small area and the brief time span in which he lives. Given that, what he needs to worry about is not total blindness, but acute myopia. Of this one becomes conscious when young people who have never reflected on the nature and destiny of man airily dismiss the Middle Ages — the whole millennium — as "superstitious" and "dark."

The trouble is that the more one moves about in space or forward in time the more frequently individual experience proves inadequate to one's needs, and these days we are more and more often forced to move out of our space-time neighborhoods. More and more often we have to know where we stand in relation to more and more strangers. This used to be taken as a reason for formal education about all sorts of strangers — for World History in brief. Constraints of time, however, render the enterprise of World History pedagogically absurd. Emphasizing the differences among the many cultures the world has known and knows, World History spreads the net of knowledge wide and therefore exceedingly thin. So thin, indeed, does the net become that it fragments into useless, senseless bits. Surely if a firm grasp of the meaning of other cultures should turn out to be necessary, our chances of getting such a grasp when we actually need it is better if we are solidly planted in our own civilization than if we are afloat amid eddies of ignorance with the debris of trivia.

As those last words come off my pen I realize that they come from a time warp, from the thirties when I was first getting my intellectual feet under me — graduation from college, Great Depression, Communism and Nazism, graduate school, unemployment, first job, World War II. In those days in a wash of cultural relativism one tried not very effectively to convince oneself that there might be some glimmer of redemptive value in the civilization of the West that was not about to be obliterated by triumphant fascist barbarism or wholly outshone by the rising sun of the Communist experiment. Those were the days when Contemporary Civilization sequences wound up with a semester "comparative" course called Fascism, Capitalism, Socialism, Communism, and the instructor entertained the wistful hope that the oscillations of the political pendulum in the real world might stop at the third alternative where it had never actually stopped before. . . .

It is time to wake up and sing a new song. Any ICCINAH but Western Civilization has stopped making sense. Now Western Civilization is the only game in town. Currently two versions of the game are being played. One is the incompetent planned version dealt with a stacked deck from behind the Kremlin walls and within the other walls and the barbed wire — we may think of it as Russian roulette. Most of the people playing the game that way, however they got into it in the first place, end up playing it with a gun at their heads. The other version is a rackety, risky, open deal with some folks trying to slip one off the bottom of the deck often enough to keep the players watchful. Mainly it is played with a straight deck properly shuffled by the rule — the rule of law. It turns out that within the rules the harder all people play to win the more winnings there will be to spread around. That is the way it has come out after a half-century of rivalry between the two versions of the Western game, the only versions seriously engaging any people with big bucks. In 1985 that is the way it stands between what in 1935 were called the "Soviet experiment" and the "confused liberal" way of arraying Western institutions and values. That is the way it is nearly seventy years after the Russian Revolution: the Soviet Union has broken eggs all over the place but come up with scarcely an omelette. And there are twelve or fifteen million shot or starved and frozen to death in the Arctic and Siberia — the Gulag — in exchange for somewhere between twelfth and fifteenth place in per capita net income among the powers of the world and not a hope of catching up with the West's confused liberals or confused conservatives — labels that do not make all that difference in the West anymore.

Western Civilization got pried loose from the college curriculum in the late sixties and early seventies by hysterical and ignorant young people screaming "relevance" at college faculties who lacked the moral courage to state their doubts about the durable relevance of a pathetic corner of Southeast Asia. And now, alas, off the back corridors and in the dusty corners of academe the musty offices and underemployed professors of Southeast Asian Area Studies moulder toward an academic extinction that will scarcely leave a mark to warn the next batch of innocents away from similar errors.

No such danger faces the Western Civ course. Someday perhaps a quasi-alternative civilization like that of Russia in the thirties will emerge from the surviving fragments of some older disintegrating culture — fundamentalist Moslem? Hindu? Confucian Chinese? Only then need the world wonder whether such a civilization can digest the elements of Western Civilization indispensable to any emergent culture's viability and survival. Only then need responsible academics wonder whether in the role of ICCINAH they need to consider an alternative to Western Civilization. In the meantime those responsible academics concerned to restore the devastated foundations of a proper college education can move confidently in the area of ICCINAH. The thing, and the only thing, to do therefore is to institute or restore as a graduation requirement the sort of Western Civilization course described earlier in this paper and to watch like a hawk those charged with offering it, lest they succumb to the sloth and slackness that are the constant companions of monopoly. For this no justification is necessary beyond the one offered here. After all, since those we are teaching are bound to take part in the only game in town, they had better know what chips they have and what the chips are worth. And we had better remember that with the kind of open market game Western Civilization is in the West, the value put on the different kinds of chips fluctuates. Still as chancy and as complex as the game is, it is not all blind luck. As little as they know, the corps of teachers in the Western Civilization courses know more than the eighteen-year-olds in their classes who are hobbled by inexperience and blinkered by the defects of their prior formal education. They have not a clue about how the game got to be what it is. So let us begin. We have nothing to lose but our educational incoherence.

JACOB NEUSNER

It Is Time to Stop Apologizing for Western Civilization and to Start Analyzing Why It Defines World Culture

When we argue about what should be taught in schools and colleges, our conception of the world is at stake. For as educators, we transmit not information but concepts. Our view of the world tells us what to teach and what to ignore.

The debates that were precipitated by former Secretary of Education William J. Bennett's important and public criticism of Stanford's revised Western-culture curriculum centered upon the university's decision to include works by members of formerly ignored groups. But how are we to present in a cohesive way the disparate cultures of Africa, Asia, Latin America, and the Pacific?

Purely political arguments either for or against affording a full hearing to neglected parts of the world are beside the point. If Africa, Asia, and Latin America are important (and they are), they belong in the curriculum; if not, then institutional politics should not make any difference. But what defines importance? The real question is not *how* to include all cultures but *why* we should include any of them, Eastern or Western. There has to be a single conception of the whole, of what has made the world that we propose to explain and hand on to the coming generations.

I think we should continue to emphasize the history and culture of the West, while encompassing the rest, because the West has in fact made the world we know. Anyone who wants to participate in the world community in the coming century had better know precisely how and why the West has defined, and will continue to define, world civilization. Why do I say that? Because everybody wants what we have: science and technology, prosperity, and democracy — that is, our philosophy, our economics, our politics.

It is the simple truth that science and technology emerge out of Western philosophy, not out of the philosophy of India or China or say of the African nations. However, those and other non-Western countries all form part of the one world we want the coming generations of Americans to understand. At issue in academic debate in the next half-century will be the place of the West in that world.

Jacob Neusner, "It Is Time to Stop Apologizing for Western Civilization and to Start Analyzing Why It Defines World Culture," *Chronicle of Higher Education*, 15 February 1989, B1–B2.

Since it is a fact that people everywhere aspire to the material advantages that flow, uniquely I think, from the modes of social organization that the West has devised — its economics, its science and technology, and also its politics and philosophy — I think it is time to stop apologizing and start analyzing what has made Western civilization the world-defining power that it is.

Study Africa, India, China, Japan, Latin America? Of course. But what is it that we want to know? A critical question that demands our study of other cultures is why it is that the West has created what the rest of the world now wants. Why did capitalism not begin in India, for example? Why is there no science in Africa? Why has democracy only been grafted onto the political structures in Asia? And, conversely, why are all of them to be found indigenously in the West? To answer such questions, we must begin where science, economics, politics, and technology began and from whence they were diffused. They uniquely flourished in the West, and, to begin with, in Western Europe.

People nowadays rightly want to find a place in the academic study of civilization for cultures indigenous to every region and land. To do so, however, we need to frame a global program of thought and reflection. And, if we are not merely to rehearse the facts about this culture or that one, we shall require modes of comparison. That is not a recipe for relativism; it is an invitation to analyze and compare and contrast cultures, all of them honored and each of them placed in relationship with the others. The basis for comparison lies in the shared and universal concerns represented by philosophy, economics, and politics.

Since the West has defined those concerns, and since all other social systems measure themselves by Western civilization's capacity to afford people both the goods of material wealth and the services of political power, the indicative traits of Western civilization demand close study. These are, I think, the following: in philosophy, the modes of thought and inquiry that we call scientific; in economics, capitalism; and in politics, the distribution of power in political structures and systems. They will dictate the shape of the curriculum, because they adumbrate the structure of world civilization today.

That doesn't mean we have nothing to learn from other cultures. On the contrary, we have much to learn, once we have established our common questions and perspectives. There is no understanding the world without the West, and there is no understanding the rest of the world without first grasping the relationship of the West, and its unique achievements in science, economics, politics, and philosophy, with the non-Western world.

In short, not all things are equally important and some things are going to receive more attention than others. West is not "best," but there are things in the West that are valued everywhere, and those are the traits of Western civilization that join the study of the West with learning about the rest. In composing a curriculum addressed to world civilization in philosophy, economics, and politics, we must hold together East and West, South and North, and, it goes without saying, both sexes as well. There can be such a curriculum, once we recognize that there really is a single world civilization, important to us all.

Democracy, capitalism, anti-colonialism, science, technology, ever-rising productivity in industry and agriculture — these essentially Western and quintessentially American values are now universal. And they define what there is to know about everyone, everywhere — beginning, of course, with ourselves.

SELECTED BIBLIOGRAPHY

Dunn, Ross E. "Multiculturalism and World History." *World History Bulletin* 8 (1992): 3–8. An appeal to abandon reductionist arguments over whose culture is to be included or not included in the curriculum in favor of a culturally neutral approach that privileges the search for world-historical problems to investigate.

Hodgson, Marshall G. S. "World History and a World Outlook." *The Social Studies* 35 (1944): 297–301. Reprinted in *Rethinking World History: Essays on Europe, Islam, and World History*, edited by Edmund Burke III, 35–43. New York: Cambridge University Press, 1993. In this early essay Hodgson's premonitory outline of the world history to come is uncanny.

Ianetti, John E. "Has the World History Course Arrived?" *World History Bulletin* 12 (Winter/Spring 1996): 6–12. The author surveys developments in the 1980s and 1990s that portend world history's acceptance as a standard teaching field in both high schools and colleges.

McNeill, William H. "A Defense of World History." *Transactions of the Royal Historical Society*, 5th ser., 32 (1982). Reprinted in *Mythistory and Other Essays*, 71–95. Chicago: University of Chicago Press, 1986. By the time he wrote this essay, McNeill was moving from the firm civilizational orientation of *The Rise of the West* to a more expansive vision of transcivilizational change. Here he argues that world history as he understands it subscribes to the same critical methods and evidentiary rules that all other subfields of the discipline acknowledge. Its questions are simply of a larger scale.

Stavrianos, L. S. "Teaching World History." *The History Teacher* 3 (November 1969): 19–24. Writing a decade after his plea in the *Journal of Modern History*, he declares that "we are better prepared for teaching and writing world history than at any time in the past." It's a matter of historians being willing to change along with the times.

———. "World History for the 21st Century." *World History Bulletin* 13 (Spring/Summer 1997): 4–9. Stumping for world history as rousingly as he did forty years earlier, Stavrianos calls on world history teachers to shoulder moral responsibility for helping young citizens distinguish between the perils and promises of High Technology.

Von Laue, Theodore H. "Major Points to Be Considered in Teaching World History." *World History Bulletin* 7 (Fall/Winter 1989–90): 33–34. A passionate advocate of world history since the 1970s, Von Laue expresses his sense of urgency about contradictory world trends — a drift toward ever more complicated social interrelationships and the continuing danger of military or environmental self-destruction. He wants a world history "adequate for the needs of the historical condition in which we find ourselves."

———. "A World History for the Future." *World History Bulletin* 11 (Spring/Summer 1994): 5–12. Von Laue takes the controversial position that the West's triumph of power and the "clash of cultures" are the main global dynamics in modern times. However, neither aggressive Westernization nor cultural conflict are inevitable. "A morally alert future-oriented global history" can help move humanity toward equality and peace.

PART THREE

REDEFINING WORLD HISTORY: SOME KEY STATEMENTS

If teaching world history in the age of superpowers, new nations, and television were to be something more than a rerigging of Western Civ to incorporate "non-Western" civilizations, then new historical hypotheses, categories, vocabularies, and principles of selection would have to be formulated. The problem coming into focus by the 1960s was not convincing educators and the public that broader definitions of world history were a good idea. Rather, it was how to lay the conceptual ground for writing and teaching about historical developments whose dimensions fit badly into the classificatory schemes of nation-state or civilization. The incessant restructuring of human relations that characterized the postwar world, together with the huge diversification of research, made historians and social scientists more aware than they had ever been of the interconnectivity of human experience over centuries and millennia. What new spatial and chronological architecture would have to be invented to properly situate the study of such phenomena as disease pandemics, trade diasporas, transoceanic migrations, or social transformations linked to worldwide deforestation? What fresh vocabulary was required to write about Africans, Asians, and Native Americans as creative agents of change and about their meetings with Europeans as historical encounters rather than occasions when history first arrived? If states and societies were to be located in geosocial contexts larger than themselves, then what names to give those frameworks when nothing in the conventional lexicon seemed to apply?

Academic ruminations over these questions involved, and still involve, a continuous and remarkable intermingling of the concerns of scholars and teachers. Debates in the past few decades over the epistemology and methodology of research in world history have been consistently tied to discussions of how to make the subject intelligible to students. How, for example, could world history scholarship be freed of confining presuppositions and categories without the teaching project either congealing into social scientific abstractions or vaporizing into clouds of unconnected data? Not all world history conceptualizers have talked about teaching. But whether they have or not, teachers, especially those in the college survey brigades, have quickly seized on any new formulation that might help them and their students make sense of the global past.

This chapter presents what I believe are seminal statements on the reimagining of world history. All these articles have frequently been cited in the historiography of world history, some for many years and some more recently. Other writings that historians would regard as equally influential are also included in this book, but they are placed in other sections following my own judgment about how to group the selections. The channels of intellectual cross-fertilization among the following five writers are quite complex. Some of these connections will be apparent in the essays, though I have resisted the temptation to try to organize the selections in a way that traces a single genealogy of thought.

According to Edmund Burke, Marshall Hodgson's precocious vision of world history is to be attributed to the powerful combination of his Quaker universalism, his residence in the intellectual hothouse of the University of Chicago, and his singular perceptions of Islam as a trans-Hemispheric cultural system.[1] In the mental arena that pitted fashionable modernization theory and Chicago's Europe-centered "great books" tradition against his universalist and cosmopolitan sensibilities, Hodgson worked out his views of world history. "Hemispheric Interregional History as an Approach to World History" is an elaboration of an unpublished essay that he drafted as an undergraduate at the age of nineteen.[2] The revision reprinted here represents one of the early published statements of his new conceptualization. He explains his idea of the Afro-Eurasian ecumene as a unitary spatial framework not only within which civilizations interacted (the dynamic William McNeill emphasized) but also within which developments occurred that might alter human relationships across the entire trans-Hemispheric region. Hodgson and McNeill at Chicago, plus L. S. Stavrianos at Northwestern University twenty miles to the north, reinforced one another's independent work in establishing the idea of the intercommunicating Afro-Eurasian zone as a useful theoretical tool. This opened new possibilities for releasing scholarly inquiry, and therefore world history teaching, from the conventional categories of nation and civilization.

Geoffrey Barraclough, who succeeded to Arnold Toynbee's professorship at the University of London in 1956, was a brilliant medievalist who saw the inadequacy of nation-state history to explain modern global developments. In arguing for a more panoramic view of the human past, he questioned the value of totalizing approaches that seek to comprehend all in a "continuous narrative." He also had doubts about grand designs such as UNESCO's *History of Mankind*, which was written by committees of experts. Distancing himself from Toynbee, he believed that a world history most useful to present global circumstances "does not call for a synthetic reconstruction of the whole of the past, but rather for the study of the processes of development of human society in different environments and different civilizations." In *Main Trends in History,* a reflection on the directions the discipline might be taking as of the mid 1970s, he considers the "prospects of world history." This book and other writings of his were important reference points for teachers and scholars of those years who were searching for persuasive language to strengthen and justify the world history project. Barraclough's most conspicuous contribution to the field was his editorship of the *Times Atlas of World History,* which defined history more inclusively than any earlier atlas and offered teachers fresh perspectives on the human landscape.[3]

Owing to his eclectic Marxism and consequent privileging of economic relationships, Eric Wolf might be placed along with Immanuel Wallterstein and Andre Gunder Frank in the broad category of "world systems" scholar (see Part Five). However, in the introduction to his 1982 book *Europe and the People without History,* Wolf made a key theoretical statement that exposes the ways in which prevailing definitions of "societies" and "cultures" inhibit rather than assist a clearer understanding of world-scale processes in modern times. Employing a conceptual vocabulary quite different from that of Hodgson or McNeill, Wolf critiques the foundational postulate of modern sociology that societies are "static, disconnected things," a strategy that has led directly to "a model of the world as a global pool hall in which the entities spin off each other like so many hard and round billiard balls." Though in *Europe and the People without History* Wolf did not speak directly to teaching issues, he made the most sophisticated case up to that time for abandoning presumably self-contained social bodies as units of world-historical knowledge. He argued rather that "cultures" are really

> only cultural sets of practices and ideas, put into play by determinate human actors under determinate circumstances. In the course of action, these cultural sets are forever assembled, dismantled, and reassembled, conveying in variable accents the divergent paths of groups and classes.

Philip Curtin is a pioneer of world history whose philosophy is largely implicit in his numerous writings on comparative and interregional themes. As Craig Lockard has pointed out (see Part One), Curtin has not, in contrast to Hodgson, McNeill, or Andre Gunder Frank, attempted to devise a conceptual architecture that might encompass the full sweep of the human past. Moreover, he has serious doubts about the value of survey courses that stress global coverage. Rather, he has adopted a world-scale frame for investigating the social and cultural history of migration, trade, and disease, drawing mainly on a methodology of inductive comparison. In his presidential address to the American Historical Association in 1983 he offers some general reflections on his approach. Like McNeill eight years earlier (see Part Two), he worries that excessively narrow graduate training and professional expertise are contributing to the flight of college students from history. Scholars have an obligation, he argues, not only to specialize but also to synthesize from "a wider span of historical knowledge." The profession must do a better job of formulating historical problems that Americans will care about and find interesting. This involves identifying the "universe of data" pertinent to the problem under investigation rather than allowing the nation-state or some other geographical convention to determine what problems can be studied or to limit the range of inquiry. Curtin offers several examples of how a proper fit between a problem and the "relevant aggregate" of human beings and data can illuminate world-historical processes and prevent interpretive distortions.

An essay by William McNeill is the last rather than one of the first key statements because for nearly half a century he has continued to refine his views on the shape of world history. Indeed, he has been remarkably self-conscious about the corrections he has made in his own intellectual course.[4] The statement offered here is part of an article he published in 1995 in an issue of *History and Theory* devoted to world history. He admits that his understanding of civilizations has changed, that he now regards them as "rather pale, inchoate entities in themselves." He has moved to the position that "a proper world history ought to focus primarily upon changes in the ecumenical world system, and then proceed to fit developments within separate civilizations, and within smaller entities like states and nations, into the pattern of that fluctuating whole." He proposes an interpretation focusing on dynamic, shifting "communications nets" that carry not only goods and money but armies, migrants, missionaries, and all kinds of cultural messages from one part of the earth to another. Like most other world historians who look for patterns far above the local and national, he recognizes that ever more intense intercommunication produces no happy drift toward cultural accord or confluence of interests. Rather, global interchange only heightens the urgency of communal identification, which allows local groups to huddle together against the gales of change. "How to reconcile membership in vivacious primary communities with the imperative of an emerging cosmopolitanism is," according to McNeill, "the most urgent issue of our time."

Notes

1. Marshall G. S. Hodgson, *Rethinking World History: Essays on Europe, Islam, and World History*, ed. Edmund Burke III (Cambridge: Cambridge University Press, 1993), x–xi.

2. See Hodgson, *Rethinking World History*, xi–xii.

3. Geoffrey Barraclough and Geoffrey Parker, eds., *The Times Atlas of World History*, 4th ed. (Maplewood, N.J.: Hammond, 1993).

4. See William H. McNeill, "*The Rise of the West* after Twenty-five Years," *Journal of World History* 1 (Spring 1990): 1–21.

MARSHALL G. S. HODGSON

Hemispheric Interregional History as an Approach to World History

The term "world history" is often used in schools (at least in the United States) to designate a course designed to tell something of as many different foreign nations as possible. As a serious field of study, however, we expect "world history" to reflect not just a wide range of facts, but in some sense an overall development in the human past. The philosophical possibility of such an overall history has been questioned. I do not intend to discuss the problem on that level. Rather, I want to remind us of a particular field to history too generally neglected, which may not itself be strictly world history, but the examination of which at least forms the principal part of any possible world history.

If a world history is philosophically possible, it will in any case be subject to two important limitations. It is unlikely to deal with all or even most of the events that have troubled mankind from the beginning, and it is unlikely to bear the type of human meaning which a sensitive history of a particular community can have. For it will deal with only such themes as are too broad in their ramifications to be conveniently handled within the limits of nations and cultural regions. Such themes are unavoidably somewhat impersonal. But admitting these restrictions, I believe that research on the world-historical level is not only possible, but exceedingly important. Indeed, its cultivation is already under way, many detailed problems of interregional history having been fruitfully approached in monographic terms, and many treatments of its overall problems having been suggested. But for its further progress now such world-historical research needs far wider recognition of its importance and its problems as an independent field.

WHAT WORLD HISTORY IS AND IS NOT

During the last decade or so (at least in the United States) we have become increasingly aware of our need for history of a world scope. But what goes by the name of world history and tries to satisfy this need is still essentially Western

Marshall G. S. Hodgson, "Hemispheric Interregional History as an Approach to World History," *Journal of World History/Cahiers d'Histoire Mondiale* (UNESCO) 1, no. 3 (1954): 715–23.

history amplified by a few unrelated chapters on other parts of the world, notably India, China, and Japan. Even such non-Westerners as write "world history" seem to have been stirred to little better than this, except for an amplification of the chapters dealing with their particular region. This sort of thing is not world history; no more than a history of France, or of Germany, supplemented by occasional chapters on other countries, would be European history. Nor is world history merely the sum of separate histories of the nations or regions of the world; no more than European history is the sum of the separate histories of the European nations. European history, rather, traces those developments which have involved large parts of Europe in common, and have determined the overall posture of affairs. It deals with the Renaissance, the rise of nation-states, the Industrial Revolution. Similarly world history must be expected to trace those developments which proceeded on a stage too wide for any more local history to cover other than fragmentarily, and which determined the cultural possibilities of mankind as a whole, or the greater part of it.

During the last three thousand years there has been one zone, possessing to some degree a common history, which has been so inclusive that its study must take a preponderant place in any possible world-historical investigations. From at least the first millennium B.C., the various lands of urbanized, literate civilization in the Eastern Hemisphere, in a continuous zone from the Atlantic to the Pacific, have been in commercial and commonly in intellectual contact with each other, mediately or immediately. Not only have the bulk of mankind lived in this zone, but its influence has long emanated into much of the rest of the world. (Thus, we are learning that the history of Bantu Africa cannot be adequately traced in isolation from the wider agricultural and commercial history to its North.) As these civilizations expanded during the millennia, their heirs, in one way or another, have come to dominate the globe; so that at least ninety per cent of the world's population now traces its history to some segment of this zone of nations; and the remainder must recognize the dominance of its cultural heritage. A history of interregional developments among the literate urban civilizations of the Eastern Hemisphere, developments transcending cultural regions like Europe, the Middle East, India, or the Confucian lands, will go far toward meeting our needs for world history.

THE PROBLEM OF ORGANIZING THE HISTORICAL MATERIAL

The attempt to study such a history is plagued with many problems, but we can set aside at least some that have been supposed to plague a universal history. We need not be deterred, of course, by the sheer quantity of past events in so wide an area. We are not concerned, after all, with each of the events that have happened in each nation, but only with those which have involved major segments of mankind, and so set a framework to all our historical experience. Those, while very important, can be presumed to be relatively few. For purposes of perspective (these need not be the only purposes of a world history, but surely they are important), a slim volume may be of more value than a fat one.

Further, we can at least postpone the insuperable problem of finding a universal scheme into which all history will fit — whether in terms of progress or of cycles, of a master-race or of a revelation. History is so rich, that almost at the first touch it yields an overabundance of suggestions of pattern. We will find this true even for so broad a zone as we are concerned with. The historian needs not fix upon a pattern for his whole field of inquiry before beginning his detailed work of criticism and exploration.

The great problems we do have to face are those of appropriately reorienting our historical and geographical attitudes, and then organizing the relevant historical material for purposes of study. We must first (as we shall see) learn to orient ourselves adequately to the Hemisphere as a whole rather than to one — or, in the case of non-Westerners, two — particular parts of it. Once the vision is caught, this is perhaps the easier of the two problems. For when we come to organizing the historical material, we must find ourselves without the frames of reference we are accustomed to in work of lesser scope. We cannot organize an interregional investigation in terms of political continuity, as is usual in the case of nations; nor even in terms of a multiple institutional continuity, as in the history of Western Europe as a whole. For the various cultural regions of the Hemisphere shared directly very few institutions — no common church, no common legal commitments, no common schools of art or literature. Yet history, to be meaningful in interpreting our past to us, must be more than a disconnected listing of events and movements, selected arbitrarily because they happened to occur on a large scale.

Interregional Historical Developments

The following approach I conceive as adapted to organizing the material with a minimum of presuppositions as to the patterns of history. Events may be dealt with in their relation to the total constellation of historical forces of which they are a part — a method not limited to world history, but perhaps likely to be especially appropriate in this case. This means that we are to consider how events reflect interdependent interregional developments. Then we are to trace these developments as they affect one another and their common geographical, cultural, and economic setting in the world as a whole.

An interregional development of this sort, relatively simple in form, is the rise, spread, and disruption of the Mongol power in the thirteenth century — in connection with which the political and even the economic life of remote parts of the Hemisphere were made to interact quite directly. But probably more important are those developments which involved no consciousness of their remoter ramifications on the part of the actors in them. Thus in the Middle Ages Chinese mathematicians learned from Muslims in Turkestan, and European mathematicians learned from Muslims in Spain. The Muslims were aware of each other's existence as scholars, but the Chinese and Europeans scarcely so. Yet we in our day need not therefore be unaware of their participation in a common tradition. This tradition had received impetus from the Aegean and the Indus and beyond, before the Medieval Muslims gathered it together again for a new dispersion; we can look at what these scholars, scattered in time and space, were doing as a whole — and so avoid more than one error of perspective and of fact. We can do the same regarding the distant spread of Hellenistic artistic inspiration; or of Indian monasticism.

But we must study those interregional developments in a common historical context, if only to avoid overlooking the clues this can afford as to the bearing of evidence in regard to any one development. (For data regarding Hellenistic art or commerce may take on quite new meaning as we become aware of the state of civilization in all the regions affected — and unaffected.) Among these unconsciously interregional developments, then, should be noted especially those which, even if appearing independently region by region, converged in their effects to alter *the general disposition of the Hemisphere.* Thus the gradual expansions into the northern parts of Eurasia by Chinese, Europeans, and others, combined to reduce steadily the range of the Eurasian nomads, and to alter their relation to all the surrounding societies. One may compare the invasions of the pre-Christian Indo-Europeans in the Middle East, when the civilizations appeared almost surrounded by uncultivated peoples ready to submerge them; then the invasions of the time of Attila, when the outsiders themselves were in a large measure submerged; then finally compare the time of Genghis Khan, when the nomads in their turn might rightly feel surrounded; their freedom of motion being cut off by great empires penetrating their very deserts; but the skills of civilization lying also at hand, to help destroy the great empires themselves with a vast success undreamed of by former nomads. One might analyze analogously, if there were more data, the results in interregional commerce of the southward expansion of the civilizations, especially around the Indian Ocean.

This gradual expansion of civilized territory over the Hemisphere, which so altered the role of the nomads, was only one part of the constant cumulative acquisition, in all parts of the world, of new techniques and discoveries. All these acquisitions resulted, in sum, in radical changes in the possibilities of further development anywhere. Of a slightly different sort are those developments taking place in particular regions, but which became of interregional consequence when they came to alter the relationships, economic or otherwise, among the regions of the world. The economic weakness of the pivotal Middle East by the end of the Middle Ages, for instance, seems to have been a decisive factor in the economic and political disposition of the world into which Europe was about to expand.

THE INTERREGIONAL HISTORICAL CONSTELLATION

In tracing the Hemispheric context of these interregional developments, we find some elements relatively constant from age to age. For instance, up to 1500 A.D. the Middle East is the only great region in direct commercial relations with all parts of the Hemisphere. Likewise the other regions persist in playing distinctive roles: the restless Mediterranean Basin, and later the eccentric Western Europe; Central Eurasia struggling with nomadism; India, harbor of wealth and exiles; Indo-China and Malaysia, crossroads of trade; the relatively isolated Far East of China and Japan. But from time to time the general posture changes greatly in point of cultural resources and dominant activities. After the rise of the early valley civilizations occurred a spread and cosmopolitan mingling of urban cultures — which produced a new total picture by the time of the great Indo-European invasions, and of the use of iron. Then among Greeks, Hebrews, Assyrians, Persians, Indo-Aryans, and Chou Chinese arose still another historical climate, different from either the age of the early river civilizations or the cosmopolitan age of Tell el-Amarna; a new age reflected surely in such matters as the new coinage, but most obviously in the great classical sages from Thales and Isaiah to Mencius. This was a cultural climate far readier for the subsequent great expansion of Hellenism than the world had been a thousand years before. In yet another thousand years, yet another world had been ushered in, not only by Hellenism but by the various activities of missionary Buddhism which sometimes mingled with it; and by the impact of several major regional empires such as Rome and the Han in China, empires which reflected to some degree the work of the classical sages. But not the least significant change which that world of Mohammed's time had undergone was the rise to political power everywhere of a new type of scriptural religion of personal salvation: either in the form of *ad hoc* faiths like Christianity or Mahayana Buddhism, or of old faiths made over like Rabbinical Judaism, and the Hindu Shaivism and Vaishnavism. Though their answers differed widely, the questions they posed were largely the same as those which Islam for a time seemed to answer more effectively than any of its older rivals. Within five or six centuries Islam was reaching into most parts of the Hemisphere. But before Islam could absorb the world, the scene changed yet again. By the time of the Mongol outburst there had intervened at least the usual cumulative improvement militarily, scientifically, in financial technique and commercial expansion; and, as if to settle old problems and clear the way for new, there had intervened scholastic syntheses of philosophy and religion from Shankara to Chu Hsi. For new problems were indeed threatening: the far Western nations of Europe were becoming unwontedly active. The stage was being set, not only in the technical means, but in the human disposition of the Eastern Hemisphere, for the modern world. Then between the Mongol victories and the Western conquest of the Oceans intervened not only certain key inventions, but a number of political and economic changes which left the crucial Indian Ocean open to Western power. Then between the days of Vasco da Gama and the French and Industrial Revolutions, the evolution of Western power in relation to each of the major world cultural regions had already set the form of the subsequent world order; which in turn began to collapse not only in Europe but throughout the world in the second decade of this century.

The purpose of this sketch of the historical constellation of the Hemisphere is to suggest some of the major watersheds, after which history throughout the Hemisphere must take account of new factors in the total situation. I have had to allow the reader to fill in the details on the canvas, and have attempted therefore rather to evoke memories than to demonstrate data. What is important is the recognition not only that there is a whole range of problems which require treatment in terms which cross all regional boundaries; but then that there has been some sort of developing pattern in which all these interregional developments can be studied, as they are affected by and in turn affect its elements as constituted at any one time.

I am sure that alternative methods of organizing these interregional materials are to be had. Jacques Pirenne, while concentrating his attention on the West, has attempted in some measure a general world history centered on the fortunes of the cosmopolitan cultures he calls "maritime" over against the more ingrown "continental" ones. Toynbee's method of tracing connections among great "civilizations," while not intended to yield world history, in effect does so. Other significant studies could be named. But there are some approaches that can be labelled blind alleys. Some have tried to list the most prominent *national* events side by side chronologically, and then deduce *interregional* patterns; this naturally does not succeed. One anthropologist, Kroeber, seems to have assumed in an early work that any world history must exhibit an *independent* parallelism of development in various regions, and used statistics to show that such does not appear. (But his statistics, in fact, suggest a striking amount of parallelism if it need not be supposed to be independent.)

Whatever one's general orientation to world history, however, the monographic problems will be similar. These world-historical problems require treatment independently, over and beyond the treatment they may incidentally receive by specialists in this or that region. Interregional history deserves attention upon its own merits. There must be more studies of "influences," of course, and generally of relationships among cultures. But these will not fully serve the purpose so long as they are limited in outlook to only one region — e.g., how has India influenced *Europe*? Yet regarded from a world view-point, even these limited studies will have a place among the innumerable studies of every sort that must arise in tracing interregional affairs. For many of all these will be pursued within a very local field; only the purpose which informs the inquiry will be world-historical. What matters is that this purpose emerges with clarity. To this end, scholarship in interregional history must become more aware of its special problems and outlook.

THE PROBLEM OF WORLD-ORIENTATION

Having indicated thus briefly the position of Hemispheric interregional history, I must turn even more briefly to certain obstacles in our way. Before any adequate sort of organization of the historical material can be found, we must accustom ourselves to seeing the world as a whole from a more interregional viewpoint. This is in some ways a psychological rather than a historical problem. Our attempts at a world-wide perspective are too often subtly vitiated by habitual distortions in our ideas of mankind dating from the days of Western world dominance. In Western thinking — and this thinking still dominates too greatly other parts of the world as well — the West was the center of the world; and the world at large was to be regarded, historically most especially, in the light of its effect upon and contributions to the modern West. Is not the world now Westernized? — we have justified ourselves; not noticing that (even if this were true) there is a great difference of historical structure and perspective between even such a world and the West itself. All too often men of other regions also have tacitly accepted the Western criterion, trying to show the supremacy of their own region by showing how much it helped to form, or is worthy to alter, the West. Such an explicit orientation is now being sloughed off; but it has left innumerable traces in our thinking which do not disappear so easily.

A peculiarly important example of the results of this attitude is the concept of "the Orient." The word has meant many things; as used by historians it has come to mean, if taken generally, all those urbanized and literate countries of the Eastern Hemisphere, whether south or east of Europe, which were eventually subjected in various degrees to the West-European expansion after 1500. There is no internal point of unity among these peoples, apart from their relation to Europe, which they do not share as much with Europe itself as among one another; the term is therefore a negative one, like "foreign"; it has meaning only in a common contrast to the triumphant West.

Yet repeatedly it is taken to have a substantive content. One hears not only general remarks about the "Oriental" character, bred of the same ignorance in the West as similar general remarks about "foreigners." One hears mention of "Oriental" philosophy, or art, or even race. Such mentions, in practice, usually refer to some particular region, rather than the formless conglomerate that would result from an attempt to lump the greater part of civilized man together in a single cultural pattern. But the more inclusive expectations they foster are nevertheless often taken seriously — often even by "Orientals" themselves; it is not rare for a native of Egypt or some equally Mediterranean country to take the credit for the best lives of India on the one hand and China or Japan on the other over three thousand years, as proof of "Oriental" superiority over the materialistic modern West. The root fallacy is to take "Orient" and "Occident" for two equal halves of the world. A Mercator projection map of the world, which frankly exaggerates the Western countries in comparison to more southerly lands like India, may encourage this. (One wonders how much less tenacious the conception would be if mapmakers could be persuaded to drop that mischievous projection altogether!) But the new global maps, as well as the briefest study of linguistic and historical variation, will remind us that the West is historically simply one among several regions in the Eastern Hemisphere, each of the same order as itself in size, populousness, and cultural wealth.

The elimination of catch-all categories like "Orient" — and the very similar "Asia" — will automatically rid us of many absurdities in daily conversation (at least in the United States). For instance, that one or another gathering is truly world-wide because it has members from "all the continents" — so many from

North America, so many from South America, so many from Europe, a couple from Africa, and even one or two from "Asia." Or the fatuous remark of a popular "world" historian, that Europe progressed and "Asia" did not, because Europe's rivers flowed from the heart of the continent out to the sea, whereas "Asia" had no such rivers. The Narbadda is roughly as long as the Rhine, and the Ganges as the Danube, and waters lands as diverse.

But even in serious history such absurdities take their toll. It is very hard to persuade a historian of "world literature" that it is misleading to give a chapter to each of the little literatures of Europe, and then one chapter to that of "India" — as if he shared the supposition so often found among the uninformed that one should learn "Indian" before going to live there. If it is worthwhile treating *world* literature at all, then Tamil and Bengali and Maratha should have chapters as distinct from Sanskrit as are the Italian and German from the Latin; if this should show up a cultural poverty in Bengali or Maratha, that would already be a point gained. But in any case, for the purposes of comparison and of perspective, it would reflect the position of India as an understandably complex sub-continent — not as one incomprehensibly vast "country" in "Asia" roughly answering to Italy in the more comprehensible Europe. Throughout the serious work of scholars we find "international" affairs in Europe treated as matters of *world* import, while relations between parts of Africa or even between India and China come under the head of *regional* studies; a war among Western powers is a "world" war, while one between China and Japan is "localized"; a new language based on all European tongues claims to be a "world" language, while a threatened alliance of Russia, China, and India could be referred as merely an "Asian bloc." However in the current situation each such instance might be justified in itself, together they reflect a pattern of thinking which makes constructive interregional history very difficult for us; and particularly just that interregional history which I am suggesting is crucial to world history — that of the literate zone of the Eastern Hemisphere. For we are psychologically still not very distant from the times in which the Greco-Persian wars and the Crusades could be regarded as episodes in an unending struggle between East and West as two halves of mankind. These unfortunate habits of thinking, not challenged as they would have been by a balanced world history, have so multifariously woven themselves into scholarly thinking that their uprooting is an important prerequisite to the writing of world history itself. Otherwise, the very categories necessary to interregional inquiry will escape us, and the "vast mass" of Africa and Asia must remain "inscrutable."

The Westward Distortion in History

Finally, I shall turn to an illustration of how important a more explicit cultivation of interregional history can be to our historical understanding generally. For a particular historical form of this Westward distortion of our view of mankind has tended to vitiate most of our popular conceptions of general history. The most significant error Westerners have made lies not in ascribing to themselves too much glory or virtue in any particular comparisons with other peoples. More dangerous has been the West's practice of reading the very structure of history in a distorted fashion, for this has been carried over unconsciously even by non-Westerners. I will review briefly some of the more unfortunate systematic errors which our lack of an adequate framework of interregional history has led us into.

True to the principle of judging all the world by its effect on the West, Western history used to set about tracing civilization from its earliest times in Egypt and Babylon only up to a point — only so long as these lands remained the nearest direct antecedents of the modern West. We ceased tracing civilization in those countries almost as soon as Greece and Rome came to have a literate history, concentrating on each of them, in turn; ignoring each time any further history in the lands farther east (except when forced to pay attention, by their role in a more westerly story). So soon as northwestern Europe came to have an independent story, all lands east of the Adriatic dropped from sight, and the very words we used suggested that henceforth the West was the world.

Something like this might have been legitimate if done consciously; but generally no recognition was made that the focus of our vision had been shifted in the process. The whole story commonly ran as if (as Westerners have indeed actually believed) civilization itself had been moving steadily west. From this false impression of the story's continuity arose a number of illusions, which continue to have their effects after the grosser aspects of the above process have been abandoned.

First, it came to be supposed that after the early years the more eastern nations had in fact little significant history. This impression was early extended from Egypt and Iraq to other lands; reinforced by a number of accidents, including the habits of Indians and Chinese of glorifying, and exaggerating, the antiquity of their institutions. A variant of the same notion, encouraged by the rapid rate of change in the modern West, and by illusions of distance, was that of the static, changeless East. Second, a different and more persistent illusion produced by the pattern was that of a certain historical discontinuity — recurrent degeneration, followed by a new start. Not that such degeneration has never in fact happened; but in the westward historical pattern the contrast between one age and another was confused and compounded with that between places, as our attention moved west. This occurred especially when the focus was shifted from the Mediterranean Roman Empire, in which Rome was a *western* outpost from the cultural and even economic point of view, to the Latin Christendom of the Western Middle Ages, in which Rome was a *southeastern* outpost on the very edge of Greek and Muslim territory. A relative decline intervened in the Imperial lands between the age of the Antonines and that of Justinian and the Hagia Sophia; the shift of attention meanwhile from the seaways of the Mediterranean to the forests of Germany and Gaul magnified this decline into the fall of the Roman Empire and the Dark Age of civilization!

Pervasive Results of the Distortion

The grosser misconceptions which have accompanied the Westward pattern of history are now being done away with; we are now less inclined to judge the fate of Greek culture by its eclipse in Merovingian Gaul. But the illusions which it fostered were a strong influence making possible the nineteenth-century theories of history which still tend to hold sway. The idea of inevitable and triumphant progress probably owes something to the practice of watching only those nations, as civilization spread, which were just taking on its graces: a partly borrowed progress always seems fast. Those conceptions of history which reduce it to stages or cycles owe far more to these illusions. The famous fall of the Roman Empire seems to be the kernel from which such conceptions have grown. Spengler decried a West-centered history, yet accepted the limitations imposed by the Westward pattern, allowing no history to India or China in the last two millennia. Toynbee is anxious to recognize the continuing evolution of the non-Western nations; yet he seems to have used the "Fall of Rome" as his starting point, and hence involved himself in a system of distinct societies, definitively rising and falling, which naturally bristles with fundamental anomalies. Thus the distortion has infected his work, even though he guarded explicitly against the illusion of the "static East," as well as escaping the imposing list of those whose data suffers a displacement in *space* which they treat as if it were a change merely in *time*.

Perhaps a more significant evidence of the pervasive effect of the Westward distortion in what we have called world history, is its effect upon so great a historical analysis as the Marxist. Like others, the Marxists have envisaged stages of evolution, appearing in a predictable order. Thus the slavery "stage" of the Roman Empire must be followed by the manorial serfdom "stage" of Carolingian Gaul. But the picture becomes awkwardly complicated if the Syrian or Anatolian provinces are focussed on, rather than Gaul: for the Abbasid and Byzantine societies represent alternative sequels to the Roman. Accordingly, as the historical vision of Victorian Europe has widened, Marxism has been faced with the need to patch up its theory, and possibly to revise it thoroughly, allowing for more varied elements in and outcomes of the dialectical process; it is my impression Marxists have not yet adequately met the problem.

It will be noticed that even our conception of the West in particular has suffered — it has been a rather dubious practice to eke out early Western history with excised portions from the development of certain more easterly lands such as Greece. More important from the present point of view, a Western history which has tried to make itself self-sufficient in this way gives a false estimate of the role of the West in the world — both passive and active. But one of the greatest tasks of world history is surely precisely to clarify the role of the West in the world. This is doubly true with regard to the literate zone of the Eastern Hemisphere. Some will have the impression that in advocating an interregional history of this zone, I am advocating not world-*oriented* history, but just *Oriental* history. Not quite: a history of "Asia" without Europe could conceivably resemble a history of Western art or letters without France. (Yet I will confess that just as a history of Europe without France would better deserve the name of European history than one of France without Europe, so a history of "Asia" without the West could be more readily called a world history, than the reverse.) The point is that *from a world-historical point of view*, what is important is not European history in itself, however important that be for us all, but its role in interregional history. This role has latterly been momentous; but our very concentration on internal Western history has commonly obscured our view of the West as one dynamic region among others in the wider world.

The problem of reorienting ourselves to a more interregional viewpoint, then, is psychologically far-reaching, and must be solved along with that of organizing the historical material. The problem of reorientation is precisely the greatest in the case of that Hemispheric history which I recommend as a major avenue to world history. But this fact only emphasizes the central importance of such history in the building of a world-historical approach free from Westward distortions. The interregional history of the Eastern Hemisphere is one of the most important to which young historians with a reasonable linguistic equipment can contribute their monographs and their vision.

GEOFFREY BARRACLOUGH

The Prospects of World History

Awareness of the need for a universal view of history — for a history which transcends national and regional boundaries and comprehends the entire globe — is one of the marks of the present. As early as 1936, the great Dutch historian, Huizinga, pointed out that "our civilization is the first to have for its past the past of the world, our history is the first to be world-history,"[1] and subsequent events have only confirmed his verdict. As since 1945 the world has moved into a new phase of global integration, the demand for a history which reflects this new situation has become more insistent. It is, particularly at a pedagogical level, a practical demand. How can we, in the world as constituted today, safely teach a history nine-tenths of which is devoted to a quarter of the world's inhabitants? As E. H. Dance has pertinently pointed out, so long as every people remains ignorant of the basic ideals and cultures of other peoples, disaster will always be just round the corner; and "yet there are no world histories in any language which give one-fifth, let alone the just four-fifths, of their space to the great 'coloured' civilisations, living and dead."[2]

Geoffrey Barraclough, *Main Trends in History* (New York: Holmes and Meier, 1991), 153–63.

The case for world history is undoubtedly very powerful. The world history of mankind, as Schieder has said, is no longer a speculative goal towards which the history of past events is directed, but is a living experience calling for corroboration in and through history.[3] The very forces which have transformed our view of the present — above all, the emergence of the greater part of mankind from political subjection to political independence and political influence — have compelled us to widen our view of the past. As recently as 1955 it was still necessary to plead that China should not "be regarded as outside the mainstream of human history."[4] It is a measure of the progress achieved in a short space of time that no one today would question this proposition. But the more the conviction of the need for an overall vision of world history has grown, the more historians have become aware of the problems and practical difficulties involved in writing it. There appears to be general agreement that few attempts to write universal history so far have been really successful, but there is still no consensus about aims and methods.

The prevalent view of universal or world history conceives of it as a continuous narrative, in one or more volumes, linking together as an intelligible whole the story of mankind from its earliest beginnings, two million years before civilization, to the present day. The practical difficulties of encompassing such a task, given the complexity of the subject-matter and the rapid accumulation of new knowledge — particularly knowledge of the history of the extra-European world — need no emphasis. No single historian can hope to write with authority on every area and every phase of human endeavour. The current tendency is therefore to have recourse to collective histories, written by teams of specialists; and since the appearance in 1963 of the first volume of the six-volume UNESCO *History of Mankind*, there has been a steady output of such composite or co-operative histories, mainly but not exclusively in the European languages. It is generally conceded that they serve a useful purpose; but their reception by professional historians has for the most part been cool and sceptical. They "cull out," in William McNeill's words, "much interesting data"; but on an intellectual level they "have conspicuously failed to provide any clear, intelligible pattern."[5] Precisely because they are written by teams of specialists, they tend to fall apart into a series of loosely linked chapters or monographs, and this — even where, as in the ten-volume Soviet world history, the collaborators share a common *Weltanschauung* — is no substitute for the unitary vision of the individual historian. Hence, in spite of the contemporary propensity for more or less encyclopaedic collective histories, the individual work continues to hold its own; and some of the most stimulating attempts in recent years to re-write history on a global scale and in a global perspective have been the work of individual historians, among whom L. S. Stavrianos and W. H. McNeill are perhaps the best known.

This is not the place for a detailed criticism of the various world histories which have appeared in the last decade. Whatever their shortcomings, there is no doubt that they represent a distinct advance, in conceptualization and in breadth of vision, on similar works of an earlier date, and this without doubt reflects the global perspectives of the world in which we live. On the other hand, it is important to consider, however briefly, the criticisms — or at least the limitations — of the conception of world history which they all, in one degree or another, represent. On a practical level, in the first place, they are open to a twofold criticism: either, because they are compilations, based on secondary knowledge, they lag behind the current level of research and, in order to encompass the whole world, reduce history to broad and vague generalizations, or, on the contrary, they simply present a mass of relatively undigested and unrelated factual knowledge. Furthermore, with rare exceptions the existing world histories continue the old tradition of narrative history, simply transferring it from the national arena to the world stage. If, as I have suggested elsewhere, history is to be regarded not as a sequence of happenings but as a series of problems, this is evidently unsatisfactory; it dulls rather than stimulates and creates the illusion of a body of generally accepted fact rather than encouraging the student to probe the great unresolved problems. The better historians, of course, are aware of these criticisms and have sought to meet them. Nevertheless, while it is generally agreed that world history is, or should be, at once something more and something less than an aggregate of national histories, and should be approached in a different spirit and manner, the problem of how to construct such a history has not yet been satisfactorily solved.

Perhaps more important than the practical difficulties are the theoretical problems involved in this type of world history. The former may conceivably be overcome with the passage of time and with increasing experience and knowledge; the latter are inherent. The first, and most insistent problem, as W. T. de Bary has pointed out, is that "we have no convenient and accepted framework in which to present world civilization as a whole."[6] There is, after all, no reason to assume that the view of world history from the Tarim basin and the view of world history from the Thames valley will ever be even broadly identical. Stavrianos claims that the standpoint he adopts is "that of an observer perched on the moon, surveying our planet as a whole, rather than that of one who is ensconced in London or Paris, or for that matter, in Peking or Delhi."[7] But in reality his approach, though more objective than that of most other writers, is distinctly western-centred. Nor is this implicit Eurocentrism exceptional. It is hard, for example, to believe that an Indian or African Marxist would wholeheartedly endorse a periodization of world history which hinges, like E. M. Zhukov's, on the "British bourgeois revolution" of the seventeenth century, the French revolution of 1789, and the Russian revolution of 1917, as the decisive steps in "the logical road of the advancement of mankind."[8] If Zhukov's views are representative, it would seem that the Soviet conception of world history is no less Eurocentric than that of non-Marxist western historians, and it is not surprising that Asian historians, such as Naito Torajiro, Miyazaki Ichisado, and Maeda Naonori, have sought to replace such views by a periodization of world history which does justice to eastern culture as a whole. How successful these attempts have been, we do not need to consider. It is sufficient in the present context to recognize that world history looked at from Peking or Cairo may well be very different from world history looked at from Paris or Chicago or Moscow.

Stavrianos is not alone in postulating that the history of man "to an over-whelming degree" is a history of the "Eurasian civilizations" and that from 1500, as a participant in the Twelfth International Congress of Historical Sciences put it, "the evolution of Europe" was the "determining" event in the course of world history.[9] African and Asian historians who might have contradicted this view were conspicuously absent; but E. H. Carr was surely right when he wrote that a view of history which treats the four hundred years between Vasco de Gama and Lenin "as the centre-piece of universal history, and everything else as peripheral to it, is an unhappy distortion of perspective."[10] On the other hand, it would be equally presumptuous to suppose, as traditional Chinese historiography did, that the whole of history is enshrined in the Middle Kingdom, and the rest is periph-eral. It may be true that the history of Asia in modern times cannot be under-stood without reference to the Western impact, but it is equally true that Western history cannot be understood without reference to the impact of Asia on the West. So far, however, the former has received far more attention than the latter.

In addition to the problem of finding a more or less universal consensus as to the shape and proportions of world history, there is the almost equally elusive question of an organizing principle. Granted that world history is more than a loosely articulated sum or aggregate of national histories, the historian is imme-diately faced by the problem of establishing a criterion of what is, and what is not, of "world-historical" importance. Here also there is no consensus of opin-ion. For many historians the distinctive feature of world history is that it deals not with nations, but with continents and civilizations. One has only to recall the criticism of A. J. Toynbee's attempts to draw up a list of the world's civiliza-tions to see that this hypothesis raises as many problems as it answers. For J. L. Talmon, on the other hand, the criterion of world history is that it "should be concerned with a meaningful totality,"[11] but this leaves open the question of the criterion of meaningfulness.

If it is to offer a coherent, meaningful and comprehensive pattern, world history cannot, as Marx pointed out, be "devoid of premises,"[12] and these premises may be classified broadly as idealist or materialist. Among the former, we may instance Lord Acton's conception of liberty as "the central thread of all history,"[13] or the views of more recent Christian writers, such as Christopher Dawson or Herbert Butterfield, for whom the unifying factor in history is the working out of divine providence. Such views, however, are more frequently found today among theologians and religious thinkers than among professional historians, among whom the prevalent tendency is to adopt a broadly materialist position, in the sense that their central theme is man's conflict with his environ-ment. This is the position of William McNeill, for whom (it would appear) technological advance (in agriculture, in warfare, etc.) is the key factor in human development, and J. H. Plumb has explicitly stated that "the material progress of mankind" is "the one aspect of the human story which both makes sense of it and also gives some slender grounds for the hopes of men."[14]

The prevalence of a materialist interpretation of world history is, no doubt, due in part to the ubiquitous influence of Marxism; in addition, it probably owes something to the influence of archaeology and pre-history, with their insistence upon the importance of human artefacts as a main source of historical knowledge, and to the current emphasis on social and economic rather than political history. But the main reason for its widespread acceptance is probably simply its evident heuristic potency. Not only does a materialist interpretation, as Marx pointed out,[15] substitute "real premises" for "arbitrary ones," but it also emphasizes the unifying features of human history. Whereas a synthesis of world history based on political events tends to be concerned, in Seizo Ohe's words, "with the features which differentiate the respective subject-cultures,"[16] an interpretation whose central theme is the growth of man's control over his environment not only postulates an organizing principle which is common to the whole of mankind, but also establishes a measurable criterion of progress and direction, without which — at least for the great majority of people — world history would be meaningless. It also provides the historian with a standard for deciding what is and what is not important from a global perspective, for selecting those particular facts and events which should and which should not be included. In particular, it shifts the emphasis from events on a national or local level, which affect only one people or ethnic group, to broad movements — for example, the Neolithic agricultural revolution — which involve the whole of mankind. Karl Jaspers, for example, has postulated an "axial period" in which a decisive historical breakthrough in the basic conditions of life and thought occurred at the same time in all the major civilizations of the world.[17]

The assumptions upon which this structure of world history is based are nevertheless less self-evident than is sometimes assumed. No one is likely to question the fact that mankind as a species is everywhere basically the same; but the relevant question, as Bodo Wiethoff has pointed out, is whether this is true of man as a social and historical being.[18] Furthermore, the very idea that world history has purpose, direction and a goal, is a peculiarly western tradition, and it is well known that many of the world's great civilizations have taken a different view, seeing the meaning and goal of human existence outside history. It is also at least questionable whether "the story of man," in Stavrianos' words, "from its very beginnings has a basic unity that must be recognized and respected."[19] No doubt, all human groups everywhere are motivated from the start by the need to cope with the material facts of life, but this is a tenuous basis for assuming that their historical development is, or can plausibly be reconstructed as, a single unitary process. As Troeltsch pointed out many years ago, it is one thing to speak of points of contact between different civilizations and different cultural groups, and quite another to suppose that their histories are linked by a real causal connexion which makes them subordinate parts of a single historical process.[20] Marx himself took the view that the unity of world history only came into existence gradually, and apparently at a relatively late stage, as a result of "intercourse and the division of labour between nations"; this was what transformed history — i.e., the history of separate peoples — into world history.[21]

But if it is granted that history only gradually becomes a single historical process, other difficulties arise. One is the familiar one, to which Zhukov among others draws attention, that even if there is a progression through economic stages in the mode of production, this progression does "not necessarily" take place "in a straightforward way."[22] Partly for this reason Soviet historians, like most other European and American historians, have fallen back upon the conventional European division into "ancient," "medieval" and "modern" history as a scheme for grouping and ordering events. But the validity of this schematization, even for Europe, is highly controversial, and its applicability to Asia and Africa is even more questionable; in fact, most competent historians of Asia have rejected it out of hand.

Nor is it by any means as clear as its advocates sometimes imply that the weight of evidence supports a "linear and unitary" view of world history, "in the sense that interactions across relatively large distances even in very ancient times are sufficient to make mankind's history a single, if loosely articulated, whole." The foremost proponent of this common assumption is W. H. McNeill, but even McNeill is forced to concede, at the very beginning of his work, that the Neolithic agricultural revolution, which allegedly began in the Middle East and spread from there into Europe, India, China and parts of Africa, may have been less than universal, and that "the Americas, monsoon Asia, and west Africa may have seen the independent inauguration of agriculture."[23] On present evidence, in other words, what McNeill calls "the segmented, pluralistic view of the human past" cannot be rejected out of hand. No one would deny, for example, the existence from an early date of relations and interactions between the Chinese and the Mediterranean peoples, and Joseph Needham in particular has conclusively demonstrated their importance. But these relations were the exception rather than the rule and the development of China and the Mediterranean lands over the course of centuries followed virtually independent paths. If we attempt to force them into a single mould, the resulting reconstruction is likely to do violence to the historical truth.

The other main objection to a "diffusionist" interpretation of world history — i.e., to a conception which sees the unifying thread as the spread of culture and cultural innovation from one or more centres — is its teleological overtone. The danger of any such approach, as F. M. Powicke once wrote, is its inherent tendency to arrange the past "as a process in which the most significant things are those which are most easily appropriated by the present," or which seem to have immediate present relevance.[24] In particular, it views history as a progressive movement leading by stages to the contemporary world, and since the contemporary world has largely been shaped by the West, it results in a marked, if subconscious, western ethnocentrism, centering on the belief that the social forms developed in Europe (including Russia) and North America during the present century are in some sense the "goal" towards which history has been working. But the "one world" of today, shaped and structured by the West, may, for all we know, be as impermanent and transitory as the Hellenistic *oikoumene*, or the Middle Kingdom which Confucian historians thought of as the culmination of history. In any case, a view of world history which makes "the rise of the

West" its central theme — as W. H. McNeill has done — is unlikely to be regarded as the last word by historians in other parts of the world.

These critical observations are intended to indicate some of the reasons why a growing number of historians today have begun to question the intellectual assumptions upon which most recent attempts to write world history rest. In their view, world history is concerned with points of contact and inter-relationships; it does not call for a synthetic reconstruction of the whole of the past, but rather for the study of the processes of development of human society in different environments and different civilizations. Their argument is not merely that attempts to systematize the whole of known history and set it out in chronological sequence are premature, when so little has been done to examine specific phases or problems in depth, but rather that the "linear" conception of world history itself is stultifying and misconceived. Raghavan Iyer has called upon historians to "discard the unitary view of civilisation" and "accept the irreducible plurality of civilisations,"[25] and Satish Chandra has urged the need to "abandon the concept of centre and periphery" — whether the centre is identified with Washington, Moscow or Peking — and replace it by "a concept of the multi-focal growth of human civilisation."[26]

The implication is that the subject-matter of world history is not the sequence of civilizations — "according" (in Lord Acton's well known formulation) "to the time and degree in which they contributed to the common fortunes of mankind"[27] — but rather the study of the differences between different countries, areas and civilizations, and of their interactions. When the past is viewed in a world-wide perspective, "history becomes" — as R. F. Wall has written[28] — "not a study of facts, but a study of inter-relationships: cultural, social and commercial, as well as diplomatic and religious." And E. Hölzle has suggested that what is necessary for an understanding of world history is not "grandiose conceptions" covering the whole of known history, but specific, concrete research "concerned with establishing historical relationships, material and ideal, between the continents."[29]

The study of world history in this sense is still in its beginnings. Because it cuts into the past at a different angle from other types of history, it cuts across the lines they have traced. The very fact that it asks new questions — questions, for example, about the processes by which ideas, inventions and products are transmitted between the various regions of the world — means that it requires not only a new approach but also the mobilization of a body of material and knowledge which, on the whole, historians concerned with one area or a single continent have neglected. World history in its contemporary connotation is not a synthesis of known fact or a juxtaposition of the histories of different continents or cultures, arranged in some sort of order of relative importance; rather it is a search for the links and connexions across political and cultural frontiers. It is concerned not so much with development in time or with the goal and meaning of history — western preoccupations which non-western cultures for the most part do not share — as with the perennial problems which have assailed mankind everywhere and with the different responses to them. This, for an increasing number of historians today, is the stuff of world history, and it has turned their attention, as we shall see, away from linear development, from the thread allegedly running through history from its earliest beginnings to the present day, to the comparative study of the institutions, habits, ideas and assumptions of men in all times and places.

Notes

1. "A definition of the concept of history," p. 8 in Klibansky and Paton (eds.), *Philosophy and History* (1936).
2. Dance, *History of the Betrayer: A Study of Bias* (1960), 26, 48, 125.
3. Schieder, Th., *Staat und Gesellschaft im Wandel unserer Zeit* (1958), 197.
4. Pulleyblank, *Chinese History and World History* (1955), 36.
5. Ballard, ed., *New Movements in the Study and Teaching of History* (1970), 23.
6. *Approaches to Asian Civilizations* (1961), x.
7. *The World to 1500* (1970), 3.
8. "The periodization of world history," *Rapports, XIe Congrès International*, vol. 1 (1960), 79–83. In fact, the application of western concepts of periodization, "Marxist or non-Marxist," to Asia was explicitly repudiated by T. Yamamoto (and others); ibid., *Actes* (1962), 64.
9. Stavrianos (1970), 5; cf. *Proceedings* of the XIIth International Congress, 1965, (1968), 539.
10. E. H. Carr, *What Is History?* (1961), 146.
11. *Proceedings* of the XIIth International Congress, 530.
12. Marx-Engels, *German Ideology*, 47.
13. Gooch, *History and Historians in the Nineteenth Century* (2d ed., 1959), 360.
14. Plumb, "The historian's dilemma," 32, in Plumb, ed., *Crisis in the Humanities* (1964), and the general preface at the beginning of each volume in the series *The History of Human Society*, which Plumb edits.
15. *German Ideology*, 42.
16. Ohe, "Toward a Comparative and Unified History of Human Culture, with Special Reference to Japan," 197, in *International Symposium on History of Eastern and Western Cultural Contacts* (1959).
17. Jaspers, *Vom Ursprung und der Geschichte* (1949), 19–20.
18. Wiethoff, *Grundzüge der älteren chinesischen Geschichte* (1971), 19.
19. *The World to 1500* (1970), 4.
20. Troeltsch, *Gesammelte Schriften* 3 (1920): 609.
21. *German Ideology*, 58, where Marx adduces the famous example of a machine invented in England "which deprives countless workers of bread in India and China and overturns the whole form of existence of these empires," and thus "becomes a world-historical fact."
22. "The Periodization of World History," 76 in *Rapports, XIe Congrès International* (1960), vol.1.
23. *A World History* (1967), 1. This, McNeill adds, is "not certain." McNeill's formulation betrays his prejudice, for evidently, on the basis of his own reasoning, it would be equally true to describe the "migrations and borrowings" on which his whole account is based, but "few of which" (he concedes) "can be reconstructed by modern scholars," as

"not certain." This having been said, it is perhaps worth adding that my sympathies are with McNeill. But it is also true, if the evidence, as McNeill admits, is less than conclusive, that any such judgment is no more than tentative and a weak foundation for a whole interpretation of world history.

24. Powicke, *The Christian Life in the Middle Ages* (1935), v.

25. Iyer, 19 in Iyer, ed., *The Glass Curtain between Asia and Europe* (1965).

26. Satish Chandra, "A Note on the Decentring of History," 4, 12, 19 of typescript. This paper was specially prepared by Professor Chandra for the present undertaking, and I should like to express my gratitude to him for his valuable observations.

27. Lord Acton, *Lectures on Modern History* (1906), 317.

28. "New Openings: Asia," 302 in *New Ways in History* (*Times Literary Supplement*, 1966).

29. Hölzle, *Idee und Ideologie* (1969), 81.

Eric R. Wolf

Connections in History

The central assertion of this book is that the world of humankind constitutes a manifold, a totality of interconnected processes, and inquiries that disassemble this totality into bits and then fail to reassemble it falsify reality. Concepts like "nation," "society," and "culture" name bits and threaten to turn names into things. Only by understanding these names as bundles of relationships, and by placing them back into the field from which they were abstracted, can we hope to avoid misleading inferences and increase our share of understanding.

On one level it has become a commonplace to say that we all inhabit "one world." There are ecological connections: New York suffers from the Hong Kong flu; the grapevines of Europe are destroyed by American plant lice. There are demographic connections: Jamaicans migrate to London; Chinese migrate to Singapore. There are economic connections: a shutdown of oil wells on the Persian Gulf halts generating plants in Ohio; a balance of payments unfavorable to the United States drains American dollars into bank accounts in Frankfurt or Yokohama; Italians produce Fiat automobiles in the Soviet Union; Japanese build a hydroelectric system in Ceylon. There are political connections: wars begun in Europe unleash reverberations around the globe; American troops intervene on the rim of Asia; Finns guard the border between Israel and Egypt.

Eric R. Wolf, *Europe and the People without History* (Los Angeles: University of California Press, 1982), 3–9.

This holds true not only of the present but also of the past. Diseases from Eurasia devastated the native population of America and Oceania. Syphilis moved from the New World to the Old. Europeans and their plants and animals invaded the Americas; the American potato, maize plant, and manioc spread throughout the Old World. Large numbers of Africans were transported forcibly to the New World; Chinese and Indian indentured laborers were shipped to Southeast Asia and the West Indies. Portugal created a Portuguese settlement in Macao off the coast of China. Dutchmen, using labor obtained in Bengal, constructed Batavia. Irish children were sold into servitude in the West Indies. Fugitive African slaves found sanctuary in the hills of Surinam. Europe learned to copy Indian textiles and Chinese porcelain, to drink native American chocolate, to smoke native American tobacco, to use Arabic numerals.

These are familiar facts. They indicate contact and connections, linkages and interrelationships. Yet the scholars to whom we turn in order to understand what we see largely persist in ignoring them. Historians, economists, and political scientists take separate nations as their basic framework of inquiry. Sociology continues to divide the world into separate societies. Even anthropology, once greatly concerned with how culture traits diffused around the world, divides its subject matter into distinctive cases: each society with its characteristic culture, conceived as an integrated and bounded system, set off against other equally bounded systems.

If social and cultural distinctiveness and mutual separation were a hallmark of humankind, one would expect to find it most easily among the so-called primitives, people "without history," supposedly isolated from the external world and from one another. On this presupposition, what would we make of the archaeological findings that European trade goods appear in sites on the Niagara frontier as early as 1570, and that by 1670 sites of the Onondaga subgroup of the Iroquois reveal almost no items of native manufacture except pipes? On the other side of the Atlantic, the organization and orientations of large African populations were transformed in major ways by the trade in slaves. Since the European slavers only moved the slaves from the African coast to their destination in the Americas, the supply side of the trade was entirely in African hands. This was the "African foundation" upon which was built, in the words of the British mercantilist Malachy Postlethwayt, "the magnificent superstructure of American commerce and naval power." From Senegambia in West Africa to Angola, population after population was drawn into this trade, which ramified far inland and affected people who had never even seen a European trader on the coast. Any account of Kru, Fanti, Asante, Ijaw, Igbo, Kongo, Luba, Lunda, or Ngola that treats each group as a "tribe" sufficient unto itself thus misreads the African past and the African present. Furthermore, trade with Iroquois and West Africa affected Europe in turn. Between 1670 and 1760 the Iroquois demanded dyed scarlet and blue cloth made in the Stroudwater Valley of Gloucestershire. This was also one of the first areas in which English weavers lost their autonomy and became hired factory hands. Perhaps there was an interconnection between the American trade and the onset of the industrial revolution in the valley of the

Stroud. Conversely, the more than 5,500 muskets supplied to the Gold Coast in only three years (1658–1661) enriched the gunsmiths of Birmingham, where they were made (Jennings 1976: 99–100; Daaku 1970: 150–51).

If there are connections everywhere, why do we persist in turning dynamic, interconnected phenomena into static, disconnected things? Some of this is owing, perhaps, to the way we have learned our own history. We have been taught, inside the classroom and outside of it, that there exists an entity called the West, and that one can think of this West as a society and civilization independent of and in opposition to other societies and civilizations. Many of us even grew up believing that this West has a genealogy, according to which ancient Greece begat Rome, Rome begat Christian Europe, Christian Europe begat the Renaissance, the Renaissance the Enlightenment, the Enlightenment political democracy and the industrial revolution. Industry, crossed with democracy, in turn yielded the United States, embodying the rights to life, liberty, and the pursuit of happiness.

Such a developmental scheme is misleading. It is misleading, first, because it turns history into a moral success story, a race in time in which each runner of the race passes on the torch of liberty to the next relay. History is thus converted into a tale about the furtherance of virtue, about how the virtuous win out over the bad guys. Frequently, this turns into a story of how the winners prove that they are virtuous and good by winning. If history is the working out of a moral purpose in time, then those who lay claim to that purpose are by that fact the predilect agents of history.

The scheme misleads in a second sense as well. If history is but a tale of unfolding moral purpose, then each link in the genealogy, each runner in the race, is only a precursor of the final apotheosis and not a manifold of social and cultural processes at work in their own time and place. Yet what would we learn of ancient Greece, for example, if we interpreted it only as a prehistoric Miss Liberty, holding aloft the torch of moral purpose in the barbarian night? We would gain little sense of the class conflicts racking the Greek cities, or of the relation between freemen and their slaves. We would have no reason to ask why there were more Greeks fighting in the ranks of the Persian kings than in the ranks of the Hellenic Alliance against the Persians. It would be of no interest to us to know that more Greeks lived in southern Italy and Sicily, then called Magna Graecia, than in Greece proper. Nor would we have any reason to ask why there were soon more Greek mercenaries in foreign armies than in the military bodies of their home cities. Greek settlers outside of Greece, Greek mercenaries in foreign armies, and slaves from Thrace, Phrygia, or Paphalagonia in Greek households all imply Hellenic relations with Greeks and non-Greeks outside of Greece. Yet our guiding scheme would not invite us to ask questions about these relationships.

Nowhere is this myth-making scheme more apparent than in schoolbook versions of the history of the United States. There, a complex orchestration of antagonistic forces is celebrated instead as the unfolding of a timeless essence. In this perspective, the ever-changing boundaries of the United States and the repeated involvements of the polity in internal and external wars, declared and undeclared, are telescoped together by the teleological understanding that thirteen colonies clinging to the eastern rim of the continent would, in less than a century, plant the American flag on the shores of the Pacific. Yet this final result was itself only the contested outcome of many contradictory relationships. The colonies declared their independence, even though a majority of their population — European settlers, native Americans, and African slaves — favored the Tories. The new republic nearly foundered on the issue of slavery, dealing with it, in a series of problematic compromises, by creating two federated countries, each with its own zone of expansion. There was surely land for the taking on the new continent, but it had to be taken first from the native Americans who inhabited it, and then converted into flamboyant real estate. Jefferson bought the Louisiana territory cheaply, but only after the revolt of the Haitian slaves against their French slave masters robbed the area of its importance in the French scheme of things as a source of food supply for the Caribbean plantations. The occupation of Florida closed off one of the main escape hatches from southern slavery. The war with Mexico made the Southwest safe for slavery and cotton. The Hispanic landowners who stood in the way of the American drive to the Pacific became "bandits" when they defended their own against the Anglophone newcomers. Then North and South — one country importing its working force from Europe, the other from Africa — fought one of the bloodiest wars in history. For a time the defeated South became a colony of the victorious North. Later, the alignment between regions changed, the "sunbelt" rising to predominance as the influence of the industrial Northeast declined. Clearly the republic was neither indivisible nor endowed with God-given boundaries.

It is conceivable that things might have been different. There could have arisen a polyglot Floridian Republic, a Francophone Mississippian America, a Hispanic New Biscay, a Republic of the Great Lakes, a Columbia — comprising the present Oregon, Washington, and British Columbia. Only if we assume a God-given drive toward geopolitical unity on the North American continent would this retrojection be meaningless. Instead, it invites us to account in material terms for what happened at each juncture, to account for how some relationships gained ascendancy over others. Thus neither ancient Greece, Rome, Christian Europe, the Renaissance, the Enlightenment, the industrial revolution, democracy, nor even the United States was ever a thing propelled toward its unfolding goal by some immanent driving spring, but rather a temporally and spatially changing and changeable set of relationships, or relationships among sets of relationships.

The point is more than academic. By turning names into things we create false models of reality. By endowing nations, societies, or cultures with the qualities of internally homogeneous and externally distinctive and bounded objects, we create a model of the world as a global pool hall in which the entities spin off each other so many hard and round billiard balls. Thus it becomes easy to sort the world into differently colored balls, to declare that "East is East, and West is West, and never the twain shall meet." In this way a quintessential West is counterposed to an equally quintessential East, where life was cheap and slavish multitudes groveled under a variety of despotisms. Later, as peoples in other climes began to assert their political and economic independence from both West and East, we assigned these new applicants for historical status to a Third World of underdevelopment — a residual category of conceptual billiard balls — as contrasted with the developed West and the developing East. Inevitably, perhaps, these reified categories became intellectual instruments in the prosecution of the Cold War. There was the "modern" world of the West. There was the world of the East, which had fallen prey to communism, a "disease of modernization" (Rostow 1960). There was, finally, the Third World, still bound up in "tradition" and strangled in its efforts toward modernization. If the West could only find ways of breaking that grip, it could perhaps save the victim from the infection incubated and spread by the East, and set that Third World upon the road to modernization — the road to life, liberty, and the pursuit of happiness of the West. The ghastly offspring of this way of thinking about the world was the theory of "forced draft urbanization" (Huntington 1968: 655), which held that the Vietnamese could be propelled toward modernization by driving them into the cities through aerial bombardment and defoliation of the countryside. Names thus become things, and things marked with an X can become targets of war.

The Rise of the Social Sciences

The habit of treating named entities such as Iroquois, Greece, Persia, or the United States as fixed entities opposed to one another by stable internal architecture and external boundaries interferes with our ability to understand their mutual encounter and confrontation. In fact, this tendency has made it difficult to understand all such encounters and confrontations. Arranging imaginary building blocks into pyramids called East and West, or First, Second, and Third Worlds, merely compounds that difficulty. It is thus likely that we are dealing with some conceptual shortcomings in our ways of looking at social and political phenomena, and not just a temporary aberration. We seem to have taken a wrong turn in understanding at some critical point in the past, a false choice that bedevils our thinking in the present.

That critical turning point is identifiable. It occurred in the middle of the past century, when inquiry into the nature and varieties of humankind split into separate (and unequal) specialties and disciplines. This split was fateful. It led not only forward into the intensive and specialized study of particular aspects of human existence, but turned the ideological reasons for that split into an intellectual justification for the specialties themselves. Nowhere is this more obvious than in the case of sociology. Before sociology we had political economy, a field of inquiry concerned with "the wealth of nations," the production and distribution of wealth within and between political entities and the classes composing them. With the acceleration of capitalist enterprise in the eighteenth century, that structure of state and classes came under increasing pressure from new and "rising" social groups and categories that clamored for the enactment of their rights against those groups defended and represented by the state. Intellectually, this challenge took the form of asserting the validity of new social, economic, political, and ideological ties, now conceptualized as "society," against the state. The rising tide of discontent pitting "society" against the political and ideological order erupted in disorder, rebellion, and revolution. The specter of disorder and revolution raised the question of how social order could be restored and maintained, indeed, how social order was possible at all. Sociology hoped to answer the "social question." It had, as Rudolph Heberle noted, "an eminently political origin. . . . Saint Simon, Auguste Comte, and Lorenz Stein conceived the new science of society as an antidote against the poison of social disintegration" (quoted in Bramson 1961: 12, n. 2).

These early sociologists did this by severing the field of social relations from political economy. They pointed to observable and as yet poorly studied ties which bind people to people as individuals, as groups and associations, or as members of institutions. They then took this field of social relations to be the subject matter of their intensive concern. They and their successors expanded this concern into a number of theoretical postulates, using these to mark off sociology from political science and economics. I would summarize these common postulates as follows:

1. In the course of social life, individuals enter into relations with one another. Such relations can be abstracted from the economic, political, or ideological context in which they are found, and treated sui generis. They are autonomous, constituting a realm of their own, the realm of the social.

2. Social order depends on the growth and extension of social relations among individuals. The greater the density of such ties and the wider their scope, the greater the orderliness of society. Maximization of ties of kinship and neighborhood, of group and association, is therefore conducive to social order. Conversely, if these ties are not maximized, social order is called into question. Development of many and varied ties also diminishes the danger of polarization into classes.

3. The formation and maintenance of such ties is strongly related to the existence and propagation of common beliefs and customs among the individuals participating in them. Moral consensus, especially when based on unexamined belief and on nonrational acceptance of custom, furthers the maximization of social ties; expectations of mere utility and the exercise of merely technical reason tend to weaken them.

4. The development of social relations and the spread of associated custom and belief create a society conceived as a totality of social relations between individuals. Social relations constitute society; society, in turn, is the seat of cohesion, the unit to which predictability and orderliness can be ascribed. If social relations are orderly and recurrent, society has a stable internal structure. The extent of that structure is coterminous with the intensity and range of social rela-

tions. Where these grow markedly less intense and less frequent, society encounters its boundary.

What is the flaw in these postulates? They predispose one to think of social relations not merely as autonomous but as causal in their own right, apart from their economic, political, or ideological context. Since social relations are conceived as relations between individuals, interaction between individuals becomes the prime cause of social life. Since social disorder has been related to the quantity and quality of social relations, attention is diverted from consideration of economics, politics, or ideology as possible sources of social disorder, into a search for the causes of disorder in family and community, and hence toward the engineering of a proper family and community life. Since, moreover, disorder has been located in the divergence of custom and belief from common norms, convergence in custom and consensus in belief are converted into the touchstone of society in proper working order. And, finally, the postulates make it easy to identify Society in general with a society in particular. Society in need of order becomes a particular society to be ordered. In the context of the tangible present, that society to be ordered is then easily identified with a given nation-state, be that nation-state Ghana, Mexico, or the United States. Since social relations have been severed from their economic, political, or ideological context, it is easy to conceive of the nation-state as a structure of social ties informed by moral consensus rather than as a nexus of economic, political, and ideological relationships connected to other nexuses. Contentless social relations, rather than economic, political, or ideological forces, thus become the prime movers of sociological theory. Since these social relations take place within the charmed circle of the single nation-state, the significant actors in history are seen as nation-states, each driven by its internal social relations. Each society is then a thing, moving in response to an inner clockwork.

Works Cited

Bramson, Leon. 1961. *The Political Context of Sociology.* Princeton: Princeton University Press.

Daaku, Kwame Yeboa. 1970. *Trade and Politics on the Gold Coast, 1600–1720: A Study of the African Reaction to European Trade.* Oxford: Clarendon Press.

Huntington, Samuel P. 1968. "The Bases of Accommodation." *Foreign Affairs* 46.

Jennings, Francis. 1976. *The Invasion of America: Indians, Colonialism, and the Cant of Conquest.* New York: W. W. Norton.

Rostow, Walt Whitman. 1960. *The Stages of Economic Growth: A Non-Communist Manifesto.* Cambridge: Cambridge University Press.

PHILIP D. CURTIN

Depth, Span, and Relevance

The discipline of history has broadened enormously in the postwar decades, but historians have not. We teach the history of Africa and Asia, but specialists in American history know no more about the history of Africa than their predecessors did in 1940. We have specialists in black history, women's history, and historical demography, but people outside these specialties pay little attention to their work. Where the field of history grew broader and richer, the training of historians grew narrower. The proportion of new Ph.D.'s that can easily teach the standard "Western Civ" course is smaller in the 1980s than it was in the 1950s. The new Asianists and Africanists know next to nothing about European or American history. Americanists know less European history than they did thirty years ago. At the level of course offerings, the old surveys in European and American history lost popularity. Departments offered a greater number of specialized courses, while history enrollments declined over all.

In recent years, the idea of a broad survey has begun to recover — with some uncertainty about what it ought to be about. A rejuvenated Western Civ is one possibility. A new world history with real concern for the history of non-Western world is another. Ironically, one reason the world history movement has not gained momentum is that few historians have the background necessary to take it on. Many world history courses are "team taught," a reasonable solution to begin with. But the very fact that they *are* is a sad admission. Even those who have recognized the need have also realized how few of their colleagues have the breadth of knowledge required — even for an introductory undergraduate course.

Nor is our failure to help graduate students gain a world-historical perspective just of concern to the history departments that train them. What we teach passes to a broader public, and members of that public make political decisions that are crucial for us all. From the heights of power in the White House, we find portrayed a simplistic, tripartite division of the world into ourselves, our enemies, and the rest — who do not count, even though they form the vast majority of the world's population. Historians did not do this all by themselves, of

Philip D. Curtin, "Depth, Span, and Relevance" (presidential address delivered at the Ninety-Eighth Annual Meeting of the American Historical Association, San Francisco, 28–30 December 1983). *American Historical Review* 89 (February 1984):1–9.

course; the rest of the educational system carries as much responsibility. Nor is everyone in the federal government as badly informed as Mr. Reagan's circle of advisers. But, if one of our responsibilities as historians is to explain how the world came to be as it is, either our answers are not very good, or they are not communicated to the national leadership. In fact, both are the case. The government has enormous resources in short-term intelligence data, but the national leadership lacks long-term understanding of historical change. Without that, its evaluation of the short-term evidence has the fallacious quality we see week in and week out. Perhaps this problem is no worse than it was when an earlier generation of leaders led us into the Vietnam war, but official American reactions to affairs in Central America and talk about preparing to "prevail" in a nuclear war suggest deterioration at the top levels.

In one sense, all this criticism amounts to is the statement that a liberal education is better than ignorance. Historians have been on the right side of that one all along. Their professional failing has been something else — to forget that one of the prime values of a liberal education is breadth, not narrow specialization. Even before the explosion of new kinds of historical knowledge, historical competence required a balance between deep mastery of a particular field and a span of knowledge over other fields of history. Depth was necessary to discover and validate the evidence. Span was necessary to know what kind of evidence to look for — and to make some sense of it, once discovered.

We find the tendency toward specialization not only in graduate requirements and course offerings but also in our professional associations. We have an American Historical Association, and the Association also has seventy-five affiliated societies, each with a special concern with some particular field of history. Many other professional associations, like the Medieval Academy of America and the Organization of American Historians, are not even affiliated, although we work together in many different ways. The clear fact seems to be that many, perhaps most, historians value their personal contacts with fellow-specialists more than they value their contacts with historians in general. This is somewhat understandable. Historians can talk with many different specialists in their own schools, colleges, and universities. But to find someone in precisely the same subfield or specialty, they have to look elsewhere. A common complaint about the annual meeting of the AHA is that too few sessions are concerned with these particular research interests. The dissatisfied drift away from the AHA toward more specialized associations. This tendency is strongest outside old-line, Western history. Most Latin Americanists, Africanists, and Asianists have stronger ties to their own subfields than they have to history as a whole. This in turn makes it hard for a program committee to organize panels in these fields, thus increasing the sense of alienation.[1] Many Asianists already regard the AHA as just another specialized organization for European and American history.

In time, these trends could be serious for the Association, but they are far more serious for the profession. They are the expression, not the cause, of intellectual splintering that has been going on for decades. The old-time, mainline fields like European and American history have been, to put it mildly, unenthusiastic about the growth of non-Western history. The Americanists were — and are — the most parochial, almost by definition, because they study the past of their own society. But Asianists and Africanists have often reacted by cultivating their own kind of parochialism — sometimes seeking refuge in area-studies programs. These, in turn, have been far more successful in opening interdisciplinary communication within the area than they have been in keeping open interarea communication within history.

But the fundamental problem is still overspecialization. It is just as ubiquitous and just as deplorable in almost any other field of knowledge. But what to do about it? One way to begin looking for answers is to step back and consider what the study of history might be expected to accomplish. Every historian will have his own answer, but many of these answers can be grouped roughly under three headings — in rising order of general importance. Each heading can be set off as a question: (1) How did we come to be as we are? (2) How did the world come to be as it is? And (3) how and why do human societies change over time?

The "we" in the first of these questions can be somewhat variable, from family history on to local history and on up to national history or even the history of Western civilization, which remains ethnocentric despite its broad scale. History, considered as one's own past, is both the most common and the most problematic approach. Self-knowledge is no doubt a good thing, but self-knowledge by itself is also a form of selfishness that can be dangerous to social health. In the nineteenth century and too far into the twentieth, history was consciously one-sided; it was not supposed to be even-handed but designed instead to promote patriotism and glorify the nation. These tendencies reached a kind of apogee with the overblown patriotic fervor of the First World War. They have declined somewhat since, but only slowly and not in all parts of the world.

I have already suggested the second category under the question, How did the world come to be as it is? This, too, is a form of self-knowledge, useful information to guide all kinds of decisions that have to be made by people both inside and outside the circles of power. This kind of history is just now beginning to challenge the more self-centered variety for a place in high school and college curricula. But the contest is no longer a simple choice between the traditional Western Civ and another, broader survey of world history. It involves complex problems at several levels in the educational process. One problem is what to teach students who will take only one or two history courses, at most. A second is what to offer to undergraduate history majors who will not become professional historians. A third is what span of knowledge to demand of graduate students in addition to the depth of specialized knowledge they will need for their research.

The choice of formats for historical study is pretty much what it has been for some time: survey courses like Western Civ or U.S. history, backed by a second level of more specialized courses set in the familiar time-span segments — Germany from Barbarosa to Bismarck, the American South from 1860 to 1876, the history of China to 1910. Off in the wings, a potential world history survey is ready to compete for the present position of Western Civ, but that competition is still uncertain. Meanwhile, we continue with time-span segments. We have to trust that students will be able to put them together into some kind of synthesis. That may sometimes happen, but it leaves the burden with the student. It may be a useful challenge, but only for students capable of creative learning — and most are not.

Perhaps we, the professional historians, should attempt to meet the challenge by trying to create our own syntheses of historical knowledge. For myself, I doubt that a world-history survey course will be even as satisfactory as Western Civ was in its day. What we need is a new kind of course that will have the perspective of world history — will ask and try to answer the question, How did the world come to be as it is? — by treating topics selectively, with examples detailed enough to be comprehensible, rather than by surveying the entire panorama too superficially to be worth remembering. Different teachers will no doubt see the world from different points of view, but the important thing is to seek a genuine world perspective. Historians have not yet tried this approach very much, but Eric Wolf's *Europe and the People without History* (1982) can stand as useful example, by an anthropologist, of the kind of broad synthesis we should be doing ourselves.

If we move in some such direction, history may well appear relevant again to far more students than we now reach. But this will not be easy, and our graduate education is largely to blame. We train people to do research on narrow subjects. We make them acquire the kind of background knowledge that appears necessary for such research. They emerge with a Ph.D. and teaching competence adequate to a narrow time-space framework. With a good deal of self-education, most will work their way outward enough to teach Western Civ or the American survey. Graduate schools, with very few exceptions, do nothing at all to prepare history teachers to handle the kind of courses students need in order to understand the world they live in.

Which brings me to the third kind of history — the kind that asks how and why human societies change over time. The main difference between this question and the second, on world-centered history, is that the answers here require an understanding of human beings in general. But human beings in general are too amorphous to be investigated directly. Obviously, we have to begin with some part of the whole — but what part? This question is nearly identical to the one Arnold Toynbee posed a half-century ago in the first volume of his *A Study of History:* What is the correct, objective "intelligible field of historical study?" His answer, of course, was that it could not be the European nation-state, the framework historians used far too commonly in his time, as in ours. He opted instead for units he called societies, of which the familiar Western civilization is the clearest example.[2] He was right in wanting some field of study other than the nation-state, but his identification of "civilizations" as the prime actors on the historical stage led to new problems. Civilizations are hard to identify. Their borders in time and space are shifting and uncertain, and we lack clear criteria to demarcate one from another. Toynbee's own choice of religion as the marker of civilization was, moreover, not universally accepted — or acceptable.

Rather than seeking a single "intelligible field of historical study," we need, more prudently, to go part way along the road Toynbee mapped out, without stopping precisely where he did. Toynbee believed that each configuration of historical events can be separated fairly clearly in time and space from other, different configurations. And he dealt at length with the limits of his civilizations in space and in time. We can each go through the same exercise and reach different conclusions by centering on a problem to be solved. Just as a "civilization" has its limits in time and space, so too each historical problem has a universe of data necessary to its solution.

Social scientists sometimes talk about a relevant aggregate. An individual, for example, can simultaneously form part of many different groupings — by family, social class, income, ethnic background, race, and so on. The task is to find which of these groupings is the significant aggregate for the problem at hand. One of the worst mistakes social scientists ever made was to assume that race is the most important determinant of human action in society or in history. That mistake led to the nineteenth-century rise of pseudo-scientific racism. Yet, to solve historical problems, we do first have to identify the relevant aggregates and discover their limits in time and space. Sometimes the correct answers are so obvious as to present no difficulty. At other times, discovering the correct aggregate requires rare breadth of knowledge, depth of insight, and plain luck. The point, however, is that the relevant body of data to be examined is not a free choice. It is dictated, ultimately, by the problem to be solved. Failure to identify it correctly can lead to errors that range from minor misunderstandings to completely wrong conclusions.

Let me take a few examples from the history of the Atlantic basin — a region badly treated by historians until recent decades, mainly because it has been partitioned among specialists in European, North American, Latin American, and African history. None of these groups paid much attention to the work of the others. The result was a range of misunderstanding from trivial to deadly. On the trivial side, I discovered, when working on the history of the Atlantic slave trade, that most Americans thought then (and probably still think) that a large majority of the slaves transported from Africa to the New World arrived in the present territory of the United States. In fact, those that came to the United States were only about 6 percent of the whole. I have no idea what teachers of U.S. history actually tell their students, but I do not think that they set out consciously to misinform. More likely, most simply stay within the limits of the assigned aggregate, the history of the United States — and thereby leave out any mention of the other 94 percent of the Atlantic slave trade. And students, unfortunately, take silence to mean absence. The result is a major misunderstanding of the role of the United States in the larger history of the Atlantic basin — and of the migrations that have formed so much of its history over the past four centuries.

A far more serious — indeed, deadly — misunderstanding underlay the early nineteenth-century idea of some philanthropic (and not-so-philanthropic) Americans that it would be both humane and convenient if freedmen of African descent could return to Africa. Recent history, as it was then understood, showed that people of European descent died of disease on the African coast at astronomical rates — in an environment in which adult Africans appeared to be reasonably healthy. This "lesson of history" suggested that, since black Americans looked like Africans and had African ancestors, Afro-Americans would be safe from African diseases. But it was wrong. The relevant factor was not race but childhood disease environment. The retransported settlers from America died at rates nearly as high as those of North Europeans. In many cases, the move to Liberia was an unintended death sentence.[3]

A third example comes from the demographic history of the American side of the ocean and concerns the comparative demographic patterns of slave populations in the U.S. South, the Caribbean islands, and Brazil. The error began with the failure of U.S. historians to look beyond the political boundaries of the United States. Historians of the South paid no special attention to the mortality and fertility rates of the antebellum slave population. In general, the numbers looked a lot like those for the white population in the same regions — with a slightly lower rate of population growth, as one might expect of a people with a lower standard of living than free people had. In this narrow framework of North American history, there seemed little to explain. Meanwhile, the Latin Americanists and Caribbeanists knew that slave populations in the tropics had such high death rates and low birth rates that population increase was rarely possible. Rates of net natural decrease could run to 2 or 3 percent, occasionally even more. But that, too, seemed explicable for the region. The white populations also suffered a net natural decrease, at least among those who were newly arrived from Europe. Only in the past two decades or so have historians of the United States looked further afield and found that the demography of the slave population here was highly unusual. What first appeared to be no problem at all now called for explanation — once it was set in the larger aggregate of New World slave demography.

These three examples, all taken from Atlantic demographic history, show an aggregate misidentified on grounds of race or from overly narrow regional specialization. Other conventions of historical discourse, even more commonplace, can lead to similar misunderstandings. One of the most deceptive is our conventional approach to divisions of time and space. Reigns and dynasties, centuries and decades are convenient short cuts for dealing with chronology, but these man-made markers can also take on the appearance of reality. Just think of the thousands of students who still associate Queen Elizabeth I with Shakespeare's plays, simply because we tolerate the label "Elizabethan drama." Some escape is possible by petty distortion, like beginning the nineteenth century in 1815 and ending it with the outbreak of the First World War. But the conventions sometimes get out of control, like the former habit of dating the Industrial Revolution in England from 1760 to 1820 — partly because those dates mark off neat decades and partly because they are the regnal dates of George III, who, of course, had nothing to do with it.

Mapping conventions are far more serious in their unintended — sometimes their intended — influence on historical thought. The Mercator projection is a prime example. Even though we know distortion is necessary in order to show the surface of a sphere on a flat piece of paper, we become conditioned to accept the convention as reality. As a result, most well-informed people "know" that the European subcontinent of the Eurasian landmass is considerably larger than the Indian subcontinent, when in reality they are nearly the same size. This misperception arises not only because the Mercator projection enlarges all northern territories but also because we use the Urals as the conventional eastern boundary of Europe, when a line drawn from the White Sea to the Black Sea makes much more sense geographically.[4] For similar reasons, most Americans imagine the Indonesian archipelago as about the same size as the Antilles. In fact, Indonesia from east to west stretches a good deal farther than the distance from Maine to California.

The conventional hemispheres cause still more serious distortions. Anyone who bothers to think about such things knows that the potential number of hemispheres is infinite, simply because the earth can be viewed from an infinite number of points in space. Knowing our ethnocentric traditions, we might expect conventional hemispheres in school atlases to center on the United States, and the newer books often show some such thing. But the older convention respects the earth's rotation and shows the north pole at the top and the south pole at the bottom. Hemispheres are thus viewed from above the equator. If the United States is then placed in the middle between east and west, the result is a conventional hemisphere that actually centers approximately on the Galapagos Islands off the coast of Ecuador. This is, of course, the hemisphere that served as a basis for "hemispheric solidarity." It conveniently puts the Asians and the Europeans halfway around the world — and on another page. Another hemisphere, centering on Omaha, would show that parts of Siberia and northwest Europe are comparatively close neighbors. Even parts of Africa would be included, while Argentina would not appear at all.

The hemispheric misconception is obviously associated with the political hemispherism of the Monroe Doctrine, the Good Neighbor Policy, and American isolationism before the Second World War. But even historians are still led astray. A recent book on the North American fur trade argues that a particular combination of Native American religious ideas joined the commercial impact of European fur traders to produce the depletion of fur-bearing animals in North America between the early seventeenth and the early nineteenth century.[5] Both the author and his opponents have argued their case without seriously considering that the depletion of fur-bearing animals belongs not to the Galapagos-centered hemisphere but to a polar-centered hemisphere. Over these same centuries, the phenomenon stretched from Finland east to the Saint Lawrence. The few miles of the Bering Straits made no real difference to the Russian fur traders, who followed their prey into Alaskan waters and on south to California. The obvious aggregate is the depletion of fur-bearing animals in northern latitudes in these centuries. The rule of parsimony suggests that similar events, wherever they occur, have similar causes. It can hardly be legitimate to leave out the culture and psychology of the Native Siberians, which might have been quite different from those of Native Americans — even though the Siberians killed their animals with about the same speed and timing as the Native Americans did.

In this case, then, the relative aggregate was split in two by geographical convention. Much the same is sometimes done for political reasons. The treatment of Canadian history in U.S. schools and universities provides a striking example. In the broadest sweep of world history over the past four hundred years, the most important thing that happened in the history of northern North America was its repopulation by settlers from Europe. These settlers founded new societies of overseas Europeans, beginning about the same time in Canada and the United States. This pattern of blanket settlement by Europeans, also prevalent in southern South America, was clearly different from two other kinds of settlement over these same centuries: the settlement of some Spanish and Portuguese among the surviving Indians of the tropics, especially in the highlands, and the settlement of the predominantly African slave populations in the tropical lowlands.

It can be argued that the fullest understanding of New World history requires a comparative study of what went on in all three of these zones. What is hard to justify is dividing the zone of blanket settlement in two by a political boundary. For school and university teaching, it seems self-evident that Americans need to know how Canada came to be there and how the Canadian historical experience differs from our own. In fact, Canadian history adds a whole new dimension and range of understanding to U.S. history seen in this comparative context. Comparison is valuable for illuminating differences as well as similarities, as the example of slave demography demonstrates. Regionalism in politics has been important in the political life of both Canada and the United States, but it has taken different forms. Both countries have a federal constitution — but one is parliamentary and the other presidential. Both countries have experienced severe regional conflicts — but one led to a major civil war and the other did not. One country has faced a severe problem of linguistic nationalism while the other has not. Yet our old emphasis on political history, with a healthy carry-over from the patriotic goals of an earlier historical tradition, makes it possible for historians on both sides of the border to deny the immense explanatory value that a broader history of North America would have had.

Examples can be multiplied. Nor is the problem limited to history as an intellectual discipline. The underlying problem is the proliferation of all knowledge in this century. The historians' solution, in common with that of other disciplines, has been to multiply the fields of specialization. To some degree, that is unavoidable. But its very unavoidability imposes an obligation. We must try even harder to balance the depth of our own specializations against a wider span of historical knowledge — to make sure we are asking the most important questions and seeking answers in the framework of the relevant aggregates. I can close by recalling two time-honored aphorisms that are still worth remembering:

Some of those gaps in our knowledge belong there.

An elegant answer to an irrelevant question is still irrelevant.

Notes

1. The journal of the Association experiences the same difficulties as the Program Committee. The *Review* cannot publish what it does not receive, and on several occasions in the last few years the editors have had to plan special issues and call for papers in those fields in order to receive articles in Asian, Latin American, and African history.

2. Toynbee, *A Study in History*, 2d ed. (London, 1935), 1:17–181.

3. Tom W. Shick, "A Quantitative Analysis of Liberian Colonization from 1820 to 1834, with Special Reference to Mortality," *Journal of African History* 12 (1972): 45–59.

4. The area of Europe, exclusive of Iceland and any part of the Soviet Union, is approximately 1,820,000 square miles; the area of the Indian subcontinent, exclusive of Ceylon and Burma, is roughly 1,680,000 square miles. Including that part of the Soviet Union west of 40 degrees east longitude (a line drawn essentially from Archangel to Rostov) would add roughly 675,000 square miles to the area of Europe: including Burma (often considered geographically a part of the Indian subcontinent) would add approximately 260,000 square miles.

5. Calvin Martin, *The Keepers of the Game: Indian-Animal Relationships and the Fur Trade* (Berkeley and Los Angeles, 1978). Also see Shepard Krech III, ed., *Indians, Animals, and the Fur Trade: A Critique of* Keepers of the Game (Athens, Ga., 1981).

WILLIAM H. MCNEILL

The Changing Shape of World History

When I wrote *The Rise of the West* I set out to improve upon Toynbee by showing how the separate civilizations of Eurasia interacted from the very beginning of their history, borrowing critical skills from one another, and thus precipitating still further change as adjustment between treasured old and borrowed new knowledge and practice became necessary.

My ideas about the importance of cultural borrowing were largely shaped by social anthropology as developed in the United States in the 1930s. Clark Wissler had studied the diffusion of "culture traits" among the Plains Indians with elegant precision; and Ralph Linton's textbook, *The Tree of Culture*, adduced other persuasive examples of far-reaching social change in Africa and elsewhere as a result of cultural adaptation to some borrowed skill. But the man who influenced me most was Robert Redfield. He constructed a typology of

William H. McNeill, "The Changing Shape of World History," *History and Theory* 34 (May 1995): 14–26.

human societies, setting up two ideal types: folk society at one extreme, civilized society at the other.

Folk society was one in which well-established customs met all ordinary circumstances of life, and fitted smoothly together to create an almost complete and unquestioned guide to life. Redfield argued that a remote Yucatan village he had studied approached his ideal type of folk society. Nearly isolated from outside encounters, the people of the village had reconciled their Spanish Christian and Mayan heritages, blending what had once been conflicting ways of life into a more or less seamless whole. Conflict and change were reprehensible, checked by the sacralizing power of binding custom.

Civilized society, exemplified by Yucatan's port city of Merida, was at the opposite pole. There Catholicism clashed with residual pagan rites, and continual contacts among strangers meant that customary rules binding everyone to a consistent body of behavior could not arise. Instead, conflicting moral claims provoked variable, unpredictable conduct. Social conflict and change was obvious and pervasive, feared by some and welcomed by others.

Armed with ideas like these, it seemed obvious to me in 1954 when I began to write *The Rise of the West*, that historical change was largely provoked by encounters with strangers, followed by efforts to borrow (or sometimes to reject or hold at bay) especially attractive novelties. This, in turn, always involved adjustments in other established routines. A would-be world historian therefore ought to be alert to evidence of contacts among separate civilizations, expecting major departures to arise from such encounters whenever some borrowing from (or rejection of) outsiders' practices provoked historically significant social change.

The ultimate spring of human variability, of course, lies in our capacity to invent new ideas, practices, and institutions. But invention also flourished best when contacts with strangers compelled different ways of thinking and doing to compete for attention, so that choice became conscious, and deliberate tinkering with older practices became easy, and indeed often inevitable. In folk society, when custom worked as expected, obstacles to most sorts of social change were all but insuperable. But when clashes of customs created confusion, invention flourished. Civilization, as Redfield defined it, was therefore autocatalytic. Once clashing cultural expectations arose at a few crossroads locations, civilized societies were liable to keep on changing, acquiring new skills, expanding their wealth and power, and disturbing other peoples round about. They did so down to our own day, and at an ever-increasing pace as the centuries and millennia of civilized history passed.

Approaching the conceptualization of world history in this fashion, separate civilizations became the main actors in world history — accepting or rejecting new ways come from afar, but in either case altering older social practices, since successfully to reject an attractive or threatening novelty might require changes at home quite as far-reaching as trying to appropriate it. Over time, civilizations clearly tended to expand onto new ground; and as they expanded, autonomous neighboring societies were engulfed and eventually disappeared. Such geographical expansion meant that in the ancient Near East what had begun as separate civilizations in Mesopotamia and Egypt eventually merged into a new cosmopolitan whole, beginning about 1500 B.C.; and, I concluded, an analogous cosmopolitanism began to embrace all the civilizations of the earth after about 1850, when the effective autonomy of China and Japan came to an end.

But when I wrote *The Rise of the West* I was sufficiently under Toynbee's spell to note these instances without diverting the focus of my attention from the separate histories of separate civilizations. The idea of a Eurasian (eventually also African and then global) ecumenical whole, embracing all the peoples, civilized and uncivilized, who were interacting with one another, dawned very slowly. Only after I convinced myself, while writing *The Pursuit of Power* (1982), that Chinese commercial expansion energized the sudden upthrust of trade in Latin Christendom after about 1000 A.D., did I realize, with Wallerstein and Dunn, that a proper world history ought to focus primarily upon changes in the ecumenical world system, and then proceed to fit developments within separate civilizations, and within smaller entities like states and nations, into the pattern of that fluctuating whole.

A weakened sense of the autonomy of separate civilizations went along with this alteration of my outlook. In *The Rise of the West* I had defined civilization as a style of life, to be recognized by skilled and experienced observers in the way an art critic discerns styles of art. But that analogy is not a good one. Works of art are tangible; whereas "life" is too multifarious to be observed in the way art critics can observe and more or less agree about stylistic affinities. In particular, within any civilization different groups lived in very different ways. What principally held them together was their common subjection to rulers, whose continued dominion was much assisted by the fact that they subscribed to a set of moral rules embodied in sacred or at least semi-sacred texts. This, it now seems to me, is the proper definition of a "civilization." Rulers who knew how to behave — paying lip service to prescribed canons of conduct and acting with a more or less exactly agreed upon disregard of the letter of those rules — could and did cooperate smoothly enough to keep a lid on turbulent subordinates for centuries on end across scores, then hundreds and, eventually, thousands of miles. Privileged ruling classes thus constituted a sort of iron framework within which a civilization could thrive. But among subordinated groups widely diverse local, occupational, and sectarian ways of life prevailed. All that united them was the fact that each group had some sort of tacit (or, occasionally, explicit) understanding with other groups, and especially with the politically dominant segments of society, so that they could act as they did without suffering too many nasty surprises.

In such a view, civilizations become rather pale, inchoate entities in themselves. Internal diversity looms large and merges almost imperceptibly into the diversity of neighboring peoples who retained varying degrees of local autonomy but still entered into negotiations which civilized rulers and traders, and, perhaps, with missionaries, craftsmen, refugees, and sometimes with colonizing settlers as well. No single recognizable style of life can be imputed to such a social landscape. Diversity, conflict, and imprecise boundaries, yes; coherence and uniformity, no.

Even the canon of sacred writings, to which dominant segments of civilized society subscribed, was full of discrepancies. Consider the Bible, Buddhist and Hindu sacred writings, and the Confucian classics! It required judicious commentary to educe a practicable guide to life from such diverse materials; and, of course, initial diversity implied perennial flexibility, inviting commentators to adjust to ever-altering circumstances by appropriate reinterpretation, age after age, while claiming, characteristically, to be restoring the true, original meaning to the sacred texts. This was the primary function of the literate (often priestly) classes; it explains why new, discrepant data were (and still are in many branches of learning) so persistently disregarded.

If civilizations were as internally confused and contradictory as I now believe them to have been, it puts them very much in tune with the confusion and complexity of the Eurasian ecumenical world system. That system was larger in geographic area, of course, and more attenuated in its internal structure, being without any articulated, overriding canon of conduct because it embraced a plurality of civilizations (and interstitial peoples) each with its own literary definition of moral principles and its own political and cultural rulers. But, for all that, the ecumene was not so very different from the diversity to be found within the borders of any of the larger civilizations that by 1500 were participating in the Eurasian and African circle of exchange and interaction.

The reason was that mercantile practice had, in fact, slowly created a workable code of conduct that went a long way towards standardizing encounters across cultural boundaries. Even the arcanum of religion made room for outsiders and unbelievers, since the principal religions of the Eurasian world — Christianity, Confucianism, Buddhism, and Islam — all agreed in exhorting the devout to treat strangers as they would wish to be treated themselves. Thus, despite the fact that no single set of rulers had ever exercised political sovereignty across the whole Eurasian-African ecumene, a bare-bones moral code did arise that went a long way towards reducing the risks of cross-civilizational contact to bearable proportions. Little by little across the centuries, local rulers of every stripe learned that they could benefit mightily by taxing instead of plundering strangers. Subordinate classes also learned to tolerate outsiders — even alien merchants, whom hard-working peasants and artisans regularly regarded as dishonest exploiters who reaped profit unjustly, since what they sold dear was exactly the same as what they had previously bought cheap from honest men, that is, from themselves. All the same, the poor gradually got used to being cheated by outsiders in the marketplace, just as their forerunners at the dawn of civilization had gotten used to surrendering unrequited rent to self-appointed, strong-armed landowners.

As these attitudes became general, so that an enforceable (and remarkably uniform) merchant law arose in the ports and other great urban centers of Eurasia, and was supplemented by an informal body of customs for dealing with strangers that extended into the rural hinterland, the structure of the ecumenical world system approximated very closely to that of the separate civilizations embraced within it. Accordingly, students of world history should make it the object of conscious investigation, for this is what gives cohesion and structure to their subject in quite the same way that governmental acts and policies give cohesion and structure to national histories. Or so I now believe.

What, then, were the major landmarks in the historical evolution of this, the largest and, eventually, world-dominating framework of human experience?

As one would expect, if I am right in claiming that encounters with strangers were the main drive wheel of social change, the earliest complex societies arose on the river flood plains of Mesopotamia, Egypt, and northwest India, adjacent to the land bridge of the Old World, where the largest land masses of the earth connect with one another. Continental alignments and climatic conditions made this region the principal node of land and sea communications within the Old World, and it was presumably for that reason that civilization first broke out there.

Sumerian literary tradition accords with this notion, since it held that the founders of their civilization had come by sea from the south and subdued the "black headed people" who were indigenous to the banks of the lower Tigris-Euphrates. The newcomers eventually learned to irrigate the swamp lands that bordered the rivers, and thanks to regular and assured harvests were then able to erect earth's first cities on an alluvial plain that lacked timber, metals, and other essential raw materials the Sumerians needed. From their inception, therefore, shipping, supplemented by overland caravans, kept the cities of the Mesopotamian plain in touch (directly or indirectly) with distant sources of raw materials and diverse peoples living within a radius of several hundred miles. And, before long, inhabitants of Egypt and of the Indus valley erected civilizations of their own, thanks partly to borrowed skills and ideas acquired through contact with Mesopotamia, and by doing so promptly established their own zones of interaction with peoples round about, just as the Sumerians had done before them.

Initially, water transport was the main link across long distances. When, at an early but unknown date, human beings discovered the use of sails, the coastal waters of the Indian ocean and its adjacent seas became an especially easy medium of transport and communication. Winds blew equably throughout the year, and their direction reversed itself with each monsoon. This made safe return from lengthy voyages exceptionally easy, even for ships that could not sail against the wind. If Sumerian tradition is to be believed, the founders of the world's first civilization emerged from this sea-room, bringing with them superior skills that had been accumulated, we may surmise, before the dawn of recorded history thanks to contacts with strangers provoked by sea travel.

About 4000 B.C. sailing ships also began to ply the Mediterranean, where comparably benign (though not quite so convenient) sailing conditions prevailed in summertime when the trade winds blew gently and steadily from the northeast. Safe return to home base often required going against the prevailing wind. Rowing was one possibility, and remained important in Mediterranean navigation until the seventeenth century A.D. Taking advantage of short-lived offshore winds created by differential heating of sea and land was another possibility. Ship and sail design that permitted tacking into the wind was a more satisfactory solution, but was not fully attained until the late middle ages. Yet ships that moved up-wind with difficulty, and could not sail the stormy seas of winter safely, were quite enough to provoke and sustain the emergence of Minoan, Phoenician-Carthaginian, and Greco-Roman civilizations. Borrowings from Egypt and Syria were critical at the start — and most such contacts were by sea.

Geographically speaking, the south China sea was about as hospitable to early sailing ships as the Mediterranean. But the possibility of seasonal navigation in southeast Asia and among adjacent offshore islands did not lead to the early development of cities and literate civilizations, perhaps because no developed civilized centers were at hand from which to borrow critical skills and ideas. Similarly, the most congenial sea spaces of all the earth were the vast tradewind zones of the Atlantic and Pacific oceans; but they too were not exploited until large ships that could tack against the wind had been invented, though Polynesian canoes did carry human settlers to remote islands of the Pacific throughout the tradewind zone. The North Atlantic and North Pacific were far more formidable for early sailors since stormy, variable winds were further complicated by high tides.

Thus climate and wind patterns set definite limits to early shipping, though it is worth noting that small coracles, made of wickerwork and hides, did begin to fish the coastal waters of the North Atlantic in the fourth millennium B.C. Fishermen also embarked from the shores of Japan from an unknown but presumably early date. Accidental drift voyages across the breadth of the oceans must have set in as soon as fishing boats started to venture onto these stormy waters. Drift voyages of Eskimo kayaks from Greenland that fetched up in Scotland in the seventeenth century, and Japanese fishermen who came ashore in Oregon in the nineteenth century, offer a well-attested sample of the random, ocean-crossing dispersals suffered by small craft lost at sea.

A few resemblances between Amerindian artifacts and those of east Asia may result from drift voyages; but fishermen did not carry much cultural baggage with them, even when they survived weeks of exposure; and it is unlikely that the real but trivial transoceanic contacts (including Norse settlements in North America) had enduring consequences of any importance before 1492. Instead, a separate ecumenical system arose in the Americas, centered in Mexico and Peru; but in the absence of an extended literary record, we know far less about its development, and, since archaeology is inherently local, connections among separate sites frequently remain obscure.

Eurasian ecumenical history is far more accessible, even though historians have not yet studied its growth and consolidation in detail. Nonetheless, it is clear enough that the initial primacy of sea transport and communication in holding the ecumene together was gradually modified by improvements in transport overland. Human beings, of course, were rovers from the start: that is how they populated the earth. With the development of agriculture, the diffusion of useful crops set in. Slash and burn cultivators, for example, carried wheat from the Near East to China, where it arrived before 2000 B.C. Rice spread from somewhere in southeast Asia and became an important crop in both India and China about a thousand years later. Other, less important crops spread as well, altering human life profoundly wherever they began to provide a new source of food for the population.

Before the dawn of literacy, human portage and wandering had been supplemented, at least in some parts of the world, by caravans of pack animals, which made carrying goods much easier. Long-distance exchange became routine in Sumerian times, when donkey caravans brought metals and other precious commodities from as far away as the Carpathian mountains of Rumania and distributed textiles and other manufactured goods in return. Caravan trade thus came to resemble trade by sea, with the difference that carrying valuable goods through inhabited lands required the negotiation of protection rents with every local ruler, whereas ships usually only had to pay tolls at their ports of destination. Since risk of plunder by some local ruffian was far higher than the risk of piracy at sea, costs of caravan transport remained comparatively high, so that only precious goods could bear the cost of long-distance land transport.

Overland contacts took a decisive new turn after about 1700 B.C. when light, maneuverable chariots were invented somewhere in the Mesopotamian borderlands. A team of horses hitched to such a vehicle could carry driver and bowman across open country faster than a man could run; and, when new, an array of charging chariots proved capable of overwhelming opposing infantry with ease. As a result, charioteers overran the river valley civilizations of the Near East and India before and after 1500 B.C. Others penetrated Europe and China, where the earliest archaeologically well-attested Chinese dynasty, the Shang, established itself about 1400 B.C. with the help of war chariots. As the spread of wheat (and of some pottery styles from western Asia) shows, swift wheeled transport and the military superiority of charioteers that resulted did not initiate trans-Asian encounters, but the establishment of the Shang dynasty through the exploitation of military techniques that originated in the Mesopotamian borderlands apparently did inaugurate many of the historical forms of Chinese civilization. This is strikingly attested by inscriptions on oracle bones discovered at the Shang capital of Anyang which are directly ancestral to the characters of contemporary Chinese writing.

Communication between China and western Asia remained sporadic and indirect for many centuries after 1400 B.C. Even when Chinese imperial initiative inaugurated more or less regular caravan trade after 100 B.C., goods that survived the long journey remained mere curiosities and expensive luxuries. A few fashionable Roman ladies did indeed clothe themselves in semi-transparent silks from China; and the Chinese emperor did succeed in importing large-boned "blood sweating" horses from Iran, only to find that the scrawny steppe ponies, with which Chinese soldiers had already come to terms, were so much hardier and cheaper to keep that the imported breed could not displace them for anything but ceremonial purposes.

Yet the inauguration of more or less regular caravan trade across Asia did connect east and west as never before; and when, after about 300 A.D., camels were brought into general use, caravans became capable of crossing previously inhospitable deserts. The effect was to incorporate vast new areas of Eurasia and Africa into an expanded trade and communications network. Tibet, Arabia, and the oases of central Asia, on the one hand, and sub-Saharan West Africa on the other entered firmly into the ecumenical system, which simultaneously expanded northward by penetrating the whole of the steppes from Manchuria to Hungary, and even filtered across mountain passes and along river courses into the forested fastnesses of northern Europe.

New and highly lethal epidemic diseases and the so-called higher religions were the two most significant novelties that spread through this expanded caravan world from shortly before the Christian era to about 1000 A.D. Material exchanges, like the spread of southeast Asian fruits and other crops to the Middle East with the elaboration of oasis agriculture, or the diffusion of Greco-Roman naturalistic sculptural styles to India, China, and even Japan were trivial by comparison with the epidemiological and religious changes that this transport system precipitated.

This balance between economic/technological and cultural/biological exchanges altered after about 1000 A.D. when the ecumenical world system began to respond to innovations within China that expanded the role of market behavior by bringing poor peasants and urban working classes within its scope for the first time. What made this possible was cheap and reliable transport within China, resulting from widespread canal construction. Most canalization was initially undertaken to regulate water supplies for the expanding carpet of rice paddies upon which China's food more and more depended. Then with the construction of the Grand Canal in 605, linking the watershed of the Yang-tse with the Yellow River system, accompanied and followed by other engineering works designed to facilitate navigation through the Yang-tse gorges and other critical bottlenecks, the most fertile parts of China came to be linked by easily accessible and easily navigable waterways. Under the distant sovereignty of the Emperor, canal boats could carry comparatively bulky cargoes across hundreds of miles with minimal risk of shipwreck or robbery. This, in turn, meant that even small differences in price for commodities of common consumption made it worthwhile for boatmen to carry such goods from where they were cheap to where they were dear.

Then, when, soon after 1000, the Sung government found it more convenient to collect taxes in cash instead of in kind, as had always been done previously, common people, including the poorest peasants, were forced onto the market so as to be able to pay their taxes. This enormously accelerated the spread of market behavior throughout China. Thereupon, to the general surprise of officialdom, whose Confucian training classified traders as deplorable social parasites, the advantages of specialized production, which Adam Smith was later to analyze so persuasively, started to come on stream throughout the varied landscapes of China.

Wealth and productivity shot upwards. New skills developed, making China the wonder of the rest of the world, as Marco Polo and other visitors from afar soon realized. Among the new Chinese skills, some proved revolutionary: most notably for Europe, the trinity of gunpowder, printing, and the compass, all of which reached Europe from China between the thirteenth and fifteenth centuries.

China's westward reach was enhanced by the development of ocean-going all-weather ships, capable of tacking against the wind and of surviving most storms. Such ships, based mainly along the south China coast, where inland canal construction was checked by the mountainous interior, allowed enterprising merchants to extend a new (or perhaps only intensified and expanded) trade network across the South China Sea and into the Indian Ocean. There stoutly-built Chinese vessels had to compete with the light craft and experienced mercantile population indigenous to those waters. As happened subsequently when European ships penetrated the Indian Ocean by circumnavigating Africa, local shipping and trading networks proved capable of undercutting the higher costs borne by large, all-weather, stout-built intruders. But all the same, a comparatively massive infusion of Chinese commodities and Chinese demand for spices and other Indian Ocean products gave a fillip to the markets of the southern seas that soon slopped over into the Mediterranean and helped to stimulate the remarkable revival of European trade in the eleventh century and subsequently, with which historians have long been familiar.

Traders' needs, in turn, provoked Europeans to develop all-weather ships that were capable of traversing the stormy, tide-beset seas of the North Atlantic with a reasonable chance of getting back to home ports safely. Inventions introduced between about 1000 and 1400, such as double planking nailed to a heavy keel-and-rib frame, powerful stern post rudders, decked-over holds, and multiple masts and sails, made this possible. European shipbuilding followed a course of its own, independent of Chinese or any other foreign model, even though European sailors were always ready to borrow anything that worked in practice, like compass navigation from China and triangular sails from the Indian ocean.

Their most fateful borrowing and adaptation, however, was the marriage European seamen made between stout-built, oceangoing ships and cannon developed initially to knock down castle walls on land. Such big guns, once adapted for use on shipboard, provided European ships with an armament far superior to anything previously known. As a result, when European ships began to sail across all the oceans of the earth, just before and after 1500, they were remarkably safe against attack by sea; and could often overwhelm local resistance on shore with wall-destroying broadsides.

The recoil from such guns was so powerful that only heavy ships could sustain it without shaking apart. The Chinese might have matched European ships in this respect, but for reasons of imperial politics the Chinese government prohibited the construction of oceangoing ships after 1434, and made private Chinese oceanic enterprise illegal. Operating as pirates systematically handicapped Chinese (and Japanese) sailors thereafter, and deprived them of any chance of arming their vessels with heavy guns like those European traders carried routinely.

The consequences of European oceanic discoveries are well known, as are the consequences of the extraordinary improvements of transport and communication that came after 1850, when European, American, and more recently also Japanese inventors utilized mechanical and electrical forms of energy for railroads, steamships, telegraph, and then for airplanes, radio, TV, and most recently, for the transmission of computer data as well. The most obvious effect of these successive transformations of world communications was to expand the reach of the Eurasian ecumene throughout the globe, engulfing the previously independent ecumenical system of America, together with less well-known social complexes in Australia and in innumerable smaller islands. The shock was enormous, and the world is still reverberating to the ecological, epidemiological, demographic, cultural, and intellectual consequences of the global unification of the past five hundred years.

Among other things, global communication and transport made world history a palpable reality. Historians, being the faithful guardians of every level of human collective identity, are beginning to adapt to that circumstance, almost half a millennium after it began to affect human life everywhere. That is why the World History Conference was called — a bit belatedly one might suppose. Yet that is not really the case, since, as I pointed out already, the historical profession still clings to more local (and more sacred) forms of history, and has not yet agreed upon how to approach the human adventure on earth as a whole.

In struggling with this question, it seems appropriate to emphasize two distinct levels of human encounters that took place across the centuries within the communications networks I have just sketched for you. First is biological and ecological: how human beings fared in competition with other forms of life, managing not only to survive but to expand their share of the earth's matter and energy, age after age, and in a great variety of different physical environments. No other species comes near to equalling humanity's dominating role in earth's ecosystem. Major landmarks are obvious enough, starting with an initial diffusion of hunters and gatherers from Africa, followed by intensified broad-spectrum gathering leading to agriculture; and then the rise of civilizations with enhanced formidability *vis à vis* other societies due to their military specialists on the one hand and their adaptation to crowd diseases on the other. The growing importance of the Eurasian ecumenical world system then takes over, diffusing diseases, crops, and technological skill across larger and larger areas, until after 1500 the process became global. Each time a previously isolated population entered into contact with the ecumenical world system, debilitating exposure to unfamiliar diseases, ideas, and techniques ensued, often with disastrous results for the previously isolated peoples and their cultures.

Uniformity never emerged, and there is no reason to suppose it ever will. Differences of climate and other circumstances require different behavior, and being both intelligent and adaptable, human beings act accordingly. Some forms of life have been destroyed by the human career on earth; many more are endangered, as we all know. Others have been carried into new environments and made to flourish as never before. Some disease organisms and weed species still defy human wishes successfully, but domesticated plants and animals have been radically altered and some entirely new species of plants and animals have been invented to nourish us and serve our wants (and wishes) in other ways.

What makes the human career on the face of the earth so extraordinary from a biological/ecological point of view is that in becoming fully human our predecessors introduced cultural evolution as soon as learned behavior began to govern most of their activity. The consequent cultural attainments of humankind, and their variability in time and space, thus constitute the second level of world history. Attention has traditionally and quite properly centered here because what has been learned can change whenever something new and attractive comes to conscious attention. And since consciousness is extremely motile, cultural evolution immediately outstripped organic evolution, introducing a radically new sort of disturbance into earth's ecosystem.

Yet in some respects cultural evolution still conforms to the older patterns of organic evolution. Initial, more or less random, variation and subsequent selection of what works best is enough to set the process in motion. Contacts among bearers of different cultural traditions promoted further change; but as I have argued already, changes were often initiated to defend local peculiarities rather than to accept what was perceived as an alien, and often threatening, novelty. It follows that even the instantaneous communication that prevails today is unlikely to result in any sort of global uniformity. Human groups, even while borrowing from outsiders, cherish a keen sense of their uniqueness. The more they share, the more each group focuses attention on residual differences, since only so can the cohesion and morale of the community sustain itself.

The upshot has always been conflict, rivalry, and chronic collision among human groups, both great and small. Even if world government were to come such rivalries would not cease, though their expression would have to alter in deference to the overriding power of a bureaucratic world administration. In all probability, human genetic inheritance is attuned to membership in a small, primary community. Only so can life have meaning and purpose. Only so can moral rules be firm and definite enough to simplify choices. But membership in such groups perpetuates the gap between "us" and "them" and invites conflict since the best way to consolidate any group is to have an enemy close at hand.

Until very recently, rural villages constituted the primary communities that shaped and gave direction to most human lives. But with modern communications and the persistent spread of market relations into the countryside, this has begun to change. Multiple and often competing identities, characteristic of cities from ancient times, have begun to open before the astonished and often resentful eyes of the human majority. How to choose between the alternative collective identities, and how to reconcile conflicting obligations that different identities impose is the perennial moral problem of all human society. In the past, most rural communities worked out more or less unambiguous rules for making such choices, so that moral behavior was usually obvious to all concerned. In urban contexts, friction and uncertainty were far greater; and today, as urbanity expands into the countryside, ambiguity and uncertainty multiply everywhere.

How to reconcile membership in vivacious primary communities with the imperatives of an emerging cosmopolitanism is, perhaps, the most urgent issue of our time. The material advantages of global exchange and economic special- ization are enormous. Without such a system, existing human populations could scarcely survive, much less sustain existing standards of living. But how firm adhesion to primary communities can be reconciled with participation in global economic and political processes is yet to be discovered. Religious con- gregations of fellow believers emerged in antiquity in response to analogous needs; perhaps something similar may happen again. But contemporary com- munications expose the faithful to a continual bombardment by messages from outsiders and unbelievers. Moreover, if that could somehow be successfully counteracted, rival religious communities might then clash, with results as di- sastrous as those arising from the twentieth century's clash of rival nations.

I suspect that human affairs are trembling on the verge of a far-reaching transformation, analogous to what happened when agriculture emerged out of broad-spectrum gathering, and village communities became the principal framework within which human lives were led. What sort of communities may prove successful in accommodating their members to global communications, worldwide exchanges, and all the other conditions of contemporary (and future) human life remains to be seen. Catastrophe of unprecedented proportions is al- ways possible. We are all aware of potential ecological disasters, due to pollution of land, air, and water. Social breakdown due to deficient or misguided nurture is perhaps no less threatening.

But human ingenuity and inventiveness remain as lively as ever. I suppose that satisfying and sustainable inventions will indeed occur locally and then spread, as other inventions in times past, having proved themselves in practice, also spread through imitation and adaptation, thus adding to the sum of human skills and enlarging the scope of human life, age after age, through emergency after emergency and crisis after crisis, from the beginning of the human career on earth to our time. Risks may be greater than ever before, but possibilities are correspondingly vast.

We live, whether we like it or not, in a golden age when precedents for the future are being laid down. It seems apparent to me that by constructing a per- spicacious and accurate world history, historians can play a modest but useful part in facilitating a tolerable future for humanity as a whole and for all its differ- ent parts. The changing shape of world history has been the principal profes- sional concern of my life. I commend it as a worthy and fascinating pursuit, apt for our age, and practically useful inasmuch as a clear and vivid sense of the whole human past can help to soften future conflicts by making clear what we all share.

SELECTED BIBLIOGRAPHY

Bentley, Jerry H. *Old World Encounters: Cross-Cultural Contacts and Exchanges in Pre-Modern Times*. New York: Oxford University Press, 1993. The opening chapter sets forth the author's idea of "modes of social conversion" as a conceptual scheme for investigating cross-cultural interaction in Afro-Eurasia from Han-Roman times to the sixteenth century. This book works well in undergraduate courses on world history up to 1600.

Blaut, J. M. *The Colonizer's Model of the World: Geographical Diffusionism and Eurocentric History*. New York: Guildford Press, 1993. The author pays little attention to world history as an academic field and finds some of its leading practitioners theoretically deficient. Even so, he pounds several heavy nails into the coffin of Eurocentrism and its teleological and essentialist assumptions about the course of modern history.

Chaudhuri, K. N. *Asia before Europe: Economy and Civilisation of the Indian Ocean from the Rise of Islam to 1750*. Cambridge: Cambridge University Press, 1990. This sequel to the author's *Trade and Civilisation in the Indian Ocean* (1985) opens with a lengthy theoretical statement on the writing of comparative and interregional history. Inspired by Braudel's *Mediterranean and the Mediterranean World*, Chaudhuri employs mathematical set theory, perhaps not as lucidly as one might have hoped, to address the huge complexities of the Indian Ocean basin as a field of human interchange across space and time.

Crosby, Alfred W. Jr. *The Columbian Exchange: Biological and Cultural Consequences of 1492*. Westport, Conn: Greenwood Press, 1972. Effects on the human community of the migrations of plants, animals, and microorganisms that accompanied the great global linkup of the fifteenth and sixteenth centuries. An early and important stimulus to world history teaching, this book was (and still is) congenial to undergraduates. It taught them that "unconscious" forces, flowing through the biosphere, explained much about the modern world that philosophy, politics, and civilizations could not explain. The author's *Ecological Imperialism: The Biological Expansion of Europe, 900–1900* (1986) had a similar impact on the field.

Curtin, Philip D. *Cross-Cultural Trade in World History*. Cambridge: Cambridge University Press, 1984. A model of world history scholarship as inductive comparison. The book was one of the fruits of the author's teaching in the Comparative Tropical History program at the University of Wisconsin.

Jones, E. L. *The European Miracle: Environments, Economies, and Geopolitics in the History of Europe and Asia.* Cambridge: Cambridge University Press, 1981. An important work because it set the momentous developments of the sixteenth century in a comparative world-historical frame. Like Michael Mann, Jones came under fire for attempting to explain economic change in terms of special conditions or seminal attributes found in Europe. However, in a subsequent book, *Growth Recurring: Economic Change in World History* (1988), Jones substantially modified his own views, arguing that societies around the world, not just Europe, tended to economic growth if not otherwise thwarted.

Mann, Michael. *The Sources of Social Power.* 2 vols. Cambridge: Cambridge University Press, 1986, 1993. A historical sociologist's interpretation of how, over the long span of history, social power became concentrated in Europe. This monumental work, though not terribly well known among world history teachers, has been one of the larger stones on which scholars such as James Blaut and Andre Gunder Frank have sharpened their anti-Eurocentrist axes.

McNeill, William H. *Plagues and Peoples.* Garden City, N.Y.: Doubleday, 1976. A global history of infectious diseases and their impact on humanity. This book, together with Crosby's *The Columbian Exchange* published a few years earlier, confirmed that the intimacy between human groups and microparasites was an important historical subject that only a world-scale approach could encompass.

——. *The Pursuit of Power: Technology, Armed Force, and Society since* A.D. *1000.* University of Chicago Press, 1982. Turning from microparasites to macroparasites, McNeill explores how and why particular groups have succeeded in attaining control over and pumping revenue from large populations of ordinary folk. He also offers a diffusionist explanation of why such power centers shifted from region to region over time. This book was seminal for world history in two major respects: 1) it threw into relief the global scope of technological change and no doubt inspired many of the books on the subject that followed; 2) it built on the earlier work of Mark Elvin (*The Patterns of the Chinese Past,* 1973) and Joseph Needham (*Science and Civilization in China,* 1954–), which revealed the centrality of China to any explanation of trans-hemispheric commercial and technological developments between 1000 and 1500 C.E.

——. *The Rise of the West: A History of the Human Community.* Chicago: University of Chicago Press, 1963. The book that, more than any other, made world history respectable and put the new subdiscipline in motion. A diffusionist view of the human past but also one against which all subsequent conceptualizations have been obliged to measure themselves.

——. "*The Rise of the West* after Twenty-five Years." *Journal of World History* 1 (Spring 1990): 1–21. McNeill's fascinating self-critical reappraisal of the historical premises that governed the writing of his monumental history. He acknowledges that world system analysis and the new environmentalism have been especially important influences on his later scholarly career.

Stavrianos, L. S. *Global Rift: The Third World Comes of Age.* New York: William Morrow, 1981. The author calls his book "an integrated Third World history," and it was indeed the first book of its kind to survey the past five hundred years. If undergraduates were not likely to digest all of its 890 pages, teachers found it a treasury of ideas as they labored to transcend the nation-based orientation of most earlier scholarship on economic and social relationships between the industrialized and developing regions. This book, together with Daniel Chirot's *Social Change in the Twentieth Century* (1977) and *Social Change in the Modern World* (1986) have probably had the most influence on world history teachers who have tried to think through modern social transformation as a global issue.

Wallerstein, Immanuel. *The Modern World-System.* Vol. 1, *Capitalist Agriculture and the Origins of the European World-Economy in the Sixteenth Century.* New York: Academic Books, 1974. The book that launched the great "world systems" debate, which over the past quarter century has obliged teachers to come seriously to grips with global economic history, conventional assumptions of Europe's centrality, and the historical agency peoples of Africa, Asia, and the Americas. Volumes 2 and 3 of *The Modern World-System* have had much less impact on the world history field, partly because of the avalanche of critical responses to volume 1 and partly because world systems history has gone off in several interesting directions (see Part Five).

PART FOUR

INTERREGIONAL AND SUPERREGIONAL HISTORY

The new world history of the past quarter century is by definition a subject that addresses macro-level problems. This does not mean that most world historians are totalizers. Relatively few have aimed to encompass the entire human scene or to discover a new global "mainstream" of development to replace the Eurocentric one. The rising interest in environmental history is likely to encourage imaginative research on very large-scale, species-centered themes. For the most part, however, world historians have targeted tractable, middle-scale problems that demand fresh configurations of time and space. "The imperative of discussing distant parts of the world within the same temporal framework," write Martin Lewis and Kären Wigen, "has forced scholars in this field to pay explicit attention to issues of geographical scale and to the relationships between places over time. . . . Attempts to write about global processes have pushed historians into a long search for appropriate regional categories."[1]

When scholars adopt geographical categories that transcend or cut across the conventional ones of state, culture, continent, and civilization, they position themselves to explain the implications of events more comprehensively, pull together fragments of data that reveal new patterns, and open fresh lines of comparative study. They construct *superregions* appropriate to the scale of the problem at hand, and they undertake *interregional* modes of analysis that favor what Steven Feierman calls "a flexible and situationally specific understanding of historical space."[2] A few of the scholars whose works have attained the status of "classics" as distinctive models of interregional history include Fernand Braudel on the Mediterranean world, Alfred Crosby on the "Columbian exchange," Philip Curtin on the Atlantic-centered "plantation complex," William McNeill on Old World disease pandemics, K. N. Chaudhuri on the economic history of the Indian Ocean, and Jerry Bentley on processes of cultural conversion across Afro-Eurasia. Several studies that variously employ "world system" analysis also qualify as good examples of interregional history. This approach is the topic of Part Five.

Some of the works mentioned above exemplify an interregional category that we might call "basin history." Beginning with Braudel's famous book on the Mediterranean, investigations of long-distance patterns of trade, capital flow, and labor migration have revealed the extent to which change has occurred in local communities because of their situation on coasts, estuaries, or islands of an ocean or sea. Study of economic transformations, slave migration, micro-organic exchange, and cultural conversion whose focal point is the middle of the Atlantic Ocean has become a mature subfield within the historical discipline. Indian Ocean interregional history is developing rapidly, and Pacific rim studies, though still suffering from definitional inconsistencies, have been a hot topic of the 1990s. The Sahara, the world's greatest "desert sea," is also an intriguing category for exploring patterns of trade, conquest, and Islamization that have involved people on both sides of that wilderness in shared experience. The Sahara basin, however, has yet to find its Braudel.[3]

The first essay in this section invites a further look at Marshall Hodgson, who drew on the ideas of both A. L. Kroeber and Arnold Toynbee to work out the earliest detailed conception of Afro-Eurasia as a place in the world with a history of its own. Edmund Burke, a long-time student of Hodgson's methodology, describes the moral and intellectual convictions that informed the scholar's work. Burke also makes clear why world history teachers should give Hodgson's formulations a long second look.

For Hodgson and McNeill, world history's center of gravity up to 1500 is the Afro-Eurasian land mass. For Lynda Shaffer it is a band of land and sea extending across the equatorial and subequatorial climes of the Eastern Hemisphere. Writing on subjects as diverse as ancient China, Byzantium, and Mississippian North America, Shaffer is a leading expositor of the new world history. In "Southernization" she argues that the region encompassing South and Southeast Asia, plus associated bays and seas, emerged by the fifth century C.E. as the world's most important center of agrarian, technological, and scientific innovation. Major advances in this region in mathematics, maritime technology, commercial crop production, and long-distance trade gradually affected and transformed neighboring regions, first China and Southwest Asia, later the Mediterranean basin and northwestern Europe. Shaffer posits "southernization" between the fifth and eighteenth centuries as a very large-scale, very long-term process that can fairly be compared to the "westernization" of the modern era. She is not interested in inventing a "South" that displays core characteristics mirroring the essential, anthropomorphized qualities some scholars have ascribed to the West. Rather, she focuses entirely on southernization as a fluid, dynamic process in which developments concentrated at first in the superregion of South-Southeast Asia eventually drew in a much larger part of the hemisphere and finally the whole world.

John Voll, in an essay published here for the first time, reflects on Shaffer's interregional model, pointing out some possible dangers of pushing the analogy between "southernization" and "westernization" too far. On the other hand, he find's Shaffer's approach, which postulates a permeable, ever-restructuring world, more convincing than Samuel Huntington's recent thesis, which envisions a world, past and future, of competing civilizational blocks.[4]

David Christian's article shifts us northward again to the superregion he labels Inner Eurasia. Mesmerized for a long time by the cultural weight and achievements of the agrarian Great Traditions, historians tended to dismiss the vast Eurasian prairie rather as Gertrude Stein did Oakland, California: "There's no *there* there." College history curricula and textbooks have usually represented Inner Eurasia has nothing more than a place on the way to somewhere else. Christian contends that even though the history of Inner Eurasia was closely intertwined with that of the far more densely populated Outer Eurasia to the east, west, and south, the region possessed not only geographical and ecological unity but also distinguishing patterns of political and economic history. Christian published his article in 1994, just when the emergence of five new states stretching across the Eurasian steppe, some of them possessing oil and nuclear weapons, obliged the world to think again about the historical significance of this part of the world.

An interregional approach to the past may sometimes reveal patterns of great significance that scholars never previously saw at all. This has certainly been the case in the study of slavery and the Atlantic slave trade. Philip Curtin has noted (see Part Two) that the Atlantic basin as a superregion "has been badly treated by historians until recent decades, mainly because it has been partitioned among specialists in European, North American, Latin American, and African history. None of these groups paid much attention to the work of the others." Among the historians who have helped correct this myopia is Patrick Manning. Here he examines the African, American, and global dimensions of the Atlantic slave trade, presenting his case for interregionality in a way readily transferable to the classroom. He proposes, for example, that the movements of both Africans and Europeans to the Americas were world-scale migrations worthy of comparative analysis. Such a study project will make sense, however, only if the Atlantic basin, not a country or continent, is established in the minds of students as a primary conceptual category.

Notes

1. Martin W. Lewis and Kären Wigen, *The Myth of Continents: A Critique of Metageography* (Los Angeles: University of California Press, 1997), 125.

2. Steven Feierman, "African Histories and the Dissolution of World History," *Africa and the Disciplines: The Contributions of Research in Africa to the Social Sciences and Humanities*, edited by Robert H. Bates, V. Y. Mudimbe, and Jean O'Barr (Chicago: University of Chicago Press, 1993), 172.

3. E. W. Bovill came close to suggesting an interregional history of the Sahara back in 1958. His classic study has recently been reprinted: *The Golden Trade of the Moors: West African Kingdoms in the Fourteenth Century* (Princeton, N.J.: Marcus Weiner, 1995).

4. Samuel P. Huntington, *The Clash of Civilizations and the Remaking of World Order* (New York: Simon and Schuster, 1997).

EDMUND BURKE III

Marshall G. S. Hodgson and the Hemispheric Interregional Approach to World History

Writing in the first issue of this journal, Gilbert Allardyce surveyed what he called the "Chicago school of world history": William H. McNeill, Louis Gottschalk, and Leften S. Stavrianos.[1] Missing from his list was a fourth Chicago-based world historian, Marshall G. S. Hodgson, whose biography is intertwined with theirs, even as his ambitious efforts to devise a methodologically self-conscious and epistemologically grounded world history distinguishes his approach from theirs.

Marshall Hodgson's influential articles on world history are widely scattered, and the world history manuscript he left upon his death in 1969 is unpublished, so it is perhaps understandable that he should have been neglected. Otherwise, Hodgson is primarily known as the author of a three-volume history of Islamic civilization, *The Venture of Islam*.[2] Because of the significance of Hodgson's efforts to devise a hemispheric interregional world history and his personal relations with McNeill and Gottschalk, both of whom were University of Chicago colleagues, one might have expected Allardyce to discuss his work as well. (Hodgson's relations with Stavrianos, who taught at Northwestern University, remain unknown.) With the posthumous publication of his *Rethinking World History*, one can see his importance more clearly.[3] As the editor of this work, in the present article I seek to place Hodgson in the Chicago context and to introduce his ideas on world history to a larger audience.

Hodgson's originality and methodological self-consciousness, unusual in the 1950s and 1960s when he was writing, as well as the ways in which his thought anticipates recent efforts to reconceptualize the place of Europe in world history, are compelling reasons to heed his voice. His perspective, though flawed in certain respects, nonetheless provides a basis for evaluating the recent debates over "Europocentrism" (as he called it) and multiculturalism. His hemispheric interregional approach to world history breaks decisively with previous Europe-centered approaches to world history. His view of modernity as a world historic process is equally innovative. While the breakout to modernity might have occurred in many other regions, he argues, it was centered, for particular

Edmund Burke III, "Marshall G. S. Hodgson and the Hemispheric Interregional Approach to World History," *Journal of World History* 6 (Fall 1995): 237–50.

reasons, in northwestern Europe. Finally, Hodgson's humanistic conscience and commitment to the moral discipline of world history (unfashionable in his age as in our own) provides a powerful argument for the field against epistemological nihilists and moral agnostics.

MARSHALL HODGSON: AN INTELLECTUAL AND HIS TIMES

Allardyce's important essay argues that the American roots of world history are to be sought in the affinity between world history and certain internationalist and pacifist strands of early twentieth-century American culture. Gottschalk, McNeill, and Stavrianos came to world history from a sense of the folly of war and the need for international understanding as a remedy to chauvinistic national histories. World history was seen by those who shared this viewpoint as a school for global citizenship. Allardyce's intuition appears validated in Hodgson's case, as well.

Like his three Chicago colleagues, Hodgson was a committed internationalist who saw in world history a means of combating ignorance, prejudice, and ethnocentrism. In Hodgson's case, his convictions derived from his membership in the Society of Friends. Indeed, Hodgson's first publication bears the dateline Camp Elkton, Oregon, where he was interned along with other conscientious objectors (most of them Quaker) during World War II.[4] As a young man, Hodgson was influenced by Wendell Wilkie's "world federalism" and was an ardent early supporter of the United Nations. Several of his earliest articles were published in journals sponsored by UNESCO, when presumably they could have found other, more scholarly outlets. The epigraph to Hodgson's *Venture of Islam* is drawn from the eighteenth-century American Quaker, John Woolman, a pacifist and antislavery activist: "To consider mankind otherwise than brethren, to think favours are peculiar to one nation and exclude others, plainly supposes a darkness in the understanding."[5] For Hodgson, it was axiomatic that "the individual sensibility, focused in a point of conscience, is one of the ultimate roots of history." I have argued at length elsewhere that Hodgson's Quakerism is a leitmotif that can be traced throughout *The Venture* — and indeed through most of the rest of his published work.[6]

Following the war, Hodgson was appointed to the University of Chicago, where as a young instructor he served for a time as an assistant to Gottschalk in the early phases of the UNESCO world history project. (He later became disenchanted with the project and quit, alleging that it lacked a coherent historical vision and a willingness to uphold intelligible standards of inquiry.) Later, disabused by the ways in which the United Nations was enlisted in the Cold War, his youthful expectations for that organization dropped by the wayside. An interesting footnote to his early career is that Hodgson briefly shared an apartment with Andre Gunder Frank in 1953 and 1954 while he was working on his germinal article, "The Interrelations of Societies in History." Frank is best known for his work on economic dependency and world-systems analysis.[7]

Hodgson's approach to world history is as much the product of a particular time and place as of a particular man. Hodgson had deep intellectual roots at the University of Chicago, where he had been an undergraduate and graduate student in the 1940s during the latter phase of Robert Maynard Hutchins's remarkable experiment, and where in the 1950s and 1960s he served as a faculty member.[8] In this period, the undergraduate program at Chicago was organized around the study of world civilizations through their "great books." Originally, the program had been limited to the study of Western civilization, but it was broadened in the postwar era to include surveys of the civilizations of India, China, and Islam under the intellectual leadership of the younger Robert Redfield and Milton Singer. The course on Islamic civilization was developed by Hodgson, then a young assistant professor. It was to remedy the absence of a suitable textbook for this course that he wrote *The Venture of Islam*. Successive generations of Chicago undergraduates read mimeographed manuscripts of *The Venture*, along with a class reader of Islamic writings in English translation.

It was Hodgson's work as a world historian, however, and not his orientalist writings, that earned him a faculty appointment at Chicago. Even though Hodgson is today primarily known as an Islamicist, he was a member of the Committee on Social Thought (where he had done his Ph.D. work) rather than the Oriental Institute (then as now primarily concerned with classical archaeology and prehistory). In the 1950s and 1960s, the Committee on Social Thought was a unique interdisciplinary graduate program of broad and eclectic scope, and not yet the fossilized repository of Eurocentrism it became in the 1980s. At the time of his death, Hodgson was chairman of the committee.

In the company of John U. Nef, Mircea Eliade, and Edward Shils, Hodgson sought to rethink the philosophical and historical traditions of Western civilization. With his vast erudition and enormous self-confidence, Hodgson was a formidable figure. Other Chicago colleagues included Gustave von Grunebaum, Muhsin Mahdi, Robert McC. Adams, Wilfred Madelung, Clifford Geertz, Lloyd Fallers, and Reuben Smith (who saw the manuscript of *The Venture of Islam* through to publication after Hodgson's untimely death). Simply to list the names reminds one of how remarkable an intellectual environment Chicago was in those days.

Although Hodgson's world federalism faded with the years, his moral commitments did not. His pacifism and prickly vegetarianism were renowned among his peers. (One catches echoes of them in Saul Bellow's *To Jerusalem and Back*.)[9] Hodgson was involved in the effort of liberal faculty to bridge the chasms of misunderstanding between the university and the black community of Hyde Park in the late 1950s and 1960s, especially with the Nation of Islam. Finally, Hodgson was one of the first faculty members at Chicago to publicly oppose the Vietnam war in a period before opposition became widespread. Other important aspects of his personality remarked by those who knew him were his Quaker insistence on the recognition of the common humanity of all people, and his natural curiosity about how others lived.

From the foregoing sketch, several things stand out. One is that Hodgson was a pure product of the University of Chicago. From his undergraduate years before World War II until his death in 1968 at the age of forty-six, he lived within its institutional confines, shaped by its intellectual traditions and human concerns, yet always also in rebellion against them. His critique of the Eurocentric assumptions of Hutchins's "great books" approach to civilizational studies was grounded in a thorough understanding of its strengths and weaknesses. Similarly, his critique of 1950s modernization theory was based in his daily interactions with the members of the Committee for the Comparative Study of New Nations, a Chicago interdisciplinary faculty seminar that included scholars such as David Apter, Leonard Binder, Bernard S. Cohn, Morris Janowitz, McKim Marriot, Suzanne and Lloyd Rudolph, Milton Singer, and Aristide Zolberg, as well as Edward Shils, Clifford Geertz, and Lloyd Fallers, among others.

Rethinking World History

Hodgson's conceptual approach to world history derives from an essay written when he was a nineteen-year-old undergraduate at Chicago. For the next twenty-five years he continually reworked this early piece, which went through several different forms, always changing, always deepening.[10] Over those years his thoughts on reconceptualizing world history and the place of Europe in it were published in several seminal articles, as well as in *The Venture of Islam.* Versions of these essays as well as chapters 11–13 of Hodgson's unpublished manuscript entitled "Unity of World History" are now available in *Rethinking World History.*

For purposes of this essay, one can usefully group Hodgson's contributions to world history under three main headings: his methodologically self-conscious attempt to examine the epistemological presuppositions of the writing of world history; his effort to resituate European history in the hemispheric interregional context of what he called Afro-Eurasia; and his vision of world history as the center of a reinvigorated historical discipline.

For Hodgson, the difficulty with most world histories was that they either consciously conceived of their mission as inscribing a Hegelian teleological narrative — the story of history as a tale of progress, with the West in the starring role — or they presented an insufficiently examined Eurocentric history as if it were world history. Anticipating in many ways the current concern with the politics of location, he believed that it was epistemologically necessary to recognize that all works are the products of their authors' (often unacknowledged) "scholarly precommitments," or fundamental orientations. For Hodgson, precommitments included not only religious affiliations but also Marxism and (more surprisingly) what he called *Westernism.* Westernists were "those whose highest allegiance is to what they call Western culture, as the unique or at least the most adequate embodiment of transcendent ideals of liberty and truth" (*RWH,* p. 78).[11] While Hodgson does not mention gender, ethnic identity, or class position in his list of precommitments, he would surely recognize their shaping influence on scholarly production as well.

The idea of precommitments was Hodgson's way of recognizing that the writing of history always necessarily brings the concerns of the present to the task of finding meaningful patterns in the past. At the same time, he believed that a historian by systematic and self-conscious effort could to a degree transcend the limitations of any personal and time-laden perspective. More clearly than many more recent authors, Hodgson did not presume to be speaking from some epistemologically sanitized space, in which one is liberated from having one or more precommitments. Rather, he assumed that we all have precommitments that both enable and constrain our understanding in various ways. Although there is no likelihood that we will ever escape the constraints of this situation, this does not mean that no human knowledge is possible.

A second fundamentally shaping scholarly orientation of which Hodgson was aware was the textualist approach to world civilizations. Here perhaps we may see a critique of the University of Chicago undergraduate core program of civilizational studies of which he was a product and in which he taught. The idea that civilizations have essences that can best be observed in their "great books" was anathema to Hodgson. For him, *civilization* as an organizing principle was constantly undercut by the fact that societies were never closed wholes and that they always contained fields of activity that were only superficially molded by the central tradition in question. "Different sorts of lettered tradition mingled in different degrees in different societies," he argued (*RWH*, p. 14), and multilingualism and multiculturalism were always present to some degree. In *The Venture of Islam* he turned this into a notable critique of what he argued was the Arabistic bias of Islamic history. Arabistic bias viewed anything written in Arabic as a product of "Arab culture," even though the lands of Islam were culturally cosmopolitan, most members of the elite were familiar with more than one language, and many ethnically non-Arab authors wrote in Arabic (*RWH*, pp. 81–85).

THE HEMISPHERIC INTERREGIONAL APPROACH TO WORLD HISTORY

Hodgson's hemispheric interregional approach to world history (as he called it) is most clearly spelled out in his 1963 article "The Interrelations of Societies in History."[12] In it, he made several important conceptual points aimed at establishing world history on a more reliable footing, against the shallowness and Eurocentrism of earlier, less methodologically self-conscious approaches.

What fascinated Hodgson was the possibility of telling the tale of humanity from the perspective of global history and not in a skewed, Western, self-justificatory version. A more adequate world history, he argued, would have to begin with the proposition that rather than privileging a particular regional civilization, the history of human literate society should take interregional developments on a hemisphere-wide basis as its focus.

Hodgson's comparative interregional approach contrasts sharply with the model proposed in McNeill's *Rise of the West,* currently dominant in the field.[13]

McNeill had seen as his task the development of an approach at once simpler and less idiosyncratic than that of Arnold Toynbee, the reigning figure in the field in the 1930s and 1940s. To this end, McNeill reduced the number of civilizations from Toynbee's nineteen to four: Europe and the Mediterranean, the Middle East, India, and China. He also retained Toynbee's idea that the civilizations of Afro-Eurasia were part of a broad intercommunicating zone, which he referred to as the *ecumene* (in place of the Greek *oikoumene* favored by Toynbee). From American cultural anthropologists Redfield and Alfred Kroeber, McNeill borrowed the concept of cultural diffusion. Where in Toynbee's approach the evolution of each civilization was largely autonomous, the working out of an encoded essence, McNeill insisted that the motor of world history was the cultural interaction of civilizations with one another. In this way, McNeill appeared to have solved the problem of connecting the separate histories of individual civilizations into a single narrative. He also appeared to have eluded the problem of essentialism that had long plagued world history and civilizational studies generally.[14]

For Hodgson, McNeill's world history was flawed in its basic conception.[15] Far from being a breakthrough, Hodgson asserted, McNeill's reliance upon cultural diffusionism was philosophically naive, because it made unacknowledged moral judgments about the relative importance of civilizations based upon their supposed contributions to the emergence of modern Europe. Moreover, since diffusionist approaches were readily assimilable by *Westernist* ones, Hodgson argued, in spite of McNeill's stated efforts to the contrary, his world history was permeated by a persistent Western exceptionalism. Long before J. M. Blaut, Hodgson had a developed critique of the diffusionism that underlay most attempts at developing a world history. He was also deeply aware of the ways in which the Mercator projection map presented a geographical encoding of a colonizer's map of the world.[16]

By contrast, Hodgson's interregional approach sought to situate developments in particular civilizations against the background of the disposition of the entire ecumene, the better to grasp their true significance. Hodgson's emphasis upon the interconnections between civilizations and upon the cumulative development of the common stock of human techniques and cultural resources across the whole of Afro-Eurasia is one of his most important ideas. He argued that the history of the interconnecting band of agrarian, cited societies from China to Western Europe is necessarily an Asia-centered history and that world history must focus upon interdependent, interregional developments on a hemisphere-wide basis:

> Historical life, from early times at least till two or three centuries ago, was continuous across the Afro-Eurasian zone of civilization; that zone was ultimately indivisible. The various regions had their own traditions; important social bodies arose, sometimes within a regional framework, sometimes cutting across regional life, which molded much of the cultural life of their constituents. But all these lesser historical wholes were imperfect wholes. They were secondary groupings. Local civilized life could go on without full participation in any of

them; some of the most creative of historical activities, such as that of natural science, cut across their boundaries. The whole of the Afro-Eurasian zone is the only context large enough to provide a framework for answering the more general and more basic historical questions that can arise. (*RWH*, p. 17)

The constant cumulative transformation of interregional conditions led to the broadening of the range of human activity from the beginning of human history. Thus, for example, the emergence of new agricultural techniques transformed the internal balance of population and economic power within given regions and cumulatively within the interregional configuration itself. But "the Afro-Eurasian historical complex was not merely a framework for mutual borrowings and influences among organizationally independent civilizations; it was a positive factor with its own proper development" (*RWH*, p. 26). With the expansion of the size of the interconnected zone and the multiplication of the historical components in Afro-Eurasia, particular developments in any given civilization (such as Arabic numerals, paper, the compass, gunpowder weapons) were soon paralleled in other societies throughout the ecumene, cumulatively affecting future possibilities everywhere.

Hodgson believed that one could not understand developments in any given civilization without considering their relationship to the interregional context as a whole. A few examples may make the stakes clear. The emergence of Greek science has one meaning seen in the context of the origins of a putative "Western" tradition, but quite another when situated against the achievements of the civilizations of the eastern Mediterranean with which it was intertwined in a complex way, as Walter Burkert has recently argued.[17] Similarly, the sixteenth-century Portuguese voyages of discovery in the Indian Ocean as seen by historians of Westernist inclination appear (tendentiously) as the beginning of a period of modern European advance, when they are more properly viewed as "one more venture within an essentially agrarianate historical complex, which was rather readily contained in the course of the 16th century by the other peoples in the Indian Ocean" (*RWH*, p. 93).

Hodgson was quick to point up the fundamental fault of such attitudes: while apparently cosmopolitan, they assume that "the modern West is the only significant end point of progress; that developments leading to present conditions in other lands have no meaning" (*RWH*, p. 290). Instead, he argued, "we must force ourselves to realize what it means to say that the West is not the modern world, gradually assimilating backward areas to itself; but is rather the catalyst, creating new conditions for other forces to work under (though in this case, to be sure, the West itself is also thoroughly transformed)" (*RWH*, p. 290).

A major purpose of Hodgson's interregional approach was to resituate modernity and to unhook it from Western exceptionalism. Seen in this light the European Renaissance, far from signaling the onset of modernity, marks instead the attainment by Western Europe of the cultural level of the other major civilizations of Afro-Eurasia in the period. Hodgson's rejection of Max Weber's tradition/modernity dichotomy and his insistence that all periods be accorded equal weight by historians made it possible to rehistoricize the premodern pe-

riod as something more than an antechamber to the rise of the West and to restore its integrity as a period interesting in its own right. (At one point he aptly
queried historians' use of the term *tradition*, defined as cultural stasis, and
pointed out that "traditional" societies are always changing and that the maintenance of institutional forms and values requires quite as much purposive energy
as changing them.) Progress-oriented histories (involving the rise of the West or
similar teleologies) ultimately draw connections where none exist. The line that
allegedly connects the ancient Greeks to the Renaissance to modern times, he
pointed out, is a moral judgment, not a historical one. By resituating European
history and modernity in a hemispheric interregional context, Hodgson permitted us to see that what is striking about European history are its profound discontinuities, not its continuity.

The Discipline of World History

Hodgson's hemispheric interregional approach to world history is part of his
overall vision of the potential role of world history. For him, world history was
the necessary disciplining frame for all history, with its own appropriate concepts and methodology. In the final section of his unpublished "Unity of World
History," reproduced in *Rethinking World History*, Hodgson sought to delineate
the types of historical thinking specific to world history, and he insisted that
"world history, interpreted as interregional history, must form the core of the intellectual organization of the historical profession" (*RWH*, p. 247).

Hodgson's sense of history as a discipline was grounded, in part, in a 1950s
sense of the division between the social sciences and history. Thus he saw the
role of history as exceptionalizing and that of the social sciences as typicalizing.
Other nontypicalizing disciplines included philosophy and art. (In the wake of
the new social history and the linguistic turn, such a division of the human sciences seems no longer tenable.) What is the domain of history? he asked. In
what ways are historical questions about the exceptional interdependent? How
do they form a field? History is a field, he argued, not because history possesses a
distinctive method but because the questions historians ask are substantively interrelated (*RWH*, pp. 252–53).

Not only is history a field, Hodgson maintained, it is a public discipline
whose basis is the asking of large-scale questions that make comparisons based
upon the many-faceted character of historical contexts. Since the question asked
often determines the answer, he continued, we need to know that the questions
asked are legitimate. Similarly, the categories one uses determine the questions
asked. Thus, he reasoned, world history requires agreement on the concepts and
terminology used before its claim to be a discipline can be recognized.

The point of Hodgson's argument is that the concepts and questions that historians use must be subjected to careful scrutiny; otherwise, they can unwittingly
smuggle in important biases. In particular, questions about origins or the filiation
of ideas or techniques are vulnerable to inadvertent biases. This is why Hodgson
included a lengthy section on methodology in Islamic studies as part of the

introduction to *The Venture of Islam* (included as chapter 6 in *Rethinking World History*). It is crucial, he argued, that we develop a methodology for determining what are significant questions — what is and what is not a problem. "The choice of terms determines what categories one uses; the categories determine the form and limits of the questions posed; and the questions posed determine the answers that can be expected. But since the comparison must be over the whole field, categorization must form a complete system: perceiving the relations and discontinuities over all mankind in time and space" (*RWH*, pp. 268–69).

In an effort to devise appropriate concepts for interregional study, Hodgson in typical fashion devised an elaborate matrix of units of analysis, including "interregional motifs," "historical complexes," new periodization schemes, and the like. His interregional motifs included large-scale events, such as the Indo-European migrations or the Black Death, and "paralleled developments" (he proposed the development of supragovernmental law as an example). As part of this same effort he also criticized the use of terms such as "the West" and "the East," which he saw as freighted with heavy and generally unacknowledged ideological baggage. His critique of the biases of the Mercator projection map, in chapter 1 of *Rethinking World History*, provides an example of how such unacknowledged racism can infiltrate even so neutral-seeming a thing as a map.

On what basis can one proceed to do world history? Hodgson made three suggestions:

> First, we must recognize the field, distinguishing it on the one hand from an extended Western history, which at present is commonly meant by the term "world history"; and on the other hand from a series of regional histories, however much value they may have in themselves. . . .
>
> Second, we must, negatively, free ourselves from various older ways of thinking of broader problems of history, which interfere with an interregional approach. We must recognize the limited role in history of our West, as one region among others, during much of its development distinctly peripheral; and even in modern times, as not the substance of the age, into which other lands are merging insofar as they are significant at all, but instead as the center of important events affecting both the West and other lands, and significant from an interregional point of view in their interregional rather than their local aspect. As a corollary of this placing of the West, we must leave behind the Westward pattern of history and the "East and West" dichotomy in studying the development of the Oikoumenic Configuration; and we must free our theorizing of the turns of thought which arise from assuming the Westward pattern.
>
> Third, positively, we must go on to developing means of organizing the various types of interregional history, particularly within literate times, finding the scope and value as organizing elements of various interregional motifs, and studying from a consciously interregional point of view various circumstances of significance. At the same time, we must look toward synthesizing hypotheses, making use of all the contributions already under way in the field, each for its particular aspect of the problem involved. (*RWH*, p. 292)

Although I am not convinced by some of the more abstract formulations proposed by Hodgson in his quest to develop a methodology for disciplining interregional comparisons — his motifs, for example, smack too much of Toynbee's categories — the attempt to devise a methodology is obviously of central importance to the development of world history as a field. The point of his motifs is that they overlap regional cultures and provide a necessary corrective to generalizations that arise from the consideration of a particular civilization's experiences (*RWH*, pp. 270–77). Hodgson's self-conscious attempt to develop a methodology appropriate to world history is the only one known to me.

At another level, interregional history as proposed by Hodgson is inadequate to the extent that it neglects the history of Africa, the Americas, and Oceania. This is indeed a major defect. Before sounding the trumpets of political correctness, however, it would be well to realize that Hodgson's world was one in which African independence was newly minted and African history as an academic discipline in its infancy. None of the other members of the Chicago school who were his contemporaries was notably more astute on this point. An Asia-centric interregional history is still a vast improvement methodologically over the "four civilizations" model, as indeed it is over all other approaches that do not put human interactions at their center. Certainly Hodgson was on the right track, for the interregional approach can be modified and extended to encompass Africa, the Americas, and Oceania.[18] If world history is to flourish as a field, then similar carefully reasoned parallel efforts to think through the difficult conceptual and methodological issues must be encouraged.

Elsewhere I have commented on the extent to which even Hodgson's approach is not exempt from a residual Westernist bias. This is apparent in his formulation of the "Great Western Transmutation" and the central role he gives to a putative Western *technicalism*. (These terms are, of course, fully defined: one expects nothing less from Hodgson.)[19] Given that most of Hodgson's writings on world history date from before 1965, it is remarkable that despite the heightening of historians' self-consciousness and the expansion of the field — the new social history, women's history, minority history, and environmental history all date from after his death — the basic insights of his interregional world history remain relevant. The challenge of devising a methodology for disciplining large-scale generalizations has yet to be addressed. Nourished by the Hodgsonian example, we need a methodologically self-conscious and conceptually rigorous discussion and debate about the basic concepts and frameworks appropriate to world history.

Notes

1. Gilbert Allardyce, "Toward World History: American Historians and the Coming of the World History Course," *Journal of World History* 1 (1990): 23–76.

2. Marshall G. S. Hodgson, *The Venture of Islam: Conscience and History in a World Civilization*, 3 vols. (Chicago: University of Chicago Press, 1974).

3. Marshall G. S. Hodgson, *Rethinking World History: Essays on Europe, Islam and World History*, edited by Edmund Burke III (Cambridge: Cambridge University Press, 1993).

4. "World History and a World Outlook," *The Social Studies* 35 (1944): 297–301.

5. John Woolman, *The Journal, and Other Writings* (New York and London: J. M. Dent and Sons, 1952).

6. Edmund Burke III, "Islamic History as World History: Marshall Hodgson and

The Venture of Islam," *International Journal of Middle Eastern Studies* 2 (1979): 241–64, reprinted in *Rethinking World History*, 301–28.

7. Personal communication, Andre Gunder Frank, 8 December 1989.

8. For a portrait of the University of Chicago in this period, see William H. Mc-Neill, *Hutchins' University: A Memoir of the University of Chicago, 1929–50* (Chicago: University of Chicago Press, 1991).

9. Saul Bellow, *To Jerusalem and Back: A Personal Account* (New York: Macmillan, 1976), 105–9.

10. The Hodgson papers at the Department of Special Collections of the Joseph Regenstein Library at the University of Chicago allow us to follow this evolution in detail. The essay "World History and a World Outlook," which dates from 1944, was the first published expression of Hodgson's distinctive approach to world history. In 1945, inspired by the title of an article by Margaret Cameron, he planned to call his world history "There Is No Orient." Its purpose was "to combat western provincialism." By October 1960 he was calling the book "The Structure of World History: An Essay on Medieval and Modern Eurasia." In 1962, the chapter outline resembled the table of contents of his eventual "Unity of World History" unpublished manuscript (the last three chapters of which are reprinted in *Rethinking World History*). By examining the gradual transformations of the project, we see the maturing of a young scholar into an established professional.

11. When cited parenthetically in the text, *RWH* refers to Hodgson's *Rethinking World History.*

12. Reprinted as chap. 1 of *Rethinking World History.* An earlier version appeared in the UNESCO journal of world history: "The Hemispheric Interregional Approach to World History," *Cahiers d'histoire mondiale* 1 (1954): 715–23.

13. William H. McNeill, *The Rise of the West: A History of the Human Community* (Chicago: University of Chicago Press, 1963).

14. McNeill discusses Toynbee's work and its relationship to his own in his *Mythistory and Other Essays* (Chicago: University of Chicago Press, 1986), chaps. 7 and 9. See also his intellectual biography of Toynbee: William H. McNeill, *Arnold J. Toynbee: A Life* (Oxford: Oxford University Press, 1989).

15. Hodgson was critical of many aspects of McNeill's approach, though for the most part he kept his thoughts to himself. His deep reservations come out in a letter he wrote to John Voll in 1961, reprinted in *Rethinking World History*, chap. 6.

16. J. M. Blaut, *The Colonizer's Model of the World: Geographical Diffusionism and Eurocentric History* (New York: Guilford, 1993).

17. Walter Burkert, *The Orientalizing Revolution: Near East Influence on Greek Culture in the Early Archaic Age* (Cambridge, Mass.: Harvard University Press, 1992).

18. Ross E. Dunn, "Central Themes for World History," in *Historical Literacy: The Case for History in American Education*, ed. Paul Gagnon (New York: Macmillan, 1989), 216–33.

19. See especially *Rethinking World History*, chap. 4. For my critique, see "Islam and World History: The Contribution of Marshall Hodgson," *World History Bulletin* (Fall 1988–89): 6–10.

LYNDA SHAFFER

Southernization

The term *southernization* is a new one. It is used here to refer to a multifaceted process that began in Southern Asia and spread from here to various other places around the globe. The process included so many interrelated strands of development that it is impossible to do more here than sketch out the general outlines of a few of them. Among the most important that will be omitted from this discussion are the metallurgical, the medical, and the literary. Those included are the development of mathematics; the production and marketing of subtropical or tropical spices; the pioneering of new trade routes; the cultivation, processing, and marketing of southern crops such as sugar and cotton; and the development of various related technologies.

The term *southernization* is meant to be analogous to *westernization*. Westernization refers to certain developments that first occurred in western Europe. Those developments changed Europe and eventually spread to other places and changed them as well. In the same way, southernization changed Southern Asia and later spread to other areas, which then underwent a process of change.

Southernization was well under way in Southern Asia by the fifth century C.E., during the reign of India's Gupta kings (320–535 C.E.). It was by that time already spreading to China. In the eighth century various elements characteristic of southernization began spreading through the lands of the Muslim caliphates. Both in China and in the lands of the caliphate, the process led to dramatic changes, and by the year 1200 it was beginning to have an impact on the Christian Mediterranean. One could argue that within the Northern Hemisphere, by this time the process of southernization had created an eastern hemisphere characterized by a rich south and a north that was poor in comparison. And one might even go so far as to suggest that in Europe and its colonies, the process of southernization laid the foundation for westernization.

THE INDIAN BEGINNING

Southernization was the result of developments that took place in many parts of southern Asia, both on the Indian subcontinent and in Southeast Asia. By the time of the Gupta kings, several of its constituent parts already had a long

Lynda Shaffer, "Southernization," *Journal of World History* 5 (Spring 1994): 1–21.

history in India. Perhaps the oldest strand in the process was the cultivation of cotton and the production of cotton textiles for export. Cotton was first domesticated in the Indus River valley some time between 2300 and 1760 B.C.E.,[1] and by the second millennium B.C.E., the Indians had begun to develop sophisticated dyeing techniques.[2] During these early millennia Indus River valley merchants are known to have lived in Mesopotamia, where they sold cotton textiles.[3]

In the first century C.E. Egypt became an important overseas market for Indian cottons. By the next century there was a strong demand for these textiles both in the Mediterranean and in East Africa,[4] and by the fifth century they were being traded in Southeast Asia.[5] The Indian textile trade continued to grow throughout the next millennium. Even after the arrival of European ships in Asian ports at the turn of the sixteenth century, it continued unscathed. According to one textile expert, "India virtually clothed the world" by the mid-eighteenth century.[6] The subcontinent's position was not undermined until Britain's Industrial Revolution, when steam engines began to power the production of cotton textiles.

Another strand in the process of southernization, the search for new sources of bullion, can be traced back in India to the end of the Mauryan Empire (321–185 B.C.E.). During Mauryan rule Siberia had been India's main source of gold, but nomadic disturbances in Central Asia disrupted the traffic between Siberia and India at about the time that the Mauryans fell. Indian sailors then began to travel to the Malay peninsula and the islands of Indonesia in search of an alternative source,[7] which they most likely "discovered" with the help of local peoples who knew the sites. (This is generally the case with bullion discoveries, including those made by Arabs and Europeans.) What the Indians (and others later on) did do was introduce this gold to international trade routes.

The Indians' search for gold may also have led them to the shores of Africa. Although its interpretation is controversial, some archaeological evidence suggests the existence of Indian influence on parts of East Africa as early as 300 C.E. There is also one report that gold was being sought in East Africa by Ethiopian merchants, who were among India's most important trading partners. The sixth-century Byzantine geographer Cosmas Indicopleustes described Ethiopian merchants who went to some location inland from the East African coast to obtain gold. "Every other year they would sail far to the south, then march inland, and in return for various made-up articles they would come back laden with ingots of gold."[8] The fact that the expeditions left every other year suggests that it took two years to get to their destination and return. If so, their destination, even at this early date, may have been Zimbabwe. The wind patterns are such that sailors who ride the monsoon south as far as Kilwa can catch the return monsoon to the Red Sea area within the same year. But if they go beyond Kilwa to the Zambezi River, from which they might go inland to Zimbabwe, they cannot return until the following year.

Indian voyages on the Indian Ocean were part of a more general development, more or less contemporary with the Mauryan empire, in which sailors of various nationalities began to knit together the shores of the "Southern Ocean," a Chinese term referring to all the waters from the South China Sea to the eastern coast of Africa. During this period there is no doubt that the most intrepid sailors were the Malays, peoples who lived in what is now Malaysia, Indonesia, the southeastern coast of Vietnam, and the Philippines.[9]

Sometime before 300 B.C.E. Malay sailors began to ride the monsoons, the seasonal winds that blow off the continent of Asia in the colder months and onto its shores in the warmer months. Chinese records indicate that by the third century B.C.E. "Kunlun" sailors, the Chinese term for the Malay seamen, were sailing north to the southern coasts of China. They may also have been sailing east to India, through the straits now called Malacca and Sunda. If so they may have been the first to establish contact between India and Southeast Asia.

Malay sailors had reached the eastern coast of Africa at least by the first century B.C.E., if not earlier. Their presence in East African waters is testified to by the peoples of Madagascar, who still speak a Malayo-Polynesian language. Some evidence also suggests that Malay sailors had settled in the Red Sea area. Indeed, it appears that they were the first to develop a long-distance trade in a southern spice. In the last centuries B.C.E., if not earlier, Malay sailors were delivering cinnamon from South China Sea ports to East Africa and the Red Sea.[10]

By about 400 C.E. Malay sailors could be found two-thirds of the way around the world, from Easter Island to East Africa. They rode the monsoons without a compass, out of sight of land, and often at latitudes below the equator where the northern pole star cannot be seen. They navigated by the wind and the stars, by cloud formations, the color of the water, and swell and wave patterns on the ocean's surface. They could discern the presence of an island some thirty miles from its shores by noting the behavior of birds, the animal and plant life in the water, and the swell and wave patterns. Given their manner of sailing, their most likely route to Africa and the Red Sea would have been by way of the island clusters, the Maldives, the Chagos, the Seychelles, and the Comoros.[11]

Malay ships used balance lug sails, which were square in shape and mounted so that they could pivot. This made it possible for sailors to tack against the wind, that is, to sail into the wind by going diagonally against it, first one way and then the other. Due to the way the sails were mounted, they appeared somewhat triangular in shape, and thus the Malays' balance lug sail may well be the prototype of the triangular lateen, which can also be used to tack against the wind. The latter was invented by both the Polynesians to the Malays' east and by the Arabs to their west,[12] both of whom had ample opportunity to see the Malays' ships in action.

It appears that the pepper trade developed after the cinnamon trade. In the first century C.E. southern India began supplying the Mediterranean with large quantities of pepper. Thereafter, Indian merchants could be found living on the island of Socotra, near the mouth of the Red Sea, and Greek-speaking sailors, including the anonymous author of the *Periplus of the Erythraean Sea*, could be found sailing in the Red Sea and riding the monsoons from there to India.

Indian traders and shippers and Malay sailors were also responsible for opening up an all-sea route to China. The traders' desire for silk drew them out into dangerous waters in search of a more direct way to its source. By the second century C.E. Indian merchants could make the trip by sea, but the route was slow, and it took at least two years to make a round trip. Merchants leaving from India's eastern coast rounded the shores of the Bay of Bengal. When they came to the Isthmus of Kra, the narrowest part of the Malay peninsula, the ships were unloaded, and the goods were portaged across to the Gulf of Thailand. The cargo was then reloaded on ships that rounded the gulf until they reached Funan, a kingdom on what is now the Kampuchea-Vietnam border. There they had to wait for the winds to shift, before embarking upon a ship that rode the monsoon to China.[13]

Some time before 400 C.E. travelers began to use a new all-sea route to China, a route that went around the Malay peninsula and thus avoided the Isthmus of Kra portage. The ships left from Sri Lanka and sailed before the monsoon, far from any coasts, through either the Strait of Malacca or the Strait of Sunda into the Java Sea. After waiting in the Java Sea port for the winds to shift, they rode the monsoon to southern China.[14] The most likely developers of this route were Malay sailors, since the new stopover ports were located within their territories.

Not until the latter part of the fourth century, at about the same time as the new all-sea route began to direct commercial traffic through the Java Sea, did the fine spices — cloves, nutmeg, and mace — begin to assume importance on international markets. These rare and expensive spices came from the Moluccas, several island groups about a thousand miles east of Java. Cloves were produced on about five minuscule islands off the western coast of Halmahera; nutmeg and mace came from only a few of the Banda Islands, some ten islands with a total area of seventeen square miles, located in the middle of the Banda Sea. Until 1621 these Moluccan islands were the only places in the world able to produce cloves, nutmeg, and mace in commercial quantities.[15] The Moluccan producers themselves brought their spices to the international markets of the Java Sea ports and created the market for them.[16]

It was also during the time of the Gupta kings, around 350 C.E., that the Indians discovered how to crystallize sugar.[17] There is considerable disagreement about where sugar was first domesticated. Some believe that the plant was native to New Guinea and domesticated there, and others argue that it was domesticated by Southeast Asian peoples living in what is now southern China.[18] In any case, sugar cultivation spread to the Indian subcontinent. Sugar, however, did not become an important item of trade until the Indians discovered how to turn sugarcane juice into granulated crystals that could be easily stored and transported. This was a momentous development, and it may have been encouraged by Indian sailing, for sugar and clarified butter (ghee) were among the dietary mainstays of Indian sailors.[19]

The Indians also laid the foundation for modern mathematics during the time of the Guptas. Western numerals, which the Europeans called Arabic since they acquired them from the Arabs, actually come from India. (The Arabs call them Hindi numbers.) The most significant feature of the Indian system was the invention of the zero as a number concept. The oldest extant treatise that uses the zero in the modern way is a mathematical appendix attached to Aryabhata's text on astronomy, which is dated 499 C.E.[20]

The Indian zero made the place-value system of writing numbers superior to all others. Without it, the use of this system, base ten or otherwise, was fraught with difficulties and did not seem any better than alternative systems. With the zero the Indians were able to perform calculations rapidly and accurately, to perform much more complicated calculations, and to discern mathematical relationships more aptly. These numerals and the mathematics that the Indians developed with them are now universal — just one indication of the global significance of southernization.

As a result of these developments India acquired a reputation as a place of marvels, a reputation that was maintained for many centuries after the Gupta dynasty fell. As late as the ninth century 'Amr ibn Bahr al Jahiz (ca. 776–868), one of the most influential writers of Arabic, had the following to say about India:

> As regards the Indians, they are among the leaders in astronomy, mathematics — in particular, they have Indian numerals — and medicine; they alone possess the secrets of the latter, and use them to practice some remarkable forms of treatment. They have the art of carving statues and painted figures. They possess the game of chess, which is the noblest of games and requires more judgment and intelligence than any other. They make Kedah swords, and excel in their use. They have splendid music. . . . They possess a script capable of expressing the sounds of all languages, as well as many numerals. They have a great deal of poetry, many long treatises, and a deep understanding of philosophy and letters; the book *Kalila wa-Dimna* originated with them. They are intelligent and courageous. . . . Their sound judgment and sensible habits led them to invent pins, cork, toothpicks, the drape of clothes and the dyeing of hair. They are handsome, attractive and forbearing, their women are proverbial, and their country produces the matchless Indian aloes which are supplied to kings. They were the originators of the science of *fikr*, by which a poison can be counteracted after it has been used, and of astronomical reckoning, subsequently adopted by the rest of the world. When Adam descended from Paradise, it was to their land that he made his way.[21]

THE SOUTHERNIZATION OF CHINA

These Southern Asian developments began to have a significant impact on China after 350 C.E. The Han dynasty had fallen in 221 C.E., and for more than 350 years thereafter China was ruled by an ever changing collection of regional kingdoms. During these centuries Buddhism became increasingly important in China, Buddhist monasteries spread throughout the disunited realm, and cultural exchange between India and China grew accordingly.[22] By 581, when the Sui dynasty reunited the empire, processes associated with southernization had already had a major impact on China. The influence of southernization continued during the Tang (618–906) and Song (960–1279) dynasties. One might even go so far as to suggest that the process of southernization underlay the revolutionary social, political, economic, and technological developments of the Tang and Song.

The Chinese reformed their mathematics, incorporating the advantages of the Indian system, even though they did not adopt the Indian numerals at that time.[23] They then went on to develop an advanced mathematics, which was flourishing by the time of the Song dynasty.[24] Cotton and indigo became well established, giving rise to the blue-black peasant garb that is still omnipresent in China. Also in the Song period the Chinese first developed cotton canvas, which they used to make a more efficient sail for ocean-going ships.[25]

Although sugar had long been grown in some parts of southern China it did not become an important crop in this region until the process of southernization was well under way. The process also introduced new varieties of rice. The most important of these was what the Chinese called Champa rice, since it came to China from Champa, a Malay kingdom located on what is now the southeastern coast of Vietnam. Champa rice was a drought-resistant, early ripening variety that made it possible to extend cultivation up well-watered hillsides, thereby doubling the area of rice cultivation in China.[26] The eleventh-century Buddhist monk Shu Wenying left an account explaining how the Champa rice had arrived in China:

> Emperor Cheng-tsung [Zhengzong (998–1022)], being deeply concerned with agriculture, came to know that the Champa rice was drought-resistant and that the green lentils of India were famous for their heavy yield and large seeds. Special envoys, bringing precious things, were dispatched [to these states], with a view to securing these varieties. . . . When the first harvests were reaped in the autumn, [the emperor] called his intimate ministers to taste them and composed poems for Champa rice and Indian green lentils.[27]

In southern China the further development of rice production brought significant changes in the landscape. Before the introduction of Champa rice, rice cultivation had been confined to lowlands, deltas, basins, and river valleys. Once Champa rice was introduced and rice cultivation spread up the hillsides, the Chinese began systematic terracing and made use of sophisticated techniques of water control on mountain slopes. Between the mid-eighth and the early twelfth century the population of southern China tripled, and the total Chinese population doubled. According to Song dynasty household registration figures for 1102 and 1110 — figures that Song dynasty specialists have shown to be reliable — there were 100 million people in China by the first decade of the twelfth century.[28]

Before the process of southernization, northern China had always been predominant, intellectually, socially, and politically. The imperial center of gravity was clearly in the north, and the southern part of China was perceived as a frontier area. But southernization changed this situation dramatically. By 600, southern China was well on its way to becoming the most prosperous and most commercial part of the empire.[29] The most telling evidence for this is the construction of the Grand Canal, which was completed around 610, during the Sui dynasty. Even though the rulers of the Sui had managed to put the pieces of the empire back together in 581 and rule the whole of China again from a single northern capital, they were dependent on the new southern crops. Thus it is no coincidence that this dynasty felt the need to build a canal that could deliver southern rice to northern cities.[30]

The Tang dynasty, when Buddhist influence in China was especially strong, saw two exceedingly important technological innovations — the invention of printing and gunpowder. These developments may also be linked to southernization. Printing seems to have developed within the walls of Buddhist monasteries between 700 and 750, and subtropical Sichuan was one of the earliest centers of the art.[31] The invention of gunpowder in China by Daoist alchemists in the ninth century may also be related to the linkages between India and China created by Buddhism. In 644 an Indian monk identified soils in China that contained saltpeter and demonstrated the purple flame that results from its ignition.[32] As early as 919 C.E. gunpowder was used as an igniter in a flame thrower, and the tenth century also saw the use of flaming arrows, rockets, and bombs thrown by catapults.[33] The earliest evidence of a cannon or bombard (1127) has been found in Sichuan, quite near the Tibetan border, across the Himalayas from India.[34]

By the time of the Song the Chinese also had perfected the "south-pointing needle," otherwise known as the compass. Various prototypes of the compass had existed in China from the third century B.C.E., but the new version developed during the Song was particularly well suited for navigation. Soon Chinese mariners were using the south-pointing needle on the oceans, publishing "needle charts" for the benefit of sea captains and following "needle routes" on the Southern Ocean.[35]

Once the Chinese had the compass they, like Columbus, set out to find a direct route to the spice markets of Java and ultimately to the Spice Islands in the Moluccas. Unlike Columbus, they found them. They did not bump into an obstacle, now known as the Western Hemisphere, on their way, since it was not located between China and the Spice Islands. If it had been so situated, the Chinese would have found it some 500 years before Columbus.

Cities on China's southern coasts became centers of overseas commerce. Silk remained an important export, and by the Tang dynasty it had been joined by a true porcelain which was developed in China sometime before 400 C.E. China and its East Asian neighbors had a monopoly on the manufacture of true porcelain until the early eighteenth century. Many attempts were made to imitate it, and some of the resulting imitations were economically and stylistically important. China's southern ports were also exporting to Southeast Asia large quantities of ordinary consumer goods, including iron hardware, such as needles, scissors, and cooking pots. Although iron manufacturing was concentrated in the north, the large quantity of goods produced was a direct result of the size of the market in southern China and overseas. Until the British Industrial Revolution of the eighteenth century, no other place ever equaled the iron production of Song China.[36]

THE MUSLIM CALIPHATES

In the seventh century C.E. Arab cavalries, recently converted to the new religion of Islam, conquered eastern and southern Mediterranean shores that had been Byzantine (and Christian), as well as the Sassanian empire (Zoroastrian) in what is now Iraq and Iran. In the eighth century they went on to conquer Spain and Turko-Iranian areas of Central Asia, as well as northwestern India. Once established on the Indian frontier, they became acquainted with many of the elements of southernization.

The Arabs were responsible for the spread of many important crops, developed or improved in India, to the Middle East, North Africa, and Islamic Spain. Among the most important were sugar, cotton, and citrus fruits.[37] Although sugarcane and cotton cultivation may have spread to Iraq and Ethiopia before the Arab conquests,[38] only after the establishment of the caliphates did these southern crops have a major impact throughout the Middle East and North Africa.

The Arabs were the first to import large numbers of enslaved Africans in order to produce sugar. Fields in the vicinity of Basra, at the northern end of the Persian Gulf, were the most important sugar-producing areas within the caliphates, but before this land could be used, it had to be desalinated. To accomplish this task, the Arabs imported East African (Zanj) slaves. This African community remained in the area, where they worked as agricultural laborers. The famous writer al Jahiz, whose essay on India was quoted earlier, was a descendant of Zanj slaves. In 869, one year after his death, the Zanj slaves in Iraq rebelled. It took the caliphate fifteen years of hard fighting to defeat them, and thereafter Muslim owners rarely used slaves for purposes that would require their concentration in large numbers.[39]

The Arabs were responsible for moving sugarcane cultivation and sugar manufacturing westward from southern Iraq into other relatively arid lands. Growers had to adapt the plant to new conditions, and they had to develop more efficient irrigation technologies. By 1000 or so sugarcane had become an important crop in the Yemen; in Arabian oases; in irrigated areas of Syria, Lebanon, Palestine, Egypt, and the Mahgrib; in Spain; and on Mediterranean islands controlled by Muslims. By the tenth century cotton also had become a major crop in the lands of the caliphate, from Iran and Central Asia to Spain and the Mediterranean islands. Cotton industries sprang up wherever the plant was cultivated, producing for both local and distant markets.[40]

The introduction of Indian crops, such as sugar and cotton, led to a much more intensive agriculture in the Middle East and some parts of the Mediterranean. Before the arrival of these crops, farmers had planted in the fall to take advantage of autumn rains and harvested in the spring. In the heat of the summer their fields usually lay fallow. But the new southern crops preferred the heat of the summer, and thus farmers began to use their fields throughout the year. They also began to use a system of multiple cropping, a practice that seems to have come from India. This led to an increased interest in soil fertility, and to manuals that advised farmers about adding such things as animal dung and vegetable and mineral materials to the soil to maintain its productivity.[41]

Under Arab auspices, Indian mathematics followed the same routes as the crops.[42] Al-Kharazmi (ca. 780–847) introduced Indian mathematics to the Arabic-reading world in his *Treatise on Calculation with the Hindu Numerals*, written around 825. Mathematicians within the caliphates then could draw upon the Indian tradition, as well as the Greek and Persian. On this foundation Muslim scientists of many nationalities, including al-Battani (d. 929), who came from the northern reaches of the Mesopotamian plain, and the Persian Umar Khayyam (d. 1123), made remarkable advances in both algebra and trigonometry.[43]

The Arab conquests also led to an increase in long-distance commerce and the "discovery" of new sources of bullion. Soon after the Abbasid caliphate established its capital at Baghdad, the caliph al-Mansur (r. 745–75) reportedly remarked, "This is the Tigris; there is no obstacle between us and China; everything on the sea can come to us."[44] By this time Arab ships were plying the maritime routes from the Persian Gulf to China, and they soon outnumbered all others using these routes. By the ninth century they had acquired the compass (in China, most likely), and they may well have been the first to use it for marine navigation, since the Chinese do not seem to have used it for this purpose until after the tenth century.

After their conquest of Central Asia the Arabs "discovered" a silver mine near Tashkent and a veritable mountain of silver in present-day Afghanistan, a find quite comparable to Potosi in South America. The Arabs mined and coined so much silver that by 850 its value, relative to gold, had fallen from 10:1 to 17:1.[45] By 940 the ratio had recovered to 12:1, in large part because the Arabs had access to larger quantities of gold. After the conquest of North Africa they had discovered that gold came across the Sahara, and they then became intent on going to Ghana, its source.

Thus it was that the Arabs "pioneered" or improved an existing long-distance route across the Sahara, an ocean of sand rather than water. Routes across this desert had always existed, and trade and other contacts between West Africa and the Mediterranean date back at least to the Phoenician period. Still, the numbers of people and animals crossing this great ocean of sand were limited until the eighth century when Arabs, desiring to go directly to the source of the gold, prompted an expansion of trade across the Sahara. Also during the eighth century Abdul al-Rahman, an Arab ruler of Morocco, sponsored the construction of wells on the trans-Saharan route from Sijilmasa to Wadidara to facilitate this traffic. This Arab "discovery" of West African gold eventually doubled the amount of gold in international circulation.[46] East Africa, too, became a source of gold for the Arabs. By the tenth century Kilwa had become an important source of Zimbabwean gold.[47]

DEVELOPMENTS AFTER 1200: THE MONGOLIAN CONQUEST AND THE SOUTHERNIZATION OF THE EUROPEAN MEDITERRANEAN

By 1200 the process of southernization had created a prosperous south from China to the Muslim Mediterranean. Although mathematics, the pioneering of new ocean routes, and "discoveries" of bullion are not inextricably connected to locations within forty degrees of the equator, several crucial elements in the process of southernization were closely linked to latitude. Cotton generally does not grow above the fortieth parallel. Sugar, cinnamon, and pepper are tropical or subtropical crops, and the fine spices will grow only on particular tropical islands. Thus for many centuries the more southern parts of Asia and the Muslim Mediterranean enjoyed the profits that these developments brought, while locations that were too far north to grow these southern crops were unable to participate in such lucrative agricultural enterprises.

The process of southernization reached its zenith after 1200, in large part because of the tumultuous events of the thirteenth century. During that century in both hemispheres there were major transformations in the distribution of power, wealth, and prestige. In the Western Hemisphere several great powers went down. Cahokia (near East St. Louis, Illinois), which for three centuries had been the largest and most influential of the Mississippian mound-building centers, declined after 1200, and in Mexico Toltec power collapsed. In the Mediterranean the prestige of the Byzantine empire was destroyed when Venetians seized its capital in 1204. From 1212 to 1270 the Christians conquered southern Spain, except for Granada. In West Africa, Ghana fell to Sosso, and so did Mali, one of Ghana's allies. But by about 1230 Mali, in the process of seeking its own revenge, had created an empire even larger than Ghana's. At the same time Zimbabwe was also becoming a major power in southern Africa.

The grandest conquerors of the thirteenth century were the Central Asians. Turkish invaders established the Delhi sultanate in India. Mongolian cavalries devastated Baghdad, the seat of the Abbasid caliphate since the eighth century, and they captured Kiev, further weakening Byzantium. By the end of the century they had captured China, Korea, and parts of mainland Southeast Asia as well.

Because the Mongols were pagans at the time of their conquests, the western Europeans cheered them on as they laid waste to one after another Muslim center of power in the Middle East. The Mongols were stopped only when they encountered the Mamluks of Egypt at Damascus. In East Asia and Southeast Asia only the Japanese and the Javanese were able to defeat them. The victors in Java went on to found Majapahit, whose power and prestige then spread through maritime Southeast Asia.

Both hemispheres were reorganized profoundly during this turmoil. Many places that had flourished were toppled, and power gravitated to new locales. In the Eastern Hemisphere the Central Asian conquerors had done great damage to traditional southern centers just about everywhere, except in Africa, southern China, southern India, and maritime Southeast Asia. At the same time the Mongols' control of overland routes between Europe and Asia in the thirteenth and early fourteenth centuries fostered unprecedented contacts between Europeans and peoples from those areas that had long been southernized. Marco Polo's long sojourn in Yuan Dynasty China is just one example of such interaction.

Under the Mongols overland trade routes in Asia shifted north and converged on the Black Sea. After the Genoese helped the Byzantines to retake Constantinople from the Venetians in 1261, the Genoese were granted special privileges of trade in the Black Sea. Italy then became directly linked to the Mongolian routes. Genoese traders were among the first and were certainly the most numerous to open up trade with the Mongolian states in southern Russia and Iran. In the words of one Western historian, in their Black Sea colonies they "admitted to citizenship" people of many nationalities, including those of "strange background and questionable belief," and they "wound up christening children of the best ancestry with such uncanny names as Saladin, Hethum, or Hulugu."[48]

Such contacts contributed to the southernization of the Christian Mediterranean during this period of Mongolian hegemony. Although European conquerors sometimes had taken over sugar and cotton lands in the Middle East during the Crusades, not until some time after 1200 did the European-held Mediterranean islands become important exporters. Also after 1200 Indian mathematics began to have a significant impact in Europe. Before that time a few western European scholars had become acquainted with Indian numerals in Spain, where the works of al-Kharazmi, al-Battani, and other mathematicians had been translated into Latin. Nevertheless, Indian numerals and mathematics did not become important in western Europe until the thirteenth century, after the book *Liber abaci* (1202), written by Leonardo Fibonacci of Pisa (ca. 1170–1250), introduced them to the commercial centers of Italy. Leonardo had grown up in North Africa (in what is now Bejala, Algeria), where his father, consul over the Pisan merchants in that port, had sent him to study calculation with an Arab master.[49]

In the seventeenth century, when Francis Bacon observed the "force and virtue and consequences of discoveries," he singled out three technologies in particular that "have changed the whole face and state of things throughout the world."[50] These were all Chinese inventions — the compass, printing, and gunpowder. All three were first acquired by Europeans during this time of hemispheric reorganization.

It was most likely the Arabs who introduced the compass to Mediterranean waters, either at the end of the twelfth or in the thirteenth century. Block printing, gunpowder, and cannon appeared first in Italy in the fourteenth century, apparently after making a single great leap from Mongolian-held regions of East Asia to Italy. How this great leap was accomplished is not known, but the most likely scenario is one suggested by Lynn White, Jr., in an article concerning how various other Southern (rather than Eastern) Asian technologies reached western Europe at about this time. He thought it most likely that they were introduced by "Tatar" slaves, Lama Buddhists from the frontiers of China whom the Genoese purchased in Black Sea marts and delivered to Italy. By 1450 when this trade reached its peak, there were thousands of these Asian slaves in every major Italian city.[51]

Yet another consequence of the increased traffic and communication on the more northern trade routes traversing the Eurasian steppe was the transmission of the bubonic plague from China to the Black Sea. The plague had broken out first in China in 1331, and apparently rats and lice infected with the disease rode westward in the saddlebags of Mongolian post messengers, horsemen who were capable of traveling one hundred miles per day. By 1346 it had reached a Black Sea port, whence it made its way to the Middle East and Europe.[52]

During the latter part of the fourteenth century the unity of the Mongolian empire began to disintegrate, and new regional powers began to emerge in its wake. Throughout much of Asia the chief beneficiaries of imperial disintegration were Turkic or Turko-Mongolian powers of the Muslim faith. The importance of Islam in Africa was also growing at this time, and the peoples of Southeast Asia, from the Malay peninsula to the southern Philippines, were converting to the faith.

Indeed, the world's most obvious dynamic in the centuries before Columbus was the expansion of the Islamic faith. Under Turkish auspices Islam was even spreading into eastern Europe, a development marked by the Ottoman conquest of Constantinople in 1453. This traumatic event lent a special urgency to Iberian expansion. The Iberians came to see themselves as the chosen defenders of Christendom. Ever since the twelfth century, while Christian Byzantium had been losing Anatolia and parts of southeastern Europe to Islam, they had been retaking the Iberian peninsula for Christendom.

One way to weaken the Ottomans and Islam was to go around the North African Muslims and find a new oceanic route to the source of West African gold. Before the Portuguese efforts, sailing routes had never developed off the western shore of Africa, since the winds there blow in the same direction all year long, from north to south. (Earlier European sailors could have gone to West Africa, but they would not have been able to return home.)

The Portuguese success would have been impossible without the Chinese compass, Arabic tables indicating the declination of the noonday sun at various latitudes, and the lateen sail, which was also an Arab innovation. The Portuguese caravels were of mixed, or multiple, ancestry, with a traditional Atlantic hull and a rigging that combined the traditional Atlantic square sail with the lateen sail of Southern Ocean provenance. With the lateen sail the Portuguese could tack against the wind for the trip homeward.

The new route to West Africa led to Portugal's rounding of Africa and direct participation in Southern Ocean trade. While making the voyages to West Africa, European sailors learned the wind patterns and ocean currents west of Africa, knowledge that made the Columbian voyages possible. The Portuguese moved the sugarcane plant from Sicily to Madeira, in the Atlantic, and they found new sources of gold, first in West Africa and then in East Africa. Given that there was little demand in Southern Ocean ports for European trade goods, they would not have been able to sustain their Asian trade without this African gold.

THE RISE OF EUROPE'S NORTH

The rise of the north, or more precisely, the rise of Europe's northwest, began with the appropriation of those elements of southernization that were not confined by geography. In the wake of their southern European neighbors, they became partially southernized, but they could not engage in all aspects of the process due to their distance from the equator. Full southernization and the wealth that we now associate with northwestern Europe came about only after their outright seizure of tropical and subtropical territories and their rounding of Africa and participation in Southern Ocean trade.

In the West Indies and along the coast of South America, the Dutch, the French, and the English acquired lands where for the first time they were able to become producers of sugar and cotton, though with African labor on Native American land. In West Africa the Dutch seized the Portuguese fort at Elmina, Portugal's most important source of gold. And in the East Indies, the Dutch seized Portuguese trading posts in the Moluccas and in 1621 conquered the Banda Islands, thereby gaining a stranglehold on the fine spices. Without such southern possessions the more northern Europeans had been unable to participate fully in the southernization process, since their homelands are too far north to grow either cotton or sugar, much less cinnamon, pepper, or the fine spices.

Even though the significance of indigenous developments in the rise of northwestern Europe should not be minimized, it should be emphasized that many of the most important causes of the rise of the West are not to be found within the bounds of Europe. Rather, they are the result of the transformation of western Europe's relationships with other regions of the Eastern Hemisphere. Europe began its rise only after the thirteenth-century reorganization of the Eastern Hemisphere facilitated its southernization, and Europe's northwest did not rise until it too was reaping the profits of southernization. Thus the rise of the North Atlantic powers should not be oversimplified so that it appears to be an isolated and solely European phenomenon, with roots that spread no farther afield than Greece. Rather, it should be portrayed as one part of a hemisphere-wide process, in which a northwestern Europe ran to catch up with a more developed south — a race not completed until the eighteenth century.

CONCLUSION

The patterns of southernization become apparent when one considers "the long duration," more or less from the fourth century to the eighteenth. It began as a Southern Asian phenomenon and spread through the warmer latitudes of the Eastern Hemisphere north of the equator. Both in China and in the Middle East it stimulated new developments and acquired new elements, and its potential continued to unfold. After 1200 the radical transformations throughout the Eastern Hemisphere brought about by the Mongolians and many others created conditions that led to the spread of southernization to Europe and Europe's colonies in the Western Hemisphere. Ultimately it transformed East Asia, the Middle East, Africa, the Mediterranean, northwestern Europe, and portions of the Western Hemisphere, more or less in that order.

Southernization was not overtaken by westernization until the Industrial Revolution of the eighteenth century. At that time the nations of northwestern Europe were catapulted into a position of global dominance, an event marked by the British takeover of Bengal and other parts of India. By the nineteenth century, using the new "tools of empire" provided by the Industrial Revolution, the northern powers for the first time were capable of imposing their will and their way on the rest of the world.[53]

Both the ocean crossing that knit together two hemispheres and the Industrial Revolution were indeed unprecedented. But their roots are inseparable from the process of southernization. Only after the northwestern Europeans had added to their own repertoire every one of the elements of southernization did the world become divided into a powerful, prestigious, and rich north and an impoverished south perceived to be in need of development.

Notes

1. Andrew Watson, *Agricultural Innovation in the Early Islamic World: The Diffusion of Crops and Farming Techniques, 700–1100* (Cambridge: Cambridge University Press, 1983), 32.

2. Mattiebelle Gittinger, *Master Dyers to the World: Technique and Trade in Early Indian Dyed Cotton Textiles* (Washington, D.C.: Textile Museum, 1982), 19. For a discussion of the significance of cotton textiles in Indonesia, see Gittinger, *Splendid Symbols: Textiles and Tradition in Indonesia* (Washington, D.C.: Textile Museum, 1979).

3. Moti Chandra, *Trade and Trade Routes of Ancient India* (New Delhi: Abhinav Publications, 1977), 35.

4. Ibid., 126.

5. Gittinger, *Splendid Symbols*, 13, 19.

6. Ibid., 15.

7. Paul Wheatley, *The Golden Khersonese: Studies in the Historical Geography of the Malay Peninsula Before A.D. 1500* (Westport, Conn.: Greenwood Press, 1973), 188.

8. D. W. Phillipson, "The Beginnings of the Iron Age in Southern Africa," in *UNESCO General History of Africa*, vol. 2, *Ancient Civilizations of Africa*, ed. G. Mokhtar (Berkeley: University of California Press, 1981), 679–80, 688–90. In the same volume, see also M. Posnansky, "The Societies of Africa South of the Sahara in the Early Iron Age," 726. Phillipson indicates that there is evidence of exchange between Zimbabwe and the coast in this early period, and Posnansky refers to the work of R. F. H. Summers who believes that early prospecting and mining techniques in East Africa reveal Indian influence. The description of Ethiopian merchants seeking gold in East Africa is from Steven Runciman, *Byzantine Style and Civilization* (Middlesex, England: Penguin Books, 1975), 132. Information about the monsoon is from A. M. H. Sheriff, "The East Africa Coast and Its Role in Maritime Trade," in *Ancient Civilizations of Africa*, ed. Mokhtar, 556–57.

9. Anthony Reid, *Southeast Asia in the Age of Commerce, 1450–1680*, 2 vols. (New Haven: Yale University Press, 1988–93), 1:4.

10. Keith Taylor, "Madagascar in the Ancient Malayo-Polynesian Myths," in *Explorations in Early Southeast Asian History: The Origins of Southeast Asian Statecraft*, ed. Kenneth Hall and John Whitmore (Ann Arbor: University of Michigan, Center for South and Southeast Asian Studies, 1976), 39. An excellent source on the early spice trade is James Innes Miller, *The Spice Trade of the Roman Empire, 29 B.C. to A.D. 649* (Oxford: Clarendon Press, 1969).

11. Taylor, "Madagascar," 30–31, 52.

12. George Hourani, *Arab Seafaring in the Indian Ocean in Ancient and Medieval Times* (Princeton, N.J.: Princeton University Press, 1951), 102.

13. Kenneth Hall, *Maritime Trade and State Formation in Southeast Asia* (Honolulu: University of Hawaii Press, 1985), 20.

14. Ibid., 72.

15. Henry N. Ridley, *Spices* (London: Macmillan, 1912), 105.

16. Hall, *Maritime Trade and State Formation*, 21.

17. Joseph E. Schwartzberg, *A Historical Atlas of South Asia* (Chicago: University of Chicago Press, 1978). The date 350 C.E. appears in "A Chronology of South Asia," a pocket insert in the atlas.

18. For a discussion on its domestication in southern China by the ancestors of the Southeast Asians, see Peter Bellwood, "Southeast Asia before History," in *Cambridge History of Southeast Asia*, ed. Nicholas Tarling (Cambridge: Cambridge University Press, 1992), 1:90–91. Also see Sidney W. Mintz, *Sweetness and Power: The Place of Sugar in Modern History* (New York: Viking, 1985), 19. Mintz agrees with those who argue that sugar was domesticated in New Guinea. He also suggests that crystallized sugar may have been produced in India as early as 400–350 B.C.E.

19. Chandra, *Trade and Trade Routes of Ancient India*, 61.

20. Georges Ifrah, *From One to Zero: A Universal History of Numbers*, trans. Lowell Blair (New York: Viking, 1985), 382, 434. This is an excellent book that explains many mysteries and contradictions in the literature. Even those who are not mathematically inclined will enjoy it.

21. 'Amr ibn Bahr al Jahiz, *The Life and Works of Jahiz*, trans. from Arabic by Charles Pellat, trans. from French by D. W. Hauter (Berkeley: University of California Press, 1969), 197–98.

22. See Liu Xinru, *Ancient India and Ancient China: Trade and Religious Exchanges, A.D. 1–600* (Delhi: Oxford University Press, 1988).

23. Ifrah, *From One to Zero*, 461.

24. Joseph Needham, *Science and Civilisation in China*, 6 vols. to date, vol. 3: *Mathematics and the Sciences of the Heavens and Earth* (Cambridge: Cambridge University Press, 1959), 40–50.

25. Lo Jung-pang, "The Emergence of China as a Sea Power during the Late Sung and Early Yüan Dynasties," *Far Eastern Economic Review* 14 (1955): 500.

26. Ho Ping-ti, "Early-Ripening Rice in Chinese History," *Economic History Review* 9 (1956): 201.

27. Ibid., 207.

28. Ibid., 211–12.

29. Ibid., 205–6.

30. Ibid., 206.

31. Thomas Francis Carter, *The Invention of Printing in China and Its Spread Westward* (New York: Columbia University Press, 1955), 68, 38–40.

32. For a reference to the Indian monk, see Arnold Paley, *Technology in World Civilization: A Thousand Year History* (Cambridge, Mass.: MIT Press, 1991), 16. Other information on gunpowder included here comes from Joseph Needham, "Science and China's Influence on the World," in *The Legacy of China*, ed. Raymond Dawson (Oxford: Oxford University Press, 1964), 246. This article is an excellent brief account of Chinese science and technology and their global significance. James R. Partington's *A History of Greek Fire and Gunpowder* (Cambridge: W. Heffer, 1960), is still useful.

33. Lo, "The Emergence of China as a Seapower," 500–1.

34. Lu Gwei-Djen, Joseph Needham, and Phan Che-Hsing, "The Oldest Representation of a Bombard," in Joseph Needham, *Science and Civilisation in China*, vol. 5, part

7: *Military Technology: The Gunpowder Epoch* (Cambridge: Cambridge University Press, 1986), appendix A, 580–81. (I am indebted to Robin Yates for this information.)

35. Lo, "The Emergence of China as a Seapower," 500. Other useful articles by Lo include: "Maritime Commerce and Its Relation to the Song Navy," *Journal of the Economic and Social History of the Orient* 12 (1969): 57–101; and "The Termination of the Early Ming Naval Expeditions," in *Papers in Honor of Professor Woodbridge Bingham: A Festschrift for His Seventy-Fifth Birthday,* ed. James B. Parsons (San Francisco: Chinese Materials Center, 1976), 127–41.

36. Robert Hartwell, "A Revolution in the Chinese Iron and Coal Industries during the Northern Sung, 960–1126 A.D.," *Journal of Asian Studies* 21 (1962): 155; and Hartwell, "Markets, Technology, and the Structure of Enterprise in the Development of the Eleventh-Century Chinese Iron and Steel Industry," *Journal of Economic History* 26 (1966): 54. See also Hartwell, "A Cycle of Economic Change in Imperial China: Coal and Iron in Northeast China, 750–1350," *Journal of the Social and Economic History of the Orient* 10 (1967): 102–59. For an excellent overview of the transformations in Tang and Song China, see Mark Elvin, *The Patterns of the Chinese Past* (Stanford: Stanford University Press, 1973).

37. Watson, *Agricultural Innovation in the Early Islamic World,* 78–80.

38. Sheriff, "The East African Coast," 566.

39. William D. Phillips, *Slavery from Roman Times to the Early Transatlantic Trade* (Minneapolis: University of Minnesota Press, 1985), 76.

40. Watson, *Agricultural Innovation in the Early Islamic World,* 29, 39–41.

41. Ibid., 123–25.

42. Ifrah, *From One to Zero,* 465.

43. R. M. Savory, *Introduction to Islamic Civilization* (Cambridge: Cambridge University Press, 1976), 116–17.

44. C. G. F. Simkins, *The Traditional Trade of Asia* (Oxford: Oxford University Press, 1968), 81.

45. Sture Bolin, "Mohammed, Charlemagne, and Ruric," *Scandinavian Economic History Review* 1 (1953): 16. In the past, Sture's interpretation of the Carolingians has been disputed. The article has, however, stood the test of time. For example, see the assessment of it in Richard Hodges and David Whitehouse, *Mohammed, Charlemagne and the Origins of Europe* (Ithaca: Cornell University Press, 1983). The information about Scandinavia's relationship with the caliphates is especially valuable.

46. Anthony Hopkins, *An Economic History of West Africa* (New York: Columbia University Press, 1973), 82.

47. F. T. Masao and H. W. Mutoro, "The East African Coast and the Comoro Islands, in *UNESCO General History of Africa,* vol. 3, *Africa from the Seventh to the Eleventh Century,* ed. M. El Fasi (Berkeley: University of California Press, 1988), 611–15.

48. Robert S. Lopez, "Market Expansion: The Case of Genoa," *Journal of Economic History* 24 (1964): 447–49. See also Lopez, "Back to Gold, 1252," in *Economic History Review* 9 (1956): 219–40. The latter includes a discussion of the relationship between western European coinage and the trans-Saharan gold trade.

49. Ifrah, *From One to Zero,* 465, 481. See also Joseph and Frances Gies, *Leonardo of Pisa and the New Mathematics of the Middle Ages* (New York: Crowell, 1969).

50. Bacon is cited in Needham, "Science and China's Influence on the World," 242.

51. Lynn White, Jr., "Tibet, India, and Malaya as Sources of Western Medieval Technology," *American Historical Review* 65 (1960): 515–26. This is an important, if little known, article.

52. William H. McNeill, *Plagues and Peoples* (Garden City, N.Y.: Anchor Press, 1976), 133, 145.

53. The term comes from Daniel Headrick's excellent book, *The Tools of Empire: Technology and European Imperialism in the Nineteenth Century* (New York: Oxford University Press, 1981).

JOHN OBERT VOLL

"Southernization" as a Construct in Post-Civilization Narrative

"Civilization" has been a very important concept in organizing the study and presentation of world history. Much of the broader history of the human experience in the past three to four thousand years has been described in terms of the great civilizations and their developments. This is true not only of the works of major macrohistorians ranging from Arnold Toynbee to William McNeill, but also of many of the specific studies of countries, regions, and societies which assume the existence of "civilizations" as an important element defining the context within which the actors are seen to be functioning. The "civilization narrative" is a crucial component in the historical methods and approaches of the modern era.

The possible weaknesses of the civilization narrative in examining the nature of the contemporary world have been apparent to many scholars for some time. It is recognized that the "emerging global mass culture reassembles goods from all parts of the world. Syncretism, the fusion of dissimilar artifacts, and processes of creolization, nonauthentic fusion of disparate elements into one among many microexperiences, this is the key expression of our time."[1] Michael Geyer concludes this analysis with the observation that "This moment of extraordinary creativity of humankind, much of it imposed on people in their struggle for survival, consists in piecing together a human existence *beyond the imagination of civilizational studies.*"[2]

It is within this context that I wish to respond to the remarkable paper by Professor Lynda Shaffer on "Southernization."[3] While many people might agree that "civilizational studies" are difficult to sustain in the context of the contemporary world, they might still argue that civilization narrative is, despite its

John Obert Voll, "'Southernization' as a Construct in Post-Civilization Narrative" (paper presented at the meeting of the New England Historical Association, October 1994).

problems, more effective than any other available conceptualization. This is especially true, in this viewpoint, when one moves out of contemporary history and into those eras traditionally labeled as "ancient" and "medieval."

Shaffer provides a challenge to that complacency (intellectual languor) in her discussion of the influence and impact of developments in South Asia in the eastern hemisphere from the fifth through the twelfth centuries C.E. She is not explicitly debating with Samuel Huntington or other current articulators of the civilization narratives, but her conclusions might be viewed as undermining the validity of that style of narrative as well as indicating foundations on which alternative narratives can be built.

The publication of Samuel Huntington's article on the clash of civilizations and the subsequent debate[4] finally persuaded me that the utility of the civilizational narrative for world historical analysis must be seriously debated. When a paradigm makes it seem logical to exclude Greece from Western civilization (as is the case with Huntington's presentation),[5] it is time to examine more closely the basic assumptions of the paradigm itself, rather than simply argue with details of the analysis. From the immediately contemporary context of Huntington's analysis, it seems difficult, if not absurd, to exclude from "The West" a country that is a member of the North Atlantic Treaty Organization (NATO) and also a member of the European Community. This would be true even if the country were not Greece, but it becomes ridiculous when you are excluding from the West the country that is felt by most people in the West to be the homeland and origin of Western Civilization. The most exclusivist interpretation of the basic canon of Western Civilization starts with a full dose of Greek writings and history.

Similarly, if one examines carefully the inventory of "civilizations" that is used by scholars like Huntington in their analyses, one can see a number of units which are not really "civilizations" in the normally accepted definition of the term. "Islam," for example, is clearly not a unit that is most effectively called a "civilization."[6] It includes significant parts of a number of different civilizations and, historically, the Islamic world included areas that were not part of the traditional regional civilizations.

Even "The West," in the context of modern history, is clearly not, in the way that Huntington uses the term as synonymous with "modern," a civilization, in the meaning that is usually associated with the term in discussions of world history. Huntington himself speaks of civilizations as cultural entities and says that they "are differentiated from each other by history, language, culture, tradition and, most important, religion."[7] In his discussion, it is not clear what he sees as "*the* language" or "*the* religion" of Western Civilization that makes it a single cultural entity. I am not arguing that "The West" does not exist or that it is not, in some way, a meaningful historic entity worth identifying for purposes of understanding world and local histories. I am only suggesting that "The West," as discussed by Huntington and the rest of us, is probably not most effectively described or analyzed as "a civilization."

It is in this context that the article on "southernization" by Lynda Shaffer represents a welcome breath of fresh air and analysis utilizing a possible new paradigm. Huntington was absolutely right to ask his critics, "if not civilization, what?" The summary of his response states his perspective clearly: "It's all very well to point to scattered events that the 'civilizations' paradigm does not explain. But there is still no better framework with which to understand the post–Cold War world."[8] There has to be some basic organizational concept for analysis of global history, whether in ancient, medieval, or modern times.

Professor Shaffer directs our attention, in her article, to a new style of conceptualization which, I think, is an appropriate foundation for the post–"civilizational narrative" era of world historical analysis. In this approach there are a couple of dimensions among many possible that I want to highlight and discuss: (1) the multi-dimensionality of the relationships among major human units; (2) the non-simultaneity of the geographic aspects of these different dimensions. My conclusion is that Shaffer provides us with an important and useful perspective. However, the term "southernization," while attention-getting, may not be the most effective label for the complex matrix of developments that she describes.

Multi-Dimensionality of Relationships

In describing the grand processes of "southernization," Shaffer examines a variety of aspects of hemispheric relationships. She notes at the outset that even though she is going to discuss a number of strands of development, there are important ones — the metallurgical, the medical, and the literary — which she will not cover. However, the discussions of the spread of cotton production, the search for bullion, the spice trade, maritime technology, the development of sugar as a bulk trade good, the spread of the use of the concept of zero, and many other specific developments show that the grand developments of intersocietal relationships in the era covered have many different dimensions. There is more than simply military conquests, the wanderings of religious "missionaries," and the activities of a few cosmopolitan merchants. Southernization requires thick description if it is to be understood in the way that Shaffer proposes.

This thick description demands that grand categories of factors not simply be viewed as aggregations of things. Too often people will recognize the importance of "trade" in inter-societal relations in the pre-modern era, but "trade" is often dealt with as an aggregated dimension. The different major products are grouped together under the generic heading of "trade relations" in a single dimension. Shaffer reminds us that the nature of the products and the development of their production are important elements in themselves. It is not enough simply to say that there was significant trade *among* the societies clustered around the South Asian center. The products and the exchanges created broad regions of similarities which distinguished one distinctive "world" from another. Thus the "world of cotton producers" emerges in Shaffer's presentation as a unit with interacting elements rather than a series of separate "worlds" that have relationships with each other. This might be said for many of the other dimensions touched on by Shaffer: one might think of the "world of zero" or the "world of crystallized sugar," etc.

This presentation differs considerably from the standard civilization narrative. Rather than multiple worlds of interaction, the civilization narrative approach identifies grand, inclusive units, "civilizations," which interact. In anthropomorphic ways, they "borrow" from one another or they clash with one another. In such a narrative, it is difficult to see the processes of southernization described by Shaffer. In the modern (post-modern?) context, the civilization narrative makes it difficult to see the "world of FAX" or the "world of CNN," or the general multidimensionality of global interactions.

The cassette "revolution" in media technology has created what one might call the "cassette world." This cassette world is one of localized diversity as well as global familiarity. Inexpensive recordings make it possible for truly global performance stars to emerge, but it also makes it possible for every local performer to have a special audience. A study of "cassette culture" in north India notes the importance of this communications technology in breaking down centralized monopolies of information and power. Peter Manuel states that the "new media render the Orwellian vision of monolithic consciousness control a possibility of the past rather than the future; 1984, indeed has come and gone."[9]

My point here is not to examine the history of media technologies. What I am saying is that the multidimensionality of Shaffer's approach represents an important style of analysis which can be more effective in examining such things as the contemporary cassette world than the old monolithic civilization narratives were.

NON-SIMULTANEITY OF BOUNDARIES

The many different interacting networks of relationships described by Shaffer do not have the same geographic boundaries. This is a simple commonsense statement, but it has importance for the development of an effective globally-oriented paradigm for historical analysis. World historical study using "civilizations" as the basic units of analysis assume that most important dimensions of identity and interaction will have essentially simultaneous geographic boundaries. This was succinctly stated by the great French historian, Fernand Braudel: "Civilizations, vast or otherwise, can always be located on a map."[10] Braudel goes on to discuss civilizations as "cultural zones" and observes that the "stability of these cultural zones and their frontiers does not however isolate them from cultural imports. Every civilization imports and exports aspects of its culture."[11] In this perspective, "civilizations" are clearly distinctive units which can import and export (or in other terminologies, "borrow") various elements but their basic identity remains as a constant unit which can be found on a map.

In the modern world, the civilization paradigm makes it difficult to see or analyze major networks similar to the sugar trade, the spice trade, and other aspects of the world of southernization presented by Shaffer. Shaffer's paradigm gives us a much better chance of understanding the global drug trade in the 1990s, for example, than the Huntington paradigm. Rather than a world made up of large, clearly identifiable blocks, called civilizations, Shaffer's approach makes it possible to see a world with many different overlapping networks of relationships of varying degrees of intensity. One might still have "civilizations" as concentrations of overlapping elements but the world would look more like a grand matrix or Venn diagram. If things like the world of crystallized sugar or interacting gunpowder empires (Western and "non-Western") or cataphract systems of warhorse feudal defense represent important aspects of historical relationships, then it is important to go beyond the relatively static structures of the civilization narrative. Shaffer shows us a way of doing this.

The Problem of the Term Itself

Shaffer's analysis provides many important insights and suggestions for further development of world historical analysis. However, there may be a difficulty with the specific term of "southernization." This term has an attention-getting quality relating to a sense of seeing parts of the world other than the West as having real significance. However, the term carries some baggage of implied assumptions which may not be Shaffer's assumptions.

Shaffer notes that the "term *southernization* is meant to be analogous to *westernization*" (p. 1). Within Shaffer's own frame of reference, this is consistent with her relatively non-civilizational approach. The indication is that Shaffer has a broader view of "Westernization" than simply being a process whereby other civilizations "borrowed" from the West. It is a more global process of major transformations which tended to occur first in western Europe and then spread to other areas. In this framework, it might be possible to assert, as I have, that "it may be that the first 'traditional' civilization to be destroyed by the processes of modernization was Western Civilization. What we now call 'Western Civilization' is identified with modernity and this is something strikingly different from the society and life style of the Europe of the medieval papacy, the great Gothic cathedrals, the Crusades, the Magna Carta and other pillars of traditional Western Civilization."[12] The modern processes of transformation which Shaffer has identified as Westernization have been called "technicalization" by Marshall Hodgson,[13] in a usage that does not make "modern" appear to be identical with "Western." If Shaffer does not see "Western" and "modern" as identical, then the analogous usage of the term "southernization" might be misleading because it seems to me that Professor Shaffer is doing more than simply tracing the expansion of Indian influence throughout the Eastern Hemisphere.

In this context, the "South" is an awkward term, however nicely it balances the negative connotations of the usage of that term in analyses of contemporary world developments. The terminological question points to a further issue that will require attention if the analysis of Shaffer is pursued further. It is important for Shaffer and the rest of us to deal explicitly with the question of what are the basic units of our analyses and what are the nature of these units.

I would like to suggest that Shaffer's approach clearly points out the need for analytical units which are not single and monolithic. Instead, the boundaries have to be flexible, dependent upon the specific issues being examined. The challenge becomes finding a way of conceptualizing the relationships among these developments. "Southernization" suggests one open-ended way of combining all of the various dimensions that need to be considered, but there is a possible misunderstanding, with people seeing this as a way of showing that "The South" dominated "The West" before the West dominated the South. Such a perspective would be useful to avoid since it could involve the same problems that the civilization narrative, as narrated by Huntington, is currently having.

One must think of such conceptualizations of Wallerstein's World-System analysis and its current revisions by Andre Gunder Frank. For part of the period considered by Shaffer, one might also look at the "world-systems" approach of Leila Abu Lughod. In a different mode, the global and hemispheric approaches suggested by Marshall Hodgson might also provide fertile ground for our search for broader, more flexible narratives that utilize the important characteristics of Shaffer's presentation, multi-dimensionality and fluidity of geographic units. Shaffer is to be congratulated for bringing together in the small space of her article so many constructive and thought-provoking suggestions.

Notes

1. Michael Geyer, "Multiculturalism and the Politics of General Education," *Critical Inquiry* 19 (Spring 1993): 529.

2. Ibid. Emphasis added.

3. Lynda Shaffer, "Southernization," *Journal of World History* 5 (Spring 1994): 1–21.

4. Samuel P. Huntington, "The Clash of Civilizations?" *Foreign Affairs* 72 (Summer 1993): 22–49; responses by various authors appeared in *Foreign Affairs* 72 (Sept./Oct. 1993): 2–26; Huntington's reply was Samuel P. Huntington, "If Not Civilizations, What?" *Foreign Affairs* 72 (Nov./Dec. 1993): 186–94.

5. Huntington, for example, reprints a map which clearly places Greece outside of the area of what he is basically describing as Western Civilization, and in his discussion identifies the world of Orthodox Christianity with Islam, not the West. Huntington, "The Clash of Civilizations?," 29–31.

6. I have explored this line of analysis more fully in "Islam as a Special World-System," *Journal of World History* 5 (Fall 1994): 213–26.

7. "The Clash of Civilizations?," 25.

8. *Foreign Affairs*, November/December 1993, table of contents, p. iii.

9. Peter Manuel, *Cassette Culture: Popular Music and Technology in North India* (Chicago: University of Chicago Press, 1993), 2.

10. Fernand Braudel, *A History of Civilizations*, trans. Richard Mayne (New York: Allen Lane, Penguin, 1994), 9.

11. Ibid. 14.

12. John Obert Voll, "The End of Civilization is Not So Bad," *Middle East Studies Association Bulletin* 28 (July 1994): 5.

13. Marshall G. S. Hodgson, *Rethinking World History*, ed. Edmund Burke III (Cambridge: Cambridge University Press, 1993). See especially chapter 4, "The Great Western Transmutation."

DAVID CHRISTIAN

Inner Eurasia as a Unit of World History

What are the basic units of world history? For those interested in what used to be the Soviet Union, this question involves several others: Are there large units of analysis that are simple but capable of illuminating the history of this entire region over long periods? Can such units also help explain the crisis the region is undergoing today? Can they reveal the larger shape of the region's history? Now is a good time to pose these large questions, for the breakup of the Soviet Union has devalued many old units of analysis. It forces us to look for fresh ways of approaching old questions. This essay is a contribution to what will doubtless be a long and complex discussion. In it I describe a large historical unit that I call "Inner Eurasia." I argue that "Inner Eurasia" constitutes one of the basic units of Eurasian and of world history.[1]

Ever since history emerged as a distinct discipline in nineteenth-century Europe, most historians have treated the national state as their main unit of analysis. This is hardly surprising, for history emerged as a scholarly discipline in a period of violent nation building. But is the national state the best unit of analysis for world history today? Is Russia the most important unit for the historian of what used to be the Soviet Union? A Ukrainian historian, or a historian of Turkmenistan or of Mongolia, will surely argue that it is not. Yet would Ukraine, Turkmenistan, or Mongolia do any better? The emergence of new nations will certainly encourage the writing of new national histories.[2] Yet these will do little to help us understand the larger history of this region.

The trouble is that the national state is a recent, and often artificial, creation. All too many national states have been assembled mechanically from loose groupings of tribes, peoples, religions, and lifeways. As a unit of analysis, the national state assumes that ethnicity, language, culture, and politics normally coincide. Yet this is rarely true. What is self-evident for the historian of modern Africa is only slightly less obvious for the historian of the former Soviet Union. If there is a larger shape to the history of this region, we must look beyond the national state to find it.

David Christian, "Inner Eurasia as a Unit of World History," *Journal of World History* 5 (Fall 1994): 173–84.

Empires, such as the Mongol or Soviet empires, or those of Kievan Rus' or the Scythians, provide convenient units, but only for limited historical periods. Religions, languages, cultures, and lifestyles are so diverse and so changeable in the area that interests us that they can provide only local and temporary signposts for historical analysis. Residual categories, such as Siberia, Inner Asia, or Central Asia, are no more helpful.[3]

Recently, historians have taken up a much larger category: the world-system. Immanuel Wallerstein first introduced the concept in 1974.[4] He argued that since 1500 a system of interacting polities and economies had emerged that was more important than the sum of its parts. Recently, Andre Gunder Frank and Barry Gills have tracked Wallerstein's world-system back to the very beginnings of civilization, some 5,000 years ago.[5] For historians interested in a particular part of the world, however extensive, the world-system is too large a unit of analysis. Yet we can no longer ignore it. Any regional unit of analysis must now take this larger unit into account and seek a place within it.

In this paper, I propose a large regional unit of analysis based mainly on geography.[6] I call it Inner Eurasia to contrast its history with that of Outer Eurasia, which includes the rest of the Eurasian landmass. Inner Eurasia includes the lands ruled by the Soviet Union in 1990, together with Mongolia. More hesitantly, I would also include parts of China's most western region, the Autonomous Region of Xinjiang. Along the southern rim of Inner Eurasia, mountains form a natural border. The mountains were thrown up during the last 40 million years, as India and Africa collided with Eurasia in their journeys north from Gondwanaland. A few natural gateways breach this border through the Balkans, Persia, and northern China. To the east and west, the flatlands of Inner Eurasia break up less dramatically, and the borders are less clear-cut. Does Poland, Hungary, or Manchuria belong within Inner Eurasia? In a short paper, it is sufficient to describe such regions as borderlands.[7] They belong partly to Outer Eurasia and partly to Inner Eurasia. To the north, the tundra and the Arctic Ocean form clearer borders.

Within these borders has existed an immense variety of climates, landscapes, lifeways, languages, and religions. The most striking of these divisions is that between the forests of the north and the steppes and deserts to the south. Despite this variety, it is helpful to think of Inner Eurasia as a single, coherent historical unit. To defend this claim, I offer three distinct arguments, political, geographical, and ecological. Ecology and geography have combined to give a distinctive shape to Inner Eurasian history from prehistory to the present, by posing distinctive problems that required distinctive solutions. As a result, the histories of Inner and Outer Eurasia have run on parallel but different tracks for a very long time. The Paleolithic of Inner Eurasia was dominated by hunting rather than gathering, its Neolithic by pastoralism rather than farming, the era of state formation by pastoral nomadism rather than irrigation agriculture. These ancient contrasts can help us explain the twentieth-century division between a largely capitalist Outer Eurasia and the command economies that dominated Inner Eurasia.

The Distinctiveness of Inner Eurasian History

Political History

The first hint of underlying coherence to this vast region is political. Unlike Outer Eurasia, Inner Eurasia has periodically been united within single, over-arching empires. In the twentieth century, the Soviet Union dominated most of Inner Eurasia. Soviet influence also extended to the two regions of Inner Eurasia that were never included formally within the USSR: Mongolia, which was a vassal state of the Soviet Union, and Xinjiang, which nearly became a vassal state. If China had remained divided, the Soviet Union might well have absorbed Xinjiang, as it did the more western parts of Central Asia.

Of course, the emergence of the Soviet empire may have been a historical accident. Perhaps, like the British empire in the late nineteenth century, the Soviet empire was the arbitrary product of imperial wars. What suggests that deeper factors are at work here is the repeated appearance of huge, if fragile, empires in Inner Eurasia.

The Soviet Union did not create an empire; it inherited one. The Russian empire had already united most of Inner Eurasia since the seventeenth century. Furthermore, Russia's empire was not the first, but at least the third woven on this particular loom. In the late sixth century C.E., Türk tribes from the Altai region created the first empire to embrace most of the southern half of Inner Eurasia. For a decade or two, the Türk empire dominated the steppes from Manchuria to the Volga. Though the empire soon split up, its successor states dominated large areas of Inner Eurasia for two centuries. In the early thirteenth century, the Mongols created the second great empire of Inner Eurasia. For a time, their empire controlled most of the steppes of Inner Eurasia, and its influence extended well into the northern forests. Briefly, the Mongols even added China to their domains. The Muscovite empire was the third polity to embrace most of Inner Eurasia, and the Soviet Union was the fourth.

No other region of the world can boast such a history of huge empires. Of the three largest empires ever created, two, the Mongol empire and the Russian empire (respectively the second and third largest), both emerged in Inner Eurasia.[8] By measuring the area under a graph plotting size against time, R. Taagepera has argued that the combined Russian-Soviet empire constitutes the most substantial empire ever created. The area under such a graph for Muscovy-Russia-USSR is:

> 65 million square-kilometer-centuries . . . while the closest runners-up (British, and post-Mongol Chinese, from Ming to Mao) are around 45, followed by Rome, Baghdad, Han China, Sassanid Persia, Sung-T'ang China and the Mongol Empire at 30 to 20 million square-kilometer-centuries. As far as the impact of an empire depends on how much land it controls for how many centuries, Muscovy-Russia-USSR already holds the record in world history. While the combined Chinese empires, from Han to Mao, add up to much more, they are separated by long breakdown periods compared with which Russian times of trouble have been negligible.[9]

Such regularities over 1,500 years suggest that there is, indeed, an underlying coherence to Inner Eurasia. The geography and ecology of the region suggest why this should be so.

Physical Geography

The geographical coherence of Inner Eurasia appears clearly on a physical map of the world. The region is dominated by the largest unified area of flatlands in the world. The ancient habit of treating the Ural Mountains as a border between Europe and Asia has long obscured this point. Yet the Urals offer no serious barrier to movement. As the Slavophile writer Danilevskii asked, what was it about the Urals that could

> confer upon them alone, out of all the mountains on the face of the earth, the honor of serving as the boundary between two continents — an honor which in all other cases is granted only to oceans, and rarely to seas? In terms of its altitude, this mountain range is one of the most insignificant of all, and in terms of its traversability one of the easiest. In the middle section, around Ekaterinburg, people cross them . . . and ask their driver: but tell me, brother, just where are these mountains?[10]

Between the Yenisei and Lena rivers lies the raised mid-Siberian plateau. East of the Lena and Lake Baikal the land is more mountainous. Yet even here, and in the more broken landscapes of northern Xinjiang and Mongolia, there was enough movement from one area to another to allow for close economic and political ties. Topographically, Inner Eurasia is therefore different from Outer Eurasia, which geography has divided into distinct regions, separated by seas or mountain chains.

The flatness of most of Inner Eurasia had great military and political significance. While land armies dominated warfare, natural features such as mountains or seas were the main barriers to military expansion. The absence of such barriers explains the size of the polities that have emerged in Inner Eurasia. Successful armies met no serious barriers until they reached the western, southern, or eastern borderlands of Inner Eurasia. Hints of this expansionist potential appear as early as the second millennium B.C.E., with the emergence of pastoralist cultures whose influence reached across huge areas of the steppes. From late in the fourth millennium B.C.E. there appears complex but powerful evidence of large, warlike migrations by pastoral nomadic societies. A striking example is the so-called "Seima-Turbino" phenomenon of the mid-second millennium B.C.E. This refers to a series of archaeological sites that seem to indicate a rapid, warlike migration of an entire people from the Altai region, along the northern borders of the steppes, and into southeastern Europe.[11] Migrations such as this prefigure the great eastern invasions of the first and second millennia C.E.

The absence of major barriers to military expansion makes Inner Eurasia a natural unit of military history and hence of political history as well.

Ecology

As the British geographer H. J. Mackinder pointed out, the Eurasian "world-island" divides into two main regions. To the west, south, and east lie the well-watered coastal "promontories" of Outer Eurasia. In the center of this landmass lies the drier, continental "heartland" of Inner Eurasia.[12]

Within Outer Eurasia, I include Europe, the Mediterranean basin, Southwest Asia, the Indian subcontinent, Southeast Asia, and China. The seas that surround Outer Eurasia provide plenty of rainfall and reduce temperature extremes. Southern latitudes keep climates warm. (Europe is a partial exception, for the waters of the Gulf Stream keep it warm despite its higher latitudes.) Abundant water, moderate climates, and plenty of sunlight make for high ecological productivity in much of Outer Eurasia.

The heartland of the Eurasian landmass is very different. It is, in the first place, "inner." Interiority condemns Inner Eurasia to aridity and to great seasonal fluctuations in temperature. The frozen seas of Inner Eurasia's northern coasts can neither moderate its climates nor provide much rainfall. Second, Inner Eurasia is northerly. Northern latitudes mean colder climates and less sunlight, with less photosynthesis and shorter growing seasons. Third, Inner Eurasia is flat. It lacks the broken topography that helps moderate the climates of Outer Eurasia. Flatness, size, and interiority explain the extreme continentality of its climates.

Aridity, high latitudes, and extreme continentality reduced the natural productivity of much of Inner Eurasia. This is true of both the main ecological regions into which Inner Eurasia divides: the arid belt of steppe and desert to the south, and the forest and tundra to the north. In the south, aridity makes for a land of desert and grasslands. Average precipitation varies from 25 to 50 centimeters.[13] The soils are often extremely rich, particularly in the western and central parts of the steppes, where they formed from the composting of grasses over thousands of years. However, erratic and limited rainfall has made farming difficult. In the northern regions, the soils are poorer than in the steppes. Rainfall, though more generous than in the south, is only moderate. Average rainfall exceeds 50 centimeters only in Belarus, northern Ukraine, and European Russia, along the southern parts of the eastern Siberian coast, and in pockets in Siberia. The contrast with Outer Eurasia is striking. There, regions with average rainfall of less than 50 centimeters are unusual, and in many regions average rainfall is well above 100 centimeters a year.

Harsh climates compound the effects of low rainfall. Northerliness and continentality make for greater extremes of temperature than in Outer Eurasia, for long winters and hot summers. Taken together, these factors have depressed the ecological productivity of most of Inner Eurasia. The differential in natural productivity between Inner and Outer Eurasia has shaped the history of Eurasia in profound ways and over long periods. Its effects have been subtle and complex.

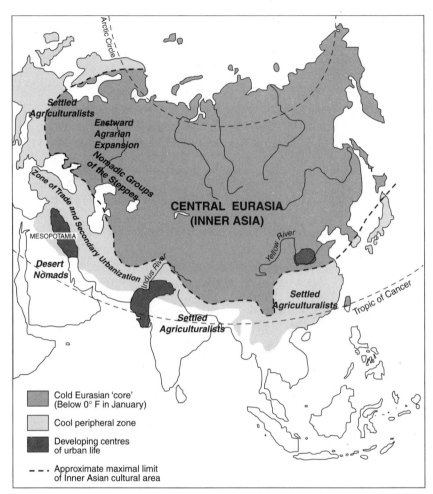

Figure 1. A map of "Central Eurasia" or "Inner Asia."

From Denis Sinor, ed., *Cambridge History of Early Inner Asia* (Cambridge: Cambridge University Press, 1990), p. 6. Sinor's "Inner Asia," defined here by average January temperatures, is similar to "Inner Eurasia" as defined in this paper. The major difference is that this map includes parts of eastern Europe and northern China that I exclude from Inner Eurasia, and it excludes parts of southern central Asia that I include in Inner Eurasia.

Ecology, Geography, and History

The most striking consequence of Inner Eurasia's relatively low ecological productivity has been demographic. Even today, Inner Eurasia is a region of lower average population density than Outer Eurasia. Historically, the concentrations of people that were the foundation for early urban civilizations and early states appeared relatively late in most of Inner Eurasia. It is tempting, therefore, to regard low natural productivity as the main shaper of Inner Eurasian history. It certainly helps explain why agrarian civilizations appeared later there than in Outer Eurasia. And that in turn explains why historians have tended to neglect the region. All too often, they have treated Inner Eurasia as a marginal region, of interest only when its barbarian peoples conquered their civilized neighbors in Outer Eurasia. This view is misleading.

In reality, ecological and demographic poverty has not confined Inner Eurasia to a marginal role in Eurasian history. Despite everything, Inner Eurasia has played a pivotal role in Eurasian and world history. It has done so because of its geographical position at the center of the Eurasian landmass. Outer Eurasia consists of a series of regions divided from each other by seas and mountain ranges. Before the sixteenth century, the main links between them passed through the southern borderlands of Inner Eurasia, along the routes known as the "silk roads." If the history of the Eurasian landmass has coherence, it arises because genes, commodities, ideas, and diseases have all traveled through the Inner Eurasian borderlands.

Exchanges occurred most freely during those periods when empires controlled large areas of Inner Eurasia. Some of these empires, such as Han China or Achaemenid Persia, originated in Outer Eurasia. However, Outer Eurasian empires never achieved a firm grip over the communication routes of Inner Eurasia, because they lacked the special skills needed to adapt to the difficult terrain of Inner Eurasia. Trade flourished when Inner Eurasian empires emerged that were capable of protecting large stretches of the silk roads. This allowed societies of Inner Eurasia to have a profound impact on the history of Outer Eurasia.[14] As a result, the political history of Inner Eurasia shaped the rhythms not just of Inner Eurasia but of the entire Eurasian world-system.

The emergence of extensive steppe empires coincided with the first appearance of a flourishing trade route across Inner Eurasia. William H. McNeill argued that the second century B.C.E. saw the first "closure of the Eurasian Ecumene."[15] In more recent jargon, it marks the first appearance of a Eurasia-wide world-system. Contacts had been made across the Eurasian ecumene for thousands of years, but this was the first time they were vigorous enough to justify talk of an emerging world-system.

The Türk empire of the sixth century C.E. linked eastern and western Eurasia for a second time. Though the original empire fragmented rapidly, successor states continued to protect the main trans-Eurasian trade routes. As a result, the Türk empire recreated for a while the Eurasian world-system of the classical era.

> In the space of a single generation, the Turks built a vast empire of their own, which covered nearly the entire Eurasian steppe and impinged on the borders of all of the great Old World civilizations, including the Central Asian city-states and India. The Turks made it their first order of business to inform their neighbors to the east and west that they were vitally interested in trade. When the Turks annexed most of the Central Asian city-states — great centers for the east-west and north-south caravan trade — in the second half of the sixth

century, they also removed the political obstacles to relatively high volume transcontinental trade.[16]

The Mongol empire of the thirteenth century played a similar role. It provided such effective protection for the major trade routes across Eurasia that it created a single economic, cultural, and epidemiological world-system.[17] This in turn contributed to the economic and cultural expansion of the Middle Ages.

For several millennia, then, Inner Eurasia was the pivot of Eurasian history. Inner Eurasia therefore counts as a vital, if neglected, unit of world history. Despite its ecological poverty and its small populations, Inner Eurasia has not been a region "without history," in Eric Wolf's phrase.[18]

This combination of ecological poverty and a pivotal geographical position has given the history of Inner Eurasia its distinctive shape. As a region of low ecological and demographic productivity, Inner Eurasia might have played a marginal role in world history. Yet because of its position, its societies were touched by, and had to react to, the most powerful currents of Eurasian history. This was particularly true of those societies closest to the borders with Outer Eurasia. To survive in competition with the more productive societies of Outer Eurasia, societies throughout the huge southern arc of Inner Eurasia had to find ways of compensating for low productivity. The distinctive solutions they found to this problem helped shape the history of the lands to their north.

This line of argument suggests an abstract way of defining what is distinctive about the history of Inner Eurasia. The societies that dominated the history of Inner Eurasia did so by evolving distinctive ways of concentrating and mobilizing the scarce human and material resources of a region of relatively low natural productivity. All societies concentrate and mobilize ecological, demographic, and economic resources. In Inner Eurasia, however, low ecological productivity combined with proximity to the more productive societies of Outer Eurasia forced societies to concentrate and mobilize scarce resources to an exceptional degree. This distinguishes their history from that of Outer Eurasia.

Notes

1. An essay such as this can defend the use of such a unit only at a general level. I will offer a detailed history of Inner Eurasia in a forthcoming volume of Blackwell's History of the World Series, ed. R. I. Moore. [See Selected Bibliograpny.]

2. Examples of influential recent national histories are Orest Subtelny's *Ukraine: A History* (Toronto, 1988) or works by the Turkmen historian, Marat Durdyiev, such as his pamphlet, *Turkmeny* (Ashkhabad, 1991).

3. However, "Inner Asia" or "Central Eurasia," as defined by Denis Sinor, are more useful categories, and are close to the definition of "Inner Eurasia" offered below. See *The Cambridge History of Early Inner Asia*, ed. D. Sinor (Cambridge, 1990), "Introduction" and "The Geographic Setting." See also the useful discussion in Larry Moses and Stephen A. Halkovic, Jr., *Introduction to Mongolian History and Culture* (Bloomington, 1985), 3–10.

4. I. Wallerstein, *The Modern World-System I: Capitalist Agriculture and the Origins of the European World-Economy in the Sixteenth Century* (London, 1974).

5. See A. G. Frank and B. K. Gills, eds., *The World System: From Five Hundred Years to Five Thousand Years* (London and New York, 1992); and Frank and Gills, "5,000 Years of World System History: The Cumulation of Accumulation," in *Precapitalist Core-Periphery Relations*, ed. C. Chase-Dunn and T. Hall (Boulder, 1991), 67–111.

6. There are superficial similarities between this argument and those of the "Eurasianists." These were a group of historians and geographers inspired by some of the writings of N. Ya. Danilevskii. Their "manifesto" was N. S. Trubetzkoy's emigre work, *Evropa i chelovechestvo* (Sofia, 1920), reprinted in N. S. Trubetzkoy, *The Legacy of Genghis Khan, and Other Essays on Russia's Identity*, ed. A. Liberman, Michigan Slavic Materials (Ann Arbor, 1992).

7. However, R. P. Lindner has argued that at least during the era of pastoral nomadism, the Carpathians marked a very clear ecological border. See his "Nomadism, Horses and Huns," *Past and Present* 92 (1981): 3–19.

8. R. Taagepera, "An Overview of the Growth of the Russian Empire," in *Russian Colonial Expansion to 1917*, ed. M. Rywkin (London and New York, 1988), 4–5. The largest empire ever created was the British empire, but it lasted only slightly longer than the Türk empire of the sixth century.

9. Taagepera, "An Overview," 6, and graph on p. 5.

10. N. Ya. Danilevskii, *Rossiya i Evropa. Vzglyad na kul'turnye i politicheskie otnosheniya Slavyanskogo mira k Germano-Romanskomu*, 5th ed. (St. Petersburg, 1895), 56–57; cited from Mark Bassin, "Russia between Europe and Asia: The Ideological Construction of Geographical Space," *Slavic Review* 50 (1991): 10.

11. See E. N. Chernykh, *Ancient Metallurgy in the USSR: The Early Metal Age* (Cambridge, 1992), 215–32.

12. I use some of Mackinder's ideas and categories, but my argument differs from his in many ways. The best introduction to Mackinder's writings is his *Democratic Ideals and Reality*, ed. A. J. Pearce (New York, 1962).

13. R. N. Taaffe, "The Geographic Setting," in *The Cambridge History of Early Inner Asia*, ed. Sinor, 35.

14. See A. G. Frank, *The Centrality of Central Asia* (Amsterdam, 1992); and H. J. Mackinder, "The Geographical Pivot of History," *Geographical Journal* 23 (1904): 421–37.

15. W. H. McNeill, *The Rise of the West* (Chicago, 1963), 295.

16. Christopher Beckwith, *The Tibetan Empire in Central Asia* (Princeton, 1987), 178–79.

17. The pioneering study of the epidemiological unification of Eurasia is W. H. McNeill, *Plagues and People* (Garden City, N.Y., 1976). J. L. Abu-Lughod describes the pivotal role of the Mongol empire in the thirteenth-century world-system in *Before European Hegemony: The World System, A.D. 1250–1350* (New York, 1989).

18. An allusion to the title of Eric Wolf's superb *Europe and the People without History* (Berkeley, 1982).

PATRICK MANNING

Migrations of Africans to the Americas
The Impact on Africans, Africa, and the New World

The movement of Africans to the Americas from the seventeenth to the nine-teenth centuries may be accounted as mankind's second-largest transoceanic migration. This migration, along with the concurrent African migration to the Middle East and North Africa, was distinct from other major modern migrations in its involuntary nature, and in the high rates of mortality and social dislocation caused by the methods of capture and transportation. A related migratory pat-tern, the capture and settling of millions of slaves within Africa, grew up in eigh-teenth- and nineteenth-century Africa as a consequence of the two patterns of overseas slave trade.

These three dimensions to the enslavement of Africans — which I have elsewhere labelled as the Occidental, Oriental, and African slave trades — were interrelated, so that there are advantages to treating them as an ensemble.[1] At the same time, my purpose here is to focus on migration to the Americas, where Africans interacted with native American inhabitants and with European set-tlers. This paper is therefore divided into three sections, considering the migra-tion of Africans to the Americas first in an American perspective, then in an African perspective, and finally in a global perspective including the Americas, Africa, and the Atlantic.

To simplify the presentation, I have restricted the quantitative data to the period from 1600 to 1800. The earlier slave trade, before 1600, was quantitatively small but socially significant. The later slave trade, after 1800, was large and sig-nificant, bringing nearly three million slaves (roughly one fourth of the total) to the Americas; African captives reached the shores of Cuba and Brazil into the late 1860s.[2] Still, the patterns I describe below for the period 1600–1800 apply, in large measure, to the entire period of the Atlantic slave trade.

Patrick Manning, "Migrations of Africans to the Americas: The Impact on Africans, Africa, and the New World," *The History Teacher* 26 (May 1993): 279–96.

THE AMERICAN PERSPECTIVE

David Eltis posed, in a 1983 article, a striking contrast in the population history of the Americas.[3] By 1820, there had been about 8.4 million African immigrants to the Americas, and 2.4 million European immigrants. But by that date the Euro-American population of some 12 million exceeded the Afro-American population of about 11 million. The rates of survival and reproduction of African immigrants were, apparently, dramatically lower than those of European immigrants. Eltis's contrast drew attention to the range of demographic comparisons necessary to make sense of this puzzle: the rates of fertility and mortality, the timing and location of immigration, the sex ratios and the social identification of persons.

The table below shows estimated numbers of immigrants from Africa up to 1800, by the region to which they immigrated. These figures, despite their apparent precision, are very rough indeed: they involve a number of assumptions, extrapolations and interpolations, including the inevitable confusion between numbers of slaves exported from Africa and imported to the Americas. As a result, all the figures, and particularly the smaller ones, must be seen as having margins of error of perhaps twenty percent. Nonetheless, they are worth presenting for the clear patterns they reveal. The table accounts for a total of about 7.6 million immigrant slaves up to 1800; nearly three million more slaves would arrive, principally to Brazil and Cuba, during the nineteenth century.[4]

To display some of the immigration data in schematic form, I have prepared Figure 1, which gives estimates, for various regions of the Americas, of the

African Immigrants, by Period and Place of Arrival (All figures in thousands of persons.)					
Region	to 1600	1600– 1640	1640– 1700	1700– 1760	1760– 1800
North America (Br, Fr, Sp)	—	1	20	171	177
Caribbean — non-Spanish	—	9	454	1623	1809
British Caribbean	—	8	255	900	1085
French Caribbean	—	1	155	474	573
Other Caribbean	—	—	44	249	151
Spanish America	75	269	186	271	235
Spanish Caribbean	7	20	14	27	140
Mexico & Central America	23	70	48	13	5
Venezuela-Colombia-Peru	45	135	93	160	60
La Plata-Bolivia	—	44	30	71	30
Brazil	50	160	400	960	726
Total	125	439	1060	3025	2947
Annual average, in thousands	1	11	18	50	70

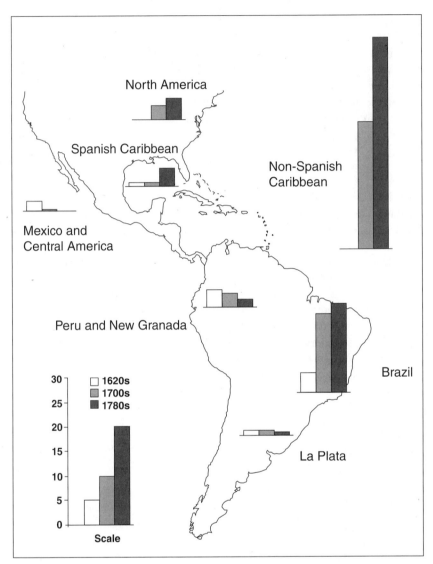

Figure 1.
Immigrants from Africa (1620s, 1700s, 1780s), in thousands per decade.

numbers of African immigrants in the 1620s (before North European entry into the trade), in the 1700s (once the Caribbean sugar trade had become fully established and the prices of African slaves had risen sharply), and in the 1780s (at the height of the Atlantic slave trade).

The figure, while it indicates the wide geographical distribution of African slaves throughout the Americas, also emphasizes their concentration in the English and French Caribbean. There, on the sugar plantations of the eighteenth century, over three million slaves were consigned to oblivion. The African-descended population of the Caribbean is today about twenty-five million, or less than a fifth of the more than one hundred and fifty million people of African descent in the Americas.

The migratory history of African slaves, once they landed in the Americas, sometimes continued for several further stages. The initial period of seasoning can be considered as migration through a change in status. Further, many slaves were physically transshipped, often over considerable distances. Slaves brought by the Dutch to Curaçao and by the English to Jamaica were transshipped to Cartagena, Portobelo, and on to various Spanish colonies. From Cartagena, some slaves were settled down in Colombia. A large number of slaves went to Portobelo in Panama, walked overland, and then went by sea to Lima. Most remained there, but some went into the highlands. Slaves landed in the Rio de La Plata went overland for 900 kilometers to Tucuman and then on for another 600 kilometers to the silver mines at Potosi. In Brazil, with the gold rush in Minas Gerais at the turn of the eighteenth century, slaves were sent overland to the mining areas, 300 kilometers from Rio and a much longer distance overland from Bahia. Slaves entering the Chesapeake and South Carolina came, in significant proportion, after stopping in Barbados. A final stage in the migration of some slaves was their liberation — either by emancipation, by self-purchase, or by escape.

One reason for emphasizing the number of distinct stages in the migration of Africans is to draw attention to the distinct rates of mortality and fertility at each stage. The mortality which is best known is that of the Atlantic crossing. (Crude mortality rates averaged about fifteen percent per voyage. While slave voyages averaged from two to three months in length, mortality is usually calculated on an annual basis. If slaves had encountered Middle Passage conditions for a full year, their mortality rate might have come to over five hundred per thousand per year. We will return below to Middle Passage mortality.) The point here is that slaves who survived the crossing had then to undergo various other types of elevated mortality: that of further travel within the Americas, that of seasoning in the locale where they were settled, and that of daily existence in slave status, where mortality was generally higher than for equivalent persons of free status. To this list must be added the fact that most slaves were settled in low-lying tropical areas where the general level of mortality was greater than in higher, temperate regions.

Fertility rates were generally lower for populations of slave status than for free populations. Fertility rates for slaves in the course of transportation, while not recorded in any detail, were certainly at an exceptionally low level. Most studies on fertility of African-American populations have focused, as is traditional and simplest, on the fertility of women. But because of the large excess of men among immigrant Africans, and because they did have children not only with African women but also with Indian and European women, there is an argument for more systematic consideration of the fertility of male Africans and African-Americans than has been undertaken thus far.[5]

A thorough accounting of the migration of Africans to the Americas would include the regional African origins — even the ethnic origins, age and sex distribution — of those disembarking in each American region. Such an accounting could now be estimated, based on recently developed evidence, though I will not attempt such an estimate here. In this regard, it is perhaps of interest that in recent years, and especially for the eighteenth and nineteenth centuries, scholars have given more attention to regional breakdowns and global synthesis in migratory movements on the African side of the Atlantic than to the equivalent details of immigration to the Americas.[6]

To give but two of the many examples that could be given of the specificity and change in African origins of American populations: In Louisiana, the initial slave population settled by the French in the early eighteenth century drew heavily on Bambara men from the upper Niger valley. This male slave population maintained and passed on its traditions because the Bambara men married Native American women, also enslaved. After 1770, the larger number of slaves entering Louisiana under Spanish rule was dominated by slaves from the Bight of Benin, including a large minority of women; these slaves brought the religion of vodoun to Louisiana. Second, while slaves from Congo and Angola were numerous among those imported to all regions of the Americas, they were virtually the only slaves imported to Rio de Janeiro from the seventeenth into the nineteenth century. The black populations of Rio, and to a lesser extent of Minas Gerais, had a degree of cultural homogeneity unusual for slaves in the Americas.[7]

The debates of the 1960s and 1970s focused on the total number of slaves crossing the Atlantic, and obscured questions of the distribution of African migrants over time, by age and by sex. The steady assemblage of slave trade data is permitting these issues to be addressed in increasing detail, and clear patterns have now come to light (Figure 2). With the passage of time from the seventeenth to the nineteenth centuries, the proportion of adult male slaves shipped increased slightly, the proportion of adult female slaves shipped decreased significantly, and the proportion of children shipped, both male and female, increased over time.[8]

For slave men, women, and children, the rate of labor force participation was generally high, as compared to free populations. Most of the work of slaves could be categorized into the occupations of mining, plantation work, artisanal work, transport, and domestic service. In Spanish America, slaves were concentrated most visibly in mining and artisanal work until the late eighteenth century, when sugar and tobacco plantation work began to dominate Cuba while slavery declined elsewhere. In Brazil, sugar plantation work dominated the sixteenth and seventeenth centuries, while mining work expanded greatly in the eighteenth century. The English and French Caribbean focused on sugar production, though coffee and livestock occupied significant numbers of slaves. Tobacco production occupied large numbers of slaves in Bahia and North America; cotton production expanded from the 1760s in Maranhão, and later in North America.

The rise to profitability of this succession of industries seems to have provided the main "pull" factor driving the movement of slaves to the Americas from Africa. The demand for sugar workers in sixteenth-century Brazil, the seventeenth-century Caribbean and nineteenth-century Cuba brought a supply response from Africa. Similarly, the demand for mine workers in eighteenth-

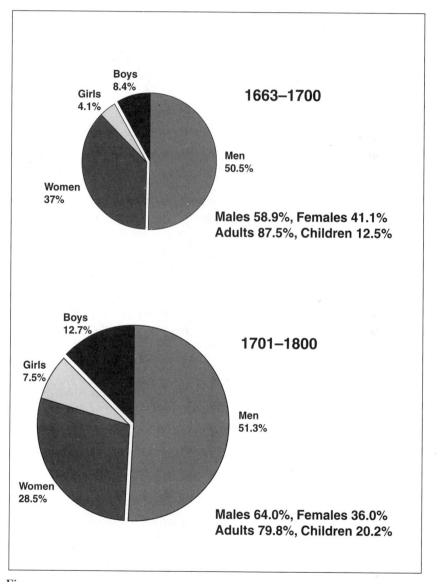

Figure 2.

African immigrants by age and sex, seventeenth and eighteenth centuries (source: Eltis and Engerman).

century Minas Gerais and New Granada brought an African response. Overall, the African and African-descended population of the Americas grew steadily through the seventeenth and eighteenth centuries, though it went into decline for as much as several decades whenever and wherever the import of additional slaves came to a halt.

THE AFRICAN PERSPECTIVE

From the standpoint of the African continent, the slave trade to the Americas interacted with other migratory movements, including slave trading within Africa. Before the seventeenth century, sub-Saharan African societies lacked the powerful states and the lucrative trade routes necessary to support an extensive system of slavery, so that slavery in Africa was almost everywhere a marginal institution. The exceptions were the large states of the Saharan fringe, notably Songhai. The trade in slaves to Saharan oases, to North Africa and West Asia took an estimated ten thousand persons per year in the sixteenth century. The oceanic slave trade from Africa in the sixteenth century was dominated by the movement of slaves to Europe and to such Atlantic islands as the Canaries and São Thome.

By the mid-seventeenth century the migration of slaves to Europe and the Atlantic islands had declined sharply, and the trans-Atlantic trade had expanded to the point where it exceeded the volume of the Saharan trade. The expansion of the Occidental trade brought, as a by-product, the development of an African trade: growth in slave exports led to the creation of expanded networks of slave supply, and these permitted wealthy Africans to buy slaves in unprecedented numbers.

In the eighteenth century, the continued expansion of the Occidental trade brought a substantial growth in the African trade, particularly as female slaves were held within African societies. The effects of this slave trade were felt mostly in West Africa and West Central Africa. Then, late in the eighteenth century, the slave trade expanded to much of Eastern Africa. Occidental merchants began purchasing slaves from Mozambique. Growing Middle Eastern demand for slaves (occasioned by an apparent growth in Middle Eastern economies that is still not well explained) led to expansion of the slave trade in modern Sudan, the Horn, and the Indian Ocean coast of Africa. Expanded slave exports in turn stimulated the development of enslavement within Eastern Africa, a development which accelerated sharply during the nineteenth century.[9] These general movements provide the context for the examples of African emigration to the Americas given in Figure 3.

The movement of so many slaves to the African coast for export entailed large-scale capture and migration. Distances for the movement of slaves to the coast could be small (an average of less than 100 kilometers for the large number of slaves from the Bight of Benin in the early eighteenth century), or they could be immense (some 600 kilometers for the Bambara slaves from West Africa who formed the nucleus of the Louisiana slave population; similar distances for slaves of the Lunda who passed through Angola on their way to Rio). These distances, travelled slowly and over long periods, brought elevated mortality with them.

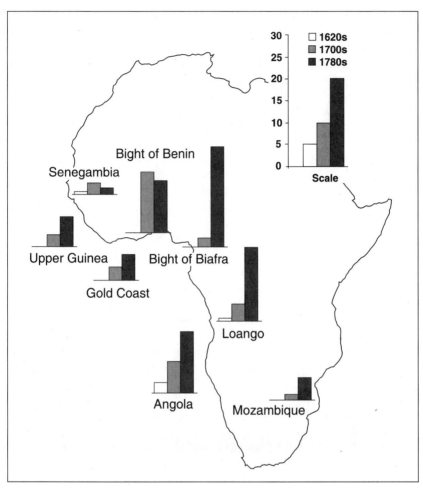

Figure 3.
African emigrants to the Americas (1620s, 1700s, 1780s), in thousands per decade.

Overall, then, the mortality of slaves within Africa was high, and their fertility was low. The considerations summarized above, with regard to the fertility and mortality of slaves in the Americas as they passed through transportation, seasoning, slave life and occasional liberation, apply in equivalent terms to the roughly equal numbers of persons in slave status at the same time in Africa. It must be emphasized that the high levels of mortality applied not only to the slaves delivered to the coast to be exported across the Atlantic; but to the nearly equal number of persons (most of them female) captured, transported to distant areas, and purchased as slaves within Africa.

This grim tale of slave mortality is not the whole of the story, of course, in that the purpose of the slave trade was to deliver live workers to the purchasers.

We should therefore mention, at least, the economic network developed for supply of the trade in Africa. Considerable labor and investment were required to provide transport, finance, food, clothing, lodging, guards, and medicine for the slaves. These systems of slave delivery, though they differed from region to region, became a significant element in the African economic landscape.[10]

The slaves held within Africa, numerous though they were, did not become readily visible to outside observers until the nineteenth century. This was because, along the western coast of Africa, most eighteenth-century slaves were women: they were held within families, and their productivity was mainly aimed at expanding the family economy. However, the Scottish explorer Mungo Park, travelling in the Senegal and Niger valleys at the end of the eighteenth century, found large proportions of the population to be held in slavery.[11] He encountered a type of economic system that was to spread widely through the continent in the nineteenth century. Adult males as well as females were held in slavery in large numbers, and slave men and women now tended to live apart from their masters as a slave class; their productivity was focused on marketable commodities. These included such African exports as palm oil, peanuts and coffee, but were more focused on yams, grains and cotton for the domestic market.

The evidence of transformation in African economic life through the expansion of slavery gives some hint of the accompanying social and ideological changes. Classes of merchants and monarchs rose with the export trade, and classes of landowners rose with the nineteenth-century growth of market-oriented slavery. Values emphasizing hierarchy arose in the societies holding and trading in slaves; egalitarian values were reaffirmed in societies resisting enslavement.[12]

The most obvious "push" factors sending African slaves across the Atlantic were war and famine. The savanna areas of marginal rainfall — Angola and the grasslands extending from Senegambia east to Cameroon — underwent periodic drought and famine, and in these times desperate families sold both children and adults.[13] The relation between warfare and enslavement is in one sense obvious, but on the other hand there have been two centuries of debate over whether the African wars broke out for purely domestic reasons, or whether the European demand for slaves stimulated additional wars.

Overall, the export of slaves from Africa halted and then reversed growth of the continent's population. During the seventeenth century, such population decline took place in restricted areas of coastal Senegambia, Upper Guinea and Angola. After about 1730, the decline became general for the coast from Senegal to Angola, and continued to about 1850. The decline was slow rather than precipitous. Even though the number of slaves exported averaged little more than three per thousand of the African regional population, and even though the trade took more males than females, the combination of the mortality of capture and transportation with the concentration of captures on young adults meant that Africa lost enough young women to reverse an intrinsic growth rate of five per thousand. The same processes transformed the structure of the population, causing the adult sex ratio to decline to an average of 80 men per 100 women.[14]

A GLOBAL PERSPECTIVE

Despite — indeed, because of — the immigration of Europeans and Africans, the total population of the Americas declined in the sixteenth and seventeenth centuries. While estimates of the pre-Columbian populations must remain speculative, the population of the Americas fell to perhaps as little as five million persons during the seventeenth century.[15]

The threatened void of population in the Americas encouraged the transformation of African slavery from a marginal institution to a central element in a global system of population and labor. The global market for slaves encompassed the Americas, Africa, the Indian Ocean and Western Asia in the eighteenth and nineteenth centuries; it interacted more broadly with the regimes of population and labor in the Americas, Europe and Western Asia. When slave prices rose sharply (as they did at the turn of the eighteenth century) or fell significantly (as they did in the eastern hemisphere in the early nineteenth century), slave laborers were moved in new directions in response to economic incentives. Free workers on every continent moved, similarly, in response to these changes in the value of labor.

Before 1600, African migration to the Americas, while it may have exceeded European migration, was small in magnitude. During the time when the Indian population was declining but still large, Africans in the Americas, while usually in slave status, were nonetheless often persons of relatively high value, serving in the military and in artisanal tasks. In Brazil, large-scale enslavement of Indians for work on sugar plantations characterized the late sixteenth century. African laborers, concentrated at first in the skilled occupations on the plantations, gradually displaced the disappearing Indians at all levels of work.

In the seventeenth century, the scarcity of Indian laborers made Africans appear, by comparison, more plentiful. Still, for much if not all of the century, the addition of African and European immigrants and their progeny was insufficient to offset the decline in Indian population.

By the eighteenth century, all the major population groups — those of Indian, European, African, and mestizo or mulatto ancestry — were growing, though from a very sparse base. However, in this period the large-scale removal of Africans from their homes to serve as slaves in the Americas, with all its attendant carnage, brought population decline for region after region in Africa, and finally for the western African coast as a whole. Consequently, the African addition to the population of the Americas (both by immigration and by natural reproduction) was insufficient to make up for the loss of population in Africa.

The centrality of African labor was costly to the slaves, and was costly in the longer run to their societies of origin. In the eighteenth and nineteenth centuries the populations of Europe, the Americas and Asia grew at unprecedented rates, apparently as a result of improved immunities, certain social changes, and perhaps improved public health conditions. In the nineteenth century these rapidly growing populations spun off millions of migrants, who searched near and far for the means to make a better living. For Africa, in contrast, the population remained stagnant or in decline, and labor migration mostly took place, even within the continent, by the forcible means which interfered with population growth.

If we link the American pull and African push factors noted above, we find that they do not yet cohere into a full theory for the migration. Three main factors have been advanced, by different groups of scholars, to explain the migration more generally. The first factor is epidemiology: the relative immunity of Africans to the diseases of the tropics enabled them to survive at a greater rate than Americans or Europeans. Hence they were more valuable and more sought after as plantation laborers. Second is relative productivity. Given the technical limits of African hoe agriculture in comparison to the more productive plow agriculture of Europeans, even a highly productive laborer in Africa could not produce as much food as an ordinary laborer in Europe. In these terms, the value or price of a European laborer was greater than that of an African. European merchants, therefore, were able to buy slaves by paying Africans more than the value of an average laborer in Africa, yet bring laborers to the Americas that were far cheaper than European laborers. The third factor is transportation costs. When Africans sought to buy goods on the world market, they had to offer local goods in exchange. Such export goods needed a high ratio of value to weight, or the high costs of transportation would consume all profits. Africa did export gold, but lacked minerals in many regions; African textiles and art work were not recognized as luxury goods overseas. Slaves were the next most valuable commodity, and so they came to dominate Africa's export trade. (In the nineteenth century, as transportation became more inexpensive, Africans turned steadily from the slave trade to exporting peanuts, palm oil and other agricultural commodities.)[16] The prices of slaves reflect the sum of these three factors, and perhaps others as well. Slave prices, however, have yet to be studied in a fully comparative and comprehensive fashion. We may hope that further studies will reveal more of the relative dominance and the interplay of these three factors — or, more simply, more of the reasons why the slave trade continued so long.

One way to signal the cost to Africa of this sort of participation in the world economy is to estimate the number of persons who died in the Middle Passage. Since the mortality schedule for the Middle Passage was somewhere between five and ten times higher than the normal mortality schedule, one is not too far off by saying that all the deaths taking place on slave ships would not otherwise have taken place. Rough estimates of the cumulative total of deaths at sea come to a total of sixty thousand for the period before 1600, three hundred thousand for the seventeenth century, a million for the eighteenth century, and half a million for the nineteenth century. To get the total excess mortality brought about by the slave trade, aside from that of the condition of slavery itself, one would have to add the deaths in the course of African capture and transportation, and those in the course of resettlement and seasoning in the Americas.[17]

On the other hand, we may choose to emphasize life rather than death. As of the mid-eighteenth century, when the population of the Americas had rebounded to perhaps as much as ten million, that total included roughly two million black slaves and another million free persons of color, with the latter concentrated in the Portuguese and Spanish territories. Two million free whites and five million Indians rounded out the total. The regional distribution included a million inhabitants in the Caribbean, the most densely populated area. North America and Brazil each had populations of roughly one and one-half million, and the Spanish mainland colonies had roughly five million inhabitants. The Americas grew rapidly in population during the eighteenth century, but trailed the Old World distantly. The population of sub-Saharan Africa totaled some fifty million persons, about twenty million of whom lived in the areas of the western coast of Africa from which slaves were dispatched across the Atlantic. Western Europe's population, far denser and in a smaller area, totaled roughly one hundred million.[18]

The European and African migrations to the Americas shared a number of characteristics in the seventeenth and eighteenth centuries. The migrants were dominantly male, and they suffered elevated levels of mortality. But several distinctions between European and African migration stand out. Africans had no pattern of return migration eastward across the Atlantic parallel to that of the Europeans, and Africans were not able to repatriate earnings to their home societies. Thus, while emigration strengthened the external trade of Africa, it did so with a weaker multiplier than that for Europe.[19] African migrants underwent an extra mortality cost in Africa and in the Middle Passage because of the violence of enslavement.

African rates of emigration were substantially higher than those of Europe. For the eighteenth century, the overall rate of emigration from the affected areas was three to four per thousand per year; this figure rose to as much as thirty per thousand per year for the Bight of Benin in the early eighteenth century. Since many more males than females left Africa, the sex ratio and marriage patterns on both sides of the Atlantic felt new pressures. In Africa, the relative surplus of adult women seems certain to have expanded the rate of polygynous marriage, and to have changed the sexual division of labor. In the Americas, very few men were able to have more than one wife, and many were unable to find a mate. This suggests a further contrast between African and European migrants: European males, because of their higher social status, had a wider range of choices of women among European, African and Indian populations, and were thus more likely to have offspring than African men.

To return to the puzzle posed by David Eltis, we can now recapitulate, though not yet in rank order, the factors responsible for the differential growth in American populations of European and African origin. Africans went in larger proportion to the high-mortality areas, the tropical lowlands. They arrived later than Europeans, on average, so that those populations which did become self-sustaining had less time to grow.[20] In addition, the condition of slavery increased the mortality and reduced the fertility of African immigrants. Finally, it may well be that the populations known as "white" and "mestizo" today include larger components of African and Indian ancestry than is now realized.

The transatlantic migration of slaves brought a rich African contribution to the culture of the Americas — in religion, cuisine, dress, language and philosophy. In language the African impact can be seen in two main ways. First is in the development of Creole languages, such as Haitian Creole, Jamaican Patois, Papiamento of the Dutch West Indies, and Gullah of South Carolina. In these languages the vocabulary is both European and African, and the grammar is mostly African. Haitian Kreyol is now a written official language of the country, and the similar Creole of the French Antilles is becoming the leading language of a new wave of multicultural music. Second is the impact of African speech on English, Spanish, French, and Portuguese as spoken in the Americas. The single biggest reason for the differences in these languages on the two sides of the Atlantic is the contribution of African expressions in the Americas.

These and other cultural patterns of the migration can be looked at in two ways. The first is in terms of survivals: that is, the continuity of West African religion in the vodoun of Haiti, or of West African cuisine in the gumbo or hot barbecue sauce of the American South. But we can also see African contributions to New World culture in patterns of change and innovation. Here the obvious example is in jazz music, which by definition is always in change, but where the rules for musical innovation can be traced back to Africa.

In addition to the heritage from Africa, the heritage of slavery created distinct patterns of community for Africans in the Americas. Other immigrants, arriving as free persons, had the opportunity to establish their own communities, in which people of similar linguistic and cultural background built up strong local units, usually maintaining some contact with the homeland — these ranged from Swiss farming towns in the American Midwest to Cantonese merchant communities to rural Japanese communities in Brazil. African communities in the Americas were largely prevented from recreating their home societies in this way because they were not free to move, and people of varying ethnic groups were often mixed purposely by their owners to reduce solidarity. As a result, inhabitants of African settlements in the Americas tended to refer back to Africa in general rather than to particular African regions, they thought of a romanticized African past rather than of the latest news because they were cut off from home, and they constructed a new, creolized culture out of the traditions available to them rather than maintain the traditions of a particular Old World region. Quite logically, therefore, the idea of the unity of Africa grew up in the Americas.

Most of the slaves died early and without progeny. In the Americas, much of their produce was exported, consumed and soon forgotten. Still, we can find ample remains of the investments of slaves in the construction of cities and the clearing of farms. I want to give particular emphasis to the value of the work done by African slaves — in the Americas, in Africa, and in the Orient — because the tradition of racist ideology in the last 150 years has done so much to deny their importance in constructing the world we live in, as well as to deny that the underdevelopment of Africa resulted in part from their forced migration. The very term, "Western Civilization," which we use to describe the continents of Europe, North and sometimes South America, reflects this denial of Africa's role in the modern world. The term carries with it the implication that the wealth and the achievement of these continents springs solely from the heritage of Europe. The migration I have discussed above is one of many ways to demonstrate that there is more to the modern world than the expansion of Europe.

Notes

1. Patrick Manning, *Slavery and African Life: Occidental, Oriental, and African Slave Trades* (Cambridge, 1990).

2. For two excellent studies of early slavery, see Frederick Bowser, *The African Slave in Colonial Peru, 1524–1650* (Stanford, 1971); and Colin Palmer, *Slaves of the White God: Blacks in Mexico, 1570–1650* (Cambridge, Mass., 1976). The fullest quantitative study of nineteenth-century Atlantic slave trade is David Eltis, *Economic Growth and the Ending of the Transatlantic Slave Trade* (New York, 1987). For a survey of the abolition of the slave trade and slavery in the Americas and in Africa, see Manning, *Slavery*, 149–67. For an important review of recent literature contrasting the experiences of Atlantic Africa and Islamic Africa, see Janet J. Ewald, "Slavery in Africa and the Slave Trades from Africa," *American Historical Review* 97 (1992): 465–85.

3. David Eltis, "Free and Coerced Transatlantic Migrations: Some Comparisons," *American Historical Review* 88 (1983): 278.

4. The main sources for the table are Philip D. Curtin, *The Atlantic Slave Trade: A Census* (Madison, 1969); Paul E. Lovejoy, "The Volume of the Atlantic Slave Trade: A Synthesis," *Journal of African History* 23 (1983): 473–501; and David Richardson, "Slave Exports from West and West-Central Africa, 1700–1810: New Estimates of Volume and Distribution," *Journal of African History* 30 (1989): 1–22. On the distribution of slaves within Spanish America, I used Enriqueta Vila Vilar, *Hispanoamérica y el comercio de esclavos* (Seville, 1977); Herbert S. Klein, *African Slavery in Latin America and the Caribbean* (New York, 1986); Marisa Vega Franco, *El tráfico de esclavos con América (Asientos de Grillo y Lomelin, 1663–1674)* (Seville, 1984); and Colin Palmer, *Human Cargoes: The British Slave Trade to Spanish America, 1700–1739* (Urbana, 1981).

Despite the error margins, one may seek and may hope to find further detail: various scholars are coding up records ship by ship, which may give us immigration in decennial or even annual terms, showing African region of origin, the carrying nation, the age and sex composition of the slave cargo, and their rates of morbidity and mortality during the voyage.

5. The changing terms by which populations identify themselves provide writers with repeated challenges. In this presentation, I have used the term "Africans" to refer to those born in Africa, "African-Americans" to refer to persons of African descent born in the Americas, and "Indians" to refer to native American peoples of South and Central America, as I think the term "Native American" is used mainly by people of the U.S.

On fertility rates of slave and free persons, see Stanley L. Engerman and B. W. Higman, "The Demographic Structure of the Caribbean Slave Societies in the Eighteenth and Nineteenth Centuries," forthcoming in Franklin W. Knight, ed. *UNESCO General History of the Caribbean*, vol. 3.

6. Richardson, "Slave Exports"; Manning, *Slavery and African Life*; Joseph C. Miller, *Way of Death: Merchant Capitalism and the Angolan Slave Trade, 1730–1830* (Madison, 1988); David Geggus, "Sex Ratio, Age and Ethnicity in the Atlantic Slave

Trade: Data from French Shipping and Plantation Records," *Journal of African History* 30 (1989), 23–44; Paul Lovejoy, "The Impact of the Atlantic Slave Trade on Africa: A Review of the Literature," *Journal of African History* 30 (1989): 365–94. The exception, for the nineteenth century, is the work of David Eltis which has addressed both sides of the Atlantic. See his *Economic Growth and the Ending of the Transatlantic Slave Trade* (New York, 1987), and "The Nineteenth-Century Transatlantic Slave Trade: An Annual Time Series of Imports into the Americas Broken Down by Region," *Hispanic American Historical Review* 67 (1987): 109–38.

7. Gwendolyn Hall, *Africans in Colonial Louisiana; The Development of Afro-Creole Culture in the Eighteenth Century* (Baton Rouge, 1992); Miller, *Way of Death.*

8. David Eltis and Stanley L. Engerman, "Was the Slave Trade Dominated by Men?" *Journal of Interdisciplinary History* 23 (1992): 237–57. For early statements of the importance of age and sex distribution in the slave trade, see John Thornton, "The Slave Trade in Eighteenth Century Angola: Effects of Demographic Structures," *Canadian Journal of African Studies* 14 (1980): 417–27; and Patrick Manning, "The Enslavement of Africans: A Demographic Model," *Canadian Journal of African Studies* 15 (1981): 499–526.

9. Gervase Clarence-Mathew, ed., *The Economics of the Indian Ocean Slave Trade in the Nineteenth Century* (London, 1988).

10. Miller, *Way of Death,* 173–283; David Northrup, *Trade Without Rulers: Precolonial Economic Development in South-Eastern Nigeria* (Oxford, 1978), 69–76.

11. Mungo Park, *Travels.*

12. These generalizations are explored in Manning. *Slavery and African Life,* 118–25, 131–41.

13. Joseph C. Miller, "The Significance of Drought, Disease and Famine in the Agriculturally Marginal Zone of West-Central Africa," *Journal of African History* 22 (1982): 17–61; Charles Becker, "Notes sur les conditions écologiques en Sénégambie au 17e et 18e siècles," *African Economic History* 14 (1985): 167–216.

14. Manning, *Slavery and African Life,* 72.

15. For a dependable review of the complex issues in estimating populations of early Spanish America, see Noble David Cook, *Demographic Collapse: Indian Peru, 1520–1620* (Cambridge, 1981).

16. Philip D. Curtin, "Epidemiology and the Slave Trade," *Political Science Quarterly* 83 (1968): 190–216; Manning, *Slavery and African Life,* 30–37; Stefano Fenoaltea, *The Atlantic Slave Trade: An Economic Analysis,* forthcoming from Princeton University Press.

17. Estimates of cumulative Middle Passage mortality are 15 percent of the export figures given in Lovejoy, "Volume of the Atlantic Slave Trade," 478. For an estimated mortality schedule for the Atlantic crossing, see Patrick Manning and William S. Griffiths, "Divining the Unprovable: Simulating the Demography of the Atlantic Slave Trade," *Journal of Interdisciplinary History* 19 (1988).

One important disadvantage of cumulative demographic totals such as this — whether it be for those who reached the Americas or for those who died on the way — is that they do not have a dimension of time (except that of per century), and are thus difficult to compare to standard stocks and annual flows of population.

18. On estimated mid-eighteenth-century population in the Americas, see Engerman and Higman, "Demographic Structure"; Angel Rosenblat, *La población indígena y el mestizaje en América* (Buenos Aires, 1950); Dauril Alder, "The Population of Brazil in the Late Eighteenth Century: A Preliminary Survey," *Hispanic American Historical*

Review 43 (1963): 191, 196; Klein, *African Slavery in Latin America*. On Africa, see Manning, *Slavery and African Life*.

19. In this regard, it would be of interest to compare the imports of Africa and of Europe in the seventeenth and eighteenth centuries, and to learn of their relative composition in luxury goods, general consumer goods, money, and goods useful in investment.

20. From the vantage point of the twentieth century, this comparison is reversed. Because so many European immigrants arrived in the late nineteenth and twentieth centuries, it is now the case that the ancestors of the average European-American arrived in the New World more recently than the ancestors of the average African-American.

Selected Bibliography

Adshead, S. A. M. *Central Asia in World History*. New York: St. Martin's Press, 1993. A discerning introduction to the history of Inner Asia as the bridge, at least from the Mongol conquests to the mid-seventeenth century, which linked together all the citied regions of Eurasia and made possible a remarkable degree of economic, cultural, and biological unification before the modern technological revolution.

Bentley, Jerry H. "Hemispheric Integration, 500–1500 C.E." *Journal of World History* 9 (Fall 1998): 237–54. Further elaboration of themes introduced in his 1993 book *Old World Encounters*. Recent research on long-distance commercial, biological, and cultural interchange in the millennium before Columbus reveals far more extensive integration among peoples of Afro-Eurasia than "modernocentric" historians have been willing to recognize.

Chaudhuri, K. N. *Trade and Civilization in the Indian Ocean: An Economic History from the Rise of Islam to 1750*. Cambridge: Cambridge University Press, 1985. The author tests Fernand Braudel's approach and methodology by applying it to the history of the Indian Ocean basin and its diverse peoples. The result is an immensely rich study and a validation of interregional analysis as the most sensible way to understand large-scale economic change in that part of the world. This book is a run-up to Chaudhuri's wider-ranging and more theoretically oriented study *Asia before Europe* (see Part Three Selected Bibliography).

Christian, David. *A History of Russia, Central Asia and Mongolia*. Vol. 1, *Inner Asia from Prehistory to the Mongol Empire*. Oxford: Blackwell, 1998. The author elaborates in full detail his conception of Inner Asia as a coherent unit of historical investigation. This is the first volume of a projected two-volume work in the Blackwell History of the World series edited by R. L. Moore. Christian sums up his main themes in the question: "How did the ecological conditions of Inner Asia affect the relationship between lifeways and social structures, and the ways both lifeways and social structures evolved in this region?"

Curtin, Philip D. *The Rise and Fall of the Plantation Complex: Essays in Atlantic History*. Cambridge: Cambridge University Press, 1990. Like *Cross-Cultural Trade in World History*, this book is a product of Curtin's long career of innovative teaching in comparative world history. An excellent vehicle for introducing students to the birth of the Atlantic economy and to one of modern history's abiding puzzles: Why did the accumulation of riches in the Atlantic world rest so heavily on the forced transport of millions of Africans thousands of miles from their homes?

Dunn, Ross E. "The Challenge of Hemispheric History (1000–1500 A.D.)." *The History Teacher* 18 (May 1985): 329–38. A call to teachers to explore more seriously the conceptual possibilities of the Afro-Eurasian intercommunicating zone, or ecumene, as a superregional unit of analysis. Textbooks fail to convey the significance of Islam's transhemispheric expansion between 1000 and 1500 because all treatment of Muslim civilization is squeezed into the conventional category "Middle East."

Fletcher, Joseph. "Integrative History: Parallels and Interconnections in the Early Modern Period, 1500–1800." *Journal of Turkish Studies* 9 (1985): 37–57. Discussion of seven "sub-surface trends and developments" that demonstrate global congruence after 1500. A strong argument for a unified history of Afro-Eurasia, which Fletcher might one day have written had he lived to synthesize his considerable knowledge.

Hodgson, Marshall G. S. *Rethinking World History: Essays on Europe, Islam, and World History.* Edited by Edmund Burke III. Cambridge: Cambridge University Press, 1993. When Hodgson died, he was still working on a full statement of his interregional framework for world history. In this volume Edmund Burke brings together most of Hodgson's published essays, plus three chapters of his unpublished work, "The Unity of World History." Burke's introduction and conclusion masterfully sum up Hodgson's remarkable global vision.

Jones, Eric, Lionel Frost, and Colin White. *Coming Full Circle: An Economic History of the Pacific Rim.* Boulder, Colo.: Westview Press, 1993. Focusing on long-term economic change, the book argues that the Pacific basin has come "full circle" from 1000 C.E., when China was the world's leading economic powerhouse, to the late twentieth century, when East Asian economies have surged again. Since the Pacific has until recent times had no integrated life of its own, the authors wisely do not attempt to write the sort of "histoire totale" that Braudel or Chadhuri did for their respective "rims." However, the discussion encompasses the southern Pacific region from South America and Australia, as well as the larger economies of the north.

Lewis, Martin W., and Kären Wigen. *The Myth of Continents: A Critique of Metageography.* Berkeley: University of California Press, 1997. Essential reading for world history teachers. The book breaks down and historicizes all the metageographical constructs, including the "seven continents," that have for so long set the rules for defining which historical problems were susceptible to investigation and which were not. The analysis of East, West, First World, Third World, Europe, Middle East, and so on draws on most of the social scientific disciplines, including the new literature of world history.

McPherson, Kenneth. *The Indian Ocean: A History of People and the Sea.* Delhi: Oxford University Press, 1993. An important book for teachers exploring the idea that the Indian Ocean has a history of its own. Emphasis on relationship between commercial and cultural interactions.

Özveren, Y. Eyüp. "A Framework for the Study of the Black Sea World, 1789–1915." *Review* 20 (Winter 1997): 77–113. The author argues that "an abstract comparison" of the Ottoman and Russian empires "as if they did not share a common geography will make us overlook the dynamic exchanges between them." A basin-centered analysis reveals the extent to which the Black Sea constituted an economic unit in this period despite continuous conflict and competition among states.

Thornton, John. *Africa and Africans in the Making of the Atlantic World, 1400–1800,* 2d ed. Cambridge: Cambridge University Press, 1998. Because this book explains persuasively and engagingly why Africans played the parts they did in the development of the Atlantic basin, it makes an excellent choice as supplemental reading for world history students. The second edition includes a new chapter on the eighteenth century.

PART FIVE

WORLD SYSTEMS AND WORLD HISTORY

The first volume of Immanuel Wallerstein's colossal study *The Modern World-System* appeared in 1974, about the same time that introductory world history courses were appearing on college campuses in sufficient numbers to be noticed. Wallerstein's thesis excited many world history novitiates. He argued that state and nation were the wrong units of analysis for understanding the inception of the modern capitalist age. Rather, a "world-system" of unequal economic relationships emerged in the sixteenth century, a system that superseded the "world empires" of premodern times and eventually encompassed the globe. This system was unlike any preceding one because it involved "a structural priority given and sustained for the *ceaseless* accumulation of capital."[1]

Wallerstein's schematic model depicted a world organized in three concentric circles: rich, powerful, and commercially innovative states at the center, which was Europe; "middling or intermediate" states in the semi-periphery; and poor, structurally dependent societies, some of them European colonies, in the outer ring. Wallerstein saw the world-system as evolving dynamically from the sixteenth century onward. The fundamental structure of relationships, however, has remained the same and explains the severe maldistribution of wealth and living standards in the world today. Wallerstein particularly challenged the "modernization theory" prevalent in the 1950s and 1960s, which was a progressivist way of looking at the global economy derived from traditional conceptions of Western nation-states as the makers of world history. By contrast, Wallerstein envisioned an early modern world united in a single process of comprehensive, systemic change, albeit one that produced drastically unequal relations of power and economic well-being.

The Modern World-System provoked a raucous academic debate, and one of the consequences was a rapid cooling of expectations that Wallerstein's model would provide an integrated framework for teaching world history. For one thing, the book could not practicably be assigned to first year college students unprepared for its dense exposition and Marxian-sociological vocabulary. At the conceptual level the book presented several problems. The model focused too heavily on economic and materialist history to appeal to instructors who preferred to accent cultural change. It offered too little scope to consider the historical initiatives and innovations of peoples outside Europe. It had little to say about global developments before 1500 C.E. And most troublesome of all, it retained a decidedly Europe-centered angle of vision on the spinning globe. Wallerstein's thesis made good copy for a lecture or two, especially as a counterpoint to modernization theory, but it was no magic bullet for world history teachers struggling with problems of choice, coherence, and thematic unity.

By the late 1980s, however, something interesting was happening. Scholars continued to debate, revise, modify, and enlarge upon the world systems approach. As a result, the term itself acquired broader, more flexible meanings. World historians began to apply the concept to dimensions of time and space and to spheres of human experience that were beyond what Wallerstein saw as crucial. Any phenomenon that involved human aggregates linking themselves together, consciously or not, across state, ethno-racial, or civilizational boundaries in relationships of cause and effect might potentially qualify as a world system. This wider, more pliable application of the concept has proved useful to world history teachers partly because the term signifies world-historical process rather than static cultural essence, and it offers a heuristic frame for exploring all sorts of developments not easily shoved into civilizational or national boxes.

"World system" has indeed proved a multifunctional tool. In *Before European Hegemony* (1989) Janet Abu Lughod nudged the inception of the world system back to the thirteenth century and improved on Hodgson's sketch of hemispheric interregional history by depicting a vast network of interlocking economic relationships that ultimately linked the Baltic to the North China Sea in the age of Mongol dominance. Andre Gunder Frank and Barry Gills then proceeded to up the ante, arguing for a "millennial world system" that came into being five thousand years ago. Numerous other scholars have applied the world system framework to the study of production and trade in ancient and medieval times. Moreover, criticism of the theory's Eurocentric bias has stimulated scholars to pay more attention than ever to evidence of Africans, Asians, and Latin Americans acting as independent historical agents rather than being mere casualties of a remorseless core-periphery machine for extraction and accumulation.

In recent years William McNeill has come round to the view that "world system," if the term is defined elastically, has more explanatory power than "civilization" at the macro-historical level. However, he would like to reconcile the two concepts by enclosing them together within the even broader category of "communications net." All interchange within villages, states, civilizations, or world systems depends on human ingenuity in devising means for traveling, transporting, signaling, and conversing. Therefore, the communications net is a good place to start when creating a structure for thinking about and teaching world history:

... markets and trade constituted only part of the communications network that crossed political, civilizational and linguistic boundaries. Soldiers and missionaries as well as refugees and wanderers also linked alien populations together, and carried information that sometimes altered local ways of life as profoundly as entry into market relationships did.

I conclude, therefore, that if the notion of a world system were tied more explicitly to a communications network and if more attention were paid to changes in that network as new means of transport and communication came into use, the notion of a "world system" would gain great clarity and power. Moreover, the polarity between the terms "civilization" and "world system" would disappear and the language of world-historians might gain greater precision if communications networks were to become the focus of attention.[2]

The fact is that the definition of world system has become notably *less* precise since Wallerstein first proposed it. Ironically, the concept's new-fashioned fuzziness probably commends it as a useful device for organizing a world history course.

In the first selection, excerpted from *The History Teacher* Craig Lockard, examines both the world system idea and the "modernization theory" that it aimed to supersede. He wrote this article in 1981 when the merits of Wallerstein's approach over the older model were still a subject of hot debate. As a covering explanation for the evolution of the world since 1500, modernization theory, which Cyril Black, Walter Rostow, and other scholars expounded in the 1950s and 1960s, no longer carries much intellectual weight. Lockard's comparison of world system and modernization theory, however, is still useful to teachers. There is no doubt that many young Americans continue to enter college professing vague opinions about the world being a better place if only the underdeveloped countries would pull themselves together and do what America did to achieve democracy and consumer prosperity. Which model offers a more convincing explanation of the present condition of the world — modernization theory, the world-system paradigm, or some modification of either? This is still an engaging topic for classroom debate.

For readers unfamiliar with Wallerstein's model, Lockard provides a concise summary of the leading ideas set forth in volume one of *The Modern World System*. I have chosen to represent Wallerstein in this volume with a brief statement he made in 1985 that raises questions about college teaching. These remarks appeared alongside essays by Philip Curtin, William McNeill, Kevin Reilly, and L. S. Stavrianos in a special section of *The History Teacher* titled, "What Is an Attainable Global Perspective for Undergraduates in History?" Wallerstein describes three "socially constructed" premises that he believes have informed history education since the nineteenth century. He recommends that students revisit these premises with a critical eye. He also proposes five new questions derived from his research on the world economy that should be incorporated into introductory history.

As Lockard tells us, the "*Annales* School" of historical method, particularly the work of Fernand Braudel, was one of the main intellectual currents that fed Wallersteinian theory. First formulated in France in 1929 with publication of the journal *Annales d'histoire économique et social*, the *Annaliste* approach has given world historians several important conceptual tools for macro-historical analysis. Though Braudel and other *Annaliste* pioneers, grounded as they were in the European historical and geographical tradition, drew mostly on documentary source material for that region, their mode of questioning lent itself to any regional or superregional investigation. Braudel's classic work, *The Mediterranean and the Mediterranean World in the Age of Philip II*, demonstrated that deep geographical and climatic structures, together with the invisible, magma-like flow of economic and social currents, have shaped the long-term course of human affairs more decisively than the actions of states, nations, and armies. Such a postulate leads inescapably to world history since sub-surface forces impelling change in human life over the long term are as identifiable and susceptible to analysis on the interregional and global level as they are within the relatively narrow bounds of Europe and the Mediterranean basin.

"Economies in Space" presents some excerpts from the opening chapter of *The Perspective of the World*, the third and final volume of Braudel's magisterial work, *Civilization and Capitalism: 15th–18th Century*. Here the author specifically addresses the idea of the world-economy (*with* hyphen) as a spatially bounded set of economic, and in Braudel's view, cultural relationships. The *Annaliste* School, with its preference for multi-layered historical description, cannot be casually lumped together with the world-systems scholars, who have been far more concerned with rigorous sociological argumentation. Even so, Braudel sets forth his theoretical ideas about historical space in terms that draw explicitly on *The Modern World System*, whose first volume had been published five years earlier. Both Braudel and Wallerstein assume Europe to be the early modern world's dynamic center, though in *Perspective* Braudel was clearly moving toward a more world-scale vision.

Andre Gunder Frank, whose concept of the "development of underdevelopment" as applied to Latin America influenced Wallerstein's work, has in recent years become a forceful spokesman for world history. He has written extensively on the subject, including the 1992 essay included here. At that time, Frank, in collaboration with Barry Gills, was developing the hypothesis that the world-system emerged neither in the sixteenth nor thirteenth century but in very ancient times. Frank has also expanded richly on Hodgson's idea that until the nineteenth century the center of gravity for production, trade, and innovation in Afro-Eurasia was not western Europe but a point much further east on the Eurasian land mass. In this regard Frank has parted ways with both Wallerstein and Braudel. In the article reprinted here he presents twenty "issues and theses" regarding the directions the world history field should consider taking.

Like both McNeill and Braudel, John Voll recommends that world historians consider a broader definition of "world system" to encompass cultural and ideological relations. In an article in the *Journal of World History* Voll exposes the inadequacy of the term "civilization" to characterize the network of cultural communication that linked Muslim communities all across Afro-Eurasia. He then proposes applying the "world-system" tool to this phenomenon, though in a different sense from the one Wallerstein intended. The Islamic world-system, Voll argues, was "built on the shared sources of the Islamic experience, which provide the basis for mutually intelligible discourse among all who identify themselves as Muslims within the Dar al-Islam." He views networks of colleges, peregrinating scholars, Sufi associations, and institutions of the pilgrimage — all of these intertwined with mercantile enterprise — as constituting a single trans-Hemispheric "community of discourse" whose evolution was itself a major development in world history. Combining the world-system idea with an interregional and supra-civilizational approach to Islam, he offers an integrated model for teaching Afro-Eurasian history, especially the period 1000 to 1800 C.E.

Notes

1. Immanuel Wallerstein, "World System Versus World Systems: A Critique," in *The World System: Five Hundred Years or Five Thousand,* ed. Andre Gunder Frank and Barry K. Gills (New York: Routledge, 1993), 293.

2. William H. McNeill, Foreword to Frank and Gills, *World System,* xii.

CRAIG A. LOCKARD

Global History, Modernization, and the World-System Approach

A Critique

While global historians seeking to comprehend trans-continental developments obviously find their most fertile material in the past five centuries or so, there is still, perhaps inevitably, great disagreement about the meaning and dimensions of early modern and modern history and of trans-regional and trans-societal interactions. Historians like McNeill and Stavrianos have laid a foundation for a new generation of global, macro-level, or comparative historians to build upon in order to raise our level of understanding, especially about the modern period of history. A number of scholars have searched for a principle or analytical tool on which to base a world-oriented study. It may be worthwhile to examine several of the most interesting results, without in any sense suggesting that this analysis provides comprehensive coverage of the field.

Most writers on modern world (and regional) history (the period since 1500) — including many "diffusionist" historians — have implicitly or explicitly organized their material around the concept of "modernization" or the "modernizing process." Thus, Edward R. Tannenbaum contends that "during the past 100 years and for the foreseeable future, modernization is the dominant force in the world."[1] There is an implicit assumption that all societies can be divided into traditional and modern, and that the idea of modernization can be applied universally. Many authors and teachers use the concept without applying any very rigorous definition. Indeed, a disconcerting number of historians and other scholars seem to use "modernization" without defining it explicitly. Many historians believe a reasonably accurate description of the modernization concept of historical development might be reduced to the following summary propositions developed by an innovative history department in a small New England university:[2]

Craig A. Lockard, "Global History, Modernization, and the World-System Approach: A Critique," *The History Teacher* 14 (August 1981): 496–515.

1. The last two centuries or so represent a wholly exceptional period within the overall sweep of human history. During this period, the inhabitants of such regions as Europe, the United States, and Japan have passed through a profound transition. This transition has broken them loose from patterns of economic, social, political, and intellectual life that man has lived for millennia. It has carried them to what amounts to an entirely new and radically different order of existence, or level of civilization, which is without counterpart in the past.

2. Hence, we can distinguish in history two broad patterns or ideal-types of civilization: the "traditional civilization" that obtained everywhere up to the eighteenth century, and the 'modern civilization' that increasingly has become the norm since then . . .

3. The transition from "traditional" civilization to "modern" civilization, or the process of "modernization," began in Western civilization. Subsequently, it has been carried outward into non-Western civilizations. In this set of facts — that it was Western civilization that first entered upon the transition to modernity, and that the consequences of its modernization have forced modernization upon the remaining traditional civilizations of the world — lie the uniqueness and the importance of Western history.

If this quote accurately summarizes the modernization approach as perceived by historians, the concepts are not altogether objectionable or unreasonable; but some scholars would disagree. Some readers may consider the following criticism superfluous; many Latin American, Middle Eastern, and African historians as well as a few Asianists, Europeanists, and North Americanists, have in the past few years rejected the modernization approach as an adequate guide to understanding modern history. But intellectual trends percolate slowly through the compartmentalized historical discipline. Though there have been many challenges in recent years, especially from Marxist and neo-Marxist scholars, modernization is far from "dead"; it continues to reign supreme as the predominant paradigm among globalists, Asianists, and Europeanists while still enjoying some popularity among Africanists as well as a diminishing number of Latin Americanists. Apparently it is also gaining popularity among Americanists, especially social historians. Books and articles employing a modernization framework appear in astonishing numbers, confirming that it still dominates American academic thinking, most strongly perhaps in political science.

Critics charge that the modernization theory fails to explain adequately the complex interconnections and interactions of societies working through various international networks and processes. Instead it encourages a bland ethnocentrism which develops little sympathy or understanding among Americans for the aspirations and plight of Third World peoples. Indeed it fails to address the sources of the contemporary world's international and intersocietal tensions. Coming into prominence in the 1950s and early 1960s, it complemented as well as justified the naive American notion that the selfless United States would help the rest of the world to wealth, progress, and democracy. Furthermore, the framework is utterly ahistorical, failing to allow for diverse and uneven continuities from the past, although to be fair some modernization theorists seem to be aware of this deficiency. The implied notion that all societies are progressing toward the same fate ("convergence") constitutes another problem, for some Third World societies now seek different futures far removed from the model of America's affluent consumer society.

Most historians (including the writer) would probably agree that, in a broad sense, concepts such as "modern" or "modernization" have some value in differentiating the rapidly changing, technologically more complex world of the past several centuries from those of the earlier periods (what are called "traditional" societies). Perhaps they also help indicate a process of technological change and development, a process not necessarily correlated with changes in human relationships and consumption patterns as some writers believe. As L. E. Shiner has noted:

> So long as the "tradition/modernity" concept is used in the limited, primarily heuristic way ideal types are meant to be used, it may continue to have its place . . . If they were treated as loose designations for a set of problems and interests rather than as operative concepts by which to guide research, they should not do much harm.[3]

Unfortunately, a large number of scholars, particularly since the late 1950s, have taken the concept somewhat further without necessarily making clear the ideological assumptions (a bias toward liberal democracy, capitalism, a Western lifestyle, high-consumption living standards, and the notion of progress) which support it or the non-universality of some of its features; indeed, for many scholars, "modernization" is a coherent theory postulating polar types of societies with wholly different characteristics. C. E. Black, an historian, represents this viewpoint when he notes:

> "Modernity" has come to be rather widely employed to describe the characteristics common to countries that are most *advanced* [emphasis mine] in technological, political, economic, and social development, and "modernization" to describe the process by which they acquired these characteristics.[4]

Obviously then to be "modern" is to be "advanced," to occupy a higher rung on the ladder of progress toward a better, more satisfying world. Political scientist Daniel Lerner goes even further: "Modernization is . . . the process of social change whereby less developed societies acquire characteristics common to more developed societies."[5]

The modernization theorists, progressing considerably beyond description, postulate some universal features of the modernizing process, including the notion of parallel stages (with their beginning and end points), and of easily defined characteristics of "modern" and "traditional" societies. Some have even developed sometimes often questionable strategies for bringing development and modernity to Third World societies based on the spread of "modern" (i.e., Western) value orientations, world views, political systems, and socioeconomic structures. The essentials of this theory have been summarized by two critics as follows:

> This perspective assumes as its basic premise that the theoretical unit for the study of social change is "society" in the abstract. Accordingly, the world is said to consist of a number of related but basically autonomous "societies" . . . each moving upward along an essentially similar path of development. Some, of course, started their ascents earlier than others, thereby showing the way to late-starters; and some proceeded at times more rapidly than others, suffering accordingly from forcing historical change. But they all trace broadly parallel lines of development. . . . The task of the social scientist is . . . to construct, and test out, explanations as to why some "societies" started earlier than others, why some developed faster than others, and why those currently lagging behind are lagging and what they must do in order to catch up to those already developed.[6]

Not all of the modernization literature fits into this mould, but one can certainly find prominent examples which well represent this approach.

This is not the place to criticize in detail the modernization theory's problems or ideological suppositions (much of which is based on Western experience and cultural biases), for that has been done in detail elsewhere; but we should note that an increasing number of historians, and their social science colleagues, have questioned the wisdom of relying too heavily or exclusively on the modernization concept (particularly its more vulgar manifestations) as an interpretation of, or analytical tool for the study of, recent historical development either in the entire world or for Third World societies in particular.

Teachers of history should be concerned that modernization theory reinforces — rather than challenges — Americans' sense of their own superiority over other peoples and cultures, since it assumes that the United States has been at the cutting edge of historical development or progress. Global historians who choose, implictly or explicitly, to employ an unmodified modernization framework have selected a paradigm that is incapable of explaining the complex interrelationships of societies in the nineteenth and twentieth centuries. As historian Theda Skocpol writes: "Modernization is best conceived not only as an *intra* societal process of economic development accompanied by lagging or leading changes in non-economic institutional spheres, but also as a world-historic *inter* societal phenomenon."[7] Students educated from a modernization perspective will certainly have difficulty comprehending the recent radical developments in countries like Iran, Chile, Vietnam, or Zimbabwe, for the theory is utterly deficient in explaining Third World revolution and counterrevolution.

The challenge to the modernization approach with subsequent development of alternative approaches has come from several directions. The most exciting and influential ideas on modern global history now come from those historians and social scientists, associated with the "world-system" approach, who view the modernization theorists' emphasis on relatively autonomous societies progressing toward a common goal as seriously deficient. Pioneered by both

First and Third World scholars, and particularly by sociologists, this approach has received increasing attention from scholars, including historians with varied backgrounds and interests. As the best-known exponent of the world-system concept, American sociologist Immanuel Wallerstein, writes about the challenge to modernization theory:

> These scholars (the world-system theorists) raised into question the presumptions of parallel "societal" development, positing instead a view of a world-economy or world system that itself "develops," but whose segments or parts in no way follow parallel paths over historical time — indeed quite the contrary.[8]

Since it offers no comprehensive interpretation of modern history, the world-system approach developed by Wallerstein and other scholars is not global history in the sense that McNeill or Stavrianos present it — perhaps macro-history is a better term — but it is not unrelated either. The global historian and world-system theorist agree that the whole is greater than the sum of its parts, while at the same time affirming that the parts cannot be properly understood without reference to the whole. There is also a common emphasis on the interaction of societies. Essentially the world-system scholars, taking a systemic and structural view of world development over the past several centuries, have established a holistic explanation for the social, political, and economic structure of, and interaction in, the contemporary world. As sociologist Daniel Chirot argues:

> Studying social change without studying its international context is theoretically unsound, and also dangerous, because it leads to the illusion that a contemporary society is the complete master of its fate.[9]

In many respects the world-system scholars are writing within a broad framework that can be termed global political economy.

Essentially the world-system approach views the modern world as a macro-system — more complex and rapidly changing but not necessarily superior to the earlier, less universal, network of societies — and takes into account a wide variety of factors — the political economy factor being the most critical — in studying this world and its evolution. To Wallerstein, in the last several centuries capitalism has defined the dominant force in the emerging world economy and a process as much as an economic system. Advocates of this approach stress that the world has become highly interdependent but that this exchange relationship is generally an unequal one favoring certain capital-rich societies at the expense of others. Historian Basil Davidson — a specialist on Africa — has succinctly summarized a variant of this theme far removed from the notions of "modernization" theorists:

> The development of the industrialized countries continues to imply the stagnation — now, even the regression — of the non-industrialized. The strong continue to feed upon the weak, and the weak continue to grow weaker; and it is to this, far more than to anything else, that one must refer the troubles and up-

heavals . . . of the newly independent regimes [in the Third World]. Not until this system and relationship begin to be radically changed will there be, or can there be, any resolution of a crisis which threatens now to become catastrophe.[10]

Modern global history from the world-system approach might be briefly summarized as follows: The world-system originated in the fifteenth century, with the growth of capitalism and of commercial agriculture in Western Europe; expansion was essential to the process and led eventually to the direct control of most of the non-Western societies by certain powerful Western countries. The capitalist economy of Western Europe continued to evolve and later spread to European settlement colonies like the United States. By the late nineteenth century, the modern world-system had become firmly established and universal as the powerful Western societies took advantage of industrial revolution; most of the world was drawn into the orbit of West European and North American capitalism, more likely than not through direct colonization, depriving the majority of societies of some or all of their autonomy. Colonialism served as a variously successful system for developing the Western core powers while at the same time bringing underdevelopment to most Third World societies. The development of geographically and culturally distinct regions was therefore part of an increasingly interlocked process of change with global implications. The twentieth century has witnessed some alterations in this integrated system (including the rise of both the United States and a challenging Communist world), but the heritage of the earlier world-system is still with us, including the continuation of a diminished autonomy for many societies.

Immanuel Wallerstein's work is essential to understanding the world-system approach. Wallerstein defines a world-system as "a unit with a single division of labor and multiple cultural and political systems";[11] furthermore, he stresses that various societies depend on economic exchange with others for their survival. His analysis postulates three types of societies developing in the modern world and defined by their position in the world-system at various periods: core-rich and powerful; peripheral — poor and underdeveloped; and semiperipheral intermediate. Wallerstein has developed a paradigm — a broad, loose but nonetheless coherent explanation that generates models which can be tested by other scholars. One of Wallerstein's students, Daniel Chirot, offers a slightly modified form of the world-system approach. Chirot sees a world-system as consisting "of a set of interconnected societies. The state of being of each of these societies depends to some extent on its relative position in the world-system, which has strong, middling, and weak members."[12] Chirot's more flexible approach avoids some of the pitfalls, sometimes attributed to Wallerstein's work, without sacrificing the basic insights of the interpretations and concepts.

Wallerstein's ideas on the nature of the modern world grew out of his desire to make connections and understand relationships. His research on contemporary Africa convinced him that he must comprehend better the colonial past if he wished to understand the post-colonial present; to do so he realized he needed to grasp the broader context as well, abandoning the sovereign state as a "social system." In other words, he concluded that the world as a whole must be considered in order to understand developments within its parts. Historians seeking to come to grips with the colonial experience and its legacy in Southern Asia, Africa, and the Caribbean can certainly sympathize with Wallerstein's dilemma. As Kaye points out,[13] Wallerstein drew inspiration from two intellectual sources important for global history: Fernand Braudel and the interdisciplinary *Annales* French school of history; and the dependency theories developed by scholars like Andre Gunder Frank.

Braudel and those of his French colleagues whose work appears mainly in the journal *Les Annales* seek to write "total" history; their approach marks a revolt against a dominant historiography that emphasized political, diplomatic, and military history and that focused on important personalities and events. The *Annales* historians, and their followers outside of France, did not entirely reject political history but they devoted more attention to social and economic developments. Braudel and his colleagues — writing what some called "geohistory" — synthesized historical and social science approaches and emphasized long-term patterns rather than what Braudel labels "eventism." For example, in his work in the Mediterranean world (a trans-national unit) in the later sixteenth century, Braudel describes the sea basin as a complex mosaic; he analyzes a bewildering variety of topics, including landscape, climate, cultural ecology, patterns of migration and trade, town life, diet, crafts, festivals, the lives of peasants, the activities of merchants, and demography. The preoccupations of most historians — diplomatic maneuvering, dynastic marriages, treaties, political conflicts, wars — occupy only about a fourth of Braudel's text and are seen as less important than such matters as economic patterns. Although Braudel and the *Annales* historians have not tried to write global history, their multi-faceted and integrated — although certainly imperfect — approach seems to offer much to global historians.

Wallerstein also draws heavily on Andre Gunder Frank's concept of the "development of underdevelopment," which stresses interregional relationships and processes. Frank argues that the process of underdevelopment in the "periphery" of Latin America resembled the same process generating development of the core countries of the industrialized West; the capitalist development of Western Europe and later the United States, developed at the expense of the underdevelopment of the Third World societies. Latin America specialist Keith Griffin, a supporter of the Frank thesis, at least in its broad outlines, believes that:

> The automatic functioning of the international economy which Europe dominated first created underdevelopment and then hindered efforts to escape from it. . . . Underdevelopment is a product of historical processes.[14]

According to this thesis, "underdevelopment" and "undevelopment" are qualitatively different phenomena. Frank charges that:

> Even a modest acquaintance with history shows that underdevelopment is not original or traditional and that neither the past nor the present of the underdeveloped countries resemble in any important respect the past of the now developed countries. The now developed countries were never *underdeveloped,* though they may have been *undeveloped.*[15]

Underdevelopment, in other words, implies a position of weakness and lack of autonomy in the world economy, what some scholars term "dependency." Thus, there is an unequal exchange relationship, in which some societies have direct or indirect influence over others lacking full control of their destinies. For specialists on Africa or Southern Asia, this approach stresses the redistributive rather than modernizing aspects of colonialism and neo-colonialism. This is a far cry from the assertion of modernization theories that countries commence the journey from tradition to modernity with the adoption of "rational" (i.e., Western) forms of education, government or economic patterns.

There are serious problems with both Frank's historiography and his formulations. And, while dependency theory or its variants has become influential in Latin American and African studies, difficulties abound in applying the framework to the entire Third World or even to some countries. But the basic point of dependency theory — that "the interplay between the internal . . . structures and international structures is the critical starting point for an understanding of the process of development. . . . "[16] — seems reasonable for much, although perhaps not all, of Latin America, and certainly has some applicability to Africa, Southern Asia, and the Caribbean. Therefore, if accepted undogmatically, and allowing for many variables, the concepts of "dependency" and "development of underdevelopment" can assist global historians who emphasize long-term patterns, causation, and trans-social relationship.

Wallerstein also is convinced of the relationship between the development of capitalism in Europe and the underdevelopment of the Third World; fundamentally, his concept of the world-system involves economic exchange relations of a world market economy. Many, although not all, of Wallerstein's formulations — for example, his views on capitalism and unequal exchange — are influenced by Marxian and neo-Marxian thought and his work does fall broadly, although not dogmatically, within the neo-Marxist tradition. The appeal should not be restricted to Marxian-influenced scholars, however. Such a thoroughgoing and broad-based formulation — especially as presented in his book on the origins of the world system in sixteenth and early seventeenth century Europe — may also engender great criticism and controversy. A few scholars totally reject Wallerstein's work, and others, including some with a Marxist orientation, criticize it in part. Some critics consider Wallerstein's analysis as too mechanical, even perhaps corrupted by economic determinism. The most incisive and detailed critic is Theda Skocpol, who finds Wallerstein's historiography and theory-building somewhat deficient although she admires his overall attempt at designing a coherent framework for studying modern world history. Her comments are worth quoting at length:

> Wallerstein's arguments are too misleading theoretically and historically to be accepted at face value.... Like other important pioneering works, Wallerstein's *Modern World-System* overreaches itself and falls short of its aims.... No one should suppose, however, that I am suggesting that we dismiss or ignore Wallerstein's ongoing study of the world capitalist system.... On the contrary, I can think of no intellectual project in the social sciences that is of greater interest and importance. Even if Wallerstein has so far given imperfect answers about the historical development of capitalism, still he has the unequalled boldness of vision to raise all the important issues. Even the shortcomings of this effort, therefore, can be far more fruitful for the social sciences than any minute successes by others who attempt much less.[17]

It is interesting that only a few historians and sociologists have found the analysis of the broader paradigm to be altogether unconvincing, especially in regard to the Europe–Third World relationship. Most of the reviews by historians have certainly found flaws, mainly of detail, in his treatment of European history, but the majority of reviews — including some by non-Marxists — accord his book either whole-hearted or qualified approval. A fuller critique of the entire scheme awaits completion of the remaining volumes in the series, when Wallerstein's conceptions will be more fully developed. It should also be noted that Wallerstein has invited debate about his work and has not attempted to impose any particular orthodoxy on those who find the broad framework useful. In his view the bare essentials of the world-system approach include an emphasis on "political economy" and the notion of a working social system, world economy, larger than any state; both themes are grounded in Marxism but certainly do not appeal solely to Marxists. Within this broad framework there remains much room for debate on both theoretical and empirical matters. Global historians, then, need not uncritically accept Wallerstein's research to find utility in the general paradigm of an interconnected world-system developing over time and having an essentially economic base.

Although the world-system approach is increasingly influencing both historians of the Third World and of Europe, particularly younger scholars, it is still far from becoming the dominant mode of interpretation on the development of the modern world. Nor has it, unlike modernization theory, penetrated the pages of world history textbooks or other broad studies of global history. This results in part from the pioneering nature of the existing work, but also may be due to the theoretical and ideological orientations of the world-system scholarship, heavily influenced by Marxism, and its undermining of the "Western civilization" bias.

It is possible that Chirot's recent and stimulating book on the sociology of world politics and the evolution of the world-system in the twentieth century may alter that situation, although it has so far received little attention from historians (but not sociologists, political scientists, and anthropologists). Chirot's carefully developed and well-documented sociologically-oriented analysis is not without problems and controversial interpretations. While the author sometimes too easily formulates generalizations from his data, his historiography and grasp of a wide range of sources are impressive. More modest in his goals and scope than Wallerstein, he has nonetheless succeeded in developing a coherent, and in many respects, a persuasive interpretation of recent history that emphasizes interrelationships. He also offers a truly macro and frequently comparative perspective focusing on key themes rather than details. Chirot effectively integrates the recent histories of Europe, North America, and the Third World in attempting to comprehend the relationship between internal and international social, economic, and political change. His book is aimed at understanding "the changing world system and how the shifting balance of international economic, political and cultural forces, shape and are shaped by changing class structures within the core, semi-peripheral and peripheral societies."[18] Like Wallerstein he sees the main differences between core and peripheral societies as not that of industrialization and value orientations — the emphases of the modernization theorists — but of wealth and specialization. Of particular interest are his thoughts on the continuing evolution of and rapidly changing balance of power in the world-system. He believes that Third World societies will increasingly reject emulation — as modernization theorists believe — but to close themselves off from the economically powerful states, forcing the Western societies to seek a future less dependent on the control of resources in poor countries.

Chirot's ambitious and flexible approach utilizes history, politics, economics, and sociology and is inspired by Wallerstein, but his work is more synthetic of mainstream scholarship and constitutes a modification of Wallerstein's perspective. It may thus receive a more sympathetic reception among non-Marxist scholars. Chirot's work may be too sociological for historians uninterested in social science perspectives or methodology. Although it ranges widely over a variety of themes, is superbly written for undergraduates, and is especially strong on socioeconomic patterns. Those advocating the modernization approach will find many of his interpretations most discomforting. Although I do not agree with all of his ideas, Chirot's analysis of modern history appears to explain the modern world and its tensions more convincingly than modernization-oriented historians. Chirot's ideas also frequently differ from many Marxist scholars, who will probably find his work interesting but inadequate.

The world-system approach (or paradigm) has its imperfections and limitations, including sometimes excessive oversubordination of micro-level to macro-level analysis and the neglect of cultural and ethnic factors. No paradigm will probably ever explain modern world history in a fully satisfactory manner and the world-system approach — at least as presently constituted — is weak in several areas. However, it seems to offer considerably more possibilities than modernization theory (shackled with too many Western biases) and in any case still stands at a formative stage of development. The paradigm adds a systemic and structural theoretical formulation for the study of recent global history; moreover this framework is strongest in explaining relationships between societies and regions, one of the patterns Americans seem least able to understand. In doing so it helps to challenge the ethnocentrism and parochialism of the American world view. Utilization of a world-system perspective in an undogmatic form helps students understand that the world consists of interdependent units of uneven influence and power. It gives them insights into the nature of international interaction and the structure of international relations and the world economic system. A world-system approach situates the United States within a broader context of historical processes and change. It remains to be seen whether, like modernization theory, the world-system paradigm — grounded to some extent in neo-Marxism — is riddled with implicit Western biases. In any case, it does in many respects provide the sort of "clear and distinct idea" that McNeill calls for to help us define what is relevant. As such the general approach, if used critically, provides a useful pedagogical as well as analytical tool for global history. Surely it provides a basis for American students to obtain a clearer, more realistic picture of the relationships between the United States and the rest of the world (not just of Western Europe) and of their own place in that world. Increasingly, global or other historians will need to deal with the questions and interpretations raised by the world-system approach.

Notes

1. Edward R. Tannenbaum, *A History of World Civilizations* (New York: Wiley, 1973), v.

2. "The Study of History at the University of Hartford: A Statement Prepared by the Department of History" (Hartford, Conn., ca. 1971), 2.

3. L. E. Shiner, "Tradition/Modernity: An Ideal Type Gone Astray," *Comparative Studies in Society and History* 17 (1975): 252.

4. C. E. Black, *The Dynamics of Modernization: A Study in Comparative History* (New York: Harper & Row, 1966), 6.

5. Daniel Lerner, "Modernization: Social Aspects," *International Encyclopedia of the Social Sciences* (New York: Macmillan, 1968), 386.

6. Terence K. Hopkins and Immanuel Wallerstein, "Patterns of Development of the Modern World-System: Research Proposal," *Review* (Fall 1977): 111–12.

7. Theda Skocpol, "France, Russia, China: A Structural Analysis of Social Revolutions," *Comparative Studies in Society and History* (April 1976): 179.

8. Immanuel Wallerstein, "The Tasks of Historical Social Science," *Review* (Summer 1977): 7.

9. Daniel Chirot, *Social Change in the Twentieth Century* (New York: Harcourt Brace Jovanovich, 1977), 256.

10. Basil Davidson, *Can Africa Survive: Arguments against Growth without Development* (Boston: Little, Brown, 1974), 29.

11. Immanuel Wallerstein, "The Rise and Future Demise of the World Capitalist System: Concepts for Comparative Analysis," *Comparative Studies in Society and History* (September 1974): 390.

12. Chirot, *Social Change*, 13.

13. Harvey Kaye, "Totality: Its Application to Historical and Social Analysis by Wallerstein and Genovese," *Historical Reflections* (Winter 1979): 408–9.

14. Keith Griffin, "Underdevelopment in History," in *The Political Economy of Development and Underdevelopment*, ed. Charles K. Wilber (New York: Random House, 1979), 78.

15. Andre Gunder Frank, *Latin America: Underdevelopment or Revolution* (New York: Monthly Review Press, 1969), 4.

16. Philip J. O'Brien, "A Critique of Latin American Theories of Dependency," in *Beyond the Sociology of Development: Economy and Society in Latin America and Africa*, ed. Ivor Oxaal, Tony Barnett, and David Booth (London: Routledge & Kegan Paul, 1975), 25.

17. Theda Skocpol, "Wallerstein's World Capitalist System: A Theoretical and Historical Critique," *American Journal of Sociology* (March 1977): 1075–89.

18. Chirot, *Social Change*, 14.

IMMANUEL WALLERSTEIN

World-Systems Analysis
Five Questions in Search of a New Consensus

The traditional general education in history in the United States (but also in western Europe) has laid emphasis on teaching the history of one's own country plus teaching the history of something that has been called the Western world (and/or civilization). In the U.S., the latter has generally meant some knowledge concerning the history primarily of Great Britain, France, and Germany in the nineteenth and twentieth centuries, of England from the sixteenth to eighteenth centuries, of the "Renaissance" and "Reformation" and also some dabbling in that of the Middle Ages as well as in that of classical Greece and Rome.

In the period since the Second World War, there has emerged some criticism of such curricula as being too "Eurocentric." Attempts have therefore been made, with very limited success, to add some instruction in what might be thought of as the "great civilizations of the East" — India, China, Japan, occasionally the Arab caliphates. Whatever gain has been achieved by this broadening of geography (which has not been too widely adopted) has probably been more than offset by the decline in standard history instruction, both at the college and high school levels. One cannot simply presume today that a college graduate has a working elementary knowledge of, for example, the French Revolution.

However, neither a plea for patchwork additions to the old curriculum (a smattering of Chinese history on top of Western history) nor a general deploring of lowered intellectual requirements in our educational system is really to the

Immanuel Wallerstein, "World-Systems Analysis: Five Questions in Search of a New Consensus," *The History Teacher* 18 (August 1985): 527–32.

point. A more fundamental question is arising. The way we teach history today is part and parcel of the intellectual consensus that emerged in Europe during the nineteenth century in the wake of the social issues laid bare by the expansion of the urban-industrial sector and the heritage of the French Revolution. And this consensus itself is being called into question. The point therefore is to see what was the consensus and what were it social roots, why it has come to be questioned and in what ways, and what are the implications for instruction in "history."

The consensus arrived at in the nineteenth century is not too difficult to describe; by definition it is familiar to everyone, although (as is the case for most intellectual consensus) people tend to think of these presumptions as obvious or factual rather than as socially-constructed perspectives. I will limit myself here to three basic premises, although they scarcely exhaust the picture.

Premise No. 1. The history of the modern (Western) world is the history of the rise of the "middle classes" (economically, politically, culturally) in the wake of the steady expansion of the market-centered organization of production, and the slow but steady urbanization process. This phenomenon has been accompanied in the political arena by the steady decline in the arbitrariness of political authorities. It has involved in the social sphere an overall increase in human welfare and of popular participation in decision-making. The slow process reached a decisive and positive turning-point in the twin key events of the late eighteenth century: the Industrial Revolution in England and the French Revolution.

Premise No. 2. The units within which these changes have occurred, and therefore the key units for historical analysis, were the (national) states. It was "England" that had an "industrial revolution" between 1780 and 1840; it was "Germany" which failed to have a bourgeois (or democratic) revolution in 1848–49. The explanations are to be sought in the prior history of these areas. We look therefore at "German" or "Italian" history of the eighteenth, the fifteenth, and even the tenth centuries to understand why "unification" of these two "nations" occurred so "late." In any case, the history of all national states has been a history of internal homogenization, of lessening loyalties of citizens to "traditional" entities or groups (e.g., "ethnic" or religious groups) and increasing loyalty to the "national" group.

Premise No. 3. The story told under premises 1 and 2 is a story of human progress. It is the story of the search for human freedom, a relatively successful search. Furthermore, the search for progress is continuing. If there seem to be setbacks, they are temporary. If there are phenomena which do not fit the picture they are anomalous. Finally, such progress is not only empirically real but theoretically inevitable.

Finally, there was a derived proposition from these premises that concerned "world history." The story of human freedom was a discovery of (a product of the particular history of) the Western world. One of its consequences was the rise of a technology which enabled the Western world to expand "overseas."

This expansion itself represented the progress of "civilization," since its basic impact was "civilizing."

To be sure, baldly stated like this, the viewpoint seems a bit caricatural, and no doubt there have been innumerable caveats, dissents, and nuances expressed. Still, a reading of high school textbooks in Western countries written between say 1850 and 1950 would doubtless confirm the generality of this consensus about how the modern world should be interpreted.

The social roots of this consensus seem very clear. The hegemony of Great Britain in the world-system in the mid-nineteenth century combined with the dramatic expansion of applied scientific technology, lent itself to this view of the world which might be seen to be a reasonable explanation of the existing realities combined with an ideological justification of the privileges of the powerful. Although many detailed changes in world realities occurred thereafter, it could be argued that the system continued to seem to thrive (even despite the two world wars of the twentieth century, and despite the Russian Revolution) until perhaps the 1960s. That being so, the particular intellectual consensus continued as a basis of both academic and public social analysis.

The ways in which this social reality began to change radically can be seen in the simultaneous occurrence of three seemingly separate developments in three different parts of the world. In the non-European zones of the world, the rise of nationalist movements did not in itself challenge the assumptions of the consensus, since it could be argued they represented the fulfilment of the process. There was, however, a fly in the ointment. It was the phenomenon of the so-called growing gap between industrialized and Third World countries. Political independence of former colonial areas did not seem in practice to overcome world inequalities or necessarily bring the automatic benefits of political and cultural "progress." Explanations that were sought in the prior "history" of these "nations" did not seem *to them* very satisfactory. They therefore pushed in two directions. One was to look for explanations in some supra-national processes. The other was to raise "civilizational" questions, posing the concept of civilizations (plural) against that of civilization (singular), which translated into doubts about universalistic assumptions built into Western historical reasoning.

At the same time, that zone of the world with Communist governments, running from central Europe to east Asia, began to experience seismic internal political difficulties. In some way, the Russian Revolution of 1917, particularly once it came into its Stalinist phase, had not really challenged the premises of the consensus. In a sense, the Communists presented themselves as the heirs of the process that had occurred over long historical time in the Western world and as its logical fulfilment. What began to come into question, among the participants of the social movements in power in these countries themselves, was the degree to which progress had really been achieved (the issues of "revisionism" on the one hand and of "terror" on the other). Once again, explanations sought in the immediate or long-term history of these "nations" did not seem very satisfactory to the people there, and alternative explanatory schema were sought. The impact of these developments was even greater perhaps elsewhere in the world. The "disillusionments" experienced were disillusionments in the face of predictions derived from the consensual framework of analysis. This led many to reappraise the premises.

Finally, in the Western world itself, the 1960s represented the institutionalization of a new kind of social turmoil which was not easily explained by the consensual premises. In particular, the premise of the reality and desirability of a process of national homogenization was called into doubt. Many groups proclaimed that they had been *entirely* left out of the process hitherto described as universal: women, all kinds of low-status "ethnic" and "national" groupings, persons of particular sexual inclinations, the handicapped, etc. To some extent, to be sure, this represented merely one more set of demands within the framework of the established process which could be accommodated, but to some extent it increasingly represented a challenge to the "assimilationist" model implicit in the old consensus, which is why these "new social movements" have aroused such strong emotional resistance. In order to pursue their objectives, these movements have consequently been forced increasingly to question intellectual premises and not merely current policies.

The intellectual outcome of the past twenty years has been to create a situation in which the premises described previously no longer represent a consensus, but merely one set of premises among actively contending sets. There is in some sense a search going on for a new consensus. This is one of the reasons why projects such as this one are being generated.

It is too early to institutionalize a new model in the university. Rather, what is incumbent on us in the present era is to construct curricula in which these premises are brought to the fore as open intellectual questions. This seems to me both eminently feasible and desirable. It would entail a more "difficult" curriculum, of course, since it is always more difficult for teacher and student to discuss uncertainties rather than to learn "transmitted knowledge." But in fact there is considerable evidence in the real world that people are sufficiently uncomfortable about received verities to be somewhat willing to engage in this more difficult mode of learning.

In particular, I suggest that five questions have to be incorporated into the basic teaching of history (first at the college level, later at the high school level), as open questions.

1. What is the meaningful unit of social analysis? Does "Germany" have a history between 1500 and 1800? There are various alternative assumptions, for example. Between 1500 and 1800, "Germany" was merely a linguistic zone within the European world-economy. Or Prussia had a history, but not Germany. Or "central Europe" had a history. I am not debating this issue here. I merely wish to suggest that the debate should not be considered an esoteric one for advanced scholars but a fundamental one for beginning students.

2. Where is the "world"? Is "world history" the history first of the "West" which then came to encompass the globe? Alternatively, is it the sum of "high

civilizations" — the West plus China plus India plus . . . ? Is the concept of "civilization" properly speaking used in the singular or the plural?

3. What is appropriate periodization? This is of course an old debate. The original division of Western historiography into Antiquity, the Middle Ages, and Modernity reflects well-known premises. The breakpoints of the "Agricultural Revolution" and the "Industrial Revolution" reflect not too different ones. But insofar as questions 1 and 2 get discussed, a systematic discussion of alternative periodizations seems eminently on the agenda.

4. Are the "groups" we use to discuss history, particularly modern history, appropriate ones? "Middle classes" and "aristocrats" are obviously different groups. So are "workers" and "peasants." Is this distinction so sure? A good deal of the empirical work of the last twenty years has called precisely these two obvious categorizations into question. If they do not "hold," much of modern history has to be radically rewritten.

5. How can progress be measured, and within what units (question no. 1 again)? Was everything that occurred later progress over that which was earlier? And was it inevitable? This has of course been a favorite question for parlor philosophy. Can it be made into an empirical/theoretical question open to careful historical analysis? I believe so.

The reader of this paper may be thinking: This is all very well, but can students discuss such questions without prior concrete historical knowledge? But the "prior knowledge" comes wrapped mostly in premises that presume answers to these questions. The trick is to wrap the knowledge in such a way as to leave the premises open. This will be harder for the professorate than for the students. But it is the minimum necessary if one wants to give undergraduates a "global perspective," and it is quite attainable if we wish to do it.

FERNAND BRAUDEL

Economies in Space
The World-Economies

Geographical space as a source of explanation affects all historical realities, all spatially-defined phenomena: states, societies, cultures and economies. Depending which of these "sets"[1] we choose, the significance and role of space will be modified accordingly — though not unrecognizably so.

I should like first to single out the economies of the world. Then I shall try to define the area and influence of the other "sets." To begin by looking at the economy is not only appropriate to the plan of the book: of all the ways of apprehending space, the economic is the easiest to locate and the widest-ranging, as we shall see. And its significance is not confined to the material aspects of world time: all the other social realities, whether favourable to it or not, are concerned in the working of the economy, constantly intervening and being in turn influenced by it — to put it mildly.

WORLD-ECONOMIES

To open the discussion, I should elucidate two expressions which might lead to confusion: *the world economy* and *a world-economy*.

The world economy is an expression applied to the whole world. It corresponds, as Sismondi puts it, to "the market of the universe,"[2] to "the human race, or that part of the human race which is engaged in trade, and which today in a sense makes up a single market."[3]

A *world-economy* (an expression which I have used in the past as a particular meaning of the German term *Weltwirtschaft*)[4] only concerns a fragment of the world, an economically autonomous section of the planet able to provide for most of its own needs, a section to which its internal links and exchanges give a certain organic unity.[5]

Fernand Braudel, *Civilization and Capitalism, 15th–18th Century*, vol. 3, *The Perspective of the World*, translated by Siân Reynolds (New York: Harper and Row, 1984), 21–22, 24–26, 27, 30, 32, 34–35, 39, 44, 634–35.

I have in the past, for instance, studied the Mediterranean in the sixteenth century as a *Welttheater* or *Weltwirtschaft*[6] — a world-theatre or world-economy — meaning by this not merely the sea itself but the whole area stimulated by its trading activities, whether near its shores or far away. I have treated it in short as a world in itself. The Mediterranean region, although divided politically, culturally and indeed socially, can effectively be said to have had a certain economic unity, one imposed upon it from above on the initiative of the dominant cities of northern Italy, Venice foremost among them, but also Milan, Genoa and Florence.[7] This Mediterranean economy did not however represent the *whole* of the economic life of the sea and its surrounding regions. It was so to speak the highest plane of the economy, whose activity, more or less intensive depending on place, was to be found along all the coastlines and sometimes deep inland. Such activity ignored the frontiers of empires — whether the Spanish Empire completed by Charles V (1519–1555) or the Turkish Empire which had begun its expansion well before the capture of Constantinople (1453). It also ignored the well-marked and strongly-felt boundaries between the civilizations which divided up the Mediterranean: Greek civilization lying humiliated and in disarray under the increasingly heavy Turkish yoke; Muslim civilization centred on Istanbul; Christian civilization with its twin poles of Florence and Rome (the Renaissance and the Counter-Reformation). Islam and Christendom faced each other along the north–south divide between the Levant and the western Mediterranean, a line running from the shores of the Adriatic to Sicily and then on to the coast of present-day Tunisia. All the great battles between Christians and Infidels were fought on this line. But merchant vessels sailed across it every day.

For it was precisely a characteristic of this singular world-economy — that of the sixteenth-century Mediterranean — that it bestrode the political and cultural frontiers which each in its own way quartered and differentiated the Mediterranean world. So in 1500, Christian merchants would have been found in Syria, Egypt, Istanbul and North Africa; while Levantine, Turkish and Armenian merchants later reached the Adriatic. The economy, all-invading, mingling together currencies and commodities, tended to promote unity of a kind in a world where everything else seemed to be conspiring to create clearly-distinguished blocs. Even society in the Mediterranean can roughly be divided into two types: Christian society with a predominantly hereditary seigniorial system; and Muslim society where the system of livings predominated, that is life-holdings bestowed as rewards for men who distinguished themselves in battle. On the death of the holder, the living or title reverted to the state and was reallocated.

In short, from studying a particular case, we may deduce that a world-economy is a sum of individualized areas, economic and non-economic, which it brings together; that it generally represents a very large surface area (in theory the largest coherent zone at a given period, in a given part of the globe); and that it usually goes beyond the boundaries of other great historical divisions.

There Have Always Been World-Economies

There have been world-economies if not always, at least for a very long time — just as there have been societies, civilizations, states and even empires. If we take giant steps back through history, we could say of ancient Phœnicia that it was an early version of a world-economy, surrounded by great empires. So too was Carthage in its heydey; or the Hellenic world; or even Rome; so too was Islam after its lightning triumphs. In the ninth century, the Norman venture on the outer margins of western Europe laid down the lines of a short-lived and fragile world-economy which others would inherit. From the eleventh century, Europe began developing what was to be its first world-economy, afterwards succeeded by others down to the present day. Muscovy, connected to the East, India, China, Central Asia and Siberia, was another self-contained world-economy, at least until the eighteenth century. So was China, which from earliest times took over and harnessed to her own destiny such neighbouring areas as Korea, Japan, the East Indies, Vietnam, Yunan, Tibet and Mongolia — a garland of dependent countries. Even before this, India had turned the Indian Ocean into a sort of private sea, from the east coast of Africa to the islands of the East Indies.

Might it not in short be said that here was a process of constant renewal as each configuration gave way almost spontaneously to another, leaving plentiful traces behind — even in a case, at first sight unpromising, like the Roman Empire? The Roman economy did in fact extend beyond the imperial frontier running along the prosperous line between Rhine and Danube, or eastwards to the Red Sea and the Indian Ocean. According to Pliny the Elder, Rome had a deficit of 100 million sesterces in its trade with the Far East every year. And ancient Roman coins are still being dug up in India today.[8]

Some Ground Rules

The past offers us a series of examples of world-economies then — not very many but enough to make some comparisons possible. Moreover since each world-economy lasted a very long time, it changed and developed within its own boundaries, so that its successive ages and different states also suggest some comparisons. The data available is thus sufficiently plentiful to allow us to construct a *typology* of world-economies and at the very least to formulate a set of rules or tendencies[9] which will clarify and even define their relations with geographical space.

Our first concern, in seeking to explain any world-economy, is to identify the area it occupies. Its boundaries are usually easy to discover since they are slow to change. The zone it covers is effectively the first condition of its existence. There is no such thing as a world-economy without its own area, one that is significant in several respects:

  — it has boundaries, and the line that defines it gives it an identity, just as coastlines do a sea;

  — it invariably has a centre, with a city and an already-dominant type of *capitalism*, whatever form this takes. A profusion of such centres represents either immaturity or on the contrary some kind of decline or mutation. In the face of pressures both internal and external, there may be shifts of the centre of gravity: cities with international destinies — *world cities* — are in perpetual rivalry with one another and may take each other's place;

— it is marked by a hierarchy: the area is always a sum of individual economies, some poor, some modest, with a comparatively rich one in the centre. As a result, there are inequalities, differences of voltage which make possible the functioning of the whole. Hence that "international division of labour," of which as P.M. Sweezy points out, Marx did not foresee that it "might harden into a pattern of development and under-development which would split mankind into haves and have-nots on a scale far wider and deeper than the bourgeois–proletarian split in the advanced countries themselves."[10] All the same, this is not in fact a "new" division, but an ancient and no doubt an incurable divide, one that existed long before Marx's time.

So there are three sets of conditions, each with general implications.

RULE ONE: THE BOUNDARIES CHANGE ONLY SLOWLY

The limits on one world-economy can be thought of as lying where those of another similar one begin: they mark a line, or rather a zone which it is only worth crossing, economically speaking, *in exceptional circumstances.* For the bulk of traffic in either direction, "the loss in exchange would outweigh the gain."[11] So *as a general rule,* the frontiers of a world-economy are quiet zones, the scene of little activity. They are like thick shells, hard to penetrate; they are often natural barriers, no man's lands — or no-man's-seas. The Sahara, despite its caravans, would have been one such, separating Black Africa from White Africa. The Atlantic was another, an empty expanse to the south and west of Africa, and for long centuries a barrier compared to the Indian Ocean, which was from early days the scene of much trade, at least in the north. Equally formidable was the Pacific, which European explorers had only half-opened to traffic: Magellan's voyage only unlocked one way into the southern seas, not a gateway for return journeys. To get back to Europe, the expedition had to take the Portuguese route round the Cape of Good Hope. Even the first voyages of the Manila galleon in 1572 did not really overcome the awe-inspiring obstacle posed by the South Sea. . . .

RULE TWO: A DOMINANT CAPITALIST CITY ALWAYS LIES AT THE CENTRE

A world-economy always has an urban centre of gravity, a city, as the logistic heart of its activity. News, merchandise, capital, credit, people, instructions, correspondence all flow into and out of the city. Its powerful merchants lay down the law, sometimes becoming extraordinarily wealthy.

At varying and respectful distances around the centre, will be found other towns, sometimes playing the role of associate or accomplice, but more usually resigned to their second-class role. Their activities are governed by those of the metropolis: they stand guard around it, direct the flow of business toward it, re-distribute or pass on the goods it sends them, live off its credit or suffer its rule. Venice was never isolated; nor was Antwerp; nor, later, was Amsterdam. These metropolises came accompanied by a train of subordinates; Richard Häpke coined the expression "an archipelago of towns," an evocative image. Stendhal was under the illusion that the great cities of Italy had treated the lesser cities kindly out of generosity.[12] But how could they have destroyed them? They certainly subjugated them, but no more, since they needed their services. A world-city could not reach and maintain its high standard of living without some sacrifices, willingly or unwillingly made by other large towns, which it resembled — a city is a city is a city after all — but from which it stood out: the metropolis was a super-city. And the first sign by which it could be recognized was precisely its retinue of assistants and subordinates. . . .

RULE TWO (CONTINUED): CITIES TAKE IT IN TURNS TO LEAD

Dominant cities did not dominate for ever; they replaced each other. This was as true at the summit as it was at every level of the urban hierarchy. Such shifts, wherever they occurred (at the top or half-way down), whatever their causes (economic or otherwise) are always significant; they interrupt the calm flow of history and open up perspectives that are the more precious for being so rare. When Amsterdam replaced Antwerp, when London took over from Amsterdam, or when in about 1929, New York overtook London, it always meant a massive historical shift of forces, revealing the precariousness of the previous equilibrium and the strengths of the one which was replacing it. The whole circle of the world-economy was affected by such changes and the repercussions were never exclusively economic, as the reader will probably already suspect. . . .

RULE TWO (CONTINUED): THE POWER
AND INFLUENCE OF CITIES MAY VARY

The reference to dominant cities should not lead us to think that the successes and strengths of these urban centres were always of the same type: in the course of their history, these cities were sometimes better or worse equipped for their task, and their differences or comparative failings, when looked at closely, oblige one to make some fairly fine distinctions of interpretation.

If we take the classic sequence of dominant cities of western Europe — Venice, Antwerp, Genoa, Amsterdam, London — which we shall presently be considering at length—it will be observed that the three first-named did not possess the complete arsenal of economic domination. Venice at the end of the fourteenth century was a booming merchant city; but possessed no more than the beginnings of an industrial sector; and while she did have financial and banking institutions, this credit system operated inside the Venetian economy, as an internal mechanism only. Antwerp, which possessed very little shipping of her own, provided a haven for Europe's merchant capitalism: operating as a sort of bring and buy centre for trade and business, to which everything came from outside. When Genoa's turn came, it was really only because of her banking supremacy, similar to that of Florence in the thirteenth and fourteenth centuries; if she played a leading role, it was firstly because her chief customer was the king of Spain, controller of the flow of bullion, and secondly because no one was quite sure where the centre of gravity really lay between the sixteenth and seventeenth centuries: Antwerp fulfilled this role no longer and Amsterdam was not yet ready: the Genoese supremacy was no more than an interlude. By the time Amsterdam and London took the stage, the world-cities possessed the whole panoply of means of economic power: they controlled everything, from shipping to commercial and industrial expansion, as well as the whole range of credit. . . .

RULE THREE: THERE IS ALWAYS A HIERARCHY OF ZONES WITHIN A WORLD-ECONOMY

The different zones within a world-economy all face towards one point in the centre: thus "polarized," they combine to form a whole with many relationships. As the Marseille Chamber of Commerce put it in 1763, "All trades are linked and join hands so to speak."[13] A hundred years earlier in Amsterdam, an observer was already concluding from the Dutch example "that there was such a close connection between all the parts of commerce in the universe that to be ignorant of one was to be ill-informed of the others."[14]

And once such connections were established, they lasted. . . .

RULE THREE (CONTINUED): THE SPATIAL ARRANGEMENT OF THE WORLD-ECONOMY

Every world-economy is a sort of jigsaw puzzle, a juxtaposition of zones interconnected, but *at different levels*. On the ground, *at least* three different areas of categories can be distinguished: a narrow *core*, a fairly developed middle zone and a vast *periphery*. The qualities and characteristics of the type of society, economy, technology, culture and political order necessarily alter as one moves from one zone to another. This is an explanation of very wide application, one on which Immanuel Wallerstein has based his book *The Modern World-System* (1974).

The centre or *core* contains everything that is most advanced and diversified. The next zone possesses only some of these benefits, although it has some share in them: it is the "runner-up" zone. The huge periphery, with its scattered population, represents on the contrary backwardness, archaism, and exploitation by others. This discriminatory geography is even today both an explanation and a pitfall in the writing of world history — although the latter often creates the pitfalls itself by its connivance. . . .

RULE THREE (CONCLUSION):
ENVELOPE AND INFRASTRUCTURE

A world-economy is like an enormous envelope. One would expect *a priori*, that given the poor communications of the past, it would have to unite considerable resources in order to function properly. And yet the world-economies of the past did incontestably function, although the necessary density, concentration, strength and accompaniments only effectively existed in the core region and the area immediately surrounding it; and even the latter, whether one looks at the hinterland of Venice, Amsterdam or London, might include areas of reduced economic activity, only poorly linked to the centres of decision. Even today, the United States has pockets of under-development within its own frontiers.

So whether one considers a world-economy in terms of its area on the face of the globe, or in terms of its depth at the centre, one's astonishment is the same: the machine seems to work and yet (especially if one thinks of the earliest outstanding cities in European history) it seems to have such a modest power supply. How was such success possible? The question will keep cropping up throughout the book, and we shall never be able to give a categorical answer: Dutch trade successfully penetrated the hostile France of Louis XIV; England gained control of an immense country like India, and these are indeed achievements bordering on the incomprehensible.

But perhaps I may be allowed to suggest one explanation, by the artificial device of an image.

Think of a huge block of marble, chosen by Michelangelo or one of his contemporaries from the quarries of Carrara,[15] an immensely heavy weight which was nevertheless cut out by primitive means and moved with very modest energy sources: a little gunpowder (which had already been used for some time in quarries and mines), two or three levels, perhaps a dozen men if that, ropes, a haulage team, wooden rollers if it was to be taken any distance, an inclined plane — and there it was. The whole thing was possible because the giant slab was helpless on the ground with its own weight: it represented a huge force, but one inert and neutralized. Cannot this analogy be applied to the great mass of elementary economic activities which was also trapped, imprisoned, unable to move from the ground, and therefore more easily manoeuverable *from above*? The devices and levers that made the achievement possible in this case consisted of a little ready money, the silver coin that arrived at Danzig or Messina, the tempting offer of credit, a little "artificial" money or a rare and coveted product; or even the market system itself. The high prices at the far end of a trading chain were a continual lure: the word got round and the whole chain went into motion.

Notes

1. See volume 2, chapter 5 of *Civilization and Capitalism* on the use of the term "set."

2. Simone de Sismondi, *Nouveaux Principles d'économie politique,* ed. Jean Weiller, 1971, 19.

3. Ibid., 105, n. 1.

4. I first found this word used in the special sense employed here in Fritz Rörig's book, *Mittelalterliche Weltwirtschaft, Blüte und Ende einer Weltwirtschaftsperiode,* 1933. Hektor Ammann, in *Wirtschaft und Lebensraum der Mittelalterlichen Kleinstadt,* n.d., 4, rightly qualifies this as "eine Art Weltwirtschaft," "a sort of world economy."

5. Léon-H. Dupriez, "Principles et problèmes d'interprétation," 3, in *Diffusion du progrès et convergence des prix. Etudes internationales,* 1966. The ideas expressed in this chapter have much in common with those of I. Wallerstein, *op. cit.,* although I do not always agree with him.

6. Fernand Braudel, *La Mediterranée, . . . ,* 1st French ed., 1949, 325, 328 ff.

7. Fernand Braudel, *The Mediterranean and the Mediterranean World in the Age of Philip II,* English trans., 2 vols., 1972–73, 1:387 (hereafter referred to as *Medit*; all page references are to the English edition of 1972–73, published by Collins, which is a translation of the second French edition of 1966).

8. A. M. Jones, "Asian Trade in Antiquity," in *Islam and the Trade of Asia, op. cit.,* 5.

9. I have used the expressions "rules" or "tendencies," following the example of Georges Gurvitch (*règles tendancielles*) to avoid using the stronger "laws."

10. Paul Sweezy, *Modern Capitalism,* 1974, 143.

11. Immanuel Wallerstein's expression.

12. *Medit.,* 1:282.

13. Charles Carrière, Marcel Courdurié, *L'Espace commercial marseillais aux XVIIe et XVIIIe siècles,* typescript, 27.

14. A.N., Marine, B7 463, 11 (1967).

15. Christiane Klapisch-Zuber, *Les Maîtres du marbre. Carrare 1300–1600,* 1969, 69–76.

ANDRE GUNDER FRANK

A Plea for World System History

INTRODUCTION AND PROCEDURE

I plead for writing a world history that is as comprehensive and systematic as possible. It should offer a more humanocentric alternative to western Eurocentrism. This history should seek maximum "unity in the diversity" of human experience and development. Therefore, we should not only make comparisons over time and space, we should also seek more connections among distant and seemingly disparate events at each historical point in time. Moreover, we should systematically seek to systematize both the comparisons and the connections. Thus, our historical inquiry may well find more than comparative commonalities among parts of the whole. We may also discover common features and relations among historical events, which are derived from their common participation in a whole. For the long period before 1492, this "whole" world history should concentrate on the unity and historical interrelations within the Asio-Afro-European "old" "eastern" hemispheric ecumene, stretching from the Pacific to the Atlantic — before Columbus (again) crossed the latter.

The principal idea I advance is the principle, indeed the imperative, of doing a "macro" world *system* history. The main reason to do so is that, as the old adage goes, this historical whole is more than the sum of its parts. This holistic principle does not deny the necessary "micro" history of its parts. However, it is necessary to remember that all the parts are also shaped by — and can only be adequately understood in relation to — their participation in the whole and their relations with other parts. Such "comprehensive" macro attention to the whole and its essential structure and dynamic must, of course, give short shrift to many "micro" details. However, these can be supplied by specialists, whose also necessary study will in turn help amend and reshape our vision of the whole.

For reasons of expository convenience (for me) and clarity of communication (with the reader), I proceed to pose selected (and numbered) either/or issues. Then, I give my own positions on these issues in the form of theses. Of course, I do not think that all historical reality is so simply reducible to such alternative choices. Nor do I claim to cover all possible or even all important such

Andre Gunder Frank, "A Plea for World System History," *Journal of World History* 2 (Spring 1991): 1–28.

alternatives and issues. My selection of issues, and their phrasing below, is governed by my own positions, whose arguments I wish to pose for the reader.

Therefore for reasons of exposition and communication, I will frequently resort to brief citations or quotations of arguments of mine, which are elaborated more fully elsewhere. I will also "appeal to authority" (and anti-authority by my lights) by citing and quoting authors who have long-standing claim to authority (even if, to their credit, they would disclaim the same). Of course, I do not expect the reader to accept my arguments on the basis of appeals to any authority, least of all my own. On the contrary, my purpose in making these appeals is only to incite readers ever more to "seek truth from (the authority of) facts" and to appeal to "the authority" of their own (re)interpretations of them.

TWENTY ISSUES AND THESES

On Eurocentrism and Its Alternatives

1. Should *world* history continue its recent western Eurocentric bend, or should it seek to liberate the world from it(self) — even in the west? *World* history should be a reflection and representation of the full diversity of human experience and development, which far exceeds the limited and limiting recent bounds of the "west." Indeed, the "west" does not exist, except by reference to the "east." Yet the historical existence of "east" and "west" is only a figment of "western" imagination.

A few generations ago, a different perspective was still counseled even by some western historians. For instance, in 1918 Frederick Teggart criticized "Eurocentric" history and pleaded for a single "Eurasian" history in which "the two parts of Eurasia are inextricably bound together. Mackinder has shown how much light may be thrown on European history by regarding it as subordinate to Asiatic. . . . The oldest of historians (Herodotus) held the idea that epochs of European history were marked by alternating movements across the imaginary line that separates East from West" (Teggart 1977, 248).

Yet since Teggart's 1918 plea, western domination in power and technology has further extended the domain of its culture and Eurocentric western perspective through proselytizing religion, mass media, language, education, "world" history writing and teaching, and using the (in)famous Mercator projection maps. Nonetheless, homogenization has proceeded less far and fast than some hoped and others feared, and many people around the world are seeking renewed and diverse self-affirmation and self-determination.

2. Should and need western Eurocentric world history and its distortions be replaced by "equal time" for the history of all cultures? Or need we admit (a variety of competing) other centric histories, be they Islamo-, Nippo-, Sino- or whatever other centric? No, we can and should all aspire to a non-exclusivist *humano*centric history. This world history can be more than a

historical "entitlement program," which gives all (contemporary) cultures or nationalities their due separate but equal shares of the past. Instead, a humanocentric history can and must also recognize our historical and contemporary *unity* in and through diversity beyond our ideological affirmations of cultural self. The UNESCO project on the *History of Mankind* (including its *Journal of World History*, published under the main title *Cahiers d'histoire mondiale*, begun in 1954!) and more recently the UNESCO "Integral Study of the Silk Roads" project have made valiant efforts in this direction. Gilbert Allardyce (1990) has reviewed the trials and tribulations of some attempts by UNESCO and others to move "toward world history" through both "entitlement" and "globaloney" programs, at least in the United States and its postwar cultural dependencies. The American leader of the UNESCO project, Louis Gottschalk, finally gave up this "mission impossible." So should fools rush in the footsteps of the daring McNeill (1963, 1990) and Stavrianos (1970) where most angels fear to tread? Why not?

3. If we should not aspire to "equal time" in history of everybody in the world, should such a world history be limited to, or concentrate on, the addition of representative "non-western civilizations" and cultures to western ones? Should we limit our study to the comparative examination of their distinctive and common features? This is the procedure of most (literally) so-called courses and textbooks. Some examples of these approaches and their internal contradictions and limitations are examined in Frank (1990a). Two well-known examples examined are the comparative studies of civilizations by Toynbee and Quigley. Another example is the approach to "Civilization as a Unit of World History" by Edward Farmer (1985) and Farmer et al. (1977).

I argue that our world history can and should also make efforts to *connect and relate* the diversity of histories and times to each other. It may be empirically possible, and in that case it is historically important, to uncover all sorts of historical connections among peoples and places, not only over time but especially at the *same time*. These connections would lend additional meaning to our comparisons. One cue among others to this kind of historiography is Philip Curtin's *Cross-Cultural Trade in World History* (1984). Another approach was used by Frederick Teggart in his *Rome and China: A Study of Correlations in Historical Events* (1939). Teggart correlated and connected diverse political and economic events (particularly wars, "barbarian" invasions, and interruption or resumption of trade) in these two geographical areas and others in between. Teggart made these *connections among contemporaneous events* "for the purpose of gaining verifiable knowledge concerning 'the way things work' in the world of human relations . . . in the spirit of modern scientific work, on the study of World History" (Teggart 1939, v, xii, and see below). Teggart also proposed a similar inquiry into the possible connections among the often observed almost simultaneous rise in the sixth century B.C. of the religious and other movements associated with Zoroaster, Confucius, Buddha, Ezekiel, and Pythagoras.

On World Historical Comparisons,
Connections, Nexuses, and System(s)

4. Need or should world historians then limit themselves to only connecting and comparing different peoples, places, and times as they appear to them at first sight? Or can and should a *one world* history also seek systematically to systematize these connections and relations, as well as comparisons, into an analysis of a *world system* history? This is now the opinion of our contemporary dean of world history writing, William McNeill (1990). In *"The Rise of the West* after Twenty-Five Years," he reflects and concludes that

> the central methodological weakness of my book is that while it emphasizes interactions across civilizational boundaries, it pays inadequate attention to the emergence of the ecumenical world system within which we live today. . . . Being too much preoccupied by the notion of "civilization," I bungled by not giving the initial emergence of a trans-civilizational process the sustained emphasis it deserved. . . . Somehow an appreciation of the autonomy of separate civilizations (and of all the other less massive and less skilled cultures of the earth) across the past two thousand years needs to be combined with a portrait of an emerging world system, connecting greater and greater numbers of persons across civilizational boundaries.
>
> To make this a feasible enterprise, one needs a clear and distinct idea of the emergent world system as manifested first in the ancient Middle East and a second time in the modern world, and one must reflect on how these intersected with the more local civilizational and cultural landscapes they impinged upon. . . . In the ancient Middle East, the resulting interactions among peoples living in different landscapes, with diverse languages and other outward signs of civilized diversity, led to the emergence of a cosmopolitan world system between 1700 and 500 B.C. . . . There is a sense, indeed, in which the rise of civilizations in the Aegean (later Mediterranean) coast lands and in India after 1500 B.C. were and remained part of the emergent world system centered on the Middle East. . . . All three regions and their peoples remained in close and uninterrupted contact throughout the classical era. . . . [Moreover] one may, perhaps, assume that a similar [to the modern] primacy for economic exchanges existed also in earlier times all the way back [to] the earliest beginnings of civilization in ancient Mesopotamia (McNeill 1990, 9–10, 12–14).

Thirty-five years earlier, Marshall Hodgson had already pleaded:

> The point is that *from a world-historical* point of view, what is important is not European history in itself, however important that be for us all; but its role in interregional history. . . . The problem of reorienting ourselves to a more interregional viewpoint, then, is psychologically far-reaching, and must be solved along with that of organizing the historical material.
>
> During the last three thousand years there has been one zone, possessing to some degree a common history, which has been so inclusive that its study must take a preponderant place in any possible world-historical investigation. . . . The various lands of urbanized, literate civilization in the Eastern

Hemisphere, in a continuous zone from the Atlantic to the Pacific, have been in commercial and commonly in intellectual contact with each other, mediately or immediately. Not only have the bulk of mankind lived in this zone, but its influence has emanated into much of the rest of the world.

[In] the following approach . . . events may be dealt with in their relation to the total constellation of historical forces of which they are a part — a method not limited to world history, but perhaps likely to be especially appropriate in this case. This means that we are to consider how events reflect interdependent interregional developments (Hodgson 1954, 716, 717, 723).

A few years later, Hodgson would add that "few scholarly tasks are more urgent than that of learning to see the various historical backgrounds of our common world in relation to each other" (1960, 879).

Allardyce (1990, 62, 67, 69) quotes others to the effect that what world history "needs is a simple, all-encompassing, elegant idea, which offers an adequate conceptual base for a world history." I suggest that the basic elements of this idea may be found in the foregoing quotations from Hodgson and McNeill. The central concept of this all-encompassing idea is the world *system* and the historical *process* of its development. What we need is a world system history, please.

The attempt to help advance this "urgent task" is also the main intent of Frank (1990a, b, c, d) and Gills and Frank (1990), although they were largely written before reading these quotations from McNeill and Hodgson. However, the major works by both authors were important inputs. Frank (1990a) concentrates on a critique of many quoted and otherwise cited civilizationists, world and other historians, historical macro sociologists, economic historians, political economists, and others. These scholars mostly do not even consider such a world system history before 1500. Or they consider it, and then deny its practicability or even its utility. Even those few who would welcome a world system history in principle, in their own practice still neglect to pursue it themselves. In each case, I first examine their arguments and procedures. Then, I conclude that their objections or reservations to such a world system history are theoretically invalid and empirically unfounded. Among the authorities, anti-authorities, and others critiqued, and in some cases recommended as partial models, are Abu-Lughod (1989), Amin (1988), Anderson (1974), Chase-Dunn (1986, 1989), Childe (1942), Curtin (1984), Farmer (1985), Farmer et al. (1977), Gernet (1982), Hodgson (1974), Lattimore (1962), Lombard (1975), McNeill (1963, 1982, 1990), Mann (1986), Needham (1961), Quigley (1961), Schneider (1977), Stavrianos (1970), Taylor (1987–88), Tilly (1984), Toynbee (1946), Wallerstein (1974, 1988), and Wilkinson (1987, 1988).

The conclusions of Frank (1990a) and Gills and Frank (1990) argue why and how such a world system history can and should be undertaken — even if "world history in world-system style is likely to appear . . . as downright subversive" (Allardyce 1990, 69). But then so have been all new systemic departures. The idea of a world system since 1500 has indeed gained ground in recent years.

However, its principal protagonists and others resist the extension of this idea backwards before 1500 (for Immanuel Wallerstein 1974, 1989) or 1250 (for Janet Abu-Lughod 1989). However, the historical empirical evidence and especially its internally contradictory treatment by these authors vitiate their arguments of a systemic historical break around 1450 to 1500, as per Wallerstein, or around 1250 to 1350, as per Abu-Lughod. This is what I try to demonstrate in Frank (1990b and c) and below. The conclusions derived from my argument challenge the very idea of "transition," especially from the supposed "modes" or "systems" of feudalism to capitalism and on to socialism. No wonder a world system history could appear downright subversive, if it rejects the adequacy of "to each his own" or "equal time to all" cultural histories. It may be even more subversive if it *also* challenges most people's "scientific" ideologies, according to which their favorite eternal or transitional political economic "mode" or "system" has exceptional virtues, thanks to God.

    5. Is world history limited to that of sedentary "civilizations" and their relations? Or must it also include "barbarian" nomads and others, and especially the multifarious relations among the former and the latter? Frank (1990a) follows Lattimore (1962) and others to make a strong plea for more study of central and inner Asian "nomadic" and other peoples, their continuous trade and political relations with their "civilized" neighbors, and the recurrent waves of migratory and invasory incursions from central and inner Asia into east, south, and west Asia, and Europe. Therefore, I argue for greater attention to the possible centrality of central and inner Asia and the dynamics and relations of its peoples with others in world history. Similarly, the nomadic tribes of the Arabian peninsula before the time of Muhammad merit more attention. Moreover, it is time to drop and take exception to the now pejorative term "barbarian." There is much reason to doubt the supposed difference between peoples who have been so labeled and those supposedly more "civilized." There is even reason to doubt the verity and utility of the supposed distinctions between "nomad" and "sedentary" peoples. However that may be, there can be little doubt about the central roles of central Asia in world (system) history (Frank 1990d).

    Africa has also received less attention than it merits in world (system) history. Curtin has done pioneering work on trade and migration in Africa, but in his *Cross-Cultural Trade in World History* (1984), he has not sought to pursue the African connection in Afro-Asia as far back in history as it may deserve. The southeast Asian peoples and their history were intimately related to and also influential on those of China and India, yet Southeast Asia is often largely omitted from even those world histories that give their due to China and India. Relations between the "eastern" and "western" hemispheres, across both the Atlantic and the Pacific, even if they may not have been "systematic," long predate those (re)initiated by Columbus.

    Exceptional geographical, topological, ecological, natural, or human resources have lent a select few regions in the world very special strategic, military, political, economic, and cultural importance in the establishment and maintenance of the world system and relations within it. Gills and Frank argue that three magnets of attractions for political economic expansion stand out. One is sources of human (labor) and/or material inputs (land, water, raw materials, precious metal, etc.) and technological inputs into the process of accumulation. The second is markets to dispose of one zone's surplus production to exchange for more inputs, and to capture stored value. The third, and perhaps most significant, are the most privileged nexuses or logistical corridors of interzonal trade. Bottle-neck control over the supply routes of raw materials, especially of metals and other strategic materials, plays a key role in attracting hegemonical powers to such areas, or in providing a basis upon which to make a bid for hegemony. Especially here, economic, political and military conflict and/or cultural, "civilizational," religious and ideological influence also offer special advantages for tapping into the accumulation and the system of exploitation of other zones in benefit of one's own accumulation (Gills and Frank 1990, 24).

Gills and Frank identify three such corridors and logistical nexuses between the Mediterranean and Asia:

> 1. The Nile-Red Sea corridor (with canal or overland connections between them and to the Mediterranean Sea, and open access to the Indian Ocean and beyond).
> 2. The Syria-Mesopotamia-Persian Gulf corridor (with overland routes linking the Mediterranean coast through Syria, on via the Orontes, Euphrates and Tigris rivers, to the Persian Gulf, which gives open access to the Indian Ocean and beyond). This nexus also offered connections to overland routes to Central Asia.
> 3. The Aegean-Black Sea-Central Asia corridor (connecting the Mediterranean via the Dardanelles and Bosporus to the overland "Silk Roads" to and from Central Asia, from where connecting routes extended overland to India and China) (Gills and Frank 1990, 24).

However, there were other such logistical nexuses in various maritime straits, such as those of Ceylon, and overland portages such as Kra on the Malay Peninsula. Along the overland invasory and silk routes in inner Asia, and its connections to China, India, and Persia, other bottleneck and crossroad nexuses played strategic roles. Among these were the Gansu (Haxi) Corridor between China and Dunhuang at the desert's edge, and the Karakorum and other passes across the Pamirs southwestward from Kashgar to Taxila, and across the Tian Shan Mountains northwestward to Samarkand and Bukhara. All of these and other nexuses deserve special attention in the study of world (system) history. Have they been special bones of political and economic contention militating against their long-term control by any one power?

On World Historical Times and Timing

6. Should we treat historical diversity and comparisons as we often do, and as Anderson explicitly defends, by arguing that "there is no such thing as a uniform temporal medium: for the *times* of the major Absolutism . . . were precisely, enormously diverse . . . no single temporality covers it"? (Anderson 1974,

10). Or can and should the systematization of inter-regional world history also realize, as Hodgson argued, that "what is important is the recognition . . . that there has been some sort of developing pattern in which all these interregional developments can be studied, as they are affected by and in turn affect its elements as constituted at any one time" (Hodgson 1954, 719).

In Frank (1978b) I argued that

> Anderson's apparent attempt to make historiographic virtue out of empirical necessity when he argues that the historical times of events are different though their dates may be the same must be received with the greatest of care — and alarm. For however useful it may be [comparatively] to relate the same thing through different times, the essential (because it is the most necessary and the least accomplished) contribution of the historian to historical understanding is successively to relate different things and places at the same time in the historical process. The very *attempt* to examine and relate the simultaneity of different events in the whole historical process or in the transformation of the whole system — even if for want of empirical information or theoretical adequacy it may be full of holes in its factual coverage of space and time — is a significant step in the right direction (particularly at a time in which this generation must "rewrite history" to meet its need for historical perspective and understanding of the single world historical process in the world today) (Frank 1978a, 21–22).

Teggart, alas unbeknownst to me, had long since

> establishe[d] (for the first time) the existence of [temporal] *correlations in historical events* . . . which exhibits the relationship between contemporaneous disturbances in several areas . . . [and] awareness of the concurrrence of events in different regions. . . . The study of the past can become effective only when it is fully realized that all peoples have histories, that these histories run concurrently and in the same world, and that the act of comparing is the beginning of knowledge. . . . It at once sets a new problem for investigation by raising the question of how the correspondences in events are to be accounted for (Teggart 1939, 239, 243, 245).

7. Did world history discontinuously jump from one place and time to another? The usual western Eurocentric rendition jumps from ancient Mesopotamia to Egypt, to "classical" Greece and then Rome, to medieval western Europe, and then on to the Atlantic west, with scattered backflashes to China, India, et cetera. Meanwhile, all other history drops out of the story. Or peoples and places never even appear in history, unless they are useful as supposedly direct descendants of development in the west. Instead, any *world* history should try to trace and establish the historical *continuity* of developments between then and now in the world systemic whole and all its parts. Hodgson and McNeill already emphasized this continuity. David Wilkinson (1987) supports Hodgson's early suggestion, which Wilkinson probably did not know. Wilkinson demonstrates convincingly (to me) that "Central Civilization" has a continuous and expanding (I would say world system) history since Mesopotamia and Egypt established relations in about 1500 B.C.

Gills and Frank (1990) argue that these relations extend even farther out and further back. During another millennium from 2500 B.C. or earlier already, peoples established relations with each other around and from the Mediterranean to the Levant, Anatolia, Mesopotamia, the Persian highlands, and the Indus Valley, as well as with many central Asian "nomads" and others. Gordon Childe (1942) already argued for the recognition and analysis of these and even earlier and more widespread relations.

Some two millennia later, China, Manchuria, Korea, and Japan in the northeast, and southeast Asian peoples developed (systematic?) relations with each other and with other peoples across and around Asia. Systemic relations around the beginning of the Christian era among Han China, Kushan Pakistan/India, Parthian Iran, the Roman empire, and parts of Africa are well documented and analyzed by among others Hudson (1931), Teggart (1939), and with regard to technological diffusion more recently again by Needham (1961). Several recent authors quote Pliny's lament about the fiscal crisis in his native Rome, which was due to its balance of trade deficit with Parthia and through it with China. Teggart went further. He quoted Cicero to the effect that "the credit of the Roman money-market is intimately bound up with the prosperity of Asia; a disaster cannot occur there without shaking our credit to its foundations" (Teggart 1939, 74). Odani (1990) suggests that, since Roman and Asian coins were of exactly the same weight and therefore interchangeable, a single international monetary system may have existed.

Teggart also correlated and compared the timing of wars and barbarian invasions in Rome and China to demonstrate that for the period 58 B.C. to A.D. 107 alone, "even in briefest summary it must be pointed out that, of the wars in the Roman East, eighteen followed wars in Chinese Turkestan, so that of the forty occasions on which outbreaks took place in Europe, twenty-seven were traceable to the policy, or rather changes of policy, of the Han government [in China]" (Teggart 1939, viii).

Teggart pioneered this analysis and suggested that

> it is to be seen that peoples in no way concerned with the silk route might yet be connected with the interruptions of trade on that route through the hostilities which the interruptions precipitated between Parthia and Rome.
>
> Thus the effects of wars which arose out of interruptions of the great "silk route" through Persia are plainly visible in the internal history of Rome. . . . Seemingly there could be no better illustration of interdependence of nations than the consideration that a decision of the Chinese government should have been responsible for a financial panic in the capital of the Roman empire. . . .
>
> It follows, therefore, that knowledge which is indispensable for an historical account of Roman affairs . . . can be obtained in no other way than by the comparison of events throughout Eurasia. Thus, apart from any wider interest, the comparisons of histories is necessary for a comprehension of what has actually happened within the borders of any national state (Teggart 1939, x, 241, 243).

Actually, Teggart himself did not limit his inquiry to correlations and comparisons. He also inquired into what he called their "connections" and knowledge concerning "the way things work" in what we might call "the world system." Moreover, Brooks Adams (1939) long ago pleaded for the recognition of this world historical unity and continuity.

8. However, since when can we accurately refer to "China," "India," "Persia," "Central Asia," or elsewhere as particular peoples or civilizations? Alternatively, how long were (or still are?) these only geographical loci in and through which different peoples came and went, mixed, and developed cultural, social, political, and economic institutions and relations, which also came and went? Most civilizations, empires, ethnicities, "races," and of course nations only *temporarily developed here and there out of a mixture of peoples.* Some peoples among them took or gained enough of a temporary upper hand to put their temporary imprint and name on the civilization, dynasty, or empire, et cetera. Perhaps the longest still living civilization is that of the Chinese. Yet for half of "China's" history, it has been ruled by non-"Chinese." Historians conventionally study the "dynastic" history of China. Civilizationists generally focus on this and other (supposedly self-contained) "civilizations." Thereby, both have detracted attention from the more important, but often changing, ecological or economic units, empires, states, and (inter)state *systems,* and their *relations* with each other over much of the world. Moreover, the fact that peoples and their institutions have come and gone over the world stage of history does not mean that there was no systemic rhyme or reason to their coming and going. On the contrary, the very coming and going of different peoples, their institutions, and their relations with each other may systematically, and not only exceptionally, have obeyed some systemic "laws" of world system development and history. We should inquire into these.

9. Should we then start our world historical (system) inquiry at some arbitrarily or conveniently selected date? Or should we instead permit the historical evidence *to take us back as far as we can* go? Should we move forwards or backwards in our historical inquiry? Both! John King Fairbank, the contemporary dean of American historians of China, wrote from his experience that "the rule seems to be, if you want to study the mid-period of a century, begin at the end of it and let the problems lead you back. *Never* try to begin at the beginning. Historical research progresses backward, not forward" (Fairbank 1969, ix).

This has been my experience as well, and I recommend Fairbank's rule to others with two reservations. One is that real historical development, of course, moved forward in time, and our scientific rendition of it must respect this fact. The other is that however heuristically useful it may be for us to inquire backward, we can still turn around to relate and present our findings and history itself forward in time.

On Cumulation of Accumulation and Ecology in World System History

10. Is world (system) history only continuous (since when?), or is it also cumulative? Has there been, is there still, a *cumulative historical development?* Civilizationists and cultural historians have long since presented much of human knowledge and culture as cumulative. Childe (1942) and others have

also presented technology as substantially cumulative (little re-invention of the wheel). If that is so, can we not theoretically argue and empirically demonstrate that world (system) history includes a long process of economic accumulation, including skills and technology, but also infrastructural, productive, and financial accumulation? That is the argument of Gills and Frank (1990) under the title "The Cumulation of Accumulation."

11. Is this process of accumulation, and the associated production, trade, finance, and their political organization independent of ecological possibilities and limitations? Just posing this question seems to answer it, especially in this age of heightened ecological degradation and awareness. Human social, economic, and political history have always been *adaptations to ecological circumstances and changes.* Ecological possibilities and limitations helped determine the development of alluvial valley agricultural civilizations like ancient Sumer and Egypt. Their ecology also affected their needs for commerce and political influence over highland sources of metals and other mineral raw materials and wood. Similarly, ecological realities and their changes also impacted on grassland nomadic and other peoples and their trading, migratory, and invasory relations with sedentary civilizations. Of course, hunting, migration, agriculture, industry, political and military institutions and activities, and many cultural ones have also in turn impinged on and altered the physical environment. Today, but also at some times and places in the past, this human ecological impact has been damaging to the physical environment and to human welfare. A world history must devote more attention to human and social ecology, especially now.

12. Are these ecological and social adaptations and transformations often renewed independent inventions (as of the wheel) at different times and places in the world? Or are many of them also the result of migratory, invasory, trade, political, and cultural *relations and diffusion around the world*? Or both? The easy answer would seem to be both by simple addition of renewed invention here and there and diffusion from here to there. However "necessity is the mother of invention." Therefore, much of the renewed "(in)dependent" invention and innovation there was also "diffused" from here. That is, invention was stimulated there by the necessity of competition with here, where its use offered a competitive advantage. Moreover, this process of diffusion and emulation of invention and innovation was not limited to things (bronze) or technology (smelting) but extended to social institutions and cultural forms.

Philip Curtin and William McNeill are among those who subscribe to and offer empirical evidence for the diffusionist thesis, both simple and competitive. Every day, archaeologists uncover, and reinterpret, additional evidence for maritime and overland diffusion over the longest distances, and at earlier and earlier times. Diffusion spread, among other things, foodstuffs; agricultural, industrial, transport, and military technology; culture and religion; language and writing; mathematics and astronomy; disease, first plague deaths and then resistance to the same, and medicine; and, of course, genes. See, for instance, McNeill's *Plagues and Peoples.* The more we look for diffusion, the more we find. The place of diffusion in a truly world-embracing history is assured, if we would only admit more of it.

13. A particularly important open question is whether the all too widespread socio-cultural institution of *patriarchy* was indigenously invented by many societies or diffused from a few to many. Feminist archaeologists and historians (thank Goddess for them!) have begun to dig up or reinterpret a paleolithic and neolithic past supposedly governed by non-patriarchal "partnership" relations. However, these relations were found to be "indigenous" particularly in Catal Huyuk and Hacilar in Anatolia, the site of Jericho in the Levant, later in Minoan Crete, and in the Balkans (Eisler 1987). Figurines that suggest non-patriarchal goddess worship have also been found farther eastward into India. The feminist scholars argue that these societies, and by extension western Judeo-Christian society, only switched to patriarchy later after armed invaders from inner and central Asia brought warfare, military technology, oppression, and therewith the "diffusion" of patriarchy. Thus, these feminist scholars suggest that western patriarchy is the result of its (unwelcome) diffusion from farther east in inner Asia.

(Re)writing history from a more gender-balanced or feminist perspective is very welcome. We particularly need more "feminist historical materialist" analysis of different and changing gender and family relations, accumulation, politics, and culture/ideology. Much of history has been dominated by men in their own interest and written by them from their own perspective. However, the above-cited feminist version of history seems less than satisfactory. It focuses rather selectively on some circum-Mediterranean societies with supposedly indigenous partnership societies and sees patriarchy as having been only belatedly diffused there from inner Asia. These primarily Euro-Mediterranean centered feminist historians would do well to expand their scope to that of the world, if not also to the world system, as a whole.

James DeMeo (1987, 1990), for instance, claims that "matrist" (but not matriarchal), democratic, egalitarian, sex-positive, pleasure-oriented, gentle, and non-violent society was "original" in much more of the world while it was wetter and greener until six thousand years ago. Then, Arabia and central Asia dried up about 4000 to 3500 B.C.; desertification expanded through what he calls the thousand-mile-wide Saharasian belt stretching eight thousand miles from Africa through inner Asia to China. As a result, many of its inhabitants suffered famines and were obliged to become pastoralist nomads. The harsh and competitive realities of this *new* lifestyle then fostered "patrism," including patriarchy, which DeMeo characterizes through at least thirty-five socio-cultural variables. These include harsh child rearing and especially infant swaddling and induced cranial deformation to enhance parents' mobility, sexual repression, patrilocal residence, patrilineal descent and inheritance, various forms of subordination of women, organized and specialized priesthood, high class stratification, high bellicosity, and frequent warfare. DeMeo finds these and other characteristics of patrism auto-correlated among each other and correlated with Saharasian and neighboring regions, as well as in some similar regions in the western hemisphere.

Thus, like the above-cited feminists, DeMeo also sees the subsequent *diffusion* of patrism by migrants and invaders escaping from dry regions to other wetter ones with previously matrist societies. However, he also tries to account for patrism as a prior widespread adaptation to changing environmental-economic conditions in the Saharasian belt. Moreover, DeMeo tries to demonstrate how, once it is introduced anywhere, patrism is reproduced, reenforced, and perpetuated inter-generationally, irrespective of subsequent patterns of climate, food supply, or settlement. Perhaps this approach offers additional scope and method for the study of endogenous invention/diffusion of patriarchy and other socio-cultural characteristics. On the other hand, like Eisler, DeMeo seems to disregard evidence and theory in support of indigenous development of patriarchy in agriculturally based ancient states and civilizations. Moreover, all those students of Asian nomads whom I have questioned say that on the evidence available to them, the status of women was higher and gender relations were more equal among nomadic than among sedentary peoples. Thus, the question remains open and calls for much more research.

On World System Characteristics and Transitions before and after 1500 A.D.

14. Are systematic and systemic relations of trade, not to mention migration and invasion or military conflict over the same, only recent developments in world (system) history, which bear study merely since the twentieth century, or the nineteenth, or the sixteenth? Or must we more systematically trace all of these political economic relations, no less and maybe even more than cultural ones, back farther and farther in a wider world (system)? I propose the latter and offer some indications on how to proceed in Frank (1990a, b, c, d) and Gills and Frank (1990). For millennia already, these systemic relations of peoples and localities combined a mixture of systematic trade relations and recurrent migrations far beyond the confines of any state or empire. Diplomatic expeditions, military excursions, and shifting alliances among states and empires were expressions of systematic and systemic relations. So were the diffusion and invention or adaptation of technological advances, social institutions, and cultural forms in response to changing ecological, economic, political, and often competitive necessities and opportunities in the wider world system.

15. Can the principal systemic features of the "modern world system" also be identified earlier than 1500 or not? Wallerstein (1988) and Modelski (1987) argue that the *differentiae specificae* of our world system are new since 1500 and essentially different from previous times and places. Christopher Chase-Dunn (1986) and others find parallels in "other" and prior world systems. Wilkinson (1987) discovers at least some of these features in his "Central Civilization" and elsewhere. However, he sees historical continuity, but no world system. Abu-Lughod (1989) sees a "thirteenth-century world system," but she regards it as different from the world system since 1500 or before 1250. Moreover, she is not so interested in comparing systemic features or characteristics. Gills (1989) and Gills and Frank (1990) combine all of the above into an analysis, or at least

an identification, of the principal features of *this* world system over several thousand years of its history and development, which are detailed below.

16. According to Wallerstein (1988, 1989, and elsewhere) and many students of world capitalism, the *differentia specifica* of the modern world system is the accumulation of capital: "It is this ceaseless accumulation of capital that may be said to be its most central activity and to constitute its *differentia specifica*. No previous historical system seems to have had any comparable *mot d'ordre*" (Wallerstein 1989, 9).

But was capital accumulation absent or minor or irrelevant elsewhere and earlier? Or, on the contrary, did capital accumulation exist and even define this (or another?) world system before, indeed long before, 1500? Gills and Frank (1990) emphatically argue for this latter position and point to considerable empirical evidence to back up the argument. For millennia and throughout the world (system), there has been capital accumulation through infrastructural investment in agriculture (e.g., clearing and irrigating land) and livestock (cattle, sheep, horses, camels, and pasturage for them); industry (plant and equipment as well as new technology for the same); transport (more and better ports, ships, roads, way stations, camels, and carts); commerce (money capital, resident and itinerant foreign traders, and institutions for their promotion and protection); military (fortifications, weapons, warships, horses, and standing armies to man them); legitimacy (temples and luxuries); and of course the education, training, and cultural development of "human capital."

The drive to produce, accumulate, distribute, and consume capital provided much of the economic, social, political, and cultural motor force in history. This was the case, for instance, of the development of Song and earlier Tang China, Byzantium, the expansion of Islam, Gupta India, and other regions in "medieval" times. However, the same may be said equally of the earlier "classical" Rome, Parthian Persia, Kushan India, and Han China; of the still earlier Hellenistic world and Persia; and so on back through world history. The mere mention of these "political" entities, not to mention their many peripheries, hinterlands, and countless nomadic migrants and invaders, should suggest that the same drive to accumulate was instrumental, if not largely determinant, for the competitive economic, political, and military rivalry and occasional opportunist alliances among and within contemporaneous political entities. That is, the quest for achievement and subsequent renewed loss of *competitive advantage (and disadvantage) within the process and pressures of competitive accumulation* have marked the economic, political, social, and cultural development of human and world system history through the ages.

17. Are other characteristics, in particular a *core-periphery structure*, of the modern world system also unique to it since 1500? Or are they also identifiable elsewhere and earlier? In a short list of three main characteristics of his modern world system, Wallerstein (1988) argues that "this descriptive trinity (core-periphery, A/B [cycle phases], hegemony-rivalry) as a pattern maintained over centuries is unique to the modern world-system. Its origin was precisely in the late fifteenth century" (Wallerstein 1988, 108).

Wallerstein (1989) also makes a list of twelve characteristics of his modern world capitalist system since 1500. Frank (1990c) argues why *all* of them also apply earlier. Frank (1990a) and Gills and Frank (1990) argued the same even before seeing Wallerstein's lists of characteristics. To avoid tiring the reader here, however, we limit the present review to Wallerstein's holy trinity alone.

The first characteristic is the core-periphery structure. Christopher Chase-Dunn and Tom Hall (1990 forthcoming) are editing a book on *Precapitalist Core/Periphery Relations*. Chase-Dunn (1986) himself has found many examples and so has Gills (1989). Wilkinson (1987) surveys core-periphery relations over five thousand years of world system history, which Ekholm and Friedman (1982) argued earlier. Therefore, Gills and Frank (1990) contend that core-periphery structures and relations have been prevalent throughout geographical space and historical time. Conceptually, however, they also need to be extended to hinterlands and a center-periphery-hinterlands (CPH) complex.

> The hinterland is not directly penetrated by the extracting classes of the center, but nevertheless it has systemic links with the center-periphery zone and its processes of accumulation. Wallerstein's use of the term hinterland to mean external to the world system is insufficient, because it neglects the structural and systemic significance of zones, which are "outside" of, but nonetheless related to, the center-periphery complex. These CPH relationships have been insufficiently analyzed. The CPH complex does not refer to mere geographical position, nor only to unequal levels of development. CPH also refers to the relations among the classes, peoples and "societies" that constitute the mode of accumulation. The CPH complex is the basic social complex upon which hegemony is constructed in a larger systemic context (Gills and Frank 1990).

18. Another of the three world system characteristics mentioned by Wallerstein is *hegemony-rivalry*. But is this feature limited to the world since 1500? Or did it also exist elsewhere and earlier? Or, indeed, does it also characterize the *same* world system earlier? Wallerstein himself discusses the rise and fall of mostly economically based hegemony only since 1500. Modelski (1987) and Thompson (1989) analyze largely politically based and exercised hegemony since 1494. Paul Kennedy (1987) wrote a best seller about the *Rise and Fall of the Great Powers* but without connecting them in any systematic way. The decline in the hegemony of a great power gives way to an interregnum of competitive economic, political, and military rivalry among others to take its place.

Gills and Frank (1990) argue that hegemony-rivalry has also characterized the world system for thousands of years. As suggested above, hegemony is not only political. It is also based on center-periphery relations, which permit the hegemonic center to further its accumulation of capital at the expense of its periphery, hinterland, and its rivals. After a time, not the least through the economic-military overextension signalled by Kennedy, the hegemonic empire loses this power again. After an interregnum of rivalry with other claimants, the previous hegemonical power is replaced by another one. Shifting systems of economic, political, and military alliances, reminiscent of those featured by George Orwell in his *1984*, are instrumental in first creating, then maintaining, and finally losing hegemonical imperial power.

Gills and Frank (1990) not only argue that there have been numerous and repeated instances of hegemony and rivalry at imperial regional levels. They also suggest that we may be able to recognize some instances of overarching "super-hegemony" and centralizing "super-accumulation" at the world system level before 1500. The Mongol empire certainly, and Song China perhaps, had a claim to super-hegemony. Thus, very significantly, the later rise to super-hegemony in and of western Europe, Great Britain, and the United States after 1500 were not unique first instances in the creation of a hegemonic world system. Instead, as Abu-Lughod persuasively argues, "'the fall of the East' preceded the 'Rise of the West'" (Abu-Lughod 1989, 338) and resulted in an hegemonical shift from east to west. This shift came at a time — and perhaps as a result — of over-extension and political economic decline in various parts of the east, which suffered a period of cyclical economic decline so common to them all as to have been world system wide. Thus the "Rise of the West," including European hegemony and its expansion and later transfer to the "new world" across the Atlantic, did not just constitute a new Modern World Capitalist System. This development also — and even more so — represented a new but continued development and hegemonic shift *within an old world system*.

19. The third characteristic of Wallerstein's world system after 1500 is *long economic cycles of capital accumulation*. Their upward "A" and downward "B" phases generate changes of hegemony and of position in the center-periphery-hinterland structure. These cycles, and especially the Kondratieffs, play important roles in the real development of the world system and in its analysis by Wallerstein (1974), Frank (1978a), Modelski (1987), Goldstein (1988), and Thompson (1989). All emphasize the relations among cycles in the economy, hegemony, and war. However, are these cycles limited to modern times, or do they extend farther back? Frank (1990c) tries to demonstrate that this same cyclical pattern definitely extends back through the eleventh century and that it could be traced further back as well. Gills and Frank (1990) go on to argue that these long cycles extend much farther back in world system history. Even Wallerstein notes that

> it is the long swing that was crucial. . . . The feudal system in western Europe seems quite clearly to have operated by a pattern of cycles of expansion and contraction of two lengths: circa 50 years [which seem to resemble the so-called Kondratieff cycles found in the capitalist world economy] and circa 200–300 years. . . . The patterns of the expansions and contractions are clearly laid out and widely accepted among those writing about the late Middle Ages and early modern times in Europe. . . . It is the long swing that was crucial. Thus 1050–1250+ was a time of the expansion of Europe (the Crusades, the colonizations). . . . The "crisis" or great contractions of 1250–1450+ included the Black Plague (Wallerstein 1989, 33, 34).

Thus, even according to Wallerstein, there was systematic *cyclical continuity* across his 1500 divide — in Europe. But Abu-Lughod (1989), McNeill (1982) and others offer and analyze substantial evidence that this same cycle was in fact world system wide. Again, even Wallerstein perceives some of the evidence:

> The collapse of the Mongols [was a] crucial non-event. . . . The eleventh-century economic upsurge in the West that we have discussed was matched by a new market articulation in China. . . . Both linked up to a Moslem trading ecumene across the Middle East. China's commercialization reinforced this model [why not system?]. . . . The Mongol link completed the picture. What disrupted this vast trading *world-system* was the pandemic Black Death, itself quite probably a consequence of that very trading network. It hurt everywhere, but it completely eliminated the Mongol link (Wallerstein 1989, 57, 58, my emphasis).

Moreover, all these developments were driven by the motor force of capital accumulation. The "crucial long swing" was a cycle of capital accumulation. It seems likely, however, that the rise and decline of different empires in medieval, "classical" Roman-Parthian-Kushan-Han, and even ancient times can and should be fit into such cyclical patterns of their own. Moreover, these regional cycles may in turn fit into, or indeed be partially derivative from, a single world system wide cycle of capital accumulation, hegemony, and development.

20. So do these characteristic similarities with the "modern-world-capitalist-system" extend only to "other" earlier empires, state systems, regional economies, or different "world systems"? Or do *similar characteristics extend backwards through time in the same world system*, which itself also extends much farther back in time? I believe the historical evidence supports, and our analytical categories should promote, this second interpretation.

How can we extend the essential features of the "modern-world-capitalist-system" of Wallerstein (1974), Frank (1978a), Modelski (1987), Goldstein (1988), Thompson (1989), and others, and of the "other" world systems and civilizations of Chase-Dunn (1986, 1989), Wilkinson (1987, 1989), and others *back in time through the same world system*?

The argument in Frank (1990a) and Gills and Frank (1990) is, in its essence, that this same world system was born at least five thousand years ago out of the confluent relations of several "civilizations" and other peoples. As mentioned above, these included at least peoples in Egypt, the Levant, Anatolia, Mesopotamia, Persia, India, and central Asia. They and other peoples have ever since been continuously and cumulatively related through center-periphery-hinterland structures, relations of hegemony and rivalry, and cycles. These have been regional and probably world system wide. Since Wallerstein's *differentia specifica* is *not* specific only to modern times, we can and should extend the identification of his single most important defining characteristic of this world system back through time: *Capital accumulation and interpenetrating transfer of surplus* have long characterized and related different parts of the same world system.

Gills and Frank (1990) schematically define this criterion of world system identification and bounding as follows:

> The capture by elite A here (with or without its redistribution here) of part of the economic surplus extracted by elite B there means that there is "interpenetrating accumulation" between A and B. This transfer or exchange of surplus connects not only the two elites, but also their "societies" economic, social, political, and ideological organization. That is, the transfer, exchange or "sharing" of surplus connects the elite A here not only to the elite B there. Surplus transfer also links the "societies" respective processes of surplus management, their structures of exploitation and oppression by class and gender, and their institutions of the state and the economy. Thus, the transfer or exchange of surplus is not a socially "neutral" relationship, but rather a profoundly systemic one. Through sharing sources of surplus, the elite A here and the classes it exploits are systemically inter-linked to the "mode of production," and even more important, to the mode of accumulation in B there. By extension, if part of the surplus of elite B here is also traded, whether through equal or more usually unequal exchange, for part of the surplus accumulated by elite C there, then not only B and C but also A and C are systemically linked through the intermediary B. Then A, B and C are systemically connected in the same overarching system of accumulation. This means that surplus extraction and accumulation are "shared" or "inter-penetrating" across otherwise discrete political boundaries (Gills and Frank 1990, 27).

The argument is that these system-defining relations have persisted continuously and grown cumulatively albeit cyclically on a system wide basis throughout much of the world for thousands of years. For instance, such systemic relations not only characterized, but probably motivated, many Akkadian and Sumerian Mesopotamian economic ties, political institutions, and military excursions into Anatolia and Persia from the time of Sargon in the 2300s B.C. Lattimore (1962), Eberhard (1977), Gernet (1982), and many others have documented and analyzed the later recurrently continuous, systematic, and systemic exchanges of surplus and other relations among sedentary "civilized" people in China and nomadic "barbarian" peoples from central Asia (and with those who were intermittently one or the other in between). Similar, if perhaps more tenuous or at least less researched, overland and maritime relations developed among Chinese and southeast Asian peoples. Farther west, the near simultaneous birth and spread of major religions after 600 B.C. and later Persian-Hellenic rivalry probably responded not only to contemporary similar, but to perhaps also *related* conditions in different "parts" of the world. As noted above, the birth of Christ, expanding systemic relations, and interpenetrating exchange of surplus characterized and *helped shape* all of Han China and its military conquests and economic dependencies through central Asia, Kushan and then Gupta south Asia, Parthian Persia, imperial Rome, and its African and European outposts. Indeed, the subsequent near simultaneous and coordinated imperial declines from Han China to western Rome and the renewed "barbarian" incursions ultimately emanating out of central Asia should be analyzed as the interconnected expressions of a single dynamic in a single world system.

CONCLUSIONS

To Reject Fashionable Transitions and Modes

Given this argument and the historical evidence to sustain it, is it still possible or sensible to argue that there was a qualitatively different "transition" to and creation of a "modern-world-capitalist-system" around 1500? Or that this "transition" arose essentially out of the "transition from feudalism to capitalism" in Europe? No! and No again! It is time to relegate the latter debate to the parochial European history to which it rightly belongs. We may still wish to debate whether there was a significant "transition" in the world as a whole around 1500, and whether this transition was more "significant" than earlier or subsequent ones. However, in this debate it would be useful and clarifying for all participants to understand that the real world (system) essence of a transition is a transition from a transition to a transition! Then we can see which transitions, if any, are more equal than others, for instance in the light of the dramatic supposedly "world shaking" transitions taking place, as I write, in eastern Europe.

Then, is it still sensible to hold on for dear life to the supposedly scientific historical categories of, and ideological preferences for, feudalism, capitalism, socialism — or indeed any such "scientifically" defined "modes of production" or ideologically defined "systems" and "isms"? I believe NOT! (and so argue in Frank 1990a, c). However, the beliefs in either the virtues or the vices, or both, of *"capitalism"* and also of *"socialism"* are still very irrationally cherished, strongly held, and widely shared (literally) right and left all around the world. Therefore, scarcely anyone is yet ready to abandon them, no matter how strong the historical evidence nor how logical the argument. Even readers who have followed and may accept my argument through the first twenty points may resist these conclusions. Nonetheless, the historical and contemporary evidence strongly suggests — and may increasingly persuade more people — that these virtues and vices are systematically ingrained in the world system itself, and not in any of its transitionally varying or variably transitional mixed up "modes."

Those who still cannot liberate themselves from their "modal" and "modish" thinking should at least examine the historical evidence that *all* "modes" share virtues *and* sins, even if the shares of some may be more equal than others. Moreover, the absolute and relative virtues and sins vary over historical time and perhaps over the "life cycles" of "modes" and their implementation or application in (different parts of) the world system. Indeed, it might be said that it is through the virtues and sins of its various and varying "modes" that the system expresses its own structural and dynamic characteristics, operation ("function"), and development (evolution). In that case however, the insistent reification of "modes" is a case of "misplaced concreteness." If we want to reify anything, we would do better (less badly) to reify the world system itself (like me?). Yet even then, we should regard the system like a three-legged stool, supported equally by its ecological/economic, political/military, and cultural/religious/ideological legs.

World system history is long (and cyclical!), and I can wait for this idea's time to come (again!). In the meantime, as throughout world system history in the past, people — today (again) actively including many more women — will unite in a myriad of ever changing social movements to continue their ever-lasting struggle for their just demands and rights. More power to them! A Luta Continua!

Author's Note: After co-authoring our above-cited joint article, Barry K. Gills also helped me improve this one.

Works Cited

Abu-Lughod, Janet. 1989. *Before European Hegemony: The World System* A.D. 1250–1350. New York: Oxford University Press.

Adams, Brooks. [1903] 1939. *The Law of Civilization and Decay: An Essay on History.* Reprint. Berkeley: University of California Press.

Allardyce, Gilbert. 1990. "Toward World History: American Historians and the Coming of the World History Course." *Journal of World History* 1:23–76.

Amin, Samir. 1988. *L'eurocentrisme. Critique d'une idéologie.* Paris: Anthropos.

———. 1989. "Le système mondial contemporain et les systèmes antérieurs." Unpublished manuscript.

Anderson, Perry. 1974. *Lineages of the Absolutist State.* London: New Left Books.

Braudel, Fernand. 1981–84. *Civilization and Capitalism.* 3 vols. New York: Harper and Row.

Chase-Dunn, Christopher. 1986. "Rise and Demise: World-systems and Modes of Production." Unpublished manuscript.

———. 1989. "Core/periphery Hierarchies in the Development of Intersocietal Networks." Unpublished manuscript.

Chase-Dunn, Christopher, and T. Hall, eds. 1990. *Precapitalist Core/periphery Systems.* Boulder: Westview Press.

Childe, V. Gordon. 1942. *What Happened in History.* London: Pelican Books.

Curtin, Philip D. 1984. *Cross-Cultural Trade in World History.* New York: Cambridge University Press.

DeMeo, James. 1987. "Desertification and the Origins of Armoring: The Saharasian Connection." *Journal of Orgonomy,* vols. 21–23.

———. 1990. "Origins and Diffusion of Patrism in Saharasia: Evidence for a Worldwide, Climate-linked Geographical Pattern in Human Behavior." *Kyoto Review,* no. 23.

Eberhard, Wolfram. 1977. *A History of China.* Rev. ed. London: Routledge and Kegan Paul.

Eisler, Riane. 1987. *The Chalice and the Blade: Our History, Our Future.* San Francisco: Harper and Row.

Ekholm, Kajsa, and John Friedman. 1982. "'Capital' Imperialism and Exploitation in Ancient World-Systems." *Review* 4.

Fairbank, John King. 1969. *Trade and Diplomacy on the China Coast*. Stanford: Stanford University Press.

Farmer, Edward L. 1985. "Civilization as a Unit of World History: Eurasia and Europe's Place in It." *The History Teacher* 18:347–63.

Farmer, Edward L., et al. 1977. *Comparative History of Civilizations in Asia*. Reading, Mass.: Addison-Wesley.

Frank, Andre Gunder. 1978a. *World Accumulation, 1492–1789*. New York: Monthly Review Press; London: Macmillan Press.

———. 1978b. *Dependent Accumulation and Underdevelopment*. New York: Monthly Review Press; London: Macmillan Press.

———. 1990a. "A Theoretical Introduction to Five Thousand Years of World System History." *Review* 13.

———. 1990b. "De quelles transitions et de quels modes de production s'agit-il dans le système-monde réel? Commentaire sur l'article de Wallerstein." *Sociologie et Sociétés* 22. English version: "What Transitions and Modes in the Real World System? A Comment on Wallerstein." *Review*, forthcoming in 1991.

———. 1990c. "The Thirteenth-Century World System: A Review Essay." *Journal of World History* 1:249–56.

———. 1990d. "Eurasian World System History: The Centrality of Central/Inner Asia." Paper presented at the UNESCO Seminar on Land Routes of the Silk Roads, Urmuqi, Sinkiang, 19–21 August.

Gernet, Jacques. 1982. *A History of China*. Cambridge: Cambridge University Press.

Gills, Barry K. 1989. "Hegemonic Transition in East Asia: A Historical Materialist Perspective." Unpublished manuscript.

Gills, Barry K., and Andre Gunder Frank. 1990. "The cumulation of accumulation. Theses and research agenda for 5,000 years of world system history." *Dialectical Anthropology* 15; and in Christopher Chase-Dunn and Tom Hall, eds. *Precapitalist Core/Periphery Systems*. Boulder: Westview Press.

Goldstein, Joshua S. 1988. *Long Cycles: Prosperity and War in the Modern Age*. New Haven: Yale University Press.

Hodgson, Marshall G. S. 1954. "Hemispheric Interregional History as an Approach to World History." *Cahiers d'histoire mondiale* 1:715–23.

———. 1960. "The Unity of Later Islamic History." *Cahiers d'histoire mondiale* 5:879–914.

———. 1974. *The Venture of Islam*. 3 vols. Chicago: University of Chicago Press.

Hudson, G. F. 1931. *Europe and China*. Boston: Beacon Press.

Kennedy, Paul. 1987. *The Rise and Fall of the Great Powers*. New York: Random House.

Lattimore, Owen. 1962. *Inner Asian Frontiers of China*. Boston: Beacon Press.

Lombard, Maurice. 1975. *The Golden Age of Islam*. Amsterdam: North Holland.

Mann, Michael. 1986. *The Sources of Social Power*. Vol. 1. Cambridge: Cambridge University Press.

McNeill, William. 1963. *The Rise of the West. A History of the Human Community*. Chicago: University of Chicago Press.

———. 1976. *Plagues and Peoples*. Garden City, N.Y.: Doubleday.

———. 1982. *The Pursuit of Power: Technology, Armed Force and Society since A.D. 1000*. Oxford: Blackwell.

———. 1990. "*The Rise of the West* after Twenty-five Years." *Journal of World History* 1:1–22.

Modelski, George. 1987. *Long Cycles in World Politics*. London: Macmillan Press.

Needham, Joseph. 1961–. *Science and Civilisation in China*. 7 vols. to date. Cambridge: Cambridge University Press.

Odani, Nakae. 1990. "Some Remarks on the Kushan Coins Found in the Western Chinese Regions." Paper presented at the UNESCO Seminar on Land Routes of the Silk Roads, Urmuqi, Sinkiang, 19–21 August.

Quigley, Carroll. 1961. *The Evolution of Civilizations. An Introduction to Historical Analysis*. New York: Macmillan.

Schneider, Jane. 1977. "Was There a Pre-Capitalist World System?" *Peasant Studies* 6:20–29.

Stavrianos, L. S. 1970. *The World to 1500: A Global History*. Englewood Cliffs, N.J.: Prentice-Hall.

Taylor, Alistair M. 1987–88. "Comment on the Shape of the World System in the Thirteenth Century by Janet Abu-Lughod." *Studies in Comparative International Development* 22:39–53.

Teggart, Frederick. 1939. *Rome and China: A Study of Correlations in Historical Events*. Berkeley: University of California Press.

———. [1918] 1977. *Theory and Process of History*. Reprint. Berkeley: University of California Press.

Thompson, William. 1989. *On Global War: Historical-Structural Approaches to World Politics*. Columbia: University of South Carolina Press.

Tilly, Charles. 1984. *Big Structures, Large Processes, Huge Comparisons*. New York: Russell Sage Foundation.

Toynbee, Arnold. 1946. *A Study of History*. 2 vols. Abridged by D. C. Somervell. Oxford: Oxford University Press.

Wallerstein, Immanuel. 1974. *The Modern World-System*. Vol. 1. New York: Academic Books.

———. 1984. *The Politics of the World-Economy*. Cambridge: Cambridge University Press.

———. 1988. *The Modern World-System*. Vol. 3. New York: Academic Books.

———. 1989. "The West, Capitalism, and the Modern World-System." In *Science and Civilisation in China*. Vol. 7, *The Social Background*, part 2, sect. 48, edited by Joseph Needham. Cambridge: Cambridge University Press.

Wilkinson, David. 1987. "Central Civilization." *Comparative Civilizations Review* 17:31–59.

———. 1988. "World-Economic Theories and Problems: Quigley vs. Wallerstein vs. Central Civilization." Paper delivered at Annual Meetings of the International Society for the Comparative Study of Civilizations, May 26–29, at the University of California, Berkeley.

JOHN OBERT VOLL

Islam as a Special World-System

Islam is identified as a religion, a civilization, a way of life, and many other things. Some of this is simply a result of the confusion created by using the same term for different phenomena. As Marshall Hodgson noted twenty years ago, the terms *Islam* and *Islamic* are used "casually both for what we may call religion and for the overall society and culture associated historically with the religion."[1] Confusion is also created by attributing to Islam the characteristics of terms that are thought to be generic but in fact have distinctive cultural or historical referents. This is sometimes clear in discussions that speak of Islam as a "religion" and may also be the case when we speak of "Islamic civilization." It may be useful to ask whether the complex of social relations that is often called Islamic civilization can be most effectively conceptualized for purposes of world historical analysis as a civilization or whether there are more useful identifying terms.

The current transformation of major social formations on a global scale provides the opportunity to reexamine our understanding of the nature of some of the basic units. In particular, it opens the way for examining the large-scale networks of relations that are the major units of contemporary global interactions. I propose to start with a well-known reconceptualization of global interactions, the world-system concepts that have been articulated by Immanuel Wallerstein, and to see if this framework can help define the global Islamic entity more usefully and clearly.

World-system theory is not a simple, monolithic explanation of global human history and society. Even as initially defined by Wallerstein, it was a complex cluster of approaches to understanding a wide variety of experiences. The world-system conceptualization has now become the basis for many different perspectives and interpretations, as the articles in issue after issue of the *Re-*

John Obert Voll, "Islam as a Special World-System," *Journal of World History* 5 (Fall 1994): 213–26.

view of the Fernand Braudel Center illustrate. Recent articles in that journal by Samir Amin and Andre Gunder Frank and a thought-provoking retrospective by Wallerstein all suggest the luxuriant productivity of this perspective.[2]

Within this very broad field of concepts, it is difficult in a short discussion to do justice to the full relevance of world-system theory to an understanding of the Islamic historical experience. Therefore, I take one aspect of the early formulations of Wallerstein and explore its implications for the study of Islamic history. At the same time I consider the implications of Islamic history for world-system theory, because I think that the Islamic experience represents a special case that suggests a different way to formulate a world-system analysis.

In his early presentation of the world-system approach, Wallerstein argued that

> thus far there have only existed two varieties of such world-systems: world-empires, in which there is a single political system over most of the area . . . and those systems in which such a single system does not exist over all, or virtually all, of the space. For convenience and for want of a better term, we are using the term "world-economy" to describe the latter. . . . Prior to the modern era, world-economies were highly unstable structures which tended either to be converted into empires or to disintegrate. It is the peculiarity of the modern world-system that a world-economy has survived for 500 years and yet has not come to be transformed into a world-empire. . . . This peculiarity is the political side of the form of economic organization called capitalism.[3]

This general presentation of the differences between modern and premodern world-systems is appealing both for its clarity and for what we know about the history of the major world civilizations. The alternations between grand imperial unifications and politico-economic disintegration in China, India, the Middle East, and Western Europe are important parts of the world historical narrative. The pattern described by Wallerstein of incipient world-economies that result either in imperial unifications or disintegrations seems to fit the history of the Middle East in the Islamic era. There is the period of the great imperial unification begun by the Arab-Muslim conquests in the seventh century and continued by the Umayyad and Abbasid caliphates. This imperial unification is part of the long line of great world-empires that brought the Middle Eastern and Mediterranean world-economy (or world-economies) under the control of one or two major imperial systems. This series began as early as the Phoenician-Greek-Persian network of the seventh century B.C.E. and stretched through the Hellenistic state system created by the conquests of Alexander the Great to the later Parthian-Sasanid and Roman-Byzantine empires.[4]

The standard account notes the disintegration of the Islamic imperial system under the Abbasid rulers of the tenth and eleventh centuries C.E. and its replacement by a decentralized network of smaller states ruled by military commanders, or sultans, who replaced the imperial caliphs as the effective rulers of Muslim areas by the twelfth century. The final act in this process of disintegration was the destruction of Baghdad, the Abbasid capital, by Mongol forces in

1258. Journalistic accounts speak of the era of "backwardness and stagnation that afflicted the Moslem world between the fall of Baghdad . . . and the renaissance of the twentieth century."[5] In the scholarly terms of his influential book, *The Arabs in History*, Bernard Lewis notes that at this time took place the "transformation of the Islamic Near East from a commercial, monetary economy to one which, despite an extensive and important foreign and transit trade, was internally a quasi-feudal economy, based on subsistence agriculture."[6]

This gloomy picture is correct in some very specific and limited ways. The imperial political unity of the Islamic world was irretrievably destroyed by the middle of the thirteenth century, and in many areas the effectiveness of the urban-based commercial monetary economy was significantly reduced. In the terms of Wallerstein, in the absence of an effective world-empire, the old world-economy of the Middle East seems to have disintegrated. At this point one might simply state that the history of the premodern Islamic world-system appears to bear out Wallerstein's formulation.

However, the standard gloomy picture of the Islamic world following the Mongol conquest of Baghdad is not the only possible picture, as the works of scholars like William H. McNeill, Marshall G. S. Hodgson, Ira Lapidus, and others show. The gloomy picture does not prepare the observer for the actual world situation at the beginning of the sixteenth century. As McNeill has noted,

> We are so accustomed to regard history from a European vantage point that the extraordinary scope and force of this Islamic expansion [in the period 1000–1500 C.E.], which prefigured and overlapped the later expansion of western Europe, often escapes attention. *Yet an intelligent and informed observer of the fifteenth century could hardly have avoided the conclusion that Islam, rather than the remote and still comparatively crude society of the European Far West, was destined to dominate the world in the following centuries.*[7]

In this so-called era of stagnation, the size of the Islamic world virtually doubled from what it had been in the days of the glories of the Abbasid caliphs. By the middle of the sixteenth century, major Muslim imperial states had been established in the Mediterranean world, Iran, South Asia, Central Asia, and sub-Saharan Africa. The power and glory of the Ottoman, Safavid, Mughal, Uzbek, and Songhai empires more than matched the emerging Iberian empires of the day and outshone the smaller dynastic states of Western Europe. In addition, Islam was actively winning converts beyond the boundaries of these empires in Southeast Asia, southeastern Europe, and elsewhere.

The world of Islam was, in fact, dynamic and expanding, not static and stagnating, or disintegrating. As a global unit, however, it is difficult to define in the standard terms of world-systems theory. It stretched from the inner Asian territories of the Manchu empire in China and the small sultanate of Manila in the Philippines to the Muslim communities growing in Bosnia and sub-Saharan Africa. Whatever the unit was, it was not a world-empire and had no prospect of becoming one. At the same time, it was not disintegrating and collapsing. Neither of the alternatives posed by Wallerstein for premodern world-systems seems to be applicable to the Islamic entity in world history in the period just before modern times.

Part of the problem may lie in the way we look at this Islamic entity as it emerged in the centuries following the collapse of effective Abbasid imperial power in the tenth century. The term most frequently used is *civilization,* as in "classical (or medieval) Islamic civilization." This is an awkward term because it implies a civilizational coherence similar to other historic civilizations. As long as the Muslim community was primarily or exclusively Middle Eastern, it could be thought of as the most recent phase of the long-standing tradition of civilization in the Middle East. In the half-millennium after the Abbasid collapse, however, Islam became an important component in many societies outside the Middle East. Some, like India, themselves represented significant traditions of civilization, and this civilizational identity was not eliminated by the introduction of Islam. As a result, by the sixteenth century, the Islamic entity was an intercivilizational entity, not an autonomous "civilization." Further, this expanding Islamic entity now included areas where the complex urban structures characteristic of traditions of civilization were not the dominant modes of social organization. The Islamic entity included both urban-based and pastoral nomadic communities.

This Islamic entity was a vast network of interacting peoples and groups, with considerable diversity and yet some sufficiently common elements so that it is possible to speak of these diverse communities as being part of "the Islamic world." I hasten to add that the problem of understanding the "unity and diversity" found within the Islamic world is a major and continuing one for scholars of Islam.[8] It is tempting to think of this Islamic world as a premodern world-system. In terms of Wallerstein's early definition, it is possible to see this vast network of interacting peoples and groups as "a social system . . . that has boundaries, structures, member groups, rules of legitimation, and coherence."[9]

The real foundation of this world-system does not appear to be a world-economy in the precise sense of the term as used in the analyses of Wallerstein and others. The primary sense of a self-contained identity and the meaning of the boundaries and legitimations do not lie predominantly in the world of trade, production, and exchange. In the current debates over the nature of world-systems and such issues as whether or not there is one world-system extending over 5,000 years, as Frank argues, most people engaging in the discourse of world-systems theory are speaking about the material world and economic forces.

Perhaps a foundation of economic ties does bind the Muslim communities of West Africa, Central Asia, the Middle East, and Southeast Asia. Unfortunately, there has been little examination of the trade patterns within the Muslim world in the centuries following the Abbasid collapse. Recent research by Janet L. Abu-Lughod shows how important such studies can be. She presents a picture of "a long-standing, globally-integrated 'world-system,' to which Europe had finally attached itself." She notes that this world-system of the thirteenth century had three or four core areas and states that "no single cultural, economic, or imperial system was hegemonic. Indeed, a wide variety of cultural systems coexisted and cooperated, most of them organized very differently from the West."[10] It is noteworthy that the trade of the three major "core" zones in Abu-Lughod's analysis (the Middle East, Central Asia and China, and the Indian Ocean basin) tended to be dominated by Muslim-controlled groups or Muslim communities. However, it was not trade or economic exchange that gave this Islamic entity its identity or basic cohesion.

In a recent article, Wallerstein noted that scholars dealing with world-systems analysis face the challenge of "elaboration of world-systems other than that of the capitalist world-economy."[11] I suggest that to understand the premodern entity of the Islamic world as a world-system, it is necessary to define world-systems in ways that are not as closely confined to the economic and material dimensions of history as the conceptualizations of almost all world-systems scholars. For example, Wallerstein insists that the networks and boundaries that define a world-system must be related to material exchanges and the economic dimensions of social systems.[12]

The Islamic world had a dimension of social legitimation and boundary definition that made it possible for someone like the great Muslim traveler, Ibn Battuta, to journey in the fourteenth century from North Africa to China and yet remain largely within "the cultural boundaries of what Muslims called the Dar al-Islam or Abode of Islam."[13] This Dar al-Islam can be seen as a special example of a large-scale human group, using the definition of William H. McNeill: "What is common to all groups, surely, is a pattern of communication among members, sufficiently frequent and sufficiently standardized as to minimize surprises and maximize congruence between expectation and experience so far as encounters within the group itself are concerned."[14] This pattern of communication in the Islamic world is not primarily based upon exchange of goods, coordination of means of production, or a large network of economic activities. Instead, it is built on the shared sources of the Islamic experience, which provide the basis for mutually intelligible discourse among all who identify themselves as Muslims within the Dar al-Islam.

One can view the world of Islam as a large, special type of "community of discourse," in the sense in which that term is used by Robert Wuthnow: "Discourse subsumes the written as well as the verbal, the formal as well as the informal, the gestural or ritual as well as the conceptual. It occurs, however, within communities in the broadest sense of the word: communities of competing producers, of interpreters and critics, of audiences and consumers, and of patrons and other significant actors who become the subjects of discourse itself. It is only in these concrete living and breathing communities that discourse becomes meaningful."[15] This pattern of communication or discourse provides the basis for identifying Dar al-Islam as a social system or human group possessing boundaries, structures, coherence, and rules of legitimation.

The Islamic discourse was able to cross the boundaries between urban-based and pastoral agrarian societies and those between the different major traditions of civilization in the Afro-Eurasian landmass. Networks of personal and organizational interaction created at least a minimal sense of corporate, communal identity in the vast emerging world-system. The modern world-system described by Wallerstein is the "capitalist world-system," identified by a distinctive structure of production and exchange. Similarly, the Muslims might be said to have created the "Islamic world-system," identified by a distinctive set of sociomoral symbols for the definition of proper human relationships. I am *not* saying that the capitalist world-system is an "economic" system and the Islamic world-system is a "religious" one. Rather, I am suggesting that both are relatively comprehensive social systems that can qualify as world-systems, even though the primary identifying characteristics are drawn from different dimensions of the social system as a whole.

The emerging Islamic world-system of ca. 1000–1800 presents some interesting problems of definition, which may be helpful in the effort to elaborate world-systems other than that of modern capitalism. I suggest that the early Islamic community — the imperial community of the Umayyads and the Abbasids from the seventh to the mid-tenth century — followed the standard pattern of world-system development. The classical Muslim caliphate was an important successor state to the "universal empires" of the tradition established by the Persians and Alexander the Great. As the world-empire system disintegrated, the collapse of the Middle Eastern world-economy seemed to be following suit.

If the premodern world-systems model held true, one would expect to see the disintegration of factors providing a systemwide sense of cohesion or shared identity. In political terms, this was clearly the case, as a variety of dynasties claimed the title of caliph, and even the fiction of loyalty to a single "successor to the Prophet" disappeared. However, although the sense of community-connectedness changed its form and organizational expression, it did not disappear. New-style organizations of legitimation and identity emerged, which were not directly dependent upon the political structure or state system. These were elaborations in concrete social forms of Islamic concepts and symbols providing a sociomoral foundation for transregional communal identity.

This transformation of the Islamic world-system can be described by paraphrasing Wallerstein's words concerning the distinctiveness of the modern world-system. He noted: "It is the peculiarity of the modern world-system that a world-economy has survived for 500 years and yet has not come to be transformed into a world-empire — a peculiarity that is the secret of its strength."[16] I suggest that a similar statement can be made about the Islamic world-system since 1000 C.E.: It is the peculiarity of the Islamic world-system that a world-society survived for almost 1000 years and yet has not become transformed into either a world-empire or a world-economy — a peculiarity that is the secret of its strength and ability to survive.

The new Islamic world-system of the post-1000 era had distinctive organizational characteristics that contrast with the traditional Islamic world-empire. In the world-empire state, personal piety took many forms but tended not to become institutionalized. Respected figures led exemplary lives and established what is now called Sufism. For the first five hundred years of Islamic history,

Sufism was a mood of pious and often ascetic devotion reflecting the lives and teachings of highly respected individuals. Not until the effective collapse of imperial unity, however, did this devotional tradition come to be manifested in the great social organizations called the *tariqahs*, which are the brotherhoods of every Muslim society.

In the twelfth century, the great *tariqah* organizations began to take shape.[17] In the context of the political disintegration of the Muslim world, the *tariqahs* assumed increasing importance as the vehicle for social cohesion and interregional unity. The "sufi movement was based on its popular appeal, and its new structure of religious unity was built on popular foundations. . . . While many *tariqahs* had only local significance, the greatest orders . . . spread over the whole or a large part of Islamic territory. Thus they contributed . . . to maintain the ideal unity of all Muslims. . . . Teachers and disciples journeyed from end to end of the Muslim world, bearing the seeds of interchange and cross-fertilization within the sufi framework."[18]

This great network of teachers and students provided one of the most important vehicles for the expansion of Islam in sub-Saharan Africa and Southeast Asia. The *tariqahs* gave people an identity that could be recognized throughout the Islamic world. Thus, a member of the Naqshbandiyyah Tariqah from northwest China could find brothers all along the road to Mecca. For example, in the eighteenth century this was the path followed by Ma Ming Xin, who studied with Naqshbandi *shaykhs* in Central Asia, India, Yemen, and the Holy Cities. On his return to China, his new approach led him into revivalist revolution that had ties with *tariqah*-related holy wars in many other parts of the Islamic world of the time. These *tariqah* networks provided an important foundational bond for the postimperial Islamic world-system.

In addition to shared teachings and identity, the *tariqahs* also provided physical support for travel throughout the Islamic world. After the development of the major widespread *tariqahs*, the wandering Sufi could turn to fellow members of the *tariqah* for spiritual support and also for shelter in the buildings of the order. Most *tariqah* centers had facilities for long-term students and more temporary travelers as well as areas for the practice of pious ritual. The visitors' facilities were known by various names throughout the Islamic world, such as *zawiyah*, *khanqah*, and the like, but they all performed comparable functions in making pious travel possible.[19]

Wandering scholars provide a similar vehicle for systemwide interactions. Muhammad is reported to have said, "Seek knowledge, even unto China," and Muslim scholars were great travelers. These were not simple sightseeing adventurers. Their goal was to gain greater knowledge within the framework of Islamic understanding. Travel for the sake of religious scholarship became "a normative feature of medieval Muslim education" and an important part of the definition of scholarship.[20] The great traditions of legal opinion became the great "schools of law," with standardized texts to be taught and passed on. Study of the texts of law and traditions (*hadith*) of the Prophet and the other major disciplines provided the program for the travelers. By the twelfth and thirteenth centuries, a standard set of works defined the major schools of law and the accepted collections of traditions of the Prophet, and these provided a common "canonical syllabus of learning" for scholars anywhere within the postimperial Islamic world-system.[21]

The changing organization of travel in search of knowledge reflects the postimperial institutions of the Islamic world. The development of instructional centers went from individualized instruction, especially in particular mosques (*masjids*) that were not mosques for the Friday congregational prayers, to *masjids* with accompanying structures specifically for lodging out-of-town students and travelers (usually called *khans*). These were followed by formal institutions of Islamic learning, called *madrasahs*, which emerged by the eleventh century in Southwest Asia, especially in the Seljuk domains, but rapidly spread throughout the Islamic world. It was in these *madrasahs* that the "canonical syllabus" was presented to scholars traveling in search of knowledge.[22]

The vocabulary underwent a parallel evolution. The Arab terms for "travel" (*rihla*) and "seeking knowledge" were used almost interchangeably in early writings. Later they were separated, with *rihla* applying to pilgrimage and the other terms keeping the basic meaning.[23] "This change may reflect the institutionalisation of the *madrasa* system in place of the formerly more individualized, orally-oriented relationships which prevailed between students and teachers in the early medieval centuries of Islamic history. Thus, Ibn Battuta [in the fourteenth century] usually looks for buildings — i.e., colleges of Islamic law and Sufi convents — rather than the solitary but renowned scholar here and there on his itinerary."[24]

How the networks of Sufi teachers and itinerant scholars were related to the flows of economic goods is not clear. These people followed the same paths as wandering merchants, and Muslim merchants and Sufi teachers are frequently mentioned together as important elements in the nonmilitary expansion of Islam in many regions. It is clear, for example, that the two worked together in the Islamization of what is now the northern Sudan in the seventeenth and eighteenth centuries.[25] In some cases, different branches of great families combined with *tariqahs* to provide a basis for networks of exchange of knowledge, political influence, and trade goods. For example, by the sixteenth century the Aydarus family of south Yemen had established a far-flung network of trade contacts, *tariqahs*, and scholarly centers throughout the Indian Ocean basin. Notables in this family held high positions in the courts of Indian princes and also acted as *tariqah* leaders and scholars of *hadith*.[26]

Clearly, people who traveled in the Islamic world of the post-imperial era — whether they were Sufi disciples, students of law, or merchants — were moving within a comprehensible unit that transcended the boundaries of regional traditions of civilization. Many were in the same situation that Sam Gellens notes for Ibn Battuta: "Ibn Battuta may not have known the local languages of the places he visited, but he did know the cultural language of Muslims and hence felt at home."[27] They were moving within the framework of a hemispheric community of discourse, or discourse-based world-system.

This sense of community is symbolized and emphasized in the belief system through the general requirement of the pilgrimage to Mecca. Every year a large gathering of believers from throughout the Islamic world assembles in the central sanctuaries of Islam on the holiday of the pilgrimage. This requirement to travel and come together has had enormous significance in giving professing Muslims a sense of belonging to an entity that transcends particular civilizations or societies. It provides a way of communicating across boundaries that might exist within the community of Muslims. In Mecca during the pilgrimage it is possible to have a sense of a shared discourse that affirms the authenticity of the Islamic message, much like what Ibn Battuta experienced as he traveled in the various parts of the Islamic world. In contemporary times, the account of the pilgrimage by Malcolm X shows the continuing vitality of this experience of a special community of discourse.[28]

The strength of this Islamic world-system is reflected in the fact that even at the peak of the hegemonic power of the modern capitalist world-system, Sufi teachers, merchants, and scholars continued to be successful in winning converts to Islam in Africa and Southeast Asia. Dutch commercial and imperial interests may have controlled the islands of Southeast Asia for centuries, but this control did not prevent the steady advance of Islam in those same islands. A similar situation can be seen in both West and East Africa, where the modern colonial state established an institutional framework that provided "new possibilities of expansion" for Sufi orders and Muslim teachers and traders.[29]

This double level of world-system operation, even in the nineteenth and twentieth centuries, suggests the need for a broader conceptualization of *world-system*. World-systems may compete and also may operate in different dimensions of a social system in ways that force a changing definition of *hegemonic*. Wallerstein has suggested that the world-system perspective needs to be "unidisciplinary" and not just "interdisciplinary" or "multidisciplinary" in method and approach, but he recognizes the difficulty of this task.[30]

The issues raised by considering the Islamic world-system may help in developing a broader approach. I suggest that the modern capitalist world-system was not the first long-lasting world-system without a world-empire. The Islamic community had already developed such a world-system in the centuries following the collapse of the Abbasid state by the tenth century C.E. This nonimperial world-system was not based on a world-economy. Instead it was a discourse-based world-system tied together by interactions based on a broad community of discourse rather than by exchange of goods. The capitalist world-system strongly influenced this Islamic world-system, but it did not destroy it. The interpretation of the capitalist and Islamic world-systems represents a subject of study that tests even the most talented unidisciplinary scholars of modern history.

Notes

1. Marshall G. S. Hodgson, *The Venture of Islam*, 3 vols. (Chicago: University of Chicago Press, 1974), 1:57.

2. Samir Amin, "The Ancient World-Systems versus the Modern Capitalist World-System," *Review* 14 (1991): 349–85; Andre Gunder Frank, "A Theoretical Introduction to

5,000 Years of World System History," *Review* 13 (1990): 155–248; and Immanuel Wallerstein, "World-Systems Analysis: The Second Phase," *Review* 13 (1990): 287–93. Frank has also discussed these issues in "A Plea for World-System History," *Journal of World History* 2 (1991): 1–28; and in "The Thirteenth-Century World System: A Review Essay," *Journal of World History* 1 (1990): 249–56.

3. Immanuel Wallerstein, *The Modern World-System*, 3 vols. to date (San Diego: Academic Press, 1974–), 1:348.

4. A clear summary description of this long tradition of cultural and sometimes imperial unity is presented in Amin, "The Ancient World-Systems versus the Modern Capitalist World-System," pp. 357–59.

5. Thomas W. Lippman, *Understanding Islam* (New York: New American Library, 1982), p. 78.

6. Bernard Lewis, *The Arabs in History*, rev. ed. (New York: Oxford University Press, 1993), 174.

7. William H. McNeill, *The Rise of the West* (Chicago: University of Chicago Press, 1963), 485 (emphasis added).

8. See, for example, the classic collection of essays by Gustave E. von Grunebaum, *Unity and Variety in Muslim Civilization* (Chicago: University of Chicago Press, 1955); and the thought-provoking review article by Andrew C. Hess, "Consensus or Conflict: The Dilemma of Islamic Historians," *American Historical Review* 81 (1976): 788–99.

9. Wallerstein, *Modern World-System*, 1:347.

10. Janet L. Abu-Lughod, "Restructuring the Premodern World System," *Review* 13 (1990): 275–76. For her full presentation, see Abu-Lughod, *Before European Hegemony: The World System*, A.D. 1250–1350 (New York: Oxford University Press, 1989).

11. Wallerstein, "World-Systems Analysis: The Second Phase," 291.

12. Discussions at the plenary session of the New England Historical Association, 19 October 1991.

13. Ross E. Dunn, *The Adventures of Ibn Battuta, A Muslim Traveler of the Fourteenth Century* (Berkeley: University of California Press, 1986), 6.

14. William H. McNeill, "Organizing Concepts for World History," *Review* 10 (1986): 215. For his discussions of the problems of defining appropriate basic units for world historical analysis, see also McNeill, "The Rise of the West after Twenty-Five Years," *Journal of World History* 1 (1990): 1–21.

15. Robert Wuthnow, *Communities of Discourse* (Cambridge, Mass.: Harvard University Press, 1989), 16.

16. Wallerstein, *The Modern World-System*, 1:348.

17. A helpful account of the emergence of the orders is J. Spencer Trimingham, *The Sufi Orders in Islam* (London: Oxford University Press, 1971).

18. Hamilton A. R. Gibb, "An Interpretation of Islamic History," in *Studies on the Civilization of Islam* (Boston: Beacon Press, 1962), 29–30.

19. A discussion of the development of these institutions can be found in Trimingham, *The Sufi Orders of Islam*, chap. 6.

20. Sam I. Gellens, "The Search for Knowledge in Medieval Muslim Societies: A Comparative Approach," in *Muslim Travellers*, ed. Dale F. Eickelman and James Piscatori (Berkeley: University of California Press, 1990), 55 and passim.

21. Ibid.

22. This discussion of the institutional evolution is based on the important works of George Makdisi, especially *The Rise of Colleges, Institutions of Learning in Islam and the West* (Edinburgh: Edinburgh University Press, 1981) and his revision of J. Ped-

ersen, "Madrasa," in *The Encyclopedia of Islam,* new ed. (Leiden: E. J. Brill, 1985), 5:1122–34.

23. Gellens, "The Search for Knowledge," 53.

24. Ibid.

25. See, for example, the very important study of the evolution of the Funj state in the central Nile valley: Jay Spaulding, *The Heroic Age in Sinnar* (East Lansing: African Studies Center, Michigan State University, 1985).

26. The information on this family is drawn from my unpublished research.

27. Gellens, "The Search for Knowledge," 51.

28. *The Autobiography of Malcolm X* (New York: Ballantine Books, 1973), chap. 17.

29. Donald B. Cruise O'Brien, "Islam and Power in Black Africa," in *Islam and Power,* ed. Alexander S. Cudsi and Ali E. Hillal Dessouki (Baltimore: Johns Hopkins University Press, 1981), 160–61.

30. Wallerstein, "World-Systems Analysis: The Second Phase," 292–93.

SELECTED BIBLIOGRAPHY

Abu-Lughod, Janet L. *Before European Hegemony: The World System* A.D. 1250–1350. New York: Oxford University Press, 1989. The modern world system emerged not out of events centered in Europe in the sixteenth century but from the consolidation of a trans-hemispheric network of trade and finance in the thirteenth. This book has had influence on world history teaching, partly because it describes the routes, cities, technology, and institutions of the commercial net so well, partly because it awakened more teachers to the fascinating interregional questions associated with the Mongol Age and the subsequent era of plague pandemic. Sudanic and tropical Africa are excluded from the analysis, leaving a large hole.

Braudel, Fernand. *Civilization and Capitalism, Fifteenth–Eighteenth Century.* 3 vols. New York: Harper and Row, 1981–84. Volumes 1 (*The Structure of Everyday Life*) and 2 (*The Wheels of Commerce*) epitomize the *Annaliste* approach, but volume 3 (*The Perspective of the World*) will be most instructive for global history teachers.

Chase, Lawrence. "Teaching All There Is to Know: The *Annales* 'Paradigm' and the World History Survey Course," *The History Teacher* 18 (May 1985): 409–22. A good brief introduction to the *Annales* School philosophy and method, including several lessons teachers can learn from the *Annalistes* and adapt to world history classrooms.

Chase-Dunn, Christopher K., and Thomas D. Hall. *Rise and Demise: Comparing World-Systems.* Boulder, Co.: Westview Press, 1997. Chase-Dunn, a sociologist, has been a major expositor of world systems theory. He and Hall compare world systems, small, middling, and large, over the centuries in an attempt to explain the emergence of the modern global capitalist economy. Key reading for very serious students of the world systems approach.

Frank, Andre Gunder, and Barry K. Gills. *The World System: Five Hundred Years or Five Thousand?* New York: Routledge, 1993. Starting from the premise that Afro-Eurasian history is whole and indivisible, Frank and Gills postulate that the world system and the long economic cycles that have occurred within it extend back to the third millennium B.C.E. One implication of their model is a much more Asia-centered view of Eastern Hemispheric history over the long span of time. Nine scholars contribute to this volume, which is in fact a multisided debate of the merits of the Frank-Gills thesis. Contributors included William McNeill (the Foreword), Janet Abu-Lughod, and Immanuel Wallerstein, as well as David Wilkinson, formulator of the idea of a "central civilization" in world history.

Jones, E. L. *Growth Recurring: Economic Change in World History.* Oxford: Clarendon Press, 1988. An alternative to the world systems approach in which the author posits the idea of "ever-present impulses for growth" in many parts of the world, not only Europe. A self-critical sequel to *The European Miracle* (see Selected Bibliography for Part Three).

Shannon, Thomas Richard. *An Introduction to the World-System Perspective.* Boulder, Co: Westview Press, 1989. A good primer for students written in fairly plain language. Dated now, however, because the world-systems debate broadened so much after this book was published.

Wallerstein, Immanuel. *The Modern World-System.* 3 vols. New York: Academic Press, 1974–1989. The author's full, detailed account of the modern economic paradox: a world-system that requires both continuous capital accumulation and bitter poverty. Vol. 1: *Capitalist Agriculture and the Origins of the European World-Economy in the Sixteenth Century* (1974); vol. 2: *Mercantilism and the Consolidation of the European World-Economy* (1980); vol. 3: *The Second Era of Great Expansion of the Capitalist World Economy, 1730–1840s* (1989). The author has restated and elaborated his 1974 thesis in numerous publications.

PART SIX

TEACHING REGIONS
AND CIVILIZATIONS
IN WORLD CONTEXT

Nearly everyone who plunges into world history teaching brings to the experience special expertise in one or two academic fields. Because of the prevailing structure of graduate education, this usually means that the instructor has had advanced training in one or more of the conventionally defined world regions. The typical world history teacher, in other words, is in the first instance an Africanist, Americanist, Europeanist, Latin Americanist, or some variety of Asianist. Middle and secondary school teachers who do not hold graduate degrees in history nevertheless have strengths and interests in particular fields and periods usually defined along the same regionalist lines. Inevitably, world history novices build on their existing fund of knowledge and are likely, at least at first, to emphasize topics having to do with the macroregions they know most about. Teachers who offer a course several years running will necessarily extend their range of knowledge into new regions, exploring the literature in fields far from their own professional bailiwick.

Tooling up for world history, however, is not merely a matter of accumulating layers of knowledge about new parts of the world. The instructor must also work out conceptual schemes for placing regional histories within larger hemispheric or global settings. Four of the writers in this section offer ideas for integrating the macroregions they know best into the world-scale scene. They do not argue for privileged consideration of "their area," but they do contend, at least implicitly, that world history education is impoverished if any major part of the globe is excluded, slighted, or folded into a crude generalized category such as the "Orient," the "Free World," or the "non-West." The final two selections reflect on the perennial epistemological and pedagogical problem of how to move beyond a Europe-centered vision of world history without adopting in its place a scheme of multiple "centrisms" that limits the subject to the stories of four or five big civilizations.

Some courses and textbooks that profess enthusiasm for correcting the traditional magnification of Europe's place in history may also drastically abbreviate attention to large chunks of the globe, most often Southeast Asia, sub-Saharan Africa, and the Americas. World history syllabi often reveal one or two gaping regional holes, sometimes owing to the labor required if an instructor is to bone up on a new area, sometimes because of a civilizational bias that leaves nonurban, though densely populated, parts of the world on the global fringe. According to the teacher-scholars included here, the best strategy for transcending the problem is not simply to learn enough about a region to be qualified to add a "unit" about it but to identify a range of historical questions and problems for investigation that will inevitably embrace all parts of the inhabited earth to one degree or another. World history teachers, for example, are likely to think they have neither the time nor the inclination in a busy semester to develop an individual unit on aboriginal peoples of Australia and New Zealand. Indeed, teachers would be ill-advised to represent these peoples as isolated and largely static "cultures." On the other hand, it is not hard to think of a number of interregional or comparative questions in world history whose investigation would be diminished if Aborigines or Maoris were not included among the significant actors: the problem of the peopling of the earth in Paleolithic times, the problem of migration and settlement in the Pacific basin, the problem of early encounters between European settlers and indigenous populations, and the problem of social change amid rapid urbanization in the twentieth century.

We do not have to venture to the southern antipodes, however, to find examples of how world history can help combat the marginalization and "otherizing" that may result from rigid regionalist approach. In the first selection, Julia Clancy-Smith, an authority on Muslim North Africa, notes the irony of the fact that the Middle East, the region next door to Europe, has as a result of orientalist presuppositions been rendered "most foreign, strange, exotic, and thus remote" in Western consciousness. She argues that a good way to override this outdated heritage is to "localize global history," that is, to examine events of world-scale importance as they are played out in concrete and dramatic ways in the Middle East. In doing so the teacher must stay alert to cross-regional parallels as well as to historical anecdotes and life stories that illuminate cultural connections. Such a strategy gives humane substance to the actors in Middle Eastern history and helps students de-exoticize their perceptions of Muslims, Arabic-speakers, and other groups in the region.

William Sater, an expert on Chile, offers similar advice about locating Latin American history in the wider world over the past five hundred years. The instructor can do this, he contends, not by trying "to cram all of Latin America into a world history course" but by paying more attention to broad interconnective trends and to opportunities for comparison with developments in Europe, North America, or other regions. At all costs the teacher must avoid getting bogged down in a country-by-country survey.

John F. Richards reflects on the place of the Indian subcontinent in world history during the early modern period, a time of accelerating global change. He identifies "six distinct but complementary large-scale processes" that characterize the centuries between the late fifteenth and early nineteenth. After describing these patterns, he asks, "Do they apply to South Asia?" In showing that they do indeed apply, he distances himself from the still common conceptualization of India as a "world culture" manifesting ageless attributes or as a setting for a picturesque narrative of the Mughal dynasty. He argues, rather, that the world changed India, and India changed the world. Like Clancy-Smith, he concludes that scholars must "move seamlessly between the particulars of local and regional histories to broader South Asian and world description and analysis."

Tara Sethia, who writes on India in the colonial period, is less concerned than Clancy-Smith, Sater, or Richards with relating a particular macroregion to global processes and more interested in applying comparative analysis to civilizational developments. She especially wants students to understand the distinctive aspects of Indian religion, politics, and literate culture as a platform for thinking creatively about similarities and differences in cultural trends in other regions. She also wants students to consider the cultural implications for South Asia of British rule and postcolonial economic globalization.

In contrast to the regionalist issues these authors raise, the persistent problem with Europe as a social and spatial construct has not been its adequate integration into world history as much as the dogged intellectual tradition that allows the Western meganarrative to set the terms by which all other regions and civilizations are represented. The idea that Western history equals world history, at least modern world history, still has its proponents (see the essay by Jacob Neusner in Part Two). More common today, according to Donald Johnson, are scholars and educators he calls "universalists." They champion genuine global history in principle but nevertheless "share a view of humanness which is based on a technological and economic definition of man, or *homo economicus*. They all tend to look upon contemporary Western liberal values and institutions as desirable and perhaps inevitable for all the world's people." In the universalist ranks Johnson lists liberal utilitarians, nineteenth-century evolutionists, modernization scholars, world-system theorists, and advocates of contemporary global education.

Against this category Johnson sets the "particularists," scholars who imagine the world in a different way. For them, "it is the distinct group, whether tribe, nation or cultural group, that is the operative level of human behavior." Cultural particularism is rooted in older traditions of American and British anthropology and includes semiologists such as Clifford Geertz who define cultures as distinctive systems of symbolic meaning. Johnson finds that despite the particularism inherent in American or in any other nationalist ideology, the universalist model has dominated social and history education. Americans, including the majority of educators, tend to regard their own national values as universal: they "see the world outside the West as destined to replicate western civilization in some future homogeneous rational culture."

Johnson believes that the study of world history suffers if it is the servant of either model. He argues rather for a humanistic history that transcends both the economic/technological preoccupations of the universalists and the pinched particularist vision that fails to see the forest of world-scale change for the trees of enclosed cultural systems. The image of universal *homo economicus* must be in balance with the undeniable realities of cultural difference from region to region. Like Sethia, Johnson favors comparative civilizational studies that teach about these traditions "not on the basis of power or potential, but because they have long histories and have engaged in great human experiments which might offer us deeper understanding of what it means to be human."

Johnson is also perfectly aware of the dangers of imagining world history as synonymous with the rolling of civilizations across time. The civilizationist tradition running from Oswald Spengler and Arnold Toynbee to William McNeill (and including the civilizationist philosophy and social science represented by such writers as Carroll Quigley and Mathew Melko) has proven in recent years to be an inadequate conceptual frame. It cannot sort out and make sense of the huge range of cross-cultural phenomena that area studies research, the new social history, neo-Marxist critiques, interdisciplinary methodologies, and the diversification of the historical profession have been uncovering. These intellectual currents have indeed had a profound impact on McNeill, who in 1990 reflected candidly on what he thought were the defects of *The Rise of the West*, published a quarter-century earlier.

> it seems to me now that the book is flawed simply because it assumes that discernibly separate civilizations were the autonomous social entities whose interactions defined history on a global scale. . . . Thus . . . the central methodological weakness of my book is that while it emphasizes interaction across civilizational boundaries, it pays inadequate attention to the emergence of the ecumenical world system within which we live today. Instead of organizing the book solely around the notion of a series of efflorescences, first in one, then in another separate civilization, I should have made room for the ecumenical process.[1]

In the last selection, an excerpt from *The Myth of Continents*, the geographer Martin Lewis and the historian Kären Wigen expose two of the traps into which excessive civilizationalism can lead. The first is that it privileges four or five Eurasian "Great Traditions," leaving other regions of the world where huge numbers of human beings have lived for millennia in "a limbo of interstices, hinterlands, repositories of barbarism, or . . . doomed areas of less-advanced civilization." The second pitfall is the all too easy temptation to ignore what fragile, ineffable social constructs civilizations are and to speak and write of them as if they were hard, round social entities knocking and crashing against one another. Lewis and Wigen single out for criticism the ideas of Samuel Huntington, who has resurrected the decidedly particularist idea of civilizations as bounded cultural structures competing with one another for advantage and who in fact recommends basing American foreign policy on this premise.

Note

1. William H. McNeill, "*The Rise of the West* after Twenty-five Years," *Journal of World History* (Spring 1990): 8–10.

JULIA CLANCY-SMITH

The Middle East in World History

If our own past is for us a foreign country, then the past of other civilizations is, perhaps, doubly foreign and thus all the more difficult to comprehend. Teaching about the Cultural Other is a daunting task. And teaching about the History of Others on a global scale may appear all the more formidable. Nevertheless, by localizing, in a sense, the past experience of non-Western peoples and regions, we can arrive at a global big picture. And paradoxically, the end result may be a more satisfactory understanding of what the problematic term the "West" itself means.

Let me use as an example of this the area known, for want of more precise nomenclature, as the Middle East in the era prior to 1500. The "middle periods" — roughly from the eighth century on — are usually given short shrift in introductory history texts, despite the fact that these centuries are, in many ways, the most instructive from a world historical viewpoint. In considering the middle periods of the Islamic ecumene, Andalusia or Muslim Spain would constitute one geocultural pole with perhaps the trans-Oxus and the Indo-Iranian worlds forming the opposite poles.

Ironically, the culture or set of cultures closest in proximity, geopolitical and historical, to Western Europe are those whose pasts have been rendered the most foreign, strange, exotic, and thus remote. Simply stated, we do not know what to do with the Middle East — or those lands on or adjoining the eastern and southern edges of the Mediterranean. This is particularly true after the so-called rise of Islam. Despite propinquity — or perhaps because of it — many people are uncertain as to where the Middle East is and, therefore, what it is.

I have heard even globally minded scholars state the following: "Asia, Africa, AND the Middle East." In strictly geographical terms, this is redundant. What is usually understood by the term Middle East today IS Southwest Asia and northern or Mediterranean Africa, plus Iran. Although, if three specialists on the region were asked to define its precise limits, three different answers might be forthcoming.

Julia Clancy-Smith, "The Middle East in World History" (paper read at the conference on "Rethinking World History . . . " 7–9 November 1991 at the University of Virginia). *World History Bulletin* 9 (Fall/Winter 1992–93): 30–34.

But there is more at stake here than mere geographic confusion or spatial disarray. In addition to making that which is geographically near remote, we have also rendered the Middle East culturally and historically distant through patterns of discourse. The words "exotic" and "fanatic" have become virtually synonymous for the Middle East and/or for Islam or Muslims; this is true both in scholarly and popular speech and writing. Both words create intellectual distance. What is remote and alien thereby becomes also monolithic, unchanging, and by extension unintelligible.[1]

To provide an illustration. Pick up any general treatment of the Crusades and you will read that the "crusaders developed a taste for Eastern spices, precious gems, silks, and satins, and other exotic attractions." Another example pertains to the use of the terms "occupation" and "invaders/invasion" for regions once under Islamic rule. These words also work to substitute intellectual remoteness for what was in fact historical propinquity. Let me provide an illustration of this.

The history of Islamic Spain spanned more than seven centuries — from the early 700s until 1492. It was an epoch that witnessed major advances in agriculture, science, philosophy, medicine, literature, etc. Yet these 700 years are reduced in scholarly discourse to naught but an occupation. Most texts ignore Andalusia in the main. When Muslim Spain is dealt with, we often find that in "1492, the Moorish invaders were expelled." Significantly, the Roman interlude in Iberia is never described as a mere invasion nor are the Visigoths portrayed as "occupiers." Looking at Andalusian history in the longue durée, we find that Spain was under Islamic rule for approximately the same number of centuries that it was under both Roman and Visigothic domination taken together.

This summer a Moroccan historian published a revealing study of historical memory and forgetfulness regarding Andalusia in the literary supplement to the Moroccan daily newspaper, *Le Matin du Sahara et du Maghreb* (Sunday, 23 June, 1991). According to the study, Spanish history textbooks for high school students still claim that Andalusia's more than 700-year existence was once again no more than an occupation. Thus, the past of one of the most brilliant and tolerant civilizations for its time is reduced to a moment, a short-term foreign residency without historical meaning.[2]

This despite the fact that Muslim Spain — and not the Crusades — was the main cultural conveyor belt between the rest of Western Europe and the Mediterranean/Southwest Asian Islamic ecumene. The knowledge and learning of the ancients, along with the tremendous advances made by Middle Eastern, North African, and Spanish scholars, literati, and scientists — of whatever religious persuasion — found their way to Europe via Andalusia and to a lesser extent via Islamic Sicily. This process however, is usually neatly excised from the West's collective historical memory and along with it a vast number of connections and relationships between Western Europe and the Islamic world in the middle periods.[3]

Why then this historical amnesia when it comes to our cultural neighbors who, of course, were also the West's long-time rivals and opponents for Eurasian supremacy?

One major difficulty in teaching the history of the Middle East has to do with how we conceive of, and teach, our own history. The Western civilization approach has erected artificial and arbitrary boundaries around something called the WEST. The West is implicitly or explicitly built around a historical and cultural antithesis — the EAST. It is instructive to consider those elements which distinguish a Western civilization from a European civilization or history course. Paradoxically, what makes the former "Western" is the inclusion of the Near East. Simply stated, the Orient makes the West, the West, but only for selected periods.

All survey textbooks — whether for secondary schools or college level courses — include the ancient Near East as part of the Western heritage. Indeed, Mesopotamia, Pharaonic Egypt, and to a lesser degree Persia, are eagerly and eternally claimed as part of the West's heritage. The Near East then disappears, for the most part, from intellectual horizons and historical narrative only to reappear briefly centuries, if not millennia, later.

Let's take a college-level text — the Burns, Lerner, and Meacham book entitled *Western Civilizations: Their History and Their Culture* — as a representative illustration.[4] Most of part I (four chapters out of five) deals with the Near East. Nothing more is heard from this part of the Western heritage, except for a brief discussion of the birth of Islam and Islamic Empires. Then 800 pages and many centuries later a few paragraphs are devoted to the region in the World War II aftermath in a section entitled "From Muhammad to Khomeini" — we find largely blank pages, with one exception.

But perhaps blank pages are preferable to what we find on page 264: "For those who approach Islamic civilization with modern preconceptions, the greatest surprise is to realize that from the time of Muhammad until at least about the year 1500, Islamic culture and society were extraordinarily cosmopolitan and dynamic." After allowing that Jewish culture flourished in Muslim Spain, the authors felt compelled to modify this apparently too favorable picture by launching into a dark discussion of women in Islam (page 265), which is not only largely inaccurate but also anachronistic. Finally, the single paragraph devoted to the half millennium of the Abbasid Caliphate reads thus: "This is the world described in the Arabian Nights, a collection of stories of dazzling Oriental splendor written in Baghdad under the Abbasids. The dominating presence in those stories, Harun al-Rashid . . . behaved as extravagantly as he was described" (page 263). I use this example not to denigrate the Burns, Lerner, and Meacham text but only to suggest that it represents a deeply embedded pattern of both scholarly and popular thinking and discourse about our — the West's — cultural next-door neighbors.

What is to be done?? Are there any solutions to the intellectual challenges posed by the Middle East? One modest proposal will sound at first paradoxical. In order to globalize history, in this case the history of the Middle East in the middle periods, we might think about localizing it. That is, to de-exoticize what has been seen as remote and hopelessly alien, and rediscover historical, cultural, and intellectual links which, in many cases, have always been there. In order to see linkages — to relearn what has been forgotten — we have to disconnect the presumed intrinsic link between romantic exoticism and the Middle East.

Mercifully, the world history or world civilization texts for secondary education are frequently more sophisticated than the college Western civilization texts in striving to re-think and thus re-link the Western historical experience with the Afro-Asian.

The *History and Life* textbook written by Wallbank, Schrier, Maier, and Gutierrez-Smith, gives extended and systematic coverage to the Middle East — Southwest Asia and northern Africa — as does the text by Dunn *Links Across Time and Place.*[5] Neither work falls into what I would call the exoticist trap; the word "exotic" appears, as far as I can tell, nowhere in the many pages devoted to this part of the globe. Moreover, each text seeks integration rather than mere juxtaposition. Unit three of the Wallbank text is entitled "The era of regional civilizations, Christendom and Islam to A.D. 1500." This is clearly an attempt to establish parallels — historical and intellectual proximity — between two worlds hitherto portrayed as apart, distant, and hostile.

However, I do have at least one quarrel with the Wallbank text, one which further illustrates my point regarding the fact that we still do not know what exactly to do with Islam and the Middle East. While the authors' characterization of Christendom as a regional civilization in this period is probably accurate, one could argue that Islam was a tri-continental civilization soon after 700; by 1500 the Islamic ecumene was a hemispheric phenomenon, and no longer just a regional civilization.

The hemispheric approach is what distinguishes *Links across Time and Place* from the others; for the authors have gone the farthest in employing that perspective to restitch the various historical strands making up Afro-Eurasia. Rather than dealing with Islam and the Middle East in separate discussions, we find provocative titles for chapters 12 through 14, for example: "Asia and Europe Develop, 750–1000"; "Power Centers in Asia and Europe, 1000–1200"; and "Eurasian Sea Trade Exchanges, 1000–1400." And here "Asia" does indeed include the Middle East.

Secondary school world history texts such as the two just cited represent a much needed counterpoise to the Arabian Nights fable of the Middle East. Moreover, the various Quincentenary celebrations are creating an auspicious environment, a felicitous climate, in which to rethink not only the past, but more significantly our images of the past and of Others. Nevertheless, much remains to be done. Obviously some sort of sustained dialogue has to be initiated between the authors and audiences of the Western civilization approach to history and those of the world history school.

Allow me to offer three modest suggestions for localizing global history as it pertains to the Middle East in the era immediately prior to the Columbian encounters and exchanges. By avoiding the Oriental exoticist paradigm — and the cultural distance it imposes — we can proceed along more useful paths to reconnecting Middle Eastern history with both world and Western history. But what should we substitute for that paradigm? Three methods can provide alternatives:

1) using specific examples of direct interconnections between the West and the Middle East to rediscover historical processes which have been erased from Western historical memory; 2) employing unsuspected historical parallels between the two regions to demonstrate similar historical patterns and paths; and 3) greater use of biography in which the life stories of individuals serve as metaphors for larger relationships and complexities.

I am not opposed to talking about the 1,001 Nights, the lovely Scheherazade, or the resplendent court of Harun al-Rashid. Nevertheless, if the *Arabian Nights* is used as a device to study another culture in another age, why not discuss instead the stories of Sinbad the Sailor? In the Sinbad cycle of tales, the sophisticated maritime knowledge of the Middle Eastern sea captains about the Indian Ocean is clearly reflected, although within the conventions of literature. Undergirding the European voyages of discovery were earlier voyages and vast knowledge of the earth, seas, and heavens accumulated by Middle Easterners. It was no accident that the region formerly known as Andalusia was in the vanguard of European overseas explorations due to the superior science and learning characterizing Muslim Spain. In this respect, the American Historical Association's newsletter, *Perspectives*, of November 1991, endorsed the Quincentenary manifesto on teaching the Columbian encounter. Statement number six has direct bearing for what we are considering:

"Columbus's voyages were not just a European phenomenon but rather were a facet of Europe's millennia-long history of interaction with Asia and Africa. The discovery of America was an unintended outcome of Iberian Europe's search for an all-sea route to the Indies.... Technology critical to Columbus's voyages, such as the compass, the sternpost rudder, gunpowder, and paper originated in China. The lateen sail, along with much of the geographical knowledge on which Columbus relied, originated with or was transmitted by the Arabs."

This is an improvement over previous treatments of seafaring technology and science which inevitably claimed that the voyages of discovery were due to NEW navigational aids, such as the compass, astrolabe, quadrant, and sailing charts. These technologies were new to Europeans but in no way new to the Middle East or other parts of Asia. Nevertheless, the last part of the AHA statement contains several problematic assertions which illustrate once more what I am saying.

The term "Arab" is, as always, deceptive. A large number of leading scientists and scholars from the middle periods were not Arabs at all but employed the lingua franca of the age — Arabic, and to a lesser extent Persian — to communicate with other members of the intelligentsia found in multiple urban centers from Andalusia to India. Moreover, the notion of transmission is also misleading since it implies that knowledge, whether from antiquity or from other regions of Eurasia, was merely passed on, conveyed, or passed down — that these shadowy "Arabs" were but the passive bearers — an archive or lending library — of someone else's wisdom. Thus, the idea of transmission of knowledge — as opposed to increasing the fund of global learning — is part of the process of Western historical excision, upon which the myth of innate Western culture superiority vis à vis the rest of the globe depends.

If we take a careful, historically specific look at the astrolabe, for example, we find a somewhat different story from that broadbrush statement by the AHA. An astronomical instrument of ancient Greek invention, the astrolabe was improved by the Egyptian geographer Ptolemy, and subsequently perfected by Middle Eastern scientists in the early centuries of Islam. Sometime in the tenth century, the astrolabe came to Europe. However the earliest dated instrument extant today was made in 984 by two masters, Ahmad and Mahmud, sons of Ibrahim, a Persian astrolabist of Isfahan — not Arabs by any stretch of the imagination and certainly not mere transmitters of knowledge. Let us return to the Indian Ocean and Persian Gulf trade and the themes of distance and remoteness as opposed to propinquity and interconnections.

After his circumnavigation of Africa in 1498, Vasco de Gama reached Malindi on the east coast of Africa. Yet it was an Arab pilot, possessed of a very good sea map and of refined maritime instruments, who showed the Europeans the way to southwest India. Both Portuguese and Arabic sources name the pilot — Ahmed b. Majid — although the Arabic sources claim that the hapless pilot was only induced to direct the Portuguese further east after having been made drunk. While this part of the story is probably fictitious, it reveals that Muslim and other traders realized the full import of the Europeans' arrival in the Indian Ocean.

When Vasco de Gama finally reached Calicut on the Malabar coast in 1498, an individual from his landing party was greeted in one of the Italian dialects — Genoese — as well as in Castilian by two Tunisian merchants. The Tunisians were part of the large resident Arab trading community or diaspora in the Indian Ocean Basin, one which had been established there for many centuries. "May the Devil take thee!! What brings you hither??" exclaimed the Tunisians, astonished — and perhaps dismayed — to see their neighbors from just across the Mediterranean this far from home and trading in territory that had long been their commercial bailiwick.

While this anecdote may seem just too anecdotal — too local — for a global curriculum it can illustrate a number of significant points for students of world history at whatever level. First, Middle Eastern navigators prior to the late fifteenth century possessed adequate maritime knowledge, perhaps, to discover the Americas. Yet, they had no reason or impetus to do so since they already were there — in the Indian Ocean trade zone — and had long dominated international commerce in that part of the globe. Moreover, the Islamic Mediterranean world had for centuries been integrated with the Indian Ocean system due to the activities of resident merchant communities from places like Tunisia. If the Columbian voyages eventually created an Atlantic world by linking continents, the advent of the Europeans in the Indian Ocean also linked parts of Eurasia previously distinct — Western Europe with South Asia. Finally, and ironically, the maritime technologies developed by Middle Eastern peoples — once in the hands of Europeans who further advanced that technology —

ultimately were employed to establish Western commercial hegemony in a region that had previously been a "Muslim Ocean."

A second example — a historical parallel — might also localize yet globalize; this one is related to another dimension of the Columbian legacy.

The *Seeds of Change* exhibition is a luxuriant celebration of exchange, diffusion, and borrowing across continents and oceans. The discussion of the transcontinental agricultural transactions triggered after 1492 would do well to consider another, much earlier green revolution which spanned three continents. I am referring to the agrarian revolution set in motion by the establishment of the Abbasid common market, centered in Baghdad after 750. This common market — the product of an Islamic commonwealth — stretched by the ninth century to the trans-Oxus region, the Indus Valley, the Indian Ocean, and as far west as the Spanish Umayyad Caliphate — to the gateway of Europe. Middle Eastern and North African–Spanish geographers, authors of farming manuals, and scholars working in the natural sciences wrote from the tenth century on of tremendous changes already under way in the countryside.[6]

Most notably, new crops, or ennobled types of old crops, were grown from Spain to India, and new techniques of cultivating both old and new crops had been introduced. These profound transformations began shortly after the Arab-Muslim conquests of the seventh and early eighth centuries and were largely completed by the eleventh century. By 1400, a writer by the name of Ansari stated that in the immediate vicinity of a small town on the North African coast, sixty-five kinds of grapes, thirty-six kinds of pears, and twenty-eight types of figs were cultivated. The range and variety of useful plants had increased astronomically in the previous centuries.

Here we find an instructive historical parallel to slightly later and larger global transformations so beautifully dealt with in the *Seeds of Change* catalog. A parallel such as this one renders the Middle East and Islam less extrinsic and distant in their relationships to both Western and global histories. Moreover, this may be more than mere parallel. It could be argued that the agrarian revolutions sparked by the Columbian exchanges succeeded to the extent that they did because of the prior green revolution occurring in Spain, Mediterranean Africa, and Southwest Asia from the eighth century on.

A third even more specific method for "localizing the global" is the use of biography in world history, something which may at first blush appear contradictory to the philosophy of world studies. Ross Dunn's work on a globe-trotting Moroccan scholar, Ibn Battuta who lived in the fourteenth century, employs the biography of an individual to explore an entire cultural universe and in fact much of Afro-Eurasia itself.[7] Ibn Battuta's life then becomes a metaphor for a whole class of itinerant scholars, pilgrims, and merchants who moved between one pole of the Islamic ecumene and the other, creating a common Islamic world order. Our Moroccan friend's biography gives a face and a voice to the Middle Eastern "Other," veiled until now by Oriental exoticism. By presenting Ibn Battuta as the Muslim equivalent of Marco Polo, foreign peoples and places previously viewed as intrinsically different become less so.

One caveat should be issued, however, in our search for historical parallels, cases of direct linkages between East and West, or for individuals whose lives offer metaphors for larger sets of phenomena or more familiar cultural land-scapes. We should not commit the error that Antoine de Saint-Exupéry cites in his elegant little parable, *Le Petit Prince*, when describing the discovery of Aster-oid B 612. This asteroid was first detected in 1909 by an Ottoman Turkish as-tronomer. When the Turkish scientist presented his findings to the Interna-tional Congress of Astronomy, no one believed him since he wore his traditional Oriental garb. In 1920, when Western clothing became mandatory in the as-tronomer's country, he presented his same discovery, this time wearing a Euro-pean suit; everyone believed him. The point is not to make the diverse peoples of the Middle East — or any non-Western peoples — "just like us" in order to understand the cultural Other. While World History and the Quincentenary ex-plore the processes of joining and coming together, both also celebrate hu-mankind's diversity.

Notes

1. Endless examples from scholarly and popular literature could be provided, such as this piece written while France and Algeria confronted each other in one of Africa's cruelest colonial wars: "In the eyes of most Americans, Algeria used to be a far-off desert where Foreign Legion types defend Beau Geste forts against howling Arabs on camels. Then there was the Casbah . . . dark ladies, exotic music. . . . Last week (1960), however, Americans were beginning to realize that Algeria could easily become another Korea" (*Newsweek*, November 1960).

2. The marvelous exhibit put together by the National Gallery of Art, Washington, D.C., *Circa 1492: Art in the Age of Exploration*, devotes no attention to Andalusia, save to note that the Nasrid dynasty of southern Spain was nothing but "an Islamic outpost."

3. The French historian, Jacques Attali, notes this process of excision whereby Western Europe denied its intellectual and scientific indebtedness to the Middle East in his *1492* (Paris: Fayard, 1991).

4. Edward McNall Burns, Robert E. Lerner, and Standish Meacham, *Western Civi-lizations: Their History and Their Culture*, 10th ed. (New York: W. W. Norton, 1984).

5. T. Walter Wallbank, Arnold Schrier, Donna Maier, and Patricia Gutierrez-Smith, *History and Life*, 4th ed. (Glenview, Illinois: Scott, Foresman and Company, 1990); and Ross E. Dunn et al., *Links Across Time and Place: A World History* (Evanston, Ill.: McDougal, Littel, 1990).

6. Andrew M. Watson, *Agricultural Innovation in the Early Islamic World: The Dif-fusion of Crops and Farming Techniques, 700–1000* (Cambridge: Cambridge University Press, 1983); and his "A Medieval Green Revolution: New Crops and Farming Tech-niques in the Early Islamic World," in *The Islamic Middle East, 700–1900: Studies in Economic and Social History*, ed. A. L. Udovitch (Princeton: The Darwin Press, 1981), 29–58.

7. Ross E. Dunn, *The Adventures of Ibn Battuta: A Muslim Traveller of the Four-teenth Century* (London: Croom Helm, 1986).

WILLIAM F. SATER

Joining the Mainstream
Integrating Latin America into
the Teaching of World History

After countless hours of labor, I have concluded that it appears almost foolhardy to try to cram all of Latin America into a world history course. The term Latin America is itself a misnomer: the area extending south from the Rio Grande to Tierra del Fuego derives only a portion of its culture from the Iberian nations. And while many people speak either Spanish or, in Brazil, Portuguese, large numbers still use a variety of Indian languages, including Quechua, Aymara, or Nahuatl. In short, the nations of Latin America may occupy the same continent, but significant racial and cultural differences distinguish them. Talking about Latin America is about as accurate as talking about Europe which, although smaller in size and population, continues to be considered more diverse than other regions of the world. Thus, rather than utilizing geopolitical terms, teachers might divide Latin America into four racial blocs: the largely Indian nations of Bolivia, Peru, Paraguay, and Ecuador; the mestizo countries, like Mexico, Chile, El Salvador, and Colombia; states with large black or mulatto components, such as Brazil and some Caribbean islands; and the predominately white societies of Uruguay and Argentina. This way, instructors could acknowledge Latin America's diverse population while still integrating it into world history courses.

CONQUEST AND SETTLEMENT

What makes Latin America unique is that the European nations not only integrated it economically, but legally incorporated it into their royal patrimonies. To understand this process, particularly the role of the state and the individual explorers, teachers should study the Spanish *Reconquista* as well as the

William F. Sater, "Joining the Mainstream: Integrating Latin America into the Teaching of World History," *Perspectives* (American Historical Association) 33 (May/June 1995): 19–22, 37.

Pre-Colombian Indians. Various authors give some insight into the three most populous Indian cultures — the Aztecs, Mayas, and Incas — as well as those of Brazil, which were neither as large nor perhaps as culturally advanced as those of Mexico and the Pacific side of South America.[1] Since the European presence — race, language, religion, and culture — is more deeply imprinted in the Western Hemisphere, Latin America shares more in common with the United States than with Asia or Africa where colonists arrived later and where the impact does seem not as permanent. Spain and Portugal, after all, controlled portions of North and all of Central and South America for approximately 300 years.

Students might benefit from reading some of the European accounts of the conquest and settlement of Mexico, Peru, or other parts of what became Spain and Portugal's empires. Although the explorers that came to these areas may have caused great destruction, the experiences of these audacious conquistadores certainly constitute one of the great human adventures. Students, for example, could compare the exultant letters of Cortes or Bernal Diaz, describing their exploits, with the experiences of those who settled the United States, Canada, and Africa or Asia. Teachers can also use recent scholarship that documents the less than enthusiastic Indian response toward those Europeans who seized their lands and who, in some cases, literally eradicated their culture.

The conquest of the Western Hemisphere changed both Latin America and Europe. In exchange for the potato, tomato, corn, as well as precious metals, Latin America received European religion, technology, languages, and culture. Perhaps the most important initial European contribution was disease: not merely smallpox and tuberculosis, which also annihilated the Europeans, but also the presumably more benign ailments of influenza, measles, mumps, and chicken pox. Without any natural immunities and often abused or ill fed, the Amerindian population perished by the millions. Teachers might compare the devastating demographic impact of the smallpox pandemic, which annihilated up to 90 percent of the Amerindian population, with the effect of European exploration on Africa or Asia. Disease traveled both ways across the Atlantic: just as malaria devastated European settlers in Africa, the Americas retaliated by giving their unwelcome guests syphilis.

Some Europeans migrated to Spanish and Portuguese America, as they did to England's American colonies, but not in sufficient numbers to compensate for the loss of native life. How the Europeans coped with labor shortages is yet another interesting topic. Early in the sixteenth century, Spanish colonists created first the *repartamiento* and then the *encomienda*, institutions that recruited and allocated Indian labor to till the fields and work the mines.[2] When the local population succumbed either to disease or abuse, Europeans first supplemented and then replaced the Indians with other Indians or with slaves from Africa. Again, this process seems to have occurred on a larger scale in Latin America than in British America, or the rest of the world. Slavery, moreover, permeated all of Latin America, although later the slaves tended to be concentrated more heavily in areas that produced valuable agricultural products or minerals where their labor was most needed. In some countries, such as Chile, the black population slowly disappeared through the process of miscegenation; in others, like Brazil, which did not abolish slavery until the end of the 19th century, blacks constituted a significant portion of the population. Teachers could compare the Latin American slave trade with the transfer of blacks across the North Atlantic, the Indian Ocean, the Mediterranean, as well as their movement within Africa. Additionally, there are various examples of indentured servitude. For example, many of the Spanish came to the Americas as indentured laborers, which can be contrasted with the experience of contract labor in the United States or the British Empire.

Christianity, particularly the Roman Catholic Church, remains one of the most enduring of the European legacies to Latin America, as it is to the United States. While the Church transferred pernicious institutions like the Inquisition to the Americas, it also provided most of the culture that existed in the colonies. Religious communities, moreover, operated orphanages, hospitals, foundling homes, schools, and universities. Religious holidays became social occasions. The Latin American Church cultivated its pocketbook as well as ministering to the soul. Over the decades, the Church accumulated land that it sometimes organized into haciendas. It also received tithes and donations, which it lent out to those in need of capital. While clearly tied to the elites, it was the Church, as an arm of the Spanish state, that afforded the Indians the little protection they received. Bartolome de las Casas and others defended Indian rights in the Spanish court; the regular orders, the Franciscans, Dominicans, Augustinians, and Jesuits, charged with converting the Indians, tried to protect their charges from the rapacious European settlers.

Although lacking the current allure of social history, economic topics present the classroom instructor with a particularly useful area for exposition. Latin America provided more resources to Europe, and for a longer period of time, than Asia, Africa, or what became the United States. Peruvian and Mexican gold and particularly silver funded Spain for decades. While not as lucrative, cultivating the land provided its owner with some wealth and more prestige. The new colonial masters created agricultural units — called, depending on the region, haciendas, *fundos, estancias, fazendas* — that produced commercially important crops like sugar or pastoral products, such as meat, hides, and tallow; other units raised horses and mules for commercial use. Happily, teachers can easily obtain information not merely on the evolution of the hacienda economy, but also on specific estates, some of which were enormous, almost self-sufficient economic entities. The development of a plantation system can be contrasted with a similar process in the United States, Africa, or Asia, which also raised raw materials for export. In addition, there were smaller farms, the ranchos, as well as self-sufficient Indian communities, which evolved into an important component of the colonial economy. These agricultural units generally began to satisfy the needs of nearby urban administrative or mining centers and slowly started to export their produce to other portions of the empire and, eventually, to Spain or Portugal. Finally, local industries and artisanal workshops manufactured consumer goods, like textiles or shoes, and prepared foods for local markets as well as for other colonies. The traffic in the produce of the mines, haciendas, and factories spawned a network of commercial houses that acted as intermediaries both within the Americas and between the colonies and Europe. More than the English or the Portuguese, the Spanish developed cities which, as the economy grew, became a source of employment for administrators and service industries. Teachers certainly could compare the Latin American process of urbanization to the growth of cities in Asia, Africa, and the United States.

Thanks to the expansion of the economy, the establishment of imperial government bodies, the introduction of the military, and the presence of the Church, colonial Latin America developed a complicated social structure. Two forces shaped the colonial society: traditional European values, which tended to favor the nobility, the military, and the clergy over commerce and, of course, the peasants; and a new component: race. Certainly Latin America's racial mix was more varied than that of Europe, British America, Africa, or Asia. From the intermingling of the Amerindian, the European, and later the black and Asian, came the fruits of miscegenation — the mestizo, mulatto, *zambo*, and *chino*. If race played an important part in determining status — many felt the need to prove their *limpieza de sangre* (that their blood was untainted by inferior people) — wealth and education could also affect one's social standing. Teachers could compare how Latin America's racial minorities absorbed European values to advance socially and economically with the same process of acculturation in Africa and Asia.

Invariably, teachers should dedicate some material to studying the political development of the Iberian colonies. It might prove more useful to concentrate on the larger nations, Mexico, Peru, or Brazil, about which much has been written, rather than try to include every part of the empire.[3] While this selection process excludes the smaller countries, it provides one of the few ways to cover the material in an efficient manner. Teachers can supplement political history with material on blacks or Asians in the workforce, compare Latin American religious dissidents to those in the United States, and contrast the somewhat privileged legal and economic status of colonial Latin American women with their sisters across the oceans.[4]

INDEPENDENCE

After the United States, the nations of Latin America became some of the first former colonial possessions to become free. After centuries of putative imperial domination, Luso-Hispanic Americans developed a sense of identity that distinguished, and later alienated, them from their European rulers. Spain's eighteenth-century attempts to reassert its control over its dominions antagonized the local elites which, over the decades, had wielded substantial economic, political, and social power. The American upper class and masses objected, sometimes violently, to the Spanish crown's policies. Like the United

States, Latin America initially sought not so much independence but more local autonomy. The Napoleonic Wars, however, so diminished the Iberian nations' strength that Latin America's elites could displace their colonial masters. Depending on the area, however, this process of emancipation occurred over decades before the rebels drove Spanish forces from the mainland.

The independence process was complex and varied from country to country. Some nations fought for it; others had independence thrust upon them. Because Madrid often utilized locally recruited militias, the wars for independence became more civil struggles than movements for national liberation. This became particularly true as Latin American elites battled the masses who attempted to use the political unrest to obtain redress for their social and economic problems. A few nations, like Brazil, achieved independence in a relatively bloodless process and long after many other nations had won their freedom. Many of the Caribbean islands remained colonial possessions. Certainly students could profit from comparing the Latin American struggle for freedom, which, like that of the United States, required prolonged fighting, with that of Asia and Africa.

Given this chaotic political process, independence may have brought freedom but it did not confer stability. The oligarchy continued to wage a war on the masses and to fight each other. For many years the ever-exotic Brazil remained the continent's only monarchy. Ideological conflicts roiled the hemisphere, and while they sometimes shared general themes — arguments over the type of government, federalism versus centralism, the status of the Church, guarantees of individual rights — each nation's search for a solution appeared unique. Some countries, like Chile, established authoritarian governments that slowly, and sometimes in response to violent protest from below, evolved into more liberal states. A few countries never, in fact, became polities. Under the sometimes benign influence of what are called caudillos, areas such as Bolivia and Paraguay fluttered between chaos and authoritarianism.

THE TWENTIETH CENTURY

Eventually change came to Latin America as it did to Europe and the United States: Argentina, Chile, and Uruguay voluntarily empowered their citizens, enfranchising first all men and then, by the mid-twentieth century, women. In some countries, foreign intervention or constant civil unrest aborted or slowed the political process. These countries appeared stuck in some political limbo, but eventually even they changed. Latin American nations, unlike those in Africa, Europe, or Asia, rarely became one-party states, nor have they, with the exception of Cuba, embraced the ideas of either political extreme. Brazil's *Estado Novo* or Chile's Socialist Republic (which, in fact, was neither) might have briefly espoused totalitarian ideals, but it was nationalism that emerged as the predominant ideology. Given the number of the countries involved, a teacher would be best advised to concentrate on the hemisphere's largest nations —

Argentina, Brazil, Chile, and Mexico, about which a great deal has been written — rather than to attempt some continental analysis on political development.[5]

The history of Latin America, like that of other areas, becomes a process of
modifying traditional institutions. The abolition of slavery, for example, constitutes an important topic that a teacher can usefully compare with similar
processes in the United States, Africa, and Asia.[6] Ending slavery did not undo
the damage done to the black community since the freed slaves remained subordinated to the dominant white oligarchy in places like Brazil as well as in the
United States. Teachers can compare how Latin American nations dealt with
this issue as well as that of race.

The unequal landholding system continued to plague Latin America just as
it did other areas of the world. Agrarian reform sought to wrest control from the
landholding minority and give it to the peons, who tilled the soil and whose
conditions approximated that of serfs. In some countries, such as Mexico,
people had to fight to bring justice to the countryside. Others accomplished
similar changes peacefully. The secularization of society, which eventually led
to the separation of Church and state — sometimes preceded by the despoiling
of the clergy — offers yet another subject for historical comparisons with nations
where state support for religion seemed minimal. Diplomatic relations among
independent states, their former colonial masters, and the rest of the world offers
another fruitful area for exploration. Latin American nations, for example, often
had difficulty winning the diplomatic recognition of Spain, a problem that did
not bedevil the United States or many of the former Asian or African colonies,
and that complicated their development. Latin America, moreover, had to deal
with another colonial legacy: uncertain boundaries. For decades, frontier disputes, which occasionally blossomed into war, bedeviled the continent.

Finally, teachers might compare the experience of Latin America's women
or minority or ethnic groups with those of the United States, Asia, and Africa.
The struggle of Latin American women to become enfranchised as well as to re-
gain many of the economic rights they possessed in the colonial period can be
placed alongside the experience of women on other continents. Countless immigrants — Arabs, Germans, Italians, Chinese, Jews, and Japanese — poured
into Argentina, Chile, Brazil, and Peru. Relating their stories would allow teachers to address the issues of assimilation, a topic which could be enhanced by including the experience of the black and the Amerindian.[7]

Comparing the process of Latin America's modern economic development
is a valuable adjunct to studying Latin American political evolution. Latin
America's economies tended to adjust rapidly in response to world market conditions. Teachers can describe this process in a variety of ways. Some might attempt to trace economic change on a country-by-country basis. A better alternative is to emphasize specific economic examples rather than nations. For
instance, students can learn about tropical economies by studying the production of sugar, coffee, or bananas in Brazil, Ecuador, Central America, or Peru.
Some Latin American nations, such as Argentina, developed pastoral economies, exporting meat or cereals. As in the colonial period, the exploitation of

mineral resources — the mining of copper, nitrates, silver, or guano in Chile, Mexico, and Peru, or the exploitation of oil in Mexico and Venezuela — proved more lucrative than tilling the ground above them.[8]

Relying on mines and fields tended to create monocultures that left Latin American producers, as it did their American, Asian, and African counterparts, at the mercy of the vagaries of world market demand. Industrialization occurred in Latin America, but not without difficulty. Latin American nations, like other nations, depended upon the customs house as their main source of income. Instituting protectionist laws, while helping nascent industries, deprived the new nations of needed revenues. By the late nineteenth century, however, countries like Chile, Argentina, and Mexico, began to build tariff walls to shelter local manufacturers. These industries provided an alternative source of employment to agriculture or mining, completing the process of economic development.

The Great Depression constituted a watershed in Latin America as it did in the United States. Various countries accepted the notion that the state should foster economic development and eventually, depending upon the situation, ownership of or, at a minimum, control over subsoil resources. As in the rest of the world, government-sponsored import substitution became the vehicle in the drive for self-sufficiency and industrialization.[9]

The growth of population and economic development accelerated the process of urbanization and stimulated the formation of unions. The development of an industrial and entrepreneurial class altered Latin America's social system. Locally trained intellectuals staffed government bureaucracies, such as Chile's CORFO, where they helped shape economic policy. Again, comparing these institutions with others, such as the TVA, can illustrate the role of the state in fomenting economic development. Post–World War II immigration, first from Europe and then Asia, increased the continent's ethnic and racial diversity.

At the end of this brief essay, we return to the starting point: how can one teach about more than twenty diverse nations, let alone compare them to Asia, Africa, Europe, or the United States? As this essay indicates, there are many topics that can easily be included in a world history course. Teachers should take care to emphasize general trends rather than become involved in a specific nation's history. Certainly Latin America's rich past and diverse population provide instructors and students with ample material for comparison with other areas of the world.

Notes

1. Frances Berdan, *The Aztecs of Central Mexico: An Imperial Society* (New York: Holt, Rinehart, and Winston, 1982) and John Hemming, *Red Gold: The Conquest of the Brazilian Indians* (Cambridge, Mass.: Harvard University Press, 1978).

2. See Lesley Simpson's *The Encomienda: Forced Native Labor in the Spanish Colonies, 1492–1550* (Berkeley: University of California Press, 1929) and *The Encomienda in New Spain* (Berkeley: University of California Press, 1950).

3. General histories for the principal areas are Jaime Rodriguez and Colin Maclachlan, *The Forging of the Cosmic Race: A Reinterpretation of Colonial Mexico*

(Berkeley: University of California Press, 1990) or Dauril Alden, *Royal Government in Colonial Brazil* (Berkeley: University of California Press, 1968).

4. Selected topics on colonial life should include a discussion on the status of various sectors. Leslie Rout, Jr., *The African Experience in Spanish America, 1502 to the Present Day* (Cambridge: Cambridge University Press, 1976) discusses the status of blacks. Asuncion Lavrin's *Latin American Women: Historical Perspectives* (Westport, Conn.: Greenwood Press, 1978) and her edited work, *Sexuality and Marriage in Colonial Latin America* (Lincoln: University of Nebraska Press, 1992), and Patricia Seed, *To Love, Honor, and Obey in Colonial Mexico: Conflict over Marriage Choice, 1574–1821* (Stanford: Stanford University Press, 1988), examine women's roles. S. Liebman, *New World Jewry* (New York: Ktav Publishing House, 1982) traces the plight of the Jews.

5. For the various countries, see David Rock, *Argentina, 1516–1987* (Berkeley: University of California Press, 1987); Ronald M. Schneider, *"Order and Progress": A Political History of Brazil* (Boulder, Colo.: Westview Press, 1991); Arthur Whitaker, *The United States and the Southern Cone: Argentina, Chile, and Uruguay* (Cambridge, Mass.: Harvard University Press, 1976); Simon Collier and William Sater, *The History of Chile* (Cambridge: Cambridge University Press, forthcoming); Frederick Pike, *The United States and the Andean Republics* (Cambridge, Mass.: Harvard University Press, 1977); and Michael Meyers and William Sherman, *The Course of Mexican History* (New York: Oxford University Press, 1983).

6. David Murray, *Odious Commerce: Britain, Spain and the Abolition of the Cuban Slave Trade* (Cambridge: Cambridge University Press, 1980) and John Lombardi, *The Decline and Abolition of Negro Slavery in Venezuela* (Westport, Conn.: Greenwood Press, 1971). Predictably, the issue of slavery became more important in Brazil, which had imported more slaves and had the largest black population of any Latin American country. See L. Bethell, *The Abolition of the Brazilian Slave Trade* (Cambridge: Cambridge University Press, 1970) and Robert Conrad, *The Destruction of Brazilian Slavery* (Berkeley: University of California Press, 1972).

7. Examples are Julie Hahner, *Emancipating the Female Sex: The Struggle for Women's Rights in Brazil, 1850–1940* (Durham, N.C.: Duke University Press, 1990); Marifan Carlson, *Feminismo! The Woman's Movement in Argentina from Its Beginnings to Eva Peron* (Chicago: University of Chicago Press, 1988); and Shirlene Soto, *Emergence of the Modern Mexican Woman: Her Participation in Revolution and Struggle for Equality, 1910–1940* (Denver: Arden Press, 1990). For an overview, see Sandra McGee Deutch, "Gender and Sociopolitical Change in Twentieth Century Latin America," *Hispanic American Historical Review* 71: 259–306 (1991). For various ethnic and religious groups, see Frederick Luebke, *Germans in the New World* (Champaign: University of Illinois Press, 1990); Ronald Newton, *German Buenos Aires* (Austin: University of Texas Press, 1977); Judith L. Elkin and G. Merkx, *The Jewish Presence in Latin America* (Boston: Allen and Unwin, 1987); and Tim Holloway, *Immigration on the Land* (Chapel Hill: University of North Carolina Press, 1980). There are also materials on the immigration of Italians, Japanese, and even the Welsh.

8. For a discussion of Latin America's mining and agrarian endeavors, see, for Chile, Thomas O'Brien, *The Nitrate Industry and Chile's Critical Transition* (New York: New York University Press, 1982). For coffee, see Mauricio Font, *Coffee, Contention, and Change in the Making of Modern Brazil* (Cambridge, Mass.: Harvard University Press, 1990); Peter Eisenberg, *The Sugar Industry in Pernambunco* (Berkeley: University of California Press, 1974); and M. Palacios, *Coffee in Colombia, 1870–1970* (Cambridge: Cambridge University Press, 1980). For agriculture and pastoral issues, see James Scobie, *Rev-*

olution on the Pampa: A Social History of Argentine Wheat, 1860–1910 (Austin: University of Texas Press, 1964) and Peter H. Smith, Politics and Beef in Argentina: Patterns of Conflict and Change (New York: Columbia University Press, 1969).

9. A good bibliography for economic topics is that of R. Conde and S. Stein, Latin America: A Guide to Economic History, 1830–1930 (Berkeley: University of California Press, 1977). For an overview, see Roberto Cortes Conde, The First Stages of Modernization in Spanish America (New York: Harper and Row, 1974) and Celso Furtado, Economic Development of Latin America (Cambridge: Cambridge University Press, 1977). For Argentina, see Carlos Diaz Alejandro, Essays on the Economic History of the Argentine Republic (New Haven, Conn.: Yale University Press, 1970); G. Di Tella and R. Dornbusch, The Political Economy of Argentina, 1946–1983 (Pittsburgh: University of Pittsburgh Press, 1989); and Jonathan Brown, A Socio-economic History of Argentina, 1776–1860 (Cambridge: Cambridge University Press, 1979). For Brazil, see Thomas W. Merrick and Douglas H. Graham, Population and Economic Development in Brazil: 1800 to the Present (Baltimore: Johns Hopkins University Press, 1979) and Werner Baer, The Brazilian Economy: Growth and Development (New York: Praeger, 1983). For Mexico, see Clark Reynolds, The Mexican Economy: Twentieth-Century Structure and Growth (New Haven, Conn.: Yale University Press, 1970) and Steven Haber, Industry and Underdevelopment: The Industrialization of Mexico (Stanford: Stanford University Press, 1989). For Chile, see Markos Mamalakis, The Growth and Structure of the Chilean Economy (New Haven, Conn.: Yale University Press, 1976). For some of the Andean nations, see Paul Gootenberg, Between Silver and Guano (Princeton: Princeton University Press, 1991); Rosemary Thorp and Geoffrey Bertram, Peru 1890–1977: Growth and Policy in an Open Economy (New York: Columbia University Press, 1978); and Linda Rodriguez, The Search for Public Policy: Regional Politics and Government Finances in Ecuador, 1830–1940 (Berkeley: University of California Press, 1985). On oil, see John Wirth, Latin American Oil Companies and the Politics of Energy (Lincoln: University of Nebraska Press, 1985) and Jonathan Brown, Oil and Revolution in Mexico (Berkeley: University of California Press, 1993).

JOHN F. RICHARDS

Early Modern India and World History

From the late fifteenth to the early nineteenth century of our present era — for convenience, 1500–1800 — human societies shared in and were affected by several worldwide processes of change unprecedented in their scope and intensity. Along with many other historians, I call these centuries the early modern period.[1] We distinguish this period from the Middle Ages that preceded it and

John F. Richards, "Early Modern India and World History," Journal of World History 8 (1997): 197–209.

from the modern nineteenth and twentieth centuries. Whether we are now in a postmodern period is a matter of conjecture, at least in my view. Contrary to many scholars, I do not regard this periodization as driven by purely Eurocentric considerations. The term *early modern* is merely an attempt to capture the reality of rapid, massive change in the way humans organized themselves and interacted with other human beings and with the natural world.[2] For South Asian history I believe it makes a good deal of sense to use the term *early modern* instead of *Mughal India*, or *late medieval India*, or *late precolonial India* for the sixteenth through the eighteenth centuries. To do so would lessen the extent to which India is seen as exceptional, unique, exotic, and somehow detached from world history. I am convinced that we must contextualize South Asian culture, civilization, and society in this way to better understand the more specific unfolding of Indian history in the sixteenth, seventeenth, and eighteenth centuries.

THE CREATION OF GLOBAL SEA PASSAGES

At least six distinct but complementary large-scale processes define the early modern world. The first of these is *the creation of global sea passages that came to link all of humanity with a transportation network of increasing capacity and efficiency*. In 1400 there were three maritime regions and seafaring traditions from which mariners were equipped to undertake long ocean voyages of discovery: the European, comprising the Mediterranean and coastal Atlantic; the Arab-Indian, covering the Indian Ocean; and the Chinese, encompassing the China Seas and Gulf of Japan. Chinese mariners had by far the largest and most reliable ships and by Sung times had already demonstrated a capacity for voyages beyond their home waters. The Zheng He expeditions of 1405–1433 sent dozens of large ships and thousands of men into the northern Indian Ocean. Had they chosen to do so, Chinese mariners could have circumnavigated Africa or sailed across the Pacific to the New World.[3] Instead, the Ming emperors rejected maritime exploration and commerce and turned their society inward after 1433. Chinese ruling elites formed and retained a deep-seated bias that prevented state investment in maritime expansion at precisely the period when European monarchs were fascinated by possible rewards from this activity.

Throughout the sixteenth, seventeenth, and eighteenth centuries, European rulers paid for and encouraged maritime exploration, mapping, and reporting that generated extensive and systematic knowledge about global geography. For the first time in human history, mariners learned that all the seas of the world are connected and navigable (save for circumpolar ice regions). As Parry puts it: "A reliable ship, competently manned, adequately stored, and equipped with means of finding the way, can in time reach any country in the world which has a sea coast, and can return whence it came."[4] For the first time in human history, European mariners created a reliable sea passage to the New World from the Old.

Europe's discovery and exploitation of reliable sea passages throughout the globe was its single most important advantage over other early modern societies.

The new maritime connections did not supersede older land routes, nor did they attract more than a portion of long-distance trade. It was European knowledge of and access to these new global routes that conferred a commercial, military, and diplomatic edge over other societies. Steady, incremental improvements in ship design and construction, navigational techniques and skills, and seaborne armaments characterized early modern European shipping fleets. Mariners routinely charted the coasts and harbors of the world's continents and islands, and identified prevailing winds and currents in the oceans. By the late 1700s European mariners even had reliable techniques for measuring longitude as well as latitude.[5]

THE RISE OF A TRUE WORLD ECONOMY

The second important large-scale process is *the rise of a truly global world economy in which long-distance commerce, growing rapidly, connected expanding economics on every continent.* The buoyant world trading system of the early modern period rested on global maritime and linking overland routes that connected all human societies. Over these routes the costs of carrying both rarities and bulk commodities, and the risks involved, declined between 1500 and 1800. At the same time, demand and supply signals moved with greater dispatch to a wider network of traders. Throughout the world increasingly sophisticated regional monetary systems based on comparable gold, silver, and copper coinage and paper-based bills of exchange facilitated trade. Annual shipments of gold and silver from New World mines gave early modern states new sources of supply for their expanding coinage needs — in sharp contrast to the metallic "famines" of earlier centuries — and helped discourage debasement of currencies.

Throughout these centuries the world trading system focused on Europe. Antwerp in the sixteenth century was the first "true general emporium" for world trade.[6] Then followed Dutch dominance of world trade, with Amsterdam at its center, between 1580 and 1740. London superseded Amsterdam for the remainder of the early modern period and thereafter well into modern times. During the period of Dutch hegemony over world commerce, Amsterdam was an active entrepôt situated at the apex of the world's markets. A confident, well-financed merchant elite in Amsterdam controlled massive shipping capital and dominant capital resources. Dutch merchants could purchase products in demand at source anywhere in the world at higher prices, bring them to Amsterdam, store them safely, add value by processing and packaging, and sell them profitably. The Dutch federal republican state, with its commercial and financial stability, intervened actively in all fiscal and marketing processes to prevent fraud and impose standards. Confidence in the state made Amsterdam's interest rates the lowest in early modern Europe.

The Dutch republic's greatest contribution lay in the creation of trading companies that were given monopolies of trade in various parts of the world.

The Dutch West Indies Company and the Dutch East Indies Company were two of the largest of these "armed politico-commercial organizations of unprecedented scope and resources not just with regard to the scale of their business operations but also in respect of their military and naval power."[7] In Asia, the Dutch East India Company, along with its English counterpart, formed the leading edge of European aggressive expansion in the early modern centuries.[8]

Commodity production for enlarged markets is a shared feature of early modern societies. Farmers and loggers in Poland, the Ukraine, and other lands around the Baltic shipped food grains and timber for the world market. Peasants in western Anatolia produced mohair yarn for export. Russians and settlers in the North American colonies sold furs and deerskins. Both North American and Latin American ranchers exported hides and dried meat to European markets. Growers in the coastal lands of eastern Brazil and the Caribbean islands supplied tons of sugar to the world market every year. Producers in Venezuela shipped cacao, while those in Guatemala, Honduras, and northern India exported indigo. The peoples of island Southeast Asia exported nutmeg, pepper, and other spices for world markets. Weavers in India produced cotton and silk textiles that found new markets in Europe. Traders in south India sold diamonds for world consumption. In addition to the world trade in material goods, European demand for cheap forced labor stimulated the export of slaves from Africa and Asia — often displacing more expensive European indentured laborers.

THE GROWTH OF LARGE, STABLE STATES

The third large-scale process that distinguishes the early modern period is *the growth, around the world, of states and other large-scale complex organizations that attained size, stability, capacity, efficiency, and territorial reach not seen since antiquity, if then.* Early modern states displayed impressive new abilities to mobilize resources and deploy overwhelming force. On the Japanese archipelago, the Tokugawa regime united the warring states of medieval Japan to form one of the world's most powerful states for the time. In Russia the czarist state consolidated power and expanded its territory. In western Europe, the French monarchy built a centralized state structure that directed colonial expansion throughout the world. On the British Isles, England forcibly assimilated Scotland and Ireland and built a vast colonial maritime empire. In the Middle East Constantinople was the hub of an expanding, confident, centralized Ottoman state, while Isfahan was the center of the rival Safavid empire. In India the Mughal empire imposed centralized rule over nearly the entire subcontinent for the first time since the Mauryas. Spanish colonial rulers imposed centralized authority over Central America and much of South America; the Portuguese did the same in Brazil. Even in China the Qing dynasty may well have controlled a more effective, powerful state apparatus than that of its predecessor, the native Ming.

THE GROWTH OF WORLD POPULATION

A fourth factor is *the doubling of world population during the early modern centuries.* Between 1500 and 1800 world population probably changed as follows:[9]

Year	World Population
1500	400–500 million
1600	500–600 million
1700	600–700 million
1800	850–950 million

Human numbers increased slowly but steadily, with an accelerating rate in the eighteenth century. According to this calculation, world population grew by 350–550 million over three hundred years. Overall, this is a slow, almost imperceptible rate of increase that masks regional variations of some consequence. Some 50 million or more inhabitants of the New World in 1492 suffered a huge die-off from previously unknown infectious disease and colonial brutality during the sixteenth and seventeenth centuries. By 1800 the total population of the New World was barely half that of the precontact total. This holocaust, however, did not deflect a strong global upward trend in the early modern period. The available direct and indirect evidence strongly supports the view that in all other regions of the world human numbers grew steadily. Some episodes of population growth were unusually rapid. The population of Japan under the Tokugawa regime went from 12 million in 1600 to 31 million by 1720.[10] The Russian population doubled from 14 million to 29 million between 1722 and 1795.[11] Nor do we see any retreat from these levels thereafter.

INTENSIFICATION OF LAND USE

The fifth important process throughout the early modern world was *the intensified use of land to expand production in numerous episodes of settler frontiers.* In addition to European settlement of North and South America and Dutch settlement of South Africa, Russia, China, eastern Europe, and parts of western Europe were engaged in substantial processes of internal colonization. Growing populations, aggressive states, and market forces combined to send pioneer-settlers into forests or savannas to reclaim land for plow cultivation or commercial pastoralism (ranching). Pioneers cleared forests, drained wetlands, and fenced grasslands. They claimed property rights over newly defined and bounded plots of land. The pioneers displaced thinly settled hunter-gatherers, horticulturists, shifting cultivators, and pastoral nomads, who were assigned a "savage" role by the intruders. Backed by the power and authority of the centralizing state, pioneer-settlers drove away, killed off, or subordinated indigenous peoples in order to claim land for cultivation or ranching. Early modern frontiersmen invariably were tied to domestic and international markets for the goods they produced. This continuing process of settlement had a windfall effect whereby abundant new resources — soil, timber, wildlife, and minerals — were put into concentrated modes of production for an expanding world economy.[12]

THE DIFFUSION OF NEW TECHNOLOGY

A final process was *the diffusion of several new technologies — cultivation of New World crops, gunpowder, and printing — and organizational responses to them throughout the early modern world.* Tobacco use and tobacco growing spread rapidly throughout Africa and Asia as a result of the New World connection. Coffee, tea, and chocolate offered new, quickly adopted stimulants as hot drinks mixed with sugar. Perhaps more significant was the adoption of maize and calorie-rich sweet potatoes. With these new cultivars, farmers could clear hill forests and profitably grow these highly productive food crops. New World food crops provided a technical breakthrough that stimulated expansion of cultivation throughout China, Japan, and Taiwan in the eighteenth century. Maize and potatoes added to the productive capacity of European, and later African, agriculture.

The early modern world saw the rapid evolution of gunpowder-related technologies. Both portable personal firearms and cannon gained ease of operation, power, and accuracy. Use of cannon on warships went through several generations of improvement in both guns and ships. The production of gunpowder, cannon founding, and musket and pistol manufacture became ubiquitous. Early modern states, confronted with the greatly increased costs of firearms, turned their attention to improving their tax assessment and collection. Military organization around firearms on land put new emphasis on infantry and mobile light field artillery in place of the medieval reliance on heavily armored mounted cavalry.

In retrospect, the most potent new technology of the period was printing with movable metal type. The new invention was especially suitable for the roman and other writing systems with a limited number of symbolic letters. Gutenberg-style printing was closely associated with European expansion and domination. China, Japan, and Korea, all of which have ideographic writing systems, remained attached to their sophisticated technology of woodblock printing, which supported wide publication of books. The Islamic and Indian worlds were slow to give up manuscripts and the pen to use less appealing metal-type printing.

THE CASE OF SOUTH ASIA

If, for the purposes of argument, we accept the validity of these broad generalizations about early modern world history, do they apply to South Asia? Does the subcontinent share in these traits of early modernity? Before answering that question it might be well to address at least two possible concerns. First, for this period (or any other period), can we treat the Indian subcontinent as a meaningful social and cultural unit? Can we make generalizations that hold throughout the entire subcontinent? Many South Asian scholars argue that only linguistic and cultural regions, such as Andhra, Maharashtra, or Bengal, can be seen as meaningful units. Others look to smaller regions or even localities as the only useful social and political units. Generalizations made for the entire subcontinent are suspect.

My own view is that the degrees of similarity in society and culture among all regions in the subcontinent are such that we can reasonably discuss and analyze South Asia as a unit. Granting fuzziness in border areas, we can look at a wide range of similarities that tie the subcontinent together. The contrast between, say, the forced-labor tax systems of the states of Southeast Asia and the land-tax systems of South Asia is but one example. The caste system is not found in Southeast Asia — or other parts of the world, for that matter — despite strenuous attempts to find analogues elsewhere. Strictly endogamous, birth-ascribed, named social units — miniature ethnicities — arranged hierarchically by principles of purity and pollution and traditional occupation and buttressed by religious dogma is a uniquely South Asian phenomenon. It is a truism that Muslim groups in South Asia have found it difficult to avoid castelike organization despite the egalitarian teachings of their faith. The caste system has certainly evolved and changed, particularly in response to new pressures, such as those generated by Islam or by colonial European rule, but the system itself is not replicated elsewhere in the world.

Travelers coming to the subcontinent from Europe, the Middle East, Southeast Asia, or other regions of the world leave no doubt about the differences between India and their home regions. The ruminations of Babur on the contrast, often drawn unfavorably, between northern India and Central Asia are well known. In addition to having customs seen as very strange, such as disposal of the dead by cremation, India was enormously productive, wealthy, and densely populated by comparison with Central Asia or even the Middle East.[13] We can also contrast the relative porosity of early modern South Asia with the impermeability of China. All manner of foreigners — traders, religious figures, adventurers — moved freely about the subcontinent. They encountered little or no state concern or control. Contrast this freedom with the strict control exerted by the Ming or Qing dynasty over any and all foreigners and over external trade by means of the tribute mission system.

The second objection to incorporating South Asia into early modern world history is that earlier scholars overestimated exogenous forces for change in this period. This bias marred the writing of South Asian history by Eurocentric scholars before 1947 and to some extent thereafter. I do not wish to return to the notion of a passive, "traditional and oriental" South Asia that only "progressed and modernized" because of influences from Europe. We cannot revert to this outworn approach. Over the last half-century historians, scholars of religion, art historians, anthropologists, literary scholars, and others have demonstrated by painstaking, detailed research the energy and dynamism of South Asian society and culture. Some of these processes came from the outside; others likely did not. The point is that these are world processes that share attributes with those in other regions but have their own unique character in South Asia.

Having at least addressed these questions, does India fit this paradigm? Yes, it does — at least in my judgment. Certainly the maritime connection is firm. Indian ports and shipping had for centuries been tied into the Arabian Sea, Red Sea, and Mediterranean system on one side and into the Bay of Bengal, Straits of Melaka, and China seas on the other. With the northern European trading companies in the lead, India after 1500 was tied into the global system of sea passages.

The role of the subcontinent in the world trading system in the early modern period was decidedly significant.[14] Throughout these centuries the subcontinent retained a favorable balance of trade with the rest of the world. Indian diamonds, pepper, handwoven cotton and silk textiles, and other commodities kept their old markets and found new outlets. Largely self-sufficient for its own needs, India was the ultimate sink for the flow of New World silver and gold.[15] Production for the world economy had more than peripheral importance. Cotton grown in the black-earth regions of western India traveled by pack bullock to Coromandel on the east coast, where it was cleaned, spun into yarn, handwoven into yards-long pieces, bleached, and printed for export. Payment for these goods took the form of imported gold and silver coins paid to merchant middlemen and ultimately to the producers themselves. Om Prakash has calculated that Dutch purchases of textiles in Bengal in the late seventeenth century likely generated 100,000 new jobs for that region.[16]

I have spent much of my career arguing that between the early sixteenth and early eighteenth centuries the Mughals conquered and ruled a dynamic, centralizing state. By 1690 the Mughal emperor was the acknowledged ruler over nearly the entire subcontinent. Simply on the basis of its ability to tax society, maintain political stability, and monopolize force, the Mughal empire must be judged a success. I have also stressed the dynamism of the imperial system, which continued to deepen and strengthen imperial institutions until structural breakup occurred in 1720. In the end the Mughal empire failed to convert the armed, warrior aristocracies of the countryside into quasi-officials in the major structural change that was needed for truly centralized rule. This was a task that the British would require a full century or more to accomplish. Despite this failure, I believe that in terms of scale, efficiency, and wealth, the Mughal empire compares favorably with the contemporary Ottoman and Safavid empires and with any state in Europe. As a recent review of my collected essays by Andre Wink points out, I have held this view with rather unimaginative consistency.[17]

Frequently over the past thirty years I have encountered arguments by colleagues that the Mughal empire had little or no impact on local societies, local lords (*zamindars*), or everyday life. Historians of southern India have stressed the decentralized nature of political power and authority in the "segmented states" of that region.[18] Historians of the Marathas have drawn our attention to the prevalence of resistance and rebellion to Mughal rule in that region by local elites.[19] Throughout, my position has been and remains that the development of unprecedented state power and political unification under the Mughals is a defining characteristic of early modern — not Mughal — India, just as it is for other regions in the world.

As far as population is concerned, most scholars postulate consider-able growth, despite spectacular famine and disease episodes. For example, McEvedy and Jones put the total population for the Indian subcontinent in 1500 at 100 million, climbing to 185 million by 1800.[20] Irfan Habib's estimates are somewhat higher; he suggests that the figure in 1600 was 140–150 million, rising to about 200 million in 1800.[21] The evidence for growth in human numbers is necessarily largely indirect since the Mughals and other early modern polities in the subcontinent did not conduct censuses. With appropriate adjustments, pop-ulation trends can be drawn from the sequence of Mughal land revenue assess-ments in the same region. The type of land-use change, settler frontier, and ex-pansion of cultivation and production described earlier does apply. In Bihar under Shah Jahan's reign, Rajput *zamindars* [landowners] in Rohtas district ex-panded cultivation with the encouragement of the state. A later description of Shahabad in this period states that "most of the zamindars during the reign of Shahjahan originated in *bankatai* or populating land after clearing forests. Those who did so became zamindars and obtained *nankars* [part of the revenue as zamindari right] for their lifetime. After the death of such zamindars, their sons obtained sanads [written orders] for the rights held by them on condition of continued service."[22]

Finally, with one exception, all of the major early modern technologies dif-fused throughout the subcontinent. New World cultivars, notably tobacco and maize, spread rapidly throughout South Asia in the seventeenth century. Oth-ers, such as chili peppers, were adopted more slowly but diffused widely. The Mughal empire succeeded in part because of its command of gunpowder tech-nology. Gunpowder, cannon, and muskets were manufactured in India in con-siderable numbers to meet military needs. Cultural resistance precluded wide-spread adoption of movable-type printing in India until the early nineteenth century. The techniques were known and demonstrated by missionaries and the European companies but did not diffuse readily or easily.

What are some of the implications of this early modern model for our study of South Asia? Certainly India's rising economic capacity should be re-assessed.[23] The economy grew simply to meet the needs of a near doubling of population as well as the intensifying demands from the world market. The ex-tent to which industrial production was a product of scattered, rural industrial operations is not well recognized. New work currently being done by Thelma Lowe combines field archaeology with documentary research to suggest wide spatial distribution of sites for steel production in the Telugu lands during the early modern centuries.[24] Indian merchants competed successfully with the Eu-ropean trading companies and traded actively with Central Asia, the Middle East, East Africa, and Southeast Asia. As Stephen Dale has shown, colonies of expatriate Indian merchants resident in Moscow carried on regular trade with the subcontinent during the seventeenth and eighteenth centuries.[25]

Most difficult and challenging is the notion of cumulative and accelerating change in early modern India. Can we infer that the circulation of people, commodities, and ideas became more dense and rapid over the early modern centuries? Surely new cultural production — manifest in the popular religious movements of northern India — increased in size, intensity, and variety. Wrapping our minds around the notion of change demands a conscious effort. Most of us still operate with an unstated assumption that precolonial India was nearly static. The statement that generalizations made for 1500 can still apply in 1750 or even 1800 is another version of "traditional" or "premodern" India. We must put aside our knowledge of the colonial outcome and look with fresh eyes at new institutions, new social forms, new cultural expression, and new productivity in the early modern period. Also difficult is the need to work up a cross-disciplinary understanding of the dynamics of change throughout the subcontinent in the early centuries.

We must generate better integrated, multidisciplinary historical research in early modern South Asia (not Mughal India), in which scholars move seamlessly between the particulars of local and regional histories to broader South Asian and world description and analysis. South Asia is too important to be consigned to the dusty shelf of oriental curios when world history is written in the future.

Notes

1. Fernand Braudel, *Civilization and Capitalism, Fifteenth–Eighteenth Century*, 3 vols. (New York: Harper and Row, 1981–84).

2. Even J. M. Blaut, the most articulate recent critic of Eurocentric world history, comments: "Africa, Asia, and Europe shared equally in the rise of capitalism prior to 1492. After that date Europe took the lead. This happened . . . because of Europe's location near America and because of the immense wealth obtained by Europeans in America and later in Asia and Africa — not because Europeans were brighter or bolder or better than non-Europeans, or more modern, more advanced, more progressive, more rational. These are myths of Eurocentric diffusionism and are best forgotten" (J. M. Blaut, *The Colonizer's Model of the World* [New York: Guilford Press, 1993], 206).

3. J. H. Parry, *The Discovery of the Sea* (Berkeley: University of California Press, 1981), 16.

4. Parry, *Discovery of the Sea*, xi.

5. Dava Sobel, *Longitude: The True Story of a Lone Genius Who Solved the Greatest Scientific Problem of His Time* (New York: Penguin, 1996).

6. Jonathan I. Israel, *Dutch Primacy in World Trade, 1585–1740* (Oxford: Clarendon Press, 1989), 405.

7. Israel, *Dutch Primacy*, 411.

8. The most complete study of the English East India Company remains K. N. Chaudhuri, *The Trading World of Asia and the English East India Company, 1660–1760* (Cambridge: Cambridge University Press, 1978).

9. My estimates are based upon population figures given in Braudel, *Civilization and Capitalism*, 1:40–49; Paul Demeny, "Population," in *The Earth as Transformed by Human Action*, edited by B. L. Turner II et al. (Cambridge: Cambridge University Press, 1990), 42–43; and Colin McEvedy and Richard Jones, *Atlas of World Population History* (London: Penguin, 1985), 349. McEvedy and Jones's figure for 1500 is revised upward to adjust for their underestimate of New World populations.

10. Conrad Totman, *Early Modern Japan* (Berkeley: University of California Press, 1993), 140.

11. Braudel, *Civilization and Capitalism*, 1:47–48.

12. John F. Richards, "Land Transformation," in Turner et al., *The Earth as Transformed by Human Action*, 163–78.

13. See, for example, Richard Foltz, "Two Seventeenth-Century Central Asian Travellers to Mughal India," *Journal of the Royal Asiatic Society*, 3rd series (1996): 367–77.

14. I have previously argued (John F. Richards, "The Seventeenth-Century Crisis in South Asia," *Modern Asian Studies* 24 [1990]: 625–38) that the fiscal crisis that seems to have overcome several large Eurasian states in the first half of the seventeenth century did not occur synchronously in Mughal India. Symptoms of crisis appeared only at the turn of the eighteenth century in the subcontinent. This argument does not necessarily undercut the notion of tightening economic ties that incorporated India into the early modern world economy. Instead, the strength of the early modern South Asian economy and trade balance precluded a fiscal crisis similar to that found elsewhere.

15. John F. Richards, ed., *Precious Metals in the Later Medieval and Early Modern Worlds* (Durham, N.C.: Carolina Academic Press, 1983), 22–23.

16. Om Prakash, *The Dutch East India Company and the Economy of Bengal, 1630–1720* (Princeton, N.J.: Princeton University Press, 1985).

17. Andre Wink, review of John F. Richards, *Power, Administration, and Finance in Mughal India* (Aldershot: Variorum, 1993), *Journal of Asian Studies* 54 (1995): 1143–47.

18. Burton Stein was the foremost proponent of this view of premodern states in India. See his *Peasant State and Society in Medieval South India* (Delhi: Oxford University Press, 1985) and *Vijayanagara* (Cambridge: Cambridge University Press, 1989).

19. For example, Andre Wink, *Land and Sovereignty in India: Agrarian Society and Politics under the Eighteenth Century Maratha Svarajya* (Cambridge: Cambridge University Press, 1986).

20. McEvedy and Jones, *Atlas of World Population History*, 185.

21. Tapan Raychaudhuri and Irfan Habib, eds., *The Cambridge Economic History of India*, 2 vols. (Cambridge: Cambridge University Press, 1982), 1:167. Habib draws on estimates made by different scholars for different dates.

22. Quoted in John F. Richards, *The Mughal Empire* (Cambridge: Cambridge University Press, 1993), 191, from Muzaffar Alam, *The Crisis of Empire in Mughal North India* (Delhi: Oxford University Press, 1986), 65–66.

23. Andre Gunder Frank, "India in the World Economy, 1400–1750," *Economic and Political Weekly*, 27 July 1996, 50–64. In this recent piece, Frank argues that "the common global expansion since 1400 benefitted the Asian centres [India and China] earlier and more than it did Europe, Africa and the Americas" (50).

24. In her dissertation in progress at the University of California, Berkeley.

25. Stephen F. Dale, *Indian Merchants and Eurasian Trade, 1600–1750* (Cambridge: Cambridge University Press, 1994).

TARA SETHIA

Teaching India in a World History Survey

India represents a core Asian tradition as well as one of the oldest strands in the fabric of world civilization. Indian religions, philosophies, art, literature, and social systems have played a fundamental role in defining the human heritage, and they merit a proper discussion in a world history survey.

Historically, India, like China, has been a seminal influence on the societies and cultures of Asia. People of the Himalayan regions, Sri Lanka, and a large part of Southeast Asia have been greatly affected by Indian culture. Buddhism, originating in India, became — and still remains — a dominant religion in several Asian countries, including China and Japan. India has also influenced the making of the modern world: Indian inventions and innovations in science, medicine, and mathematics contributed to the emergence of these disciplines. For example, the Indian discovery of zero and numerals, mistakenly referred to as Arabic numerals, revolutionized mathematical knowledge. Traditionally, Indian raw materials have been attractive to the West just as the subcontinent has been a vast market for industrial goods. And today, India is poised to become a major exporter of value-added goods and services. Hence, the study of Indian society is intrinsically important for understanding the rest of Asia and is relevant as well to a historical understanding of the emergence of the modern world.

From a more contemporary perspective, India is the world's largest democracy and a leading developing country. Its population — representing more than 850 million people of diverse cultures, languages, religions, and food habits — continues to be a growing attraction to the consumer and labor-oriented industries of the West.

The distinctiveness of Indian civilization lies not merely in its antiquity but, more importantly, in its continuity and diversity. Hindus, for example, continue to seek inspiration from traditions and concepts similar to those originally advanced by their ancestors. The *Ramayana* and the *Mahabharata*, the epics composed in ancient times, are still read and revered. In the same way, social institutions, languages, and literature show strong trends of continuity. This, however, does not mean that Indian society has been static. In fact, it is important to

Tara Sethia, "Teaching India in a World History Survey," *Perspectives* (American Historical Association) 34 (March 1996): 15–20.

note that Indian traditions have constantly evolved over the past three and a half millennia. And Indian society is perplexingly multicultural, multiethnic, multilingual, and multireligious, though officially a secular state.

AN APPROACH TO TEACHING INDIA IN WORLD HISTORY

Given such longevity and diversity, teaching about the Indian subcontinent can be both a fascinating and a frustrating experience. And, teaching about India in a world history course poses additional challenges. India has continued to be imagined and imaged in diverse ways by scholars and laypeople alike. For instance, in the past India was seen by some as the land of the maharajas, and by others as a home of snake charmers. At one time perceived as a source of fabulous and untold wealth, India today is seen as a land of abject poverty. As in the past, India continues to be associated with spirituality, metaphysical reality, mystical happenings, and the sacred cow. While some continue to romanticize and idealize the image of India, others look on it with contempt and disdain. For some, India evokes the memories of Gandhi; for others, that of the *Raj*. While contemporary India is seen by many as a land plagued with poverty and communal conflict, it is viewed by many others as a nation equipped with several sophisticated technologies of the 21st century. Thus, the challenge in teaching about India lies not so much in providing basic knowledge about India, but rather in exposing students to the connections between the images and the realities that have characterized Indian society from antiquity to the present and in enabling students to see India as a land of unity in diversity, of tradition and modernity, and of change and continuity.

There is also the challenge of time. How much time (measurable in class periods, should be devoted to the discussion of the Indian subcontinent in a world history survey? Related to the question of time is that of topic — what to discuss and what to discard? Equally important are concerns about the extent of depth and detail. And there is the difficulty of how to communicate concepts that are completely foreign to many students.

While it is difficult to arrive at specific answers to these questions and problems, it is possible to address them within the context of the general structure of and approach to the teaching of world history. If a teacher takes an integrated approach to world history, for instance, it will be hard to measure time to be spent on a specific culture in terms of class periods, just as the question of depth and detail might be subject to a given level of student-teacher interest. I emphasize a comparative approach to the study of various traditional and contemporary societies in a world historical context. This format has several advantages. It engages students in a meaningful intellectual exercise that requires them to identify the unique qualities characteristic of an individual civilization while allowing them to grasp more effectively the similarities among civilizations. This approach also enables students to focus on the larger issues and trends that characterize human history and helps to broaden their perspectives. The themes selected for discussion in this paper are not prescriptive but, rather, represent some of the broader issues in a world historical context.

As I begin to teach about India, I usually ask students to share their images of the subcontinent. This brief but informal dialogue helps me to understand how the students have come to acquire their impressions (e.g., through films, novels, newspapers, television, personal contact, or academic training). I then use this context to discuss the diverse range of scholarly and popular views about Indian society and to raise key issues related to the subject, such as the influence of dominant discourse in shaping images about other cultures. For instance, I explain how the Orientalist discourse (see Edward Said, *Orientalism*, 1979), has shaped Western images about the "Orient" and "Orientals."

LAND AND PEOPLE

A discussion of "imaginative" geography and culture explicit in terms such as "Orient" and "Orientals" is then juxtaposed with a discussion of my first important theme, the land and peoples of India. This theme allows the class to examine India's specific place in world geography, especially on the Asian land mass, and the influence of geographical features on its history and culture. The theme provides students with a thorough orientation to India's unique physical features and helps them understand how these features shaped the country's history. A brief discussion of the cultural geography of India exposes students to its numerous languages, dialects, and complex cultural contours. Time permitting, I have students (in groups) do a short class exercise of mapping India (i.e., identifying by marking on a blank map the major features of the physical and cultural geography of the subcontinent), using historical atlases and wall maps. I conclude the discussion of the theme by fleshing out the connection between geography and history. I examine how, for example, the Himalayas and monsoons have historically affected the people of the subcontinent. Teachers will find Joseph Schwartzberg, ed., *A Historical Atlas of South Asia* (1978) a good reference to consult.

The connection between geography and history can be further extended by a discussion of Indus Valley civilization in the global context of riverine civilizations, the growth and diffusion of agriculture and farming techniques, and the rise of urban trends from the dawn of history. This discussion sets the context for a comparative study of the river-based civilizations of the ancient world. It enables students to perceive similarities and differences underlying human heritage across the globe. They learn to identify the common characteristics of river-based civilizations flourishing in the Euphrates-Tigris valleys, the Indus River valley, the Nile River valley, and the Yellow River valley while appreciating the distinctive and unique characteristics of each. For example, in discussing the geographic extent of these civilizations, it can be pointed out that the Harappan (or Indus valley) civilization, which encompassed 840,000 square miles, was probably twice the size of the old kingdom of Egypt and four times that of Sumer and Akkad. Or, the connectedness of civilizations and peoples of the ancient world might be illustrated by focusing on evidence of Indian contact with the civilizations to the west. For example, the commercial contacts with the Euphrates-Tigris civilization can be demonstrated by archaeological evidence pointing to Harappan manufactures found in Mesopotamia.

The migration and movement of people, including nomadic invasions, played a significant role in defining the cultural, ethnic, and racial contours of the ancient world. In the large context of the migration of Indo-Europeans, I introduce the coming of Indo-Aryans to the Indian subcontinent. The ensuing interaction between the nomadic Indo-Aryans, equipped with horse-driven chariots, and the highly cultured people of the Indus valley lays the groundwork for the Vedic age, the second stage of civilization in India (around 1500 B.C.E.). Relying on the evidence from philology and archaeology, a majority of scholars maintain that the Aryan tribes were part of the Indo-Europeans who originated somewhere in central Asia or southern Russia. These people migrated in constant waves toward Europe and India. It is interesting to note that although Indo-Aryans and Greeks came from the same stock of people (i.e., the Indo-Europeans), they met as strangers in the sixth century B.C.E. Persian empire. The characteristics of the Greek and Aryan gods in regulating the order of nature and in banishing evil from the world can be highlighted to show their common background and heritage. However, it is important to point out that the so-called Vedic culture and civilization owed its origin not only to the Indo-Aryans, but, as recent research suggests, also to an amalgam of Aryan and Harappan cultures. (For details about key issues and controversies pertaining to the representation of ancient Indian history, see Romila Thapar's *Interpreting Early India*, 1993.)

THE EMERGENCE OF TRADITIONS: HINDUISM, JAINISM, AND BUDDHISM

Students can be familiarized briefly with the sources of Indian traditions — the Vedic and the Epic literature. Focusing on selected excerpts from *Rig Veda* (see Ainslie T. Embree, ed., *Sources of Indian Tradition*, vol. 1, 1988), one of the most ancient surviving pieces of literature, I ask students to discuss the cosmology and worldview that characterize the Indian tradition as well as the role of ritual and sacrifice. This discussion can be carried further with more concrete examples of Indian tradition and values drawn from the two epics, *Ramayana* and *Mahabharata*.

The way is now paved for a more specific discussion of the evolution of Hinduism, Jainism, and Buddhism in the historical context of the evolution of religious and philosophical traditions in the ancient world. Taking Hinduism as a case in point, I ask, What is Hinduism? Is it a religion or a philosophy? Is it earthly or metaphysical? Is it spiritual or material? Is it polytheistic or monotheistic? Is it a social practice or a complete way of life?

The discussion of Buddhism and Jainism can be used to stimulate comparative and global thinking. I also focus on how, for example, Jainism and Buddhism emerged in India in the context of changing socioreligious trends, and why Jainism remained totally inside India while Buddhism spread beyond the Indian subcontinent. The spread of Buddhism from India can be used to illustrate the connectedness of world regions during ancient times. At the same time, one can raise a question about how Buddhism posed a challenge to Hindu society during the classical period in India just as it did to the Confucian state in China. This context enables me to come back to the subcontinent and examine the changes that took place in classical (or Gupta) India, as well as to flesh out the evolutionary nature of Hinduism, by pointing out how and why Hinduism assumed the shape that it did. This can be explained by reference to the prescribed Four Ends of Man *(Dharma, Artha, Kama,* and *Moksha)* and to the Four Stages of Human Life (the Four *Ashramas: Brhmacharya, Grihastha, Vanaprastha,* and *Sanyasa).* This explanation enables students to see that Hinduism is more than just a religion or social practice, that it is a complete way of life — spiritual and material.

A related issue in this context is the relation of these religious systems to Indian social structures. Using excerpts form the *Bhagvad Gita* and the *Dhammapada,* we examine the connection between religious and moral imperatives and evolving social and political structures. Here, the Hindu sanction for social behavior (e.g., the Four Ends of Man, the Four *Ashramas),* as illustrated in the *Gita,* can be compared to the Buddhist sense of righteousness and duty, as illustrated in the *Dhammapada.* In addition to examining the role of social codes and religious sanctions, it is useful to reflect on the role and place of the individual and the family in the larger social and political structure, since a majority of our students are completely unfamiliar with social systems different from their own. Ideas of order and harmony can be examined with reference to the *Varna* (caste) system as an organizing principle in the social structure. It is, however, important to note the rigid as well as flexible nature of the caste system. For example, the founder of the first imperial age in India, Chandragupta Maurya, was not of the *khshatriya* caste (second from the top in social hierarchy and traditionally the caste of the rulers and warriors), but of the *vaishya* caste (second from the bottom, the caste of the merchants and artisans).

At the same time, the plurality of Indian traditions and their respective social and political influence can be highlighted by a discussion of the role of Jainism and Buddhism (which also represented resistance to Brahmanic authority under Hinduism and were therefore anticaste in nature) in shaping the Mauryan state in India. The classic examples are Chandragupta, founder of the Mauryan state, who renounced the world by becoming a Jain monk, and his grandson, Asoka the Great, whose polity and life were deeply influenced by Buddhism.

The global theme of the ancient empires can be used as a context to discuss the rise of Magadha, the Mauryan empire, India's first imperial unification, and the Gupta empire, the classical period of Indian history. This theme allows the teacher to demonstrate the interconnectedness of history through a discussion of empires and imperial expansion elsewhere in the ancient world. In this context, Alexander the Great's Indian expedition, just before the rise of the Mauryas, can be highlighted to point out that he was accompanied by a number of Hellenistic scholars whose purpose was to acquire knowledge about the ideas and religions of India. His staff also surveyed roads in Asia, which led to increased commercial and cultural interaction. The Mauryan king, Chandragupta Maurya, maintained close diplomatic relations with the Hellenistic kingdom. Trade with India dominated the commercial and trading relations of the Roman empire. Egypt was a valuable link between the trading worlds of the Indian Ocean and the Mediterranean.

INDIA AND THE ARAB WORLD

Contact between India and the Arab world, although starting earlier, became more pronounced and significant during the medieval period. The long-established trade between the Persian Gulf and the Indian Ocean became a subject of several notable Arabic works. The Arabs appear to have had high regard for India. *Saif-i-Hindi* (the Indian sword) was their favorite weapon. Arab interest in India is also attested by the records of numerous Arab travelers, ranging from Sulaiman the merchant to the globe-trotter Ibn Battuta. Indians were seen as "men unsurpassed in science, especially astronomy." The period between 500 and 800 was indeed remarkable for scientific activity in India, especially in astronomy and mathematics. For a long time it was believed in Europe that the symbol for zero and the decimal system of notations were of Arab origin (thus the misnomer, Arabic numerals), but it is now universally acknowledged that these passed from India to Europe through the Arabs.

The rise and expansion of Islam is a major theme for medieval world history. In this context several important questions can be raised about the advent of Islam in India. Why was the coming of Islam delayed until the 10th century, especially given historical contacts between Arabia and India? Who were the people who brought Islam to India? Why did Islam come to India not through Arabia but via the Khyber pass — a strategic passage for all invaders of India from the northwest? These questions set a comparative context and allow students to grasp what was different or unique about the Islamic onslaught in India, and how it paved the way for the establishment of the Mughal empire and a distinct Islamic art, architecture, and culture in the subcontinent. K. N. Chaudhuri's *Asia before Europe: Economy and Civilization of the Indian Ocean from the Rise of Islam to 1750* (1991) is an insightful and useful scholarly reference.

The Indian case can be compared, for example, to that of China. Both experienced invasions from the northwest between 1000 and 1300, and both cultures survived these major interventions. In India, despite several centuries of Muslim rule, Hinduism remained intact as a majority religion. Islam imbibed many cultural traits of Hinduism and vice versa. Such an exchange created change as well as synthesis. A comparative analysis of the Bhakti and Sufi movements reveals the sharing of certain common characteristics. For example, both movements aimed at unity with God through love and devotion; challenged the traditional guardians of religions, the *Pundits* and the *Ulama*; recognized the significance of *guru* and the *pir*; advocated the use of vernacular languages; appealed largely to the lower classes; and led to the fusion of cultures. An examination of selected excerpts from these movements (drawn from *Sources of Indian Tradition*, vol. 1) provides an instructive introduction to these cultural movements, and lends a different perspective to the interaction between Islam and Hinduism — one based on mutual respect, sharing, and caring.

While Buddhism was eliminated from its original homeland, the early medieval period witnessed its spread throughout central Asia, Tibet, Nepal, China, Korea, Japan, and part of southeast Asia. It was also from India that Islam spread to Southeast Asia. (Similarly the Mongol invasions of Asian land masses led to the spread of Chinese inventions, especially gunpowder and the compass, which helped Europeans to launch what became known as the Age of Exploration.) Once again, the movement of people and ideas allows students to see the interconnectedness of history.

EUROPEAN IMPERIALISM

The growth of transoceanic trade, with spices as its focus, allows us to understand the early encounters between Indians and Europeans. It is important to point out, however, that Europeans were peripheral to Asia prior to the 19th century. During the eighteenth century a more dominant trend was the revival and reform of tradition in India. Excerpts from social reform movements (see Stephen Hay, ed., *Sources of Indian Tradition*, vol. 2 1988) could be used to assess the nature of indigenous society, culture, and reform on the eve of British political intrusions into the Indian subcontinent. This discussion is particularly meaningful for understanding the images the West had of non-Western people, and vice versa, especially for considering notions of the "barbaric" and the "civilized."

Early European intrusions were primarily characterized by missionary and commercial activities in India and around the Indian Ocean. The multifaceted theme of culture and colonialism can be examined by focusing on the role played by technology in shaping the subsequent interaction between the British and the Indians. This provides a context to understand the rise of Western domination of non-Western regions and peoples. Selected portions of Daniel R. Headrick's *Tools of Empire* (1982) are useful in facilitating a broader understanding among students of the subjugation of the highly sophisticated and relatively vast civilization of India by the numerically insignificant British. For example, one can illustrate how railways in nineteenth-century India were used more as tools of imperial expansion and consolidation rather than as means of industrialization and social transformation. By focusing on the agents, missionaries, and trading corporations, such as the British East India Company, it is easy to define and distinguish various brands of imperialism: cultural, political, and economic. Similarly, the case of opium production in colonial India by the British to promote the illegal opium market in China and to get Chinese tea for the British market can help highlight the complex nature of Western imperialism, which manifested itself in different forms and led to a variety of interactions between the colonizers and the colonized. The subtleties of the nature and impact of imperialism can be demonstrated through a discussion of such novels as R. K. Narayan's *The English Teacher* (1980) or George Orwell's *The Burmese Days* (1984).

NATIONALISM AND INDEPENDENCE MOVEMENTS: INDIA AND PAKISTAN

Just as imperialism was a global trend of the nineteenth century, so also nationalism and independence movements characterized the world of the late nineteenth and twentieth centuries. The various strands of the nationalist movement in India and its diverse leadership can be illustrated through a discussion of excerpts from primary source documents (e.g., *Sources of Indian Tradition*, vol. 2). The discussion may be further accentuated by exposing students to the literature of national awakening, such as Munshi Prem Chand's *Selected Short Stories* (1980), and by critically integrating discussion of films such as *Bharat ki Khoj* (literally meaning "search of the Indian nation"). Questions about the role of leaders versus masses in the transformation of history and historical change can be explored by focusing on a novel by R. K. Narayan, *Waiting for the Mahatma* (1981) or on Raja Rao's *Kanthapura* (1989). Either novel might be juxtaposed with Shahid Amin's essay "Gandhi as Mahatma" (in Ranajit Guha and Gayatri C. Spivak, eds., *Selected Subaltern Studies*, 1988), and the film *Gandhi*. The peculiarities of Indian nationalism can be highlighted by raising and examining the question of why the national movement in India resulted in the creation of two nations: India and Pakistan. Thus, nationalism can also be discussed to understand the phenomenon of partition in India, which was as much nationalistic as it was political. India played a leading role in the national and independence movement in Asia, and was the first country after the Phillipines to become independent.

In the post–World War II period, the major problems confronting the world have been the problems of democracy and development. In the context of this large and complex theme, India again can be integrated effectively into world history. India is both the largest democracy in the world and a leading developing country. This, however, does not mean there are no challenges to the healthy survival of democracy or to the country's continuous economic development. In fact, the rise of fundamentalism — which is a global phenomenon — has posed serious challenges to the survival of Indian democracy. Moreover, the problems of poverty, population, and environmental hazards have inhibited the full realization of developmental benefits. Here India can be compared to the leading developing countries in terms of the continuing interaction between modernity and tradition. Comparisons could focus on the role of authority versus democratic institutions or on issues of poverty and population.

THE WORLD TODAY

It is useful, from the point of view of students, to explain what India is like today. This can be done through a discussion of a variety of issues, including religion, science, theater, film, literature, and the role of women and children. Teachers will find a valuable resource on contemporary India in a special issue of *Daedalus* (1989) entitled *Another India*. This issue includes brief but insightful assessments of present-day realities by some of the leading Indian intellectuals. Also useful and easy to follow are Sara Mitter's *Dharma's Daughters* (1991) and the film *Kamala and Raji* for insights into the traditional and changing role of women in India today.

A country with a rich tradition of spiritual masters, India is today rapidly becoming, among other things, a land of software mavens. In a recent commentary in the *Los Angeles Times*, Jonathan Power observed, "In Aesop's fable of the tortoise and the hare, we read one of life's repeating stories: plodding wins the race. I venture to say, by the year 2000 we'll learn this lesson again. It will be India, and not China, that will be on its way to becoming the giant of Asia and, before too much time is past, the largest economy in the world."[1] A study of India in world history survey courses is not only vital to understanding of our human heritage, it is also critical to comprehending the 21st-century world.

Note

1. *Los Angeles Times*, Sunday, 20 March 1994, M5.

Donald Johnson

The American Educational Tradition
Hostile to a Humanistic World History?

Although many leaders in American education support the new movement in global education and advocate the teaching of the world beyond Europe, deeply ingrained traditions in American education and current professional arrangements stand in the way of constructing a genuine world history. Much attention has been paid to the more obvious barriers to the teaching of an integrated world history, such as ethnocentrism in textbooks and the lack of systematic teacher training in the field. But these issues need to be seen in the larger context of American educational history and philosophy wherein the more subtle biases toward Euro-centric world views have emerged. Such analysis and changes in teacher preparation are both necessary if a truly humanistic and integrated world history is to come about in the schools.

Almost from its beginnings, historical writing in the West has been caught in a paradox. Because Herodotus and his successors were creating a new way of organizing what they saw around them, they were unaware that as they sought to record facts objectively, they were unconsciously using the norms of their own civilization as the basis for all civilizations. Herodotus presented the histories of Egypt and India as exotic deviations from Hellas. Western historical writers from Augustine to Toynbee have continued to draw that same invisible line separating the civilized West from the alien others of Asia, Africa, and the pre-Columbian western hemisphere and to employ the norms of western civilization as universal. The West is not alone in this approach. Other cultures have produced similar ethnocentric world histories. Chinese historical writing in the great tradition of Ssu-ma Ch'ien has always seen the rest of the world as a barbaric departure from the norms of Chung Kuo — the Middle Kingdom. Classical Indian scholars did not think history was a worthwhile enterprise and that long and rich civilization did not produce histories as such until the coming of the British in the seventeenth century.

In recent years there have been many conscious attempts to escape the narrowness and Western-centeredness of historical writing. Few contemporary

Donald Johnson, "The American Educational Tradition: Hostile to a Humanistic World History?" *The History Teacher* 20 (August 1987): 519–44.

scholars or educators would now argue that the world outside the West does not deserve its rightful place in historical writing and in the school curriculum. Most present-day history teachers would feel uncomfortable with the statement of one of the most widely used school textbooks in 1876 that:

> Of all the races, the White, or Caucasian, exhibits by far the most perfect type, physically, intellectually and morally. It is the race with which we shall be almost exclusively concerned, as the other two races, if we except some few nations of the Turanian stock, have not played any great part in the drama of history.[1]

However well intentioned the new efforts in global history are, the meaning of these new texts, materials, and essays by global educators is not at all clear. Certainly, few social studies teachers or college history professors would agree with Marshall G. S. Hodgson's 1963 analysis that:

> Within this vast historical complex [Africa, Asia, and Europe] Western Europe played a peripheral and, till well into the Middle Ages, a backward role. . . . Only in the High Middle Ages did Western Europeans begin truly to rise to the creative level of the core areas of civilization.[2]

Although this statement may be accurate, it is doubtful that most Western-trained historians and teachers would be willing to organize their courses or texts around such an interpretation. If the teaching and writing of world history is somewhere between Meyer's 1876 text and Hodgson's recent statement, then where along this spectrum do most of the recent world histories and school texts lie in coverage and treatment of the world beyond Europe? More important, what is the analytical framework for writing world history that informs both the scholarly and popular histories and the college and high school texts and teaching that claim to be offering a new universal world history? Do the major world civilizations now have a rightful share of space in the thoughts, teaching, and textbooks of world history, and has the conceptualization by historians, social scientists, and educators given the world beyond the West a legitimate place in our scholarly disciplines and in our college and high school teaching?

As Donald Kagan announced in 1984 in the *New York Times Book Review*, "World History Is Back." In his review of three world histories published in the past twenty-five years, Kagan traced the history of world history from Herodotus to the present and suggested that, "The new universal historians have made a good start, and their example should encourage others to have a try."[3] The first text reviewed, *History of the World* by J. M. Roberts, introduced India on page 263, covered the great Gupta age in less than two pages, and traced China from the Warring States to the Tang in five pages. India was again introduced on page 381 and its history from the end of the Guptas to the coming of the British was covered in six pages.[4] Similarly, China from the end of the Tang to the coming of the Europeans was disposed of in the same chapter in seven pages. The second of the new world histories, *A History of the World* by Hugh Thomas, devoted even less space to Asia and Africa and did not deal with

China, India, or African kingdoms as civilizations with unique cultural values and unique histories.[5]

The third book in Kagan's review was a notable exception for treating civilizations beyond Europe seriously. William McNeill's work, ironically titled *The Rise of the West*,[6] published in 1963, devoted many pages to the world views of India, China, and the Middle East and presented the distinct cultural styles developed in all the great world civilizations. McNeill also offered an intriguing historical framework of cultural diffusion which integrated all cultural centers in the Euro-Asian land mass into an interacting whole. Even so, *The Rise of the West* focused on technology, particularly military technology, as the driving force of human development. . . .

Many college and high school texts commonly deal with civilizations outside the West by dealing with their histories as area studies or cultural complexes and fail to provide the subtle development of their histories over time. Millennia of Indian and Chinese history are often summed up in one chapter. The student is given the impression that India and China were nuclear civilizations on a par with Egypt and Sumer. Often the few chapters that deal with formative Asian civilizations trace those histories right down to the sixteenth century and then Asia vanishes from view while the text resumes the real story of civilization with the introduction of Greece and Rome.[7] Asia does not reappear until the age of discovery and imperialism. During the age of European discovery, we first meet the Mayas, Incas, and Aztecs, and, when European imperialism is introduced, students often read about Africa for the first time. Students do not learn that each civilization has an on-going unbroken history, many at least as complex and of longer duration than that of the West.

High school textbook writers were often aware of their concentration on Western civilization and sometimes explained the lack of space accorded the world beyond Europe. One 1950s text explained on page 559 why human history prior to 1800 had been covered without a single mention of India or China:

> So far we have made no study of the Far East. . . . This does not mean that they were unheard of until late in history or that their people were uncivilized or not worthy of study. . . . The Far East, however, played little part in World History until modern times, when Europeans found their way to that area. Consequently, there was little reason to study these lands earlier in the course.[8]

In the consciousness of most practitioners and teachers of history in the United States the larger world and its history still remain addenda to the main body of real history which begins in the Middle East, defines itself further in Greco-Roman civilization and reaches its apex in modern Europe and the United States. This approach is not surprising when we consider that more than sixty percent of professional historians in the United States are in the field of American studies and the next largest group are scholars of European history. There is a substantial number of African, Middle East, and Asian historians scattered in numerous colleges and universities throughout the country. However, these scholars usually specialize in a narrow field such as Islamic science, Sung history, Tamil kinship, etc., making it difficult if not impossible to bring their considerable knowledge to bear on the writing and teaching of an integrated world history. This difficulty is made all the more acute because American and European historians seldom deign to work with or take seriously their fellow historians in these "exotic fields."

Even more problematic than the limited attention to the larger world in textbooks is the more complex issue of historical conceptualization. As Foucault has observed, it is the framework of "discourse" that actually reveals the genuine terms of discussion and the underlying values for any topic or concept. An eminent Asian scholar, Edward Kracke, warned many years ago, "In approaching any Asian Civilization, the greatest difficulty seems to be that of overcoming our initial preconceptions concerning the bias of a civilization and its objectives, drawn from our Western experience."[9] It is clear that most writers and publishers who are responsible for developing materials, writing new curricula, and adding new chapters to school history books have not been fully aware that our own categories, models, and methodologies are based on a specific cultural and historical tradition and that the so-called new "Global Education Movement" grows out of a specific American reform tradition.

All cultures have constructed world views and cosmologies which explain to them the nature of the universe and the place of that people within it. Western historians, philosophers, and social scientists have also constructed various images for conceptualizing the world. For the purpose of simplicity this myriad of images will be divided into two major ways of viewing the world and the people and societies within it. On one hand, there have been those who see the world as a single global system, either as an actual functioning economic and political system or as a vision of a world they yearn to see develop. This conceptualization of the world tends to see all human beings as essentially alike in aspirations and needs and proceeds to make generalizations about human behavior which can be used to describe anyone in any group regardless of geography or culture. These scholars can be referred to as the "universalists." On the other hand, there are those who see the world as composed of distinct groups and who insist that to know anything of value about human behavior we must analyze specific groups of people and see the unique culture and social structure that influence and explain their behavior. These scholars can be referred to as the "particularists."

The traditions of both the universalists and particularists go far back into human history. Those cultures which have tended to universalism have usually propounded a single set of human values which were presumed to fit all peoples everywhere. Many universalist societies such as ancient Rome forcibly annexed their neighbors to bring about a single system. Others, such as the early Christians, spread their visions of one world through vigorous proselytizing. Some thinkers from Plato and Augustine to Thomas More, Francis Bacon, and William Irwin Thompson, offered their visions of one world through utopian literature, thereby projecting their own personal values as the basis for that one world. Within the universalist group there were and are those of the *realpolitik* school who see an inevitable merging of disparate cultures under one economic and political system. Such thinkers can countenance such a change brought about either by armed intervention or by "visionaries" who eschew violence and conflict and see the future world system as a freely chosen, problem-free utopia where human compassion and expanded consciousness will replace both arms and parochialism. Sometimes, as in the case of Karl Marx, the visionaries and realists met in a single person's view of the world.

One aspect, at least, of the particularist tradition is equally long. Most early nuclear civilizations made invidious distinctions between themselves and outsiders. The Athenians could not understand the language of the people who surrounded them and gave us the word barbarian. The Chinese knew their land as Chung Kuo, the Middle Kingdom, and they clearly demarcated themselves from the outer barbarians. The early Hebrews certainly saw the Canaanites in a similar ethnocentric way. A strong thread in Western history since Herodotus has continued to hold to the particularist view. Since 1500 most Westerners have seen themselves primarily as citizens of a particular nation, and the writing of history has become even more rooted in the particular histories of nation-states. In the contemporary world, nations as far apart as Japan, Great Britain, China, and Denmark devote most of their school history instruction to the story of the students' own culture.

In our own time, both the universalist and particularist models are widely used. However, in public education and in popular culture in the United States the universalist view predominates. In view of our propensity toward nationalistic history the emphasis on universalistic history seems pardoxical, but an analysis of major texts and the teaching of so-called world history suggests that there is no perceived contradiction in the celebrating of Western superiority, particularly that of the United States, and the recent attempts to teach students about the wider world.

Our universalistic model is rooted in the first so-called "scientific" efforts to study other people seriously and professionally and is only about a hundred years old. By the middle of the nineteenth century the infant studies in social science were taking their first form. Founded in northern Europe and the United States largely by white males, these new tools for understanding human behavior owed much to their Enlightenment and liberal/utilitarian predecessors. The early social scientists were mostly universalists who looked for scientific laws to explain all human behavior everywhere. Scholars applied theories of evolution to society and saw society as a living organism with all the characteristics of biological life. They believed the social order developed, grew old, and often died. For Herbert Spencer all societies everywhere evolved from simple to complex; for Tonnies they developed from *Gemeinschaft*, interpersonal relationships, to *Gesellschaft*, or impersonal relationships. For Henry Maine all social orders progressed from status relationships to contract relationships; for August Comte, the first to use the term "sociology," history moved inexorably from religion, to philosophy, to science. His positivism claimed to unlock the final knowledge of how all people are driven by natural laws and how we at last could understand our own social patterns and behavior.

In the United States the idea of evolution of societies and history found a hospitable home, and the law of progress and evolution was the favored analytical construct. Historians such as John Fiske and the founding father of American anthropology, Lewis Henry Morgan, both agreed that the secret of human development was evolution and that every group passed through immutable stages of growth from savagery, to barbarism, to civilization. These late nineteenth-century evolutionists were modeling their ideals of the advanced society on their own western experience. Ethnocentric in the extreme, they saw in their visions of the coming world social orders moving up stairs of development which led ultimately to life as it was known at the time in London and Boston.

From the perspective of contemporary life, it is easy to see the basis for the popularity of the evolutionary model of social analysis. The early social scientists were products of the growing industrial power of the West. The colonialism they saw only proved the superiority of western culture and demonstrated its highly evolved status while the subject societies, those we now casually refer to as "Third World," were rationalized as being on a lower plane of evolution. The model of social analysis for all of the founding fathers of social science was rooted in the common premise that non-western cultures were lower or "traditional," while western cultures were advanced or "modern." Modern Europe became the pinnacle and product of all human development. Whether monotheism, the nuclear family, highly complex urban life, contractual legal relationships, or individual human rights, the apex in each category of human endeavor resembled western society. The criteria for being "civilized" was the degree of commonality with the nineteenth- and twentieth-century West.

This vision of western civilization as the acme of human development and civilization has informed textbook writing during the past one hundred years. An 1876 school text states:

> [S]till the people of this race [Asians] have made but little progress in the arts and in general culture — perhaps simply through lack of favoring circumstances. Even their languages have remained undeveloped. These seem immature, or stunted in their growth.[10]

Many contemporary high school texts still reflect this nineteenth-century evolutionary view of historical change. One widely used world history text of the adopted list for New York City explains:

> Man was first a savage, then a barbarian, and finally a civilized being. The savage depends almost entirely on nature. He secures food from wild plants and wild animals; he knows nothing of metals but makes his tools and weapons of stone, wood and bone; he wears little or no clothing; and his home is merely a cave, a rock shelter, or out of bark. Such primitive folk live in the interior of Africa and Australia. The barbarian has gained more control over nature than the savage. He plants seeds, has domesticated animals, and uses some metal implements. Most American Indians before the coming of Columbus and

most of the Negroes in Africa may be classified as barbarians. In contrast to the savage and the barbarian, the civilized man is one who, to a large extent, can change his surroundings to fit his needs and wants.[11]

The evolutionary model (from traditional culture to the modern West) of social and historical analysis attained its most sophisticated heights in the 1950s in the American school of modernization theory. By that time, America was well into what Henry Luce had proclaimed as "The American Century," and leaders saw the United States as the new bastion of western civilization. By the late 1950s and early 1960s a great number of modernization studies had been published. The modernizers were almost always from the social science disciplines and even attempts at history, such as Seymour Martin Lipset's *The First New Nation: The United States in Historical and Comparative Perspective*, promoted the example of the modern West as the inevitable future of the world. In 1967, one leader of the movement suggested, "We are confronted — whether for good or bad — with a universal social solvent. The patterns of the relatively modernized societies, once developed, have shown a universal tendency to penetrate any social context whose participants have come in contact with them."[12] Another modernization scholar explained that modernization is conceptually related to economic development but the concept is more comprehensive. He went on to define the term modernization as having:

> at least four distinct but interrelated processes. . . . (1) In the realm of technology, a developing society is changing from simple and traditionalized techniques toward the application of scientific knowledge. (2) In agriculture, the developing society evolves from subsistence farming toward the commercial production of agricultural goods. This means specialization in cash crops, purchase of nonagricultural products in the market, and often agricultural wage labor. (3) In industry, the developing society undergoes a transition from the use of human and animal power toward industrialization proper or men working for wages at power-driven machines, which produce commodities marketed outside the community of production. (4) In ecological arrangements, the developing society moves from the farm and village toward urban concentrations. Furthermore, while these four processes often occur simultaneously during development, this is not always so.[13]

Modernization theory has grown far more modest in its claims and at the same time more sophisticated and less positivistic in its approach than was the case in the 1960s. Contemporary scholars in the field such as Gino Germani, Lloyd and Sussane Rudolph, and the recent book of Baidya Varma,[14] indeed do seriously consider cultural variations and historical differences in their approaches to social change. Unfortunately, it is not the recent scholarship on modernization which informs most school texts. Rather, we usually find in these a vulgarized and simplistic view of social change which flows from the assumption that the movement of the world is toward an American norm and that a technological base making possible mass consumerism is the desired ingredient in any cultural change. This one-dimensional developmental model was found to dominate the 300 textbooks analyzed in the 1974 Asia Society study of school texts. This developmental approach, which pits traditional against modern, appeared in 89 percent of the titles, was dominant in 73 percent, and was the exclusive approach in 56 percent of the texts evaluated.[15]

The evolutionary approach usually sees religion as the culprit in standing in the way of "modernization" and assumes an inevitable movement from religiously based societies to secularization. One text from the 1920s exemplifies this model:

> The majority of the Indian people, therefore, lived in misery. Since this planet offered them very little joy, salvation from suffering must be found elsewhere. They tried to derive a little consolation from meditation upon the bliss of their future existence.[16]

The common metaphor of ahead-and-behind found in so many texts usually features contemporary western civilization as the norm for modernized states. One recent text asks rhetorically, "Why is India so far behind Japan and the countries of Europe and North America?"[17] The periodization of western civilization is also employed in this evolutionary model with particular western social organization of centuries ago used as a yardstick to denigrate contemporary Asian civilizations. One text tells us:

> Most of the people of India today live much as their ancestors did centuries ago. The organization of rural life in India closely resembles that which was found in medieval Europe a thousand years ago.[18]

The developmental approach explains social change exclusively by pointing to changes in technology and economic arrangements. Furthermore, this model denigrates other civilizations by stressing what they do not have when compared to us in technological and economic terms. One school text exemplifies this approach when it explains:

> With all the progress that has been made, however, there is still only one automobile for thousands of persons in China. The United States, by comparison, has so many automobiles that everybody in the country could go for a ride at one time.[19]

From a modernization theory which postulated all nations of the world on the march toward a civilization which replicates the modern West, it was a short step to the 1970s world systems approach developed by such thinkers as Barrington Moore and Immanuel Wallerstein. The advocates of the world systems approach come, not surprisingly, from the disciplines of political science, sociology, and economics and most owe more than a little debt to Karl Marx. In a number of books dating from the 1950s Wallerstein and his associates have elaborated on his basic premise that "A single capitalist world economy has been developing since the sixteenth century and its development has been the driving force of modern social change."[20] Wallerstein sees two aspects of the world capitalist system, the structural aspect and the developmental aspect. The "structure" of the system consists of (a) one expanding economy, (b) expanding multiple states, and (c) the capital-labor relation.[21] Wallerstein has been able to develop a model which at once traces the development of the capitalist economy in the West and relates that system to the "underdeveloped" states of Africa, Latin America, and most of Asia. The joining of western studies with so-called Third World studies was carried out by Wallerstein's rather ingenious concept of dividing the world into core and periphery areas. From its origins in northern Europe, the capitalist core has enlarged during the past three centuries to include most of Europe and the United States. The periphery of this core includes the colonial holdings and the agricultural areas of the rest of the world. From an analysis of the dynamic of the relations between the capitalist haves with the agrarian have-nots, Wallerstein was in a position to trace the developing relations between the two spheres in a provocative and exciting new way.

A second major theme of universalism, which has particular importance in America's concept of the world and which appears in many school texts, comes from the early nineteenth-century American Romanticism which had much in common with the British liberal utilitarians. The basic assumptions of liberal/utilitarian thought rested on the belief in rational man operating in a society composed of individuals, each pursuing his own happiness and avoiding pain. The utilitarian believed human problems could be solved rationally through the sacred principle of law and that a policy of "just laws and light taxes" would usher in a society where poverty would be eliminated and earthly happiness could be embraced by all people regardless of race or culture.

When the British reformers such as Thomas Babington Macaulay and James Mill applied the liberal model to Asia, they quite naturally saw the social and cultural system there as not only obsolete, but irrational and the major obstacle to a potential glorious future which the multitudes of Asia might enjoy if they gave up their backward ways. If, the British liberals reasoned, they could only convince their subjects to grow beyond Hinduism, Islam, and Confucianism, and the accretion of centuries of superstitious values, imperial teachers could build in Asia and even in Asians a sense of individualism, institute parliamentary democracy, rationalize the legal structure, and promote a consuming society.

This great progress could be accomplished in spite of the Asian people whom most liberals held in low esteem. James Mill spoke for this group when he described India and China as:

> Nations [that] are, to nearly an equal degree, tainted with the vices of insincerity; dissembling, treacherous, mendacious, to an excess which surpasses even the usual measure of uncultivated society. Both are disposed to excessive exaggeration with regard to everything relating to themselves. Both are cowardly and unfeeling. Both are in the highest degree conceited of themselves, and full of contempt for others. Both are in the physical sense, disgustingly unclean in their persons and their houses.[22]

Yet despite the low state of Asian civilization, reform would be possible if only the negative influence of religion could be overcome. A major school text published in 1972 continues to echo British liberalism of a century and a half earlier when it explains:

> Progress has also been discouraged by Hinduism, the religion followed by more than four-fifths of India's population. This religion teaches that people should accept their way of life without trying to change it. India's leaders have great difficulty convincing people that changes must be made.[23]

In a similar vein a 1975 Prentice-Hall text explains the role of Hinduism in India: "The lack of absolutes in Hinduism shows up in a disregard for time, apathy towards work, and what might appear to be carelessness. These attitudes are considered normal and proper by most Indians."[24]

As disciples of Lockean psychology, the utilitarians believed that by restructuring the environment through education the benighted Asians could be uplifted and their superstitious ways overcome. After 1835, these values were made concrete with the introduction of English as a medium of instruction in India and the establishment of English colleges. The objective of this decision, as Macaulay explained, was to "form a class of persons, Indian in blood and color, but English in taste, in opinions, in morals, and in intellect."

This old concept which saw the civilized West as playing schoolmaster to the benighted Asian has been a constant theme in American textbook writing. A 1904 textbook instructed our students that:

> Although we find obscure notices of India in the records of the early historic peoples of western Asia, yet it is not until the invasion of the peninsula by Alexander the Great in 327 B.C. that the history of the Indian Aryans comes into significant contact with that of the progressive nations of the west.[25]

One of the most popular textbooks of the 1920s taught the reasons for the backwardness of Asian nations and even offered a remedy:

> The great Empire of India, almost as populous as China but only half as large in area, received the first lessons in European Civilization chiefly at the hands of England.[26]

Later on in the same text the authors explain how the ungrateful Indians reacted to their British mentors when they write: "Such was the perplexing result of India's lessons in European Civilization. She was willing to discharge her teacher."[27]

Contemporary texts are slightly less blatant in their featuring of western civilization as the teacher of Asia, but the message is the same. One text, echoing the liberal/utilitarian bias, explains:

> Back in the middle of the nineteenth century Japan was in much the same situation as China — backward industrially and greatly opposed to the Euro-

peans. . . . But Japan, unlike China, realized the practical superiority of European civilization and decided to adopt it.[28]

Another recent text echoes this "West as benign helper" idea and rationalizes colonialism by explaining:

> When the Europeans first came to Africa, they found they had to teach the Africans their way of doing things in order to bring out the riches of the mines and forests. They built roads and railroads to bring the ore and products to the sea. They brought schools and better health to many Africans. They trained Africans to run the railroads and to work in offices. They educated Africans for a certain amount of leadership. This system is sometimes described as imperialism or colonialism.[29]

Despite several major differences in approach among the liberal utilitarians, nineteenth-century evolutionists, modernization theorists, and the current world system analysts, all share a commitment to a universalist view of the world. Moreover, all of these schools share a view of humanness which is based on a technological and economic definition of man, or *homo economicus.* They all tend to see contemporary western liberal values and institutions as desirable and perhaps inevitable for all the world's people.

In sharp contrast to the universalist tradition in social science and history stands the particularist view of the world, best expressed in the disciplines of history and anthropology. Although the particularist world view has never had much legitimacy in American popular culture or education, by the 1930s this approach had come to dominate American and British anthropology. Rooted in the earlier work of Emile Durkheim, particularists such as Franz Boas mounted a strong attack on the evolutionary universalism of Lewis Henry Morgan and Karl Marx and by the 1920s had worked out a theoretical basis for their analysis.

For the particularist, it is the distinct group, whether tribe, nation or cultural group, that is the operative level of human behavior. Durkheim raised the crucial question for the particularists: Why is it that all peoples everywhere throughout time have seen themselves as members of specific groups? For Durkheim each society is moral in the sense that it creates its own consciousness and imparts those values to each of its members as shared meanings and rules. For the particularists like Durkheim, the world is a collection of small social and cultural units from which individuals derive their personal identity.

Much of twentieth-century anthropological scholarship has been a reaction to the evolutionary model of Morgan and his contemporaries. In America, Franz Boas launched a counter-attack against universal evolutionists by arguing that each society was different and had to be studied and understood in the context of its own norms. One culture, he suggested, had little to say about the validity of another. Boas's stature as a teacher soon brought him a group of students who became followers of his approach. Among these early students were Margaret Mead and Ruth Benedict, who not only argued for cultural pluralism but saw culture as the dominant factor in shaping personality. This view offered a counter-position to the dominant Freudian psychology of the time.

Following the lead of Boas and his students, A. R. Radcliffe-Brown and Bronislaw Malinowski developed the school of structural-functionalism in the 1920s. The new analytical system, which also owed much to Durkheim, saw rites, rituals, and other seemingly exotic behavior and beliefs as in fact the crucial elements which bonded any given society together as a social system. Rain dances, sacrifices, joking relationships, and avoidance taboos all took on new meaning under the scrutiny of the structural-functionalists who focused on the small unit as the key to social organization. Any society could fly into fragments, they argued, and therefore each society had to provide for constant renewal of its social system and cultural values through ritual, sport, festival, and other social dramas.

Following the particularism of the structural-functionalists are the semiotic scholars of our own time such as Victor Turner, Mary Douglas, and Clifford Geertz. The semiologists share the Boazian tradition of concentrating on specific cultures as the unit of analysis and in utilizing rigorous field work to determine the cultural system of a particular group. The semiologists break sharply with the evolutionists in their definition of being human. For the semiotic school, man is not essentially the tool maker or economic creature of Adam Smith and Karl Marx but a maker of meanings or symbols. This system of symbols, created from human imagination, then structures social relationships, economic systems, and other human behavior.

Clifford Geertz, the eminent American symbolic anthropologist, speaks eloquently for particularism when he writes, "To be human is thus not to be everyman; it is to be a particular kind of man and of course men differ: 'Other fields,' as the Japanese say, 'other grasshoppers.'"[30] This "other grasshoppers" approach has come to stand for the efficacy of analyzing specific cultures as the best way to understand how the world actually works. The secret of human understanding, as Geertz explains, is not to look for some universal man beneath his cultural overlays but to seek out culture with a small "c," the thousands of small particular cultures each with its own map, set of meanings, and distinctive way of believing and acting. As Geertz explains:

> Becoming human is becoming individual, and we become individual under the guidance of cultural patterns. . . . And the cultural patterns involved are not general but specific — not just marriage but a particular set of notions about what men and women are like, how spouses should treat one another, or who should marry whom; not just religion but belief in the wheel of karma, the observance of a month of fasting, or the practice of cattle sacrifice.[31]

History, like anthropology, has largely followed the course of particularism in its approach to the world. Daniel Boorstin has emphasized that the study of American history demonstrates its uniqueness, and he further suggests that this particular experience cannot be replicated and has little use as a model for development in other nations.[32] Perry Miller has also emphasized the inner life of the Puritans and concluded that "The Errand into the Wilderness" gives to American history a solitary quality to be understood best by seeing the culture within its own peculiar framework.[33] Contemporary historians such as John Fairbank would agree with Geertz that the best way to gain an understanding of the world is through the study of specific histories of China, Japan, or Vietnam. Historians such as the late Paul Mus criticized American involvement in Vietnam on the basis that policymakers tended to universalize the conflict and saw it as an example of international communism rather than perceiving it as a nationalistic and cultural event rooted in Vietnamese history.

The particularist approach to the world, best expressed in the disciplines of history and anthropology deriving from the influence of Durkheim, has never had the appeal in mass American culture and public education that universalism has enjoyed. American culture, ironically, has seen itself as culture-free and a civilization based on law and equal treatment of each individual regardless of cultural origins. Most Americans have seen in their experiment a hope for the world and a model of integration of any individual who was willing to work hard. Of course, the American ideals of law, the ethic of hard work, self-reliance and even individualism itself were all products of a specific northern European cultural ethos. Despite this fact, Americans pictured themselves as "culture-free" and as a group of rational "can do" problem solvers. It is this longstanding educational and popular cultural world view of universalism based on rational individualism and on an economic definition of humanness that became both the basis for popular culture and the mainstream of American educational philosophy.

Charged with the responsibility for the major socialization of young citizens, American schools have found that the universalist model of culture has fit well with the school's function of integrating all youngsters into the American way of life and has also served well as an agent for the assimilation of millions of immigrants into the social system. There is a firmly rooted tendency among American educators to see the world outside the West as destined to replicate western civilization in some future homogeneous rational culture.

In the mass culture of the United States, liberal utilitarianism and its optimistic world view found a hospitable home and was never tempered by a more tragic view of history which the British and other Europeans increasingly accepted in the late nineteenth century. In America, the major values of British liberalism lived on in the philosophy of Pragmatism. James, Dewey, and other Pragmatists retained the value of rationalism as the vehicle for human reform. Thanks to large doses of the newly discovered psychology and language taken from the new natural sciences, America had found a philosophy of individualism, law, and economic growth which would validate liberalism and offer an alternative to the ideologies of class consciousness and cultural conflict growing in Europe. In no other American institution did Pragmatism find such a welcome home as in education.

In Pragmatism American educators had found a philosophy of reform which rested on the beliefs that human beings are rational, economic growth is primary, individualism is the basis for the social order, and that evolutionary progress through inevitable stages of growth toward the "better life" is made possible through increasing consumer abundance, all of which is the desirable and inevitable script for the future of the world. The reformers also retained the promise that the technological and economic determinants of history would eventually overwhelm and dissolve so-called "traditional cultures" and create a homogeneous world which would replicate the modern West.

The influence of Pragmatism, particularly as enunciated by John Dewey and his followers, has been enormous. With the growing emphasis after 1930 on instrumental citizenship education as the major objective of schooling, the place of history and the humanities in the public schools, and especially in teacher education, was seriously eroded. The past would have no significant role in creating the rational global community of the future and neither would the great variety of cultures and civilizations which make up the world outside western industrial culture. Thus, study both of other civilizations and of history were of scant interest to the reformers. Students were to be taught to look to the future and to learn to cope with more pressing world problems such as population, world trade, ecological imbalance, and food production, and to play a role in bringing about a "better world." The role of culture, especially religion, was often presented as a source of needless conflict which would eventually be replaced by rationalism. This liberal, evolutionary, universalistic view of the world is not a philosophy which supports studying the past for its own sake or of studying non-western civilizations for their own truth and beauty. If history is to be included in this type of curriculum, it serves to illustrate stages of desired social change and lends itself to an instrumental citizenship training and is not to be seen as a humanistic enterprise in and of itself.

Yet another reason that professional education clings to universalistic, deterministic, and instrumental models of culture lies in the nature of education as a profession. Since the 1930s education has undergone constant professionalization, and even the academic subjects taught in the schools have their own professional associations, such as the National Council of the Social Studies (NCSS). Since their founding these associations have become increasingly separate from academic departments and from professional organizations like the American Historical Association and the American Philosophical Society. Furthermore, scholarly, discipline-based professional organizations have moved dramatically away from their earlier involvement in teaching and curriculum development and from teacher education in general. The result has been the unfortunate fossilizing of approaches to history, social science, and humanities in the schools which were dominant in the Progressive period.

This strong and continuing legacy of technological determinism mixed with liberal utilitarian philosophy modified by John Dewey has continued to influence American education in the twentieth century. The majority of graduates of teacher-training institutions have been socialized as positivists and evolutionists who believe technology will dissolve all older values and usher in an increasingly economically interdependent and culturally homogeneous world.

Education tends toward positivism as a method of scientific legitimacy for itself, and, as a consequence, professional education clings to a system of research which emphasizes weighing, measuring, and quantification. Ethnography and other humanistic approaches have been slow to gain acceptance as legitimate methods of research in teacher education and, except for history, are seldom choices for graduate research. This tradition in teacher education has militated against any serious desire to study civilizations outside the West, except as they represent stages of some future world system. In the few education courses dealing with the world outside the United States students are often taught that if people from various world cultures just get together for face-to-face, "rational" communication, they could solve many of the world's problems.

The new global education movement is the latest example of a long and continuing world view in American education. The global education movement derives essentially from traditional American liberalism and 1950s modernization theory, with a vague connection to Immanuel Wallerstein's world systems approach. The global education movement in its present form stresses more a universalism of civilization than the particularism offered by anthropology or history. In addition, global education still tends to stress technological and economic factors as explanations of social change almost to the exclusion of cultural values, history, and the other humanities. Consequently, the new movement which one might expect would take other civilizations and particular cultures seriously may do just the opposite.

Instead of promoting the study of specific cultural areas and their various histories, many global educators advocate a generalized study of the world in its present form and in its future, presumably homogeneous state. Most global educators present people as citizens of a global system, and they stress economic relationships and usually down-play any cultural differences which divide the human community. The everyman of the imagined impending global culture is the rational man who draws his identity from his economic behavior. Many leading global educators argue that the world is moving rapidly toward this single word culture. As one leader in the field writes:

> The point is that today most human beings live out their lives in a cocoon of culture whose circumference equals the circumference of the globe. In a word, there is a global culture.[34]

Elsewhere, the same author, in arguing against the study of specific cultures, writes that "the conception of global education as education about foreign societies and cultures is inadequate, for it obscures the fact that all of humanity is part of a planet-wide system."[35]

The new global approach is our own liberal idea of a rational life which implies that to be human means to acquire property and consumer goods, in brief, the western way of life. The view is often expressed in school texts as well:

> Western Civilization developed in Europe among men of the Caucasoid race.
> The fact tended to give Caucasoids a belief in their own superiority because

they had better ships, weapons and technology than the non-caucasoid peoples they conquered. But Western Civilization is a culture factor, not something biological. It can be learned, and is being learned by people of every race. Western Civilization is becoming World Civilization.[36]

Although there may be a superficial truth in the above statement, we are more likely living out an historical paradox which places two contradictory trends before us. One road, paved with technology and economic interdependence, is taking all of us toward a world of homogeneity and interdependence — a genuine universalism. The other road, paved with culture-specific values and primordial loyalties, is leading us into greater subdivisions based on particularistic cultural meanings and values.

Clearly, there is a move in the world toward economic interdependence, and there is a startling commonality of popular culture all around the world. American music and blue jeans can be found in most countries; some forms of yoga are as familiar here as in India. But facile statements such as "We are all human" or "We all want the same things in life" may be not only irrelevant but dangerous. The oversimplification of life which reduces humans to the role of producers and consumers of economic goods is one of the great temptations to those trying to make sense out of an increasingly culturally complex world. However, as trade and travel increase and bring individuals into contact with other individuals all over the globe, the urge for cultural identification and the drive for survival of one's religious and linguistic group appears to grow stronger.

Catholics and Protestants are killing each other in Northern Ireland; in Iran the Bahais are being systematically slaughtered; the Sikhs' desire for a Khalastan has cost India thousands of lives, including that of its prime minister. Jews and Arabs do not recognize they are cultural cousins and relate to one another in hatred; whites in South Africa think their black citizens are less civilized; French-speakers in Canada and Spanish-speakers in New York vociferously insist on maintaining their languages and cultures; fundamentalist Christians in America would legislate their own values into universal law if they could. Even in the "rational" West there is no single transcendent value around which all nations and cultural groups can rally. How much more diverse is the whole world in which we live.

Clifford Geertz celebrates this seeming paradox in modern life. He reminds us that at the same time that the world is becoming more economically interrelated, it is also becoming more primordial.[37] Every cultural group fights to preserve its unique identity of race, language, religion, and customs. Celebrating the paradox, we should not have to choose between universalism or cultural particularism; we need to integrate both models into our world view. Of course, we need to study the shrinking of the world, brought closer through communication, trade, and travel, but at the same time we also need to teach about the unique cultural styles and values which grow out of long, unique historical experiences and give all of us personal identity and meaning in an increasingly alienating world.

And it is a humanistic and integrated world history which might bridge the gap between these two dimensions of modern life. History with a strong humanities core can bring together both the universalism and particularism of contemporary scholarship. The humanities consider similar fields of scholarship around the world, but they present unique creations in each field. In addition, it is the mission of the humanities to see the human behind often reified concepts like modernization, technology, and complex organizations. The humanities in schools, and especially in teacher training institutions, must go back to its basic understanding of itself and its vision of reality: the humanly created world. If this can be done, the humanities can serve in a creative adversarial role to challenge those advocates of a consumer religion based on notions that technology and economic interdependence are rapidly transforming the world into a great market place where idiosyncratic cultural styles are becoming obsolete.

In an increasingly pluralistic world, a legitimate world history rooted in the humanities could broaden global education because it would set a humanistic, particularistic paradigm alongside a model of economic and technological determinism. Humanistic history is at its best in the concrete; it sticks our nose in differences and will not let us retreat behind superficial and abstract statements about a "common world culture." Study of the humanities evokes immediate and emotional responses and helps us to see specific meanings in larger abstractions. When we hear a koto, we know it is not a violin or guitar. When we see an Ardhanarisvara, we cannot convert it into something familiar like our uni-sex advertisements; we must confront a new reality. Literature gives us flesh and blood portraits of differing people with different values, and we cannot escape that reality with clichés. By confronting unique aesthetic experiences, we are forced to recognize that Japanese, Indians, and Nigerians actually do think and feel differently than we do. In the words of the 1980 Commission on the Humanities:

> Finally, though slowly, the meaning of cosmopolitanism has broadened, and with it the idea of citizenship. We cannot afford to look parochially at other cultures as curiosities, "like us" only insofar as their members have converted to Christianity or studied at Oxford or Yale.[38]

If the approach of humanistic world history were to be taken seriously in American education, then civilization and its humanistic creations could no longer be seen as imprisoned by the borders of western culture. To break out of this mind-set, a genuine attempt would have to be made to include each of the great civilizations of the world as equals in the schools. In studying history in this way, all major civilizations have to be awarded a history and not treated as an area study. Each civilization must be developed chronologically so students realize that civilizations outside the West have histories and cultures that are worth studying. Concepts such as ancient, medieval, and modern should be replaced by periodization which takes into account the various centers of civilization. The spotlight shining on the golden ages of world history shifts from Egypt to Greece and Rome, then to the Mauryan, Han, and Gupta dynasties. During the European

Middle Ages, it shines on the Tang and Sung of China and on the great expanse of Islamic civilization as well as on the flowering of the West African kingdoms.

The process of introducing this kind of approach to world history and the inclusion of non-western history in the school curriculum will not become a reality in the curricula of teacher training institutions unless new linkages of cooperation are established and new systems of working together are developed. Most graduates in teacher education have had no systematic training in non-western languages, history, or literature, and there is little prospect that this will change. In most history departments there is presently insufficient personnel to offer non-western history, and, with the hiring freeze and the propensity to fill the few existing vacancies with professors who can teach the new technologies, there is little hope that those who can teach Asian and African art, literature, language, and history will be hired in the foreseeable future.

What can be done to break the vicious cycle of Western ethnocentrism? Although it is doubtful that institutions of teacher education presently have the faculty who could take such an approach to world civilization and the humanities, other resources are available. Often the large research universities house NDEA area studies centers specializing in the languages and culture of South and East Asia, the Middle East, Latin America, the Soviet Union, and Africa. All of these NDEA centers are required by federal law to devote a part of their budgets to "out-reach" activities. These centers could make a very practical and longlasting contribution by taking responsibility for aspects of the world history course offered to students in teacher education programs. Unfortunately, at this time the NDEA centers have little articulation with colleges of education, even those within the same university. Crossing the street that separates schools of education and the area centers would be one concrete and useful step that many teacher training colleges could take immediately.

For the smaller colleges of education which are not in proximity to NDEA centers, the opportunity still remains to forge linkages with these area studies centers. The centers are spread all over the nation. Small teacher training schools could form alliances with the centers and request the center personnel to travel to the teachers' colleges to offer courses or parts of courses. Creative scheduling such as Friday-to-Sunday courses several times a year might facilitate this type of cooperation. Professors in colleges of education could also be offered seminars with professors from the area studies centers. American universities have more faculty who know more about more cultures and the humanistic creations of these cultures than perhaps any other county in the world. In many cases these scholars are only a block or two away from the teacher training centers. Yet, paradoxically, these experts are seldom called upon by professional educators. An alliance, which admittedly will initially be difficult, must be forged between the area studies specialists and professors of education if future teachers are to have the humanistic education they will require to pass on a more realistic world view than the one which now dominates American teaching.

If the large integrated world civilization course cannot be mandated for students who will become teachers, the next best option would be to require every student in a teacher-training program to take at least two courses in non-western culture. In large universities this could be easily accomplished by drawing upon the existing offerings in departments of music, art, anthropology, history, and comparative literature. Most universities offer at least a few such courses, and some of them could be required of all potential teachers. For those enrolled in teacher training institutions not part of a large university system, the same relationship can be forged with nearby larger universities which willingly supply visiting scholars in various non-western humanities to teach courses or parts of courses. It is imperative that this training be systematic and presented as any other course work would be offered and not given as a weekend workshop or one day in-service program.

Another solution to help alleviate the absence of existing personnel in teacher education and the parochialism of approach in those institutions would be for teacher training colleges to hire some of the young scholars who have been trained in non-western humanities and area studies but who are not able to get teaching jobs at the university level in the areas of their specialization. There are competent young scholars ready to work in Indian languages and literature, Chinese history and philosophy, Arabic literature, Latin American culture, and many other fields of non-western studies. Hiring these individuals in teacher training colleges would demonstrate a beginning commitment to non-western studies and would add a dimension in teacher education not previously experienced. It would be an adventure for both the young scholars and the type of faculties that presently dominate most teacher training institutions.

Because department and program organization and structure in teachers colleges are generally more flexible than in liberal arts colleges, there is a great possibility of creating new configurations for courses and teaching. The common foundations, usually required of all students, such as philosophy and history, could easily become more comparative and incorporate materials and paradigms from China, India, Japan, and Africa. Alternate models of education and philosophy could help stretch our understanding of education and teaching. Even in educational sociology and psychology, bastions of western ethnocentrism, material on stratification, the self, personality, and child development could just as easily be chosen from cultures outside the West, and these case studies would broaden both future teachers and the disciplines themselves. In methods courses, systems of socialization and teaching used in other civilizations such as the guru-shishya system of India or the relationship between Zen master and pupil in Japan could be considered by future teachers as possible models.

Students who graduate from teacher-training institutions must feel comfortable in dealing with material from all the world's civilizations or they will never willingly teach about them. This means we must systematically introduce the whole world into teacher-training institutions and then insist that a culturally pluralistic curriculum be the context for those offerings. "The Cloud Messenger" has to be required along with "Hamlet." Tu Fu and Li Po have to be taught alongside Blake and Byron. Chartres has to be compared to

Meenakshi. The Acropolis and Ajanta should stand aesthetically side by side. Cheever and Mishima must both be read, and Subalaxmi and Kathleen Battle must both be heard.

We ought to accept the wider world in the school and college curricula with more than ghetto status, even if it means reducing our attention to western European and American studies. If we were to take the history of all civilizations seriously, we would have to make a substantial revision in the way we treat the world in the schools and colleges. We would have to deal with the great civilizations of Asia, Africa, and the Middle East, not on the basis of power or potential, but because they have long histories and have engaged in great human experiments which might offer us deeper understanding of what it means to be human. We should want to know about China, India, Japan, Southeast Asia, the Middle East, Africa, and the Americas, not as tools in the cold war or instruments for our own good life because they contain minerals and markets for us, but because they were and are important in their own rights and are heirs to a long and rich history.

Perhaps the most significant value of a real world history approach would be to place before our students alternate paradigms of civilization. If the world of the future is to be richer in meaning, our students should have more choices available. Maybe the centuries of effort that the Chinese have invested in human relations, the millennia of collective wisdom the Indians have amassed on the inner self and the vast experience the West African tradition offers of more politically active roles for women all could enrich our own lives.

Louis Dumont, a scholar who has spent most of his life studying India, suggests that we are facing a crisis of modern western ideology.[39] Since that crisis involves the very way we think, it is particularly difficult for us to define the crisis. However, Dumont tells us that "to isolate our ideology is a *sine qua non* for transcending it, simply because otherwise we remain caught within it as the very medium of our thought." One way out of this dilemma, Dumont suggests, is to attempt a comparative approach, to imagine the perspective of a radically different culture and use it to look back on our own.

Dumont argues that modern western ideology is unique. It differs not only from Indian culture but from all other cultures including our own historic tradition. What Dumont calls this aberrant world view, which we so casually take for granted as natural, is an economic view of human history. This economic ideology makes the relation of the isolated individual and nature primary and builds up the concepts of society and culture from that. Most other societies take society and relations among individuals as primary and derive concepts of economics and individualism from them. Dumont questions whether it is not the modern West which is out of step with the world. He forces us at least to recognize that our identification of humanness in economic terms, *homo economicus*, means we are creating models of humanity based on our unique categories of value which are not implicit in the "nature of things."

Part of our teaching and learning always has to be an awareness of the very categories we think in. That is education in its deepest sense. Philosophy, history, the concept of civilization itself, are all terms created by humans. They are subject to amendment and change by human beings. By including the humanistic traditions outside the West in our teacher education and for all students, not as an add-on, but as a source of questions and answers perhaps fundamentally different from our own western tradition, we teach critical thinking not only about specific civilizations but also about the nature of our own thought patterns and value systems. We make it possible for students to understand and question the very disciplines in which we are engaged. The comparative approach has to be a part of American education, and, if we are to get beneath the convenient clichés of a common humanity and are to take the larger world in which we live seriously, then world history should lead the way.

Notes

1. Philip V. N. Meyers, *Ancient History* (Boston, 1876), 109.

2. Marshall G. S. Hodgson, "The Inter-relations of Societies in History," *Comparative Studies in Society and History* 5 (1963): 248.

3. *New York Times Book Review*, 11 November 1984, 1, 42.

4. J. M. Roberts, *History of the World* (New York, 1976).

5. Hugh Thomas, *A History of the World* (New York, 1979).

6. William H. McNeill, *The Rise of the West* (Chicago, 1963).

7. See, for example, Gerald Leinwand, *The Pageant of World History* (Boston, 1983).

8. William Neff and Mabel Planer, *World History for a Better World* (New York, 1953), 559.

9. As quoted in Milton Singer, "The Asian Civilization Program at the University of Chicago," ed. *Asian Studies in Liberal Arts Colleges* Ward Morehouse (New York, 1966), 31.

10. Meyers, *Ancient History*, 4.

11. Wesley Roehm and Morris Burke, *Record of Mankind* (Boston, 1970), 6.

12. Marion J. Levy, "Social Patterns and Problems of Modernization," *Readings on Social Change*, ed. in Wilbert E. Moore and Robert Cook, (Englewood Cliffs, N.J., 1967), 150.

13. Neil Smelser, "The Modernization of Social Relations," in *Modernization*, ed. Eva and Amitai Etzioni, (New York, 1966), 110–11.

14. Baidya Nath Varma, *The Sociology and Politics of Development* (London, 1980).

15. Bonnie Crown et al., *Narrative Report of the Asia Society to the Ford Foundation on Textbook Evaluation Project* (New York, 1975), 92.

16. Hendrick Van Loon, *The Story of Mankind* (Garden City, N.Y., 1921), 245.

17. L. S. Stavrianos et al., *A Global History of Man* (Boston, 1974), 504.

18. Roehm and Buske, *Record of Mankind*, 40.

19. Clarence Sorensen, *A World View* (Morristown, N.J., 1968), 300.

20. Immanuel Wallerstein, *The Modern World System*, vol. 1, *Capitalist Agriculture and the Origins of the European Economy in the Sixteenth Century* (New York, 1974). Also, Terence K. Hopkins and Wallerstein, *World System Analysis: Theory and Method* (Beverly Hills, Calif., 1982), 39–83.

21. Hopkins and Wallerstein, *World System Analysis*, 42–44.

22. Quoted in Michael Edwardes, *Raj* (London, 1966), 74–75.

23. T. A. Raman, W. A. Fisher, and Margaret Fisher, *India and Southeast Asia* (Grand Rapids, Mich., 1971), 116.

24. Fred R. Holmes, *India: Focus on Change* (Englewood Cliffs, N.J., 1972), 40.

25. Meyers, *Ancient History*, 109.

26. Carlton J. Hayes and Parker Moon, *Modern History* (New York, 1924), 668.

27. Ibid., 673.

28. Suzanne Sankowsky and Claire Hirschfield, *Mainstreams of World History* (New York, 1974), 372.

29. Melvin Schwartz and John O'Connor, *The New Exploring the Non-Western World* (New York, 1976), 205.

30. Clifford Geertz, *The Interpretation of Cultures* (New York, 1973), 53.

31. Ibid., 52.

32. See, for example, Daniel Boorstin, *The Americans*, 3 vols. (New York, 1965).

33. Perry Miller, *Errand into the Wilderness* (New York, 1956).

34. Lee Anderson, *Schooling and Citizenship*, 268.

35. Lee and Charlotte Anderson, "Global Education in Elementary School: An Overview," *Social Education* 41 (1977): 35.

36. Stephen Jones and Marion Murphey, *Geography and World Affairs* (New York, 1971), 30.

37. Geertz, *Interpretation of Cultures*, 255–311.

38. Report of the Commission on the Humanities, *Humanities in American Life* (Berkeley, Calif., 1980), 11.

39. Louis Dumont, *From Mandeville to Marx* (Chicago, 1977).

Martin W. Lewis
Kären E. Wigen

Geography in the Historical Imagination

Structuring a discussion of premodern history around a handful of large-scale civilizations has much to recommend it. The high level of congruence between historians' civilizations and geographers' world regions (at least within Eurasia) suggests that universalistic religious communities have in fact demarcated areas of intense and enduring interaction (as discussed in chapter 6). The problem with most global histories is not that they adopt a civilization-

Martin W. Lewis and Kären E. Wigen, *The Myth of Continents: A Critique of Metageography* (Berkeley: University of California Press, 1997), 130–2, 134–5.

centered framework. Rather, it is that they perpetuate Toynbee's tendency to overstress the internal coherence of such regions (following area specialists in downplaying interregional connections),[1] while abandoning his ecumenical reach (settling instead for a focus on a few "primary" areas). What has been lost is Toynbee's insistence on giving equal attention to *all* civilizations. As a result, the standard cartography of premodern world history has been radically contracted, simplified, and prioritized — with some disturbing ideological implications.

The best place to see this schematization at work is in general-interest books on world history. The typical single-volume work begins on the eve of European expansion (circa 1500), highlighting four cultural zones across Eurasia: the realms of Christian, Islamic, Hindu, and Confucian civilization. The rest of the world is relegated to a limbo of interstices, hinterlands, repositories of barbarism, or (in the case of the Americas) doomed areas of less-advanced civilization. A stripped-down example of this standard metageography can be seen in L. S. Stavrianos's *The World Since 1500*.[2] Stavrianos begins his work with a tour of the major world civilizations immediately prior to European expansion. Here, three principal Eurasian cultural zones — Europe, the Muslim world, and the Confucian world — are contrasted as a group with the more isolated cultural spheres of sub-Saharan Africa, the Americas, and Australasia. The exclusions created by Stavrianos's definition of the Muslim world are revealing. Effectively, it comprises three great empires: the Ottoman (in Turkey and the Balkans), the Safavid (in Persia), and the Mogul (in India). This formulation subsumes predominantly Hindu India into the culture of its ruling elite; it also places Islamic societies of the Sahel outside the Muslim world, and leaves the Islamic regions of Central and Southeast Asia — along with their Buddhist neighbors — off the map altogether. Nor is the reduction of the community of Islam during this period to the three "gunpowder empires" unusual. Such important sixteenth-century Islamic polities as the Uzbek Khanate are rarely discussed in world history textbooks, even in the minimal sense of acknowledging their existence. The resulting image of the world in 1500 is one where a handful of powerful states are lit up on an otherwise dark canvas.

A more sophisticated regionalization scheme can be seen in a newer work, J. M. Roberts's *History of the World*.[3] Roberts's scope is impressive. The most comprehensive section of his work (Book IV, "The Age of Diverging Traditions") includes chapters on Islam and the Arab Empires, Byzantium and Russia, the Turks and the Mongols, Western Europe, India, China, Japan, the Americas, and sub-Saharan Africa. The latter may be accorded only five pages, but at least it is recognized as a civilization in its own right. Yet even Roberts omits any discussion of Southeast Asia prior to European colonialism. The conventional cellular view of Eurasian historical geography — one that discerns only Europe, the Islamic world, India, and China, perceiving all other areas as merely the fuzzy edges of these great "civilizations" — evidently still does not have room for a complex and hybrid region like Southeast Asia.[4]

HISTORICAL ATLASES AND SINOCENTRISM

If a simplified framework of civilizations remains the mainstay of world history texts, a similarly flattened geohistorical conception remains the frame of reference for most historical atlases of the world. The limitations of such a vision can be seen particularly well in the way these atlases depict eastern Asia. Paralleling the Eurocentricity of their overall conception, most historical atlases exhibit a secondary, but no less pronounced, Sinocentrism in their vision of East Asia. This perpetuates three distortions. First, a multinational world region — comparable in many respects to Europe — is represented as though it were composed of a single state comprising a unitary civilization. By focusing almost exclusively on the territorial extent of the Chinese Empire under its various dynasties, historical cartographers implicitly reduce East Asia to the scale of a single country, whereas Europe is allowed to play the role of a culture area of continental scope. In the process, they also unwittingly obscure the fact that present-day China is more an empire than a nation-state, holding in its tight embrace extensive territories in Central Asia that were conquered by the Manchus but never fully assimilated to Chinese ways of life.[5]

Second, the intimate connections between China and its closest cultural neighbors — Japan, Korea, and Vietnam — are obscured. Japan is most often pictured by itself on separate maps, a move that highlights internal Japanese developments without showing the archipelago's deep historical connections to the mainland. (The effect would be like that of excluding Britain from all maps of Europe.) Korea, by contrast, is simply ignored. In most English-language historical atlases, the peninsula is either excluded from view altogether, portrayed as a mere appendage of China, or reduced to a blank outline, as if it were bereft of history.[6] Although Korea is a country the size of Britain, with a language of its own and a long, intricate, and well-documented political, social, and cultural history, it is rarely considered significant enough to merit depiction in English-language historical atlases. (The major exception here comes in treatments of the Korean War, an era of obvious interest to American audiences.) As a result, such important Korean kingdoms as Silla, Paekche, Koguryo, and Po-Hai are effectively excluded from our historical-geographical consciousness.[7] When it appears at all, Korea is reduced in the American historical-cartographical imagination to little more than a parade ground for foreign invaders. . . .

GEOPOLITICAL REIMAGINATION AND THE HUNTINGTON THESIS

As the foregoing discussion suggests, the conviction shared by Toynbee and others that discrete civilizations were the fundamental units of human organization has had a marked impact on world history tests and atlases. Outside of the field of history, however, this vision has been less influential. The regional structure of the world in 1500, on the eve of European expansion, is obviously not that of the late twentieth century. Especially in the Americas, the lines of cultural cleavage and the circuits of interconnection have been completely reconfigured; the pre-Columbian map is of little account in formulating policy for the contemporary United States or Brazil. Even within the "Old World" ecumene, major cultural assemblages have been substantially transformed and spatially rearranged. Indeed, the dominant social science view in the post–World War II decades held that cultures across the globe were converging toward a single Westernized modernity.

Recent events, however, have conspired to bring civilizations back into view, even in policy circles. With the breakup of the Soviet Union, the end of the Cold War, and the dissolution of the midcentury trinity of First, Second, and Third Worlds, deeply rooted divisions based on older cultural distinctions are returning to view. In the Eastern Hemisphere, the religious groupings and other large-scale social entities identified by world historians have proved remarkably persistent. Moreover, while there have been some significant spatial shifts, the core territories of each regional civilization have endured. History now appears more relevant than social scientists of the postwar period imagined.

In an effort to grasp the new lines of fracture in the volatile post-1989 world, the political theorist Samuel Huntington has proposed a remapping of potential high-level conflict zones based on the persistence of major civilizations. Huntington proposes a distinctive metageography of global warfare, which he sees as having been socially and spatially structured along different lines in four successive eras. Wars between princes in the Middle Ages gave way, in his view, to wars between modern nation-states, which in turn yielded at midcentury to conflicts between ideological blocks. In the 1990s, Huntington sees the beginning of the next era, one in which major battles — those with the potential for significant escalation — will be fought less between states or ideological alliances than between discrete civilizations.[8]

Huntington's thesis deserves serious consideration. The enduring reality of macrocultural divisions has already proven militarily significant, and may well become more so in the near future. As the recent fighting in Bosnia attests, political struggles across major civilizational boundaries have assumed a special intensity in this decade. Equally cogent is Huntington's insight that eastern and western Europe are more significantly divided by the old split between Orthodox and Latin Christianity than by the Iron Curtain, which already lies in a rusted heap. Yet Huntington errs in the same way that Toynbee did, by ignoring both the numerous crosscutting groupings and the deep internal subdivisions that fractionate each of the world's major civilizations. The European Union notwithstanding, there is no reason to believe that western Europe has irrevocably abandoned its legacy of internecine conflict. Similarly, any notion that China, the two Koreas, Vietnam, Japan, and Singapore will find grounds for a military entente in their common Confucian heritage is dubious at best. Most doubtful of all, however, is Huntington's vision of an impending Islamic-Confucian alliance threatening the West (a scenario based primarily on evidence of recent arms sales between Pakistan and China). If the development of a united Confucian block is unlikely, the emergence of a workable alliance between Islamic and Confucian civilizations is even more so. Centuries-old religious ties may indeed have a place on our contemporary world maps,[9] but it would be simplistic to ignore the competing claims of economic class, local community, transnational commercial exchange, and nationalism.

Notes

1. As K. N. Chaudhuri (1990, page 11) writes, "The specialist historians of Asia, each examining his own narrow chronology and field, are often unable to see the structural totality of economic and social life and they are inclined to treat the experience of their own regions as unique or special." In compensation, Chaudhuri deliberately blurs the boundaries between each civilization in his own work, to good effect.

2. See Stavrianos 1975.

3. Roberts 1993.

4. Southeast Asia fares poorly in many recent college textbooks on world history. F. Roy Willis (1982), for example, attempts to transcend the Eurocentrism once typical of the genre by examining India, China, and the Middle East as well as Europe. In one chapter (9), Southeast Asia is granted a short discussion, yet it is not considered on its own terms; Willis describes premodern Cambodia and Java, for example, as merely exemplars of a "reinvigorated Indian culture" (page 384).

Archibald Lewis (1988), who displays a nearly global sweep in his impressively synthetic *Nomads and Crusaders*, similarly bypasses the region. Lewis opens this book with the assertion: "In the year 1000 five great civilizations existed in the world of Africa and Eurasia: the East Asian, the Indic, the Islamic, the Byzantine-Russian, and the western European" (page 3). While Lewis seems to be adopting the same tired roster of discrete social systems, he does acknowledge the existence of areas, such as Tibet, that do not fit into this scheme, and he is in general highly sensitive to subtle variations in geographical patterning of macrocultural affiliation. Still, the eclipsing of Southeast Asia is noteworthy.

5. China has managed to retain far more of its early modern empire than have its European counterparts. In the mid-eighteenth century — just as Russia was advancing in the Kazakh steppes, Britain was beginning to build a land-based empire in India, and the Netherlands was starting to carve out an Indonesian imperium — the Manchu rulers of China were expanding vigorously in Central Asia. The actions of the Central Kingdom there were as brutal as those of any European imperialists; it virtually exterminated the Zunghar Mongols, for example (see Bergholtz 1993, page 402). Therefore it is a considerable falsification of history to argue, as Chiang Kai-shek did, that "Xinjiang is Chinese not as a result of Qing [Manchu] conquest . . . but due to 2,000 years of assimilation" (quoted in Millward 1994, page 446). The most ardent Chinese nationalists actually claim that China should rightfully control all territories that ever paid homage to it — including Kazakhstan, Nepal, Russia's far east, and virtually all of mainland Southeast Asia (see Lamb 1968, page 39). For more on China's imperial conquests in Central Asia, see Lattimore 1988, Bergholtz 1993, and Jenner 1992.

6. In the eighteenth and nineteenth centuries, European atlases often portrayed Korea as a portion of Tartary (see, for example, Palairet 1775; Woodbridge 1824); with the disappearance of this region it was usually simply transferred to China. A few atlases of the late 1800s and early 1900s did, however, portray Korea as an autonomous geographical unit (Bartholomew 1873, map 28; W. Johnston 1880, map 19; *Hammond's Modern Atlas of the World* 1909, map 95; Cram 1897, page 188).

7. Most of the people of Po-Hai (more properly, in Korean, Parhae) were speakers of Tungusic languages rather than Korean, but the kingdom's rulers were Korean, and they "clearly regarded their state as representing a revival of Koguryo" (Lee 1984, page 72).

8. See S. Huntington 1993. Huntington's thesis bears a certain resemblance to the arguments put forward by geographer Donald Meinig in a little-known 1956 article. Meinig's piece, which is concerned with the "evolution from nationalism to cultural-ism," remains in many respects more insightful than that of Huntington.

9. It also seems likely, however, that Huntington — like many other scholars in the field — has exaggerated the religious nature of civilizations, as well as the historical depth of animosity across religious-civilizational boundaries. Barbara Metcalf (1995), for example, convincingly shows that the "civilizational" divide separating Hindus from Muslims in South Asia is largely a modern invention.

Works Cited

Bartholomew, John. 1873. *A Descriptive Hand Atlas of the World.* Philadelphia: Zell.

Bergholtz, Fred W. 1993. *The Partition of the Steppe: The Struggle of the Russians, Manchus, and the Zunghar Mongols for Empire in Central Asia.* New York: Lang.

Chaudhuri, K. N. 1990. *Asia before Europe: Economy and Civilization of the Indian Ocean from the Rise of Islam to 1750.* Cambridge: Cambridge University Press.

Cram, George. 1897. *Cram's Universal Atlas.* New York: Cram.

Hammond's Modern Atlas of the World. 1909. New York: Hammond.

Huntington, Samuel P. 1993. "The Clash of Civilizations." *Foreign Affairs* 72:23–49.

Jenner, W. J. F. 1992. *The Tyranny of History: The Roots of China's Crisis.* London: Penguin.

Johnston, W. 1889. *The World: An Atlas.* Edinburgh: Johnston.

Lamb, Alastair. 1968. *Asian Frontiers: Studies on a Continuing Problem.* London: Pall Mall Press.

Lattimore, Owen. 1953. "The New Political Geography of Inner Asia." *Geographical Journal* 119:17–32.

Lee, Ki-baik. 1984. *A New History of Korea.* Cambridge: Harvard University Press.

Lewis, Archibald. 1988. *Nomads and Crusaders, 1000–1368.* Bloomington: Indiana University Press.

Metcalf, Barbara D. 1995. "Too Little and Too Much: Reflections on Muslims in the History of India." *Journal of Asian Studies* 54:951–67.

Millward, James A. 1994. "A Uyghur Muslim in Qianlong's Court: The Meaning of the Fragrant Concubine." *Journal of Asian Studies* 53:427–58.

Palairet, John. 1775. *Bowles's Universal Atlas.* London: Bowles.

Roberts, J. M. 1993. *History of the World.* New York: Oxford University Press.

Stavrianos, L. S. 1975. *The World since 1500: A Global History.* Englewood Cliffs, N.J.: Prentice-Hall.

Willis, F. Roy. 1982. *World Civilization.* Vol. 1. *From Ancient Times through the Sixteenth Century.* Lexington, Mass.: Heath.

Woodbridge, William C. 1824. *Modern Atlas of Universal Geography.* Hartford: Cook.

SELECTED BIBLIOGRAPHY

Embree, Ainslie T., and Carol Gluck, eds. *Asia in Western and World History: A Guide for Teaching.* Armonk, N.Y.: M. E. Sharpe, 1997. A product of Columbia University's Project on Asia in the Core Curriculum, this book presents an extensive collection of essays on teaching world history with particular reference to Asia. Carol Gluck contributes a thoughtful general introduction on the emergence of world history as a scholarly field.

Farmer, Edward L. "Civilization as a Unit of World History: Eurasia and Europe's Place in It." *The History Teacher* 18 (May 1985): 345–63. An argument for studying European history in a comparative framework of Eurasian civilizations.

Farmer, Edward L., Gavin R. G. Hambly, David Kopf, Byron K. Marshall, and Romeyn Taylor. *Comparative History of Civilizations in Asia.* 2 vols. Reading, Mass.: Addison-Wesley, 1977. Out of print now, this textbook is still well worth consulting because it tries systematically to situate all the major civilizations of Asia, including Southwest Asia, into a framework of cross-cultural processes.

Guzman, Gregory G. "A Working Definition of the Term 'Civilization' for Introductory Survey Courses." *World History Bulletin* 8 (Spring/Summer 1991): 23–27. Students should begin studying world history equipped with a concrete definition of "civilization."

Hathaway, Jane. "Early Islamic Civilization in Global Perspective." *World History Bulletin* 12 (Winter/Spring 1996): 13–19. The author, an Ottoman specialist, considers a number of themes and problems in Islam's first seven centuries to demonstrate that "Islamic history is by its very nature world history."

Hitchens, Marilynn Jo. "East Central Europe in World History." *World History Bulletin* 8 (Spring/Summer 1991): 8–10; "Russia in World History." *World History Bulletin* 9 (Fall/Winter 1992–93): 19–20; "Glasnost, Perestroika and Nationalism in Russian and World History." *World History Bulletin* 10 (Spring/Summer 1993): 43–47. In this series of three short articles written in the aftermath of the Soviet collapse, the author situates the Eastern European and Russian past in world history. Hitchens is a Russian scholar and past president of the World History Association.

Huntington, Samuel P. *The Clash of Civilizations and the Remaking of World Order.* New York: Simon and Schuster, 1997. A vigorous reaffirmation of the idea of civilizations as cultural entities, which are now, the author declares, reasserting their distinctive attributes and destinies in the absence of a bipolar Cold War. To preserve peace, he argues, Americans must accept an inherently multicivilizational world, renew and defend the "unique qualities" of Western civilization, and forsake dangerous attempts to impose our civilization on others.

Krejci, Jaroslav. *Before the European Challenge: The Great Civilizations of Asia and the Middle East.* Albany: State University of New York Press, 1990. This book focuses on the great religious traditions, offering historical profiles of the major belief systems of Eurasia.

Lockard, Craig A. "Integrating African History into the World History Course: Some Transgressional Patterns." *World History Bulletin* 10 (Fall/Winter 1993–94): 21–31. Rich ideas for developing a world history course that pays proper attention to the African past.

———. "Integrating Southeast Asia into the Framework of World History: The Period before 1500." *The History Teacher* 29 (Nov. 1995): 1–29. The author's analysis of thirteen world history texts shows that they accord an average of 5 pages to Southeast Asia compared to 175 for Western Europe. To help rectify this deplorable situation, he offers a sweeping and intelligent synthesis of the region's premodern history "as a basis on which to begin the integration of Southeast Asia into world history textbooks and courses."

McNeill, William H. "Europe in world History before 1500 A.D." *The History Teacher* 18 (May 1985): 339–44. Brief reflections on situating Europe in Afro-Eurasian history.

Melko, Matthew, and Leighton R. Scot. *The Boundaries of Civilizations in Space and Time.* Lanham, Md.: University Press of America, 1987. This volume reflects the interests of the sociologists, anthropologists, historians, and other academics who make up the membership of the International Society for the Comparative Study of Civilizations. These scholars explore the origins, classifications, systemics, and fates of civilizations, asking many of the same questions that world historians do.

Quigley, Carroll. *The Evolution of Civilizations: An Introduction to Historical Analysis.* 2d ed. Indianapolis: Liberty, 1979. A leading work of civilizationist metahistory that, like the writings of Samuel Huntington, reflects on the destiny of the West. Quigley characterizes the West as a mature, internally stable civilization, but one that nonetheless exists in a world where all civilizations have proved transient.

PART SEVEN

PERIODIZING WORLD HISTORY

Whether investigating a half-century of social change in an English village or two millennia of developments in ancient India, historians are obliged to cut the past into distinct pieces. They do so for a number of reasons. One is simply to identify and isolate chunks of time in order to study them one by one, since all periods cannot be studied simultaneously. A second is to distinguish one cluster of interrelated historical events from another in order to discover patterns of change. A third is to identify significant shifts in those patterns in terms of discontinuities or turning points, which serve as the start and end of periods. A fourth is to highlight trends or events that appear dominant or important during a particular span of time.

In his essay, Jerry Bentley declares that "periodization ranks among the more elusive tasks of historical scholarship." Indeed the three scholars whose reflections are included in this section recognize that serious quandaries about organizing time await anyone starting down a new path of world history teaching or research. They also implicitly agree that periodization is almost always less perplexing when a single nation, state, or civilization provides a container for all relevant variables than when the cultural and social backdrop is multiform and complicated. None of the essays in earlier sections of this book specifically addresses periodization, but the formulations of several of them — Shaffer's "Southernization" (Part Four), for example, or Hodgson's "Hemispheric Interregional History as an Approach to World History" (Part Three) — obviously involved imaginative rethinking of time as well as space.

As geographers and world historians know, it is impossible to project the lands and seas of planet Earth on a flat map without conceding one kind of distortion or another in depictions of size, shape, and distance. Similarly, no periodization scheme for world history can intelligibly integrate all, or even most phenomena except perhaps at the very broadest and thus least useful levels of generalization. Whether the stretch of time under investigation is short or long, any ordering of perceivable continuities and breaks is a mental construction of the historian. Consequently, a periodization that seems illuminating to one scholar is hopelessly wrongheaded to another. Turning points that demarcate a bundle of interrelated economic developments may have no bearing on contemporaneous cultural trends. A sweeping global scheme that works for Afro-Eurasia over six millennia probably won't fit the Americas. If some world-scale time fractures, such as the start of World War I, seem abrupt and obvious, many others are fuzzy and perennially contested. Period labels that highlight dynastic reigns or art styles may seem misleading to those who study price cycles or changing social relations between men and women. In short, all periodizations are in some measure biased, arbitrary, and illusory, but they are also absolutely essential tools for making sense of the constructable past.

The selections in this section, which all address the problem of *long-term* periodization on either a global or hemispheric scale, are especially relevant to instructors designing introductory world history curricula. It is noteworthy that the four periodization schemes presented here are not wildly divergent. On the contrary, world historians seem well agreed on the largest-scale turning points in history. All four frameworks, for example, designate 1500 C.E. or thereabouts as a major watershed. Most teachers would probably concur. It is an index of the vitality of the field, however, that some scholars now question whether "1500" was such a great divide after all. One argument is that the European-led seaborne global linkup of the late fifteenth and sixteenth centuries was, in terms of communications and economy, merely a global extension of the Afro-Eurasian system of production, trade, and transport that came to maturity in the thirteenth century. Another argument, put forth by Andre Gunder Frank, holds that 1400, not 1500, marked the beginning of a global demographic and economic upswing that affected human interrelations in countless ways.[1]

When world historians zero in on relatively short periods, say a few hundred years or less, contention over trends, disjunctions, and descriptive labels is likely to be lively. Debates about periodization will probably be even warmer in the years to come because new world-historical research continues to shake up conventional categories of time and space. Eco-minded historians, for example, have been stepping forward to argue that shifts in the biosphere, disease environment, or planetary climate block out more consequential periods of human experience than do the ups and downs of civilizations.[2]

In the first selection Peter Stearns proposes that teachers and textbook authors learn to be more conscious of periodization as a methodological problem, thus helping to free students from the tired notion that history is "one damn thing after another," and world history "an unusual number of damn things." Precisely because all periodizations are the cultural constructs of their inventors, students should approach this subject "as an analytical issue, perhaps the fundamental intellectual issue in historical thinking." Stearns believes that attention to the Great Traditions is very important but that textbooks more often than not pass up the challenge to devise horizontally integrated macrohistorical time frames, preferring to play it safe with multiple sets of parallel periods compatible with a civilizational text structure.

He recommends a plan in which the criteria for determining large-scale historical periods are three "graded levels of generality, each level coming closer to the character of particular societies." These three spheres — basic technological shifts, changes in patterns of commercial exchange, and development of belief systems — may be superimposed on one another and at the same time shown to intermesh in shaping the character of successive periods. In the last part of his essay, not included here, Stearns deploys his three "interacting factors" to produce a time map spanning eleven thousand years:

9000–3500 B.C.E.	Development of agriculture leading to the emergence of civilizations
3500–500 B.C.E.	Expansion of civilizations to encompass wider realms of human interchange
500 B.C.E.–500 C.E.	First major period of inter-civilizational contacts
500–1500 C.E.	Emergence of new civilizations, expanding commercial relations, and growing dominance of monotheistic religions
1500–present	Complex world economy, industrialization, and Western ascendancy

Jerry Bentley also recommends a tripartite set of criteria for large-scale periodization under the rubric "processes of cross-cultural interaction," and like Stearns, he identifies cross-regional trade as one key category. His other two choices are mass migrations and patterns of empire-building. Focusing his discussion entirely on Afro-Eurasia from paleolithic times to 1500 C.E., he tests the hypothesis that "cross-cultural interactions were intensive and extensive enough to provide frameworks for periodization" in the millennia before the great global convergence of the sixteenth century. He finds that in premodern times human interconnections having to do with migrations, trade, and imperial expansion were indeed so significant that, as Marshall Hodgson put it, "any given changes were likely to lead to new ones, and the total course of all these changes form a single story."[3]

Knowing that world history periodizers must be cautious in their claims, Bentley grants that a premodern categorization embracing the Eastern Hemisphere, Western Hemisphere, and Oceania all at once is not achievable. He also recognizes that high-flying global periodization must not be allowed to camouflage the more "finely calibrated" time divisions that speak to particular regions and societies. Even so, he says, the project to investigate history from large-scale and comparative perspectives is perfectly valid. Therefore conceptions of time are required that situate both particular historical processes and the histories of localities and regions in their broadest appropriate contexts of interactivity.

Bentley's essay presented here excludes the portion that outlines in detail his rationale for a periodization lodged in cross-cultural interaction. The following summary of his six-era outline may be compared with Stearns's design, which is different, but not drastically so:

3500–2000 B.C.E.	Age of early complex societies
2000–500 B.C.E.	Age of ancient civilizations
500 B.C.E.–500 C.E.	Age of classical civilizations
500–1000 C.E.	Post-classical age
1000–1500 C.E.	Age of transregional nomadic empires
1500 C.E.–present	Modern age

William Green is persuaded that the quest for an integrated global periodization, as opposed to the multiple time ladders of region-centered world history, is a worthwhile, indeed "inescapable pedagogical problem." However, an integrationist approach that identifies "universal epochal frontiers," not just regional ones, should be grounded in theory: "To make a cake, one needs a recipe. To divine why and how history has evolved as it has, the historian needs a theory of change. Theory does more than identify the ingredients of historical problems. It explains the process which gives those ingredients meaning."

Green warns that world history integrationists face tough questions: How can they escape the temptation to privilege the historically weightiest societies, particularly the big, interacting civilizations of Eurasia, to the neglect of peoples whose political and cultural structures are less majestic? How can they determine in what ways changes within particular societies and civilizations possess actual causal links to "common engines of change" having hemispheric or global scope? What alternatives might there be to the "progressive, evolutionary, materialist theories of change" that are so deeply embedded in the Western intellectual tradition? Reviewing existing theories of change, Green gives special attention to world-system postulates as a promising, though uncertain foundation for a global time frame.

At the end of his essay he proposes a periodization of his own, though he offers no detailed rationale. He also admits that because a convincing deductive model is not yet available, his preferences are no more theory-driven than other frameworks:

3000–1000/800 B.C.E.	Early sweep of history following Hodgson's model
1000/800 B.C.E.–400/600 C.E.	Regional efflorescences leading to demographic and migratory crises
400/600–1492 C.E.	Era of exceptional Islamic and Chinese achievement
1492–present	Multicausal transition to global integration

Sometimes teams of teachers or textbook authors find themselves having to reach consensus on a global periodization. Undoubtedly, the largest collaboration ever undertaken to partition the global past was the 1992–96 project to write National Standards for History. Led by the National Council for History Standards, whose members included William McNeill, nearly three dozen academic, professional, and public-interest organizations worked together to produce comprehensive guidelines for the historical knowledge and critical skills young Americans should possess by the time they graduate from high school. From the beginning the Council supported content standards having an explicit chronological structure. This meant coming up with provisional periodizations for both United States and world history to guide the work of the teams of K–12 and university teachers who developed the full documents. The discussions over time divisions were prolonged and sometimes contentious. Several levels of committees and task forces were involved at one point or another, and individuals variously favoring a West-centered, multiculturalist, or integrated global approach to the standards naturally enough had conflicting ideas about periodization. A modified global approach was ultimately adopted.

The world history standards, whose periodization was revised slightly in the second edition published in 1996, are meant primarily for use in public schools. Their development, however, involved remarkable teamwork among teachers and scholars, many of whom had previously given much thought to the problem of conceptualizing the global past. Indeed, Stearns, Bentley, and others whose contributions are included in this volume participated in the process to one degree or another. The final selection comprises the brief essays and rationale statements that introduced the content standards for each of nine global eras.

Notes

1. Andre Gunder Frank, *ReOrient: Global Economy in the Asian Age* (Berkeley: University of California Press, 1998), 328–29. (See Selected Bibliography in Part Eleven.)

2. See the essay by David Christian in Part Eleven.

3. Marshall G. S. Hodgson, *Rethinking World History: Essays on Europe, Islam, and World History*, ed. Edmund Burke III (Cambridge: Cambridge University Press, 1993), 19–20.

PETER N. STEARNS

Periodization in World History Teaching
Identifying the Big Changes

The welcome revival of interest in teaching and writing about world history inevitably forces an examination of the divisions of time historians characteristically employ for this vastest of all subject areas. Periodization, the conceptual tool that makes change over time a manageable topic, and therefore history teaching feasible, is unquestionably a tricky device at the world history level and perhaps for this reason more often assumed than discussed. Yet an explicit grasp of the bases of world history periodization is all the more essential for the magnitude of the range surveyed. Students need to be aware of the points at which world history shifts gears, and to this end, teachers need to be open to discussions of alternative modes of periodization and various options and criteria for choice.

For world history can become a victim of a mindless survey approach in which one factual parade follows another with few seminal events to break the flow and even fewer analytical mechanisms through which reasonably coherent chunks of chronology can be isolated and discussed. True, all of the many (often excellent) texts in the field do offer major section headings, appropriately delimited by dates; they do not force readers through 1200–1500 pages without a few key markers en route. Few, however, pause to discuss why units of time were selected as they were, what principles of differentiation were involved, or what alternatives were rejected and why. Few texts, in other words, encourage world history students to approach periodization as an analytical issue, perhaps the fundamental intellectual issue in historical thinking. Accordingly, few texts, whatever their intentions, adequately divert students from a sense that history consists of one damn thing after another, world history an unusual number of damn things, and the subject overall an occasion for memorization rather than conscious thought.

When world history teachers do turn to conceptual frameworks, their clearest tool is not a categorization of time but of place. Identifying discrete civilizations allows a sense of the world's diversity, specific points of diffusion and con-

Peter N. Stearns, "Periodization in World History Teaching: Identifying the Big Changes," *The History Teacher* 20 (August 1987): 561–74, 579–80.

tact, and a host of exercises in comparative analysis. While not all textbook treatments are as systematic in defining civilizations as might be wished, and while more comparative sketches of key topics are devoutly to be desired, a teacher can proceed to geographical or civilizational units in world history with some confidence.

This is less true, however, for units of time — and yet time is in fact the historian's chief concern, the issue most important to bring before students in any kind of history course. World history periodization is characteristically seen in terms of units of convenience or temporary parallelisms, such as the rise and fall of the classical empires, rather than widely-applicable schemas that fit more than one point in time. What is needed, in contrast, is a periodization both explicit and defendable (which is not the same as sacrosanct), that meets several criteria. It must involve attention to factors sufficiently general that they can focus recurrent discussion, seriously advancing a conceptual grasp of history including causation. It cannot rely overmuch on events or on the kinds of political change most likely to occur within rather than across civilizations. It must embrace popular as well as elite activities, as against the outdated assumption that in world history the masses can be ignored as changeless while attention rivets on elite developments. It must set a framework for periodization within individual civilizations (though it need not explain all the twists and turns) and also for topics, such as science or the conditions of women, that must be pursued across civilizational boundaries. The periodization required need not be strikingly original in the major turning points selected, but it must be livelier and more discussable than is common in the field.

This essay is intended to discuss periodization issues in a fairly concrete fashion, as they have worked in one world history course now in its fifth and reasonably successful year and in another (yes, yet another) recently-issued short text.[1] My purpose is less to push a single periodization scheme (for illustrative reasons I will sketch one with which I am comfortable) than to show how periodization — even when seemingly obvious — can and should be discussed. Following the process of dealing with several differentiating factors allows a grasp of how periodization can be used to analyze what world history is about, beyond (and, in my view, above) the level of memorization. The twin purposes of periodization in this discussion are first, to make world history itself manageable in permitting a scope of generalization and a focus on selective facts that convey processes and events of real importance but stop short of overwhelming detail, and second, to introduce into world history some sense of history's analytical excitement where, precisely because of desperate attempts at coverage, it may most be lacking.

This exercise is more than theoretical. The problems of the world history course as survey are very real. Teachers in the field, mostly self-taught because of the absence of explicit training save at a few new centers, need to raise conceptual problems beyond the strict narrative-flow, one civilization at a time, so that the basic history course can stimulate historical thinking as well as provide coverage. Furthermore, a good periodization scheme also helps integrate all major periods into the larger stream of world history. Here is, in my experience, one of the crucial tests of using periodization dynamically: to give new life and drama to developments in the world at all points and not just when the first great traditions were set or when the challenge of modern techniques, power relations, and beliefs began to force a world response.

The need for something more than simplistic periodization is, of course, a hardy perennial in survey history. Western civilization courses too often move mechanically from one time slot to another without raising issues of what key factors changed, what caused change, and whether an alternative periodization might be construed. But world history runs a particular risk of unexamined periodization not only because of its vast embrace, but because the subject does involve legitimate periodization dilemmas that single-civilization courses do not — dilemmas that can understandably, if not excusably, be sidestepped through silence.

For periodization, when it works best and most dynamically in history, involves real (and hopefully explainable) alterations in characteristics. These alterations unquestionably occur where the process of change operates within a common framework, like politics in a nation state, economies in a single market region, or ideas in a common culture zone. The world, even now and certainly before the past two centuries, has not fully provided such a framework. Relatively few events or influences have been crossed from one civilization to the next, and fewer still have involved more than two or three of the seven or more civilization areas in world history. Basic determinants of human life and institutions have operated within the context of a single civilization, or still smaller units, and changes in world dynamics have only modestly intruded. At least in the present state of scholarship, and probably as a matter of ineluctable fact, periodization at the world history level cannot be as tight or as encompassing as that within a single civilization. There is no point deluding ourselves that we can hope for as detailed a series of time slots in world history as many of us learned about, and in turn taught about, in western civilization (or Chinese, or Middle Eastern) surveys.

There is, then, an undeniable dilemma. World history courses particularly need periodization to avoid unmanageable survey qualities and to spark thought, but they also face particular problems in filling their need for the simple reason that the world has never been a single basic society, operating according to a close-knit pattern of common causation. Small wonder that many of the big survey texts opt for an implicit overall periodization, saving their real attention for units of time within the key civilizations covered.

Yet a periodization framework does exist for world history so long as we recognize that it is a somewhat loose weave within which the textures of individual civilizations set more intricate designs. The best way to approach the problem is through a series of graded levels of generality, each level coming closer to the character of particular societies.

Level one, most basic and therefore most important to establish in the classroom, is quite familiar. There have been, as popularizers such as Alvin Toffler as well as world history scholars like Leften Stavrianos have reminded us, two fundamental transformations in human world history, the first from hunting and gathering to agricultural society, the second from agricultural to industrial society.[2] Each of these transformations reminds us that the human species, for all its important animal features, is the only one thus far capable of changing fundamental subsistence systems, a change that in turn informs a host of other features of humankind's social and personal existence. For the rise of agriculture, and then of industry, involved more than technological change and a real alteration of the units of economic organization. Each transformation also forced significant shifts in political structure. Larger states normally followed from the rise of agriculture, while the advent of industry seems to spell the death of typical agricultural political forms from village government to monarchy. Each basic system affected the nature of human residence and the structure and functions of families. Each also set significant preconditions for belief systems. Hunting and gathering types of animism could nonetheless survive well into the agricultural era just as agricultural monotheisms helped shape the industrial age. Each transformation, finally, had important considerations for women's history.[3] Hunting and gathering families yielded to patriarchy with agriculture in ways that varied only in specifics from one civilization to the next.

Whatever else a world history course does, it must establish for students the basic features of agricultural and industrial societies (and the transformation from one to the other). Particular civilizations can and should be used to illustrate these features and to show how common structures — such as the limitations on state revenues and communications in agriculture — translate into important variations in specific contexts. Knowing what problems each major type of economy solves, and what new problems each creates, and what ramifications each form has on the range of human activity beyond economic organization is key to a good world history course, and additional detail should never be allowed to obscure this fundamental typology.

The first level of world history periodization, then, focuses on two periods of crucial transition: first, when agricultural societies initially developed, with the Neolithic revolution and its subsequent, gradual spread in much of Asia, Africa, and Europe and its separate establishment elsewhere; and second, when industrialization took hold in the nineteenth and twentieth centuries. There have been no more significant watersheds in the history of the species anywhere around the globe.

This said, there are, of course, several problems in relying too heavily on this basic periodization. Students may be encouraged into an unduly simple-minded technological determinism. This can be cushioned by discussing cultural and political factors that vary a society's openness to technological change, since even in the Neolithic revolution it is clear that there were determined holdouts among peoples exposed to agriculture, as well as among more isolated groups. But since American students are so inclined to believe that when you know technology, you know everything essential, a supplementary periodization is imperative. The fact is that even when technologies are exchanged from one culture to the next, or over time, they do not bring the same political or cultural structure that accompanied their birth. A periodization that rests on basic technological change alone would thus omit or falsely simplify vast areas of human endeavor.

The Neolithic Age and the industrial revolution each rivets attention on societies that make the transition early, risking a slighting or a pejorative interpretation of the "laggards." Most of us find this skewing acceptable for the Neolithic case. Societies that did not develop extensive agriculture fairly early were unable to create the sophisticated political and artistic forms, or even civilization itself, at least until relatively late. They were also characteristically sparse in demographic terms. They can be noted, particularly as they show signs of moving toward agriculture, and their rich anthropological complexity can be sampled as against facile assumptions that only people technically in civilizations are civilized in the sense of having important cultures and detailed rules of behavior.

But the fact is that the areas that developed agriculture fairly late do not count for much in the conventional terms of world history until a few laggards like northern Europe and Japan began to play catchup by around A.D. 1000. The distortions involved in looking mainly at the early converts to agriculture can encourage some misunderstandings of the achievements of non-agricultural peoples and unquestionably lead to neglect of many (if thinly-populated) parts of the world. But these distortions can be compensated for in part through deliberate attention to areas outside the key civilization zones of east Asia, southern Asia, and western Asia, together with the Mediterranean. And they are further corrected by exploration of the accession, however belated, of additional areas to the ranks of agricultural economies.

The distortions involved in a focus on industrialization are harder to correct because they involve our own world and, indeed, raise questions about the future. The distinctions between industrialized and developing nations are real, but they can be oversimplified into patterns of success and failure. Furthermore, in this case the technologically advanced areas are not the most populous; too much attention to their achievements leaves out not only most of the world geographically, but the largest demographic segments as well. Distortions can be modified by using the late nineteenth and twentieth centuries, rather than the early nineteenth, as the key point of economic divide, so that industrialization is not simply a western model but a revolution that encompasses Russia and Japan as well. Further modification comes through using measurements more sophisticated than a developed/less-developed dichotomy for twentieth-century world history. Various strategies and levels of change in most of Asia, Latin America and Africa can be properly appreciated as part of a worldwide shift, still incomplete, toward accommodation to the dictates of industrialization. The fact remains that, as with the earlier agricultural transformation, this most basic periodization in world history does focus attention on the societies that led in change, and relatedly suggests a chronology for other societies in terms of the dates and extents of their catching up. The resultant picture is not entirely inaccurate, as leaders even of laggard societies (like those of northwestern Europe during the Middle Ages) have often recognized. But it is unduly monochromatic, and it can, for modern history, feed another set of student biases about the backwardness of the world's nonindustrialized majority.

A final objection to the agricultural-industrial revolution framework might be the eager assumption by futurologists like Toffler and even some more sober world historians that we are already embarked on yet another, comparable transformation toward a post-industrial stage. This model does not, I believe, work at a world history level and is dubious even within the context of western and Japanese societies.[4] While world history does allow some exploration of post-industrial assumptions, it need not build on them. Focusing on the nature, impact, and uneven development first of agricultural societies, then of industrial systems, suffices for an initial framework for world history that covers a roughly 11,000-year span and most definitely includes our own age.

Few world history courses, however, can rest on this simple, dichotomous periodization alone. They will want, in dealing with the history of the past two centuries, to do more with the human majority than note its lag in industrialization while merrily focusing on the West, the Soviet Union, Japan, and now a few other sections of East Asia's Pacific rim. They will seek to do more with human history 9000 B.C.–A.D. 1800 than to define the principal features of agricultural society and chronicle when each major part of the world began to adopt them by moving away from hunting and gathering. A world history course needs, in sum, a more elaborate periodization than can be provided by two transformations alone, one that can, among other things, more fully express the varieties possible within a basic agricultural or industrial framework.

The first level must not be neglected, however. Admitting the inadequacies of a technological systems periodization constitutes a challenge to improve and supplement, not to replace. It remains true that, however barebones the result, a world history student needs to know and understand this first periodization more than any other, precisely because so many essential aspects of the human experience are captured through it. In a genre of history that too often overkills with detail, so that simpler outlines are obscured beyond recall, this first chronological typology must continue to shine through as the least controvertible chronological organization of the global human experience.

Within the first framework, a number of subdivisions are possible. If only for want of recorded detail, a distinction must be made between the advent of agriculture and the development of civilization proper with its establishment of cities, writing, and more formal bureaucracies. Early civilizations, like the river-valley societies of Mesopotamia, Egypt, northwest India, and northern China, can be distinguished from the larger political organizations and culture zones generated by successor societies simply on grounds of scale of achievement and impact. When to date this divide can legitimately vary, particularly for China and Mesopotamia; separation between initial river-valley culture and a later classical civilization is clearer in India and the Mediterranean part of the Middle East and North Africa. But a periodization of some sort that moves from the establishment of agriculture, to early civilization, to a fuller and geographically more extensive classical civilization works well simply on grounds of increasing complexity. The fact that disagreements exist over precise timing — whether to flow from Shang to the middle Chou dynasty or to break earlier, whether to deal with the Vedic and Epic ages in India along with the Indus River civilization or to mark the divide with the Aryan invasions — may not matter greatly in terms of essential criteria. A periodization that moves from agriculture to early civilization to more elaborate expression can be applied also to later-comers, such as Central America or Russia, though with similar organizational disputes about when to demarcate each phase.

A somewhat more general schema, still working within the agricultural and industrial revolutions framework but extending further in time, involves the interrelated criteria of commercial contacts and the economic-cultural pecking order of major civilizations. This schema does not work well for the earliest civilizations when societies developed in considerable isolation, but it gains steadily in utility from about 500 B.C. onward — that is, from the point at which a categorization of formative stages begins to lose focus in the older centers of Asia and the Mediterranean.

The fact is, despite uneven development and periodic setbacks, commercial contacts among the major, established civilizations have increased fairly steadily since the establishment of Mediterranean and Indian Ocean networks. With commercial contacts has come a general, though still more uneven, tendency for heightened commercialization within the more sophisticated agricultural economies (and then, of course, the industrial economies from their inceptions). With increased commercial links have also come other kinds of technological and cultural diffusion and, finally, a series of particularly dynamic individual civilizations able to take special advantage of the patterns of diffusion and commercial exchange. From the final centuries before Christ until after the fall of the Guptas, India played a clear leadership role, sending out and receiving cultural influences from Greece and the Middle East, China, and Southeast Asia. Then the position of dominant trader and cultural diffuser was taken over by the Islamic Middle East and more recently still, after the extraordinary Mongol interlude and the brief Chinese surge, by the West. The partial eclipse of the West during our own century as monopolizer of international commercial exchange suggests again the utility of discussing the opening of a new, but as yet rather unclear, period in world history during the past fifty years.[5]

A periodization by stages of commercial exchange, each more elaborate and far-reaching than its predecessor, and each marked by a particularly dynamic leadership civilization, thus suggests a quadripartite chronological division after the long formative stages of civilization itself: 400 B.C. to about A.D. 500; 500 to 1500; 1500 to the twentieth century; and the later twentieth century onward. Each period was brought to a close amid some disarray caused by invasion and/or cultural decline (Gupta India and Arab Islam) and internal struggle (the wars of the twentieth-century West) within the leading trading society. Each succeeding period was marked not only by an increased overall level of international trade, but also by more extensive cultural diffusion (the spread of Islam vs. the earlier spread of Buddhist and Hindu forms) and by rising levels of internal commercialization. Increased exchange, urbanism, merchant influence, and money use thus marked not only the leading traders (India, then Islam, then the commercializing West) but also other participants such as China and Japan (e.g., the trade upsurge under the Tang and Sung and then what has been dubbed a commercial revolution under the Ming and early Ch'ing).[6] The evolving pattern of trade embraces, in other words, not only economic change but also important shifts in values, social structure, urbanism, and political potential.

This subordinate periodization works within the larger, simpler technological framework of the agricultural and industrial revolutions. It recognizes that, aside from a few important advances launched mainly in China, there were no huge technological shifts between the establishment of widespread agriculture and the eighteenth century — yet there was world historical change nevertheless within the context of agricultural societies and their mutual contacts. The periodization builds on and extends backward in time one of the most fruitful general theories for world history, that of Immanuel Wallerstein and his world economy schema.[7] The rise of a western, capitalist-dominated world economy here becomes the most recent and undeniably the most extensive version of a longer-standing pattern in which trading networks expanded and in which particular civilizations were able to seize a leadership role. The periodization correspondingly puts recent world history into a fuller time perspective. By this means we can see how the West's commercial and cultural power had precedents and how societies that provided raw materials to more dynamic centers and received cultural impulses back from them are not simply a creation of modern times. The periodization, including its utilization of a generalized version of the Wallerstein approach, also helps explain the industrial revolution itself by showing how increasingly commercialized agricultural economies and the West's ability to exploit wide markets provided the technical needs, funds, and value changes necessary to produce the most recent of humankind's two great transformations.

While periodization by levels of commercial exchange also has some key deficiencies, they can be repaired without destroying the schema itself. Until the rise of the West and to an extent until the nineteenth century, such periodization leaves out a good bit of the world. The Americas and much of sub-Saharan Africa played no role in expanding trade during the periods of Indian and Arab dynamism. These societies can nevertheless be discussed, but in terms of isolation and lag that need to be handled carefully. Northern Europe and Japan were also not seriously included during the first world trading period, a point which can be used to show how isolation and backwardness need not be permanent in world history. The fact remains that, like the great technological transformations, commercial contacts did not operate smoothly or evenly around the globe. While they do focus on much of what is important in world history, they cannot be used to cover everything.

Even in societies involved in extensive commercial exchange (including the Americas and sub-Saharan Africa after 1500, but also including East Asia until recently), relationship to leading international trading patterns can skew the terms of discussion. This fact has been used, correctly to a point, in criticisms of Wallerstein's grand system. Chinese history between 1500 and 1830 simply cannot be discussed mainly in terms of its relationship to the Western-dominated world economy. China's vigor, its changes and continuities, had little to do with the fact that it was falling relatively behind the West, though this lag describes Chinese history more accurately after 1830. Even clearly dependent (or for Wallerstein, peripheral) economies must not be seen simply as reactive to outside influence, a point made increasingly about African history[8] and valid for modern Latin America as well. It does remain possible to use a periodization based on commercial levels and commercial positions to set a general world framework and then turn to the equally important peculiarities of individual civilizations. The result balances some genuine world (or civilized-world) chronology against the separate dynamics, and partially separate periodization, of the world's main constituent parts. As with the larger chronology of basic technological transformations, it is most essential to emphasize the general pattern, but it is also important, once this is established, to deal with the nuances, the extent to which major cases partly escaped the general framework. This balancing is, finally, feasible for students, once they grasp that there is a core chronology that makes the operations of the parts not entirely disconnected or random.

A periodization based on commercial levels, working within the larger technological framework may, finally, encounter the objection of being too purely materialistic. It is certainly compatible with material explanations of history, though hardly tied to a single rigorous approach such as Marxism. And it does risk encouraging students to see artistic or other cultural developments as ephemera compared to the technical and economic substratum. What does it matter to know Africa's cultural and religious patterns, when Africa links to world history mainly through technological lag and then commercial dependency? How can China's rich cultural heritage be appreciated against the more readily-assimilated fact — the fact that more clearly links China to world history from the eighth to the nineteenth century — of a tendency toward isolation? It is, again, essential to balance general chronology against the characteristics of particular civilizations while not using them simply to explain different positions in the reigning world economy. But it is also possible to use a final world-historical periodization itself to bring cultural features into sharper relief.

This final, general periodization — the third layer — involves belief systems. It treats important cases of cultural diffusion, as in the spread of Islam, but it also rests on a wider typology. There have been, after all, only three major kinds of widely-accepted belief systems in world history, though hosts of variants on each, and each kind can be roughly located in time.

Animism set a context for beliefs about self, environment, and community in all early agricultural societies, and its impetus continued into most early civilizations. Exploring the functions and logic of animism and its varieties across space and time is an essential introduction into early religious systems, but also into wider worldviews at both elite and popular levels. The evolution of animistic beliefs in societies like India and China (Chou dynasty efforts to refine prayer and sacrifice, for example) can introduce internal periodization into the early cultural history of the civilized world. At various points, but especially between the spread of Buddhism and the introduction of Islam, monotheisms — the world's second great belief system — began to cut into the animistic approach, though typically with long periods of compromise and of elite-mass divisions. This second great phase in the history of mentalities allows exploration of the wider ramifications of monotheism compared to its predecessors: monotheism extended standardized cultures over earlier regional variants, increased the separation between man and nature, and created new intellectual and emotional motivations for morality. Obviously, here, too, varieties among the great religions and their evolution over time permit internal differentiation without violating the first cut at a worldwide cultural periodization.

Finally, over the past three centuries (but with some earlier precedent, e.g., Confucianism in China) a series of secular faiths — socialism, nationalism, and indeed, recent consumerism — have in many societies displaced or modified the framework of monotheism, often with a heightened valuation of science as a backdrop.[9] As with earlier mentalities change, remnants of previous beliefs persist, even in apparently secularized cultures, and great variations have developed in the extent of secularization (Middle East vs. Eastern Europe) and among the possible secular emphases.

A general periodization that distinguishes chronologically among the major belief systems is highlighted by the cultural crises that often preceded a key transformation. Cultural turmoil in the Mediterranean world before Christianity spread widely, or in the Middle East before Islam, or, again, in the eleventh through the thirteenth centuries before the rural popularization of Islam, or in the West between the sixteenth and eighteenth centuries are crucial cases in point. The same kind of transition period (and other cases, such as the transformation of Hinduism under the impact of Muslim competition) can also be defined in terms of new relationships between a literate elite and the illiterate (or in modern times, less-literate) masses. Watersheds, in other words, are not sterile markers in a cultural progression but offer real and complex drama that helps define belief systems or amalgams on either side of the divide. In some cases, this drama extends across the boundaries of civilizations, as in the general turn to otherworldly monotheisms under the impact of the barbarian invasions between the third and sixth centuries[10] or the West's challenge to both animism and monotheism in societies like the Americas or sub-Saharan Africa from the sixteenth century onward.

Cultural periodization, as with periodization based on technology and commerce, has its drawbacks. Latin America and sub-Saharan Africa again fit into world patterns but with a pronounced delay which not only complicates a worldwide chronology but tempts dismissal of these important societies as irredeemable laggards. The full transition to monotheism is a major facet in African history still today, and it can be explored with many analogies to earlier transitions in the Middle East or Europe. Parts of East Asia fit slightly uncomfortably into the threefold cultural periodization; the distinctiveness of Confucian values, in an otherwise "monotheistic" period in world history, needs separate comment though Daoism and the Buddhist impact, as well as ongoing popular animism, fit the larger pattern of change and continuity. Indeed, Confucian and government attacks on popular cultural traditions show close resemblance to Western elite attacks between the seventeenth and eighteenth centuries, prior to a fuller secularization in each case.[11] Still, the need to adapt a valid but schematic chronology to specific cases remains a key tension in world history. This flexibility is all the more necessary given the unusual duration of transition points, particularly in the impact of significant challenges to animism at the popular level in virtually all civilizations.

Still, the idea of cultural transitions in a recognizable basic pattern adds substantially to the framework set by technological and commercial transitions. Monotheism develops within agricultural societies but is not an inevitable product thereof (quite apart from major variations among specific monotheistic religions), and while monotheism relates to commercial contacts and merchant classes, it is no automatic result of some set phase of commercial development. Robin Horton has shown that an expansion of contacts with a wider world — the logical result of commercial growth, though also possible through new political links — encourages monotheism, at least in Africa, by heightening interest in a supreme being who has already been seen to have wider organizational power than the local spirits.[12] This important link with commercial growth (which can be developed for other societies in prior centuries) does not, however, predict the exact timing or extent of a shift to monotheism, or, of course, the variety of monotheism preferred. Again, cultural variables have their own power, even if they do not operate in full isolation from commercial or technological factors.

More obvious links exist between the secular faiths and industrialization and rising commerce, as these cut into traditional community forms and produce new kinds of elites, but here, too, ideology has an independent power and may precede key technological and economic change or impede such change.

In turn, discussion of belief systems for the modern era is essential to maintain a sense of the cultural dimension. The second half of world history courses often play this aspect down in favor of economic development and issues of power politics. A third-tier periodization based on mentalities is a vital but also accurate means of maintaining a cultural theme commonly emphasized for the earlier stages of world history. The point is that the technological, commercial, and cultural periodizations provide three distinct, if related, vantagepoints on social change that describe patterns and contacts on an ultimately global basis. Without usurping the separate civilizational characteristics, the tripartite basis for world history chronology conveys vital facets of any human society, covering key changes in popular as well as elite history and describing as well vital contacts and power relations among the major civilizations. Obviously, other social institutions and behaviors must still be inserted into the framework. As noted above, political institutions, though not yet susceptible to a global periodization of their own, save perhaps in some commonsense generalizations about tendencies toward bureaucratic growth, must not be omitted in a periodization not in the first instance political. The nature of the state relates to technological and commercial activity and also to changes in beliefs; empires helped prepare the spread of monotheism, while the rise of secular faiths has crucially altered the concept of political loyalty, especially at the popular level. All three kinds of change — technological, commercial, and ideological — also set conditions for global diplomatic relations at all points, including the decades of western imperialism. The history of science, although a subordinate theme during most of world history and unquestionably a variable among civilizations, can also be fit into a periodization established by technological level and commerce as well as belief systems. Social structure, deriving first from technology, is more precisely shaped by commercial levels and beliefs, though, again, with more detailed variants according to specific civilizations and their own chronological schedules. A tripartite periodization schema, in sum, sets a stage for exploring equally important but less sweeping or less consistent factors in world history as well as encouraging more detailed inquiry into specific civilizational patterns. The schema also allows a teacher to play, on a world history stage but with concrete cases in point, on the tensions between structural determinism, large cultural trends, and civilizational diversities that replicate some of the key issues in contemporary historical thought, especially under the impetus of social history.[13]

Notes

1. Peter N. Stearns, *World History: Patterns of Change and Continuity* (New York, 1987).

2. Alvin Toffler, *The Third Wave* (New York, 1981); L.S. Stavrianos, *The Promise of the Coming Dark Age* (New York, 1976).

3. P. Hudson, *Third World Women Speak Out* (New York, 1979); Ester Boserup, *Women and Economic Modernization* (London, 1970). For an ambitious but badly flawed account, attempting a world survey of women's history, see Gerda Lerner, *The Creation of Patriarchy* (New York, 1986).

4. Daniel Bell, *The Coming of Post-Industrial Society* (New York, 1974); J. H. Servan-Schreiber, *The Knowledge Revolution* (Pittsburgh, 1986).

5. Geoffrey Barraclough, *An Introduction to Contemporary History* (New York, 1968).

6. William T. Rowe, "Approaches to Modern Chinese Social History," in *Reliving the Past: The Worlds of Social History*, ed. Olivier Zunz (Chapel Hill, N.C., 1985), 236–98.

7. Immanuel Wallerstein, *The Modern World System*, 2 vols. (New York, 1980); for an excellent introduction to teaching from Wallerstein, see Craig Lockard, "Global History, Modernization, and the World-System Approach: A Critique," *The History Teacher* 14 (1981): 489–515.

A recent article by William H. McNeill ("Organizing Concepts for World History," review essay, *World History Bulletin* 4 [1986–87]: 1–4) somewhat relatedly stresses the advent of a new ecumene around 1000 A.D., based in part on new trade levels. This fruitful concept is, however, consistent with a somewhat more graded periodization, for McNeill in this article moves rather starkly from the advent of agriculture to the coming of the ecumene with no particular dividing lines in between or after.

8. David William Cohen, "Doing Social History from Pim's Doorway," in Zunz, *Reliving the Past*, 191–235.

9. D. G. Carleton, *Secular Religions in France, 1815–1870* (London, 1963).

10. William H. McNeill, *A World History*, 3d ed. (New York, 1979), 194–210.

11. Donald Sutton, "Pilot Surveys of Chinese Shamans, 1875–1945," *Journal of Social History* 15 (1981): 39–50; James L. Watson, "Standardizing the Gods: The Promotion of T'ien Hou ('Empress of Heaven') Along the South China Coast, 960–1960," *Popular Culture in Late Imperial China*, ed. David Johnson, Andrew Nathan, and Evelyn Rawski (Berkeley, Calif., 1985), 292–324; Keith Thomas, *Religion and the Decline of Magic* (New York, 1971); Robert Muchembled, *Popular Culture and Elite Culture in France, 1500–1750* (Baton Rouge, La., 1983); Walter Ong, *Orality and Literacy: The Technology of the World* (London, 1982).

12. Robin Horton, "African Conversion," *Africa* (1971): 85–108; and "On the Rationality of Conversion," *Africa* (1975): 220.

13. James Henretta, "Social History as Lived and Written," *American Historical Review* 89 (1975): 1293–1322.

JERRY H. BENTLEY

Cross-Cultural Interaction and Periodization in World History

Periodization ranks among the more elusive tasks of historical scholarship. As practicing historians well know, the identification of coherent periods of history involves much more than the simple discovery of self-evident turning points in the past: it depends on prior decisions about the issues and processes that are most important for the shaping of human societies, and it requires the establishment of criteria or principles that enable historians to sort through masses of information and recognize patterns of continuity and change. Even within the framework of a single society, changes in perspective can call the coherence of conventionally recognized periods into question, as witness Joan Kelly's famous essay "Did Women Have a Renaissance?" or Dietrich Gerhard's concept of "old Europe."[1]

Jerry H. Bentley, "Cross-Cultural Interaction and Periodization in World History," *American Historical Review* 101 (June 1996): 749–56.

When historians address the past from global points of view and examine processes that cross the boundary lines of societies and cultural regions, the problems of periodization become even more acute. Historians have long realized that periodization schemes based on the experiences of Western or any other particular civilization do a poor job of explaining the trajectories of other societies. To cite a single notorious example, the categories of ancient, medieval, and modern history, derived from European experience, apply awkwardly at best to the histories of China, India, Africa, the Islamic world, or the Western hemisphere — quite apart from the increasingly recognized fact that they do not even apply very well to European history.[2] As historians take global approaches to the past and analyze human experiences from broad and comparative perspectives, however, questions of periodization present themselves with increasing insistence. To what extent is it possible to identify periods that are both meaningful and coherent across the boundary lines of societies and cultural regions? What criteria or principles might help historians to sort out patterns of continuity and change and to distinguish such periods?[3]

This essay suggests that efforts at global periodization might profit by examining participation of the world's peoples in processes transcending individual societies and cultural regions. From remote times to the present, cross-cultural interactions have had significant political, social, economic, and cultural ramifications for all peoples involved. Thus it stands to reason that processes of cross-cultural interaction might have some value for purposes of identifying historical periods from a global point of view. Moreover, with cross-cultural interactions as their criteria, historians might better avoid ethnocentric periodizations that structure the world's past according to the experiences of some particular privileged people. Scholars increasingly recognize that history is the product of interactions involving all the world's peoples.[4] By focusing on processes of cross-cultural interaction, historians might more readily identify patterns of continuity and change that reflect the experiences of many peoples rather than impose on all a periodization derived from the experiences of a privileged few.

Two caveats about the periodization proposed here deserve some consideration. In the first place, a periodization based on cross-cultural interaction cannot pretend to embrace literally all of the world at all times. For most of history, the Eastern hemisphere, the Western hemisphere, and Oceania were largely self-contained regions whose peoples encountered each other infrequently and sporadically, if at all. Within each of the three regions, however, cross-cultural interactions took place regularly and shaped the experiences of all peoples involved. The understanding of early interactions is particularly strong for Eurasia and much of Africa, so that the cross-cultural interactions serve well as the basis for periodization in much of the Eastern hemisphere even before modern times. From the sixteenth century forward, cross-cultural interactions provide a foundation for a genuinely global periodization of world history.

In the second place, global periodizations do not represent the only useful or appropriate frames for historical analysis. It goes without saying that developments internal to individual societies — such as the building of states, social structures, and cultural traditions — have profoundly and directly influenced the historical experiences of the lands and peoples involved. (Of course, these "internal" developments have generally taken place within a much larger context that helps to account for local experiences.) Moreover, different peoples have participated in large-scale processes to different degrees, so global periodizations often chart historical development in approximate rather than finely calibrated fashion. Thus global periodizations must allow for alternatives that are sensitive to the nuances of local experiences. Peter Brown's concept of "late antiquity," for example, has great power for the effort to understand historical development in the Mediterranean basin and Southwest Asia, even if it does not resonate on a hemispheric or global scale.[5] Periodizations of individual lands and particular regions will often be more subtle and specific than global periodizations, since they have the potential to reflect more accurately local patterns of continuity and change. Thus, while striving to understand historical development on the large scale, global historians must acknowledge that their periodizations do not always apply equally well to all the lands and regions that they ostensibly embrace.

Nevertheless, global periodizations have their place in contemporary historical scholarship. To the extent that historians consider it valuable to examine the past from global and comparative points of view, they need to identify periods of history that coherently situate historical development in large geographical and cultural contexts. Moreover, global periodizations also have the potential to establish pertinent larger contexts for the understanding of local and regional experiences. For purposes of constructing these global periodizations, the analysis of cross-cultural interactions and their results holds rich promise.

When dealing with the past five centuries, efforts at global periodization clearly must take cross-cultural interactions into account. Since the year 1492, the regions of the world have come into permanent and sustained contact with each other, and cross-cultural interactions have profoundly influenced the experiences of all peoples on earth. Legions of scholars have examined the effects of cross-cultural interactions in modern times while exploring themes such as long-distance trade, exchanges of plants, animals, and diseases, transfers of technology, imperial and colonial ventures, missionary campaigns, the transatlantic slave trade, and the development of global capitalism.[6]

For earlier periods, however, it might seem that founding a global periodization on cross-cultural interactions stretches a point beyond usefulness. Granting that the world's peoples did not live in isolated, hermetically sealed societies until 1492, it remains a legitimate question whether cross-cultural interactions were intensive and extensive enough to provide frameworks for periodization in pre-modern times. It is a reasonable concern, for example, that a periodization founded on cross-cultural interaction might accord undue privileges to that tiny fraction of humanity that undertook long-distance travel or that otherwise became directly engaged in cross-cultural interactions in pre-modern times.

Yet, even in pre-modern times, processes of cross-cultural interaction had implications that went far beyond the experiences of the individuals who took part in them. Three kinds of processes in particular had significant repercussions across the boundary lines of societies and cultural regions: mass migrations, campaigns of imperial expansion, and long-distance trade. Mass migrations had the potential to bring about political, social, economic, and cultural transformations in the lands they touched. The migrations of Indo-European, Bantu, Germanic, Turkish, Slavic, and Mongol peoples all worked profound effects across the boundary lines of societies and cultural regions. These migrations touched almost every corner of the Eastern hemisphere before modern times. Meanwhile, the migrations of ancient Siberian and Austronesian peoples led to the establishment of human societies in the Western hemisphere and the Pacific islands.

Alongside migrations, empire building also influenced historical development across the boundary lines of societies and cultural regions. The establishment of large-scale empires did not necessarily imply the extension of close, centralized supervision to all lands and peoples falling within imperial boundaries. "Heaven is high, and the emperor is far away," according to a Chinese proverb, which acknowledged a degree of *de facto* independence enjoyed by local and regional authorities of pre-modern empires. Even in the absence of effective central supervision, however, pre-modern empire building deeply influenced human societies. Quite apart from the imposition of foreign rule and taxes on conquered peoples, imperial expansion also favored the establishment of commercial and diplomatic relations between distant peoples, as well as the spread of cultural traditions.

Granting the importance of mass migrations and imperial conquests, questions might still remain about the significance of long-distance trade in pre-modern times. Traditional wisdom holds that long-distance trade in pre-modern times dealt largely if not exclusively with luxury goods of high value relative to their bulk. Traffic in such goods might make for a fascinating topic of inquiry, since it sheds light on the ingenuity of merchants and the development of markets. Nevertheless, so the traditional wisdom suggests, trade in luxury goods had limited significance for pre-modern social and economic history for several reasons: it involved a tiny proportion of the populations of producing and consuming societies, it mainly affected political and economic elites, and it did not generate a division of labor or otherwise restructure the economies and societies of trading parties.[7]

Recent research has called much of this received wisdom into question and has suggested that long-distance trade had more important effects than scholars have commonly realized. This research represents several lines of thought. One comes from the perspective of economic anthropology and draws attention to the cultural and political significance of pre-modern trade in luxury commodities. Even though trade in preciosities directly involved only small numbers of people, it involved some very important people. Apart from their economic value, exotic commodities often served as symbols of power, status, and authority. The ability to display them, consume them, or bestow them on others was crucial for the establishment and maintenance of political and social structures. Thus, even when its economic value was small, trade in luxury goods often had large political and social implications. Kingfisher feathers, tortoise shells, and rhinoceros horns might strike modern analysts as commodities of little economic significance. In pre-modern China, however, the rarity of such items conferred on them high value, which ruling elites appropriated as symbols of power, status, and authority. To the extent that trade in exotic items figured in the establishment or maintenance of political authority, it was a very important affair, regardless of its economic significance.[8]

A second line of argument emerges from studies of cross-regional commerce. It suggests that even when long-distance trade had its origins in the exchange of preciosities, it had the potential to expand rapidly and develop into bulk trade affecting large numbers of people rather than just political and economic elites. An example of this sort of development comes from trade in Buddhist paraphernalia between India and China. Buddhism reached China by the second century B.C.E., but it did not become a popular faith there until the late fifth and sixth centuries C.E. The growth of a Chinese Buddhist community generated high demand for exotic commodities such as coral, pearls, gems, crystals, semi-precious stones, glass, incense, and ivory, as well as symbolic items (such as statues or representations of the Wheel of the Law) used in Buddhist rituals or as decorations for stupas and monasteries. By the sixth century C.E., this demand had stimulated a high volume of trade in commodities that during earlier centuries had figured as luxury goods traded only in small quantities.[9] Quite apart from the cultural and political significance of the spread of Buddhism to China, this trade had important economic effects in both India and China.

A third line of research suggests that pre-modern trade occasionally became voluminous enough to push large regions toward economic integration and thus to shape economic and social structures across the boundary lines of societies and cultural regions. The Indian Ocean basin represents the most important case in which trade encouraged the economic integration of an especially large region in pre-modern times. By the seventh century C.E., large numbers of Persian merchants, soon followed by Arabs, ventured throughout the Indian Ocean basin from East Africa to India and beyond to Southeast Asia and China. By the tenth century, trade generated enormous revenues in port cities throughout the basin. More important, this trade was by no means limited to luxury goods but also involved heavy and bulky commodities. Cargoes of dates, sugar, building supplies, coral, timber, and steel crossed the ocean in large quantities. (Often, they did double duty, serving both as ballast during voyages and as marketable commodities in port cities.) As trade linked the lands of the Indian Ocean basin, comparative advantages encouraged the organization of large and sophisticated regional industries: silk textiles in China and India, cotton textiles in India, ceramics in China, steel and iron production in China, India, and Southwest Asia, and the breeding of horses, cattle, and camels by nomadic and pastoral peoples in Central Asia, Southwest Asia, and Arabia. Thus, far from being an economically insignificant affair involving exchanges of luxuries between elites, long-distance trade in the Indian Ocean helped structure economies and societies in the various regions of the Indian Ocean basin.[10]

When pre-modern societies engaged in long-distance trade on a regular and systematic basis, trade routes not only facilitated the transportation and exchange of commodities, they also served as avenues of technological and biological diffusions. In some cases, these diffusions profoundly influenced the development of societies engaged in trade, which suggests a fourth reason for the significance of long-distance trade in pre-modern times. Technologies involving transportation, metallurgy, weaponry, animal energy, and natural sources of power all diffused throughout most of Eurasia and Africa, largely along trade routes. Meanwhile, long-distance trade and campaigns of imperial expansion sometimes combined to encourage biological diffusions in pre-modern times. During the half-millennium from about 600 to 1100 C.E., for example, Islamic conquests and trade in the Islamic world sponsored a remarkable diffusion of food and industrial crops throughout much of the Eastern hemisphere, resulting in population growth and increased production from China to Europe and North Africa. Similarly, during the era of the ancient silk roads and again during the age of the Mongol empires, traffic over long-distance trade networks facilitated the spread of lethal pathogens beyond their original homes, leading to disease epidemics in much of Eurasia.[11]

Finally, besides its political, social, economic, and biological significance, long-distance trade also had implications for cultural and religious change in pre-modern times. When merchants traded regularly across the boundary lines of societies and cultural regions, they established diaspora communities and brought cultural and religious authorities from their homelands into those communities for their own purposes. Their cultural and religious traditions sometimes attracted interest among their hosts, particularly when foreign merchants came from a well-organized society possessing the capacity to provide significant political, diplomatic, military, or economic benefits for their hosts. In several notable cases, the voluntary association of individuals with the cultural and religious traditions of foreign merchants helped to launch processes of large-scale conversion, by which societies made a place for foreign cultural or religious values. Merchants played prominent roles, for example, in the processes that led to the establishment of Hinduism and Buddhism in Southeast Asia, of Buddhism, Manichaeism, and Nestorian Christianity in Central Asia, and of Islam in Southeast Asia and sub-Saharan Africa.[12]

Thus recent research has made a persuasive case for the significance of long-distance trade, even in pre-modern times. Pre-modern trade did not wield an influence approaching that of cross-cultural commerce in modern and contemporary times. In combination with processes of mass migration and imperial expansion, however, it is clear that long-distance trade had strong potential to shape historical experiences across the boundary lines of societies and cultural regions even in pre-modern times. To the extent that mass migration, imperial expansion, and long-distance trade engaged peoples of different societies in significant cross-cultural interactions, these interactions might serve as a basis for the periodization of world history in pre-modern as well as modern times.

The remainder of this essay will outline a periodization of world history consisting of six major eras distinguished principally by differing dynamics of cross-cultural interactions that worked their effects across the boundary lines of societies and cultural regions. The six eras are: an age of early complex societies (3500–2000 B.C.E.), an age of ancient civilizations (2000–500 B.C.E.), an age of classical civilizations (500 B.C.E.–500 C.E.), a post-classical age (500–1000 C.E.), and age of transregional nomadic empires (1000–1500 C.E.), and a modern age (1500 C.E. to the present).

Notes

1. Joan Kelly-Gadol, "Did Women Have a Renaissance?" orig. pub. in Renate Bridenthal and Claudia Koonz, eds., *Becoming Visible: Women in European History* (Boston, 1977), 137–64; rpt. in Joan Kelly, *Women, History and Theory: The Essays of Joan Kelly* (Chicago, 1984), 19–50. Dietrich Gerhard, *Old Europe: A Study of Continuity, 1000–1800* (New York, 1981).

2. On the last point, see Gerhard, *Old Europe*; and C. Warren Hollister, "The Phases of European History and the Nonexistence of the Middle Ages," *Pacific Historical Review* 61 (1992): 1–22.

3. Several scholars have already offered thoughtful reflections on periodization from a global point of view. Some explicitly argue or implicitly assume that human societies evolve in reasonably similar fashion, so that periodization depends on the identification of stages that all societies pass through. Apart from the large body of Marxist evolutionary scholarship, see, for example, Robert McC. Adams, *The Evolution of Urban Society: Early Mesopotamia and Prehispanic Mexico* (Chicago, 1966). Others have proposed hemispheric and global cycles as foundations for periodization: see Andre Gunder Frank, "A Theoretical Introduction to 5,000 Years of World System History," *Review* 13 (1990): 155–248; and the essays in Andre Gunder Frank and Barry K. Gills, eds., *The World System: Five Hundred Years or Five Thousand?* (London, 1993). Yet others envision periodizations based to some extent on cross-cultural interactions: see Ross E. Dunn, "Periodization and Chronological Coverage in a World History Survey," in Josef W. Konvitz, ed., *What Americans Should Know: Western Civilization or World History? Proceedings of a Conference at Michigan State University, April 21–23, 1985* (East Lansing, Mich., 1985), 129–40; Peter N. Stearns, "Periodization in World History Teaching: Identifying the Big Changes," *History Teacher* 20 (1987): 561–80; and William A. Green, "Periodization in European and World History," *Journal of World History* 3 (1992): 13–53. See also William A. Green, "Periodizing World History," *History and Theory* 34 (1995): 99–111. William H. McNeill, *The Rise of the West: A History of the Human Community* (Chicago, 1963), does not address the issue of periodization directly but nonetheless contributes to its understanding by offering an integrated history of the world from a global point of view. See also McNeill's reflections on *"The Rise of the West* after Twenty-Five Years," *Journal of World History* 1 (1990): 1–21. This essay draws inspiration from the contributions cited above, and it seeks to complement them by proposing a principle for identifying coherent periods of history from a global point of view.

4. A few examples of recent works that nicely illustrate this point about the modern world: Mechal Sobel, *The World They Made Together: Black and White Values in Eighteenth-Century Virginia* (Princeton, N.J., 1987); John E. Wills, Jr., "Maritime Asia, 1500–1800: The Interactive Emergence of European Domination," *American Historical Review* 98 (February 1993): 83–105; Edward W. Said, *Culture and Imperialism* (New York, 1993); Ronald T. Takaki, *A Different Mirror: A History of Multicultural America* (Boston, 1993); and Paul Gilroy, *The Black Atlantic: Modernity and Double Consciousness* (Cambridge, Mass., 1993).

5. Of Peter Brown's many thoughtful and penetrating works, see especially *The World of Late Antiquity, A.D. 150–750* (London, 1971); and *The Making of Late Antiquity* (Cambridge, Mass., 1978). In the form of mass migrations, of course, cross-cultural interactions were a prominent feature of late antiquity. In his own work, however, Brown has concentrated on the cultural and religious history of the Mediterranean basin, and to a lesser extent of Southwest Asia, without placing the experiences of those regions in a larger Eurasian or hemispheric context and without directly addressing the theme of cross-cultural interaction.

6. See, among others, Philip D. Curtin, *Cross-Cultural Trade in World History* (New York, 1984); Daniel R. Headrick, *The Tentacles of Progress: Technology Transfer in the Age of Imperialism, 1850–1940* (New York, 1988); Immanuel Wallerstein, *The Modern World-System*, 3 vols. (New York, 1974–89); Eric R. Wolf, *Europe and the People without History* (Berkeley, Calif., 1982); William H. McNeill, *Plagues and Peoples* (Garden City, N.Y., 1976); and two works by Alfred W. Crosby, *The Columbian Exchange: Biological and Cultural Consequences of 1492* (Westport, Conn., 1972); and *Ecological Imperialism: The Biological Expansion of Europe, 900–1900* (New York, 1986).

7. There are works that take long-distance trade seriously even in pre-modern times: see especially Curtin, *Cross-Cultural Trade in World History*; and C. G. F. Simkin, *The Traditional Trade of Asia* (London, 1968). For several works that in various ways express the view that early long-distance trade was an enterprise of limited significance — and that do so from radically different perspectives — see Wallerstein, *Modern World-System*, 1:19–21, 39–42; W. W. Rostow, *How It All Began: Origins of the Modern Economy* (New York, 1975), 14–15; Rondo Cameron, *A Concise Economic History of the World: From Paleolithic Times to the Present* (New York, 1989), 32–33, 78, 121–22; and Patricia Crone, *Pre-Industrial Societies* (Oxford, 1989), 22–24, 33–34. In the interests of fairness and precision, I would like to point out that these authors do not absolutely deny the significance of early long-distance trade: Cameron, for example, holds that it helped to integrate the economy of the Mediterranean basin under the Roman empire. In all cases, however, these authors and others convey the clear impression that long-distance trade was not an activity of large economic significance until modern times.

8. See Jane Schneider, "Was There a Pre-capitalist World System?" *Peasant Studies* 6 (1977): 20–29; and Robert McC. Adams, "Anthropological Perspectives on Ancient Trade," *Current Anthropology* 15 (1974): 239–58. For broader analyses along similar lines, see also Mary W. Helms, *Ulysses' Sail: An Ethnographic Odyssey of Power, Knowledge, and Geographical Distance* (Princeton, N.J., 1988); and Nicholas Thomas, *Entangled Objects: Exchange, Material Culture, and Colonialism in the Pacific* (Cambridge, Mass., 1991). On the political significance of long-distance trade in early Southeast Asia, see Kenneth R. Hall, *Maritime Trade and State Development in Early Southeast Asia* (Honolulu, 1985). On the taste for exotic commodities and the uses made of them in pre-modern China, see especially two volumes of Edward H. Schafer, *The Golden Peaches of Samarkand: A Study of T'ang Exotics* (Berkeley, Calif., 1963); and *The Vermilion Bird: T'ang Images of the South* (Berkeley, 1967).

9. It is impossible to calculate the value of this trade, but literary and archaeological sources make it clear that by the sixth century C.E., trade in Buddhist paraphernalia had become quite large. See Wang Gungwu, *The Nanhai Trade: A Study of the Early History of Chinese Trade in the South China Sea* (Kuala Lumpur, 1958); and Liu Xinru, *Ancient India and Ancient China: Trade and Religious Exchanges*, A.D. 1–600 (Delhi, 1988).

10. On the economic integration of the Indian Ocean basin, see especially two recent volumes of K. N. Chaudhuri, *Trade and Civilization in the Indian Ocean: An Economic History from the Rise of Islam to 1750* (Cambridge, 1985); and *Asia before Europe: Economy and Civilization of the Indian Ocean from the Rise of Islam to 1750* (Cambridge, 1990). See also George F. Hourani, *Arab Seafaring in the Indian Ocean in Ancient and Early Medieval Times* (Princeton, N.J., 1951); the first volume, with four additional volumes projected, of André Wink, *"Al-Hind": The Making of the Indo-Islamic World* (Leiden, 1990); and an article in which Wink outlines his larger vision of the Indian Ocean basin, "'Al-Hind': India and Indonesia in the Islamic World-Economy, c. 700–1800 A.D.," *Itinerario* 12 (1988): 33–72.

11. On the diffusion of technologies, see Arnold Pacey, *Technology in World Civilization: A Thousand-Year History* (Oxford, 1990); Richard W. Bulliet, *The Camel and the Wheel* (Cambridge, Mass., 1975); and Lynn White, Jr., *Medieval Technology and Social Change* (Oxford, 1962). On biological diffusions, see McNeill, *Plagues and Peoples*; Crosby, *Ecological Imperialism*; Andrew M. Watson, *Agricultural Innovation in the Early Islamic World: The Diffusion of Crops and Farming Techniques, 700–1100* (Cambridge, 1983); and Lynda N. Shaffer, "Southernization," *Journal of World History* 5 (1994): 1–21.

12. See Jerry H. Bentley, *Old World Encounters: Cross-Cultural Contacts and Exchanges in Pre-Modern Times* (New York, 1993), which examines cases of conversion encouraged by the voluntary association of host peoples with the cultural and religious traditions of foreign merchants.

WILLIAM A. GREEN

Periodizing World History

Periodization is both the product and the begetter of theory. The organizing principles upon which we write history, the priorities we assign to various aspects of human endeavor, and the theories of change we adopt to explain the historical process: all are represented in periodization. Once firmly established, periodization exerts formidable, often subliminal, influence on the refinement and elaboration of theory.

The ancient/medieval/modern formula currently in use had its origins in Italian humanist thinking, but acceptance of this tripartite model did not be-

William A. Green, "Periodizing World History," *History and Theory* 34 (May 1995): 99–107, 109–11.

come universal until the nineteenth century. Since then, tripartite periodization has griped Western academe like a straitjacket, determining how we organize departments of history, train graduate students, form professional societies, and publish many of our best professional journals. It pervades our habits of mind; it defines turf; it generates many of the abstractions that sustain professional discourse. It determines how we retain images and how we perceive the beginning, middle, and ending of things. It is insidious, and it is sustained by powerful vested interests as well as by sheer inertia.

Scholars who endeavor to formulate an acceptable periodization for world history confront far fewer practical obstacles than those who would seek to alter period frontiers in European history or in other established regional histories. World historians encounter neither an entrenched scheme of epochal divisions nor the dead weight of inertia. There is still a comparatively small professional literature self-consciously addressed to the global perspective. World history has only recently emerged as a field of concentration in a few Ph.D. programs. Consequently, there is not a large and well-established graduate faculty committed by training and tradition to a particular mode of periodization, nor are there commonly acknowledged chronological parameters — fields of preparation for comprehensive examinations — that have imposed a standard epochal division upon the field.

An important practical consideration in periodizing world history involves audience. Our primary audience is university students (usually first- or second-year undergraduates), and the chief vehicle for transmitting world history is the textbook. For practical pedagogical reasons, we are compelled to seek reasonable symmetry in our periodization, even though there are vast discrepancies in the availability of historical data for different eras and for different regions of the globe.

How we periodize world history will be influenced by our objectives in teaching the subject. World historians attempt to explain how human societies have been transformed from bands of hunters and gatherers to the types of people we are today. Even today, in an age of space exploration, hunters and gatherers survive in remote regions of the world. The organizational problems created by such diversity of human experience have occasioned different strategic approaches to writing world history.

One approach provides an integrated mainstream treatment of world history. Another emphasizes regional diversity. The integrated approach routinely focuses on the most developed and complex societies, their ups, their downs, their interactions with one another, and their troubled encounters with less complex peoples. This approach devotes paramount attention to Eurasia. Sub-Saharan Africa, pre-Columbian America, and Australasia are less heralded and, for long stretches of time, they pass largely unnoticed. Integrated mainstream world history enables historians to employ common engines of change to explain the historical process, thereby facilitating the identification of universal epochal frontiers.

Regional strategy embraces more of the world's peoples for longer periods of time whether those peoples functioned within the evolutionary mainstream or at some distance from centers of civilization. Conceived as a congeries of regional histories, this approach to world history emphasizes intercultural understanding and carries less risk of offending political sensitivities. Those who advocate a region-by-region approach are able to argue that for most of human history, really significant interaction between major world civilizations was limited and, for the most part, inconsequential. Because rates of change differ from one region to another, the regional approach discourages the use of overarching theories of change that would facilitate the adoption of universal epochal frontiers.

The burden of proof in these matters rests with the integrationists. They must demonstrate that, from an early time, the destinies of the world's peoples (or at least some significant portion of the world's peoples) have been linked. It must be shown that engines of change operating globally have been *decisive* in propelling both the rate and the direction of change across diverse and distant cultures. Unless integrationist theory is convincing on this question, a fragmented, region-by-region approach to writing (and to periodizing) world history might be the most expedient approach.

In this regard, America presents the integrationist with a significant problem. Major civilizations thrived in four regions of the Eastern Hemisphere several thousand years before the rise of an equally complex civilization in America. Lasting interactions between all the continents did not begin until after 1492. There may have been common experiences within each of the hemispheres; but, prior to 1492, history at its grandest level could only be hemispheric. A completely integrated world history is only possible after the hemispheres were in permanent contact. Unless one wishes to deny that pre-Columbian America constitutes a significant component of the human experience, some degree of fragmentation in writing and periodizing global history is inescapable.

Ideally, all periodizations should be rooted in disciplined concepts of continuity and change. Historical epochs should exhibit important long-term continuities, and moments of transition between epochs should involve the dissolution of old continuities and the forging of new ones. We must identify how powerful historical forces interacted to generate particular forms of change at particular velocities. To do this, we need a theory of change. A single general theory may suffice if we are confident that the paramount forces governing change in the social organism have been constant across the millennia. If the paramount forces of change have varied from region to region or from one age to another, no single theory will suffice. In that case, we must adjust our theory to accommodate the changes we perceive in historical circumstances. European history provides an example. A neo-Malthusian demographic model has been adopted by numerous historians to explain developments during Europe's medieval period. The utility of the model declines steeply for the eighteenth and nineteenth centuries when rapid expansion of commerce, technology, and industry raised per-capita productivity, thereby diminishing the menace of repeated positive checks.

We cannot hope to be value-free in our formulation of theory. Our theories reflect our priorities. Medieval writers assigned God a directing hand in history. Their epochal divisions were drawn at dramatic moments of divine intervention. Marx disdained concepts of divine intervention, insisting that human action has always been driven by material forces. More than any other thinker, Marx established priorities for the twentieth century. Other writers have developed alternative theories of change (often in response to Marx), but all, or nearly all, have agreed on the central importance of material forces.

Until now, the identification of period frontiers has generally taken two forms. One focuses on a coincidence of forces, the other on a leading sector. The coincidental approach identifies the convergence of numerous important developments at a single moment in history. The *circa* 1500 C.E. watershed in Western tripartite periodization rests largely on this type of observation. In the decades around 1500 numerous important events converged: the Ptolemaic perception of the universe was challenged, printing and gunpowder achieved importance, Columbus reached America and DaGama sailed to India, Constantinople fell to the Turks, Luther launched the Protestant Reformation, and the monarchies of England, France, and Spain were consolidated. Taken together, these happenings, it has been argued, dissolved old continuities and gave rise to a new epoch in Western history.

The leading-sector approach concentrates on one overwhelming source of change that exercises decisive pulling power on all others. Proponents of the leading sector might argue that the discovery of the New World with its abundant natural resources and its effect upon Old World understandings of the cosmos was an event of such monumental proportions that it drew the whole of Western society from one set of norms to another.

Both concepts identify major happenings. Both demand the application of organic theories of change. Unless we adopt the view that significant historical forces like those operating in the fifteenth century coincide randomly, we are obliged to seek a theory of change that explains why and how such coincidences occur. Similarly, we need an organic theory to explain how a leading sector becomes leading and how it is related to the powerful forces that follow in its wake. With such a theory we are like a person who wants to bake a cake but lacks a recipe. This person might identify the ingredients of a cake and place them together on the kitchen counter, but until a recipe is in hand that explains what weight to give each ingredient, how and when to fold them together, and at what temperature and for what length of time to bake them, he or she will not have a cake.

Historians stand at the opposite end of a similar process. For historians, the cake of history has already been made. The historian's task is to determine, as best he or she can, the ingredients from which it is composed, their relative weights, and the manner by which they were integrated. To make a cake, one needs a recipe. To divine why and how history has evolved as it has, the historian needs a theory of change. Theory does more than identify the ingredients of historical problems. It explains the process which gives those ingredients meaning.

Explicit theories of change were not used in the establishment of Western tripartite periodization. For its inventors the mere recognition that numerous important events converged in time was considered sufficient. In redefining European periodization, organic theory would be essential. The principal models currently in use among Western scholars — market-driven division-of-labor models, neo-Malthusian demographic models, Marxian or world-systems models — are compatible with tripartite periodization and with its sixth- and sixteenth-century epochal divides. Nevertheless; as I have attempted to show elsewhere, those same models (except perhaps world systems) would commend the eleventh and the eighteenth centuries much more emphatically than the sixteenth century as decisive moments of transition in European history.[1]

Can theories of change assist us in periodizing world history? Yes, if. . . . Yes, if before the sixteenth century one (or both) of the hemispheres was functionally interrelated to the extent that some common engine (or engines) of change exerted an integrating and profoundly transforming influence upon leading civilizations and their hinterlands. If so, how did each civilization internalize and accommodate this common engine of change? How did this common engine influence both the rate and the direction of change? Finally, how did it affect the relative position of each of the major civilizations over time?

This is no small undertaking. Identifying shared experiences among the major civilizations is not a problem. Demonstrating that a shared experience was the paramount means by which the hemisphere and each civilization within it was transformed *is* a problem. It is one thing to apply organic models to regional civilizations where we have ongoing, well-documented interaction between major historical actors (groups, institutions, individuals). It is another to apply organic models where our knowledge of the interaction between historical actors (in this case, whole civilizations) is limited and where there are few reliable data on how different civilizations responded to and were affected by common stimuli (for example, trade, disease, invasion). For the early millennia of world history, available empirical evidence is insufficient to lend strong support to any general theory of change. The most we can hope for is reasonable plausibility. Reasonable plausibility is not an insignificant or insufficient goal. It is precisely what is being sought by scholars in other areas of historical enquiry where theory is critically important, such as psychohistory.

Where do world historians stand on periodization? What theoretical orientations have they employed? In the main, modern writers of world history texts have adopted progressive, evolutionary, materialist theories of change. Their theoretical orientation corresponds to that of the leading progressive and evolutionary theorists of the nineteenth century. Both have embraced human history from its origins to the present, trying to locate critical stages in humankind's long transition from hunters and gatherers to modern world citizens. Both have assumed that there are common and universal qualities to human nature and that human nature inevitably generates social and cultural development. Both have considered change to be gradual and constant; both have identified the direction of change as evolving from homogeneous to heterogeneous, from simple

to complex; both have believed that, on balance, change has occasioned better-
ment in the quality of human life (nineteenth-century scholars were boldly confident of this; contemporary world historians make this case more subtly, sometimes even apologetically). Both have asked the same kinds of questions: how do
people become civilized?

It is modern scholars' methods, not their concept of the problem, that
chiefly distinguishes contemporary world historians from Comte and Spencer.
Nineteenth-century evolutionists placed highest priority on ethnographic evidence. Because humans were thought to have a uniform nature and because
most change was considered to be immanent to society, all humans were
thought to have evolved along a single upward gradient. Each culture studied by
anthropologists from the most primitive to the most sophisticated was thought to
represent a stage in the progressive evolution of the species. Modern world historians have redirected their emphasis from ethnographic to historical forms of
evidence. We are less disposed to uniformitarianism. Yet we persist in assuming
that human beings, by their common nature, respond to similar stimuli in similar ways. On this premise, world historians continue to seek the unifying laws
and regularities that enable them to weave the histories of disparate civilizations
together in coherent, integrated fashion.[2]

As a rule, they differentiate past societies hierarchically on the basis of their
technologies and by the degree to which invention and innovation permitted division of labor and social stratification. They perceive diffusion as the principal
mechanism by which technological progress was realized. It is a process by
which distinct civilizations dispersed their special skills, products, organization,
and culture outward into adjacent regions, just as pebbles tossed into still water
generate a concentric outward movement of ripples. The diffusion of advanced
products and modes of behavior compromised and seduced barbaric peoples on
the periphery of civilized regions. Converging cultural ripples emanating from
various distinct civilizations produced action and reaction, borrowing, change,
and adjustment between civilizations. War was one means of diffusion, but
trade was its principal vehicle.

Trade-driven division of labor theory, a modern derivative of the work of
Adam Smith, has consistently been used as a guide to explain the rate and direction of change within civilizations. This "commercial" theory aids in delineat-
ing interactions between civilized peoples and "barbarians," and it provides
insight into the manner in which contacts, great or small, among leading civilizations promoted interregional borrowings and thereby stimulated social transformation across cultural frontiers. Though widely employed, this theory has
not, in its classic form, been used to embrace all the peoples of a region or all
the civilizations of a hemisphere within a single integrated historical process. An
elaboration upon it — namely, world-systems theory — attempts to do that.

Commercial theory has provided material groundwork for a periodization
based on spiritual and intellectual breakthroughs. Having noted the rapid
growth of commerce in the first millennium B.C.E., Karl Jaspers determined that
vigorous material development generated intellectual breakthroughs in four

regions of high civilization. Jaspers called this the *axial age*, defining the break-throughs as transcendental, a search for immortality and salvation. The four breakthroughs were monotheism among Jews, rational philosophy in Greece, Confucianism and Taoism in China, Buddhism and Jainism in India.[3]

Marshall G. S. Hodgson adopted Jaspers's formulation, advocating a peri-odization that divided world history into two unequal compartments: an *agrar-ian age*, 7000 B.C.E. to about 1800 C.E., and a *technical age* since 1800. The late agrarian age was subdivided into three epochs: *preaxial* (3000–800 B.C.E.), *axial* (800–200 B.C.E.), and *postaxial* (200 B.C.E.–1800 C.E.). Rising prosperity, acceler-ated by interregional commerce, provided a fertile intellectual climate for these breakthroughs, Hodgson contended. In the amalgam of Judaic monotheism and Greco-Roman philosophy, Christianity took root. From this triad emerged Islam. Apart from these two "secondary-stage revolutions," few profound reli-gious and philosophical revolutions have arisen since the first millennium B.C.E.[4]

These axial age "breakthroughs" provoke questions about the relationship between material forces and cultural values. Did one promote the other, either directly or indirectly? Were the four transcendental breakthroughs linked in any discernible way? Do they provide evidence of interregional integration across the hemisphere? Or, were these breakthroughs distinct phenomena, connected only to the extent that they emerged in societies that possessed a literary tradi-tion and some measure of material comfort and social stratification?

These questions were addressed by two separate groups of scholars. Both concluded that transcendental breakthroughs were not the product of direct dif-fusion of ideas from one civilization to another.[5] Chinese civilization was quite insulated; transformations in India were a derivative of local conditions and cul-ture. Both Greeks and Jews were influenced by Mesopotamian and Egyptian cultures, but the different nature of their societies and the distinct character of their breakthroughs precludes the likelihood that they had a linked experience. Two great civilizations of the age did not have transcendental breakthroughs: Egypt and Assyria. The scholars who participated in these studies agreed that high material development was a necessary, if not sufficient, requisite for a breakthrough, but the only shared impulse of all axial age movements was "the strain toward transcendence."[6] Hodgson died in 1968, leaving unfinished a world history that may have adopted the axial age as a pivot of world periodiza-tion. Subsequent world historians have not pursued his insight.

In 1978 Geoffrey Barraclough observed that "Marxism is the only coherent theory of the evolution of man in society, and in that sense the only philosophy of history, which exercises a demonstrable influence over the minds of histori-ans today."[7] The appeal of Marxism has declined precipitously in recent years. World-systems theory has usurped its influence. The most noted practitioner of world-systems theory, Immanuel Wallerstein, has used it to achieve a tightly in-tegrated analysis of the Atlantic basin over the last five centuries. World systems theory, while neo-Marxist in origin, is a complex elaboration upon trade-driven division of labor theory. It is progressive, evolutionary, and materialist. Although

Wallerstein himself questions the utility of the model for pre-1460 world history, others strongly advocate its adoption as a means of integrating regional histories of the Eastern hemisphere in a single historical process. Janet Abu-Lughod has described a world system centered in the Middle East during the thirteenth century.[8] William McNeill encourages use of the world system as an overarching ecumenical process as early as 1700 B.C.E.[9] Andre Gunder Frank and Barry Gills recommend world-systems analysis as the framework for Afro-Eurasian history beginning at least as early as 2700 B.C.E.[10]

Frank is the most explicit, if most extreme, theoretician for premodern application of the world-systems approach. He discards traditional categories of analysis, challenges standard notions of periodization, and presents a new paradigm for the study of world history. For the last 5000 years — possibly more, writes Frank — a world system has operated across Afro-Eurasia based upon the transfer of economic surplus between regions. Those transfers integrated regional modes of exploitation and accumulation into an overarching, interpenetrating, competitive order. A universal drive for capital accumulation was the primary motor of change across the hemisphere. Each region possessed a hegemonic center connected to a dependent periphery and to a distant hinterland with which it interacted. The consistent outward reach of these regional systems generated increased interregional economic exchange and competition. Shifting technological advantage, among other forces, enabled first one, then another, of the great regional civilizations to exert superhegemony over others.

William McNeill does not fully endorse world-systems theory, although he finds its aspirations praiseworthy. He sees a Middle Eastern world system developing around 1700 B.C.E. After 1000 B.C.E., he would merge Greek, Middle Eastern, and Indian societies into one expansive Middle Eastern "great society." China would join this world system around 100 B.C.E. with the opening of caravan trade to Syria. Lethal diseases spread along the expanded trade routes producing severe demographic decline in both the Mediterranean and Chinese spheres in the third century C.E. The recovery that began in the sixth century was accelerated by the rise of Islam. Superhegemony passed from the Islamic regions to China around A.D. 1000 and to Europe after 1500.[11] I am not certain how these observations translate into formal periodization, if indeed that is McNeill's intention. One might presume something like the following: segment one, to 1700 B.C.E.; segment two, from 1700 B.C.E. to *circa* 300/600 C.E.; segment three, *circa* 300/600 to 1500; segment four, since 1500.

McNeill has shown us that epidemic disease has had a powerful impact on world history, notably in the demographic declines of Chinese and Mediterranean civilizations after the second century A.D., in the formation of a single hemispheric disease pool by about A.D. 1000, in the eruptions of bubonic plague in the sixth and fourteenth centuries, and in the devastation of native Americans after 1492. Still, it is hard to see how one could employ disease as the central driving force in human affairs, although disease must serve as a major factor in any episodic construction of period frontiers.

The issue of disease does provoke some doubt about the extent to which interregional exchange via the world system had integrated the Eastern hemisphere before the second century B.C.E. If the spread of lethal disease across trade routes from the Pacific to the Mediterranean at the end of the second century occasioned significant demographic decline at both ends of the system, why, it must be asked, were these catastrophic effects so long delayed? If an "overarching" and truly "interpenetrating" world system had existed for a millennium or two, is it not probable that these destructive biological effects, occasioned as they were by interregional contacts, would have been experienced earlier?

Besides world-systems theory, there are several avenues of approach that might, in time, provide an overarching theoretical foundation for world history. One, perhaps the most compelling of them all, is ecological. It would involve interpreting human experience in the context of a universal ecosystem in which people have been involved in complex patterns of interdependence with all other forms of life, animal and vegetable.[12] Some scholars have suggested gender relations as a basis for the organization of world history courses, if not for the structuring of comprehensive texts. Neither of these orientations currently commands the attention given to world systems. In fact, no general theory of change being employed by world historians today is as fully refined or as well articulated as world-systems theory. It is a powerful explanatory tool. Nevertheless, numerous problems have to be resolved in the theory; numerous questions must be answered. The jury remains out.

In the meantime, we must go on writing and teaching world history, updating texts and reorganizing syllabi. We have to make choices about coverage and about periodization. There is a strong possibility that neither world-systems theory, nor ecological theory, nor any other theory will provide a satisfactory framework for all of world history. If, in the end, we are obliged to accept some degree of fragmentation in our presentation of world history, should we not go a further step and concede to a decidedly regional approach, giving roughly equal attention to all regions of the globe? This would gratify cultural relativists and those who resent the minimal attention usually given to sub-Saharan Africa and pre-Columbian America. Here, the response should be a practical and purely sensible one. It makes no more sense endlessly to disassemble our subject than it does to erect unities where they may not exist. Some people, some places, some institutions, and some belief systems are more enduring, more significant, more universal, and more influential to the whole human experience than others. They demand primary attention. The balance being struck by most writers of world history seems to me a correct one. Peoples who functioned at great distance from the mainstream should not be ignored; neither should they serve as major elements in the presentation or periodization of world history.

Although we may lack an overarching and integrating theoretical framework for periodizing world history, we still have the practical need, as authors and teachers, to separate six millennia of human experience in chronological compartments having some measure of coherence. For the moment, we are compelled to exercise arbitrary eclectic judgments on global periodization, not unlike the writers and teachers whose judgments about European history gradually produced Western tripartite periodization. This would be regrettable. It is not disastrous. It involves our seeking a practical solution to an inescapable pedagogical problem. Most world historians have personal preferences on periodization. Few of these preferences are lodged in systematic theory, yet many of them are highly similar even though similarities may arise from different reasons.

Notes

1. William A. Green, "Periodization in European and World History," *Journal of World History* 3 (1992): 13–53.

2. For a brief comprehensive analysis of theories of progress, see Kenneth E. Bock, "Theories of Progress and Evolution," in *Sociology and History: Theory and Research*, ed. Werner J. Cahnman and Alvin Boskoff (Glencoe, Ill., 1964), 21–41.

3. Karl Jaspers, *The Origin and Goal of History*, trans. M. Bullock (New Haven, 1953), 1–21.

4. Hodgson observed that spiritual and intellectual advances since the axial age have, in the main, arisen inside the cultural traditions laid down in that period. See Marshall G. S. Hodgson, *The Venture of Islam: Conscience and History in a World Civilization*, 3 vols. (Chicago, 1974), 1:48–53, 105–20.

5. Benjamin I. Schwartz (among others who wrote on the theme), "Wisdom Revelation, and Doubt: Perspectives on the First Millennium B.C.," *Daedalus* 104 (1975); *The Origins and Diversity of Axial Age Civilizations*, ed. S. N. Eisenstadt (Albany, 1986).

6. Benjamin I. Schwartz, "The Age of Transcendence," *Daedalus* 104 (1975): 3; S. N. Eisenstadt, "The Axial Age Breakthrough — Their Characteristics and Origins," in Eisenstadt, ed., *Origins and Diversity*, 2.

7. Geoffrey Barraclough, *Main Trends in History* (New York, 1979), 164.

8. Janet L. Abu-Lughod, *Before European Hegemony: The World System, A.D. 1250–1350* (New York, 1989).

9. William H. McNeill, "*The Rise of the West* after Twenty-five Years," *Journal of World History* 1 (1990): 1–21.

10. Andre Gunder Frank and Barry K. Gills, "The Cumulation of Accumulation: Theses and Research Agenda for 5000 Years of World System History," *Dialectical Anthropology* 15 (1990): 19–42; Frank, "A Theoretical Introduction to World System History," *Review* 13 (1990): 155–248; Frank, "A Plea for World System History," *Journal of World History* 2 (1991): 1–28.

11. McNeill, "*The Rise* after 25 Years," 12–18.

12. An early attempt at such history is Clive Pointing's *A Green History of the World: The Environment and the Collapse of Great Civilizations* (New York, 1991).

NATIONAL CENTER FOR HISTORY IN THE SCHOOLS

World History Standards for Grades 5–12

ERA 1

THE BEGINNINGS OF HUMAN SOCIETY

Giving Shape to World History

So far as we know, humanity's story began in Africa. For millions of years it was mainly a story of biological change. Then some hundreds of thousands of years ago our early ancestors began to form and manipulate useful tools. Eventually they mastered speech. Unlike most other species, early humans gained the capacity to learn from one another and transmit knowledge from one generation to the next. The first great experiments in creating culture were underway. Among early hunter-gatherers cultural change occurred at an imperceptible speed. But as human populations rose and new ideas and techniques appeared, the pace of change accelerated. Moreover, human history became global at a very early date. In the long period from human beginnings to the rise of the earliest civilization two world-circling developments stand in relief:

The Peopling of the Earth: The first great global event was the peopling of the earth and the astonishing story of how communities of hunters, foragers, or fishers adapted creatively and continually to a variety of contrasting, changing environments in Africa, Eurasia, Australia, and the Americas.

The Agricultural Revolution: Over a period of several thousand years and as a result of countless small decisions, humans learned how to grow crops, domesticate plants, and raise animals. The earliest agricultural settlements probably arose in Southwest Asia, but the agricultural revolution spread round the world. Human population began to soar relative to earlier times. Communities came into regular contact with one another over longer distances, cultural patterns became far more complex, and opportunities for innovation multiplied.

"World History Standards for Grades 5–12," *National Standards for History* (Los Angeles: National Center for History in the Schools, University of California, Los Angeles, 1996), passim.

ERA 2
EARLY CIVILIZATIONS AND THE EMERGENCE
OF PASTORAL PEOPLES, 4000–1000 B.C.E.

Giving Shape to World History

When farmers began to grow crops on the irrigated floodplain of Mesopotamia in Southwest Asia, they had no consciousness that they were embarking on a radically new experiment in human organization. The nearly rainless but abundantly watered valley of the lower Tigris and Euphrates rivers was an environment capable of supporting far larger concentrations of population and much greater cultural complexity than could the hill country where agriculture first emerged. Shortly after 4000 B.C.E., a rich culture and economy based on walled cities was appearing along the banks of the two rivers. The rise of civilization in Mesopotamia marked the beginning of 3,000 years of far-reaching transformations that affected peoples across wide areas of Eurasia and Africa.

The four standards in this era present a general chronological progression of developments in world history from 4000 to 1000 B.C.E. Two major patterns of change may be discerned that unite the developments of this period.

Early Civilizations and the Spread of Agricultural Societies: Societies exhibiting the major characteristics of civilizations spread widely during these millennia. Four great floodplain civilizations appeared, first in Mesopotamia, shortly after in the Nile valley, and from about 2500 B.C.E. in the Indus valley. These three civilizations mutually influenced one another and came to constitute a single region of intercommunication and trade. The fourth civilization arose in the Yellow River valley of northwestern China in the second millennium B.C.E. As agriculture continued to spread, urban centers also emerged on rain-watered lands, notably in Syria and on the island of Crete. Finally, expanding agriculture and long-distance trade were the foundations of increasingly complex societies in the Aegean Sea basin and western Europe. During this same era, it must be remembered, much of the world's population lived in small farming communities and hunted or foraged. These peoples were no less challenged than city-dwellers to adapt continually and creatively to changing environmental and social conditions.

Pastoral Peoples and Population Movements: In this era pastoralism — the practice of herding animals as a society's primary source of food — made it possible for larger communities than ever before to inhabit the semi-arid steppes and deserts of Eurasia and Africa. Consequently, pastoral peoples began to play an important role in world history. In the second millennium B.C.E. migrations of pastoral folk emanating from the steppes of Central Asia contributed to a quickening pace of change across the entire region from Europe and the Mediterranean basin to India. Some societies became more highly militarized, new kingdoms appeared, and languages of the Indo-European family became much more widely spoken.

Era 3
CLASSICAL TRADITIONS, MAJOR RELIGIONS,
AND GIANT EMPIRES, 1000 B.C.E.–300 C.E.

Giving Shape to World History

By 1000 B.C.E. urban civilizations of the Eastern Hemisphere were no longer confined to a few irrigated river plains. World population was growing, interregional trade networks were expanding, and towns and cities were appearing where only farming villages or nomad camps had existed before. Iron-making technology had increasing impact on economy and society. Contacts among diverse societies of Eurasia and Africa were intensifying, and these had profound consequences in the period from 1000 B.C.E. to 300 C.E. The pace of change was quickening in the Americas as well. If we stand back far enough to take in the global scene, three large-scale patterns of change stand out. These developments can be woven through the study of particular regions and societies.

Classical Civilizations Defined: The civilizations of the irrigated river valleys were spreading to adjacent regions, and new centers of urban life and political power were appearing in rain-watered lands. Several civilizations were attaining their classical definitions, that is, they were developing institutions, systems of thought, and cultural styles that would influence neighboring peoples and endure for centuries.

Major Religions Emerge: Judaism, Christianity, Buddhism, Brahmanism/Hinduism, Confucianism, and Daoism all appeared in this period as systems of belief capable of stabilizing and enriching human relations across large areas of the world and providing avenues of cultural interchange between one region and another. Each of these religions united peoples of diverse political and ethnic identities. Religions also, often enough, divided groups into hostile camps and gave legitimacy to war or social repression.

Giant Empires Appear: Multi-ethnic empires became bigger than ever before and royal bureaucracies more effective at organizing and taxing ordinary people in the interests of the state. Empire building in this era also created much larger spheres of economic and cultural interaction. Near the end of the period the Roman and Han empires together embraced a huge portion of the hemisphere, and caravans and ships were relaying goods from one extremity of Eurasia to the other.

Era 4

Expanding Zones of Exchange
and Encounter, 300–1000 C.E.

Giving Shape to World History

Beginning about 300 C.E. almost the entire region of Eurasia and northern Africa experienced severe disturbances. By the seventh century, however, peoples of Eurasia and Africa entered a new period of more intensive interchange and cultural creativity. Underlying these developments was the growing sophistication of systems for moving people and goods here and there throughout the hemisphere — China's canals, trans-Saharan camel caravans, high-masted ships plying the Indian Ocean. These networks tied diverse peoples together across great distances. In Eurasia and Africa a single region of intercommunication was taking shape that ran from the Mediterranean to the China seas. A widening zone of interchange also characterized Mesoamerica.

A sweeping view of world history reveals three broad patterns of change that are particularly conspicuous in this era.

Islamic Civilization: One of the most dramatic developments of this seven-hundred-year period was the rise of Islam as both a new world religion and a civilized tradition encompassing an immense part of the Eastern Hemisphere. Commanding the central region of Afro-Eurasia, the Islamic empire of the Abbasid dynasty became in the eighth- to tenth–century period the principal intermediary for the exchange of goods, ideas, and technologies across the hemisphere.

Buddhist, Christian, and Hindu Traditions: Not only Islam but other major religions also spread widely during this seven-hundred-year era. Wherever these faiths were introduced, they carried with them a variety of cultural traditions, aesthetic ideas, and ways of organizing human endeavor. Each of them also embraced peoples of all classes and diverse languages in common worship and moral commitment. Buddhism declined in India but took root in East and Southeast Asia. Christianity became the cultural foundation of a new civilization in western Europe. Hinduism flowered in India under the Gupta Empire and also exerted growing influence in the princely courts of Southeast Asia.

New Patterns of Society in East Asia, Europe, West Africa, Oceania, and Mesoamerica: The third conspicuous pattern, continuing from the previous era, was the process of population growth, urbanization, and flowering of culture in new areas. The fourth to sixth centuries witnessed serious upheavals in Eurasia in connection with the breakup of the Roman and Han empires and the aggressive movements of pastoral peoples to the east, west, and south. By the seventh century, however, China was finding new unity and rising economic prosperity under the Tang. Japan emerged as a distinctive civilization. At the other end of the hemisphere Europe laid new foundations for political and social order. In West Africa towns flourished amid the rise of Ghana and the trans-Saharan gold trade. In both lower Africa and the Pacific basin migrant pioneers laid new foundations of agricultural societies. Finally, this era saw a remarkable growth of urban life in Mesoamerica in the age of the Maya.

ERA 5
INTENSIFIED HEMISPHERIC INTERACTIONS, 1000–1500 C.E.

Giving Shape to World History

In this era the various regions of Eurasia and Africa became more firmly inter-connected than at any earlier time in history. The sailing ships that crossed the wide sea basins of the Eastern Hemisphere carried a greater volume and variety of goods than ever before. In fact, the chain of seas extending across the hemisphere — China seas, Indian Ocean, Persian Gulf, Red Sea, Black Sea, Mediterranean, and Baltic — came to form a single interlocking network of maritime trade. In the same centuries caravan traffic crossed the Inner Asian steppes and the Sahara Desert more frequently. As trade and travel intensified so did cultural exchanges and encounters, presenting local societies with a profusion of new opportunities and dangers. By the time of the transoceanic voyages of the Portuguese and Spanish, the Eastern Hemisphere already constituted a single zone of intercommunication possessing a unified history of its own.

A global view revels four "big stories" that give shape to the entire era.

China and Europe — Two Centers of Growth: In two regions of the Eastern Hemisphere, China and Europe, the era witnessed remarkable growth. China experienced a burst of technological innovation, commercialization, and urbanization, emerging as the largest economy in the world. As China exported its silks and porcelains to other lands and imported quantities of spices from India and Southeast Asia, patterns of production and commerce all across the hemisphere were affected. At the opposite end of Eurasia, Western and Central Europe emerged as a new center of Christian civilization, expanding in agricultural production, population, commerce, and military might. Powerful European states presented a new challenge to Muslim dominance in the Mediterranean world. At the same time Europe was drawn more tightly into the commercial economy and cultural interchange of the hemisphere.

The Long Reach of Islam: In this era Islamic faith and civilization encompassed extensive new areas of Eurasia and Africa. The continuing spread of Islam was closely connected to the migrations of Turkic conquerors and herding folk and to the growth of Muslim commercial enterprise all across the hemisphere. By about 1400 C.E. Muslim societies spanned the central two-thirds of Afro-Eurasia. New Muslim states and towns were appearing in West Africa, the East African coast,

Central Asia, India, and Southeast Asia. Consequently, Muslim merchants, scholars, and a host of long-distance travelers were the principal mediators in the interregional exchange of goods, ideas, and technical innovations.

The Age of Mongol Dominance: The second half of the era saw extraordinary developments in interregional history. The Mongols under Chinggis Khan created the largest land empire the world had ever seen. Operating from Poland to Korea and Siberia to Indonesia, the Mongol warlords intruded in one way or another on the lives of almost all peoples of Eurasia. The conquests were terrifying, but the stabilizing of Mongol rule led to a century of fertile commercial and cultural interchange across the continent. Eurasian unification, however, had a disastrous consequence in the fourteenth century — the Black Death and its attendant social impact on Europe, the Islamic world, and probably China.

Empires of the Americas: In the Western Hemisphere empire building reached an unprecedented scale. The political styles of the Aztec and Inca states were profoundly different. Even so, both enterprises demonstrated that human labor and creative endeavor could be organized on a colossal scale despite the absence of iron technology or wheeled transport.

Era 6

THE EMERGENCE OF THE FIRST GLOBAL AGE, 1450–1770

Giving Shape to World History

The Iberian voyages of the late fifteenth and early sixteenth centuries not only linked Europe with the Americas but laid down a communications net that ultimately joined every region of the world with every other region. As the era progressed ships became safer, bigger, and faster, and the volume of world commerce soared. The web of overland roads and trails expanded as well to carry goods and people in and out of the interior regions of Eurasia, Africa, and the American continents. The demographic, social, and cultural consequences of this great global link-up were immense.

   The deep transformations that occurred in the world during this era may be set in the context of three overarching patterns of change.

The Acceleration of Change: The most conspicuous characteristic of this era was the great acceleration of change in the way people lived, worked, and thought. In these 300 years human society became profoundly different from the way it had been in the entire 5,000 years since the emergence of civilizations. Five aspects of change were especially prominent. Though American Indian populations declined catastrophically in the aftermath of the first European intrusions, world numbers on the whole started their steep upward curve that continues to the present. The globalizing of communications produced intensified economic and cultural encounters and exchanges among diverse peoples of Eurasia, Africa, and the Americas. Capitalism emerged as the dominant system for organizing production, labor, and trade in the world. Innovations in technology and science multiplied and continuously built on one another. European thinkers, drawing on a worldwide fund of ideas, formulated revolutionary new views of nature and the cosmos, ideas that challenged older religious and philosophical perspectives.

Europe and the World; the World and Europe: Europeans came to exert greater power and influence in the world at large than any people of a single region had ever done before. In the Americas Europeans erected colonial regimes and frontiers of European settlement that drew upon various European traditions of law, religion, government, and culture. Europeans seized relatively little territory in Africa and Asia in this era, but their naval and commercial enterprises profoundly affected patterns of production and interregional trade. The trade in human beings between Africa and the Americas to provide a labor force for European commercial agriculture was a particularly catastrophic aspect of the expanding global economy. Closely linked to Europe's far-reaching global involvement was its own internal transformation — political, social, economic, and intellectual. In this era peoples almost everywhere at some time had to come to terms with European arms and economic clout, but as of 1750 Europe by no means dominated the world scene.

Empires of Eurasia: Indeed, the greater share of the world's peoples, cities, agrarian wealth, and land-based military power were in this era still concentrated in the region stretching from the eastern Mediterranean to China. Between the late fourteenth and early sixteenth centuries four huge empires arose to dominate the greater part of Eurasia and Northern Africa. Effectively employing artillery and other firearms to expand territorially and maintain law and order among diverse populations, the Ming, Ottoman, Mughal, and Safavid states have sometimes been called "gunpowder empires." They unified such large areas of Afro-Eurasia — politically, economically, and culturally — that they contributed much to processes of globalization.

ERA 7
AN AGE OF REVOLUTIONS, 1750–1914

Giving Shape to World History

The invention of the railway locomotive, the steamship, and, later, the telegraph and telephone transformed global communications in this era. The time it took and the money it cost to move goods, messages, or armies across oceans and continents were drastically cut. People moved, or were forced to move, from one part of the world to another in record numbers. In the early part of the era African slaves continued to be transported across the Atlantic in large numbers; European migrants created new frontiers of colonial settlement in both the

Northern and Southern Hemispheres; and Chinese, Indian, and other Asians migrated to Southeast Asia and the Americas. International commerce mushroomed, and virtually no society anywhere in the world stayed clear of the global market. Underlying these surges in communication, migration, and trade was the growth of world population, forcing men and women almost everywhere to experiment with new ways of organizing collective life.

This was an era of bewildering change in a thousand different arenas. One way to make sense of the whole is to focus on three world-encompassing and interrelated developments: the democratic revolution, the industrial revolution, and the establishment of European dominance over most of the world.

Political Revolutions and New Ideologies: The American and French revolutions offered to the world the potent ideas of popular sovereignty, inalienable rights, and nationalism. The translating of these ideas into political movements had the effect of mobilizing unprecedented numbers of ordinary people to participate in public life and to believe in a better future for all. Liberal, constitutional, and nationalist ideals inspired independence movements in Haiti and Latin America in the early nineteenth century, and they continued to animate reform and revolution in Europe throughout the era. At the same time political and social counterforces acted to limit or undermine the effectiveness of democratic governments. Democracy and nationalism contributed immensely to the social power of European states and therefore to Europe's rising dominance in world affairs in the nineteenth century. Under growing pressures from both European military power and the changing world economy, ruling or elite groups in Asian and African states organized reform movements that embraced at least some of the ideas and programs of democratic revolution.

The Industrial Revolution: The industrial revolution applied mechanical power to the production and distribution of goods on a massive scale. It also involved mobilizing unprecedented numbers of laborers and moving them from village to city and from one country to another. Industrialization was a consequence of centuries of expanding economic activity around the world. England played a crucial role in the onset of this revolution, but the process involved complex economic and financial linkages among societies. Together, the industrial and democratic revolutions thoroughly transformed European society. Asian, African, and Latin American peoples dealt with the new demands of the world market and Europe's economic might in a variety of ways. Some groups argued for reform through technical and industrial modernization. Others called for reassertion of established policies and values that had always served them well in times of crisis. Japan and the United States both subscribed to the industrial revolution with rapid success and became important players on the world scene.

The Age of European Dominance: In 1800 Europeans controlled about 35 percent of the world's land surface. By 1914 they dominated over 84 percent. In the long span of human history European world hegemony lasted a short time, but its consequences were profound and continue to be played out today. Western expansion took three principal forms: (1) Peoples of European descent, including Russians and North Americans, created colonial settlements, or "neo-Europes," in various temperate regions of the world, displacing or assimilating indigenous peoples; (2) European states and commercial firms exerted considerable economic power in certain places, notably Latin America and China, while Japan and the United States also participated in this economic expansionism; (3) in the later nineteenth century European states embarked on the "new imperialism," the competitive race to establish political as well as economic control over previously uncolonized regions of Africa and Asia. Mass production of new weaponry, coupled with the revolution of transport and communications, permitted this surge of power. The active responses of the peoples of Africa, Asia, and Latin America to the crisis of European hegemony are an important part of the developments of this era: armed resistance against invaders, collaboration or alliance with colonizers, economic reform or entrepreneurship, and movements for cultural reform. As World War I approached, accelerating social change and new efforts at resistance and renewal characterized colonial societies far more than consolidation and stability.

ERA 8
A HALF-CENTURY OF CRISIS AND
ACHIEVEMENT, 1900–1945

Giving Shape to World History

On a winter's day in 1903 the "Kitty Hawk," Orville and Wilbur Wright's experimental flying machine, lifted off the ground for twelve seconds. In the decades that followed air travel was perfected, and all the physical barriers that had obstructed long-distance communication among human groups virtually disappeared. Oceans, deserts, and mountain ranges no longer mattered much when people living thousands of miles apart were determined to meet, talk, negotiate, or do business. For the first time in history the north polar region became a crossroads of international travel as air pilots sought the shortest routes between countries of the Northern Hemisphere. Radio and, at mid-century, television revolutionized communication in another way. Long-distance messages no longer had to be transported from one point to another by boat or train or even transmitted along wires or cables. Now messages, whether designed to inform, entertain, persuade, or deceive, could be broadcast from a single point to millions of listeners or watchers simultaneously.

These and other technological wonders both expressed and contributed to the growing complexity and unpredictability of human affairs. In some ways peoples of the world became more tightly knit than ever before. Global economic integration moved ahead. Literacy spread more widely. Research and knowledge networks reached round the world. However, in other respects division and conflict multiplied. Economic and territorial rivalries among nations became harsher. Laboratories and factories turned out more lethal weapons and in greater quantities than ever before. People rose up against autocratic governments on every continent. Among the turbulent trends of the era, two developments seem most prominent.

The Twentieth Century's Thirty Years War: The powers of destruction that centuries of accumulated technical and scientific skill gave to human beings became horrifyingly apparent in the two global wars of the twentieth century. In the Thirty Years War of the 1600s, one of Europe's most destructive contests, more than four million people may have died. The wars of 1914–1945, by contrast, took forty-five million lives. Since World War I sowed copious seeds of the second conflict, the complex links of cause and effect over the entire period make a compelling subject for the world history student. Though both wars engulfed Europe, the globe is the proper context for understanding them. Air power, especially in World War II, meant that no country's borders were safe, whatever the distances involved. Campaigns were fought from the mid-Pacific to West Africa and from Siberia to the North Atlantic. Combatants came from many lands, including thousands from European colonial possessions. The century's first five decades were not, however, all violence and gloom. In the midst of war and world depression heroism and ingenuity abounded. Age-old diseases were conquered or brought under control. Democracy endured in many states despite recurrent crises, and governments responded with remarkable efficiency to the demands of war-time management and welfare.

Revolution and Protest: Human aspirations toward democratic government, national independence, and social justice were first expressed on a large scale in human affairs in the 1750–1914 era. These aspirations continued to inspire revolutions throughout the first half of the twentieth century. The most dramatic political changes occurred in Russia, China, Mexico, and Turkey. In all these places jarring shifts and disturbances in economic life, both local and international, were at the root of the political crises. In all of them, moreover, contests quickly developed between the advocates of liberal, parliamentary democracy and those who championed an authoritarian or single-party state as the most efficient instrument of political and economic transformation. Apart from revolutions, relatively peaceful movements of protest and dissent forced a broadening of the democratic base, including voting rights for women, in a number of countries. The European colonial empires saw few violent risings between 1900 and 1945. There was, however, no colonial "golden age." Resistance, protest, and calls for reform, drawing heavily on the liberal and nationalist ideals that the Western powers proclaimed, dogged imperial regimes all across Africa and Asia.

ERA 9
THE TWENTIETH CENTURY SINCE 1945:
PROMISES AND PARADOXES

Giving Shape to World History

The closer we get to the present the more difficult it becomes to distinguish between the large forces of change and the small. Surveying the long sweep of history from early hominid times to the end of World War II, we might reach at
least partial consensus about what is important to the development of the whole
human community and what is not. The multifarious trends of the past half-
century, however, are for the most part still working themselves out. Therefore,
we cannot know what history students one or two hundred years from now will
think was worth remembering about the decades after World War II. Clearly,
the era has been one of tensions, paradoxes, and contradictory trends. Some of
these countercurrents provide students with a framework for investigation and
analysis.

Democracy and Tyranny: In the three decades following World War II, a multitude of new sovereign states appeared around the world. The breakup of the
Soviet Union that began in 1990 introduced fifteen more. Triumphant nationalism, in short, has radically transformed the globe's political landscape. Even so,
peoples on every continent have had to struggle persistently for democracy and
justice against the powerful counterforces of authoritarianism, neo-colonialism,
warlordism, and stolid bureaucracy. Many of the newer independent states have
also faced daunting challenges in raising their peoples' standard of living while
at the same time participating in a global economic system where industrialized
countries have had a distinct advantage. The political, and in some places economic, reform movements that bloomed in Africa, Eurasia, and Latin America
in the 1980s are evidence of the vitality of civic aspirations that originated more
than two centuries ago.

War and Peace: World War II ended amid anxious hopes for genuine world
peace. In 1945, however, the Cold War was already underway. For forty years recurrent international crises and the doubtful consolations of mutually assured
destruction dominated world affairs. The European colonial empires were dis-
mantled and power transferred to new nationalist leaders with less violence or
acrimony than anyone might have expected — with some exceptions. Nationalists waged protracted anti-colonial wars in Vietnam, Algeria, Angola, and
Mozambique. When the Soviet Union collapsed, the threat of catastrophe re-
ceded and the world sighed in relief. On the other hand, local wars and terrorist
assaults multiplied as ancient enemies settled old scores and ethnic or nationalist feelings rose to the surface. Amid the ruthless confrontations of the second
half of the century, people of good will have continued to seek peace. The
achievements and limitations of the post–World War II settlements, the United

Nations, the European Economic Community, Middle East negotiations, and numerous other forms of international cooperation are all worthy of serious study for the lessons they may offer the coming generation.

Global Links and Communal Identity: The transformations that the world experienced in the previous three eras appear modest in comparison with the bewildering pace and complexity of change in the late twentieth century. The revolution of global communication has potentially put everyone in touch with everyone else. Business travelers, scientists, labor migrants, and refugees move incessantly from country to country. Currency transfers ricochet from bank to bank. The young men and women of Bangkok, Moscow, and Wichita Falls watch the same movies and sport the same brand of jeans. In economy, politics, and culture the human community is in a continuous process of restructuring itself. Global interdependence, however, has a flip side. As the gales of change blow, people seek communal bonds and identities more urgently than ever. Communalism has frequently led to fear and suspicion of the "other." Even so, the institutions and values that communities share protect them in some measure from the shocks of the new and unforeseen. The social and cultural bonds of family, village, ethnic community, religion, and nation provide a framework for estimating how others will think and behave and for calculating with some confidence the pattern of affairs from day to day.

Countercurrents in the Quality of Life: The early twentieth century promised, at least in the industrialized countries, a new age of progress through science, technology, and rational policy-making. Fifty years and two world wars later, humanity was less optimistic about its future. Art and literature after 1945 starkly reported the era's skepticism and angst. Science, medicine, and techniques of human organization continued to benefit society in wondrous ways. A truly global middle class emerged, and it enjoyed rising prosperity for several decades. Several countries, notably along the eastern Pacific rim, became economic powers to be reckoned with. On the other hand, the world population explosion, persistent poverty, environmental degradation, and epidemic disease have defied the best efforts of statesmanship, civic action, and scientific imagination. Amid the distresses and dangers of the era, people have sought not only communal ties but also moral and metaphysical certainties. Spiritual quests and ethical questionings have been a vital part of the cultural history of the past half-century.

Selected Bibliography

Dunn, Ross E. "Periodization and Chronological Coverage in a World History Course." In *What Americans Should Know: Western Civilization or World History, Proceedings of a Conference at Michigan State University, April 21–23, 1985*, edited by Josef W. Konvitz, 129–40. East Lansing: Michigan State University, 1985. This essay reflects on challenges of periodizing world history, then proposes a four-part scheme for Afro-Eurasia, 1000–1600 C.E. The volume also includes an essay by Lewis W. Spitz, "Periodization and Chronological Coverage in a Western Civilization Course."

Gills, Barry K., and Andre Gunder Frank. "World System Cycles, Crises, and Hegemonic Shifts, 1700 B.C. to 1700 A.D." In *The World System: Five Hundred or Five Thousand Years?* edited by Andre Gunder Frank and Barry K. Gills, 143–99. New York: Routledge, 1993. As part of their extended argument for the emergence of world systems of capital accumulation dating to 3000 B.C.E. or earlier, Gills and Frank present a world-scale periodization whose organizing principle is transitions in economic-political hegemony. They posit four major sequences: the Bronze Age period, 3000 to 1000 B.C.E.; the Iron Age axial and classical periods, 1000 B.C.E. to 500 C.E.; the medieval and early modern periods, 500 to 1500 C.E.; and the modern world system period. They also subdivide each of these major phases into A/B cycles of economic expansion and contraction.

Green, William A. "Periodization in European and World History." *Journal of World History* 3 (Spring 1992): 13–53. The author analyzes periodization in the European intellectual tradition and measures the suitability of conventional practice for the new world history.

Manning, Patrick. "The Problem of Interactions in World History." *American Historical Review* 101 (June 1996): 771–82. A response to Jerry H. Bentley's article in the same issue, part of which is included here. Manning raises questions about the meaning of both "interaction" and "culture."

PART EIGHT

COMPARISONS AND THEMES

All world history teaching and writing that is not mere chronicle is in some measure comparative or thematic. Because, like all practitioners of the discipline, world historians work with empirical evidence, their explanations of sweeping events or huge processes must be anchored in substantive "cases" and historical moments. Otherwise, big patterns are nothing more than abstractions. The scholar who investigates a large-scale development encompassing several regions or localities — the appearance of the Mongol empire, for example — must, in order to make sense of the data, show how that development played itself out similarly or differently among a variety of groups occupying different spots on the map. The teacher who introduces students to such global phenomena of modern times as imperialism or nationalism must discuss a set of comparative cases to make the generalizations concrete and intelligible. The textbook writer embarked on a global survey of civilizations must make at least general thematic and comparative choices as a guide to selecting data and arranging them in a lucid, engaging narrative.

Most of the new world history scholarship of the past half-century has intended not to survey or synthesize the whole human record but to investigate particular subject matter. In that sense most of this literature is by definition thematic. Some of it is also explicitly and systematically comparative. Historical scholarship has been blooming in such variety in recent decades that it is difficult to decide which comparative and thematic approaches to a subject may qualify as world history and which may not. Is a book that compares a similar pattern of developments in two different parts of the world necessarily world history? Do all the new books on human evolution, paleolithic migration, and environmental adaptation fit into this category? Is a book on, say, twentieth-century transnational developments a contribution to world history even if the author never thought of characterizing it that way and may be oblivious to the emergence of the world history field? Perhaps the more pertinent question is, "Does any of this matter?" World history is, and should be, a very big tent, enveloping any topic or approach that presumes the human species to be the primal terrain of inquiry. As R. I. Moore has put it,

> World history need not, and indeed must not, aim to be encyclopedic — that can be left to encyclopedias. On the other hand, it cannot exclude anything from its purview *a priori*, as Swiss history or military history might do. . . . World history is . . . a perspective — and the only perspective — in which all events, structures, and processes must ultimately be capable of being viewed. It is, historically speaking, the set of all sets.[1]

Indeed, it is the capacity to connect one piece of monographic research to another, to reveal through comparison patterns that no one noticed before, to encourage topical specialists to talk to one another, and to identify themes that require interdisciplinarity that makes the field of world history so exciting.

Acknowledging that this field is "the set of all sets" does not of course offer much comfort to the world history teacher struggling to make comparisons and themes work in the classroom. In most introductory courses instructors probably already use comparative strategies informally and spontaneously, even if they don't design their whole course around a systematic comparative method. In assignments and lectures students may encounter a great deal of comparison and accompanying classifications, taxonomies, and generalizations without really knowing that a specific methodology is being applied.

Therefore, when the opportunity arises, teachers should make students aware of how particular authors, including textbook authors, apply comparative skills and show students how to do the same in their essays and exams. Short of that, any class activity that involves comparative thinking — a lecture that models a piece of comparative analysis, a discussion that prompts inductive reasoning from a set of cases, an exam that assesses the ability to identify relevant variables rather than merely set two or more cases side by side — may help sharpen students' critical aptitude. Comparison, and generalization from comparison, dislodges exceptionalist and parochial assumptions. It highlights the variety and complexity of human experience. It helps fit events into larger wholes. It shows how the apparently inconsequential may be significant. It uncovers possible causal relationships among events occurring in distant parts of the world. It provokes students to consider whether a particular run of events or a distinctive way of doing things in one society was inevitable or "natural." It introduces students to a basic analytical technique of the social science. It helps them recognize historical phenomena as problems rather than merely as enclosed linear sequences. As Raymond Grew has written, "comparison is a means of breaking out of the trenches dug by received conceptions. . . . Conceived comparatively, the historical problem is then more likely to determine the scope of the research — investigation that may require chronological, geographical, and social dimensions that are quite unconventional."[2]

Comparison, whether it is systematic or not, always involves specific subject areas and sets of questions; in other words, it involves themes. Broadly understood, a theme is simply a topic, a subject of discourse or discussion. Nevertheless, as pedagogical terms in world history, "theme" and "thematic" have stirred a fair amount of confusion and disagreement. In the precollegiate social studies tradition, a "thematic approach" often implies something that sets historians' teeth on edge. It may mean the decidedly presentist procedure of identifying particular "contemporary problems" for study, then searching along a narrow path into the past to find appropriate "background" material to toss into the hopper. Or it may involve tracing a particular category of phenomena across time — slavery, empires, city-building, nationalism — in a way that pays insufficient attention to the broader historical contexts of time and place in which those phenomena were embedded. Approaching a "technology theme," for example, by arguing that one invention or discovery "led to" or was exclusively causative of the next would only muddle students' understanding of the complexities of historical causation.

Most world history teachers who have been trained in the discipline stay clear of such rigid or presentist treatment of themes. Even so, it is not easy to find a workable balance between panoramic coverage of successive ages of the human past and deeper soundings of selected themes to enhance intelligibility. If empires, belief systems, trade, gender relations, epidemiology, world systems formation, cultural encounters, and monumental architecture are themes that ought to be included in an introductory course, which themes should be left out? For surely a small committee of history professors could think up interesting themes far into the night. As a general rule, teachers should choose a limited number of subject areas, because if they don't, students may wander through the course in a state of bafflement.

One sensible approach is to announce a single overarching thematic question at the start of the semester, then consider it from different angles and in comparative perspective as the course moves along, striving to relate to that question as much course data as possible. In a first-semester freshman course that runs from early times to 1500, I have posed this set of central questions: 1) What were the leading characteristics that defined the "agrarian age"? 2) What are the principal features of modern times, or modernity? And 3) What features fundamentally distinguish modernity from the agrarian age? In class we reiterate and discuss these questions in relation to whatever subject matter we are considering.

Another approach is to choose a broad subject area such as long-distance trade or changing social class relations as a thematic pole on which to hang all discussion, though flexibly enough to permit exploration of a fairly wide range of subject matter. Here the theme is a cognitive life raft to which students will be repeatedly encouraged to return. A third approach is to carry out a comprehensive, chronological survey of world history but to choose three or four "vertical" themes — such as technological change, religion and state, family and society — that weave through the "horizontal" structure of historical developments linked by specific periods and turning points.

In the first selection, Michael Adas, a graduate of the Wisconsin School of world history, reminds us how promising comparative approaches have become since the days of Toynbee and H. G. Wells. In the past few decades scholars have successfully fused comparative theory in the social sciences with empirical historical research, although reasoning inductively from cases to detect general patterns is generally more interesting to historians than formulating theoretical hypotheses to test deductively. The surge of historical knowledge about Africa, Asia, and Latin America has also given historians a much bigger, less ethnocentric world in which to search for cases worthy of comparison. *Prophets of Rebellion*, which Adas published in 1979, was an early model of a precise, systematic comparison of cases that enlarged our general understanding of the relationships between modern millenarian movements and social protest.[3] Included here is a brief excerpt from Adas's introduction to the first of a projected three-volume series of studies in global and comparative history, all originally published as booklets by the American Historical Association.

Adas was a student of Philip Curtin, and he refers to his mentor as "the leading practitioner" of systematic comparative history. Curtin's work exemplifies the point that much innovative scholarship in world history has emerged from creative teaching rather than the other way around. At the University of Wisconsin and then at Johns Hopkins University, he taught an undergraduate course originally called "The Expansion of Europe" and later, "The World and the West." Out of that course evolved much of his comparative scholarship, notably *Cross-Cultural Trade in World History* and *The Rise and Fall of the Plantation Complex*. In the second selection Curtin describes this two-semester class and its methodological premises. He regards his comparative approach as unquestionably thematic, although his themes are carefully defined historical problems, not general organizational labels. Indeed, Curtin believes that the most effective way to achieve intellectual breadth in the classroom is to investigate a series of case studies in a world-scale context rather than to aim for global coverage, which may merely produce "systematic superficiality."[4]

In her essay, Helen Wheatley, also one of Curtin's former students, explains in more detail his method of "inductive comparison," relating it to her own teaching and research. She is particularly interested in "a world comparative approach" to the Pacific Northwest in the eighteenth and nineteenth centuries. She shows how the conventional practice of associating this region with the theme of transcontinental European settlement has tended to make the Pacific Northwest a terminus of history, a place whose function was to be there when Europeans arrived from across the Rockies. The comparativist's eye, however, sees something else: the similarities in patterns of fur trapping and trading in both the Pacific Northwest and Siberia. Following Curtin's earlier work in *Cross-Cultural Trade in World History*, Wheatley tests these similarities by systematic inductive comparison of the two cases. Suddenly the scene shifts. The Pacific Northwest is no longer a peripheral area eventually incorporated into a Neo-Europe but a central part of a fur-trading system that extended across the boreal forests of North America and Siberia and that connected to larger, world-encircling trade networks.

In his world history course at the University of Wisconsin, Eau Claire, Steve Gosch also stresses long-distance trade as a unifying thematic strategy. He aims to help "students move from world history as facts and factoids to world history as patterns and processes." He does not compare cases systematically but employs a number of theoretical frameworks and conceptual tools, inviting students to examine cross-cultural trade from different intellectual perspectives and thereby to recognize its importance as a motor of history. He draws on Karl Polanyi's classification of exchange, Philip Curtin's definition of trade diaspora, and several iterations of world-systems theory. Gosch admits that his method has not succeeded with all students. But who can doubt that a course grounded in a single broad but concrete theme is more likely to yield analytical understanding among at least some students than one that skips haphazardly from one subject area to another?

Cultural phenomena lend themselves to comparative and thematic treatment as readily as economic change. David Smith, who teaches at the California State Polytechnic University, Pomona, acknowledges the special problems of introducing students to world history from 500 to 1600 c.e., a period that involved the growth and interaction of many different religious traditions. To guide students through the maze of cultural data, he has chosen four specific thematic categories through which to consider the similarities and differences among major religions as they come on the world scene and move through successive periods of expansion and transformation. His analytical categories are "legalism," the "hard struggle for salvation," "philosophic religion," and the "easy road to salvation" (or the "faith-only path"). He applies this analytical structure first to India and then to other regions and interregional processes as they arise in the general chronological framework of the course. He carefully weaves his religious themes into a general narrative of change to avoid the essentialist trap of presenting world faiths in terms of ageless cultural qualities. Both Smith and Gosch use a case-based approach that is less systematic than Curtin's or Wheatley's but nevertheless lends cognitive coherence to a freshmen introductory course.

Notes

1. R. I. Moore, "World History," in *Companion to Historiography*, ed. Michael Bentley, 948–49 (New York: Routledge, 1997).

2. Raymond Grew, "The Case for Comparing Histories," *American Historical Review* 85 (October 1980): 770.

3. Michael Adas, *Prophets of Rebellion: Millenarian Protest Movements against the European Colonial Order* (Chapel Hill: University of North Carolina Press, 1979; Cambridge: Cambridge University Press, 1987).

4. For a bibliography of 191 works on comparative and world history, see the syllabus for Philip Curtin's "Seminar in Comparative World History" (spring semester 1998) in Steven Adams, Michael Adas, and Kevin Reilly, eds. *World History: Selected Course Outlines and Reading Lists from American Colleges and Universities*, new enlarged and updated ed. (Princeton: Markus Wiener, 1998), 18–30.

MICHAEL ADAS

Global and Comparative History

Recent writers and teachers of global history have been less concerned than their predecessors with comprehensiveness or providing a total chronology of human events — though these concerns are often evidenced in world history textbooks or mandated by state school boards. In the past two or three decades global and comparative history has tended to be thematically focused on recurring processes, such as changes in military organization and patterns of colonization, or on such cross-cultural phenomena as the spread of disease, technology, and trading networks. In approaching these topics, recent scholars have more consciously employed techniques of comparative analysis than earlier writers, who tended to forage rather erratically and randomly across cultures and civilizations. In fact, one of the key advances in the writing of cross-cultural history in the past few decades has been the rigorous application of the comparative method. In contrast to virtually all earlier works on global history, where case evidence from different cultures was juxtaposed but rarely systematically compared, recent scholarship has often thoroughly integrated the techniques of comparative analysis that have been refined mostly by practitioners of the other social sciences.

Here it is important to stress that though they are routinely conflated, world and comparative history represent quite distinct approaches. Both are cross-cultural; both aim at identifying larger historical trends and recurring patterns. But while world history involves mainly questions of perspective, genuinely comparative history requires the application of a distinct methodology. Central to the comparative technique are the systematic selection of case examples and the mastery of the historical materials relevant to each of these. As Theda Skocpol and Margaret Somers have argued,[1] case selection involves testing to determine that the case contexts are in fact comparable, the identification of constants to link the different parts of the comparison, and the determination of independent (or causal) and dependent (or outcome) variables. Care must be taken that the variables are consistently employed across each of the cases — a process that involves further choices regarding the specific method of comparison an author wishes to employ. As Skocpol and Somers implicitly illustrate, historians tend to favor the contrast-of-contexts approach, which reflects a disci-

Michael Adas, ed., *Islamic and European Expansion: The Forging of a Global Order* (Philadelphia: Temple University Press, 1993), ix–xi.

plinary stress on the importance of empirical evidence, often at the expense of grand theorizing. But as numerous and influential works written on cross-cultural phenomena in the past two or three decades have shown, historians can deal effectively with macrocausal issues, develop meaningful typologies, and test hypotheses. As in the other social sciences, analytical payoff provides the main rationale for the application of the comparative technique. The key contributions that comparativists have made in recent decades to debates over slavery and revolution, for example, which have preoccupied social scientists in a variety of fields, are alone sufficient to justify the serious application of the comparative technique by professional historians.

The great proliferation of studies by area specialists in the post–World War II era has in many ways facilitated serious comparative history and cross-cultural analysis. Area specialists' monographs have provided contemporary scholars with a good deal more data on different cultures and societies throughout the globe than was available to earlier writers who attempted comparative or world history. As a result, the best recent works in these fields have displayed far greater sensitivity than earlier, more comprehensive, world surveys to cultural nuances and to the intricacies of the internal histories of the societies they cover. Sensitivity to the diversity and complexity of the human experience deters most contemporary cross-cultural and comparative historians from the search for universal laws or attempts to discern an overarching teleological meaning in world history. Their main concerns are the identification of patterns and recurring processes, and the study of the dynamics and impact of cross-cultural interaction.

Much of contemporary work on global and comparative history has been focused on non-Western cultures and societies, or the regions lumped together as the Third World before the recent collapse of the Second World and with it the credibility of Cold War ideology. The spread of Islamic civilization, European overseas expansion, the rise and decline of the South Atlantic slave trade, industrialization and the completion of Europe's drive for global hegemony, all have key European (or North American) components. But each of these processes has been grounded in the historical experiences of non-Western societies, and each in turn has been profoundly influenced by the responses of African, Asian, Latin American, or Oceanic peoples. Practitioners of the new world history have very often adopted this perspective because they see it as the most effective way of bringing the experience of the "people without history" into the mainstream of teaching and scholarship. Over the past two or three decades, global and comparative history have proved compelling vehicles for relating the development of Europe to that of the rest of the world and of challenging the misleading myth of exceptionalism that has dominated much of the history written about the United States.

Note

1. "The Uses of Comparative History in Macrosociological Inquiry," *Comparative Studies in Society and History* 22 (1980): 174–97.

Philip D. Curtin

The Comparative World History Approach

One of the most pressing problems for education in the final quarter of the century is the proliferation of knowledge. In history alone, fields of knowledge unrecognized in 1950 have new prominence. Some are new areas like Africa and much of Asia, which were either left out or kept subordinate in the typical Western Civilization courses — and rarely subject to courses on their own merits in American universities. Others are new topical approaches like women's history, the history of the family, historical demography, or Afro-American history. If these are added to what we used to expect students to learn, something we once expected will be squeezed out. Students spend less time in history courses, in any event, than they did a quarter of a century ago. History itself, in short, has already shrunk to make room for new subjects in the university curriculum.

This problem at the broadest level recurs when one tries to put together a university course in World History. Three alternative approaches are now becoming common. One is a World History survey, often confined to a rather short period of time in order to make possible a genuine world-historical perspective without an impossible level of superficiality. "The World of the Twentieth Century" would be a typical title for such a course.

A second possibility is to try for a broader perspective, but to limit that perspective to some defined part of the world. That, in effect, is what the old Western Civilization course did. Another possibility is to take something broader — the Atlantic basin, for example, so that European history is balanced to some extent by bringing in North America, South America, and Africa. Another is to use the Indian Ocean world as a way of balancing the Middle East against India and Southeast Asia.

A third possibility is to try for a global perspective by pursuing themes that occur in several parts of the world. In effect, this approach combines extremely superficial reference to many aspects of world history with deeper soundings into particular topics that are seen to have particular importance. This is sometimes known as Comparative World History, as opposed to the World History Survey.

Philip D. Curtin, "The Comparative World History Approach," *The History Teacher* 18 (August 1985): 520–27.

It is a little hard to describe how this approach works pedagogically. No texts have been written with this intent, though Eric Wolf's *Europe and the People without History*[1] would come close. Some book-length studies by historians who use the comparative world approach in their own teaching, however, illustrate the way they can pursue particular themes in a variety of cultural contexts. Michael Adas's *Prophets of Rebellion*[2] would be one example. My own *Cross-Cultural Trade in World History*[3] would be another.

Part of the problem is that comparative courses can follow a great variety of different themes. The comparative approach is simply that — an approach, not a substantive body of information. Rather than talk in generalities let me illustrate *an* approach to comparative world history with a course I have been teaching since 1953, in one form or another. The course began as one semester, then evolved and changed as it grew to two semesters and altered with the times and the need to conform to the teaching requirements of three different universities — meanwhile passing itself off under four different titles.

The current name is "The World and the West," and its central point is that, by the end of the eighteenth century, the West had become the dominant culture in the world — and was to become still more dominant politically, intellectually, and militarily as the world entered the "European Age" of the nineteenth and twentieth centuries. This may sound like the older "expansion of Europe" approach, but it is not. It assumes some knowledge of European history, and sometimes deals with European motives and attitudes, but it is fundamentally concerned with the impact of Europe on other cultures. The emphasis is on culture change among the non-Europeans.

The present version is a two-semester course, the first semester with the subtitle "The Shifting Balance" being devoted to the rise of Europe in the period from about A.D. 1000 to the beginnings of the industrial age. The end of the pre-industrial world is not taken as a strict chronological line, but rather as a transition, as some institutions characteristic of the pre-industrial period are pursued well into the nineteenth century — plantation slavery, for example, being carried down to its abolition in Brazil in 1888. The second half deals with the impact of Europe in the industrial age itself, defined roughly as 1800 to the present.

The course rests on a theoretical framework of elementary, if not to say simple-minded generalizations about culture change. One of the most basic is that aspects of culture can be transmitted either on the initiative of the donor, that of the receiver, or both. The diffusion of technology across, and between, the "intercommunicating zones" of world history is a recurrent theme in both semesters in many different circumstances. With technology, the initiative was most often that of the recipients. Religions, on the other hand, have often spread through a missionary effort by the transmitters, as is fully evident not only with the spread of Christianity and Islam through overt proselytization but also in the spread of Buddhism along the trade routes of central Asia until it reached both China and Japan.

Less intentional culture change took place, of course, and especially in the colonial settings that emerged as European power began to make itself felt overseas. In this connection, the course organization uses a number of distinctions in cultural demography. In recent centuries the dominant Europeans have found themselves in control of societies having four distinct patterns of culture.

In one, called "territorial empire," Europeans ruled an alien society through relatively small cadres of administrators and soldiers. Typically, these cadres need not have been more than 5 percent of the local population. They were often much smaller. Examples would be the Netherlands Indies, any part of tropical Africa, or the British *raj* in India.

An opposite cultural-demographic pattern came into existence when the dominant power blanketed the native inhabitants with so many settlers that the settler culture became *the* culture of the new country. Overseas Europeans, in effect, carried their way of life with them as they moved. These territories can be labelled "true colonies." The obvious examples are the United States, Canada, Argentina, Australia and New Zealand, and large parts of Soviet Asia.

Between these extremes, two other patterns have some importance. One is sometimes called "plantation society." The crucial factor, however, is not the agricultural system but the fact that the dominant power introduced settlers — not European settlers, but settlers from a third society. The most obvious example is northeastern Brazil and the Caribbean islands, where the Europeans ran the plantations but Africans worked them. Even though the percentage of Europeans was in the range common to territorial empire, the mass of the people had come as uprooted individuals, without a community other than the one they joined as slaves. This made it very difficult to retain their original culture intact. The result was the formation of a new, mixed culture of a kind often labelled "creole."

The second cultural-demographic type lying between territorial empire and true colony is commonly called a plural society — that is, a society where two cultures exist side by side, each retaining its integrity over long periods of time. The obvious examples are places like Malaysia, where Malay and Chinese cultures continue to the present alongside smaller minorities of Arabs, Indians, and Europeans. South Africa, most of Soviet Central Asia, Andean Latin America, or Algeria before 1962 are all part of the same pattern. But these societies are not necessarily indefinitely plural. Cultural integration over the long term tends to produce a growing area of common culture, even though enclaves of originally separate cultures may persist. Mexico is a good example of this kind of cultural integration over the past couple of centuries. Most Mexicans now live with an integrated culture with both Indian and European roots, even though some Spanish and many Indian communities have kept their cultural integrity into the 1980s.

These categories, however, are not designed to provide an ironclad theory or to carry much of the weight of explanation. They are a convenient framework for comparison, with the understanding that comparison will highlight differences as well as similarities. The categories are also useful as a guide to representative types of culture contact that need to be "covered" in a course that aims to achieve the perspective of world history.

The course outline proceeds through a set of topics — three to four per semester. It begins with a survey of relations between major societies over the period from about A.D. 1000 to the early sixteenth century, intended mainly to set the stage for a non-ethnocentric view of the world as it was then. Here, and throughout the course, no textbook is available to carry the main thread of narrative. When good survey material is available, as it is in this period from the works of William McNeill and Eric Wolf, reading assignments can carry the burden of continuity, while lectures can deal in greater detail with problems needing more analytical treatment. For other topics, the lectures have to carry the main line, while readings provide material for case studies.

In this first section, lectures and readings together seek to examine the resources available to the major world societies in their agricultural systems, their technology, their political organization, and their military power — going on to a survey of intersocietal relations.

The second topic has to do with the impact of Europe on maritime Asia from Japan south and west along the Indian Ocean coasts as far as Ethiopia — over the period of the sixteenth century to the late eighteenth. Its aim is to look at culture contact in a period when the impact of Western culture came mainly through trade and the missionary movement. Students read large sections of my *Cross-Cultural Trade* along with parts of regional texts like Percival Spear for India[4] or Steinberg and others for Southeast Asia.[5] The lectures deal comparatively with particular themes — such as the successes and failures of the Christian missionary movement in sixteenth-century Japan, Timor, and Ethiopia, or the economic impact of improvements in maritime technology on freight rates, hence on the possibilities of trade between parts of maritime Asia — and on the agricultural adjustments that followed.

The third and final topic for the first semester is a return to the Atlantic basin for a seven-week examination of the "Rise and Fall of the South Atlantic System." The centerpiece is the complex of slave plantations in the tropical Americas, fed by the slave trade from Africa, and intimately related to the Western societies of North America and Europe, as well as to the plural societies of nearby, non-plantation Spanish America. Although the core is culture-change within the "plantation" cultural-demographic type, the combination of lectures and readings makes it possible to survey Spanish American colonial history in a superficial way, while looking briefly at African history in the era of the slave trade and then in somewhat more detail at the revolutions that demolished the South Atlantic System. Jamaica and Haiti serve as case studies for the late eighteenth/early nineteenth century, while Brazil and Cuba are used to illustrate the final end of slavery in the Americas. One sidelight within this topic is a single lecture on the Spanish theory of empire in the sixteenth century, set alongside the English theory of empire in the early seventeenth. The purpose of this lecture is partly to bring in the importance of intentions and justifications, even when these are not in line with reality, and partly also to serve as background for two similar discussions of imperial theory in the second semester — one on the theory of overseas colonization in the early nineteenth century, a second on the theory of imperial expansion later in the century.

The second semester of this comparative world history course poses far more severe problems of organization, if only because the industrialization of western Europe and eastern North America created far greater power differentials between the West and the rest of the world. It also brought about a far more complex set of cross-cultural tensions and adjustments, as the Europeans created their territorial empires overseas.

The sub-title for the second semester is "The Revolution of Modernization." I must add a caveat immediately. I do not subscribe to the modernization theory that was so popular in social scientific circles in the 1950s and 1960s and for some time afterwards. The definition of modernization used here is strictly economic — the creation of a kind of society capable of high productivity and high mass consumption. "Industrialization" would have done just as well, but for the fear of leaving advanced agricultural economies like Denmark or New Zealand out of the picture.

The semester begins with some theoretical discussions of what modernization might and might not be taken to mean and then passes on to a four-week topic on European overseas settlement, the only topic focused directly on European activities. This approach has several purposes. One is to introduce the study of migration as a key fact of recent history — now seen on a scale more massive than the slave trade had been, and standing as background for the still more massive patterns of migration that were to follow the Second World War. A second is to highlight the fact that cultures do not change *only* because of contact with alien societies. They also change in response to new circumstances, and culture change among the overseas Europeans is a case in point. This is approached through case studies. I first look at transfrontier cultures, those of Europeans who moved beyond the frontiers of the European way of life and adopted a new culture they either invented to meet their new circumstances or borrowed from the alien people they settled among. The examples used here are: the *métis* of Manitoba up to the 1860s or so, the gaucho culture of the Argentine pampa up to the early nineteenth century, and the *trekboer* culture of eighteenth-century South Africa.

Tans-frontier cultures serve to introduce a two-week comparative study of frontier-metropolitan tensions, using Argentina and South Africa in the first half of the eighteenth century as cases in point. Here, the main line of survey is carried by sections of texts on Argentine and South African history, while the lectures carry an analytical theme drawing from the geographers' ideas about central-place theory.

Just as the first topic for the semester focused on "true colonization," the second focuses on territorial empire, beginning with a quick survey of the patterns of imperial expansion and its possible causes, but concentrating on conquest and culture change from the point of view of the conquered. Four principal examples are used here, those of Soviet Central Asia, Bengal, Java, then Mexico — concentrating there on the Maya of Yucatan and the Yaqui of Sonora. As usual, some topics can be carried by readings — Elizabeth Bacon on Central Asia,[6] Nelson Reed on Yucatan[7] — while others are more easily presented in lectures.

The third topic is called "Conversion." It too comes from the introductory typology of culture change — in this case, culture change by intent, a thread already followed in the minor theme of Western missions and non-Western responses in the first semester. The nineteenth-century missionary movement now makes its appearance in a pair of lectures on the movement in Europe and on the ground in Uganda, while the students read Robin Horton[8] and J. D. Y. Peel[9] for sociological and anthropological comparisons between the *reactions* to the missions in Uganda and Nigeria. The use of Uganda illustrates one way comparative cases can serve several purposes. Using the same time/place context in different ways allows the students to work from a body of material that begins to be familiar. Uganda in the 1880s to about 1910 is used first to show how European missions operated, second as part of a two-case example of African reactions to missionary teaching, and finally to introduce the theme of non-Western borrowing from the West as a form of "defensive modernization."

This theme of cultural change on the borrower's initiative continues in the two weeks that follow, which take up Meiji Japan and Turkey from the nineteenth-century reform movement into the period of Ataturk.

The final topic of the course departs from the original typology to look at political and intellectual pressures in the mid-twentieth century non-Western world — at the independence movements as a political manifestation of a revolt against the West, but even more as subtle reactions of ambivalence in aversion to some Western manifestations and as a continued and avid effort to get at least the kind of material resources industrial technology seems to make available. The national revolts are given a week, just as conventional "imperialism" was given a week. The first of the remaining weeks is devoted to millennial movements of an anti-Western nature, combining lectures with readings from Michael Adas's *Prophets of Rebellion*. The final two weeks use Indonesia and Ghana respectively, from the early independence movement to the fall of Nkrumah and Sukarno respectively.

A course of this scope creates some special pedagogical problems. It covers a lot of unfamiliar material in a fairly short period of time. For the past ten years or so, I have experimented with ways of doing this. One of these is the interplay of lectures and readings, so that one tends to carry the main and/or survey aspect of the course, while the other carries the analysis. This implies a different role for the lectures and readings, though the two work together. It also calls for a conscious effort to integrate the two. This is done with two periods of class discussion each week in addition to the two lectures that are normal at Johns Hopkins. To give the lecturer time to direct all class discussions himself, the lectures are on tape cassettes available in the library on loan. The readings tend to be about 100 to 150 pages each week. Each student is expected to produce at the beginning of the week a three-page "intellectual journal," giving his or her reactions to the current readings and just-past lectures. This exercise tends to prepare students for the discussions, and the students are compensated for the extra work by receiving four credits in place of the usual three.

It is obvious that a course of this kind can achieve breadth, but only at the cost of coverage. It is also necessarily idiosyncratic. No two teachers putting together a course in comparative world history will do it quite the same way. This may not be altogether bad, but the particular course outlined here also leaves some serious gaps. It tells students far too little about the last fifty years. On the other hand, teachers probably teach better what they understand better. As long as they avoid the trap of staying too close to their own research interests, both they and the students probably learn more from eclectic and uneven breadth combined with depth in sample soundings than they would have learned from systematic superficiality.

Notes

1. Eric Wolf, *Europe and the People without History* (Berkeley, Calif.: 1982).
2. Michael Adas, *Prophets of Rebellion* (Chapel Hill, N.C.: 1978).
3. Philip D. Curtin, *Cross-Cultural Trade in World History* (New York: 1984).
4. Percival Spear, *India: A Modern History* (Ann Arbor, Mich.: 1961, 1972).
5. David D. Steinberg, David K. Wyatt, John R. W. Smail, Alexander Woodside, William R. Roff, and David P. Chandler, *In Search of Southeast Asia* (New York: 1971; Honolulu, 1985).
6. Elizabeth E. Bacon, *Central Asians under Russian Rule: A Study in Culture Change* (Ithaca, N.Y.: 1980).
7. Nelson Reed, *The Caste War of Yucatan* (Palo Alto, Calif.: 1964).
8. Robin Horton, "The Rationality of Conversion," *Africa* 45 (1975): 219–35, 373–99.
9. J. D. Y. Peel, "Conversion and Tradition in Two African Societies," *Past and Present*, no. 7 (1977): 108–49.

HELEN WHEATLEY

The World and the Northwest:
The Fur Trade, Regional History,
and World History

An Essay Celebrating the Teaching
and Scholarship of Philip Curtin

Most of us face the challenge of teaching some kind of survey course, but we may not necessarily have the opportunity to teach anything like *The World and the West*. I have had both successes and failures in my efforts to translate Philip Curtin's subjects and methods into my own teaching. Oddly enough, I have had a harder time carrying his example into my freshman survey courses than into other classes that may, by title at least, have nothing to do with world history. I have pondered this seeming paradox for years now, and I would like to share my thoughts on it.

Speaking of paradoxes, let's take a look at Phil Curtin himself. Here is a man who seems to know and write about everything, yet he is a sworn enemy of dilettantes. He doesn't want us to think that world history means teaching or writing "a little bit about everything." Yet he feels perfectly comfortable describing *The World and the West* as a course "concerned with the impact of the West on the rest of the world since about 1000 C.E. — that is to say, a course spanning the globe over a millennium.[1] When it comes to the freshman world history survey, Curtin thinks it is entirely appropriate to cover about five thousand years in a couple of semesters. The key to this seeming paradox of achieving broad coverage while also demanding scholarly rigor is that he is flexible about subject matter, but firm about method. He has always had a very clear and straightforward message about teaching world history: Teach comparatively.

What is comparative method? The method is empirical. To be more specific, it is based on inductive reasoning. In a course taught in the Curtin style, you learn to generalize from case studies, moving from the particular to the

Helen Wheatley, "The World and the Northwest: The Fur Trade, Regional History, and World History: An Essay Celebrating the Teaching and Scholarship of Philip Curtin" (revised version of a paper presented at the World History Association Annual Meeting, Fort Collins, Colorado, 18–20 June 1998).

general. As an environmental historian, I think of this as a natural history method, as opposed to a laboratory method. With natural history, you refine your observation skills. You learn to search for patterns in what you observe. If you have seen them aright, these patterns might lead you to some useful theories about what caused them to develop. This is quite different from a deductive laboratory approach where you start out with a theory of causation and then develop experiments to test the theory.

Phil Curtin would argue that his inductive method is properly called comparative history. As he has explained elsewhere, his *World and the West* course uses comparative method on a number of his favorite subjects: cross-cultural trade, plantation societies, frontiers, cultural assimilation, and responses to colonialism. In his introduction to the book *Cross-Cultural Trade in World History*,[2] which was drawn from *The World and the West* course, Curtin spelled out his approach very clearly and simply. Historical work is comparative if it abstracts particular phenomena by defining a comparative subject. The method of abstraction is to observe similarities and differences.

The world dimension is added by making sure that the study is not ethnocentric. The abstracted subject itself (such as the plantation complex), rather than the historical experience of any particular society, defines the point of view. One of Phil Curtin's preferred techniques for escaping ethnocentrism is to focus upon cross-cultural phenomena. He also prefers to look at historical change over long periods of time. Like the cross-cultural approach, the long time-frame is not necessary for doing world history, but it is certainly effective.

The comparative method of teaching or research calls for a thematic design. For this reason, I have found the approach more amenable to upper division courses than to introductory surveys. The course must be defined by the comparative questions rather than by other criteria, usually some form of cultural literacy, which most often motivate institutions to offer those survey courses in the first place. This is not to say that a comparative introductory world history course is not possible or desirable. I am simply saying that a radical curriculum redesign toward comparative questions may be harder to sell to one's colleagues.

In my own teaching situations, I have found it much easier to use *The World and the West* as a model for upper-division courses. They are more open to structuring around topical themes than many introductory courses. Thematic courses such as family history lend themselves easily to comparisons across time and cultures. For example, I once taught an environmental history course that explored forest use comparatively. I used the inductive comparative method of working with case studies. My students did not know that they were taking a world history class.

Even regional history courses can be taught by structuring them around comparative themes. In the history of the American west, a subject that I have taught from time to time, I find that the comparative structure is an excellent way to escape ethnocentrism — one of Curtin's criteria for doing world history. I have been interested in designing a world comparative approach to the history of the Pacific Northwest. My environmental history course that looked at forests was an experiment in this process, since my main goal was to help my students in Seattle understand the historical dynamics of this critical industry. The course led us as far afield as Africa, Japan, and India. In investigating the fur trade, my research, true to the open spirit of Curtin's method, has led me to such seemingly unrelated matters as the lives of the Vikings and imperialism in China, among many other topics. Let us see how comparison can get us there.

If comparison is the fundamental method of world history, what does it mean to look for similarities and differences? Again, following the inductive method, it means that we use cases to look for patterns in history, and for variations in those patterns. To accomplish this, we create an abstract tool, a filter for our observations, by defining a subject area. The filter creates a model of history, rather than a mirror of history. By definition, the filter excludes many historically important events, letting in only those that are germane to the subject. The trade-off for this loss is that we are better able to see how a place (in the case of regional history) fits into a wider variety of historical patterns, depending on which comparative lens we use.

Because I am interested in the Pacific Northwest, it makes sense for me to use a comparative subject such as forestry. Another good subject for the region is the fur trade. Curtin has tackled this himself in *Cross-Cultural Trade in World History*. He has pointed out that the North American fur trade was part of an expansion of the world fur trade, which also included the boreal forests of Siberia. The American and Siberian fur trades can be compared very fruitfully. According to Curtin, areas of broad similarity between the two regions include the following:

Disease gradient: Bearers of luxurious fur, especially martens, otter, and other members of the family of *mustelidae*, exist mainly in the taiga, or boreal zone, where human populations have tended to be sparse and relatively isolated. Thus, the fur trade was also an interaction between the high-disease and low-disease areas of the intercommunicating zone. This had profound significance for the historical dynamics of the fur trade.

Depletion of fur-bearing animals: Fur animals were "open access" resources. A pattern developed of essentially "mining" the animals and moving on, rather than conserving them. Curtin himself does not go into great detail on this matter. However, William Cronon, in his book on the settlement of New England called *Changes in the Land*, made the important point that incorporation of the region into the world trade system meant that a finite resource — the local animal population — was used to supply a relatively infinite market demand.[3] This was the basis of the "mining" dynamic.

Types of animals exploited: In the Eurasian taiga, sable was the most valuable target. Luxurious pelts were deliberately associated with nobility, as shown by passage of sumptuary laws in European countries restricting the wearing of certain types of furs to the noble classes. The sea otter filled a similar luxury role in China. It is very important to look at the types of animals and the reasons why they were valued in the long-distance trade. In doing this — although again, Curtin did not take it this far in his own study — we find an important connection between fur and fashion as a display of status. Borrowing a page from Sidney Mintz's *Sweetness and Power*,[4] we can trace fashion trends in fur as a dimension of the expansion of the world trade over time: merchants, the middle class, and finally even the lower classes entered the fur-consuming market as trade grew in the pelts of cheaper and more numerous critters such as squirrels, beavers, wild hares, and muskrats.

Roles of tools/technology in the spread of hunting and trapping: Curtin observes that Europeans introduced iron and steel tools to the Americas, making it easier to kill animals and changing indigenous cultures in the process. To my knowledge, no one has done a study of the changes in the technology of Siberian hunting and the impact of technology on the "small peoples," as the Russians call indigenous societies, except perhaps investigation of the use of guns. I will note that Eurasian boreal and sub-arctic peoples were not completely isolated, and I have seen reference, for example, to an ancient north-south trade exchanging finely-crafted steel harpoons for walrus-tusk ivory. At any rate, technology gained importance for everyone in the eighteenth century and afterward, and transportation technology was especially critical. It provided access, especially to the maritime mammals, and it lowered costs. Moreover, the creation of denser networks of communication pulled the boreal and sub-arctic zones into a tighter feedback loop with global markets.

This short list of similarities is enough to illustrate the unique powers of comparative methodology to both broaden *and* refine our view of the past. When applied to regional history, its value comes from expanding the range of perspectives that can move us beyond the relatively narrow scope of nation-histories.

My concern about the teaching of Northwestern history as regional history was first aroused by my simple observation that while the maritime fur trade is of enormous historical significance to the Pacific Northwest, the subject of fur is usually treated as part of a story that I call in shorthand "White Men Move West." It centers the Northwest fur trade in the experience of European migration, starting with the so-called "mountain men" who followed the inland rivers and trails from east to west in a pattern similar to the west-to-east expansion of Russian traders into Siberia. This perspective is not averse to comparison. The pattern linking the fur trade to settler colonialism can be found in both North America and Siberia. Yet while I believe that settler colonialism might make a great third theme for a course on the Pacific Northwest, it is not the best way to view the fur trade. Precisely because my starting point is the region itself, I know that the settler colonialism model leaves out too much fur trade history. If we make the fur trade our starting point, we see a lot more of what really happened in the region.

The fur trade question is better than settler colonialism, because it gives proper account to the role of maritime trade. In particular, it unlocks the communication networks of the Pacific, a pattern that is virtually invisible when we view North American history as a "Westward Ho" sweep across the continent from the Atlantic side. The most interesting result of using the comparative fur trade model is that it actually puts the Pacific Northwest at the heart of the story during the Pacific maritime phase. By contrast, the settler colonialism model keeps the Pacific Northwest far out on the periphery.

In brief, my view of the fur trade complex is this: A significant cross-cultural trade in fur and marine mammal ivory developed in conjunction with the general rise of long-distance trade in the world. In essence, the exploitation of human beings and animals were the means by which the northern boreal zone was able to enter into world trade networks. The fur trade intersected with the Silk Road — walrus tusk ivory, for example, was used to make the hilts of Persian scimitars — and with European networks that would become increasingly important over time. The Volga River basin, which ultimately linked the Silk Road to the Baltic Sea, was the first major arterial of the long distance fur trade. This is where the Vikings enter the story, when they lay claim to a share of this trade network. As world trade expanded and intensified, so too did the range and intensity of exploitation of boreal zone and sub-arctic animals. The development of maritime trade created new dimensions of the fur trade: first in the form of Atlantic and Pacific trade networks, and second in the variety of animals opened up to exploitation and introduction to the world market, notably the North American beaver, the northern fur seal, and the sea otter.

The Pacific Northwest enters the story as a nexus of the world maritime fur trade. The Atlantic side was connected mainly through the beaver and enterprises such as the Hudson's Bay Company, which were built on exploitation of this animal. The Pacific side of the maritime fur trade was built upon the skins of sea otter and fur seals. The orientation of this trade was not toward Europe, but toward China.

Contrary to the "Westward Ho" version of Pacific Northwest history, a focus on the fur trade shows that the China trade, first developed by Russia, was the earlier and more influential means by which the region was incorporated into global networks. Native traders such as the Tlingit and the Nootka were already connected to world networks by the time Lewis and Clark walked to the Pacific shore. Russians, Americans, and Britons became intermediaries by which the eastward and westward circuits of fur trade were, by the end of the eighteenth century, closed into a global system. We might even describe a Pacific Northwest era as the first era of globalized fur trade, which lasted as long as the choice animals (sea otters, northern fur seals, and beaver) did — from the 1760s through the nineteenth century. The era reached its height in the early 1800s, just before China descended toward economic and political collapse. (It is worth noting that the cheapness and accessibility of Chinese silk was one of the things that killed demand for beaver felt.)

I have derived these observations regarding the historical course of the fur trade from inductive method, looking at particular case studies. My interest has been more in the extension of what we might call the Eastern/Pacific networks than it has in the Western/Atlantic networks. My case studies include Volga River traders, who connected Northern Eurasia to the Silk Road; the Vikings, who linked the Silk Road to Baltic trade; the Russians, who extended these networks eastward through Siberia to the Pacific; and the mixed, globalized world of the Pacific maritime trade, which incorporated the Pacific Northwest.

These case studies span time as well as space, in order to describe and evaluate the development of the fur trade complex as a whole. It bears noting that a Eurocentric approach to the question would have reached China eventually, but only when Western Europeans got there. My world-historical approach places the Pacific maritime commerce with China in the context of a long-standing fur trade between Asia and the North. This makes the case for using a world comparative approach to regional histories. Otherwise, we might easily overlook important systems of which the region is a part, because we are too wedded to viewing the region in terms of one particular systemic relationship, such as that between the Pacific Northwest and settler colonialism.

Only the inductive method could have carried us to this point. It is hard to imagine how to start out with a theorem and arrive at any linkage between Tlingits and Vikings. Yet the inductive method can carry us to that point with speed and ease. This is what is so wonderfully open and, dare I say, subversive about it.

The similarity of patterns derived from inductive method are not the same thing as *identical* patterns. The point is not to say, "See, when all these factors come together in a particular way, we get the same result." Let's face it: the chaos and complexity of life does not afford us the luxury of doing identical comparisons, especially when we are dependent on whatever detritus of evidence floats on the ebbs and tides of history and into our reach. If I want to understand the Pacific Northwest, for example, I am unlikely to find another place in the world that has the same history. What I can do is ask, how do the things that matter in the Northwest compare to other places and histories? In answering that question, regional links with world history become obvious and important.

Philip Curtin has given us a tool to model the complexity of history creatively, through an open-ended process of looking for patterns. The search for similarity and difference serves as Curtin's Ockham's razor. That fourteenth century suspect of heresy is famous for his dictum, "Multiplicity ought not to be posited without necessity." Scientists use Ockham's razor to argue that complicated explanations aren't needed where a simple one will do. Concepts such as "the plantation complex" or "the fur trade complex" allow the creation of simple groupings based on similarity. Having observed similarities, the burden of proof shifts to proving that cases are too different to belong to the same set. This has the effect of keeping the set for comparison wonderfully large, whereas a search for identical comparisons would make the set frustratingly small. Thus, Curtin's comparative questions challenge us to open up and admit that we might find comparable patterns linked across broad spans of time and space — if we start by looking.

Curtin is an avid photographer. I can think of few people who have learned to see as far and as clearly as he, but I'm sure he would be the first to say that vision gets you nowhere unless you have the right equipment to turn that vision into a work of art. The comparative method may not do everything, but as tools and techniques go, it sure does a lot. No historian should do their work in the world without it.

Notes

1. Philip D. Curtin, "Graduate Teaching in World History," *Journal of World History* 2 (Spring 1991): 81–89.
2. Philip D. Curtin, *Cross-Cultural Trade in World History* (Cambridge: Cambridge University Press, 1984).
3. William Cronon, *Changes in the Land: Indians, Colonists and the Ecology of New England* (New York: Hill and Wang, 1983). See especially chapter 5, "Commodities of the Hunt."
4. Sidney W. Mintz, *Sweetness and Power: The Place of Sugar in Modern History* (New York: Viking, 1985).

STEVE GOSCH

Cross-Cultural Trade as a Framework for Teaching World History

Concepts and Applications

The most important lesson that my world history students have taught me during the past ten years is that if my course is to work, it must be conceptually clear. "There is so much information to learn in this course," they tell me. And, they are right. There is, inevitably, a lot of information for students to absorb in a course in global history. In addition, I know that despite my best efforts at coherence, my course does at times seem to be little more than the story of "one damn thing after another." How to avoid suffocating my students in an avalanche of facts? To me, this is the great challenge presented by the world history course.

The topical approach to world history introduced by Kevin Reilly (2nd ed., 1989) in his classic textbook, *The West and the World*, is one way of meeting this challenge. Some of my most rewarding teaching experiences have come during

Steve Gosch, "Cross-Cultural Trade as a Framework for Teaching World History: Concepts and Applications," *The History Teacher* 27 (August 1994): 425–31.

the semesters when I based my course on Reilly's book. Here, however, I will offer another alternative for structuring the world history survey. I suggest that an emphasis on the theme of long-distance trade across cultural or civilizational frontiers can be a useful way of organizing courses in global history. Although the paper will focus on the premodern period, this general approach is applicable to the centuries since 1500 as well.

Recent scholarship on hunter-gatherers, Neolithic agriculturalists, and the first urban civilizations highlights the importance of long-distance trade in the distant past. Lynda Shaffer's superb book on *Native Americans before 1492* shows how indigenous peoples in the regions of the Great Lakes and Mississippi Valley developed far-reaching trade circuits long before they engaged in agriculture.[1] James Mellaart's well-known findings at Çatal Hüyük illustrate how one Neolithic community flourished, in part, because of its central role in the long-distance trade of obsidian.[2] And much of the recent work on the birth of urban civilization in Mesopotamia emphasizes the importance of long-distance trade rather than irrigated agriculture as the source of the surplus that made early city life possible.[3]

In my course I use three analytical models as ways of emphasizing the importance of long-distance trade: Karl Polanyi's typology of exchange in general,[4] the concept of the trade diaspora as defined by Philip Curtin,[5] and the world system approach employed by Andre Gunder Frank,[6] Immanuel Wallerstein,[7] Jane Schneider,[8] Janet Abu-Lughod,[9] and numerous other scholars.

Polanyi's framework of reciprocity, redistribution, and market exchange is excellent for introducing basic issues. According to Polanyi humankind engages in three main types of exchange. In egalitarian, stateless societies, the reciprocal exchange of social objects predominates. To the extent that long-distance trade takes place in societies of this kind, it is gift exchange. With the development of an economic surplus and the formation of structures of social and political power, reciprocity gives way to the collection and subsequent redistribution of social objects by elite groups. Long-distance exchange in such societies is non-market or "administered" trade and is conducted in neutral "ports of trade." Finally, in modern capitalist societies market-based exchange becomes the rule and trade is conducted in accordance with the laws of supply and demand.[10]

Polanyi's framework has led to much scholarly debate.[11] Specialists on the ancient Near East have been especially critical of Polanyi with regard to his treatment of exchange in Mesopotamia. Polanyi argued that all trade in the ancient Near East was under strict authoritarian controls; market exchange and free-lance merchants simply did not exist. However, a generation of research has established that he was wrong on this point.[12] The existence of market-based exchange in ancient Mesopotamia is indicated by evidence that the price of textiles, copper, tin, gold, silver and precious stones fluctuated over time.[13]

Although the Polanyi model must be modified to take account of more recent empirical research, I think the categories are still useful. Xinru Liu employs them as a way of sorting out the types of trade between China and India from the first century to the sixth. She sees reciprocal gift exchanges between the Chinese authorities and the nomads of central Asia as the type of transaction which inaugurated Sino-Indian trade on the Silk Road. Liu also regards the oases in the Taklamakan Desert and the special quarters for foreign merchants in the Chinese cities of Changan and Luoyang, where foreign trade was carefully supervised, as the functional equivalents of Polanyi's ports of trade. In addition, according to Liu, the existence of rich merchants in Chinese and Indian cities indicates that there was free-lance trade and that prices were somewhat shaped by the forces of supply and demand.[14]

Paul Wheatley also makes use of the Polanyi frame in his examination of the impact of Indian merchants on Southeast Asian societies during the early first millennium. Wheatley argues that prior to the arrival of the Indian traders, most Southeast Asian polities were chiefdoms within which reciprocity was the predominant mode of exchange. The long-term effect of the arrival of the Indian entrepreneurs was to induce a series of sweeping changes into Southeast Asian life. Among the most important of these changes were the simultaneous transformation of the chiefdoms into Indian-style kingdoms and the shift from exchange based on reciprocity to that based on redistribution. Wheatley's study is a vivid illustration of the connections between long-distance trade, modes of exchange, and political structures.[15]

The Indian merchant-mariners arrived in the Malay Strait each year when the monsoon winds blowing across the Bay of Bengal were favorable. It is likely that after a stay of as long as a year, some of the Indian traders returned to their "home offices" on the Coromandel coast while others remained in the Southeast Asian emporia. The result was the establishment of an Indian trade diaspora composed of three groups of merchants: permanent residents of south Indian coastal cities, semi-permanent denizens of the Southeast Asian ports, and a third group of traders that regularly moved back and forth.

Trade diasporas are the subject of Philip Curtin's valuable book, *Cross-Cultural Trade in World History*. Curtin defines trade diasporas as "communities of merchants living among aliens in associated networks."[16] His study is an examination of the importance of these networks in various parts of the world from 2000 B.C.E. to the nineteenth century. I use Curtin's volume as a second way of incorporating long-distance trade into my course.

According to Curtin, the earliest documentary records establishing the existence of a trade diaspora are the clay tablets which illuminate the activities of Assyrian merchants who traded on the Anatolian Peninsula around 2000 B.C.E. Assyrian merchants from the city-state of Ashur traveled to Anatolian cities like Kanesh (present-day Kultepe) in order to exchange Iranian tin and Babylonian textiles for locally extracted gold, silver, and copper.[17]

Like Wheatley's Indian merchants who later traded in Southeast Asian ports, the Assyrian traders in Anatolia were divided into "stayers" and "movers." The stayers became semi-permanent residents in the Anatolian cities; the movers traveled back and forth from Ashur with the caravans. In organizing this early trade diaspora, the Assyrian merchants anticipated the activities of a host of later long-distance merchants in various parts of the world: Phoenicians, Greeks, Armenians, Jews, Arabs, Africans, Indians, Chinese, Native Americans, Italians, and Portuguese.

Trade diasporas are important in world history because the merchants who participated in them were both commodity-brokers and culture-brokers; the traders facilitated the exchange of things and also served as transmitters of ideas. Xinru Liu's book on trade between India and China illustrates very clearly how economic transactions and cultural interchange often overlapped. Buddhists in India sought silk banners from China for the decoration of stupas and for ceremonial use. Chinese Buddhists looked to India as the source of the "seven jewels" (precious stones) used in worship. Monasteries in India and China were often located on key trade routes and benefited from the patronage of merchants. Sometimes the monks engaged in trade and banking themselves.[18]

I like to use traveler's accounts as a way of demonstrating the connections between commerce and cultural contacts. My students read excerpts from Herodotus on Egypt both for his observations about Egyptian life and for indirect evidence of trade between the Aegean and the Nile regions during the classical period.[19] Assignments from the travel book by Xuan Zang, the Chinese Buddhist monk who journeyed from the Tang capital to India from 629 to 645,[20] and from Marco Polo[21] are intended to illustrate other links between cross-cultural travel and trade. A lecture based on Ross Dunn's expert retelling of Ibn Battuta's amazing journeys in the Afro-Eurasian world during the fourteenth century is my attempt to help students see the overlap between cultural interchange and economic transactions within the Realm of Islam.[22]

World-system theory, my third framework for teaching about the importance of long-distance trade, constitutes one of the major growth industries in historical studies today. The contributions of Immanuel Wallerstein, Andre Gunder Frank,[23] and numerous other members of the world-system school to a new understanding of the economic relationship between Europe and the wider world since the fifteenth century are well known. Two decades after the publication of Wallerstein's first volume, it is not easy to imagine how a history of the modern world could be written without taking account of the categories of core and periphery.

One of the most interesting developments in world-system scholarship during the past decade is the application of world-system analysis to the premodern world. Jane Schneider opened this field of inquiry in her influential article "Was There a Precapitalist World System?" Schneider's central point is that prior to the fifteenth century the trade in luxuries or "prestige goods" sometimes created asymmetrical links between world regions which prefigured those analyzed by Wallerstein. For example, Schneider maintains that when Chinese silk was exchanged for European bullion, a precapitalist core-periphery relationship had come into being.[24]

Andre Gunder Frank and a growing number of scholars from various disciplines have recently begun to project the world-system framework far back in time.[25] Barry Gills and Frank argue that the modern world system originated in the Bronze Age around 2500 B.C.E. when trade relations first linked Mesopotamia, the eastern Mediterranean, Egypt, the Indus Valley, and parts of central Asia into one interconnected sphere of what they term "accumulation." According to Gills and Frank, this earliest world system contained the essential features of its modern counterpart: asymmetrical relationships between regions in the core and periphery, continuing struggles for hegemony within the core, and alternating periods of expansion ("A phases") and contraction ("B phases") in the system as a whole. Gills and Frank argue that during the past 4,500 years this original world system has expanded to embrace all of humankind.[26]

The most fully developed application of the world-system perspective to a specific period in the premodern world, and the one that is most important to my course, is Janet Abu-Lughod's justly praised book, *Before European Hegemony: The World System A.D. 1250–1350.* Abu-Lughod argues that the century from 1250 to 1350 was a crucial watershed in world history in that a vast trade circuit stretching from France to China drew together key parts of Afro-Eurasia as never before. For Abu-Lughod the thirteenth-century world system differed from its modern capitalist counterpart in that it had three cores rather than one. From 1250 to 1350 Europe, the Middle East, and Asia were roughly equal members of a great Old World network of exchange.[27]

This premodern world system was to some extent an "archipelago of towns" in which urban centers in Europe (Bruges, Ghent, Genoa, and Venice), the Middle East (Cairo, Aden, and Hormuz), and Asia (Samarkand, Calicut, Kanchipuram, Malacca, Quanzhou, and Hangzhou) were connected to one another by trade and shared in a common culture of commerce. In some of these cities manufacturing, especially the production of textiles, flourished along with trade: Ghent was a major center of woolen cloth production, Cairo produced refined sugar and cotton textiles, and Kanchipuram in south India was known for its production of cotton cloth.

After flourishing for about a century, the thirteenth century world system collapsed. Abu-Lughod's explanation for this development is one of the most interesting parts of her book. She argues that the population declines stemming from the spread of the Bubonic Plague in the fourteenth century led to a fall-off of long-distance trade. The simultaneous unraveling of the Pax Mongolica made exchange across the central Asian overland routes increasingly uncertain. Not long after this, the Ming dynasty (1368–1644) banned Chinese ships from participation in the Indian Ocean commerce. The withdrawal of Chinese vessels from the *Nanhai* trade was the final blow. The great trade net which had emerged around 1250 and, for a century, connected key regions of Afro-Eurasia in a non-hegemonic (or multi-hegemonic) world system was broken. In Abu-Lughod's striking formulation, the "fall of the East" had cleared the way for the "rise of the West."

Abu-Lughod's book is excellent for drawing together the themes of exchange, trade diasporas, and world systems as I conclude my course. But the extent to which an emphasis on cross-cultural trade is successful in helping students move from world history as facts and factoids to world history as patterns and processes remains in doubt. I must confess that the evidence from my students' papers and examinations in this regard is mixed.

Notes

1. Lynda Norene Shaffer, *Native Americans before 1492: The Moundbuilding Centers of the Eastern Woodlands* (New York: M. E. Sharpe, 1992).

2. James Mellaart, *The Neolithic of the Near East* (New York: Charles Scribner's Sons, 1975).

3. Guillermo Algaze, *The Uruk World System: The Dynamics of Expansion of Early Mesopotamian Civilization* (Chicago: University of Chicago Press, 1993); Andre Gunder Frank, "Bronze Age World System Cycles," *Current Anthropology* 34 (1993): 383–429.

4. Karl Polanyi, Conrad M. Arensberg, and Harry W. Pearson, eds., *Trade and Markets in Early Empires* (Glencoe: Free Press, 1957).

5. Philip D. Curtin, *Cross-Cultural Trade in World History* (New York: Cambridge University Press, 1984).

6. Andre Gunder Frank, *World Accumulation and Underdevelopment, 1492–1789* (New York: Monthly Review Press, 1978); "A Plea for World System History," *Journal of World History* 2 (1991): 1–28.

7. Immanuel Wallerstein, *The Modern World-System*, 3 vols. (New York: Academic Press, 1974–88).

8. Jane Schneider, "Was There a Precapitalist World-System?" *Peasant Studies* 6 (1977): 20–29; reprinted in *Core/Periphery Relations in Precapitalist Worlds*, ed. Christopher Chase-Dunn and Thomas D. Hall, 45–66 (Boulder: Westview Press, 1991).

9. Janet Abu-Lughod, *Before European Hegemony: The World System* A.D. *1250–1350* (New York: Oxford University Press, 1989).

10. Polanyi et al.; see also: George Dalton, ed., *Primitive Archaic and Modern Economies: Essays of Karl Polanyi* (Boston: Beacon Press, 1971) and Jeremy Sabloff and C. C. Lamberg-Karlovsky, eds. *Ancient Civilizations and Trade* (Albuquerque: University of New Mexico Press, 1975).

11. Curtin, *Cross-Cultural Trade*, 87–89.

12. Ibid., 70.

13. Robert McC. Adams, "Anthropological Reflections on Ancient Trade," *Current Anthropology* 15 (1974): 239–57.

14. Xinru Liu, *Ancient India and Ancient China: Trade and Religious Exchanges* A.D. *1–600* (Delhi: Oxford University Press, 1988).

15. Paul Wheatley, "Satyāntra in Suvarnadvīpa: From Reciprocity to Redistribution in Ancient Southeast Asia," in *Ancient Civilizations and Trade*, ed. Jeremy Sabloff and C. C. Lamberg-Karlovsky, 227–83 (Albuquerque: University of New Mexico Press, 1975).

16. Curtin, *Cross-Cultural Trade*, 3.

17. Ibid., 67–70.

18. Xinru Liu, *Ancient India and Ancient China.*

19. Peter N. Stearns, Stephen S. Gosch, Jay Pascal Anglin, and Edwin Griesehaber, eds., *Documents in World History*, vol. 1, *The Great Traditions: From Ancient Times to 1500* (New York: HarperCollins, 1988), 21–24.

20. Ibid., 145–49.

21. Ibid., 135–39.

22. Ross E. Dunn, *The Adventures of Ibn Battuta: A Muslim Traveller of the Fourteenth Century* (Berkeley: University of California Press, 1986).

23. See notes 6 and 7 above.

24. Schneider, "Was There a Precapitalist World-System?"

25. See notes 3, 6, and 7 above; also Chase-Dunn and Hall, eds., *Core-Periphery Relations in Precapitalist Worlds.*

26. Barry K. Gills and Andre Gunder Frank, "5000 Years of World System History: The Cumulation of Accumulation," in Chase-Dunn and Hall, eds., Core-Periphery Relations in Precapitalist Worlds.

27. Abu-Lughod, Before European Hegemony.

DAVID R. SMITH

Teaching Religions in the Medieval Period

At the California State Polytechnic University, Pomona, we offer a three quarter sequence in world civilizations according to the following format: the Ancient World to 500 C.E., the Middle Period to the seventeenth century, and the Modern Period. In many ways the second course is the most difficult to teach, partially because of the many different cultures and religions that must be treated in that course. To help organize this material and to allow comparisons to be made between these different societies, I have developed a few simple categories for the variety of religious forms that we encounter: legalism, the hard struggle for salvation, the faith-only path, and philosophical religion. In addition, I spend considerable effort in distinguishing monotheistic religions from polytheistic ones and in pointing out influences flowing from one culture to another.

The concentration on the categories came about purely by accident. Traditionally, courses treating the Middle Period first treat the successors of Rome — Western Europe, Byzantium, and Islam — and then take up the East, Africa, and America later in the quarter. In trying to make our course a truly world civilizations course, my colleague, David Levering, and I were always bothered by the obvious provincialism of treating the West first and then introducing other, more advanced civilizations. We played with the idea of starting with the East, where many cultural and technological innovations originated, and dealing with the West toward the end of the quarter. Given that perspective, we decided to introduce a change. But where to start? China or India? In my impulsiveness its seemed that China was the obvious and only logical place to begin. Did not the Chinese outpace western Europe by more than a millennium in certain inventions? According to the received tradition of twentieth century historiography on China, it was in the late Tang and Sung periods that China entered into

David R. Smith, "Teaching Religions in the Medieval Period," World History Bulletin 7 (Fall/Winter 1990–91): 23–26.

the modern era when urban life and commerce became the most important elements in civilization, an evolution that the West was to imitate only in the High Middle Ages. Levering, on the other hand, suggested that we start with India because it offered a bridge between eastern and western Eurasia and had influenced China so thoroughly in the early Middle Period.

As it turned out, I had the opportunity to experiment with the new format first, so naturally I began with China. The experiment worked well except for one little problem at the beginning. In order for the students to understand Chinese Buddhism I had to review the basic elements of Hinduism and Buddhism. Nearly everything else went very smoothly through the introduction of Chinese civilization into Japan, the Arab and Muslim contacts with India, and ultimately the other material of the quarter. Dealing with Islam naturally led to treating Africa and Byzantium. Byzantine influence and the common problem of barbarian attacks offered an introduction to western Europe, which we followed until its expansion into the Americas. We finished the course by treating the Renaissance and Reformation. The experiment had proven to be a success, but my colleague was correct about beginning with India.

Doing this, however, caused some conceptual problems owing to the extreme complexity of Hinduism. Nearly every form of religious expression developed anywhere in the world crops up there, from crude fertility cults to sophisticated logical systems. It even offers a form of trinitarianism comparable to Christianity's. To help the students come to grips with this culture, I felt compelled to simplify it. Introducing the categories of religious expression seemed to be the only way to accomplish that goal. Early experience had shown me that, indeed, monasticism commonly appeared in different areas of Eurasia in our period, and faith-only movements occurred in more than one context. So, it was only a small step to develop a set of formal categories to summarize the similarities between the various cultures' approaches to religion.

Before laying out the limited number of themes, however, a basic description of nature worship religions is necessary in order to set up the dichotomy between Hinduism and monotheistic religions. Nature worship religions offer worship to the forces of nature and thus elevate the universe itself to divine status. Many gods are contained in this kind of religion because of the many natural forces obviously at work in the universe. "Imminence" is sometimes the term used to describe this concept of the divine, for the gods remain in the world. (The term is from the Latin *immaneo*, "remain in.") Since these forces play a prominent role in the agricultural process, fertility became one chief concern, and various fertility rites developed to encourage nature to reproduce bountifully. Analogy between animal-human reproduction and plant reproduction was drawn very early, and many rites employed human sexual acts as a part of these rites. Finally, nature worship religions tend to be open to contributions from other societies. Since nature is complex, another god or several additional deities could do no harm — they might even help.

Monotheistic religions tend to be the exact opposite. There is only one God. He has created the world and therefore cannot be part of it. He has transcended nature, His creation, and thus is remote (from the Latin *transcendo*, "rise above"). Truth has been delivered by God, and other societies' deities are not acceptable. This system is closed, demanding acceptance of its own truth and excluding other systems altogether.

Monotheism makes its God remote, so the people are continually attracted to the nature gods which are close at hand and earthy. As a result, compromises appear in monotheism through introduction of saints and the borrowing of holidays and festivals of the nature cults. These adaptations usually come after the monotheistic religion has matured and begun to deal with the realities of peoples' needs and original background.

In dealing with India, a treatment of nature worship in Hinduism allows the instructor to suggest that similar religions have already been studied in the previous quarter. In the middle period, China, Japan, Korea, Southeast Asia, Africa, and pre-Columbian America have similar religions. In fact, most religions except Judaism, Christianity, and Islam are of this type. Therefore, it is very important to communicate to students some idea of the appeal these polytheistic systems had and still have.

The first category is what I call "legalism." In India, it is expressed by the term *dharma*, or law, and it is tied in with the caste system. Living up to the duties of one's caste allowed for progress up the caste ladder towards the highest caste, Brahman, after which one could hope for *moksha* or release from the cycle of existence. In this way, Hinduism becomes a social regulating system, determining the task each social group or caste was to perform and the status each was to receive. At this point, the concept of *karma*, transmigration, and *kama* are introduced or reviewed. More advanced courses treat these concepts in greater detail, but since our course is a freshman survey, it treats a great amount of material superficially.

Related to this first category is the notion of the "hard struggle for salvation." This refers to the spiritual athletes of Hinduism (and other religions) who subordinate their whole beings to the struggle for enlightenment or its equivalent in other contexts. Asceticism, yoga in both its physical and meditative aspects, and the use of mind-expanding drugs all fall into this category. Students ordinarily do not understand the term "asceticism," which has to be carefully explained. In our southern California environment, even after it is explained they are incredulous that someone could approach life from that perspective. For meditation, I usually conduct a short meditation using the mantra "so-ham" that I learned in my guru-hunting youth. Physical yoga is ordinarily understood or easily explained.

Philosophic religion is a category also derived from studying Hinduism. In India, it is so complex that I cover only a few examples. Shankara's monism, which finds unity behind the multiplicity of deities and traces it to the Upanishads, becomes India's traditional philosophical defense against monotheistic challenges. The five Hindu philosophic schools offer a logical system more elaborate than the Greeks'. Here I don't go into much detail, given the nature of our course. Ramanuja's response to Shankara in the defense of the bhakti, or devotional, sects is the final element in this area that I discuss.

The fourth category is "the easy road to salvation" which fits Amidism, the faith-only version of Buddhism, which eventually became popular in China, Korea, and Japan. Parallels here appear in Christianity in the Pauline letters, especially Romans 1:16–17, and in Islam in the first pillar. Note that in Romans 1:17, the phrase commonly translated "from faith to faith" is a Greek idiom for "faith only"; this is reflected in Luther's German translation of this verse.

Buddhism shares the fundamental concepts of Hinduism, described above, but objects to the caste system. It offers escape for everyone through acceptance of the four noble truths and following the eight-fold path. This original form of Buddhism (Theraveda or Hinayana) fits into the hard struggle for salvation category. It involves complete dedication and for that reason does not appeal to everyone. Caste, however, does not prevent one from taking this road.

Mahayana, a new form of Buddhism, developed in the second or third century B.C.E. under Hellenistic savior cult influence. Many different incarnations of Buddha, called Boddhisatvas, have appeared throughout history to offer salvation to their fellow humans. This variety of Buddhism is very complex, ranging from "hard struggle" forms which demand asceticism, meditation, and the like, to "faith only" forms such as Amidism. In all its forms Buddhism proved very adaptable to local circumstances, accepting whatever gods and religious rites it encountered. Tibetan Buddhism is a familiar example of a case where Buddhism merged with local shamanistic beliefs. Like Hinduism and other nature worship religions, Buddhism is an open system. Through the Saca tribes' contacts with China, Buddhism entered the Later Han Empire in the first two centuries C.E. It became very popular in China where it had affinities with Taoism and addressed the physical and emotional concerns that Confucianism did not. It also offered an attractive aesthetic and intellectual tradition that the Chinese adopted. In fact, Buddhism became the dominant religion until 842. At that time a reaction set in, and the imperial government suppressed and limited Buddhism. The restoration of imperial power under the Sui and Tang seems to have had something to do with this crackdown, for Confucianism made a comeback owing to the government's need for bureaucrats.

Confucianism itself, however, became transformed by the conflict with Buddhism — into Neo-Confucianism. It reached a steady state in the twelfth century with the writings of Chu Hsi who introduced the notions of *chi* (material force), *li* (principle), and the Great Ultimate. This new side to Confucianism fits the philosophic religion category. As a social organizing force, Confucianism must be classified as legalism. It borrowed ideas from the old legalist school of the first empire, and its own emphasis on rank and status also fit our legalism category.

In addition to influencing Confucianism, Buddhism also evolved several new forms in the Chinese environment, partially under the influence of Taoism. Ch'an (Zen in Japan) and T'ien Tai are two of the more prominent, both to be classified in the "hard struggle" category.

Along with other aspects of Chinese culture, Buddhism passed into Korea and Japan. I have not yet been energetic enough to work up my Korean material, so I will mention only Japan. From the sixth to the twelfth centuries esoteric Buddhist sects dominated. The native Japanese religion, Shinto, was a simple worship religion that peacefully co-existed and interacted with Buddhism. Since the esoteric sects appealed only to a few, mostly upperclass, Japanese, we must assume that Shinto remained the only religion of the commoners. The esoteric sects were of the "hard struggle" category which means that most people would not have had the time for them. This principle also applies to Zen, which became prominent in the twelfth century, but only among the upper ranks of the warrior elite. Amidism began making in-roads in the twelfth century, both among the commoners and the rank and file samurai. Monastic preachers were responsible for this phenomenon just as monks had spread Christianity in the early Middle Ages.

Similar examples of these categories could easily be cited for Islam and Christianity. For example, Islam became nearly an overly legalistic religion until Al-Ghazali successfully incorporated Sufism, a "hard struggle" element, into it. Islam also borrowed heavily from Neo-Platonic philosophy and went through a crisis of adjusting to Aristotle's ideas, a crisis that Western Christianity was also to go through in the twelfth century. Monasticism played a prominent role in the expansion of Christianity and in the development of an independent papacy in the eleventh century. Once the papacy had established itself, however, legalism came to dominate in that institution.

To contemplate why these categories appear in the various religions we have mentioned, we might consider that different needs are met by a religious tradition. As social cement, legalism tends to appear in the form of rules about how people are to relate to each other. Government is impossible without legalism, and before the modern period, as I continually remind my students, religion and politics were not separated anywhere in the world. Personal fulfillment is another aspect of religion, and that may take the form of intellectual activity that can have a religious side to it. Thus, philosophic religion. Similar rewards can also be achieved through the discipline, both physical and mental, that the hard struggle sects taught. Modern scientific studies have shown that mental and physical "highs" can be achieved through the various practices of these cults. Asceticism can produce similar results.

The problem in teaching world history is that there is far too much material to learn and teach. To overcome this obstacle, the world history teacher continually has to read and study and reorganize the material. The idea of the categories is to provide some over-riding principles for organizing the teaching of this one aspect of world history. All the particular facts and details remain, but by calling attention to the categories the similarities between various cultures' religions can be pointed out. The differences are also important, perhaps more important than the similarities, but the categories are still useful in providing a beginning on which a discussion of differences can be based.

SELECTED BIBLIOGRAPHY

Comparative Studies in Society and History 22 (April 1980). This issue of the journal offers a special section on "Approaches to Historical Comparison." Seven social scientists discuss methodological issues, including "The Uses of Theory, Concepts, and Comparison in Historical Sociology" and "The Uses of Comparative History in Macrosocial Inquiry."

Cooper, Frederick. "Race, Ideology, and the Perils of Comparative History." *American Historical Review* 101 (October 1996): 1122–38. This review of books by George M. Frederickson and James T. Campbell is also a valuable commentary on the merits and risks of two kinds of comparative analysis. One juxtaposes two cases to pull out similarities and differences, the other examines a transatlantic phenomenon as it played itself out interactively in two places.

Essays on Global and Comparative History. Edited by Michael Adas. Washington, D.C.: American Historical Association, 1990–. A superb, bargain-priced series of pamphlets (seventeen to date) presenting in succinct form a wide range of topics and historiographical issues in world history. These essays are designed, according to the AHA, to be "especially useful to college and secondary school teachers who are engaged in teaching world history in a comparative format." Ten of the essays have also been published in Michael Adas, ed., *Islamic and European Expansion: The Forging of a Global Order* (Philadelphia: Temple University Press, 1993). For a list of titles currently available, See <www.theaha.org>.

Grew, Raymond. "The Case for Comparing Histories." *American Historical Review* 85 (October 1980): 763–78. This is the lead essay in an issue devoted to comparative history. Grew discusses a number of methodological problems, but he concludes that comparative history is not "a method." Rather, "for historians to think comparatively, to compare histories, is to do what we already do — a little more consciously and on a somewhat broader plane."

McAfee, Ward. "On a Wing and a Prayer: Teaching about World Religions." *Perspectives* (American Historical Association) 33 (December 1995): 27–30. Both a historian and practicing Christian, the author takes an empathetic approach to his subject, believing that "it is important to avoid a sterile neutrality" in introducing students to the major faiths and ethical systems. His unifying theme is the mystical element he finds in all the religions, the necessity of putting off self to find true Selfhood.

Muhlberger, Steven, and Phil Paine. "Democracy's Place in World History," *Journal of World History* 4 (Fall 1993): 23–45. Important reading for any teacher who wants to use democracy and its development in the world as an analytical theme. The authors argue that the presumption of democracy as an exclusively Western invention has concealed the long history and social importance of quasi-democratic institutions, especially on the local level, in China, Sub-Saharan Africa, India, and Native North America.

Stavrianos, L. S. "Technology as a Central Theme for World History." *The History Teacher* 18 (August 1985): 513–20. In this short essay Stavrianos contends that the tumultuous world we live in today is largely a consequence of the technological transformations of the past two and a half centuries. This is reason enough to build the study of world history around six technological revolutions he believes to have occurred, beginning with tool-making.

Stearns, Peter N. "Nationalisms: An Invitation to Comparative Analysis." *Journal of World History* 8 (Spring 1997): 57–74. Explicitly addressing nationalism as a *teaching* problem, Stearns calls for "a new generation of analysis that goes beyond the stories of particular movements but cuts under the most sweeping generalizations about the phenomenon." This requires more systematic comparison of cases giving careful attention to the historical factors special to each instance.

White, H. Loring. "A Technological Model of Global History." *The History Teacher* 20 (August 1987): 497–517. White adopts a broad definition of technology to include "mental" means of accomplishing significant tasks, such as politics, education, and religion. He offers an innovative, detailed, and periodized course scheme that adheres closely but not restrictively to his central theme.

PART NINE

GENDER IN WORLD HISTORY

World history and gender-related history have thrived during the past quarter century, but until recently they have not had much influence on one another. Insofar as world history emphasized large-scale political, military, economic, and social forces, biographies of notable men or women got little attention, and the "maleness" of human action tended to be assumed. Women's history, on the other hand, drew its data from European civilization, or from other parts of the world, mainly within the analytical frame of area studies.[1] In the past decade, however, women's history and world history have intersected more systematically as the comparative range of gender studies has broadened and as globalists have become more aware of the gendered nature of much of the past and its representations.

Today, many history teachers are striving to do fuller justice to the historical experience of both men and women and to make their students understand that gender distinctions in every world region and in almost all spheres of life are socially constructed rather than "natural." Here is an example of how one group of history educators, including me, gained a more nuanced understanding of how to present issues of women and gender in the world history classroom. In the summer of 1995, two panels of distinguished educators gathered in Philadelphia to review the first edition of the National Standards for History. The Council on Basic Education, working with the National Center for History in the Schools (NCHS), convened these committees and asked them to recommend changes to the standards for both United States and world history, thereby tempering the media controversy that had flared up over them and setting plans in motion to produce a revised second edition.

Among the members of the review panel for world history was Joan Wallach Scott, a fellow of the Institute for Advanced Study and a prominent authority on labor and women's history.[2] Not surprisingly, Scott inspected the social and cultural aspects of the standards closely, especially the guidelines for the understandings that high school graduates should have about women and gender. Her written comments to the panel, which were later incorporated into the revised standards, encapsulated some of the conceptual difficulties that still needed to be overcome to bring classroom practice and textbook writing into line with the best scholarly thinking on this crucial dimension of world history.

The task force of K–12 and college teachers (in all, nineteen women and sixteen men) that had drafted the world history standards in detail in 1993–94 concurred that the content of history education must take proper account of women, family, and gender-related issues. These topics, however, were to be worked into a general thematic scheme formulated by the National Council for History Standards that emphasized the political, economic, environmental, religious, and high cultural contours of world history, types of subject matter most likely to be amply represented in existing K–12 textbooks and other resources. Social historical content would not predominate, and the "new cultural history" would be only a minor theme.[3] The task force proceeded to look for ways to draft and incorporate standards on women and gender wherever these topics seemed appropriate. The ideological sensibilities of the writers were progressive and inclusionary, and the draft standards included numerous gender-related teaching recommendations. Even so, the group was not tuned in as closely as it might have been to cutting-edge scholarship. The standards documents that emerged manifested too much of what Sarah Hughes and Judith Zinsser call the "add women and stir" approach to history education. In her perceptive critique of the world history standards Joan Scott wrote,

> Women [in the standards] are another example of an approach that . . . substitutes static and homogeneous notions for historical ones. The standards most often refer to women in terms of their roles and statuses. A typical sentence refers to changes in the status of women — and peasants or slaves or workers — as if these categories were entirely separate, as if race or occupation or social position didn't affect the roles and statuses of women, as if "women" was a fixed homogeneous category. . . . The approach that refers simply to "women" will perpetuate the very attitudes it seeks to correct. Women will be thought of as timeless beings defined by their sex and their reproductive roles; peasants or workers or aristocrats will be represented as men. . . .
>
> Having separated women from the main narrative as a group understood in terms of roles and statuses, the standards miss many opportunities to include women as individual historical actors. . . .
>
> They also systematically miss the opportunity to point to specific differences between men and women. Thus, although the standards sometimes refer to relations between men and women, the idea of "relations" (like the idea of "roles and statuses") is empty. Instead, one should ask for analyses of the different impacts of events or processes on men and women.[4]

If some of the history professionals responsible for the standards project had not quite "gotten it" before listening to Joan Scott, they were at least beginning to grasp the deficiencies she pointed out when they undertook the revisions. Along with a few other astute reviewers, she recommended a number of specific changes. As a result, many statements relating to women and gender were altered in one way or another.[5] Here, I offer four examples of standards "before and after," which may serve as cautionary data for instructors who are developing or revising world history courses. They demonstrate that sometimes minor changes — of a word or phrase — may express a more enlightened perspective and significantly modify the historical conceptions that teachers and students are likely to form:

1. *First Edition*
   [Explain] the class divisions of Greek society and the social and political roles of major classes, including slaves. [Analyze] the place of women in Athenian society.

   Second Edition
   Explain hierarchical relationships within Greek society and analyze the civic, economic, and social tasks that men and women of different classes performed.

2. *First Edition*
   [Assess] the political, social, and cultural contributions of women in the Japanese imperial court.

   Second Edition
   Assess the political, social, and cultural contributions of aristocratic women of the Japanese imperial court.

3. *First Edition*
   [Analyze] how Christian values changed the social and economic status of women in early medieval Europe.

   Second Edition
   Analyze the importance of monasteries and convents as centers of political power, economic productivity, and communal life.

4. *First Edition*
   [Analyze] the effects of industrialization and urbanization on development of class distinctions, family life, and the political and economic status of women.

   Second Edition
   Explain how industrialization and urbanization affected class distinctions, family life, and the daily working lives of men, women, and children.[6]

The three authors included in this section would certainly agree that Joan Scott's warnings were apt. In their essays they not only argue for recognition of women's historical agency and the need to transcend the "side-barring" of women as an undifferentiated category, they also affirm the potency of gender as a mode of analysis, especially the investigation of the significance of maleness and femaleness as cultural constructs in societies around the globe. In addition, they offer practical recommendations for teaching a more richly gendered world history that therefore has weightier explanatory value.

The first two selections illustrate an emerging line of scholarship: the integration of global and gender-related history through interregional and comparative analysis. The expositors of this approach avoid ethnocentrism by selecting cases for comparison from around the world. They also have a globally minded preference for investigating large-scale patterns because, as Sarah Hughes writes, gender is a "fundamental organizing principle of human societies."

In her innovative research Ida Blom applies comparative analysis to gender and the development of the nation-state worldwide. She finds that the assumption of a "natural" binary opposition between a public sphere commanded by men and a private sphere ruled by women breaks down as soon as we become conscious of the centrality of women and of gendered symbolic representations in the historical development of nation-states. Comparing inductively the diverse cases of India, Japan, Norway, and Sweden, she observes that women have adopted two gender-based strategies for gaining full membership in the national polity and community. One starts with the premise that women and men are similar in the sense that they have equal claims to natural rights and fulfillment of civic potential and should therefore have equal political rights and responsibilities. The other posits that men and women are different but that each sex has particular gifts and abilities to contribute to the making of the nation-state. Here the question is not political equality but rather the right to full participatory membership in civil society. Blom concludes that these two strategies have operated simultaneously around the world and thus constitute a global pattern of significance in the context of nation-state formation. She also demonstrates, however, that women have employed one or the other strategy in different ways, depending on a range of cultural variables. Gender analysis thus may lead to a deeper understanding of global processes and the factors that make cultural communities distinctive and special.

The second selection is the published version of a presidential address Judith Zinsser made to the World History Association in 1996. Like Blom, Zinsser targets the bland assumption that world history subject matter not specifically about women, family, or gender relations is probably either gender-neutral or connected to the doings of men. Part Eight listed technology among the useful organizing themes for a world history course, but few instructors would be quick to associate this subject with gender. Zinsser shows, however, that in research on technological change, "gendered premises affected the questions we asked, the evidence we found, and the conclusions we drew from that evidence." For a long time, she points out, assumptions of maleness governed what scholars thought might be knowable about the Paleolithic and Neolithic eras. Deconstructing these assumptions has allowed historians to "see" in the ancient past the productive tasks women performed and the tools they used. For modern history, scholars on the trail of cultural representations of gender have revealed that perceptions of women as "naturally" possessing mental or physical skills that are different from men determined divisions of labor in nineteenth-century industrial society far more than biological differences between the sexes. Undoubtedly, world history teachers could rethink many of the topics they present using the analytical tools of gender.

The next two selections take us to the classroom. Sarah Hughes reports on her methods of teaching a multisection departmental world history course to infuse the experience of women and gender. Whatever the topic, she strives to lead women from their hidden places in history. She asks, in effect, "Where were the women? What were they doing?" She challenges the notion that certain patterns in gender relations were "natural" and that when the subject is diplomacy, war, politics, production, or trade the historical actors may be assumed to be men. Finally, Judith Zinsser returns to show that even slight changes in a course's conceptual vocabulary can significantly sharpen students' consciousness of the gendered social order. By "sexing the universal" she not only brings women up front as historical agents individually and collectively, but she also encourages students to imagine the past as invariably peopled with men *and* women. Both Hughes and Zinsser offer useful ideas for readings and films.

Notes

1. These points are made in Sarah Shaver Hughes and Brady Hughes, *Women in Ancient Civilizations* (Washington, D.C.: American Historical Association, 1998), 2.

2. Scott's famous seminal essay is "Gender: A Useful Category of Historical Analysis," *American Historical Review* 5 (December 1986), 1053–75; reprinted in Joan Wallach Scott, *Gender and the Politics of History* (New York: Columbia University Press, 1988), 29–50.

3. See Part Seven for the world history standards periodization design and accompanying introductory essays. I might mention that the National Standards for United States History, reflecting classroom and textbook practice, gave greater attention to social historical issues than did the world guidelines. See *National Standards for United States History: Exploring the American Experience*, expanded ed. (Los Angeles: National Center for History in the Schools, University of California, Los Angeles, 1994). The revised U.S. and world history standards were published as *National Standards for History*, basic ed. (Los Angeles: National Center for History in the Schools, University of California, Los Angeles, 1996). To avoid confusion, note that the first edition is the *Expanded Edition*, with separate volumes for U.S. and world history. The second, revised *Basic Edition* combines U.S. and world history in one volume.

4. Joan Scott, "World History Standards Review, August 21–23 Meeting" (Communication to the Council on Basic Education Review Panel for World History, 1995).

5. The small committee that drafted language for the revised edition included Joanne Ferraro, the San Diego State University historian who writes on women and gender in early modern Italy. Judith Zinsser, at that time a member of the NCHS's Advisory Board and president of the World History Association, also reviewed a draft of the second edition.

6. *National Standards for World History: Exploring Paths to the Present*, expanded ed. (Los Angeles: National Center for History in the Schools, University of California, Los Angeles, 1994), 78, 116, 120, 212; *National Standards for History*, basic ed., 149, 159, 160, 189.

IDA BLOM

World History as Gender History
The Case of the Nation-State

World history was for long regarded as "an illegitimate, unprofessional, and therefore foolish enterprise."[1] But as gradually global integration becomes part of history, renewed academic efforts are being made within this field. These efforts may be seen as rooted in two traditions: one developing out of grand civilizational studies, the other rooted in the histories of discovery, maritime empires, etc.[2] In contrast to earlier attempts at understanding the history of the world, today's research is consciously striving at avoiding the trap of Eurocentrism. Looking for autonomous trajectories of development and interregional exchange, historians now understand the European expansion from the middle of the nineteenth century as colliding and overlapping with the dynamics of other regions.

The concerns of today's researchers of global history are studies of recurring processes and the dynamics and effects of cross-cultural interaction. Global history research has become an inter-disciplinary field involving a number of different approaches, such as anthropological and ethnohistorical insights as well as comparative macrosociology. "A fundamentally new framework of conception and inquiry, able to capture the life *in toto* of the whole of mankind since the dawn of time," is needed.[3] I will suggest that one of the latest new directions within global history, still scantily developed, may assist in creating "a fundamentally new framework of conception and inquiry,"[4] namely comparative and cross-cultural studies of women's history and gender analysis.

GLOBAL HISTORY AS GENDER HISTORY

I shall posit that one way of structuring global history is to think of the world as held together through a *gendered order, a gender system,* a basic division of

Ida Blom, "World History as Gender History: The Case of the Nation State," in *Between National Histories and Global History*, ed. Stein Tønnesson, Juhani Koponen, Niels Steensgard, and Thommy Svensson, 71–91 (Helsinki: Finnish Historical Society, 1997).

individuals according to biological sex. One of the most easily perceptible common characteristics of any society, regardless of time and space, is the division of individuals according to sex. Any social group, class, caste, ethnic group, etc., comprises girls and boys, women and men, in fact, the gender division cuts vertically through all horisontal social stratifications.

This is not a new observation. It permeated some Enlightenment attempts at writing global history. During the late eighteenth century, a number of German, French and British historians were looking for explanations for why some peoples developed "civilized" cultures, while others remained "barbaric." If they found skin-colour to be the most important criterion for the degree of sophistication of societies, their Eurocentric histories also highlighted gender-differences within cultures. Although the male adult was the central figure in these global cultural histories, analyses of everyday lives were concerned also with the lives of women and children. Some historians even wrote separate women's histories. In his four volume *Geschichte des weiblichen Geschlechts* (1788–1800) the German historian Christoph Meiners showed almost modern insights into the problems of gender history. He exhibited an understanding of the relativity of historical sciences, and of the difference that may exist between lived history and the reconstruction made by historians.[5] Other historians, in Denmark as well as in Britain, were eager to demonstrate that women's position in society was conditioned by modes of production, as well as by political and religious systems.[6]

Throughout the greater part of the nineteenth century, gender remained an important element in philosophical discussions of how to create the best society. But, rooted in grand civilizational studies, women's history lost importance as the historical sciences turned to studies of the formation of nations and nation-states, diplomacy and statesmanship. Not only the global and cultural perspectives, but also the understanding of the gendered structure of societies was lost.[7]

When, during the past decades, the interest in women's and gender history has again led to attempts to analyze the importance of gender within different cultures, historians encounter some of the same problems as their precursor. Although Asian, African and Latin American historians are now also researching the importance of gender, this approach to the historical sciences is still to some degree dominated by western researchers and by western theories of gender. A number of comprehensive syntheses of women's history through the ages have appeared, but only one — a Norwegian-Danish three volume work — attempts to cover women's history outside the western world.[8] However, cooperation among historians across cultures has been stimulated by world-wide networking, resulting in cross-cultural conferences and journals perceptive of cross-cultural gender differences.[9] Discussions among historians of different cultures, analysing world-wide phenomena from their varying perspectives stimulate analyses of cross-cultural similarities and differences. An early attempt at a gendered approach to global history has inspired this paper.[10]

CENTRAL CONCEPTS OF GENDER ANALYSIS

Women's and gender history internationally seem to have developed through methodologically and theoretically similar, though not chronologically parallel phases, and to share certain common assumptions.[11] Theories of patriarchy have been used to explain gender hierarchies, systematic differences between women and men and changes in gender relations. Patriarchal theories have gradually been broadened or even sometimes replaced by theories on interaction of cultural and biological givens. Many historians now apply theories of a "gender system" or a "gendered order."[12] Introducing poststructuralist analysis as an important tool for historians of gender, Joan W. Scott has been pivotal in the international debate on how to understand the functioning of gender. Scott defines gender as "a constitutive element of social relationships based on perceived differences between the sexes, . . . gender is a primary way of signifying relationships of power."[13] The concern of gender history, according to Scott, is not limited to highlighting women's and men's common and gender-specific histories, but should also be to analyse "the often silent and hidden operations of gender that are nonetheless present and defining forces in the organization of most societies."[14]

According to this way of thinking, gender is a basic social structure, interacting with all other social structure, be it class, race, religion, etc. In any culture, in any society, gender will have an impact on the socialisation of the individual, on distribution of work, on responsibilities and rights in the family and in society. Gender relations are at work in politics, in economics, they influence inheritance rules, etc. When societies change, so do gender relations, and changes in gender relations influence other social relations. One basic common assumption, then, is that the question of the importance of gender as an analytical category should always be raised. Consequently, gender as an analytical category should be of the utmost importance to any approach to global history.

In this paper, I shall discuss the interaction of understandings of gender and the concept of the democratic nation-state. The construction of the nation-state has mostly been studied as a phenomenon originating in western societies, spreading to the rest of the world. But as has been pointed out, the concept of the unitary nation-state was in itself an idea that became rapidly globalised and may be termed a "bearer" of globalisation, affecting people in different parts of the world during roughly the same period of time, i.e. the late nineteenth and early twentieth centuries. Images of democracy, freedom and welfare, to name but a few, have been perceived as examples of cultural flows, as *ideoscapes*, on a par with ethnoscapes, technoscapes, finanscapes and mediascapes.[15] Studying a limited number of manifestations of the construction of the nation-state, I will understand this concept as belonging to cultural flows, to global ideoscapes, influenced by different understandings of gender, and outlining one of multiple trajectories into modernity.

NATION, SEX, ETHNICITY, AND CLASS

A number of criteria have been operationalized in order to decide who should be eligible for political citizenship in democratic nation-states. A central criterion was sex, as it manifested itself in biologically determined physical characteristics. Nowhere, except in Finland, were women given the right to vote at the same time as men. Although women's reproductive capacity, their physical capacity of bearing children, was highly valued, it was never a criterion for granting them political rights.

In the USA another physical criterion also long meant exclusion from political rights, the criterion of skin-colour. One might say that physical characteristics such as the capacity to bear children and skin-colour, acted as what Eric Hobsbawm has called "visible ethnicity," dividing individuals into more or less worthy, more or less influential members of the nation. This was clearly the case within the British Empire.

But criteria were not always explicitly formulated as physical characteristics. What was made decisive was questions of economic self-sufficiency and intellectual abilities.[16] Such criteria excluded many men — servants, some workers and in some nations black men — and everywhere all women. All these individuals were in different ways economically dependent. Add to this that women and blacks were seen as reigned by emotions and intuition, not by rational reasoning, and consequently also fell short when it came to intellectual abilities, another criterion for being included in the nation through political rights.

In a global perspective, it may be ascertained that democratic rights in the nation-state were first bestowed on white men of the upper social strata, then on white male workers and peasants. Coloured men and all women, regardless of skin-colour, were, in that order, the last groups to be accepted as full citizens. It may be said that "history flows faster" in the case of men than in the case of women, although it did not flow equally fast for men of all classes.[17] The growth of democratic nation states was clearly influenced by the gender system, as well as by class and race.

Such observations seem to confirm the global working of the private/public dichotomy. In any culture, the gendered division of work and responsibilities has assigned women to the family sphere (the private), men to the wider society (the public). Although this dichotomy manifests important variations, this overall pattern seems to obtain as a global phenomenon.

But so does the deconstruction of the dichotomy of the private family and household as a feminine, apolitical arena opposed to the masculine public world of politics (and economics, etc.). As soon as the concept of politics is widened to include any action with the purpose of distributing power and resources in society, the family can no longer be seen as a private institution. It must also be perceived as a channel for political power, especially in societies where such power was restricted to a small elite.[18] This also applies to power

embedded in collective actions, where women outside elite groups had a possibility of influencing important political decisions. The construction of the
democratic nation-state strengthened the possibilities of collective actions, not
only from male-dominated fora, such as trade unions and political parties, but
also from female dominated voluntary organisations, be it suffrage organisations
or philantropical societies.[19]

These possibilities were seized by groups of women as means of working to
obtain political rights within the nation. Two different strategies, building on
two different understandings of gender, were applied.[20]

Grounded on natural rights arguments, the equal-rights-strategy was built
on the assumption that women and men were individuals with basically similar
potentials, and consequently with the same rights in the family and in the
nation-state. This led among other things to claiming votes for women on the
same conditions as for men.

The difference strategy saw women and men as basically different, but with
complementary potentials, and with equal importance to the national home.
Women were perceived as mothers and wives in the private world, men as producers, soldiers and politicians in the public world. Consequently, the two sexes
did not have the same duties and did not need the same rights in the nation. According to the difference strategy, different functions in family and society
should lead to different rights, but different rights should form the foundation of
equally important membership in the nation.

Maybe surprisingly, this dichotomous understanding of gender might also,
and in fact often did, lead to claims of equal rights. The logic behind the claim
that women and men should have the same rights in the nation would then be
that feminine elements were needed in society, in the public, to complement
masculine influence. In this thinking, the very difference between women and
men was the reason for claiming equal rights.

Both understandings of gender and both strategies should, therefore, be
seen as analytical tools, not as mutually exclusive entities. In fact, the two often
co-existed, not just within a certain group, but also within one and the same
individual.

Finally, I will argue for dissolving also the dichotomy state-nation/culture-
nation, the political as opposed to the cultural component of the nation, created
by Friedrich Meinecke.[21] Support for the political autonomy of a sovereign nation state, the civic/political perception of the concept of nation, is intimately
related to the concept of national culture. Shared national history, language and
national symbols, "rooted in a soil of recognizable traditions and forms of expression," an "imagined community," are presuppositions for a voluntarily organized society and for support of political institutions.[22]

However, understandings of gender have everywhere been central to this
"imagined community" as well as to shared national symbols. World-wide, also,
the two strategies and the two different perceptions of gender outlined above,
may be found in efforts to include women in the creation of the modern demo-

cratic nation-state. I shall attempt to support these statements with examples of construction of nation-states as different as Sweden, Norway, India and Japan.

National Symbols — and Their Political Meanings

A global metaphor for the nation-state has been the home. A Nordic audience will recognize such concepts as the Swedish *Folkhemmet* (People's home). Norwegians share the images characterising their national anthem, where "the thousand homes," defended by strong fathers and by mothers who are sometimes fighting just like men, sometimes weeping, are symbols of common history. Concepts like "fatherland" and "mother tongue" indicate the gendered family as a symbol of the nation. Women as mothers are very visible not only to French and British national rhetoric, but may also be found in Asian cultures, for instance in the widely used concept of "Mother India." In Bengal, anti-British feelings around the turn of the century were imbued with a Hindu nationalism, invoking the mother goddess Kali, also the goddess of strength, to liberate Mother India. When the British pointed to the subjugated position of Indian women as a sign of the uncivilised character of Indian culture, Indian nationalists would cite old Hindu traditions — the *shakti* — where powerful goddesses invested women with strength and steadfastness. In Japan, however, although the family was also here the symbol of the state, education and ideology stressed filial piety to the father as emperor, indicating a different expression of nationalism. The mother image, strongly supported by state-directed organisations like the *Aikoko Fujinkai* as from 1901, in the 1930s by the *Dainippon Rengo Fujinkai*, became that of the subservient figure, happy to sacrifice her sons to the needs of the emperor, or taking care of children after her husband had died on the battlefield.[23]

Within the symbolism of the family/nation-state, women were made bearers of national traditions, for instance through the gender-specific habit of wearing traditional dresses. Especially Indian, but also Japanese women, to a much greater extent than men, continued to dress in traditional ways, something that manifested itself also in Norwegian renaissance of wearing the *bunads* as from the turn of the century.[24]

No doubt, many more examples of the home, of mother and father figures, used as metaphors for the nation, may be found in national rhetoric accompanying the construction of the nation-state. My point is that a discourse built on the easily recognisable tradition of perceiving the family as the locus of loyalty, safety, closeness, at the same time clearly indicated the different positions of mothers and fathers, and consequently of women and men in the nation-state.[25] The image of the home with a gendered division of responsibilities, locating women in the private sphere and with a narrower space of action, men in public society with a much wider range of responsibilities, clearly suggested a division between the public and the private. Limited mobility for women has been expressed in a number of cultural customs, distinguishing individuals within the same social category according to their biological sex. Over the centuries, for example, groups of Chinese women had their feet bound at a very early age, and many Muslim and Hindu women observed *purdah*, some living their lives in the women's part of the house, the harem or *zenana*. In such cases, women's mobility was physically restricted. In Europe and in the Americas, ideological and psychological approaches taught women and men that respectable women must not appear unescorted except in certain well-defined areas. Failure to respect these boundaries made male aggression towards them more or less legitimate.[26] Such cultural norms affected understandings of citizenship as outlined above, and strengthened the perception of the public as an exclusively male arena. A Norwegian politician in 1890 legitimated his opposition to granting women the right to vote by stating that

> the very word "public" — for how fine and ironic language often is — there is nothing to prevent us from saying that all of us, we are public men, but we know of course that if we linked the word public with the name of a woman, it would be the utmost disgrace . . . as long as the world has existed . . . the veil is a garment that belongs to the woman, but never to the man, and that whoever tears a woman's veil is guilty of a shameless deed.[27]

For all the cross-cultural similarities in the language of symbols, it should, however, not be forgotten that where the family functioned according to a very strict patriarchal power-model, as was very evident in Japan and India, such symbols were prone to uphold women's subordinance and men's domination. Although we find globally shared national symbols, we must take cultural differences into account. The same concepts do not necessarily have exactly the same meaning within different cultures.

Two Strategies for Integrating Women in the Nation-State through Political Citizenship

The equal-rights-strategy and the difference strategy may be seen as global phenomena, occurring wherever a nation-state was being created.

At the end of the nineteenth century, some women — and men — had begun to protest against gender-based differences in democratic rights within the nation-state. From the 1880s, women members of popular rights movements in Japan raised the issue of suffrage as a universal human right, to be applied also to women. They envisaged a democratic Japan and worked to abolish gender differences in education and to promote the same economic, legal and moral rights for women as for men. The Japanese Christian Women's Temperance Union, founded in 1893, not only fought drinking problems and domestic violence, but also state-controlled prostitution, and soon came to support the claim for women's suffrage. However, the Japanese constitution of 1889 abolished women's possibilities of access to the throne, for the first time in Japanese history, and even supported polygamy for the emperor in order to secure a male line of descent. From 1890 to 1945 Japanese women were by law prohibited from taking part in party politics. Modeling its political system on Bismarck's Germany, this provision corresponded well to what was the case in a number of German states, where women were also excluded from party politics between 1852 and 1908. The equal-rights strategy did not succeed in the construction of the Japanese nation-state. Even universal male suffrage was not attained until 1925, and the lively, but short-lived women's suffrage movement of the interwar period was drowned in state-supported promotion of women as mothers and in war-time policies.[28]

In India, women's organisations such as the All India Muslim Women Conference and the Women's Indian Association, formed in 1914 and 1917 respectively, may be understood as examples of the equal-rights strategy. Support given to limited women's suffrage in some Indian provinces in the 1920s and for all India in 1935 as well as women's active participation in Gandhi's civil disobedience strategies, may further testify to the existence of equal-rights strategies in the formation of the Indian nation. So would the fact that, even to the embarrassment of Gandhi, who feared being accused of hiding behind women, many women took part in public meetings and in the big salt march of 1930.[29]

As for Europe and North America, the use of this strategy is well documented, not only in the fight for women's suffrage, but also in numerous discussions of admission of women to the same education and jobs as men. It has also been pointed out, time and time again, that the equal-rights strategy, as mentioned above, might be rooted, now in the argument that women had the same potentials as men, now in the argument that women were needed in the nation because of their different qualities from men.[30]

Examples of the difference strategy are also found world-wide. The biggest Japanese women's organisation, *Aikoko Fujinkai*, worked around the turn of the century to support Japanese authorities, among other things by attempting to make women see their sons as the sons of the emperor, and to prepare mothers to proudly sacrifice their sons for the fatherland. The Japanese tradition of the patriarchal family and the subservient wife may thus be translated into understanding women as contributing to the national good by sacrificing their sons for the nation. Also Indian nationalists argued that women had a special role as guardians of Hindu traditions. The swadeshi-movement, expressing its criticism of British sovereignty just after the turn of the century through boycott of British goods, appealed to women as consumers and organisers of protest meetings. If we move into the interwar years, Gandhi's ideas of femininity are easily translated into the difference strategy. Women should take part in the national struggle, but preferably in other ways than men. They were not too welcome in public protest marches, but all the more when they were seen busily producing Indian cotton cloth and wearing Indian costumes. Gandhi saw the goddess Sita, the faithful, self-sacrificing wife, as the ideal woman. He also found women especially well prepared for *satyagraha*, i.e., non-violent resistance.

In Scandinavia, the difference strategy manifested itself through the Swedish Women's Association for the Defence of the Nation and the Norwegian Women's Circles of the Norwegian Defence Association. In both countries, these organisations contributed to strengthening the military defence through large-scale fund-raising activities.[31] The parallel to Japan may be discerned when conservative Swedish women saw themselves as national mother figures with the duty to educate boys to become soldiers who would defend the nation. National mothers should bring up future generations to love their country, and, maybe in contrast to the Japanese *Aikoko Fujinkai*, to protect the weak, especially the children. Some conservative Swedish women stated very clearly, that even without the right to vote, they felt completely accepted as members of the nation.[32]

In Norway, the big Norwegian Women's Sanitary Organisation in the 1890s saw it as an important task to educate nurses to assist the Norwegian army in case there should be war with Sweden. The social-democrats of these two countries mobilised the masses by promoting the idea of equality and democracy as a better defence of the nation than strong military force. Gender difference was stressed when argumentation for the vote underscored women's potential for creating peace as a special legitimisation for women's vote.

However, gender-differences in the construction of the nation-state were not limited to symbols and arguments. They also resulted in different channels of influence and power. Men would give voice to their political opinions through membership in political parties, through voting and by supporting the nation as soldiers. They would form voluntary organisations to act as pressure groups for their convictions. Women only slowly gained access to party politics and voting. Voluntary organisations and communal actions, therefore, were important political instruments for women and often remained so long after women got the right to vote.[33]

GLOBAL PARALLELS

The similarities found in the importance of gender to the construction of the nation-state may tempt the historian to talk of global patterns. Gender was important for all nation building, and national symbols were imbued with gendered meanings. Central concepts like "political rights" were not gender neutral, and purposeful political action was needed to make this concept include women. Political actions mostly took different forms for men and women. This happened even in cases where political opinions were gender neutral, such as in the question of resistance to western culture in India and Japan and in Norwegian discontent with the union with Sweden, 1814–1905.

Further, two different strategies building on different understandings of gender prevailed. One understood women as basically different from men, but nevertheless as important as men to the nation. The other saw the inclusion of women in the nation with the same political rights as men, as an expression of the equal potential of the two sexes. Although the difference strategy could lead to the same conclusion, there was a tendency for this strategy to uphold existing gender hierarchies. The difference strategy consequently seems to have been the preference of conservative political forces.

How may we explain such parallels? If we see them as expressions of a universal gender order or gender system, how may the existence of that order be explained?

Cross-cultural parallels may point to universalities in human behaviour. Understandings of gender seem to rest on deep mental structures, regulating feminine and masculine behaviour and changing only very slowly. Consciously or unconsciously, these mental structures may influence expectations as to acceptable thoughts, actions and strategies by the two sexes. Basic gender relations, the very understanding of feminine and masculine identities, seem to transcend cultural differences. A universal gender hierarchy has given rise to theories of patriarchy, seeing the dichotomies man-woman, public-private, strong-weak, and so on, as universalities.

Does this mean that gender was more important to the construction of the nation-state than class, caste, ethnicity or other social categories? My answer is: sometimes yes, sometimes no. Constructing a nation-state might result in the problem of competing loyalties. Loyalty to a nation might compete with loyalty to one's class or sex. In some situations, loyalty to one's sex was stronger than loyalty to one's nation. In Scandinavia, for a long time, and despite the national crisis, leaders of the middle class women's organizations cooperated sisterly across the Norwegian-Swedish border. For women and men of the Social Democratic parties, the national conflict brought no problems of cooperation. Gender — and class — proved more important than nationality. Alliance across national borders was also important in Asian nations. Japan found inspiration for political reform in western cultures, among other things for a modern education of middle class women. The All India Women's Conference cooperated with British suffragists.

But the harder the national conflicts grew, the more problematic became alliances across national divides. Conflicts of loyalty arose. As I understand, at some point cooperation between Indian and British feminists in the question of female suffrage became extremely difficult. The heated atmosphere between the two nations made loyalty to nation more important than loyalty to sex. No doubt, western inspiration for changes in the situation of Japanese women was short-lived, and even for one of the prominent women in the Norwegian women's movement, Gina Krog, loyalty to the Norwegian nation in 1905 for a while put a stop to cooperation with Swedish women. Krog's Swedish counterparts were appalled when she characterised Sweden as "a sly, malignant robber." Scandinavian sisterly cooperation entered an extremely cool period. Conflicts between loyalty to gender — and class — and loyalty to nation were evident in a number of European nations at the outbreak of the First World War when socialists and suffragists had to choose which cause to support.

The varying reactions, some giving priority to gender, some to nation, some to class, may be explained by the concept of fractured identities. If we conceive of historical agents as individuals with a number of possible identities, and consequently with a number of latent loyalties to defend, this helps us understand changing priorities. One aspect of a person's or a social group's identity will come to the foreground the moment this aspect is threatened or otherwise activated.[34] This will explain changing reactions. As national crises activated national loyalties, gender conflicts activated gender loyalties, just as class — and in some nations caste or ethnic conflicts — brought such loyalties to the forefront.

No doubt, a number of world-wide parallels present themselves in the study of the process of constructing the nation-state. But there were also outstanding differences.

Cultural Differences

Geyer and Bright have maintained that "the crucial watershed inaugurating twentieth-century world history consisted in a series of parallel, simultaneous crises in the organisation of power, production and culture — that is, in the autonomous reproduction — of virtually every region of the world."[35] Studies of similar strategies within different cultures highlight variations of the global trajectory.

One of the main differences in the interplay of gender and nation building was the very dissimilar goals that would have to be reached in order to pave the way for women to acquire political citizenship. In Japan and India, priority was given to safeguarding women's physical and psychic integrity within a culture where the problems discussed were concubinage, child marriages, the total submission under husband and mother-in-law, and prohibition of widow remarriage. In this setting, to see women as members of the nation in the same way as men, was a distant goal for a very small part of the population.

Gender relations in Europe, and especially in Scandinavia were totally different. In a number of countries, around 1900, women had gained the right to the same education as men, and married women were no longer lawfully regarded as minors. Part of the women's emancipation movement fought for the right of married women to have an economic activity of their own outside the family, and for women to keep their national citizenship also when marrying a foreigner. The idea to include women in the nation by giving them the vote on the same conditions as men, was not a very far cry.

Consequently, despite common deep-seated ideas of gender differences, cultural variations were decisive in the way gender differences manifested themselves in the construction of the nation-state.

Is it possible to find central elements that may help understand culturally different implications of gender for national citizenship? Let me suggest as one important element the very different importance given to collectivity and to individualism.

At the risk of lumping together very disparate cultures, it may be said that hierarchical and fundamentalist religious beliefs, be it within Hinduism, Confucianism, Christianity, Judaism or Islam, are inimical to accepting women as individuals with the same potentials as men and consequently hesitant to accept women as citizens with the same rights as men.[36] In Japan and India, religion may have strengthened the concept of a stable and strongly patriarchal kinship system and a submissive wife. Add to this that where kin and family build the only safety nets in case of need, when sickness, accidents, poverty or old age threatened the individual, family and kin were the most important center for all loyalties. This would put an obstacle to any wish for individual rights. In many cases such a wish would not even arise. With a patriarchal family and kinship system, individual rights would certainly be more farfetched for women than for men.

In northern Europe, and especially in Scandinavia, on the other hand, the Lutheran religion had for a long time stressed individual freedom. Industrialisation and urbanisation had for some time also loosened the ties between family and individual. At the end of the 19th century the first steps were taken towards what would later be termed "the welfare state," gradually providing a public safety net around the individual to secure basic needs. This added to the weakening of collective kinship ties and made the road to individualism easier. But even here, this road had higher barriers for women than for men.

However, it is important not to see cultures as absolute entities. Internal fractions and conflicts over values and ideas characterise any culture, among these conflicts over gender relations. Regional differences may be of the utmost importance. The question of loyalty to the family, of collectivity versus individualism, as well as religious and economic circumstances, differed widely from northern to southern Europe, as it did within different regions of Asia and other parts of the globe. Although very different political developments of course played an important part in this question, the catholic religion and the agrarian economy of southern Europe may in part explain why women in most Mediterranean countries did not gain political citizenship till after the Second World War, while women in northern Europe and the USA attained the right to vote around the First World War.[37] As for India, small groups of women got the vote through the Government of India Act of 1935, while a proposal by the Japanese government for restricted voting rights for women in local elections, was rejected by the Upper House of the Diet. Japanese women had to wait until 1945, Indian women until 1950, to obtain the same political rights in the nation as men.[38]

CONCLUSION

Sketching gendered patterns of national symbols and looking for common strategies in the construction of nation-states as different as Japan, India, Sweden, and Norway, makes, of course, only a small and uncertain step on the way towards global gender history. A multitude of specific and comparative studies shall be needed, clarifying similarities and differences. However, the resulting patterns of thinking, I am sure, will prove extremely helpful in understanding the gendered nature of politics, nationally and internationally.

A gender analysis of global history highlights the importance of gender to central historical processes. The construction of nation-states world-wide involved both sexes, albeit in different ways. As competitive elections became part of political systems world-wide, an arena for political gender relations was created. In fact, gender relations were by some contemporaries seen as indicators of the success of nation-building. At the first session of the Indian National Congress, in 1889, one of the participants asked political reformers of all shades of opinion never to forget that "unless the elevation of the female element of the nation proceeds pari passu with their work, all their labor for the political enfranchisement of the country will prove vain."[39] Investigating the connection between "the elevation of the female element of the nation" and the construction of nation-states will result in better knowledge of the gender specific circumstances and possibilities for historical actors, and, consequently, in a better understanding of how societies and nations function.

Gender relations may be perceived as part of cultural flows, interacting with ideoscapes of democracy, freedom and welfare. Women and men, globally and within varying cultures, often based their actions on shared understandings of femininity and masculinity. Such understandings might be stable through long periods, in fact so stable that they were translated into symbols for the nation itself. Although important changes in society, such as the formation of nation-states, affected gender relations in culturally specific ways, global studies of the importance of gender to the formation of nation-states deconstructs the often suggested polarisation of women and men as actors within the private and the public arenas respectively. Although political action took gendered forms, both sexes were actively engaged in the process of nation-building, and this process comprised the home and family as well as public parliaments and political parties.

Applying gender analysis to global history indicates that although the histories of women and men have a lot in common, just like the multiple histories of the world,[40] women and men have had some gender-specific historical experiences. Consequently, to study also the hidden operations of gender is important for a thorough understanding of the complicated patterns of historical transformations, at the global as well as at all other levels.

Notes

1. Michael Geyer and Charles Bright, "World History in a Global Age," *American Historical Review* 4 (1995): 1034–60.

2. Geyer and Bright 1995, 1034–48.

3. E. Ladewig Petersen, "Reflections on Recent Trends in World-Historiography," in *Clashes of Cultures: Essays in Honour of Niels Steensgaard*, ed. Jens Christian, V. Johansen, et al. (Odense: Odense University Press, 1992), 16.

4. Jerry H. Bentley, "Shapes of World History in Twentieth-Century Scholarship," in *Essays on Global and Comparative History*, ed. Michael Adas (Washington, D.C.: American Historical Association Publications, 1996), 1–34.

5. Michael Harbsmeier, "World Histories before Domestication: The Writing of Universal Histories, Histories of Mankind and World Histories in Late Eighteenth Century Germany," *Culture and History* (Copenhagen: Akademisk forlag, 1989), 93–131, esp. 107–12.

6. Ida Blom, *Det er forskjell på folk — nå som før: Kjønn og andre former for sosial differensiering* (Oslo 1994), 16–25.

7. Diana H. Coole, *Women in Political Theory: From Ancient Misogyny to Contemporary Feminism* (Sussex: Wheatsheaf Books, 1988). See also Blom 1994.

8. Bonnie S. Anderson and Judith P. Zinsser, *A History of Their Own: Women in Europe from Prehistory to the Present*, 2 vols. (New York and London: Harper & Row, 1988). Bonnie G. Smith, *Changing Lives: Women in European History Since 1700* (Lexington and Toronto: D. C. Heath, 1989). *Histoire des femmes en Occident*, 5 vols., ed. Georges Duby and Michelle Perrott (Paris: Plon, 1991–1992). English translation 1993. *Cappelens kvinnehistorie*, 3 vols. ed. Ida Blom (Oslo 1992–1993). Vols. 1 and 2 translated into Danish 1992.

9. The International Federation for Research in Women's History was founded in 1987, and the following year accepted as an internal commission of the International Committee for Historical Sciences. At the world conferences of the historical sciences the IFRWH organizes a special program on women's and gender history and facilitates integration of this perspective into other programs. See "Foreword" and "Editorial Note" in *Writing Women's History: International Perspectives*, ed. Karen Offen, Ruth Roach Pierson, and Jane Rendall (London: Macmillan, 1991). *Gender and History* and *Journal of Women's History* are international journals exclusively devoted to the historical sciences, but historical research on women and gender is also presented in *SIGNS — Journal of Women in Culture and Society*, in *Feminist Studies*, *Women's International Studies Forum* as well as in the Nordic journal *NORA*. See also Ida Blom, En annen historie? Kvinnehistorie i et internasjonalt perspektiv *(Norwegian) Historisk Tidskrift* 4 (1990): 417–35; Blom 1994, 79–97; and Ida Blom, "Women's History towards the Year 2000 — An International Perspective" *The (Indian) Journal of Women's Studies* 1 (1996): 5–36.

10. An international conference at the University of Melbourne in 1993 resulted in four articles in *The Journal of Women's History* 4 (1995): Ida Blom, "Feminism and Nationalism in the Early Twentieth Century: A Cross-Cultural Perspective," 82–94; Aparna Basu, "Feminism and Nationalism in India, 1917–1947," 95–107; Noriyo Hayakawa, "Feminism and Nationalism in Japan, 1868–1945," 108–19, and Yung-Hee Kim, "Under the Mandate of Nationalism: Development of Feminist Enterprises in Modern Korea, 1860–1910," 120–36. See also Ida Blom, "Das Zusammenwirken von Nationalismus und Feminismus um die Jahrhundertwende: Ein Versuch zur vergleichenden Geschlechtergeschichte," in *Geschichte under Vergleich. Ansätze und Ergebnisse international vergleichender Geschichtsschreibung*, ed. Heinz-Gerhard Haupt and Jürgen Kocka (Frankfurt and New York: Campus Verlag, 1996), 315–38.

11. Ida Blom, "Global Women's History: Organizing Principles and Cross-Cultural Understandings," in Offen, Pierson and Rendall 1991, 135–49. Blom 1990. Blom 1994, 57–98. Hanne Rimmen-Nielsen, "Køn, kultar, repræsentation: Nyere tendenser i international kvindehistorisk forskning," *Den jyske historiker* 58–59 (1992): 7–34.

12. Gro Hagemann, "Kvinnehistorie — faglig blindspor eller fruktbar disiplin?" *(Norwegian) Historisk Tidskrift* 3 (1986): 343–60. Yvonne Hirdman, "Makt och kön," in *Maktbegreppet*, ed. Olof Petersson (Stockholm: Carlssons Bokförlag, 1987), 188–206. Christina Carlsson Wetterberg, "Från patriarkat till genussystem — och vad kommer sedan?" *Kvinnovetenskaplig tidskrift* 3 (1992), 34–48. Gro Hagemann, "Postmodernismen en användbar men opålitlig bundsförvant," *Kvinnovetenskaplig tidskrift* 3 (1994), 19–34.

13. Joan W. Scott, "Gender — A Useful Category of Historical Analysis," *American Historical Review* 5 (1986). Reprinted in Joan W. Scott, *Gender and the Politics of History* (New York: Columbia University Press, 1988), 29–50. Quotation from p. 42.

14. Scott 1988, 27.

15. Arjun Appadurai, "Disjuncture and Difference in the Global Cultural Economy," in *Global Culture: Nationalism, Globalization, and Modernity*, ed. Mike Featherstone (London: Sage, 1990), 295–310.

16. Leonore Davidoff, *Worlds Between: Historical Perspectives on Gender and Class* (Oxford: Polity Press, 1995), 227–76. For a stimulating analysis of changing understandings of gender and race, see Catherine Hall, "Missionary Stories: Gender and Ethnicity in England in the 1830s and 1840s," in *White, Male and Middle Class: Explorations in Feminism and History* (Cambridge: Polity Press, 1992), 205–54.

17. Petersen 1992, 25.

18. Although mostly acting as substitutes for men, reigning queens might wield decisive personal power. As mothers, wives, and lovers, other women might seriously influence male kings and princes. Even in the modern world, women may gain political leadership through family positions, such as being widows or daughters of former important politicians. (Indira Gandhi, India; Khaleda Zia, Bangladesh; Benazir Bhutto, Pakistan). See Sverre Bagge and Sølvi Sogner in Blom 1992, 1:343–59, 2:15–23, and Else Skjønsberg, in Blom 1993, 3:273–84.

19. *Women, Politics and Change*, ed. Louise Tilly and Patricia Gurin (New York: Russell Sage Foundation, 1990). See also Blom 1992, 2:511–31, and the massive discussion, especially among American scholars, on gender and social policies. See Erinn Larsen, *Gender and the Welfare State — Maternalism — A New Historical Concept?* Cand. philol. thesis at the Department of History, University of Bergen, Spring 1996. For Norway, see Tone Margrethe Birkenes, *Kvinners frivillige og organiserte samfunnsaktivitet i Kristiansand 1901–1907*, Cand. philol. thesis at the Department of History, University of Bergen, Fall 1995.

20. Joan W. Scott, "Deconstructing Equality-versus-Difference: Or, the Uses of Poststructuralist Theory for Feminism," *Feminist Studies* 1 (1988), 33–50. Rimmen-Nielsen 1992. See also Kari Melby, "Women's Ideology: Difference, Equality, or a New Femininity: Women Teachers and Nurses in Norway, 1912–1940," in *Moving On: New Perspectives on the Women's Movement*, ed. Tayo Andreasen, *Acta Jutlandica* LXVVII: 1. Humanities Series 66 (Århus: Aarhaus University Press), 138–54. Kari Melby, *Kvindelighetens strategier: Norges Husmorforbund, 1915–1940. Norges Lærerinneforbund, 1912–1940*, Dr. Philos. thesis in history, University of Trondheim, 1995, 31–61 and 381–411.

21. Øystein Sørensen, "Nasjonalisme, skandinavisme og pangermanisme hos Bjørnstjerne Bjørnson," in *Nasjonal identitet — et kunstprodukt?* ed. Øystein Sørensen (Oslo: KULT skriftserie 30/Nasjonal identitet 5, Norges forskningsråd), 1994, 211.

22. Øyvind Østerud, "Er nasjonalstaten foreldet?" *Nytt Norsk Tidskrift* 4 (1992), 351–64. Benedict Anderson: *Imagined Communities: Reflections on the Origin and Spread of Nationalism*, London: Verso, 1983. Eric Hobsbawm, *Nations and Nationalism since 1780: Programme, Myth, Reality* (Cambridge: Cambridge University Press, 1990).

23. For India, see Basu 1995, for Japan, see Hayakawa 1995. Maurice Agulhin discusses the possibility of democratic regimes being symbolised by women, authoritarian regimes by men, in *Marianne au pouvoir: L'imagerie et la symbolique républicaines de 1880 à 1914* (Paris: Flammarion, 1989), 347–49. A very helpful overview of women's history outside Europe and Northern America is Iris Berger, et al., *Restoring Women to History: Teaching Packets for Integrating Women's History into Courses on Africa, Asia, Latin America, the Caribbean, and the Middle East* (Bloomington: Organisation of American Historians, 112 North Bryan Street, Bloomington, Indiana, USA 47408–4199), 1988. Sharon L. Sievers writes on "Women in China, Japan and Korea," 63–118, and Barbara Ramusak on "Women in South and South East Asia," 1–63. Where nothing else is

indicated, the following is built on Sievers, Ramusak, and Blom 1993. See also Rosemarie Schade and Keith J. Lowther, *Gender Balancing History: Towards an Inclusive Curriculum*, vols. 1–7 (Montreal: Simone de Beauvoir Institute, Concordia University), 1993.

24. Ida Blom, "Nation–Class–Gender: Scandinavia at the Turn of the Century," *Scandinavian Journal of History* (1996), 1–16.

25. Blom in Haupt und Kocka 1996. For a closer analysis of Norwegian national symbols, see Blom 1996.

26. A long number of explanations for these customs exist in the different cultures. See Blom in Offen, Pierson and Rendall 1991. Blom 1994, 79–97.

27. C. J. Heuch, cited from Eva Kolstad, *Utsnitt av lovforslag, komite-innstillinger og debatter i Stortinget om stemmerett for kvinner* (Oslo: O. Fredr. Arnesen Bok- og Aksidentstrykkeri A/S), 1963, 163.

28. Hayakawa 1995. Yukiko Matsukawa and Kaoru Tachi, "Women's Suffrage and Gender Politics in Japan," *Suffrage and Beyond: International Feminist Perspectives*, ed. Caroline Daley and Melanie Nolan (New York: New York University Press, 1994), 171–83. Marjorie Wall Bingham and Susan Hill Gross, *Women in Japan from Ancient Times to the Present* (Minneapolis: Glenhurst Publications, 1987), 167–72.

29. Basu 1995. Ramusack in Berger 1988, 17–26.

30. Olive Banks, *Faces of Feminism: A Study of Feminism as a Social Movement* (Oxford: Martin Robertson, 1981, 61–150. Blom 1992, 2:511–31. Smith 1989, 348–57. Daley and Nolan 1994.

31. Blom 1996.

32. *Dagny* 12 (1905), 238. Quoted in Blom 1996, 8.

33. Birkenes 1995.

34. Tuija Pulkkinen, "Citizens, Nations and Women: The Transition from Ancient Regime to Modernity and Beyond," paper presented at the International Federation for Research in Women's History Symposium: *Rethinking Women and Gender Relations in the Modern State*, Bielefeld, April 1993. See also Peggy Pascoe, Introduction, and "Race, Gender and Intercultural Relations: The Case of Interracial Marriages," *Frontiers* 1 (1991), 1–18; and Gerda Lerner, "Reconceptualising Differences among Women," *Journal of Women's History* 3 (1990), 106–22.

35. Geyer and Bright, 1045.

36. Blom 1992, 514, 528.

37. In Spain, women got the vote in 1931. But that was a very special case. There had been little fight to obtain a right that was in the eyes of many radical Spaniards compromised by the existing political regime. Mary Nash, "Political Culture, Catalan Nationalism, and the Women's Movement in Early Twentieth-Century Spain," *Women's Studies International Forum*, 1–2 (1996), 45–54.

38. Mitsukawa and Tachi 1994. Basu 1995. Hayakawa 1995. Blom 1993.

39. Basu 1995, 97.

40. Geyer and Bright, 1058.

Judith P. Zinsser

Technology and History: The Women's Perspective
A Case Study in Gendered Definitions

Given the theme of the conference and my commitment to women's history, I knew that I wanted to speak to you about the significance of women's contributions to the history of technology. The topic of cloth production seemed the perfect choice. No other process has been so clearly connected with technological changes across the ages. No other product has been more closely associated with women in many different cultures through the centuries.

But as I read and started to piece together a narrative, I realized that it was 1) not very interesting and 2) not convincing at all. For, however carefully I chronicled women's activities, I knew that this story would not change your thinking or your approach. Instead, I would be up against what I have come to call the "So what" problem in women's history. "So, you've told me all of this about what women did, so what? How will that change the way I present the history of technology to my classes, or frame the questions for my research?" The answer quite simply is, it won't.

But not because women are insignificant. Giving a gender dimension to history is not just an exercise in finding room for women in a few paragraphs here and there. To engender history, to make it truly the story of women's and men's lives, we must examine the very terms of that history. In this case, how have we defined the concept of "technology"? How has this definition determined what will and will not be valued, what will and will not be included in a history of technology? How does this definition affect our analyses of the interaction between technology and society?

By way of illustration, I have chosen to describe this intersection of women's history and the history of technology in two very different eras in the history of cloth production: 1) at the beginnings of spinning and weaving in prehistory, and 2) in the nineteenth and twentieth centuries when the textile and clothing industries represented the vanguard of industrialization and modernization. In this way I will demonstrate not only the rich interplay between

Judith P. Zinsser, "Technology and History: The Women's Perspective: A Case Study in Gendered Definitions" (Presidential Address, World History Association Fifth International Conference, Pomona, Calif., 22 June 1996). *World History Bulletin* 12 (Spring 1996): 2, 6–9.

women's history and the history of technology, but also the process by which gender, concepts of the "masculine" and "feminine," have influenced those histories.[1]

PREHISTORY: VALENCED TECHNOLOGY

Archaeologists, anthropologists and historians of women have only recently begun to decipher the technology of cloth production in prehistory. That it has taken so long is not without significance and tells us about the ways in which the very concept of "technology" has been skewed, or valenced as philosophers of science say, by the gendered premises of our own culture. For many decades these premises determined our definition of "technology" and our discussions of it in prehistoric societies.[2] These premises determined the questions we asked, the evidence we found, and the conclusions we drew from that evidence.

By gendered premises of our own culture, I mean the association of certain qualities and activities with the concepts of "masculine" or "feminine" and the creation of a hierarchy of value in which those qualities and activities associated with the masculine were valued more than those associated with the feminine. "What?" I hear you saying. "How does this gendered hierarchy relate to the study of technology in prehistory?"

I appreciate that it is usual to speak of "technology" and its history as somehow "neutral," outside of any social context, almost "a force" outside of human agency and experience. As Evelyn Fox Keller and Sandra Harding have shown, however, "science" and its product "technology" cannot be neutral, unless we are to imagine them as *not* created by humans and *not* created for human purposes. Nor are they neutered, without gendered associations. Surely, we must acknowledge — and nowhere is it more evident than in the studies of prehistoric peoples — that "creators . . . [are] distinctly marked as to gender," and our decisions about what to designate "technology" more often than not have been tied to artifacts associated with perceived male activities.[3]

The most common explanation for the prevalence of descriptions of men's activities in prehistory and ascriptions of their significance has been the "durability" of the remains of those men's activities, the granite ax blade and flint arrowhead, for example. We have in fact dated all of prehistoric time in terms of the stone and metal remains, the evidence of men's activities, heralded "hunting" as essential to survival, and thus privileged that evidence and the acts they suggest. Our most common descriptions of "prehistory" have given greater significance to men, to their activities and thus to their technology. The tools of hunting, however crude, subsumed all of our definition of "technology."

More recently, the work of archaeologists like Elizabeth Wayland Barber and anthropologists like Frances Dahlberg, have caused us to rethink those descriptions, their gender-heavy exclusionary definitions of "technology," and the subjective, gendered valences they reflected.[4] With improvements in archaeological techniques and borrowing from other sciences, we have found organic remains, the evidence of activities traditionally associated with women, such as gathering and food preparation. What's more, we have given that evidence equal, if not primary, significance. For example, historians and anthropologists now speak of "gathering and hunting societies" to suggest the primary importance of gathering to the basic survival of early peoples.

More germane to this conference, in reconstructing women's activities in prehistory we have discovered, or rather expanded our definitions of "technology." Grinding stones, scraping blades, and bone needles now rank with axes and arrowheads as "inventions." Nowhere is this process of unskewing our premises, of rethinking questions, of including new evidence, and thus reformulating conclusions more evident than in our descriptions of the earliest production of cloth. Previously, spindles and looms, spinning, weaving, and the making of cloth were not included in our list of early technology and its uses. In fact, cloth production had to become mechanized thousands of years later before most historians spoke of "inventors" and technology in connection with this most basic of human activities.

Now, we have cordage from the Gravettian culture (ca. 15,000 B.C. in southern France and northern Spain) made out of grasses, and archaeologists who speak of the "String Revolution" of the upper paleolithic age and its significance to the success of the species. We have spindles with their clay whorls, and the weights for the warp threads of neolithic ground looms (7000 B.C., Jarmo, Iraq), examples of the tools that transformed organic materials into essential products. We now appreciate the importance of textiles for clothing, for exchange, and for ceremonial purposes. Thus, we have rewritten key aspects of our narrative, altered our analyses, and learned to value women's contributions to the social, economic and political activities of cultures in prehistory.[5] Finally, if we wish to, we can see the subjective myopia of gender-valenced definitions and conclusions and broaden our understanding of "technology."

THE NINETEENTH AND TWENTIETH CENTURIES: SKILL'S MANY MEANINGS

Spinning and weaving in prehistory demonstrated the ways in which a gendered hierarchy of values has affected our definition of "technology" and our ability to recognize the significance of different "technologies." Similarly, our conventional narratives of the nineteenth and twentieth century worlds of mechanized cloth production reveal gendered premises that determined our questions, clouded our understanding of evidence, and skewed our conclusions.

Let me give you an example. In this period of industrialization and economic modernization, an obvious intersection of the history of women and the history of technology comes in analyses of employment patterns, the fact of "job segregation," a phenomenon associating men with "skilled" and women with "unskilled" work. The traditional explanation given for this division of labor by sex has been access to training, specifically, training in a "skill" and the use of a "technology" that women were implicitly, if not explicitly, incapable of acquiring. I would suggest to you that we were wrong.

We misread the reasons for job segregation. We overestimated the significance of skills and technology in employment practices and patterns. Why were we wrong? Because we made the same assumptions about the term "skills," about the concepts of "skilled" and "unskilled" that we had about "technology." We assumed that they were neutral terms, imagined them defined outside of any social context. We believed them to be neutered words without any gendered associations.

Far from being neutral, however, the concept of "skill" is rich in cultural connotation. In our analyses of nineteenth and twentieth century industrialization and modernization the word has proved malleable, supple, without consistent application or meaning. Our historical uses of the word "skill," as in our uses of the word "technology" in prehistory, demonstrate how gendered premises affected the questions we asked, the evidence we found, and the conclusions we drew from that evidence. It has, in fact, not been "skill" but rather gendered images of appropriate and inappropriate "masculine" and "feminine" behavior that have more often than not dictated which of the employment opportunities created by new technologies would and would not be open to women. Cultural definitions of gender, of what is "feminine" and "masculine" have been more important in creating job segregation than either the level of technology involved or the need for training and specialized skills. A *gendered* division of labor prevailed, not a *sexual* one.[6]

Examples of the ways in which cultural mores have influenced women's and men's interactions with technology rather than any fixed understanding of the word "skill" abound in the newest research about eighteenth- and nineteenth-century European textile and clothing production. Anna Clark's study of Scottish and English textile production shows that in the cottage industry phase of production, men wove and women spun. With the introduction of mechanized spinning men left their "skilled" work to go into the factories (to jobs designated as "unskilled" in other industrializing regions, the northeastern United States, for example). There women worked the hand looms without serving apprenticeships and without any references to the presumed physical and mental limitations that had previously barred them from these men's tasks.[7] Nineteenth century entrepreneurs in a textile center in northern France gave the women weavers only the lightweight calicoes as "more suited to their [weaker] physical strength and their inferior intelligence." That men had previously woven other lightweight fabrics went unremarked.[8]

Late nineteenth-century European governments fostered this gendered division of labor with all of its inconsistencies. A French government investigative committee sent to Lorraine to study the economics of the embroidery trades decided that this "putting out" work should continue rather than be superceded by mechanized production in factories. In justifying their decision, they emphasized the social as well as the economic benefits to the region, the stability this apparently outmoded process fostered. Given the positive effects of this production system, the Committee then considered whether or not boys as well as girls should be taught embroidery — certainly a trade requiring great "skill." They decided no. It would not, they concluded, be good for "the development of [the boys'] health and their physical strength."[9] Boys should be out in the fields with their fathers even if this generated less income and required less skill than the work in the home.

Our studies of economic modernization in the last quarter of the twentieth century, of transnational corporations and their manufacturing and trade practices offer, if anything, a more obvious pattern of job segregation. For example, by the end of the 1980s 80 percent of the workers in the Bataan export processing zone in the Philippines were young women, employed in garment and electronics manufacturing.[10]

Our explanations for this worldwide sexual division of labor, as for the phenomenon in eighteenth- and nineteenth-century industrial Europe have depended on an apparently neutral and neutered definition of "skills," of a similarly neutral and neutered, analysis of the effects of new "technologies." In fact, however, the concept of "skill" has proved just as malleable, just as supple and inconsistent in definition and application in our analyses of late twentieth century modernization as it was in our narratives of European industrialization.[11]

Initially, the introduction of new "technology" was heralded as "skilled" work and as offering new opportunities for women. It meant, according to labor historians, the "integration" of "unproductive" segments of the population into the waged economy. However, a decade later in the 1980s introduction of similarly complex technology in the mills in Argentina and Brazil was referred to as "deskilling." In practical terms on this occasion the new technology eliminated women's jobs and created more managerial positions for men who lacked experience but whose basic computer training was valued more highly than the experiential knowledge and proven educability of the women workers. No one, needless to say, suggested promoting the women to these newly created job categories.[12]

It is not "skill" or "technology" that explains these patterns of employment. Rather it is the same gendered premises about the meanings of "masculine" and "feminine," about what is and is not appropriate for women and men, about what is and is not women's rightful place in an economic and social hierarchy that created this *gendered*, rather than *sexual*, division of labor. In the 1970s and 1980s Brazilian textile workers had unequal access to promotion whether or not they acquired new "skills." For example, they could be dismissed if they became pregnant.[13] An ILO (International Labor Organization) study of "trends" in labor practices from 1960 to 1980 documented the increasing numbers of younger women brought into the waged labor force. ILO found that employers kept them on for only a few years to avoid seniority precedents and gave them no benefits. In theory these workers, however highly skilled, were to leave their jobs and marry.

As in the nineteenth century, modern states have endorsed and contributed to this gendering of work as they courted new technologies and new manufacturing for their economies. The Brazilian government sponsored training sessions but gave shorter courses to women textile workers, whose average age was seventeen or less.[14] In the early 1980s the Malaysian government hoped to attract high technology United States business to its newly created export processing zones. An official brochure extolled the skills and virtues of Malaysia's young women:

> The manual dexterity of the oriental female is famous the world over. Her hands are small and she works fast with extreme care. Who, therefore, could be better qualified by nature and inheritance to contribute to the efficiency of bench-assembly production line than the oriental girl? No need for Zero Defects program here! By nature, they "quality control" themselves.[15]

GENDER AND WORLD HISTORY

By my description of the intersections of women's history with the history of technology, of the interaction of gender with definitions of "technology" and "skill," I do not mean to suggest that there are no differences between women and men. But as anthropologist Gayle Rubin has pointed out: Men and women are, of course, different. But they are not as different as day and night, earth and sky, yin and yang, life and death. In fact, from the standpoint of nature, men and women are closer to each other than either is to anything else — for instance, mountains, kangaroos, or coconut palms. Far from being an expression of natural differences, exclusive gender identity is the suppression of natural similarities.[16]

Yes, women and men are different. The phenomenon that historians are now trying to understand is the *meaning* given to that difference and the results of this "suppression of natural similarities." Feminist labor historians, like Ava Baron, write of studying how sex difference operates as a social force.[17]

The history of technology has not been immune to this social force. Technology, like science its progenitor, does not exist outside of society and human relationships. Instead, in its definition, its effects, and its applications it is subject to the cultural attitudes of particular societies. In the archaeology of early technology and tools, those attitudes led us to "discover" and value articles associated with male activities. It led us to ignore or devalue those associated with apparently female tasks.

Similarly, our discomfort with or rejection of gendered assumptions about women, men, and technology obscured our understanding of the spread of mechanization and industrialization. In cloth and textile production, our neglect of cultural attitudes about women and men, and of the significance of traditional definitions of "feminine" and "masculine," led to the wrong explanations and to incomplete formulations of the history of labor and the processes of modernization.

It was perhaps a kind of arrogance that led us to assume that technology outweighed or erased cultural traditions that were thousands and thousands of

years old. As Sandra Harding writes: "In virtually every culture, gender difference is a pivotal way in which humans identify themselves as persons, organize
social relations, and symbolize meaningful natural and social events and
processes."[18] Cultural traditions carry meanings and connotations that determine how language is interpreted, how concepts are defined, what will and will
not be valued. As world historians, we must be more aware of this and make use
of it. Gendered analyses enhance our understanding not only of the interactions
between technology and society, but of all the phenomena we seek to explain
and describe. For world history "gender" is not only "a useful category of analysis" but an essential one.[19]

Notes

1. In writing this essay, I have drawn widely from histories of technology, industry,
and labor. These provided much of the basic economic and social information. It is,
however, writings by feminist historians, those exploring women's issues and the effects
of a gender analysis — for example, Anna Clark, Ava Baron, Gail Hershatter — that have
given it whatever force it may have as a synthesis. In addition, I found the work of a number of scholars in other disciplines — Vron Ware, *Beyond the Pale* (New York: Verso,
1992), Sandra Harding, *The Science Question in Feminism* (Ithaca: Cornell University
Press, 1986), and Arturo Escobar, *Encountering Development: The Making and Unmak-
ing of the Third World* (Princeton: Princeton University Press, 1995) — key in helping me
to think about the construction of men's and women's "history" and of "technology."

2. I am accepting the definitions of "technology" from the philosophical discussion
of the 1960s; Ellul's *The Technological Society* (1964) as quoted by Carol J. Haddad,
"Technology, Industrialization, and the Status of Women" in *Women, Work, and Technology: Transformations*, ed. Barbara Drygulski Wright et al. (Ann Arbor: University of
Michigan Press, 1987). It goes as follows: "the totality of methods rationally arrived at having absolute efficiency (for a given stage of development) in every field of human activity," p. 33.

3. That "science" itself is gendered in its epistemology, methods, and practice is the
subject of studies by scientists and philosophers. I am drawing on Harding, 38–39, 15;
Evelyn Fox Keller, *Reflections on Gender and Science* (New Haven: Yale University Press,
1985) and "Gender and Science: An Update" in *Secrets of Life, Secrets of Death, Essays on
Language, Gender and Science*, ed. Evelyn Fox Keller (New York: Routledge, 1992);
Corlann G. Bush, "Women and the Assessment of Technology: To Think, to Be, to Un-
think, to Free" in *Machina ex dea: Feminist Perspectives on Technology*, ed. J. Rothschild
(New York: Pergamon Press, 1983), 154–55 and Timm Triplett, "Hebrides Women: A
Philosopher's View of Technology" in Wright et al., 148.

4. See Barber's *Women's Work: The First 20,000 Years: Women, Cloth, and Society
in Early Times* (New York: W. W. Norton, 1994) and Dahlberg's early edited collection,
Woman the Gatherer (New Haven: Yale University Press, 1981).

5. See, for an overview of the significance of textiles to cultures, the introduction by
Annette B. Weiner and Jane Schneider to their edited collection, *Cloth and the Human
Experience* (Washington: Smithsonian Institution Press, 1989).

6. This is a paraphrase of some of the very useful questions posed about women's
labor and its relation to technology by Daryl M. Hafter, "Introduction: A Theoretical

Framework for Women's Work in Forming the Industrial Revolution" in *European Women and Preindustrial Craft*, ed. Daryl M. Hafter (Bloomington: Indiana University Press, 1995). See also Ava Baron's excellent study of the printing industry, "Contested Terrain Revisited: Technology and Gender Definitions of Work in the Printing Industry, 1850–1920," in Wright et al.

7. See Anna Clark, *The Struggle for the Breeches: Gender in the Making of the British Working Class* (Berkeley: University of California Press, 1995). I am grateful to Hilda L. Smith for telling me about Edith Abbott's study of this phenomenon in the textile mills of New England. See her *Women in Industry* (New York: Source Book Press, 1970 [reprint of 1910 edition]). Research on German and Russian employment patterns in the first decades of industrialization reveal similar shifting definitions of the word "skill" and of the significance assigned to women's waged and unwaged work. See Ruth Ellen B. Joeres and Mary Jo Maynes, eds. *German Women in the Eighteenth and Nineteenth Centuries* (Bloomington: Indiana University Press, 1986) and Barbara Alpern Engel, *Between the Fields and the City: Women, Work & Family in Russia 1861–1914* (New York: Cambridge University Press, 1995).

8. Gay Gullickson, "Love and Power in the Proto-Industrial Family" in *Markets and Manufacturing in Early Modern Europe*, ed. Maxine Berg (London: Routledge, 1990), 218.

9. As quoted in Whitney Walton, "Working Women, Gender and Industrialization in Nineteenth-Century France: The Case of Lorraine Embroidery Manufacturing" in Hafter, 101.

10. Liza Largoza-Maza, "The Medium Term Philippine Development Plan Toward the Year 2000: Filipino Women's Issues and Perspectives," in *Women's Rights Human Rights: International Feminist Perspectives*, ed. Julie Peters and Andrea Wolper (New York: Routledge, 1995), 63.

11. For an overall description of these 20th century technologies, see Paula Jezkova, "Changes in Textiles: Implications for Asian Women" in *Women Encounter Technology: Changing Patterns of Employment in the Third World*, ed. Swasti Mitter and Sheila Rowbotham (New York: Routledge, 1995), 96–97. For the general effects on Asian countries, see Mitter's introduction, 7.

12. Liliana Acero, "Conflicting Demands of New Technology and Household Work: Women's Work in Brazilian and Argentinian Textiles," in Mitter and Rowbotham, 73–74. Emily Honig found the same "deskilling" in China from the 1920s to the 1940s; see *Sisters and Strangers: Women in the Shanghai Cotton Mills, 1919–1949* (Stanford, Calif.: Stanford University Press, 1986).

13. Acero in Mitter and Rowbotham, 78.

14. Acero in Mitter and Rowbotham, 79.

15. Haddad in Wright et al., 50.

16. Gayle Rubin, "The Traffic in Women," in *Toward an Anthropology of Women*, ed. Rayna Reiter (New York: Monthly Review Press, 1975), 179.

17. In this formulation I am drawing on Michelle Zimbalist Rosaldo, "The Use and Abuse of Anthropology: Reflections on Feminism and Cross-Cultural Understanding," *Signs* 5, no. 3 (Spring 1980): 400. [In this essay she reconsidered her feminist analysis of cultures' valuations of women's and men's tasks, "Woman, Culture, and Society: A Theoretical Overview" in *Women, Culture, & Society*, ed. Michelle Zimbalist Rosaldo and Louise Lamphere (Stanford: Stanford University Press, 1974). See Ava Baron, "Gender and Labor History: Learning from the Past, Looking to the Future" in *Work Engendered: Toward a New History of American Labor*, ed. Ava Baron (Ithaca: Cornell University Press), 21.

18. Harding, 18.

19. The reference is to Joan W. Scott's essay "Gender: A Useful Category of Historical Analysis" in *Gender and the Politics of History* (New York: Columbia University Press, 1988).

Sarah S. Hughes

Gender at the Base of World History

Gender is one fundamental organizing principle of human societies. As such, it should be integral to world history survey courses — as basic as economic systems, growth of cities and states, trade, conquest, or religion. Students need to learn about the changing and various distinctions of gender that have divided the lives of women and men from prehistory to the modern period. Pervasive assumptions that women have always kept house and cared for children should yield to knowledge about women's productive labor in gathering and growing crops, in weaving textiles in homes and factories, in marketing, and in providing essential social services. Considering gender reveals critical differences in the family foundations of societies — varying from how marriages were contracted and ancestry calculated to how property was transferred and classes formed. That women had no public role in classical Athens is relevant to democratic theory and to understanding why American women's demand for voting rights was ridiculed before 1920. Whether considering religion, literacy, health, art, slavery, war, or trade, gender usually mattered and to teach world history accurately, we need to explore this and explain how it mattered.

Judith Zinsser, in *History and Feminism: A Glass Half Full*, points out that it has been nearly twenty years since women historians called for systematic analysis of gender relationships as a "fundamental category of historical thought."[1] Except among pioneers like Steve Gosch, this has not happened in university world history courses.[2] Instead, a few women may be added, usually to discussions of Western societies — added to what is not human history, but men's history. If you doubt this, recollect discussions of the modern democratic state; what meaning does "democracy" have if half of adults are disfranchised? Do your students learn about women's access to basic civil and political rights in the twentieth century? Do they know that women voted in Thailand and Turkey

Sarah S. Hughes, "Gender at the Base of World History," *The History Teacher* 27 (August 1994): 417–23.

before they did in France?[3] There is, I believe, more leadership at the secondary school level, exhibited in state mandates that women be included in history courses and in curriculum transformation efforts, such as Philadelphia's "Women in World History Project," which is creating units parallel to the district model world history syllabus. A weakness of this approach is already apparent, however; it is hard to "add and stir" women into an impersonal batter. Comparative history needs rethinking to incorporate significant patterns of masculine and feminine behavior.[4]

My title, "Gender at the Base of World History," is, then, more reflective of intention, than of what I actually accomplish now working within the traditional paradigm. I teach three sections of world history each semester in a department where forty sections are scheduled; I use standard textbooks and conform to departmental guidelines of chronology, extent of reading, writing assignments, and exams. So what I propose is a pragmatic approach to incorporating gender within the framework of world history as it is now conceived. Five years ago this was difficult, but the proliferation of new resources — both theoretical and empirical — makes doing so easier each year.

I think about gender in planning courses — considering how it might fit with each topic, and about where the ordinary texts or organization omit critical gendered historical developments. Squeezing more explanatory factors into a world history syllabus is hard, and I can devote few classes only to gender. So, it is critical to establish early that discerning the social meanings of male and female is one major historical theme. This is stated in my course description and reenforced in syllabus topics.

In selecting required readings, gender is a primary focus of at least one book. It might be explicit, as in Sarah Pomeroy's *Goddesses, Whores, Wives and Slaves: Women in Classical Antiquity*, or embedded in a text like Jonathan Spence's *The Death of Woman Wang*. I find that students who have learned to look at history in gendered ways find evidence of its patterns even in books chosen to illustrate other historical factors — such as the Chinese Judge Dee mysteries. In designing written assignments based on readings, I've learned to leave open the selection of themes so that students may analyze gender, or avoid it. It is particularly important in a required general education course to avoid making male or female students believe that feminism — a feared and hated word among Shippensburg freshmen — is being forced on them. Even when I assigned Gerda Lerner's *Creation of Patriarchy*, suggested themes for papers included some gender-neutral topics.

In the classroom, I mention gender regularly in lectures and discussions. World history has a tendency to omit actual people — even most famous men — in favor of broad impersonal, but implicitly masculine, forces. I try to remind students that we are talking about women and men whose collective behavior is consequential. Seeing gender can become habitual. Teach them to look at television news shots as vignettes of people, not unlike themselves, and to see gender patterns when the street demonstrators or soldiers are overwhelmingly male or when the refugees are only women and children, as the United

Nations estimates seventy to eighty percent today are. What we have seen this past year in Somalia and Bosnia makes it easier to understand how warfare in the ancient Near East and North Africa so often led to enslavement of women. Often it takes very little class time to indicate the gender-specificity of war, slavery, education, migration, or citizenship in the state. Thorough analysis of masculinity and femininity is never possible in a survey, and generalized types are more necessary than I like, but there is usually time to be accurate in using the words human, male and female, as well as gendered pronouns.

Because students believe grades are important, gender must also be incorporated in testing. Questions of fact and analysis appear regularly in my multiple-choice items and essays. I distribute study questions prior to essay exams, and intersperse gender topics among more traditional ones. Here are samples from several semesters for the period A.D. 1300 to 1500:

(1) Were the ideals for women's behavior developed in classical Islamic societies practiced by the women of fourteenth-century Cairo?[5]

(2) If, in a previous life, you were a young, unmarried person born into a family of ordinary wealth about 1400, would you choose to have been born in (a) Western Europe, (b) Southeast Asia, or (c) Peruvian Inca society? Explain your choice of gender and geography as you compare and contrast daily life in these places.[6]

(3) Describe the character and lifestyle of a typical Italian Renaissance man. Where was he born? How was he educated? What were his values or beliefs? How did he spend his time?

These topics draw upon social or intellectual history; economic and political history are also important to the project of engendering world history.

Few issues are as critical as the division of labor, beginning with prehistoric gathering and hunting societies. Student misconceptions are so deeply entrenched that I spend one class on the importance of women's gathering to sustenance of their families, on their participation in some hunting activities, on patterns of shared childcare, and on the relative equality anthropologists find in later similar societies. *Gender and Anthropology*, published by the American Anthropological Association, has useful essays and suggestions for class projects that range from primates to modern gathering-hunting peoples.[7] The transition from foraging to agricultural societies may be included in this unit, or developed later. What is important is to stress that both women and men participated in producing vegetative and animal food. Human societies depended on productive labor by most adults, but usually divided it into male and female tasks. A book that is comparative and useful in its categorization of gendering in agriculture is Ester Boserup's *Woman's Role in Economic Development*.[8] As we encounter new regions and new crops, women's farming responsibilities can be quickly introduced. As trade develops, who owns and has the right to market various agricultural products needs to be established when possible.

Early in the first semester we also discuss food processing and cooking. Students tend to equate women's domestic work with what they know, with the spacious houses they know — that are full of appliances, furniture, linens and clothes. Before 1800, most women and men lived in small, sparsely-furnished spaces, had few clothes, and spent far more time producing rudimentary products for survival. I also introduce early in the course the variability of gender assignment of other tasks of hand manufacture: spinning, weaving, potting, leather work, building construction; but the tendency for blacksmithing and metalwork to be done by men. Slides are useful — particularly those that show African men sitting at a loom or women building a house. My intention is to shake the students' received notions of "natural" gender patterns and to make them question relationships of work and power between the sexes in any historical society.

In world history classes, I avoid several unanswerable issues of the prehistorical era. One is the role of goddesses. Another is the origin of patriarchy. I find Gerda Lerner's exploration of patriarchy's historic beginnings too narrow because of its Western focus. Furthermore, historical evidence does not suggest to me a single pattern of male oppression of women, but much more complex negotiations of power. Rather than trying to explain why or how men subjugated women, I demonstrate how patriarchy was associated with the major ancient civilizations of Mesopotamia, Persia, Greece, China, India, and Rome. We discuss how the benefits of civilized life most often arose beside domination of women, class inequalities, and slavery. Discussion of the explicit inequality of women and men embedded in law, marriage, philosophy, religion, and government is shocking to many of my students. Athens and China are important examples both because one need add only a little to the facts in textbooks and because the philosophies of Plato, Aristotle, and Confucius influenced conceptions of male and female for millennia in broad regions. In Athens, where the conception of manhood is central to the society, the intertwining of gender, age, sexuality, and power offers an opportunity to introduce homosexuality. Sarah Pomeroy's *Goddesses, Whores, Wives and Slaves* discusses gender in both Greece and Rome. Within the Mediterranean, Egyptian women had relatively high status, with more choices in marriage, work, and law than their Asian or European neighbors. Yet they were as likely to be slaves. Hatshepsut and Cleopatra had little in common with their serving women. Establishing the privileges of free women in dynastic Egypt sets a stage for showing significant Egyptian influence on women's rising status in the Hellenistic Mediterranean and East Africa.[9]

Sometime in the first semester student consternation and depression mounts over women's seeming perpetual and universal low status. This may appear among male students who are overwhelmed with guilt. There is a concomitant tendency to leap to the false conclusion that everything was terrible until the American Revolution liberated women. So, it is important to deal with societies besides Egypt in which women had high status. I rely on a unit on Southeast Asia, based largely on readings from Anthony Reid's *Southeast Asia in the Age of Commerce*. Here, women were thought to be more competent than men in business, were more often literate, and expected sexual satisfaction from men. The beauty of this picture for female students is marred by a preference for blackened teeth, tattooed bodies, and androgynous dressing, while male students may be horrified by descriptions of genital surgery to enhance men's appeal to women. Discussion of gender in Southeast Asia serves a further purpose of illustrating the selectivity of Indian and Chinese influences. If one only looks at the Buddhist temples of Pagan, Borobudor or Angkor Wat, India's influence can seem overwhelming; persistence of diametrically different ideals of masculinity and femininity suggests more complex cultural interaction. Lorraine Gesick first showed me that in medieval Thailand local women merchants enabled foreign men to maintain long-distance trade. Once observed, this practice can be found on continents beyond Southeast Asia. One day, I believe gender will transform our understanding not only of trade, but of the spread of religion and culture. Think about the meaning to be deconstructed from a textbook phrase such as "Muslim traders spread Islam as they married local women." This implies that agency or power was male, while closer scrutiny may reveal how tenuous his position as a foreigner was.

My final example concerns gender and colonialism. I find the Peruvian case useful, for Irene Silverblatt, in *Moon, Sun, and Witches*, briefly explicates how the Incas used gender to solidify their conquests of adjacent peoples and then how the Spanish imposition of European gender ideology both enhanced their control of Andean peoples and oppressed women especially. Andean women's resistance to loss of status earned them prosecution as witches in the seventeenth century. The role of gender in European conquest of the Americas can also be explored in examples drawn from Canadian Hurons or the New Mexican pueblos.[10] Kathleen M. Brown suggests considering "the relationship between gender and colonialism" as "cultural encounters . . . occurring along gender frontiers. . . ." Such gender frontiers were not distinct from economic, linguistic, political or religious confrontations, but pervaded these aspects of culture, with each society defining its gender categories as "natural." Brown concludes that "the struggle of competing groups for the power that comes with controlling definitions of 'the natural' makes gender frontiers a useful concept for understanding colonial encounters."[11] Exploring these issues might extend into the nineteenth and twentieth centuries, for Africanists have developed a significant body of work connecting European exploitation of gender with the slave trade, colonization, capitalism, and Apartheid.[12] Perhaps only the literature on women and the welfare state compares to it in significance for world history. I have scarcely touched on the modern period, because it is easier to incorporate gender as sources become more plentiful and women move from the household into the public arena. A final recommendation is perhaps the most important. The indispensable source everyone needs is a volume of short interpretative essays and bibliographies, published by the Organization of American Historians, entitled *Restoring Women to History: Teaching Packets for Integrating Women's History into Courses on Africa, Asia, Latin America and the Caribbean, and the Middle East.*[13]

Notes

1. Judith P. Zinsser, *History and Feminism: A Glass Half Full* (New York: Twayne Publishers, 1993) citing Joan Kelly's essay on "The Social Relations of the Sexes," 40.

2. Stephen S. Gosch, "Using Documents to Integrate the History of Women into World History Courses," *World History Bulletin* 5 (Fall/Winter 1987–88).

3. *The World's Women, 1970–1990: Trends and Statistics* (New York: The United Nations, 1991). Table 3 lists the year of women's gaining the right to vote in all countries, with Thailand in 1932, Turkey in 1934, and France in 1944. The volume contains extensive data on work, households, education, and health.

4. For a beginning, see Cheryl Johnson-Odim and Margaret Strobel, "Conceptualizing the History of Women in Africa, Asia, Latin America and the Caribbean, and the Middle East," *Journal of Women's History* 1 (Spring 1989).

5. Huda Lutfi, "Manners and Customs of Fourteenth-Century Cairene Women: Female Anarchy Versus Male Shar'i Order in Muslim Prescriptive Treatises," in *Women in Middle Eastern History*, ed. Nikki R. Keddie and Beth Baron (New Haven: Yale University Press, 1991), a reserve library reading, was the basis for this essay. This reading is more successful in revealing the complexity of women in Islamic cultures than others I have tried.

6. Reserve library readings from Anthony Reid, *Southeast Asia in the Age of Commerce, 1450–1680*, vol. 1; *The Lands Below the Winds* (New Haven: Yale University, 1988) and Irene Silverblatt, *Moon, Sun, and Witches: Gender Ideologies and Class in Inca and Colonial Peru* (Princeton: Princeton University Press, 1987) were the basis of this question, along with John P. McKay, B. Hill, and J. Buckler, *A History of World Societies*, vol. 1, 3rd ed. (Boston: Houghton Mifflin Company, 1992).

7. Sandra Morgen, ed., *Gender and Anthropology: Critical Reviews for Research and Teaching* (Washington, D.C.: American Anthropological Society, 1989). Kevin Reilly, ed., *Readings in World Civilizations*, vol. 1; *The Great Traditions*, 2d ed. (New York: St. Martin's Press, 1992) has a useful section.

8. Ester Boserup, *Woman's Role in Economic Development* (New York: St. Martin's Press, 1970).

9. See Gay Robins, *Women in Ancient Egypt* (Cambridge: Harvard University Press, 1993) and Sarah B. Pomeroy, *Women in Hellenistic Egypt from Alexander to Cleopatra* (New York: Schocken Books, 1984).

10. Karen Anderson, *Chain Her by One Foot: The Subjugation of Women in Seventeenth-Century New France* (London: Routledge, 1991); Ramon A. Gutierrez, *When Jesus Came, the Corn Mothers Went Away: Marriage, Sexuality, and Power in New Mexico, 1500–1846* (Stanford, Calif.: Stanford University Press, 1991).

11. Kathleen M. Brown, "Brave New Worlds: Women's and Gender History," *The William and Mary Quarterly*, 3rd series, 1 (April 1993): 318–19. This is a fine guide to gender literature of the European/African/Americas frontiers of 1500–1800.

12. Cherryl Walker, ed., *Women and Gender in Southern Africa to 1945* (London: James Currey, 1990); Elizabeth Schmidt, *Peasants, Traders, and Wives: Shona Women in the History of Zimbabwe, 1870–1939* (Portsmouth, N.H.: Heinemann, 1992); Claire Robertson and Iris Berger, eds., *Women and Class in Africa* (New York: Holmes and Meier, 1986); and Sharon Stichter and Jane Parpart, eds., *Patriarchy and Class: African Women in the Home and Workforce* (Boulder, Colo.: Westview, 1988).

13. Edited by Cheryl Johnson-Odim and Margaret Strobel in 1988, the volume is available in paperback from the Organization of American Historians for $20.

JUDITH P. ZINSSER

And Now for Something Completely Different: Gendering the World History Survey

As a high school teacher in the 1970s, I was proud of myself for changing my world history classes beyond recognition. I altered their European orientation by "including" — as we then described it, despite the paternalistic implications — units on Africa, the Americas, and Asia. You can imagine my shock when I discovered that in spite of these efforts I still had missed 51 percent of the world's population. This gender blindness — the fact that I could have simply overlooked so many millions of people throughout so much time and across so much space — remains the most frightening aspect of my training and of my early research and teaching. Women are clearly essential to every aspect of our experience, yet they were somehow made invisible.

It is not just the omission of women that is significant, but also the skewing of men's history. Men appeared unsexed and neutered as the "universal" for all human beings. The end result was a past less rich and less nuanced, only half discovered and half told. If we are to remedy this lack, how should we tell the history of men *and* women? What can we do to gender the world history survey?

First, one must remember that even more than other surveys, *any* course in world history will reflect an endless series of impossible and clearly subjective choices made by instructors, whether they teach high school, college, or graduate classes. Second, rarely will a world history course follow a simple linear narrative. Even the "marching civilizations across time" approach doubles back on itself as it describes first one cultural region and then another.

My course reflects, but does not follow, the traditional time breaks. In fact, I try to force myself and my students out of the familiar by using a big, open-ended "timeless" question as the frame for the entire course. I ask, and students answer, only one question. This year it was: What causes order in societies and what causes disorder? No culture or time period is favored with such a question. Instead, everyone's history becomes a potential case study, and traditional causal explanations like economic, social, and cultural factors become organizational devices rather than fixed answers.

Judith P. Zinsser, "And Now for Something Completely Different: Gendering the World History Survey," *Perspectives* (American Historical Association) 34 (May/June 1996): 11–12.

Breaking old patterns also helps me honor my commitment to teach about women *and* men. I do not believe that the standard narrative organization for world, European, or U.S. history makes that possible. Even the best-intentioned "add women and stir" approach (or "don't stir" depending on your perspective) highlights only a few exemplars and leaves half of humanity isolated in some apparently peripheral section of the course that everyone can see "will not be on the exam." And, most important, the old frameworks and periodizations leave history, and the men of that history, just as they have always been. No, in order to gender the survey one must rethink history in terms of actions, interactions, and reactions, by women and men, between women and men, by women, and by men.

To assure that my survey reflects gender I set three criteria for myself that I keep in mind as I write my lectures and plan discussions. These criteria influence the readings and films I choose and determine the oral and written assignments I require. My course must illustrate (1) joint actions by women and men in familiar events, (2) interactions between women and men, and (3) reactions by women and by men as separate experiences reflecting different perspectives.

To show how I use these self-imposed rules, I offer a range of examples from my course World History since 1500. In every class period, in order to indicate that the familiar events of world history consist of joint actions by women *and* men, I "sex the universal" in my lectures. That is, instead of referring to "Chinese peasants" I say "peasant women and men." Instead of "slave owners" I say "men and women slave owners." Students adopt this kind of phrasing without comment and apparently without realizing how different it sounds from what they usually hear.

The readings I assign fulfill one or more of my requirements. In my unit on seventeenth- and eighteenth-century China, students read *Emperor of China: Self-Portrait of K'ang-Hsi* (1988), which describes the thoughts of the powerful Qing emperor as constructed by Jonathan Spence. The book is very obviously about the reactions, separate experiences, and perceptions of a man. In contrast, *The Death of Woman Wang* (1979), also by Spence, offers a sense of women's *and* men's lives in rural China during the same time period. This book describes women and men as they relate to one another (Woman Wang is murdered by her husband) and as they exist as members of clans and of the village, as joint actors in familiar events. In our discussion of the "effectiveness of the imperial government in maintaining order" students comment on the differences in men's and women's experiences at K'ang-Hsi's court and in the isolated rural community described in *The Death of Woman Wang*. Without an impassioned speech on my part, they discover elite men's political power and women's vulnerability across class and culture.

The History of Mary Prince: A West Indian Slave, Related by Herself (1993), edited by Moira Ferguson, presents a description of enslavement in the early nineteenth century, but from a woman's perspective. Assigned books for the twentieth century also follow my criteria. Zareer Masani, the creator of *Tales of the Raj* (originally a radio series, 1988), made a concerted effort to include both women's and men's accounts of life in the India of the 1930s and 1940s. Journalist Jane Kramer did the same in *Unsettling Europe* (1990), her account of immigrant families in 1970s Europe.

Each of the three films I show in my survey class vividly demonstrates interactions between women and men. All are international prizewinners with strong heroes and heroines. Nine in *Red Sorghum* (about a remote rural winery in 1930s China) and Ma Tine in *Sugar Cane Alley* (about Martinique in the same time period) are the principal influences in the lives of the young boys whose stories are portrayed. *Salaam Bombay* offers at least six different plots, each rich in the survival tactics of young boys and girls and of their male and female elders.

Lastly, I also mold my oral and written assignments to fit my three criteria. I formulate propositions for debates that require students to think about men *and* women as historical agents. For example, one of my propositions is "Men and women choose order over rights." And an essay assignment at the end of the term asks students to consider women and men as joint actors in familiar events, the interactions between women and men, and women's and men's separate perceptions and experiences. This year I have offered students a choice of autobiographies by contemporary women political activists and I directed them to analyze "the roles women and men played in causing order or disorder." Two books are by Latin Americans (Domitila Barrios de Chungara's *Let Me Speak! Testimony of Domitila, a Woman of the Bolivian Mines* [1979] and *I Rigoberta Menchú — An Indian Woman in Guatemala,* edited by Elisabeth Burgos-Debray [1985]). Two other books are accounts of black and colored opposition to apartheid (Ellen Kuzwayo's *Call Me Woman* [1985] and *A Life's Mosaic: The Autobiography of Phyllis Ntantala* [1993]). Another choice is Le Ly Hayslip's *When Heaven and Earth Changed Places: A Vietnamese Woman's Journey from War to Peace* (1993) about the Vietnam War, and the last is Chen Xuezhao's *Surviving the Storm: A Memoir* (1991), about events in China from the 1930s to the present.

Clearly, there is ample material available. For me, the difficulty was not selecting new readings, rather it was changing goals and priorities. I gave up the idea that there was a fixed body of information that had to be covered. I decided that vivid encounters with a few cultures were more important than learning names and dates from many cultures. I thought about what I do as a historian and what of that experience I wanted my students to understand. The ability to imagine and think about history as both joint and separate enterprises by men *and* women is a key part of what I must pass on, not because I am a feminist, but because that's the way it happened.

SELECTED BIBLIOGRAPHY

Adas, Michael, ed. *Islamic and European Expansion: The Forging of a Global Order.* Philadelphia: Temple University Press, 1993. This volume, also cited in Part Eight, includes three important essays on gender in world history: "Gender, Sex, and Empire" by Margaret Stroble, "Industrialization and Gender Inequality" by Louise Tilly, and "Gender and Islamic History" by Judith Tucker.

Gosch, Stephen S. "Using Documents to Integrate the History of Women into World History Courses." *World History Bulletin* 5 (Fall/Winter 1987–88): 17–20. To illustrate how this integration might be achieved, Gosch discusses four primary source documents from the premodern history of India, China, and Japan. Three are folk stories about women and men, the fourth is a set of passages from the diary of a woman of the Heian royal court.

Hughes, Sarah Shaver, and Brady Hughes. *Women in Ancient Civilizations.* Washington, D.C.: American Historical Association, 1998. This contribution to the Essays on Global and Comparative History series edited by Michael Adas is an excellent conceptual and historiographical resource for teaching ancient world history that stakes out the experience and contributions of both halves of humanity.

———. *Women in World History.* 2 vols. Armonk, N.Y.: M. E. Sharpe, 1995. The introductions to these two volumes of readings raise several of the basic questions instructors should consider as they rethink the gendering of their courses.

Morris, Marilyn. "Sexing the Survey: The Issue of Sexuality in World History since 1500." *World History Bulletin* 14 (Fall 1998): 11–20. This review of several world history textbooks assesses current treatment of sexual mores across periods and cultures. Morris concludes that world history texts have made large strides in incorporating women but continue to exhibit a good deal of "squeamishness" in addressing homosexuality.

Reilly, Kevin. "Women and World History." *World History Bulletin* 4 (Summer 1987): 1–6. World history's challenge to the traditional Western Civ course must involve formulation of new historical questions that embrace the experience of both men and women. This essay was a keynote address to a

conference at Colorado State University on women in world history, probably the first major meeting on this subject ever held.

*Restoring Women to History: Teaching Packets for Integrating Women's History
into Courses on Africa, Asia, Latin America, the Caribbean, and the Middle
East,* rev. ed. Bloomington, Ind.: Organization of American Historians,
1990. So far, the OAH has published a separate spiral-bound booklet for
each of the five world regions. These volumes are a treasury of teaching
ideas. More than that, the general introduction that Cheryl Johnson-Odim
and Margaret Strobel have written for the series is a brilliant conceptual
primer on the gendering of world history.

Shaffer, Lynda N., and George J. Marcopoulos. "Murasaki and Comnena: Two
Women and Two Themes in World History. *The History Teacher* 19 (August 1986): 487–98. This essay highlights the careers of two gifted women of
the tenth to the twelfth centuries who deserve attention in world history
courses. The authors also show how teaching about these women fits into
the innovative structure of an introductory course developed at Tufts
University.

PART TEN

CONSTRUCTING WORLD HISTORY PROGRAMS AND CURRICULA

Like most curricular innovations or reforms, the movement to advance world history education has an institutional and a political dimension. World history courses represent past and present reality in particular ways, and teachers, students, and administrators, as well as public officials, are likely to have differing ideas about how those representations best serve more general educational or societal interests. Moreover, world history may have to elbow its way into an already congested curriculum, and other programs, such as Western Civ, may be shoved into oblivion. Over the past two decades many college and high school history departments have been the scene of lively contestations over which versions of the world-scale past, if any, students ought to know. Part Two presents several of the opposing arguments that have undoubtedly been heard. World history proposals, which are frequently linked to revision of core requirements or to public educational reforms, usually have to be negotiated up and down the university or school district. Sometimes politicians get into the act. Witness, for example, the legislative initiatives in Massachusetts and California to require public schools to cover the Irish potato famine.

Teachers should not be surprised when a new world history program becomes a hot rock. The innovation may not only challenge standing intellectual and ideological commitments, it may also involve reallocation of funds, redistribution of workloads, and changes in hiring plans. In most institutions world history has probably been introduced without doing lasting damage to faculty esprit. Moreover, university administrators these days tend to be enthusiastic about innovations that promise to diversify the curriculum or "globalize" the campus. Whatever the local political circumstances may be, instructors who propose a world history course should recognize that the definition of the subject and the reasons for teaching it are not self-evident. They should try to be as

481

explicit as they can about their conceptualization of the subject, the research base that justifies it, the pedagogical rationale for its acceptance, and the ideological precommitments that underlie one approach as opposed to another. It is interesting, for example, that the subject matter content standards recently developed in almost all states to guide world history teaching in public schools embody particular viewpoints about what is important in the human past and what is not. Even so, few of these documents includes concrete explanations of why teachers and students should be asked to approach the subject matter in the way the state is recommending or how teachers are to design whole courses that are coherent and intelligible. New initiatives may achieve wider support sooner when all interested parties share at least a general understanding of the objectives, significance, and difficulties of what they are doing.

Once a program gets under way, faculty should continue to review their teaching motives, successes, and deficiencies. Periodic meetings or retreats to talk about conceptual or pedagogical problems are always a good idea, especially when adjunct instructors and graduate students, as well as full-time faculty, are involved in the program. Faculty might organize an ongoing seminar to talk about new books or articles that raise conceptual or comparative issues applicable to teaching. A department might make a special effort to initiate new full-time or adjunct instructors into the program rather than assume that newcomers understand the distinctions between world history as a serious analytical construct and world history as warmed over Western Civ or a disjointed survey of civilizations. Indeed, the most persuasive advocates of Western Civ are those who also think the course must be subjected to repeated intellectual and pedagogical critique. World history teachers should ask no less of themselves, and surely students will only benefit. Frederick Buell, describing the development of a four-course "world studies" program at Queens College, writes frankly:

> The curriculum . . . is not written in stone. As self-criticism yields insights and as new scholarship dictates, the program will change. The experience at Queens has shown that, in constructing such a program out of diverse disciplinary interests and commitments, an "imagined community" of participants emerged, and this community, along with the program, can remain viable only so long as the same sort of exploration that produced it continues. . . . If there is anything that we have learned at Queens, it is that this project is a focus for many of the strongly-felt disagreements of our day — disagreements that range from what we should teach to how we should teach it. The intent of the World Studies Program at Queens is not to suppress or even resolve these disagreements, but to use them in the development of a new and challenging pedagogical experience for faculty and students alike.[1]

The seven selections in Part Ten describe courses and programs but also explain why they are a good idea and how they might benefit students. The essays by George Brooks, Michael Doyle, Jerry Bentley, Philip Curtin, and Edmund Burke and Ross Dunn consider the intellectual and pedagogical grounds for new or revitalized curriculum. Thomas Davis and John Rothney take a more introspective line, reflecting on the experiential process of getting a program up and running.

George Brooks, who has taught world history at Indiana University for many years, proposes a sequence of four one-semester world history courses designed primarily for history majors, but valuable to any student seeking a richer humanistic education. The courses are all panoramic, taking students around the globe, across millennia, or both. In justifying such an approach Brooks argues that the university's interests are best served when the experiences of particular cultural and ethnic groups are incorporated into a large world-scale frame rather than consigned exclusively to separate corners of the curriculum. The Indiana history department in fact decided not to adopt the full program proposed here, although Brooks teaches "Themes in World History," a course that in a single semester introduces students to the big patterns of change from Paleolithic times to the present.

Thomas Davis reminds us that introducing world history to the university may require a delicate touch and a thick skin. Davis took a sabbatical leave from the Virginia Military Institute to think about and design a new program, and he reflects on the career influences and milestones that attracted him to world history. His colleagues and deans, however, had not shared his journey, so when he returned to campus he still had to persuade, negotiate, and, with his colleagues' help, feel his way along. Today world history is required of all first-year students at VMI.

Like Davis, John Rothney recounts the personal adventure he undertook with colleague Carter Findley to institute a twentieth-century global history course at Ohio State University. Rothney focuses more on the intellectual than the institutional process but offers an insightful narrative of how he and Findley thought the course through and laid down a solid conceptual foundation. In fact, the two teachers planned their course so well that a successful world history textbook came out of it.[2] The essay reprinted here omits their course syllabus (a version written in the mid-1980s), as well as a detailed section on teaching techniques.

The fourth and fifth selections are a pair. Michael Doyle makes a thoughtful case for preserving and invigorating the Western Civ course, justly criticizing the "civilization-of-the-week" survey. In their response to his essay, Edmund Burke and Ross Dunn make seven counterproposals for world history curriculum that might offer something better. Doyle echoes J. H. Hexter (see Part Two) in arguing that problems of coverage and training make global history impractical and that in any case, students should learn most about "the very culture to which they belong." Doyle also contends, however, that a revitalized Western Civ would put more emphasis on the global context of European ascendancy and on what Theodore Von Laue calls the "world revolution of Westernization." Burke and Dunn question Doyle's assumption that the West or any other civilization can rightly be seen as possessing an inherent, organic mentality that neighboring groups imitate or absorb. They conclude that although the ideological premises of Western Civ as a unified construct are bankrupt, stuffing more civilizations, perspectives, achievements, and textbook chapters into the curriculum is no help in advancing world history as an intelligible endeavor.

Doyle is certainly right when he charges that too many college world history teachers are insufficiently prepared for the challenge. One response to the problem of training has been the founding of both M.A. and Ph.D. graduate programs in world history. Certainly none of these programs aims to make graduate students experts in "everything" or to transform them into young Toynbees or McNeills. None aims to subvert in-depth study of particular historical problems or meticulous research in primary source documents. Rather, they all aspire, by one approach or another, to introduce students to world history as a mode of analysis involving comparison, formulation of larger-scale questions, and use of various tools of the social sciences. Some graduate programs aspire mainly to prepare students to teach world history in public schools or community colleges. Others emphasize comparative or transnational research. Today, graduate programs having a distinct world history component exist or are under development at more than a dozen universities, including the University of Hawaii, Northeastern University, Rutgers University, Ohio State University, the University of Minnesota, the University of California at Riverside, Villanova University, New York University, the University of Texas at Arlington, the University of North Texas, Miami University (Ohio), the University of Pennsylvania, Johns Hopkins University, and the University of Manitoba. The list will undoubtedly grow longer in the next several years.

The last three selections offer models for graduate study. Jerry Bentley describes the program at Hawaii, which has flourished since its founding in 1984. Graduate students may choose world history as one of four fields in their doctoral training. The program has the threefold purpose of preparing prospective educators to teach core world history surveys, to contribute to the maturation of world history as a research field, and to "stretch the boundaries of the discipline" by integrating historical methods with those of other disciplines.

Philip Curtin pioneered world history in the late 1950s when he founded the Comparative Tropical History graduate program at the University of Wisconsin (see Craig Lockard's essay in Part One). After Curtin moved to Johns Hopkins in the mid 1970s, the program ceased, though many of its graduates went on to introduce world history in other places. In this essay Curtin outlines a program reflecting his view that the inductive comparison of cases is the best methodological strategy for equipping young scholars with world-historical sensibilities and skills. Indeed, his model has influenced the newer programs at Rutgers, Northeastern, the University of Hawaii, and elsewhere.

In the final selection Patrick Manning reports on the doctoral program in world history that was initiated at Northeastern University in Boston in 1994. In contrast to Hawaii, Northeastern offers a Ph.D. in World History, though candidates also take examinations in a regional field and in a methodological and thematic specialization. According to Manning, the program has three major objectives: "to produce teachers of world history and professors who will train teachers," "to address the many issues in transnational and transregional history," and "to develop a historical perspective on the current reconceptualiza-tion of the world." Among American research universities, Northeastern already has the largest concentration of world history Ph.D. students. Moreover, through its World History Center and associated Resource Center it has made a multitiered commitment to advancing world history research and education at the K–12, undergraduate, and graduate levels and to producing new CD-ROM and print materials for the teaching field. Other university world history educa-tors will be watching the Northeastern experiment as a promising institutional model that integrates teaching, research, outreach, and resource development.

Notes

1. Frederick Buell, "World Studies at Queens College," *Comparative Civilizations Review*, no. 26 (Spring 1992): 136–149.

2. Carter Vaughn Findley and John Alexander Murray Rothney, *Twentieth-Century World*, 4th ed. (Boston: Houghton Mifflin, 1998).

George E. Brooks

An Undergraduate World History Curriculum for the Twenty-First Century

World History is the Highest (and Last) Stage of History
(with acknowledgment to V. I. Lenin)

That American youth will live in an increasingly integrated and competitive world is obvious. Less evident is how adequately American colleges and universities are preparing students for future challenges. This paper addresses the potential contributions of college and university history departments.

Historical Perspectives

Until the 1960s, college and university history departments offered undergraduate programs that generally included introductory survey courses in American history and western civilization and upper-level offerings in United States, British, European, and ancient history. Depending on departmental size and resources, there might be courses in Asian history (reflecting the widening perspectives introduced by World War II and the Korean conflict), Russian history (propelled into the curriculum by the Cold War and Sputnik), Latin American history (due to latent American concern galvanized by Castro), and a scattering of courses on whichever parts of the globe accorded with the secondary interests of faculty and the entrepreneurship of chairpersons. The growing realization of America's irrevocable global involvement and the advent of Ford and Rockefeller grants and government-funded area studies programs and research awards in the 1950s and 1960s initiated the training of scholars specializing in Russia and eastern Europe, the Middle East, Asia, and Africa. The inauguration of the Peace Corps in the early 1960s greatly broadened student horizons, and many Peace Corps volunteers returned to the United States to seek academic careers focused on the areas in which they had worked. American involvement in Vietnam sparked student interest in yet another part of the world.

George E. Brooks, "An Undergraduate World History Curriculum for the Twenty-First Century," *Journal of World History* 2 (Spring 1991): 65–79.

The proliferation of history courses in the 1960s and 1970s reflected a congruence of different but compatible interests. Students' demands for "relevant" courses coincided with the preferences of faculty with specialized training. Burgeoning student enrollments created unprecedented demand for teachers, and one of the most effective recruiting inducements offered new history Ph.D.s was the promise that they might develop their own courses instead of teaching traditional survey courses.

As students demanded new courses focused on blacks, women, American Indians, and other hitherto neglected groups and topics, faculty hastened to accommodate these circumstances, thereby also promoting their own interests. Western civilization courses were discontinued at many institutions, and American history survey courses were depreciated in favor of topics courses catering to student and faculty concerns. The proliferation of history courses appears likely to continue in the 1990s, a practice that seems to satisfy everybody, or so it would appear. One wonders, however, whether haphazard selection from a cafeteria-style display of history courses is the optimal means of inculcating American youth with knowledge of their own heritage and that of humankind generally, or whether the time has come for historians to undertake an earnest and searching reexamination of the objectives and content of undergraduate history instruction.

When undergraduate history majors choose careers in the teaching profession and related fields in public history, libraries, and archives, they are assured of increasingly specialized graduate history programs. Departments that once mandated a broadly conceived major field (e.g., American history or European history) combined with three or even four minor fields, likewise of considerable geographical and chronological scope, have in recent years restructured their requirements. Graduate students may now focus on one aspect of a major field that may be considerably reduced in scope, while a single minor field may be a topic field integrated with the major field. Graduate students consequently seek employment in departments where they may teach courses even more specialized than those of their mentors.

The undergraduate program at Indiana University demonstrates the developments discussed above. Course options are bountiful: 34 U.S. history courses; 33 in medieval and modern European history; 17 in Russian and eastern European history; 15 in ancient and Near Eastern history; 11 in Asian history; 7 in African history; 6 in Latin American history; 6 in comparative history; 17 proseminars and special topics courses; and 4 honors courses. Some listed courses have fallen into desuetude as faculty retire or move to other institutions, and some courses are only sporadically offered. Concomitantly, special topics course numbers are routinely used to launch new courses pending approval and listing in the Arts and Sciences *Bulletin*. The courses are taught by highly qualified scholars, many of whom are strongly committed to teaching undergraduates. However, the history major mandates no required linkages — chronological, geographical, sequential, or thematic. As a result, undergraduate history students

have no common experiences regarding courses or faculty, and, more importantly, share no common professional perspectives. Only a computer could calculate all possible course permutations, and students have probably conceived
combinations even a computer would miss. It seems reasonable to assume,
moreover, that few students selecting from such course smorgasbords acquire
the global perspectives one might hope of young people facing the challenges of
the twenty-first century.

The time is overdue for history departments to review course listings and devise more structured programs, both because of the advantages afforded by the
world history perspectives discussed following, and because newly assertive university administrators are currently imposing top-down curricular changes.
Boston University's president recently mandated an old-style western civilization
curriculum that depreciates the historical roles and contributions of women, minorities, and inhabitants of the Third World, while disputatious and well-financed
Dartmouth and Stanford students and alumni are demanding similar curricular
revisions. Surely history departments will want to shape curricular changes by the
preemptive development of programs with persuasive and defensible rationales?

A WORLD HISTORY CORE CURRICULUM

Following are proposals for four one-semester core courses designed to promote
world history perspectives and wide learning about the world's peoples, to be
taken prior to students' enrollment in upper-level courses and seminars. Although the courses are designed as a sequence of offerings for history majors,
they might likewise be taken, collectively or individually, by students majoring
in other disciplines or enrolled in schools other than Arts and Sciences. There
are two organizing principles: the notion that historical perspectives inform and
civilize; and the elucidation of the shared attributes of peoples and cultures, not
their differences. The core courses address a fundamental issue raised by both
proponents and critics of area studies and minority courses: the point that their
contributions should be incorporated into curricula, not added to them, in
order to ensure that all students benefit. As in all introductory survey courses,
the intention is to promote intellectual engagement and prepare students for
upper-level elective courses and seminars.

The use of slides and map transparencies is integral to teaching world
history courses. American students (and faculty) are lamentably weak in
geographical knowledge, so course syllabi should include lists of place names,
ecological zones, ocean currents, wind patterns, and other geographical features
requisite for understanding historical developments discussed in lectures and assigned readings. Map learning should be facilitated by careful selection and by
repetition and reinforcement in more than one assignment and lecture. Thus,
for example, Manila might appear as the destination of seventeenth-century
Spanish fleets carrying silver and American cultigens from Mexico, as well as
the capital of the Philippines; Nagasaki might figure as the only Japanese port

open to foreigners during Japan's period of isolation from 1637 to 1853, and the target of an atomic bomb in World War II; and the Canary Current might come into consideration as the current that speeds the southward passage of vessels in the Atlantic Ocean, and whose cold waters are exploited by fishing fleets from nations as far distant as the USSR, the People's Republic of China, and South and North Korea.

The courses described are conceived as comprising two weekly lectures, plus a section meeting to discuss readings and lectures, administer quizzes on assignments and map work, show films, and discuss students' term papers.

1. The Shared Heritage of Humankind: World History from Paleolithic Times to the Present

This first-year, first-semester course is intended to be one of those challenging courses that high school counselors exhort students to expect, but that first-year college students are adept at avoiding should the courses exist.

The first part of the course treats such worldwide historical developments as the origins and dispersion of our shared ancestors; world language families; domestication of crops and animals and their subsequent diffusion by trade, conquest, and settlement; role specialization contributing to urbanization, state-building, and other social institutions; and patterns of religious beliefs and the spread of the major world religions.

Subsequent lectures emphasize intra- and intercontinental developments, such as: the Mediterranean Sea as linking, not separating peoples; the Indian Ocean trading complex extending from the Red Sea to south and east Asia; the silk road trade network of land routes that connected Han China with the Roman empire; Europe's growing control of the sea lanes of the world from the fifteenth century, followed by the conquest of the Americas; the development of European territoriality and the transition from estates to nation-states; and, from the late eighteenth century, the imposition of European control over Asians, Africans, and the peoples of the Pacific.

The latter part of the course discusses the progressive integration of all peoples into the modern world economy (those with some control over their lives termed it "progress"); unparalleled worldwide population growth and urbanization during the past two centuries; the consequences of World War I, the Great Depression, World War II, and decolonization; the proliferation of state controls over citizens made possible by technological advances in many fields; the Green Revolution that has negated 1950s worst-case scenarios of an overpopulated and famine-stricken planet, and has so far enabled citizens of the First World to sleep soundly in their beds at night; and the reorientation of world markets, exemplified by the progressive shift of American trade from Europe to the Pacific rim. Other lectures focus on the attributes of less developed countries and newly industrializing countries inhabited by more than three-fourths of the world's population; heedless environmental exploitation; unsolved pollution problems; and such global trends as the spread of English, world sports, and civilization diseases, including the proliferation of drugs, alcoholism, and family instability.

William McNeill's *A World History* is a fine textbook when combined with assignments on such relatively neglected areas as Africa and Latin America. There are many suitable supplementary course readings in the excellent *Time-Life* series and in issues of *National Geographic.* Students should be enjoined to read such international news journals as *The Economist* and the *Christian Science Monitor* as part of a lifelong commitment to learning, for the practical catch-their-attention purposes of improving their comprehension of lectures and assignments in the latter part of the course, and for use in a required five-page term paper describing the salient political, economic, and social attributes of a selected less-developed country. The term paper is for most students a first encounter with less-developed countries, and one hopes that the countries studied will afterwards continue to hold special interest in news broadcasts and leisure reading.

Three subsequent core courses would reinforce and expand the world history concepts and information imparted in the course on the Shared Heritage of Humankind. To gain perspective on contemporary world developments, compete successfully in the global arena, and enjoy rewarding personal relationships with Africans, Asians, Europeans, and Latin Americans, one must acquire some appreciation of their cultural heritages and what they consider unique and important about themselves — "where they are coming from," as Americans say. A course on the contemporary world addresses these concerns. Meanwhile, courses on the Eurasian and Atlantic worlds would incorporate long historical perspectives, a paramount consideration being the necessity of countering the parochialism and present-mindedness of American youth.

2. Contemporary World History: The Twentieth Century

Instead of a respite from the first semester's long march from paleolithic times to the present, students will strive anew for an understanding of the complex and baffling world of their grandparents, parents, and themselves. Besides greatly expanded coverage and analysis of topics treated in the last part of the Shared Heritage course, there would be systematic discussion of global institutions and international political and economic linkages.

Most American students know very little about United Nations agencies and programs, the World Bank, the International Monetary Fund, the General Agreement on Trade and Tariffs, the International Airline Transport Association and other shipping conferences, multinational corporations, stock markets, and the European Economic Community, although they wield enormous influence on their lives. Such institutions are properly understood in historical perspective. GATT addresses the same issues as mercantilism, exemplified by the English Navigation Acts and the French *Exclusif;* IATA and other shipping conferences represent the same monopolistic and restrictive practices as those of American transcontinental railroads that Grangers contended with during the nineteenth century; the EEC derives from Europeans' determination to harness the destructive forces that engendered centuries of warfare; and the United Nations owes much to the experiences of the League of Nations.

The foregoing is a challenging agenda, but should we not strive to prepare the next generation of Americans to be as informed and globally oriented as their counterparts in other countries?

Examples of texts and readings include William R. Keylor, *The Twentieth-Century World* (1984), *The Economist,* and as many novels as the instructor has the temerity to assign, with the foreknowledge that the hubbub will cease as soon as students get caught up in books such as Chinua Achebe's *Things Fall Apart,* which delineates the effects of European colonialism on an African society; Carolina Maria de Jesus' *Child of the Dark,* which depicts life of the underprivileged in a Sao Paulo favela; and Kamala Markandaya's *Nectar in a Sieve,* which shows the life of rural poor in India prior to the changes for good and bad associated with the Green Revolution.

A required ten-page student paper would examine the salient features of a cartel such as OPEC or the De Beers diamond trust; Unesco, UNCTAD, and other United Nations agencies; multinational economic organizations such as the Andean Pact, ASEAN, ECOWAS, and SADCC; the proliferation of toxic wastes and environmental pollutants; and such social and cultural themes as women's rights, labor migrancy, the growth of international sports competition, nationalism, music, art, dress, product design and advertising, and rivalry between youths and elders.

3. Eurasia from Indo-European Migrations to Perestroika

Indo-European speaking peoples left an indelible mark on Eurasia from the Atlantic Ocean to the Indian subcontinent; some groups ventured as far as central Asia. Their linguistic and cultural heritage was modified and enriched in subsequent millennia by the conquests and migrations of Uralic-Altaic speaking Huns, Magyars, Turks, and Mongols. Relay commerce by land over the silk roads and by sea expedited exchanges of commodities, pandemic diseases, cultigens, and cultural traditions. Hinduism, Buddhism, Judaism, Christianity, and Islam and their social and cultural patterns diffused widely. Hellenism left an indelible imprint on western Eurasia, while Chinese social and cultural patterns influenced Koreans, Japanese, and the peoples of southeast Asia. Maritime groups inhabiting the eastern rim of Asia populated the vast Pacific cosmos, introducing south Asian cultigens and domesticated animals.

The growth of maritime trade links and the relationship between cultivators and pastoralists are conspicuous themes in Eurasian history over several millennia. The Mediterranean Sea linked, not separated, the peoples dwelling along its shorelines, Indo-European speakers to the north and Afro-Asiatic speakers to the south, east, and southeast. From early times Eurasia and east Africa were connected by sea lanes navigated by, among others, Sabaean mariners along the Red and Arabian seas, Persians and Arabs who by the sixth century reached southern China, Indians and Indonesians, and Chinese and Japanese who exercised growing maritime roles from the thirteenth and fifteenth centuries, respectively.

Uralic-Altaic speaking pastoralists conquered vast areas of Eurasia several times: Huns in the fourth century, Magyars in the tenth century, Saljuq Turks in the eleventh century, Mongols and Turks in the thirteenth century. Nomads controlled the grasslands of northern Asia for millennia, coexisting and contending with Chinese cultivators who contrived to sustain larger and larger populations by means of intercropping, double-cropping, peripatetic bee-keeping, and, from the sixteenth century, the adoption of American cultigens. Mongols conquered China and expanded its boundaries during the Yuan dynasty (1280–1368), as did the Manchus during the early part of the Qing dynasty (1644–1912). From the fifteenth century, gun-wielding Cossacks conquered Uralic-Altaic speaking groups across vast territories, incorporating them into the sprawling Russian empire with imponderable consequences for the future.

The fifteenth century similarly marks a new era in Eurasian maritime history, as Ming dynasty rulers decided to forsake overseas expeditions instead of exploiting Zheng He's voyages of reconnaissance across the Indian Ocean as far as east Africa. Portuguese seafarers fortuitously entered the Indian Ocean three-quarters of a century later, within a generation achieving control of its sea lanes, to be displaced in the centuries following by Dutch, French, and English seafarers and monopolistic trading companies.

Most of the peoples of south and east Asia came under European domination before Japan's rapid modernization during the Meiji period (1868–1912), the historical pendulum being reversed with Japan's defeat of Russia in 1905. Sub-themes treated during this period include the imposition of European colonial rule, the transfer of civil and military technology, and the exploitation of millions of Indians and Chinese transported worldwide to labor on plantations, railways, and other capitalistic enterprises.

Eurasian peoples sustained great losses in population and resources during the turbulent first half of the twentieth century, bearing the brunt of two world wars and numerous lesser conflicts, Stalin's purges and contrived famines, and chronic warfare and political turmoil in China. World War II and its massive bloodlettings, including the Holocaust, Hiroshima and Nagasaki, and the dislocation of numerous populations, was closely followed by the upheavals attending decolonization, with far-reaching consequences both for the inhabitants of the European metropoles and the peoples of south and east Asia.

Nonetheless, during the third quarter of the twentieth century, many Eurasian states achieved political, economic, and social stability undergirded by the significant increases in food production made possible by the Green Revolution and by economic growth promoted by expanding world trade and stimulated by German and Japanese entrepreneurship. The restructuring of Russia and east European countries during the last quarter of the twentieth century, together with the potential stabilization of Middle Eastern affairs following the peace treaty between Egypt and Israel and the truce between Iran and Iraq, offer the promise of augmenting Eurasian economic and political cooperation and higher standards of living and increased opportunities for its peoples.

Suggested texts and readings include William H. McNeill's *Rise of the West* (1963) and *Plagues and Peoples* (1976); Eric R. Wolf's *Europe and the People without History* (1982); Immanuel Wallerstein's "The Rise and Future Demise of the World Capitalistic System: Concepts for Comparative Analysis" (1974); and Daniel R. Headrick's *The Tentacles of Progress: Technology Transfer in the Age of Imperialism* (1988). A bonus regarding the inculcation of Eurasian perspectives is enhanced appreciation of the classic travel accounts of Marco Polo and Ibn Battuta and books by contemporary travel writers such as Colin Thubron and Paul Theroux.

Term paper topics would span Eurasia, and students should be encouraged to experiment with interdisciplinary and comparative themes. Topics such as the silk roads, Eurasian pandemics, the spread and evolution of cataphract warfare, and the diffusion of cultigens, technological innovations, weapons, art styles, and religions suggest innumerable possibilities.

4. The Atlantic World from the Classic Period to the Present

American Indian civilizations flourished for more than a millennium prior to European contact and the introduction of Eurasian and African diseases that decimated their populations and irrevocably transformed the lives of survivors and their descendants. The first part of this course would focus on the remarkable achievements of Aztec, Mayan, and Inca civilizations, with subsidiary treatment of the agricultural and hunting-gathering societies adapted to environments from the Arctic to Tierra del Fuego.

A second group of lectures would provide an overview of west and west central Africa prior to the fifteenth-century European voyages of reconnaissance and commercial initiatives. Topics would include intra-African caravan, coastal, and riverine trade networks; trans-Saharan commerce; and the political, social, and cultural attributes of such states as Mali, Benin, and Kongo.

Since the main themes of European history are delineated in the Eurasian course, the next section would begin with the reorientation of western Europe to the Atlantic world during the fourteenth century, treating such topics as the inauguration of annual flotillas of galleys from Italy to Flanders, the transmission of Italian maritime skills to Portugal, and the Iberian voyages to enslave the Guanches of the Canary Islands.

European voyages to west Africa from the 1440s, and to the Americas and the Indian Ocean a half-century later, initiated a new epoch in world history with unparalleled economic, political, demographic, ecological, epidemiological, and other consequences for Europeans and for the inhabitants of other parts of the globe. More than sixty million Europeans, free and unfree, were transported to the Americas between the sixteenth and twentieth centuries, as were some ten million enslaved Africans from west and west central Africa. They imposed themselves on the remnants of Indian societies decimated by pandemics whose economies were transformed by the introduction of European, African, and Asian cultigens and domestic animals. European and African settlers and their descendants were likewise transformed by their experiences in the Americas, resulting in kaleidoscopes of ethnic, social, and cultural attributes.

Mercantilist economic policies promoted the reckless exploitation of the soils and subsoils of the Americas by means of captive, indentured, and free labor. During the nineteenth century, European rule was supplanted by indigenous oligarchies, the trans-Atlantic trade in captive African labor was gradually suppressed, and northern European economic interests, preeminently British, supplanted those of Portugal and Spain until they were in turn challenged by American entrepreneurs. Meanwhile, European imperialists partitioned the African continent and instituted direct exploitation of its resources.

Decolonization and the creation of the United Nations transformed the Atlantic world during the second half of the twentieth century. African colonies gained political independence beginning in the 1950s, but with strong economic and cultural links to former metropoles that have institutionalized the weakness of countries exporting primary products vis-à-vis industrialized countries. African and Latin American countries compete to sell minerals, coffee, cocoa, and other tropical products that are frequently in surplus in world markets. Both groups of nations are prominent in the north-south dialogue in the United Nations and other world arenas, striving for greater political and economic independence in circumstances where intimidation and debt collection by the British fleet and the American marines have been superseded by the International Monetary Fund and consortia of financial institutions.

The last part of the course would discuss ecological degradation and the catastrophic AIDS pandemic. North American and European ecologies are imperiled by acid rain and other pollutants, while the rain forests and cultivable lands of Africa and South America are being rapidly depleted by exploitative enterprises exercising few responsibilities regarding reforestation or soil conservation. AIDS poses a particular threat to the population of Africa (and potentially Latin America), with alarming morbidity projections for countries with few medical facilities.

Suggested texts and readings would include Alfred W. Crosby, *The Columbian Exchange* (1972) and *Ecological Imperialism* (1986); Philip D. Curtin, *The Atlantic Slave Trade: A Census* (1969); Joseph C. Miller, *Way of Death* (1988); Joel Garreau, *The Nine Nations of North America* (1981); and Joseph A. Opala, *The Gullah* (1987).

Students' papers would trace their family ties to Europe, Africa, Asia, or the Americas, describing the political, economic, and cultural milieus from which their ancestors migrated, including, for example, a hamlet in northern Portugal or southern Italy, a Jewish ghetto in central Europe, a Yoruba or Ibo village in present-day Nigeria, a farming community in southern China, or a secondary migration from elsewhere in the Americas, such as Mexico or Haiti.

TEAM TEACHING

History departments can institute core courses by a combination of self-motivated remedial training by overspecialized historians, by team teaching, and by inviting the assistance of faculty colleagues in other disciplines. Team teaching core courses offers an excellent opportunity to showcase faculty specializations and methodological approaches, thereby attracting better prepared students to upper-level history courses.

History departments are composed of intelligent and often widely travelled people, many of whom know a great deal about stock markets, world banking systems, international negotiations, peace and conflict studies, population issues, environmental concerns, and other matters they frequently never have the opportunity to discuss with students. Many are parents who share a concern that their children and the next generation of students should be taught more about a pluralistic world than they themselves learned in college, and with the advantage of historical perspectives.

Leadership by chairpersons and senior faculty is crucial, likewise supportive oversight by deans who can mediate interdepartmental cooperation, ensure that appropriate incentives are accorded faculty members (especially junior faculty) engaged in new and challenging teaching assignments, and disburse requisite funds for slides, transparencies, and equipment. Course planning and week-to-week administration can be delegated to one or several faculty members, with one individual responsible for coordinating each course for a three-year shakedown period.

There are numerous potential collaborators in other departments and programs (the teaching of world history is too important to be trusted solely to historians). Few students enter college with knowledge of linguistics, folklore, anthropology, sociology, or psychology, and members of these departments may welcome the opportunity to advertise their disciplines and attract students to their courses. Students are generally uninformed about Indo-European, Afro-Asiatic, Austronesian, and other world language families, and about such concepts as protolanguages and loan words. They do not know that folklorists systematically try to understand and interpret human experience through myths, folktales, and other verbal and musical expressions enriching and giving meaning to people's lives, and that much can be learned from how a society views itself and regards other groups. Anthropologists might expand these themes, explaining how their discipline contributes to an understanding of world societies, literate and pre-literate. Sociologists and psychologists could contribute perspectives on the phenomena characterized as civilization diseases, such as cancers, heart attacks, alcoholism, drug abuse, and mental breakdowns, that reflect the social and psychological tensions of modern life.

Deans of schools of business and journalism already requiring their students to take history courses could probably identify one or several of the core courses as appropriate for their students and encourage their faculty to contribute lectures. Members of schools of business or economics departments might give lectures in the twentieth-century course, discussing such topics as stock markets, GATT, OECD, world banking, international debts, multinational corporations, shipping conferences, the Great Depression, comparative advantage, and theories of economic development. Faculty in journalism and mass communications might lecture on the proliferation of technological capabilities and discuss political and institutional constraints regarding news gathering and dissemination. Political scientists could trace the development of democratic institutions and of totalitarian regimes, the League of Nations and United Nations, and the proliferation of international agencies and organizations.

Environmental degradation and pollution are not recent phenomena. In classical times, the lands along the Tigris and Euphrates rivers supported large populations until the soils became heavily impregnated with salt. The lone tree on Lebanon's flag eloquently testifies to cedar forests that once provided a major commodity of trade. Air pollution contributing to overcast skies above England's industrial heartland made rickets one of the first civilization diseases. Faculty in schools of agriculture, medicine, and public and environmental affairs might contribute lectures addressing such global concerns.

Of special significance for world history courses are the contributions of faculty associated with African, African-American, Asian, Uralic-Altaic, Jewish, Latin American, native American, Russian, and east European programs, and with religious studies, women's studies, and other programs and institutes. World history courses can and should incorporate many of their perceptions and analyses; too often the potential contributions of such programs have been unrealized for the great majority of undergraduates.

There are many possible lecture topics and themes regarding each of the four core courses, and historians associated with the core courses would share with students opportunities to add to their knowledge and interdisciplinary perspectives, the better to revise and restructure the core courses year by year. Once history faculty become familiar with the contributions of guest speakers, they may decide to appropriate salient lecture themes and reading materials for their own presentations, terminating the guest lecturers' contributions with appreciation, or request other topics suitable for the revised syllabi. Historians associated with core courses may decide to pioneer new upper-level topics courses based on interdisciplinary concepts and teaching strategies.

Historians are sometimes denigrated as birds that fly backward because they are preoccupied with where they have been rather than where they are going. However, many historians who reached maturity in the 1960s and 1970s were influenced by high school teachers who grappled as best they could with state directives mandating global history courses and with the challenges of discussing current events during the turbulent era of the civil rights movement, the war in Vietnam, and Watergate. Some served in the armed forces, some in the Peace Corps, and most have travelled more widely than their elders. Consequently, many younger historians beat their wings to different cadences and follow methodological flyways that require forward-looking perspectives to keep abreast of their peers in other disciplines. One may look to them to develop world history courses, assisted by scholars in other fields who have shared similar life experiences.

FUTURE PERSPECTIVES

College courses can only begin to implant world history perspectives. Once learned, such perspectives are expanded, deepened, and added to by personal and professional commitments to continuing self-education. Preeminently these include daily and weekly reading of such international news journals as *The New York Times, The Christian Science Monitor,* and *The Economist* and subscriptions to well edited and richly illustrated magazines like *National Geographic, Natural History,* and *The Smithsonian,* which along with the many splendid programs on public television contribute to nurturing world history perspectives among children. These encourage family attendance at museums, art galleries, and concerts. Historical perspectives, together with those of other humanities, prepare educated persons to transcend compulsive professional routines and lead richer and more satisfying lives.

One must think in terms of generations: that the sons and daughters and grandsons and granddaughters of students taught to appreciate (only) the Parthenon and Chartres cathedral may as business people and travellers seek out the incomparable Taj Mahal, Nikko's wonderfully crafted buildings, Lalibela's rock-hewn churches, and Chichen Itza's temples, not to mention the wondrous American Indian artifacts surviving in the United States — a lifetime's enrichment and delight awaits the informed traveller. Many of the travellers' children, one hopes, will become world history teachers in high schools, colleges, and universities.

Thomas W. Davis

Starting from Scratch
Shifting from Western Civ to World History

I write this essay with all the zeal of a recent convert to world history who has been academically energized by his newfound devotion to the subject. I also write with at least some awareness of the problems involved in teaching the subject.

I began my career in 1972 [at the Virginia Military Institute (VMI)] as a specialist in British history. I happily taught the required two-semester Western Civilization course for nearly twenty years. Having secured promotion and tenure, I could have continued with Western Civ until retirement. But something kept troubling me about the course. In particular, I wondered occasionally if the rumblings about world history within the profession were worth further consideration. Increasingly, the answer for me became a resounding "yes," not because of political correctness, a desire to attack Western Civ, demands for multiculturalism, or the ethnic diversity in my classrooms, but simply because of what I considered to be more "e.c." — educationally correct. It came down to a question J. H. Hexter once posed: Which of the two courses is more beneficial for our students? I like the way he phrased that question, because it can be used to validate both Western Civ and world history. But for today's students, who will be spending most of their adult lives in the twenty-first century, I came increasingly to see the advantages of world history. . . .

Institutional Support

Moving to world history becomes easier if you have the support and encouragement of your department head, academic dean, and college president. I was fortunate to have all three on my side. My experience has been that deans and presidents are often supportive of academic innovations that respond to perceived needs in higher education. In Virginia, for instance, the state has made a major commitment to implement the recommendations of an influential report

Thomas W. Davis, "Starting from Scratch: Shifting from Western Civ to World History," *Perspectives* (American Historical Association) 34 (December 1996): 27–29, 38, 39.

issued by the Commission on the University of the Twenty-First Century. One recommendation was to internationalize the curriculum to expose students to global perspectives. This shift in focus can be accomplished in many academic disciplines, but the obvious place to start for many educational leaders is with the introductory history course. Educational leaders like signs of innovation and fresh thinking in the curriculum. That does not automatically make them cheerleaders for world history, but the fact remains that the shift to global history is often seen by administrators as one positive way of responding to the educational needs of today and tomorrow. These leaders also favor innovations that do not require substantial changes in faculty staffing. I also find that boards of trustees are inclined to support the shift to global history, particularly those trustees who work in the business community and regularly think about international markets and the movement of goods and services across cultural boundaries.

DEPARTMENTAL SUPPORT

In a department that has long offered Western Civ as its basic first-year course, the idea of a transition to world history was not embraced uniformly by all the faculty with joy and eagerness. My colleagues' reactions ranged from healthy skepticism to guarded enthusiasm. I treated all responses with respect, including the view that Western Civ was the educationally preferable approach to introductory history.

A few of my colleagues expressed doubts along these lines: "My two-semester Western Civ course is already superficial, so how could I ever be satisfied if I had the entire globe to cover?" I replied by raising the issue of what we include and exclude in every course we teach, regardless of its scope. A specialist could easily conclude that a yearlong course in the American Civil War is superficial because of all that's left out. As historians, we always face issues of selection and organization, whether the scope is local or global.

Another major argument was expressed this way: "As a twenty-year teacher of Western Civ, how could I ever teach myself enough about China, India, and Africa to feel comfortable — in a sense, legitimate — in front of a class?" This is a valid concern, but there is an appropriate answer. It boils down to personal professional commitment and the willingness to make time to read more broadly. Those who conclude that world history is the better course educationally will find or make the time to prepare, especially if there is institutional support. And teachers who agree to teach world history *will* need help along the way, but I'll always remember this comment heard during my own transition: "Moving to world history will inevitably involve a lot of time devoted to reading and teaching yourself." For those who remain reluctant and daunted by the task of going global, another observation comes to mind: "Teaching world history is a lot easier than contemplating the task." In other words, "just doing it" is the way to overcome many of the anticipated problems.

TIME AND MONEY

There are many helpful people and useful resources available to faculty who want to begin teaching world history, but the journey will be immeasurably more difficult without two key ingredients. To start, colleges might consider small summer stipends to support the initial reading required to begin such a course. In addition, they might provide instructors with a reduced teaching load during the first year of offering the course. Since so many educational voices speak in favor of global awareness, institutions need to show their support in substantial ways.

In the fall semester of 1991, I took a sabbatical leave for the sole purpose of examining world history as an introductory course and making specific recommendations. I methodically worked my way through numerous books and articles, starting with selected issues of the *History Teacher* and with J. W. Konvitz's splendid collection of edited essays, *What Americans Should Know: Western Civilization or World History?* (Michigan State University, 1985). I obtained Kevin Reilly's useful *World History: Selected Course Outlines and Reading Lists from American Colleges and Universities* . . . and I reviewed readings suggested by Ross Dunn. . . . I also invited Michael Galgano of James Madison University and Carl Smith to share their world history experiences with my departmental colleagues in afternoon seminars. Teachers at James Madison University made the switch from Western Civ to world history several years ago, and I sought to benefit from their efforts.

A major boost came from my joining the World History Association and reading articles in the *Journal of World History* and the *World History Bulletin*, which are aimed at teachers wanting to get started in global history. . . .

I savored the writings of William McNeill and Peter Stearns on world history, and I believe that despite their differences (e.g., on the relative significance of cultural diffusion), the two share some thoughts in common. For instance, both contend that the study of global history prepares one for an understanding of the modern world — more so than any other introductory first-year history course. Both argue in favor of focusing initially on the major, enduring civilizations in the world and on their legacies, although McNeill stresses the contact between the regions as the primary motor that drives civilizations forward, while Stearns focuses more on the distinctive elements in different societies and on the forces that shaped their experiences. . . .

In addition to reading, I attended my first world history conference where I learned, for instance, about the effectiveness of bringing area specialists to one's college for weeklong summer seminars — e.g., engaging African or Middle Eastern experts to discuss the best books, themes, and organizing principles for teaching their subjects. I also learned from the conference where funding might be obtained for such seminars. Not incidentally, I was reminded that teaching universal history was once the norm and that the traditional Western Civ course had a definite history of its own, rising to prominence in this country only after World War I. . . .

When I completed my sabbatical, I wrote a report to the administration that outlined my conclusion: V.M.I. should initiate a two-semester world history course for first-year students as a pilot project. In the three semesters that followed, I hammered out the details of the proposed course with my colleagues, who became increasingly supportive, especially when they saw I was not trying to draft any of them as reluctant participants. Further assistance came from my department chair, Blair Turner, a Latin American historian who had taught Western Civ for years; he proved quite eager to teach the new course. In the spring of 1993, Turner and I made final plans and selected books. For the first semester (pre–1500), we chose William McNeill's *History of the Human Community*, 4th ed. (Prentice-Hall, 1993), Peter Stearns's *Documents in World History* (HarperCollins, 1988), and Ross Dunn's *Adventures of Ibn Battuta* (University of California Press, 1986). We began the course in fall 1993, and here's how we did it.

THE FIRST SEMESTER

The university registrar selected 100 first-year students from the entering class of 360 and placed them in world history; the remaining students were enrolled in Western Civ. We met with our world history students three times per week, with each week in the semester being devoted to one of McNeill's fourteen chapters. His chronological organization and emphasis on cultural diffusion provided the structure to our course and the framework for our lectures and discussions.

For the first meeting of each week, a lecture was presented to all the students. With fourteen major lectures in the course, Turner and I gave half of them, spread throughout the semester. The other seven were given by teachers in our community invited to discuss a particular aspect of each week's chapter in McNeill. For instance, a Far Eastern historian gave an overview of classical China (comparing the Yellow River communities in the north with those along the Yangtze to the south), the early Chinese dynasties, and the different philosophies espoused by the Legalists, Taoists, and Confucians. A Middle Eastern historian gave a lecture on Mohammed and the origins of Islam. Another colleague intrigued me with his talk on Africa before European contacts. I learned about Monomotapas and the city of Great Zimbabwe, and I also gained much from the lecturer who described the Mongols and their expansion over the steppes of Eurasia. During the past decade, my own department has hired several new teachers with area specialties beyond Europe and North America, a fact that helped us compose the lecture list.

In regard to my own lectures, I enjoyed researching and delivering a talk on early India and the Hindu religion and on the Kushite civilization in northeast Africa, but I think my favorite discovery was preparing a lecture entitled "The World in the Year One." I started my preparation by asking our reference librarian about calendars and differing methods of measuring time, learning for the first time what "the year one" was for the Chinese, the Jews, the Indians, and the Zoroastrians.

For the second meeting in the week, students attended one of eight discussion sections scheduled over a four-day period. Turner and I had about twelve students in each discussion group, and we expected them to be conversant each time we met on the content of the week's lecture and on the assigned chapter in McNeill's text. In our effort to improve the discussions, we emphasized techniques of good note taking, and we allowed students to consult their notes during the brief weekly quizzes that took place during our second weekly meeting. The quizzes were based solely on that week's lecture and textbook assignment.

After all the discussion sections had met, Turner and I were ready for the week's third session with our students, when we met collectively with our respective discussion sections (his three, my five) to review and expand upon the primary lessons of the week's material and to preview the coming week. We also used these meetings for periodic hour tests.

As for grades, we offered the students varied opportunities. In addition to weekly quizzes, two hourlong tests, and an examination that counted 30 percent of the final grade, we assigned two papers to be composed outside of class. The first was an essay addressing the question of why democracy developed in Greece but not in India and why the caste system emerged in India but not in Greece. The second paper required students to write an analytical review of Dunn's book. While some students complained about the difficulty of following Ibn Battuta's travels in unfamiliar parts of the world, most seemed willing to meet the cultural challenges posed by a book set in the fourteenth-century Islamic world; they also began to see the global interconnections in the Dar al-Islam. To assist students, I showed them the December 1991 issue of *National Geographic*, which featured a cover picture and major article about a modern-day replication of Ibn Battuta's journey. Somehow, reading that article and viewing a current picture of Adam's Peak in Sri Lanka seemed to help students. . . .

THE SECOND SEMESTER

For the second semester, Turner and I continued with McNeill's textbook (volume two, post–1500). We used Alfred Crosby's *Columbian Exchange* (Greenwood, 1972) and Chinua Achebe's *Things Fall Apart* (Ballantine Books, 1983, c. 1959) for outside reading and reports, plus one book on an aspect of world history that students selected themselves. Crosby and Achebe seemed particularly effective for teaching about the consequences of "culture contact" and for altering student perspectives.

CONCLUSIONS

In looking back at our initial foray into world history, Turner and I are pleased. Students accepted the course and its broad, global perspective more readily than we had expected. The final grades resembled the distribution in Western Civ.

And the two teachers were happy to have had their own intellectual batteries recharged. While favoring the format just described, we recognize that other approaches could also work (e.g., the traditional arrangement of a teacher meeting the same group of twenty-five or thirty students three times per week). Pedagogically, however, we benefited from our team approach featuring the common lecture at the beginning of each week, the common syllabus, and our working together to produce the course's common assignments and final examination.

We recognized after our first attempt at teaching the course that some areas were in need of improvement. For example, we now try to help our first-year students glean more from the weekly lectures by giving them samples of our own lecture notes and by asking all lecturers to distribute a topical outline at the start of their talks: this latter technique increases the attention level of our students as the fifty-minute lectures progress. In discussion classes, we strive to elicit more comments from the group and to have students respond to each other instead of engaging in two-way discussions with the teacher. We are seeking innovative techniques for teaching and learning more about geography, especially techniques and computer programs that take advantage of new technology in the classroom.

Although the "work-in-progress" sign is still hanging on our world history course, we are encouraged by the initial results and by a recent unanimous department vote to abandon the Western Civ course for world history. Teachers new to the subject are getting institutional support to assist their transition. As more colleagues consider making the transition from Western Civ to world history, more seem willing to "work up" a fresh lecture in a new field — as long as they can commit the time and complete the suggested readings. Visits from outside experts and discussions with more experienced world history teachers are helping novice instructors gain the confidence to "take over" new subject material.

For myself, I savor comments made by students who were asked if the course had made any difference to them. One said: "I saw the movie *Malcolm X* during the holidays and understood the parts about Islam because I'd had your course." Another remarked: "I was at home with my girlfriend during vacation, watching 'Jeopardy' on television. When the category of 'world religions' came up, I just devastated her with my answers; she couldn't believe all I knew." Another student told me that he understands China far better now, having read *The Analects* by Confucius; yet others tell me that they can read the morning newspaper with far more understanding, thanks to the course. I will gladly add those comments to my list of justifications for world history, a list headed by my favorite reason: the world is round.

JOHN ROTHNEY

Developing the Twentieth-Century World History Course
A Case Study at Ohio State

During the spring quarter of 1980, Carter V. Findley and I team-taught to some 160 Ohio State undergraduates the first experimental offering of a course in the global history of the twentieth century, entitled "Critical Issues of the 20th Century World." In 1984, this course became one of only three on our campus (the other two offered by the geography and sociology departments) which fulfill the "Contemporary World" component of the twenty hours of "History and Society" required for our Bachelor of Arts degree. During the present academic year, the large enrollments in "Critical Issues" produced by this requirement necessitated offering the course every quarter, using three separate teams of professors.

Our once-experimental course has thus proved a success, both in numbers enrolled and in the strategic place it occupies in the core curriculum of a large state university. Now that even off-campus voices are being raised in debate over the basics of American undergraduate education, it seems appropriate to offer our fellow historians a case study of how one contemporary global history course was conceived, how its syllabus was constructed, and what unusual teaching strategies were employed in presenting the material. My hope is that by indicating both possibilities and pitfalls, this account may prove useful to colleagues at other institutions who are planning similar courses. For, if history is to be "in" again, after falling from favor in the 1960s and 1970s, it is not necessary that a revived "Western Civilization" be the only basic offering. Many who are redesigning curricula will insist that courses reflecting the twentieth-century reality of global interdependence are also essential forms of preparation for young people, most of whose lives will be spent in the twenty-first century.

When we began planning our course in the late 1970s, history's place in the curriculum could not be taken for granted. Historians pondering their dwindling audience wondered whether the kind of courses being offered as undergraduate introductions might not be the cause of shrinking enrollments. Again

John Rothney, "Developing the Twentieth-Century World History Course: A Case Study at Ohio State," *The History Teacher* 20 (August 1987): 465–68, 471–76, 483–85.

and again, most notably at a crowded session of the annual meeting of the American Historical Association in 1976, William McNeill had warned that "our discipline is in danger of slipping away from the privileged position it has hitherto occupied in the college curricula." The crisis had arisen, he pointed out, with the collapse of consensus among historians on what should constitute their basic introductory course. The implicit paradigm of the "western civilization" surveys that had once fulfilled that function — that history was a story of progress culminating in the triumph of twentieth-century western industrial democracy — had been devastated not only by the horrific nature of the century's second global war but also by the decolonizing wave, ecological anxieties, and political disillusionments of the 1960s. Meanwhile, a generation of historians trained in narrowly defined regional, temporal, and functional specialties could agree on no introductory paradigm to replace that of "western civ." Consequently, McNeill declared, the historical profession "did not recognize any obligation to find something of general importance to teach all students, something all educated persons should know."[1]

To a certain extent, McNeill's strictures applied to the situation at Ohio State when Carter Findley and I began to teach "Critical Issues of the Twentieth Century World." Until the early 1970s, history enrollments had been safeguarded by a fifteen-hour, three-quarter western civilization sequence. When the history department agreed in a curricular compromise to reduce its requirement to ten hours, a catastrophic decline began. Between 1970 and 1977 enrollments fell by over fifty percent, at a rate far worse than that of English or the humanities in general.

Nevertheless, it would not be correct to say that the idea of creating this course arose from any general concern of the Ohio State history department at students' growing indifference to their discipline, or from any concerted effort to stanch an enrollment hemorrhage. The new course emerged rather serendipitously, not as History 1 or History 101 but as History 209, one of a potpourri of some twenty-six separate courses with which an OSU student in the late 1970s could fulfill what history requirement remained. The only unusual stipulation the department made about the new course was that it should always be team-taught, combining a specialist in a western culture (presumably a Europeanist) with a specialist in some non-western culture.

Thus, when Carter Findley, an Ottoman historian, and I, a French historian, agreed to teach the course for the first time in 1980, we had virtual carte blanche to design the course as we chose. Moreover, there were relatively few models on other campuses from which we could draw inspiration, though Robert Byrnes of Indiana University and Robert L. Roeder of the University of Denver had reported to the annual meeting of the AHA in 1978 on their versions of a global twentieth-century course.[2]

Starting though we were virtually from scratch, Findley and I were nonetheless guided throughout our planning of what to teach and how to teach it by our experience of the capacities of our future audience. A land-grant institution, Ohio State in the late 1970s was obliged to admit virtually any applicant who held an Ohio high school diploma. Only a little over half of these became Arts and Sciences students, the rest pursuing essentially vocational education in the Colleges of Education, Engineering, Agriculture, and Administrative Sciences (another name for business administration), among others. Students from these colleges were required only to take five hours of a "social science"; History 209, if elected, might be the only history course they would take at the college level — or anywhere — except for the minimum of one semester of U.S. history Ohio law required of high school graduates. Many of our students, then, would have recently emerged from the forty percent of U.S. high school students who believed Israel to be an Arab country and the sixty percent who believed history to be a "dull" subject.[3]

As we planned our course, then, we knew that we could take very little "background" for granted. Moreover, with students of this degree of preparation, History 209 could not possibly aspire to the lofty level of comparative abstraction and synthesis that many historians associate, whether enthusiastically or not, with the teaching of history on a global scale. Far from being a defect, indeed, chronological limitation to our own century could well prove a blessing. We could foresee that even treating its eight decades in the span of a ten-week quarter might prove a tight fit, given our goals. For we were determined that students should complete the course with both a command of the narrative outline and some capacity for interpretive generalization about their own century.

To achieve these goals, we decided, we would have to confront, from the outset, a basic dilemma. Though we wanted students to emerge from the course with the kind of comparative perspective on, for example, twentieth-century revolutions that would help them to interpret current events, we could not take for granted that they would know at the beginning of the course the basic chronology of even the Mexican or Russian revolutions. Yet, we did not want to devote all of our teaching to dispensing that kind of memorizable chronology. We were sure that one reason many students viewed history as being so indigestible was the tendency of too many of their teachers to present their subject as a series of factual increments: Latin American history after African history after East Asian history and so on through "one damn thing after another." Our dilemma, in other words, was perhaps inseparable from world history courses: how to provide sufficient depth of treatment of especially important events to avoid mere superficiality while at the same time to afford sufficient breadth of subject matter to challenge our students' inevitably parochial world view.

If our syllabus has escaped this dilemma, it is because we designed it after agreeing upon some basic ground rules.

The first of our ground rules was that we wanted our course to be genuinely global both in content and in interpretive point of view, rather than a course in twentieth-century western civilization with some exotic appendages tacked on. To realize this objective, we quickly concluded, would require real team-teaching. Findley and I could not simply split the world down the middle, western and non-western, and each go his separate way. Thus, we developed the syllabus in concert, tying it together with a set of themes that transcend the East/West or North/South divisions familiar to twentieth-century historical analyses. We attended all of each other's lectures, which had been prepared in accordance with the thematic framework for the course we had devised together. Indeed, except when on occasion we divided the class to provide smaller discussion groups, both of us were present at all the classes and shared equally in the preparation of examinations and in the grading of papers, whether on "western" or "non-western" subjects, as well as all the other activities of the course.

Such a degree of cooperation was possible because the departmental and higher administration at Ohio State gave us both full teaching credit for our roles in this single course. Some of our colleagues may have felt that we were each being unfairly relieved of responsibility for half a set of lectures, though in fact each of us, in the first few offerings of the course, probably devoted more time and effort to it than either would have to a course for which he was solely responsible. Yet, I would argue as forcefully as I can that this kind of team-teaching, pairing a western and non-western specialist, is essential to the intellectual integrity and thus to the success of a genuine world history course.

Interpretively, this pairing helped Findley and me to avoid portraying the twentieth-century world from either an exclusively western or an exclusively "Third World" perspective. Least of all, since neither of us was an Americanist, were our lectures likely to reenforce the naturally Americanocentric world views of our students. Rather, I would argue that the necessity for reconciling the sometimes quite contrasting outlooks which our differing training had given us produced from our team a rather dispassionate, "global" interpretive stance for the course as a whole. My training as a French historian and Findley's as the historian of a nation that had thrown off European dependency led us to see such an important contemporary topic as the U.S. involvement in Vietnam, for example, not merely as a tragedy of American politics or a disaster for Southeast Asian peasants, but an another chapter in the long story of the collapse of the European-dominated world system of 1914.

Our second ground rule in designing our syllabus was that the course could not attempt to "cover" all of the major areas of the twentieth-century world. Our syllabus, for example, lists no lectures about Latin America. While this may well seem an inexcusable omission, one might review the list of lectures and try to replace some existing topic with a Latin American one or two. Even if such a substitution were made, it would yield at best a lecture or two on a whole continent, at a level of generality that would make the whole exercise meaningless. "Coverage," we decided, was an historian's mirage, becoming ever more unattainable as the twentieth century lengthens and the nations of the globe proliferate.

We decided that the way to resolve this dilemma of breadth vs. depth was to give the course a thematic structure under which the characteristic problems of twentieth-century Latin America, like those of other regions, could be subsumed. Thus, in our very first lecture, we set forth five themes of international, societal, political, economic, and cultural history that seemed to us to express the most salient characteristics of each of these subdivisions of twentieth-century global history.[4] Throughout the remaining ten weeks of the course recurrent references to these themes help students link particular events they are studying to useful generalizations about their world.

The first and most important of these themes is that the world of the twentieth century forms an interdependent system whose nature has dramatically changed from the western-dominated pattern of 1914, through two European "civil wars" and a brief interlude of U.S. hegemony, to the situation of today, which we characterize as "interdependence amid scarcity." One consequence, it seems to us, of the tightening of the bonds of global integration in the twentieth century is heightened confrontation between what we call "culturally conservative" societies, taking their direction from a prescriptive past, and "change-oriented" societies that assume innovation to be the norm of the human experience. (We do *not*, it should be noted, imply that the "modernization" of non-western societies to conform to western models is the desirable or even the inevitable outcome of this global clash.)

This confrontation between "traditional" and "modern" that forms our central interpretive theme of twentieth-century global societal history has obvious implications for our third central theme, the history of political institutions. Culturally conservative societies have usually found the sanction for the exercise of political authority in the divine: the Chinese emperor, for example, was the "son of heaven," just as the sovereigns of earlier European centuries claimed to rule by the grace of God. In the twentieth century, however, the sanction for political authority almost everywhere has become the mobilized popular will, whether actually expressed through the exercise of universal suffrage or claimed to be embodied in some charismatic leader. Politically, then, our theme for the twentieth century is the process of mass political mobilization.

In the economic sphere, it seems to us that the central theme of the twentieth century has been the headlong development of technology, the supreme achievement of the change-oriented society. There are few parts of the world today that do not aspire to the standard of living associated with technological progress. More and more of the earth's peoples have learned to see the natural world not as an environment with which humankind must harmonize its existence, but as something to be mastered, exploited, transformed for human benefit, like the Amazonian rain forest. The triumph of this idea and its sometimes troubling consequences form our fourth theme of the twentieth century. The idea has not gone unquestioned, however, even in the western world which first articulated it — one symptom of the deep unease that seems to us characteristic of the mind and spirit of the twentieth century.

Our fifth theme, of cultural history, we describe as the "search for values for survival." Though we are careful to articulate no prescriptions, we do invite students to search for clues to where such values might be found. Directly, or by implication, we ask them to ponder whether the values expressed in contemporary international relations correspond to the realities of a world of "interdependence amid scarcity." Or to think: How can events in the headlines be explained as the self-defense by culturally conservative societies of values threatened by the onrush of change? What responsibility does the individual bear in a society mobilized ostensibly to reflect the will of the majority? Has humankind's exploitation of the natural world done it such damage that we should begin to question the value of "progress"? And, in general, have the value-systems that have determined the course of this century's history become inadequate to assure human survival into the next one?

These, then, are the five themes of our course: the evolution of the world system, the clash of traditional and modern, the process of mass mobilization, the ambiguous triumph of technology, and the search for viable values. Each of the ten weekly units into which the syllabus is divided is intended not only to focus in depth on a particular historical episode or pattern, but also to illustrate the unfolding of these themes. For example, the first unit compares the life of a modern metropolis at the beginning of the century with that of an impoverished colonial village on the periphery of the world system. The contrasting vignettes we present of Berlin and of the Egyptian village of Dinshawai, the site of a dramatic clash between colonizers and colonized, illustrate both the European-dominated world system of 1914 and the survival of culturally conservative attitudes together with the extent of political mobilization and technological development, and the breadth of cultural horizons in these two environments.

The second unit examines how the first global war of 1914–18 weakened the European-dominated world system. The third continues this theme, emphasizing the Russian Revolution as a challenge to the existing world order. In considering the Great Depression, in the fourth weekly unit, we emphasize the global impact of the crisis and show how various societies, ranging from liberal capitalist Western Europe and the United States to National Socialist Germany, mobilized their societies to rescue their economies. (Faithful to the world-historical dimension of the course, students are shown Franklin D. Roosevelt's New Deal not as another chapter in the familiar story of U.S. history but "in global perspective," as another *example* of the emergence worldwide of the "guarantor state.") By focusing on the spread of fascism, our fifth unit links the global economic crisis to the outbreak of the Second World War and the final collapse of the European-dominated world system.

The second half of the course begins with a sixth unit using India and the Middle East as case studies of the collapse of European dominion. Here, too, important narrative — on the emergence of the world's largest democracy and the origins of the contemporary Middle Eastern crisis — can be combined with thematic analysis: for example, how Gandhi achieved mass mobilization by skillfully amalgamating ideas drawn from both culturally conservative and change-oriented societies. After a seventh unit examines the implications of the Cold War and the "era of détente" for the evolving world system, the eighth and ninth units, by considering such selected examples as the Middle East and sub-Saharan Africa, highlight the rising self-assertiveness of the "Third World." In these units students are also introduced to the global obstacles to redefining the world system along the more "equitable" lines the Third World demands: overpopulation, food and non-renewable resource depletion.

Our two concluding vignettes, comparing and contrasting explosive urbanization in a western (Los Angeles) and non-western (Cairo) context are intended to sum up the main currents of the twentieth century. The western metropolis by 1987 is no longer in Europe but on the rim of the Pacific basin. One of Los Angeles' principal products, the video program, constitutes a renewed challenge to culturally conservative societies and a powerful tool of mass mobilization, as well as a technological triumph hardly imaginable at the beginning of the century. Whether its worldwide omnipresence is a matter for human self-congratulation or despair is a value judgment on which thoughtful citizens of the twentieth century might well disagree.

For all its characteristic problems of a Third World supermetropolis, its vast immigrant shantytowns and pathetically deficient infrastructure, Cairo is shown to be less different from Los Angeles in 1987 than Berlin was from Dinshawai in 1914. Our implicit comparisons of the two supermetropolises with the representative environments of 1914 is intended to permit the most thoughtful students to measure how the world system has changed, how culturally conservative societies have shrunk or altered, how masses have been mobilized, how western technology has been diffused, and how the world's peoples have reacted to all these changes in the course of the twentieth century.

It would be over-optimistic, of course, to assert that all students completing our course are able to relate the events about which they have studied to this kind of thematic overview. No doubt some, like some of the readers of this article, might reject our five themes as an overly schematic way of simplifying complex historical realities. The themes' chief justification is that they were conceived to make contemporary history intelligible, and thus meaningful, to college students. Above all, as we planned History 209, we wanted to break down the wall that in many students' minds separates the classroom "world," about which they take notes in lectures and write essays in examinations, from the real world in which they actually live.

I must conclude this account by saying that developing this course has been my most stimulating intellectual experience in the past decade. Like Professor McNeill, I had long been increasingly alarmed by the disparity between professional historians' estimation of what they did and the view of their significance held by the American public, especially the young. For that reason, it was a profoundly satisfying experience to develop a course that really was, as McNeill put it, "of general importance to teach all students, something all educated persons should know." We were fortunate, moreover, that the nature of our assignment precluded our attempting anything too ambitious. On occasion, history departments, rejecting the ethnocentrism of "western civilization" introductory courses, have attempted to make the whole sweep of world history the subject of their survey. Such courses must inevitably overburden students, requiring them to compare world civilizations when they hardly know the fundamentals of their own and are only beginning to acquire a sense that chronology and geography make epochs and regions distinctive. Heretical as the proposition will sound to some, I would argue that there is much to be said for an introductory course like History 209/400 that teaches very recent history, broadly, interpretively, and with maximum pedagogical flexibility.

This is not to say that using occasional alternative teaching strategies fully confronts the gravest threat to the future of humanistic disciplines like history: the submersion of the literate culture of the schools by the popular culture of the mass media. At least, however, the use of such strategies permits a bolder assertion of the claims of the humanities on the attention of the young in an environment where those claims receive little other reenforcement.

Given these potential advantages, it is surprising that more history departments do not offer a contemporary global history course. It is true that neither their training nor their professional reward structure encourages historians, particularly younger ones, to eschew monographic narrowness in favor of the breadth of synthetic imagination such a course often requires. And team teaching — the obvious remedy — may not be congenial to all historians, solitary enquirers by nature, even if administrators are willing to fund it.

Yet I am not sure that these are reasons rather than excuses. My own research interests in the history of France since Napoleon have been immensely enhanced by the reading I have had to do to teach half of the contemporary world, not to speak of what I have learned from my fellow teacher. Planning and teaching History 209/400 has been exhausting at times but also immensely exhilarating.

Beyond the dimension of personal satisfaction, moreover, there is the matter of the future of our discipline. If historians will not undertake the task of making the contemporary globe intelligible, who will? And what is it of social utility that historians will be doing instead?

Notes

1. William McNeill, "History for Citizens," *AHA Newsletter* 14 (March 1976): 4–6.

2. Robert F. Byrnes, "Organizing a New Course on the World in the Twentieth Century: The Agony and the Ecstasy," *Teaching History: A Journal of Methods* 5 (Spring 1980): 51–58; Robert Roeder, "The Twentieth Century World: An Experience in Course Development," *AHA Perspectives* 17 (November 1979): 6–7. See also Joe Gowaskie, "The Teaching of World History: A Status Report," *The History Teacher* 18 (May 1985): 365–75.

3. Fred M. Hechinger, "Council to Fight U.S. Students' Parochial View," *New York Times*, 13 March 1979.

4. These themes are also central to our textbook: Carter V. Findley and John Rothney, *Twentieth Century World* (Boston, 1986), 3–27.

Michael F. Doyle

"Hisperanto"

Western Civilization in the Global Curriculum

"What has Athens to do with Jerusalem?" asked the Christian apologist Tertullian in the second century, thereby implying that the Greek heritage had become irrelevant in the new dispensation. What possible utility could a knowledge of antiquity have to anyone in the new age? Something ominously akin to that seems to be at work in the effort to dilute, if not replace, the study of Western civilization in undergraduate education. One author has recently recounted the "Rise and Fall of the Western Civilization" course.[1] Others have referred, not exactly with the nostalgia of John Donne regarding those "bare ruined choirs," to the "last Eurocentric generation."[2] To support the continuation of Western Civ runs the risk of appearing reactionary or, worse yet, ethnocentric in this global age of inclusion.

When Clinton Rossiter wrote his *Conservatism in America*, he subtitled his text *The Thankless Persuasion*.[3] He did so because the liberal consensus seemed to be pretty much in place and accepted as a fait accompli. A similar sentiment surrounds "multiculturalism" and with it, world history. To challenge its place in the changing curriculum seems equally thankless. Not long ago, Donald Kagan, then dean of the college at Yale, told the incoming first-year students there that the study of Western civilization would be an integral part of their education. His penalty for speaking his mind was considerably less severe than that meted out to John Hus in 1415, but it nonetheless chills. Some students "hooted" him down and denounced him as a racist. In reporting the incident, the *Yale Daily News* identified Kagan as a "white male professor" who had apparently sent "what could be perceived as a dangerous message to this community."[4]

To speak of curricular issues is to step into a terrain booby-trapped with intellectual landmines. What motivates my presentation is simply this: What is best for our students? In my particular institution, a community college in New

Michael F. Doyle, "'Hisperanto': Western Civilization in the Global Curriculum," *Perspectives* (American Historical Association) 36 (May 1998): 1, 24–28.

Jersey, students arrive with only a minimum exposure to the history of Western civilization, since it is not a high school requirement. Is it best for these students to gloss the history of the world in preference to learning about the very culture to which they belong?

Several reasons are adduced for replacing Western Civ, and most of them warrant serious consideration. Students sometimes do feel unconnected to the European past; the United States is increasingly non-European ethnically; and the course itself has, at least in the past, been used to celebrate the superiority of the West and to neglect all "others." Admittedly, textbooks as well as teachers not so long ago dealt with non-European or non-American peoples only as they related to the Europeans themselves, and then normally in a cavalier and condescending fashion.

Recently, authors of textbooks, informed by research in social and cultural history, have attempted to correct such deficiencies and have responded to the valid charges that the survey of Western Civ has traditionally neglected an awful lot of people and ideas. Presently, most Western Civ textbooks are no longer guilty of such egregious errors, in part because writing a text has indeed become a "hazardous" undertaking.[5] Many in fact have used the course to swing the pendulum in a corrective fashion sometimes to the other extreme. Most, however, treat the West in its totality, revealing its many warts and scars. The days have long passed when Western Civ had as its aim "to trace the roots of American liberty and democracy back along a particular track, the railhead usually being Hammurabi, . . . which exposes the fundamental ideological nature of the course."[6] Once upon a time, that characterization would have been quite accurate, but that no longer reflects the reality of Western Civ texts or its teachers. This has been accomplished by the thoughtful and persistent insistence of some that women, minorities, and "people without history" be incorporated into the coverage. One must strenuously challenge, for example, Peter Stearns's contention that contemporary texts celebrate Athens with only "passing reference" to its slavery.[7] The more popular texts in American undergraduate education expend a great deal of energy criticizing the "democracy" of Athens as well as the "new imperialism" of late nineteenth-century Europe. A perusal of some of the more popular college texts can easily document that claim. For instance, one respected text reminds readers that slavery was in fact "commonplace" in ancient Greece, and compares it to Mesopotamian slavery. The index makes further reference in nine separate lines to the institution of slavery in Western civilization.[8]

In his textbook, Mark Kishlansky informs the student that in classical Athens, "over one-quarter of the total population were slaves" and judges it "fundamental" to Athenian culture. He includes ten additional references to that institution in his index.[9]

Lynn Hunt, in her recent contribution to the field, counts twelve general entries under slavery in the index. More to the point, she discusses at length the significance of slavery in ancient Greece, where slaves worked, tutored, and might be killed "with impunity" by their owners. She concludes that the slaves of ancient Greece certainly contributed to the economy of Greek society but received little benefit or recompense for their efforts.[10]

Likewise, the discussion of women in all of the above texts is made central and not peripheral to Western civilization. The charge of Stearns simply has no merit any longer, and an examination of the texts refutes his contention.

Thanks to the prompting of world history representatives, many textbooks now also include (and not merely as a "caboose") the important contributions made by non-Western civilizations to the development of Western civilization from its very foundations in Mesopotamia and the Mediterranean basin. In that sense, the old Western Civ course has indeed "fallen."

I should note at the outset that the proponents of world history with whom I have had the good fortune to communicate have had a profound impact on my own thinking. In fact, much of my initial hostility to world history has been dissipated; I have revised, and continue to do so, my own thinking on the subject. Judging by the feedback on the Internet to the "thread" of Western Civ or world history discussion, the issue is by no means a settled matter among my colleagues on campuses throughout the United States. I am grateful especially to Ross Dunn and Sara Tucker for their informed and judicious responses to my queries. In addition, textbook authors such as Lynn Hunt, Mark Kishlansky, and John McKay have also provided me with some useful insights into the question. After my introduction to the Internet, I discovered that this very question had been discussed in some detail in 1994. And it continues to generate much debate, which testifies to a certain vigor in our profession.

Two incidents prompted my initial interest in this question (as well as my hostility). First, our dean asked me if I thought we ought to replace our tired old Western Civ course with a more "current" offering in world history. At the time, I paid little attention (she is not a historian, I thought), merely reporting the conversation to my colleagues who, like myself, expressed concern that such a strategy would further dilute what we already believed too thin. Later, the dean of instruction likewise indicated his belief that our department ought to be more inclusive and scuttle our Western Civ course. Again, he is not a historian. I did recall reading some articles in *Perspectives* that posited the end of the European focus in history, but again I paid little attention.[11]

Some time later, I received a notice about an upcoming meeting of the mid-Atlantic branch of the World History Association. I scanned the topics and areas to be discussed and saw nothing that hinted at dissent from the idea that world history had replaced Western Civ. I received encouragement to submit a proposal that would consider the validity and advisability of so doing. Amid some protests that my doubts had already been settled and hardly warranted attention, my proposal was accepted. I proceeded to ask my former graduate school professors if indeed world history had replaced Western Civ. They were taken aback by the suggestion and offered further encouragement along with my colleagues at Ocean County College to pursue this issue.

Discovering that our students are woefully ignorant of all history, I looked at what kinds of history high school students in New Jersey studied. Most take two years of American history and one year of world history. Not surprisingly, their lack of knowledge of European history borders on the scandalous. Professor Evelyn Edson of Piedmont Virginia Community College relates a tale not atypical of today's student when she recounts a student's question, "Wouldn't Socrates have died before he was born, if he lived from 469 to 399?"[12]

Next, I investigated what colleges, especially two-year schools, are offering as history courses. Among the nineteen community colleges in New Jersey, eleven offer Western Civ; three offer both surveys; and four offer only world history. Among New Jersey four-year institutions, Trenton State and Rutgers offer world history while Stockton, St. Peter's, Seton Hall, and Georgian Court stick with Western Civ. Obviously, there is no unanimity concerning which survey best suits the needs of students. Despite the fact that Western Civ remains the overwhelming preference among most colleges and universities (and also despite my misgivings), I do imagine that world history may eventually replace Western Civ as the choice of many if not most colleges and universities in the United States (see Table 1).[13] The appeal of "global" seems too popular in the present environment to avoid this. Certainly the ever-growing movement toward a "global marketplace" strongly encourages a global preparation for the work force. However, I hope that the history of Western civilization will continue to receive the treatment that it merits. I will outline in more detail how best to accomplish and ensure that.

My objections to world history fall into two distinct categories. World history advocates have addressed them, but not satisfactorily. The issues involve logistical and philosophical problems that seem presently to be somewhat insoluble though I remain hopeful that a solution will evolve. I should reiterate that the single most important question that I keep asking myself as a professional educator is, what is best for our students? I think that transcends any philosophical or historiographical concerns we might have.

First, the logistical problem of attempting to "cover it all." Naturally, no one, even in the more limited U.S. survey, manages to do so and we probably should stop trying. To try to do so can only lead to "virtual" history. If we attempted to teach Spanish and Russian and Korean in the same language class we would only confuse the student. Some would construct an entirely artificial language like Esperanto to accomplish that "global" feel. The danger of so much coverage is that we might well hurry our students through the world like Carmen Sandiego and leave them stranded.

A survey of some of the world history texts documents this point. Students assigned *Heritage of World Civilizations* leave Europe at the end of the Roman Empire and proceed to India, Iran, Africa, China, Japan, then Iran and India again before taking up the narrative with the Franks almost 200 pages later.[14] The McKay text sticks closer to the narrative.[15] It does so by assigning 22 pages to cover over eleven hundred years of African history. The next 30 pages manage to cover India, China, and Japan during a period of over a thousand years! Those pages simply will not do justice to the subjects. In fact, they do the subject a disservice. The interesting thing about the McKay text is that the volume

Table 1. Faculty Teaching World History and Western Civ by Type of College

	U.S.2-yr	U.S.4-yr	Canada	Total
1. Teaching "Introduction to World History"				
1991	365	1,912	104	2,381
1993	442	2,115	104	2,661
1995	516	2,229	109	2,854
2. Teaching "Western Civ"				
1991	1,295	3,139	95	4,529
1993	1,316	3,174	102	4,592
1995	1,324	3,055	107	4,486

Source: CMG Information Services, "Mailing List Catalog," via H-Net.

on Western history lists the same authors as the one on world societies. Surprisingly, both texts are similar in length. In fact, the world history survey is 10 percent shorter![16] To accomplish this, some items included in the Western Civ text had to be excised, including health and medical issues in Frankish times, medieval town life, the Dominicans, and other topics.

One of the strategies employed is reduction in the coverage of Western history. One of the leading proponents of the world history movement and a recent convert to the cause, Peter Stearns, recommends a strategy of trimming, sometimes "radical" or "severe pruning."[17] Even the Renaissance lay victim to this Occam's razor, though I suspect he made that cut in jest.[18] Obviously, we all make decisions as to what to include and exclude in our surveys, which are, after all, just that. Only the publishing industry seems comfortable with this arrangement. They always miraculously manage to piece together a world history or Western Civ or American history course textbook that is fifteen chapters long; one for each week in the semester.

Some world history strategists (and realistic Western Civ teachers as well) acknowledge that covering it all is neither possible nor desirable. Therefore, the former elect to focus on "processes" or the "big events." Ross Dunn defines the latter as events big enough to have an impact on different cultures in a "shared experience."[19] Does that suggest that until an event becomes significant to a majority it lacks historical credibility? Originally, the scientific revolution had little impact beyond the couple of hundred individuals who even understood it. Yet, as one Western Civ text reminds us, this "quiet revolution" had "far-reaching implications."[20] A generation ago Herbert Butterfield argued that this revolution reduced historical movements like the Renaissance and the Reformation to the ranks of "mere episodes."[21] What of those male bastions of the medieval period — universities? Do they fail to warrant mention because of their obvious "minority" status that precluded them from being a "shared experience" for most?

Stearns argues that an "urgent need" to understand Africa and Asia exists.[22] There is no debate there, but would not a full course (taught by individuals with some expertise) better serve that need? In this, I would support Diane Ravitch who suggests a yearlong study of Western Civ and another year of non-Western civilizations.[23]

Another logistical problem is the issue of teacher preparedness. It seems that our students ought to be assured that their professor has some schooling in the areas being taught. Very few world historians, I suspect, have linguistic training in non-Western languages, which handicaps them significantly. I do not pretend to be informed and expert in all (not even most!) areas of European history, but my total lack of training in non-Western areas troubles me immensely. To "retool" seems to do a grave injustice to a field deserving of lengthy preparation. Many correspondents have indicated their willingness to undertake the challenge of so doing; but can one really keep current with developments in "world" history? (Again, I make no pretense of so doing even in my own area.) Perhaps this can be addressed by the graduate programs newly in place in institutions like the University of Hawaii, Rutgers University, and others. Specialization within the field of history (indeed within any area) does offer some virtues that have been part of the schooling of historians within the United States, and the training in world history seems to contravene that professional tradition.

Less troublesome than the simple logistics of offering world history in lieu of Western Civ and providing skilled professionals to teach it is the philosophical issue. Ross Dunn recounted a revealing incident that occurred innocuously enough while walking down the street in his own culturally and ethnically diverse neighborhood. He noticed a sea of faces, those of relative "newcomers" to America. On his way back home, he wondered if his own children would have the opportunity to learn about these immigrants and their personal reasons for leaving their natal homes and coming to California.[24] Perhaps he and I live in similar environments. Although quite sympathetic to Dunn's feelings about the wonderful opportunity to discover and understand other peoples, my own response to the incident differs (and I hope it will not be interpreted as mere ethnocentrism). I wondered if these latest groups of American immigrants would elect to learn about the culture and civilization they had chosen to live in. I also pondered what changes they might bring or attempt to effect in their new environment. I was also reminded that, for better or worse, the globe is becoming increasingly Western. How ironic to abandon the study of that civilization at what Francis Fukuyama calls, with some exaggeration, "the end of history." Still, the chief distinguishing characteristic of modernity is its "Westernness." It would seem that we ought to require our students to be conversant with the features of that civilization because of its very relevance rather than replacing it due to its perceived irrelevance!

Western Civ does, in fact, require our students to confront other cultures. A Western Civ text (and course) should present the features of that other civilization or culture, not just as they appeared to Western eyes, but on their own terms. Certainly Western Civ students should read parts of the Qur'an and understand the attitudes that produced Fanon's *The Wretched of the Earth*. Indeed, as Stearns has rightly argued, we have "to treat non-Westerners as players in their own right and not simply as recipients of Western impulses and guidance."[25] I think no Western Civ instructor could possibly dissent from such a praiseworthy goal.

Because of what Theodore Von Laue identified as the world revolution of Westernization, a Western Civ course (properly sculptured) offers the student the best background to understanding the forces presently dominating much of the world and making informed comparisons.[26] Harvard historian David Gordon argued similarly that a Western Civ course would expose the student to many "unsavory ideas" and force the student to confront important and continuing issues with a solid foundation.[27] Naturally there are only so many classes that we can require our undergraduate students to take. As historians, we would prefer to see the number of history courses increased. Given the limitations of the school year, we have to make decisions. World historians declare that their choice is the better because it connects people of the increasingly diverse population with the history they study. Others argue that our ignorance of non-Western societies will hamper us economically in the future in an increasingly complex global economy. Still others opine that without seeing the whole picture of human history we stay focused on the particular only, and consequently miss the larger landscape. All of these are excellent reasons for enlarging our vision in the survey course so that we survey not just the familiar but the "foreign" as well.

The question becomes which vehicle will best allow our students to accomplish these estimable goals. Western Civ proponents want to ensure that we study our own civilization and understand exactly how it came to be what it is. If, as some world history advocates suggest, we accord all civilizations equal time then, as William McNeill reminds us, none can be considered essential.[28]

In the existing Western Civ surveys, the students already have their hands full. To edit more from it and to add other civilizations in its place would cause us to lose the narrative and, consequently, the coherence of history. As Theodore Rabb of Princeton concluded, our first responsibility has to be teaching the fundamentals of Western Civ. Only then can the student branch out.[29] Peter Stearns's idea was to select certain themes or processes and limit them to three or four to enable the student to find patterns that allow generalizations to link all civilizations; this certainly makes the world history course "doable," but it fragments the past and risks losing the student in the process.[30]

Fritz Stern edited an instructive book a generation ago entitled *The Varieties of History* in which he offered several examples of how historians have defined their roles and philosophies of history. He was not troubled by the changing face of history. "Nothing is more characteristic of the history of the last two hundred years than the demand from within the profession that history must once again become broader, more inclusive, more concerned with the deeper aspects of human experience."[31] At the close of the century, a similar demand is being heard. What historians have to decide is how best to serve the needs of the student and the integrity of history.

In order to keep the question alive, I would like to offer some alternatives to the either/or proposition of dropping Western Civ altogether or retaining it and dropping world history. Neither, it seems, will simply disappear. Lynne Cheney recommended that students take six credits of Western Civ and six more of non-Western history, along with three credits in American history.[32] As desirable as this scheme is, it is equally unrealistic. Students will simply not accept the burden of so many history requirements.

In light of that, one recommendation to replace the "Western Civ or world history" alternative is the following. Western Civ should be reconfigured into two distinct courses. The first would focus on the ancient world to the Renaissance or Reformation, which pretty much replicates the existing "Civ One" course. The second half of the course would focus on the interaction between the West and the world. It is during this course that time could be spent developing a world perspective that would not interrupt the narrative but would in fact complete it. In his classic, *The Rise and Fall of the Great Powers*, Paul Kennedy made no apology that the book had a "heavily Eurocentric" thrust. In fact, he judged it "only natural."[33] As Jacques Ellul observed, the entire world has become "heir to the West."[34]

William McNeill, whose important work *Rise of the West* basically established the world history movement, also focused on Europe's central role in the making of the modern world.[35] Yet even he did not attempt to include "everyone" in his survey. He defended the continuation of separate national histories to supply that natural need that everyone has for a sense of history.[36]

The above solution to the present "troubles" in the discipline is actually not my first choice. I would prefer to continue two courses in Western Civ and add a required course for all students on the history of the twentieth-century world along with an additional course in a non-Western field. The recent work of Eric Hobsbawm might serve as an organizational model for such a useful and "doable" course. Like most in the discipline, however, it is regrettably a text that could be read by only a minority of our students.[37] (I haven't even mentioned the role of reading level in the choice of texts as well as courses for our students, but it certainly is an issue of increasingly important consideration.)

The needs of our students are best met by teaching them first and foremost about their own civilization and all the contributions made by others to it; this instruction needs to be an informed one. We are too much in the habit, I suspect, of applying the cant of bumper stickers to our profession: think globally, act locally. If the world history survey attempts to cover the world in the same space in which we previously covered Western Civ, the attempt must surely fail. The narrative that most students (and readers) need is sacrificed and the student is offered a smorgasbord or sampler which, like a wallpaper book, would stupefy and confuse.

My final option would be: allow the issue to be sealed in the marketplace. Colleges ought to work to offer both world history and Western Civ surveys so that educators provide the fullest spectrum of information to their students and allow each individual to determine the preferred route. My only entreaty is to focus the world option on a thorough treatment of the West as well as for Western Civ to continue to incorporate a more inclusive approach to all cultures with which it came into contact. The chief beneficiary of this would be the student, who lives in Western civilization, attends an institution founded in the West, and is presumably a part of that civilization.

Notes

1. Gilbert Allardyce, "The Rise and Fall of the Western Civilization Course," *American Historical Review* 87 (1982): 695–743. More recently see Thomas Davis, "Starting from Scratch: Shifting from Western Civ to World History," *Perspectives* (December 1996): 1.

2. John R. Gillis, quoting Caroline Walker Bynum in "The Future of European History," *Perspectives* (April 1996): 1.

3. Clinton Rossiter, *Conservatism in America: The Thankless Persuasion* (New York: Vintage Books, 1962).

4. Quoted in Richard Bernstein, *Dictatorship of Virtue: Multiculturalism and the Battle for America's Future* (New York: Alfred A. Knopf, 1994), 50.

5. Joyce Appleby et al., *Telling the Truth about History* (New York: Norton, 1994), 294.

6. Ross Dunn, e-mail to the author, 7 August, 1996.

7. Peter Stearns, *Meaning over Memory: Recasting the Teaching of Culture and History* (Chapel Hill: University of North Carolina Press, 1993), 82.

8. John McKay et al., *A History of Western Society*, 5th ed., vol. 1 (Boston: Houghton Mifflin, 1995), 87–89.

9. Mark Kishlansky et al., *Civilization in the West*, 2nd ed., vol. 1 (New York: HarperCollins, 1995), 72–75.

10. Lynn Hunt et al., *The Challenge of the West*, vol. 1 (Lexington: D. C. Heath & Co., 1995), 57–58. See also Donald Kagan et al., *The Western Heritage*, 5th ed. (Englewood Cliffs, N.J.: Prentice Hall, 1995), 46, 88–90.

11. Gillis, 1.

12. Evelyn Edson, "The Historian at the Community College," *Perspectives* (October 1996): 17.

13. In addition, Mark Kishlansky of Harvard indicated that his Western Civ text outsold his world text by roughly three to one. Personal correspondence.

14. Albert Craig et al., *The Heritage of World Civilizations* (New York: Macmillan, 1994).

15. John McKay et al., *The History of World Societies*, vol. 1 (Boston: Houghton Mifflin, 1996).

16. As one of the authors happily reports in McKay, *World Societies*, preface, xix.

17. Stearns, 181–85.

18. Stearns, 188.

19. Ross Dunn, "Central Themes for World History," in *Historical Literacy: The Case for History in American Education*, ed. Paul Gagnon et al. (New York: Macmillan, 1989), 220.

20. Hunt, 571.

21. Herbert Butterfield, *The Origins of Modern Science, 1300–1800*, rev. ed. (New York: The Free Press, 1965), 7.

22. Stearns, 8.

23. Quoted in Dunn, "Central Themes," 219.

24. Dunn, "Central Themes," 216–17.

25. Stearns, 46.

26. Subtitled *The Twentieth Century in Global Perspective* (New York: Oxford University Press, 1987).

27. "Inside the Stanford Mind," *Perspectives* (April 1992): 8.

28. William McNeill, "Pursuit of Power: Criteria of Global Relevance," in Gagnon, 107.

29. Theodore K. Rabb, "Old and New Patterns for the History of Western Civilization," in Gagnon, 214.

30. Stearns, 105.

31. Fritz Stern, ed. *The Varieties of History: From Voltaire to the Present* (Cleveland: World Publishing Co., 1956), 12.

32. Cited in Stearns, 80.

33. Paul Kennedy, *The Rise and Fall of the Great Powers: Economic Chance and Military Conflict from 1500 to 2000* (New York: Random House, 1987), xxi.

34. Jacques Ellul, *The Betrayal of the West* (New York: Seabury Press, 1978), 21.

35. William McNeill, *The Rise of the West: A History of the Human Community* (Chicago: University of Chicago Press, 1963).

36. McNeill, "What Do We Teach?" in Gagnon, 136.

37. Eric Hobsbawm, *The Age of Extremes: A History of the World, 1914–1991* (New York: Vintage Books, 1956).

EDMUND BURKE III
ROSS E. DUNN

Michael Doyle's Views on Western Civ

A Comment and Counterproposal

Michael Doyle (*Perspectives*, May 1998, pp. 1, 24–28) has thought carefully about world history as a teaching field and has exchanged ideas with colleagues who advocate it. He concludes, however, that Western Civ should not relinquish its place as the dominant model for the introductory college course. He exposes what is surely the greatest weakness of the world history survey these days: the tendency for some instructors to let the chapters of comprehensive textbooks, rather than a coherent conceptual design, guide the organization of their course and to ask students to absorb helter-skelter a great deal of information about all major world re-

Edmund Burke III and Ross E. Dunn, "Western Civ in the Global Curriculum: A Response," *Perspectives* (American Historical Association) 36 (Oct. 1998): 31–33.

gions and civilizations. Even global texts that are based on clear and imaginative principles of selection tend to include a great deal of traditionally standard information in order to pass the "wet thumb" test of prospective adopters flipping the pages looking for their favorite teaching topics.

Doyle prefers Western Civ to world history, not only because global texts try to cover too much ground but also because they make onerous demands on instructors to "retool." They also divert students from in-depth study of "their own civilization." Doyle proposes instead a modified Western Civ that would take greater account of "all the contributions made by others" to the Western tradition and that would stress, for the modern centuries, "interaction between the West and the world." He invites Western Civ teachers to rethink their courses in light of the challenge from world history. We support that recommendation. We also believe, however, that he rests his objections to world history on questionable premises and on some misunderstanding of what the movement for world history in collegiate education aims to achieve.

The Western Civ tradition to which Doyle refers has itself evolved considerably since its nineteenth-century genesis. With the advent of the Cold War, as Gilbert Allardyce has argued, the Western Civ narrative became the "history of freedom," and as such an important ideological component in the struggle against communism.[1] This civics lesson version of Western Civ was always uneasily yoked together with other, more complex understandings of the European past. Though Doyle's nostalgia for a time of greater moral and political certainty resonates for many Americans, it is unclear how his call for renewed vigor is an adequate response to the manifest differences between U.S. society of the 1950s and the 1990s.

In part this is because Doyle argues for Western Civ from assumptions that he leaves unexamined. He appears to assume that college world history may be largely defined as the study of the main narratives and distinctive characteristics of a number of different named "cultures," and that these categories may be thought of as stable, totalizable entities. From this premise, the argument follows logically enough that students should investigate "their own civilization," the one they "belong to," in greater detail than they do other civilizations.

Champions of Western Civ in both colleges and high schools, as well as educators on the political right, have often contended that civilizations, conceived as the most historically significant "cultures," may reasonably be regarded as possessing good qualities and bad qualities. They have also argued that all cultures, in one way or another, have transgressed their core values but that Western civilization's essential qualities, despite periodic outbreaks of militarism, racism, social oppression, and other anomalies, are on the whole particularly appealing and beneficial to humankind. Therefore, young Americans should be proud to belong to "the West" and should know more about it than the "non-West."

Such arguments for Western Civ rest on an ahistorical and curiously anthropomorphized conception of civilization, in which "the West," likened to an individual historical actor, performs this or that deed on the world stage: the West "gave science to the world," the West "ended slavery," the West "has committed its share of crimes," the West "is penetrating all other cultures," and so on. According to Doyle, the West has revealed "its many warts and scars," a rhetorical reification akin to claiming that Oklahoma has more "warts and scars" than Vermont or that Norway has "committed more crimes" than Portugal.

Doyle refers to the "narrative," the "fundamentals," and the "features" of Western civilization as if the historical profession generally agrees about what these things might be. In fact, they don't agree at all. If, as Doyle claims, the Western narrative is no longer simply the cavalcade of liberty, then what exactly is the story about? If our first responsibility is to teach the "fundamentals" of Western civilization, then we need to define those timeless facts or characteristics. Doyle seems to assume we all know the answers. In fact, many scholars would teach as an axiom of good historical methodology that seminal or essential cultural traits can never be ascribed to societies or civilizations, or for that matter to tribes, ethnic groups, or hunting bands.

Sometimes it seems to us as if the Western Civ and world history camps talk past one another. One side defines introductory history education as exploration of the differing traits of civilizations as revealed primarily in their respective canonical texts and other primary source documents. The other side defines it as the study of change in sundry spheres of life — social, economic, epidemiological, and so on. Defenders of Western Civ, who are often deeply committed humanists, tend to think of the field's subject matter in terms of the continuities, enduring characteristics, and intellectual/cultural achievements of civilizations. World history partisans, whose fields of specialization are more often than not tilted toward the social sciences and history of the non-Western world, have tended to see the appearance, florescence, and decline of civilizations in a broad comparative perspective and to regard all historical inquiry as an endeavor to investigate processes rather than fixities.

We have no objection to students pondering European canonical texts as part of their humanistic education. Quite the contrary — we support it. However, as academic subjects carrying general presuppositions about time and space, European history and Western Civ are not at all the same thing. Embedded in the very structure of Western Civ is the wholly teleological notion that an actual chain of cause and effect may be discerned that links Paleolithic East Africa to Sumerian Mesopotamia, Mesopotamia to republican Rome, Rome to the Italian Renaissance, and the Renaissance to global "Westernization." This view of history is a well-ordered ideological construct, but it is no longer convincing or sufficient as a way to explain how the world, or even Europe, has changed over the centuries and millennia. Indeed, it can be seen as an effort to construct an "imagined community" in order to endow the West with a uniquely privileged status, rather than to situate it alongside its sister civilizations. Designs for teaching world history are, of course, constructs as well — as indeed are all history syllabi. But these designs are not, on the whole, founded on an ahistorical quest for "origins." They recognize that change takes place in consequence of the interplay of numerous forces and circumstances prevailing at any particular moment of the past, and they offer students a more plausible

foundation for thinking about how and why change occurs in our own complicated times.

Doyle has made proposals for a more up-to-date Western Civ. We would like to offer a few counterproposals as grist for the mill when history departments in both two- and four-year institutions debate the relative merits of Western Civ and world history.

1. If a department offers or proposes to offer an introductory world history program that sweeps across the millennia from Paleolithic times to the present, then it should develop an explicit conceptual framework to guide selection and organization of content. This means adopting specific principles of selection and making clear thematic choices. The tables of contents of comprehensive global texts are no substitute for the instructor's or department's own conceptual plan. Consider assigning a comprehensive text as a reference tool rather than as the main reading. The textbook may then support rather than determine the selection and ordering of themes and topics. In place of long weekly textbook assignments, ask students to read and discuss some of the many excellent books and articles available on specific topics in world history.

2. Consider replacing the broad multicivilizational survey with courses that are emphatically comparative, interregional, or global but that embrace smaller chunks of time. Consult the periodization scheme in the National Standards for World History for ideas on designing courses around discrete time periods and major world-historical developments.[2] It is worth noting that the teachers and scholars who recently drafted a curriculum for Advanced Placement World History chose a one-year course limited to the period 1000 C.E. to the present rather than a survey starting with the Lower Paleolithic.

3. Consider, on the other hand, adopting the *very* large-scale model of "big history" as developed by David Christian, Fred Spier, and others. As Christian has written, doing big history means exploring the past on all different scales "up to the scale of the universe itself."[3] He argues that questions about human origins, evolution, and long-term impact on the natural environment are *historical* questions, and very important ones at that. Undertaking such explorations, however, demands appropriate contexts, in some cases astrophysical. For the syllabus of a course in "big history" taught at the University of California at Santa Cruz, consult the web site at http://wwwcatsic.ucsc.edu/~hist80a.

4. Reexamine critically not only the premises of Western Civ but also those of multiculturalism, which tend to support rather than challenge quasi-static descriptions of civilizations and which sometimes encourage students to reify Asian, African, and Latin American societies as grossly as they do "the West." World history teachers should invariably adopt what Andre Gunder Frank has called a "humanocentric" approach to world history. They should never be in the business of debating which civilizations were the most glorious and which committed the worst crimes.

5. Because it provides an effectual context for integrating knowledge acquired in several courses, world history seems especially suited as a capstone

course for history majors and other upper-division students. We propose two intellectually and pedagogically distinct kinds of advanced world history courses. One program would focus on the study of particular periods and developments to throw light on larger-scale, transcultural patterns of change in a variety of spheres. This program would give much attention to interactions among peoples, set civilizational change in wider interregional or global frames, and invariably address in some measure environmental and ecological issues. A second program would emphasize the study of key texts, literary works, aesthetic movements, and scientific innovations of particular times and places. Its central aim would be to illuminate the ways in which these texts, images, and discoveries speak to the human condition. While much of the content might represent the work of Europeans, the course would eschew any teleological agenda for revealing the "essence" of this culture or that. It would also present great writings and art never as "belonging" inherently to any group but always to all humanity.

6. Since more and more states are instituting academic standards that require schools to teach world history, postsecondary instructors need to address the challenge of providing a rigorous and coherent world history curriculum for future teachers. Unfortunately, most of the comprehensive textbooks published for the K–12 market embody no clear conceptual plan or world-historical point of view but aim merely to "cover" the requisite civilizations one by one in a way that balances the demands of multiculturalist and traditionalist interest groups. Therefore, prospective K–12 professionals should be given opportunities to think about globe-embracing history as a distinct field of study that involves particular conceptual problems and that presents creative, engaging angles of vision on the human past as well as investigations of particular regions. San Diego State University has recently created "World History for Teachers," a semester course whose subject matter is specifically correlated to the chronological scope and content of the world history program for grades six and seven taught in virtually all California public schools.

7. Abandon the Western Civ model entirely but urge students to study European history, as well as other regions, as part of their general education. European history, including attention to canonical texts, is a perfectly valid subject of inquiry. Students should understand, however, that a distinctive European urban and high cultural tradition arose sometime around 1000 C.E. It did not arise on the plains of East Africa three million years ago, not on the banks of the Tigris-Euphrates in the fourth millennium B.C.E., and not in ancient Athens, whose civilizational context was the Eastern Mediterranean and Black Sea basins, not Europe as conventionally defined.

Doyle has pointed out some of the failings of world history surveys and offered good ideas for making Western Civ better. Our aim in making this rejoinder is simply to carry forward the debate he initiated. We believe that the Western Civ structure is beyond repair but also that there is much more in world history's future than the comprehensive civilization-of-the-week survey.

Notes

    1. Gilbert Allardyce, "The Rise and Fall of the Western Civilization Course," *American Historical Review* 87 (1982): 695–725. See the same author's "Toward World History: American Historians and the Coming of the World History Course," *Journal of World History* 1 (Spring 1990): 23–76.
    2. *National Standards for History,* Basic Edition (Los Angeles: National Center for History in the Schools, UCLA, 1996).
    3. See David Christian, "The Case for Big History," *Journal of World History* 2 (Fall 1991): 223–38. Also Fred Spier, *The Structure of Big History: From the Big Bang until Today* (Ann Arbor: University of Michigan Press, 1997).

JERRY H. BENTLEY

Graduate Education and Research in World History

About two years ago, Professor Philip D. Curtin offered a set of reflections on graduate education in history. Alongside specialized research, which of course has reigned supreme in graduate education during this century, Curtin urged the cultivation of a broader perspective among emerging professional historians. As a practical means to this end, he briefly sketched the graduate program instituted during his term as chair in the Department of History at the University of Utopia. All the Utopian graduate students prepare four fields, chosen from at least two of the world's major cultural regions — the West, East Asia, Africa, Latin America, Southeast Asia, etc. Students in Utopia also devote one-quarter of their programs to the study of some theme or problem from a global point of view. Finally, they reflect on the broader significance of their dissertation projects and write essays on the global context of their research. As a result of this program, Utopian graduates not only acquire the specialized research skills expected of all professional historians, but also develop an appreciation for the relationship between the general and the specific — a sensitivity to the broader historical context that lends meaning and significance to the discoveries of specialized local research.[1]

    When Professor Curtin's article appeared in print, the Department of History at the University of Hawaii had just instituted a new Ph.D. field in world history. Now, the claims of travel agents notwithstanding, Hawaii is not Utopia. Yet the Ph.D. field in world history now offered in Hawaii closely resembles the graduate program available at Curtin's University of Utopia. By way of develop-

Jerry H. Bentley, "Graduate Education and Research in World History," *World History Bulletin* 3 (Fall/Winter 1985–86): 3–7.

ing this point, I would like first to outline the conception of world history that serves as a foundation for the new field, then to sketch for you the main features of the Ph.D. field in world history, and finally to mention some of the results that graduate education in world history might offer to the discipline of history as a whole.

The Nature of World History

In academic circles today, the terms "world history" and "global history" generally bring to mind an introductory survey course on the world's major civilizations — and rightly so. Educators have increasingly come to believe that courses in American history and Western civilization do not constitute an adequate foundation for responsible citizenship in the contemporary world. In these latter days, it seems only prudent to familiarize students with the various traditions of civilization and to encourage in them the development of a capacity to empathize with the foreign.[2] Indeed, in view of the fact that instruction in history has implications extending far beyond the academy, it strikes me that the historian's most important business is to develop for undergraduate students a broad and ecumenical vision of the past.

For the purposes of graduate education and research, however, world history means something different from what it does in an introductory course. At the post-graduate level, the purpose of world history is not to survey the major civilizations, not to lay a foundation for responsible citizenship, but rather to develop and apply analytical approaches appropriate for some of the problems that historians have recently begun to study. As a field of research, world history arose rather spontaneously, it seems to me, out of the recognition that a national orientation is an inadequate vehicle for much of the historian's business. In order to arrive at a satisfactory understanding of certain historical forces and phenomena, historians have found it necessary to cross traditionally recognized boundaries in carrying out their analyses. Let's explore these points in more detail.

Scholars of the nineteenth century who fashioned history into a professional discipline were entranced by the development and the capacities of the strong, centralized national state. When conducting historical analysis, they naturally concentrated on problems of national politics — matters of statecraft, diplomacy, constitutions, institutions, and the like. They produced numerous works of genuine power that stand the test of a century's time as monuments to scholarship, as works that served by their very examples to define the discipline of history. To cite but one example, Leopold von Ranke's *German History in the Age of the Reformation* will command the respect of professional historians probably forever. It bears mention also that the nineteenth-century scholars selected a useful focus for their work: the national state ranks as one of the most dynamic of all human institutions, and the effort to understand the world's development cannot afford to neglect such a powerful force in history.

During the present century, historians have vastly expanded the boundaries of their discipline. They have adapted new methods of analysis to the needs of

historical scholarship; they have turned their attention to topics previously neglected; and they have sought new ways to conceive and to explain human development through time. Especially since World War II, historians have increasingly become aware of some inherent limitations of national-oriented
historiography. A large number of powerful historical forces simply do not respect national boundary lines, but work their effects on a regional, continental,
or even global scale. As a result, they do not lend themselves to successful analysis within a national framework, but call naturally for a broader angle of vision.
These influences include — to name some of the most prominent — infectious
and contagious diseases, climatic changes, technological developments, population movements, economic fluctuations, long-distance commerce, religious
faiths, ideas, and ideals. During the past several decades, historians have undertaken to analyze these influences in increasingly systematic and serious fashion.
The result is world history — historical analysis undertaken not from the viewpoint of national states, but rather from that of the global community.

World history of this sort has developed under two general analytical rubrics.
In the first place, scholars have devoted their talents to the comparative analysis of
processes that work their influences in all parts of the world, or at least in several of
its major regions. Some of the themes recently explored by comparative analysts
include feudalism, imperial rule, racial segregation and discrimination, market-
oriented economic development, the effects of social and political change on religious faiths, and rebellion and revolution.[3] During the course of all this work, the
methods and purposes of comparative analysis have become increasingly sophisticated. Comparative analysts naturally concentrate their attention on experiences
that are to some degree similar, hence comparable. But they do not engage in a
naive, simple-minded search for regularity or uniformity across national and cultural boundary lines. Indeed, some scholars place special emphasis on differences
between various experiences, the better to highlight nuances and to understand
the particularities of historical developments. Others shift the focus somewhat and
undertake comparative study in order to illuminate large-scale processes that work
their effects across traditionally recognized boundaries.[4] In all cases, a sophisticated comparative analysis has the potential to place local developments in a
meaningful context, one that can lead to more accurate and sensitive interpretation of the local developments themselves.

In the second place, alongside comparative analysis, world historians have
devoted their attention to the results of encounters between peoples of different
civilizations or cultural regions. Some of the themes recently explored by analysts of cross-cultural contacts include long-distance trade, transfers of technology, efforts to spread ideas and values, the cultural effects of foreign conquest,
and exchanges of plants, animals, and microorganisms across cultural and even
biological boundary lines.[5] Like comparative analysis, the investigation of cross-
cultural contacts has become increasingly sophisticated in recent decades,
thanks largely to the efforts of cultural anthropologists and ethnohistorians. The
time has long passed when scholars depended upon the categories of Western "impact" and non-Western "response" to frame their understanding of

cross-cultural contacts. Recent studies of these contacts have underscored instead the accommodations made by all parties involved in cross-cultural encounter, since all found themselves confronted by new situations and new demands. Analysis of cross-cultural encounters has served to advance the understanding of history's dynamics, since cross-cultural contact ranks as one of the most effective agents of change in all human experience.

THE PH.D. FIELD IN WORLD HISTORY
AT THE UNIVERSITY OF HAWAII

During the past several decades, as a substantial body of serious literature emerged, scholars began to think about formal instruction in world history at an advanced level. A Ph.D. program in comparative world history came into being as early as the mid-1960s at the University of Wisconsin, and somewhat later the faculty of the University of California at Santa Cruz instituted an M.A. program along similar lines. On the recommendation of a faculty committee at the University of Hawaii, a new Ph.D. field in world history won endorsements in 1984, and it became available to graduate students in the fall term of 1985.

All students preparing the field in world history in Hawaii take two seminars. The first (HIST 609) is an introductory reading seminar that deals with the most important themes, theories, methods, and literature of world history as a field of research. During the early weeks of the term, the seminar examines the classic literature of world history, including works of Wells, Spengler, Toynbee, and McNeill. Discussion of these works serves two main purposes: it helps the seminar to account for the development in this century of a broad-gauged perspective on the past; and it introduces the seminar to themes of perennial importance that resonate even in the most recent literature on world history. During the remaining and larger part of the term, the seminar concentrates on several analytical and interpretative approaches especially prominent in contemporary research in world history. Reading and discussion focus on the five categories of literature that strike me as the most influential in recent work on global history. The first category includes studies that compare historical experience across the boundary lines of civilizations or cultural regions. The second and third categories include studies inspired by the two major interpretative schools — those of the modernization theorists and the world-systems theorists — that have so far emerged and that help to organize much of the thinking about world history. The last two categories represent the major new directions beyond modernization and world-systems analysis that world history currently takes. One of these deals with the material and biological foundations of history and takes inspiration from ecologists, demographers, and geographers. The other deals with the cultural dimension of the human experience and takes inspiration from cultural anthropologists and ethnohistorians. Members of the seminar evaluate all these approaches for the possibilities and limitations they hold for global history. The seminar thus offers a historiographical orientation to contemporary world history, and it prepares the members for further reading or research on themes significant for the field.

The second seminar (HIST 610) has enough built-in flexibility that it can take the form of either a reading or a research seminar, or even a combination of the two. In any case, it always concentrates attention intensively on a single theme or issue important for the understanding of history in global terms. The first time it was offered, for example, the seminar concentrated on the methodology of comparative history. Members of the seminar read theoretical and methodological works by historians and sociologists, then each wrote a research paper undertaking comparative study of some issue of global import. The second time it was offered, the seminar dealt with a different theme — the cultural results of encounters between peoples of different civilizations. Common readings focused on sixteenth-century encounters between Spaniards and Indians in Central America, experiences that have generated a large literature and that suggest ways of thinking about encounters in other locales. Written work then consisted of research papers on the results of cross-cultural encounters in parts of the world of special interest to seminar members. During the spring semester of 1988, Professor Philip Curtin will offer the seminar, which will focus on yet another theme, "The World and the West: The Revolution of Modernization." Future versions of this seminar might deal with themes like feudalism, decolonization, long-distance trade, comparative colonial experiences, or other topics of global significance — depending upon the interests of seminar members and of faculty available to teach the course.

A pair of seminars by themselves does not constitute a Ph.D. program. At the University of Hawaii, the Ph.D. in history requires preparation of four fields, selected from various subdivisions of American, Asian, European, and Pacific history, with the field of world history also available as an option. While preparing the more traditional fields divided along geographical, chronological, and topical lines, candidates acquire the specialized research skills and detailed understanding of issues universally expected of professional historians. Instruction in matters of this sort I consider crucially important for advanced students in history. During the past century, the discipline of history has developed, refined, and in some cases perhaps even perfected techniques of investigation and analysis that have deepened knowledge and improved understanding of the past. Indeed, the credibility of the discipline rests largely on historians' respect for accuracy and their insistence on fair evaluation of all relevant evidence. In whatever new directions historians take their discipline, they certainly will want to honor and preserve the high standards of scholarship observed by professional researchers. World historians in particular absolutely must respect established standards, or run the risk of discrediting a venture of great intellectual potential. For this reason, in Hawaii as in Utopia, Ph.D. candidates complete programs that equip them with the full range of research techniques and analytical skills properly expected of all professional historians.

OPPORTUNITIES OFFERED BY GRADUATE
EDUCATION AND RESEARCH IN WORLD HISTORY

But the discipline of history also stands in need of development along new lines, and graduate education in world history can serve a useful function by encouraging a timely and responsible shift in historical consciousness. In establishing the Ph.D. field in world history, the Department of History in Hawaii articulated three specific goals for the new field.

In the first place, we hope the Ph.D. field in world history will work an indirect but nonetheless important influence on instruction in introductory survey courses. Now, the purposes of the Ph.D. field and of basic research in world history of course differ considerably from those of the introductory course. Furthermore, I wish to point out that a successful introductory course by no means depends upon formal instruction in world history — as witness the numerous autodidacts who by dint of their own broad reading and creative thinking have instituted courses of genuine sophistication in world history.[6] Nevertheless, it stands to reason that — particularly for beginning instructors — exposure to the research literature on world history would prove useful in the effort to organize a coherent survey of the world's major civilizations. After all, at the level of both the introductory course and professional research, many of the same basic themes guide contemporary thinking about world history. Acquaintance with the advanced literature on genuine global themes — comparative study of processes that take effect across cultural boundary lines and analysis of contacts between peoples of different civilizations — at the very least has the potential to suggest some useful interpretative frameworks for beginning instructors designing courses in world history.

Quite apart from this indirect influence on the undergraduate curriculum, the Department of History in Hawaii hopes the Ph.D. field will contribute in more immediate fashion to the development of world history as a field of research and scholarship, as a recognized subdiscipline of the broader field of history. Preparation of the field in world history accounts for only about one-quarter of a candidate's formal Ph.D. curriculum, but it has the potential to integrate the candidate's entire program in especially significant fashion by suggesting global perspectives as the context for basic research. Already it has encouraged one candidate to frame his dissertation research in such a way as to shed light on global themes. The dissertation, now nearing completion, deals with the war in Vietnam, more specifically with the different approaches taken by American and Vietnamese strategists toward the world of nature. The thesis argues that Americans fought against the environment, while Vietnamese cooperated with the world of nature. The thesis has immediate significance for the effort to explain the course of the war in Vietnam, but it also has broader implications for those interested in global themes — such as conflicts between peoples of different civilizations, or attitudes toward the natural world held by peoples of different civilizations. Perhaps more importantly, the project has the potential also to register advances in the subdiscipline of world history itself. It deals with issues — ecology and environment — that do not figure prominently in studies inspired by modernization and world-systems theories. Due to its capacity to suggest new perspectives for basic research, then, graduate education holds considerable promise for the effort to develop and consolidate world history as a sub-field of the broader discipline of history.

Finally, from a more general point of view, the Department of History in Hawaii hopes the Ph.D. field in world history will contribute to the larger scholarly effort now underway to stretch the boundaries of the discipline of history. During the past several decades, historians have learned to profit from the work of sociologists and anthropologists, to adapt techniques of quantification to the needs of historical scholarship, to investigate hitherto neglected topics like the historical experiences of peasants and minorities, to invent methods of analyzing orally transmitted evidence. The *Annales* school and the new social historians have worked an especially deep influence on contemporary scholarship, both within the discipline of history and beyond.

The emergence of world history strikes me as a development roughly parallel to the others just mentioned. At its best, historical scholarship always consists of a dialogue between past and present. Parties to the conversation must respect each other's interests and values, must listen carefully and refrain from temptations to distort the other's intentions. But the conversation itself must necessarily advance — investigate new directions, explore new ideas, reformulate problems along new lines — or run the risk of collapsing into a boring rehearsal of worn-out lines. To me, world history represents an effort to advance the colloquy between past and present. More specifically, it represents an effort to develop a vision of the past that is appropriate for the world of the late twentieth century and beyond. Given the interdependence of the contemporary world and the intermingling of peoples within it, such a vision will inevitably emerge in any case. In all the world of scholarship, though, historians are those most sensitive to the influence of tradition, to the vagaries of change through time, and to the necessity of understanding human experiences in their proper contexts. In my opinion, then, it becomes an intellectual imperative for historians to stretch the boundaries of their discipline and frame a fresh vision of the past — one that deals responsibly with the reality of the past while also addressing issues placed on the agenda by the complicated and interdependent world of the present. This goal both defines the task and suggests the promise of graduate education and research in world history.

Notes

1. Philip D. Curtin, "World Historical Studies in a Crowded World," *Perspectives* (American Historical Association) 24 (January 1986): 19–21. See also a similar appeal for graduate education in world history by Craig A. Lockard, "The Promotion of Graduate Study and Research in World History," *World History Bulletin* 2 (Fall 1984): 6–7.

2. The most effective spokesman for introductory courses on world civilizations is William H. McNeill. See his *Mythistory and Other Essays* (Chicago, 1986) for a collection of pertinent writings. See also L. S. Stavrianos, "The Teaching of World History," *Journal of Modern History* 31 (1959): 110-17; and the essays of Kevin Reilly et al., "What Is an Attainable Global Perspective for Undergraduates in History?," *The History Teacher* 18 (1985): 501–35.

3. This list is by no means complete, but mentions only some of the most prominent themes recently studied by comparative analysts. For one example of a work dealing with each of the themes, see, respectively: Rushton Coulborn, ed., *Feudalism in History* (Princeton, 1956); Michael E. Doyle, *Empires* (Ithaca, 1986); George M. Frèdrickson, *White Supremacy* (New York, 1981); E. L. Jones, *The European Miracle* (Cambridge, 1981); Clifford Geertz, *Islam Observed* (Chicago, 1971); Michael Adas, *Prophets of Rebellion* (Cambridge, 1987); and Theda Skocpol, *State and Social Revolutions* (Cambridge, 1979).

4. A large scholarly literature deals with the methods and purposes of comparative analysis. For present purposes, see especially the following items: Raymond Grew, "The Case for Comparing Histories," *American Historical Review* 85 (1980): 763–78; Alette Olin Hill et al., "Marc Bloch and Comparative History," *American Historical Review* 85 (1980): 828–57; and Theda Skocpol and Margaret Somers, "The Uses of Comparative History in Macrosocial Inquiry," *Comparative Studies in Society and History* 2 (1980): 174–97.

5. Again, this list is by no means complete, but rather mentions the most prominent themes recently studied by analysts of cross-cultural contacts. For one example of a work dealing with each of the themes, see, respectively: Philip D. Curtin, *Cross-Cultural Trade in World History* (Cambridge, 1984); Daniel R. Headrick, *The Tentacles of Progress* (New York, 1987); Greg Dening, *Islands and Beaches* (Honolulu, 1980); Nancy M. Farriss, *Maya Society under Colonial Rule* (Princeton, 1984); and William H. McNeill, *Plagues and Peoples* (New York, 1976). On the last theme, I cannot resist mentioning also two contributions of Alfred W. Crosby: *The Columbian Exchange* (Westport, Conn., 1972); and *Ecological Imperialism* (Cambridge, 1985).

6. See the sampler of syllabi collected by Kevin Reilly, ed., *World History: Selected Reading Lists and Course Outlines from American Colleges and Universities* (New York, 1985).

PHILIP D. CURTIN

Graduate Teaching in World History

The problems of graduate training in world history are not very different from the problems of graduate training in any other field of knowledge — or from the problems of education at all levels. The crucial fact is that available knowledge is increasing at a faster rate than ever before in history, and it promises to go on increasing at a similar rate for the foreseeable future.

One reaction is to build bigger libraries with new technology for information retrieval. This is all very well, but access to information is not necessarily knowledge, much less wisdom. The recipients have to know what to do with the information: how to assimilate it to what they already know and fit it into their understanding of the world and their place in it. Libraries can be larger, but human beings have to struggle with the same limitations they have always had. Consequently, while available information grows, areas of professional specialization shrink to keep them within the bounds of human capacity. The problem of any graduate education is to combine the demands of increasing specialization with enough breadth to keep that specialized knowledge in perspective. This is true of every kind of graduate education across the whole range of arts and sciences.

For world history, as for other fields of knowledge, one theoretical possibility would be to set up graduate training for generalists, or people whose specialty would be to know a little bit about everything. No such option now exists, nor should it. Everyone who now teaches world history at the university level began with some narrower field of specialization in the history of some particular time and place, and that is the correct point of departure. Our ability to understand the nature and validity of broad generalizations depends on our knowledge of the underpinnings at scattered points. Otherwise, it would be hard to imagine what lies beneath the surface. The conventional wisdom is correct: that the best understanding comes from an appropriate combination of depth with a broad span of knowledge.

How to translate this general proposition into a particular program of training? Let us begin with the assumption that graduate students in the twenty-first century will still be asked to show knowledge of a certain limited number of

Philip D. Curtin, "Graduate Teaching in World History," *Journal of World History* 2 (Spring 1991): 81–89.

areas of history that will still be called "fields." We can assume for convenience that these students of the future will have to demonstrate proficiency in four to six fields, taking four as a convenient example.

Should one of these be a field in world history? I think not. By that time, students who have already come through primary and secondary schools and universities will already have been exposed to a variety of courses in world history — more in the twenty-first century than today. They should have adequate superficial knowledge. A slightly deeper superficial knowledge of world history is not likely to produce much gain in real understanding. The key to understanding is not in the survey, but in the way the parts are linked together, that is, comparative history.

Comparative history is a difficult concept because it has so many different meanings to different people. The kind of comparative history I have in mind crosses the boundaries of the major culture areas to pick out similarities or differences and to make comparisons in the perspective of world history. In the twenty-first century, many (perhaps most) academic historians will teach world history, but the *specialists* in world history will not be "worldists" or "globalists"; they will be "comparatists."

How might a graduate field in comparative history be organized? One component would certainly be a course in comparative world history: a course where lectures, discussions, and readings actually make comparisons that reach across the major barriers of culture, time, and space. Many models already exist. Kevin Reilly's collection of reading lists in world and comparative history, published by the World History Association in 1985,[1] illustrates the possibilities with twenty-two different undergraduate courses that would qualify as some kind of comparative world history.

My course, called "The World and the West," is concerned with the impact of the west on the rest of the world since about 1000 C.E. The basic approach is somewhat anthropological. The central theme is the way in which human ways-of-life have changed through interaction between peoples of varying cultures. The method is to consider a number of case studies as a basis for generalization. The course tries to draw on data from all of the major culture areas, but changing human culture remains at the center of the picture.

I have already raided my lectures for that course to publish two books, one on cross-cultural trade and one on plantations.[2] Other themes are concerned with the comparative movement of European frontiers overseas; the reception of western culture in places as various as Uganda, Turkey, and Japan; or the revolt against European colonialism, viewed comparatively with examples from Ghana and Indonesia. Other people's courses in comparative modernization have some of these same elements, but any such course will be most effective when instructors deal with themes that especially interest them. Variety is therefore desirable.

Comparative courses are put together in different ways. Some instructors pick a particular geographical focus. Another possibility is to consider intercommunication between culture areas across Eurasia from Japan to Europe. Still another centers on a body of water and the people who live on its shores. The Indian Ocean is one such body of water. The Atlantic after Columbus is another.

Still another approach is to choose parts of the world that have had a common experience defined in some other way. The comparative history of the tropical world is one possibility, sometimes discussed as the history of the Third World. Another possibility is a topical subject, like women's history, treated on a global basis. Still another is intentionally to choose comparisons between societies that are distinctly different — like a course on the history of the family in England and China taught at the University of Pennsylvania or one on peasant societies in France and China at Columbia.

The important point is not so much the choice of things to compare, but the way the comparisons and contrasts can be used to deepen our understanding of the way human societies change through time. Many of these comparative courses are designed for undergraduates. The University of Manitoba has a whole range from a freshman survey to graduate courses — all offered as part of a history concentration in modern world history.[3] At both graduate and undergraduate levels, the goal is the same, and such courses are an appropriate part of graduate training in world history.

A second kind of comparative training already present in American universities involves a seminar or proseminar where the students read and discuss published works in cross-cultural comparative history. This approach is used, among other places, at the University of Hawaii and at Johns Hopkins University.[4] The choice of texts is even wider than in the variety of courses in comparative world history. At the broader end of the spectrum are works that take a theme through some part of world history: McNeill's *The Rise of the West,*[5] Von Laue's *Revolution of Modernization,*[6] Eric Wolf's *Europe and the People without History,*[7] Immanuel Wallerstein's *Modern World-System,*[8] or Janet L. Abu-Lughod's *Before European Hegemony.*[9]

In another category are the worldwide histories of changing technologies. Here we have Daniel Headrick's two books on technology transfer from Europe, books that are already widely used in world history courses.[10] And, of course, McNeill comes in again with *The Pursuit of Power,*[11] along with Geoffrey Parker's more recent entry, *The Military Revolution.*[12]

Cross-cultural environmental history is still another category of comparative history, with McNeill represented this time by *Plagues and Peoples.*[13] Other examples are Alfred Crosby's *Columbian Exchange and Ecological Imperialism,*[14] and my own *Death by Migration.*[15]

The Vietnam War and other recent disturbances served as impetus for a spate of books on the comparative histories of revolutions, mostly taking in revolutions of the past two centuries, if not merely those of the recent past. Here the earlier tradition of comparative revolutionary studies in the manner of Crane Brinton[16] became cross-cultural and often worldwide, with political scientists, anthropologists, and sociologists (such as Barrington Moore, Theda Skocpol, and Eric Wolf[17]) entering alongside the professional historians.

The list of possible topics could be extended to take in comparative millennarian and nativist movements with authors like Michael Adas and Peter

Worsley.[18] Comparative frontier studies go back to Owen Lattimore on the *Inner Asian Frontiers of China*[19] and come down to Howard Lamar and Leonard Thompson in *The Frontier in History.*[20] Comparative urban histories range from Robert Adams's *Evolution of Urban Society,*[21] which compares ancient Mesopotamia and ancient Middle America, to Gilbert Rozman's studies on urban networks in Russia, China, and Japan.[22] Taken together, the discussion of these works can carry the student toward an understanding of what comparative history can and cannot do to broaden our understanding of world history as a whole.

A third approach to teaching comparative history involves another kind of seminar, which might be called a research seminar, but in a special sense of that term. Most comparative history has to rest on secondary authorities rather than basic research with source material. It is nevertheless possible and desirable to try to arrive at generalizations, even when the sources have not been explored in detail. The model I have in mind originated as the seminar in comparative tropical history at the University of Wisconsin, beginning in the early 1960s. Over a semester, a group of students worked on a single problem in comparative history. The topic had to be chosen with some care. It had to be divisible into fifteen or twenty cases for comparison, so that each student could present one or two cases for discussion during the course of the semester, and information on each case had to be available in the secondary literature. As the semester progressed, student discussions helped to refine the questions being asked of each new case. Some cases had to be rejected as inappropriate, while others did not work well for lack of sufficient evidence. If all went well, the seminar would arrive at a general statement based on the comparisons. That statement might not be the last word about the problem at hand, but it could usually tell something about the patterns, uniformities, or lack of patterns illustrated by the topic chosen.

Several different kinds of topics are appropriate for this kind of exercise. One I used was the comparative study of trade diasporas, with each student doing two papers of about ten pages, each reporting on a particular trade diaspora. Many possible topics owed their quality of comparability to the wide spread of colonial regimes to different culture areas beyond Europe. One successful topic, for example, was the comparative study of the relationships between changes in land tenure introduced by colonial regimes and the accompanying changes in social structure. The *zamindari* settlement in Bengal toward the end of the eighteenth century is a famous example, but others can be found on almost all continents.

Another kind of example is culture change among the European colonists who moved overseas or, more interesting still, culture change that took place among Europeans who settled beyond the frontier line of European control. These trans-frontiersmen could be found in the eighteenth and nineteenth centuries in places as various as the Canadian prairie provinces, the Karoo in South Africa, or among pastoralists like the gauchos of Argentina and the *llaneros* of Venezuela. Comparative forms of resistance to European rule or to the spread of European culture is another source of workable comparative topics, from comparative primary resistance to the different forms of local nationalism or group identity that appeared as colonialism faded.

Whatever the topic, the point of the exercise is not to discover truth or to produce a publishable set of papers as a conclusion to the seminar. Some comparative seminar topics can lead to publishable books: a comparative seminar on trade diasporas in 1973 became a pilot project for a book on cross-cultural trade that appeared in 1984.[23] But that is not the object. The object is to work through the problems that make comparative history one of the more frustrating and difficult forms of historical writing. Learning by doing is a significant step beyond merely reading and criticizing the comparative works that have already appeared.

To return to the Ph.D. field in comparative history. One would hope that in the twenty-first century, a program can be prepared using some combination of these existing techniques for teaching comparative history, and that more experience with the subject and with world history generally will lead to still better ways. Doctoral programs offering a field in some form of comparative world history already exist at Hawaii, Manitoba, Minnesota, and Johns Hopkins, and probably at several other universities. The further experience of these programs is bound to lead to innovations and improvements. Nevertheless, variants of the three approaches I just outlined may still be around. These are, in summary, courses incorporating comparative themes in a broad world history; second, the study of published works on aspects of comparative world history; and finally, experimental exercises in a joint effort to make comparisons the source of historical generalizations.

But the comparative field should only be one field among several in the training of historians. Historians need depth as well as span. This means, among other things, that they need detailed knowledge of some particular segment of time and space, and this includes knowledge of the techniques necessary to investigate in that field. These techniques may include languages, diplomatics, statistics, training in gathering and interpretation of oral data, or cross-disciplinary training that can reach into fields as diverse as economics, linguistics, medicine, archeology, or biology. This proposed graduate program for the next century assumes that about half a student's pre-dissertation time will be devoted to his or her major geographical area, or two of the four fields.

The fourth field should deal with another segment of time and space, and one from another culture area. Each student should be required to prepare a field from *at least two* of the major culture areas of the world: the west (including both Europe and North America), east Asia, Africa, Latin America, south Asia, and southeast Asia. That would provide world historians with a reasonable beginning toward the kind of broader knowledge they will need to master later in their careers.

So far, I have recommended in the guise of predicting, and recommending is easy. Getting recommendations accepted is a more serious problem. I must therefore hesitate before predicting that *any* of these recommendations will ever become common practice. On the other hand, world history as a fundamental course in the history curriculum seems to have an assured future, not necessarily as a replacement for the common western civilization survey, but at least as a second kind of survey. In spite of increasing specialization, enough historians seem willing to move out of their narrow specialties to staff such courses. This in itself may change attitudes, as it has at places like the University of Hawaii or the Air Force Academy, where a survey of world civilizations is required of all.

On the other hand, the explicit programs in comparative world history that once flourished at Wisconsin and Santa Cruz have since been cancelled. But closing these formal programs had some trade-offs — several of the people who had been involved in them went on doing the same kind of teaching in new settings. The variety of new comparative world history courses — without a formal program — is far more important. The full range is not well publicized; even Kevin Reilly's extensive collection of syllabi is not complete, simply because many historians who teach cross-cultural courses do not think of themselves as world history specialists, only as people with an interest in a subject like comparative urban history or the comparative industrialization of Japan and the west.

These trends suggest that a broader conception of historical study is making more progress against the dominant graduate training of the 1990s, still overwhelmingly designed to turn out specialists on narrow areas in time and space. Unless that pattern is changed, over-specialization will continue to be the easy way intellectually, and the easy way to professional advancement. Time will tell.

Notes

1. Kevin Reilly, ed., *World History: Selected Reading Lists and Course Outlines from American Colleges and Universities* (New York: Markus Wiener, 1985). A new edition is in press for 1990.

2. P. D. Curtin, *Cross-Cultural Trade in World History* (New York: Cambridge University Press, 1984); *The Rise and Fall of the Plantation Complex* (New York: Cambridge University Press, 1990).

3. T. E. Vadney, "World History as an Advanced Academic Field," *Journal of World History* 1 (1990): 209–24.

4. Craig Lockard, "World History Graduate Program: University of Hawaii," *World History Bulletin* 5, no. 2 (1988): 2–11.

5. William H. McNeill, *The Rise of the West* (Chicago: University of Chicago Press, 1963).

6. Theodore H. Von Laue, *The World Revolution of Westernization: The Twentieth Century in Global Perspective* (New York: Oxford University Press, 1987).

7. Eric Wolf, *Europe and the People without History* (Berkeley: University of California Press, 1982).

8. Immanuel Wallerstein, *The Modern World-System*, 3 vols. to date (New York: Academic Press, 1974–).

9. Janet L. Abu-Lughod, *Before European Hegemony: The World System, A.D. 1250–1350* (New York: Oxford University Press, 1989).

10. Daniel R. Headrick, *The Tools of Empire: Technology and European Imperialism in the Nineteenth Century* (New York: Oxford University Press, 1981) and *The Tentacles of Progress: Technology Transfer in the Age of Imperialism, 1850–1940* (New York: Oxford University Press, 1988).

11. William H. McNeill, *The Pursuit of Power* (Chicago: University of Chicago Press, 1982).

12. Geoffrey Parker, *The Military Revolution* (Cambridge: Cambridge University Press, 1988).

13. William H. McNeill, *Plagues and Peoples* (Garden City, N.Y.: Doubleday, 1976).

14. Alfred W. Crosby, *The Columbian Exchange: Biological and Cultural Consequences of 1492* (Westport, Conn.: Greenwood Press, 1972); *Ecological Imperialism: The Biological Expansion of Europe, 900–1900* (Cambridge: Cambridge University Press, 1986).

15. P. D. Curtin, *Death by Migration: Europe's Encounter with the Tropical World in the Nineteenth Century* (New York: Cambridge University Press, 1989).

16. Crane Brinton, *The Anatomy of Revolution*, 2d ed. (New York: Prentice Hall, 1972).

17. Barrington Moore, Jr., *Social Origins of Dictatorship and Democracy: Lord and Peasant in the Making of the Modern World* (Boston: Beacon Press, 1966); Theda Skocpol, *States and Social Revolutions: A Comparative Analysis of France, Russia, and China* (Cambridge: Cambridge University Press, 1979); Eric Wolf, *Peasant Wars of the Twentieth Century* (Englewood Cliffs, N.J.: Prentice Hall, 1969).

18. Michael Adas, *Prophets of Rebellion: Millenarian Protest Movements against the European Colonial Order* (New York: Cambridge University Press, 1987); Peter Worsley, *The Trumpet Shall Sound: A Study of Cargo Cults in Melanesia*, 2d ed. (New York: Shocken, 1974).

19. Owen Lattimore, *Inner Asian Frontiers of China*, 2d ed. (New York: American Geographical Society, 1951).

20. Howard Lamar and Leonard Thompson, eds. *The Frontier in History: North America and Southern Africa Compared* (New Haven: Yale University Press, 1981).

21. Robert Adams, *Evolution of Urban Society* (Chicago: Chicago University Press, 1965).

22. Gilbert Rozman, *Urban Networks in Russia, 1750–1800, and Premodern Periodization* (Princeton: Princeton University Press, 1976); *Urban Networks in Ch'ing China and Tokugawa Japan* (Princeton: Princeton University Press, 1973).

23. Curtin, *Cross-Cultural Trade* (n. 2 above).

Patrick Manning

Doctoral Training in World History
The Northeastern University Experience

In an April 1992 article in *Perspectives*, I described a proposed Ph.D. program focusing on world history.[1] Seven years later, I am able to report that the program
is in place, has seventeen doctoral candidates (including eleven working on dissertations), and that as many as three will complete their degrees this year.
These students are comfortable in area studies literatures and discourse, but approach their problems globally. The Northeastern University program, while
modest in size by comparison to established doctoral programs, appears already
to have gathered the largest concentration of doctoral students in world history.
A description of this program provides an occasion to ask what role doctoral programs in world history might have in the future of the historical profession.

Research in World History

As a teaching field, world history has grown dramatically during the last two
decades. World history is now one of the principal high school courses in history, along with U.S. history. At community college and university levels, world
history courses and textbooks equal in number those of Western civilization.
Still, the approach of most textbooks and courses in world history, though intended to be global, relies heavily on the national and area studies traditions in
which the teachers and authors were trained. To interpret world history as a
string of regional histories is one logical approach, but it is not the only one.

   Research in global history has also expanded during the past generation.
Global historians, in constructing a field where there was none, have created an
impressive body of scholarship, and have extended their audience from the *Journal of World History* to their share of articles in the *American Historical Review*.
The level of research, however, has lagged far behind the demands of teaching, and the contribution of doctoral dissertations to that research has been

Patrick Manning, "Doctoral Training in World History: The Northeastern University Experience," *Perspectives* (American Historical Association) 37 (March 1999): 35–38.

negligible. Research in world history has developed incrementally through the contributions of individual scholars, mostly at senior levels, working on their own.

Aside from these individuals, the leading historians and their institutions have been content to stick with the inherited national and civilizational frameworks in interpreting the past. They have implicitly joined with the globalization theorists to assume that global social phenomena are a characteristic of the present and not the past. In this still-dominant view, the rise of agriculture, the iron age, organized religion, planet-wide maritime contact, industrialization, and democratic aspirations are appropriately analyzed as local, and not as global, phenomena.[2]

The thin line of senior scholars who have taken up world history, working in their second academic language for the last 20 years of a career, are perhaps not the best-chosen group for breaking through the limits of national and civilizational paradigms. It is our view that younger scholars, whose first academic language is global and who may have up to 40 years to enunciate interpretations in its terms, could do more to develop a planetary approach to our past.

The formal training of world historians, however, has grown at a very slow rate. The expansion of training in world history has been achieved with almost no organized or consistent investment in research. Efforts at concentrated study in world history from the 1950s into the 1970s, at Chicago, Northwestern, and Wisconsin, were not sustained. In the 1980s graduate study in world history began again, notably with the work of Philip Curtin at Johns Hopkins, Jerry Bentley at Hawaii, and Carter Findley at Ohio State. Investment in global programs remained minimal. The 1996 grant of $690,000 by the Annenberg/CPB Project to Northeastern for developing the *Migration in Modern World History* CD-ROM may be the largest grant for world history, but it is far below the amount necessary to launch research in the field.

The work to be taken on by doctoral programs in world history may be identified at three levels. First is to produce teachers of world history and professors who will train teachers. Second is to address the many issues in transnational and transregional history that now appear on the historical agenda — issues in global environmental and economic history, but also in social and cultural interactions. The third level is to develop a historical perspective on the current reconceptualization of the world. Two centuries ago, scholars elaborated a new world view through a vision of progress and evolution, structured by notions of separate nations, races, and continents. Today we witness the emergence of a systemic conceptualization of the world, emphasizing interconnections among phenomena previously considered as discrete. The task of historians, in this effort, is to explore the record of global connections in the past.

THE NORTHEASTERN UNIVERSITY PROGRAM

Northeastern University's doctoral program admitted its first students in September 1994. Creating a new program provided a chance to take a fresh look at doctoral study in history. Our faculty's consensus in favor of a focus on world history has been central in getting the program through various challenges.[3] After a few years of development, the program has these general emphases:

Focus on world history with courses, bibliography, exams, and dissertations on the various aspects of world history.

Reliance on the program's linkage to the World History Center. This center, focusing on research, curriculum development, and institutional development in world history, has provided substantial support and practical applications for doctoral students.

Substantial focus on historical methodology — the analytical skills of historians, and theories and methods of disciplines on which history draws.

Articulation of global historical study with strong area studies training in the regions of each student's choice, including history of the United States and of European countries.

Exploration of the variety of approaches to world history — comparative, interactive, and synthetic.

Northeastern's medium-sized department is relatively well balanced by region and specialization. Of the fourteen full-time faculty members regularly teaching in the department, six are trained in U.S. history, four in European history, and four in history of other areas. Of the U.S. historians, two faculty members direct three doctoral students, two of the four trained in European history direct four doctoral students, and the four trained in history of other areas direct eleven doctoral students.

We have admitted from three to seven doctoral students per year. Two came to us with B.A. degrees; two more entered the doctoral program after completing M.A. degrees at Northeastern, and thirteen came to us with M.A. degrees from other institutions. Two students are from outside the United States (both from China). Three of our students received previous degrees from Ivy League institutions, three completed degrees at other private institutions in the northeast, and eight obtained degrees from public institutions from Maine to Wisconsin to Texas.

The doctoral students take courses along with M.A. and M.A.T. candidates, of whom a growing proportion focus on world history. The department offers six to eight graduate classes per term on a quarter system; students take two or sometimes three courses per term. Doctoral students take a course in global historiography, as well as introductory and advanced courses in methodology, and at least two of the seminars we offer are on global political, social, and cultural history. "Approaches to World History" is a one-quarter survey of world history, of particular interest to students in our M.A.T. program, but also taken by doctoral students. Courses such as "Gender and Colonialism," "The African Diaspora," and "The Early Modern Atlantic" are inherently global; courses in environmental history and urban history, taught by U.S. specialists, have become significantly global in reach. A course on borderlands, rather than on the Soviet Union, emphasizes regional linkages. Even explicitly regional courses, as on the Caribbean and modern China, include global dimensions.

Doctoral students select a major professor immediately and a committee of three as soon as possible. One committee member may be from outside the department or outside the university. In deliberations with the committee, the student sets a program for language study, for methodological specialization (which should consist of three courses), a dissertation topic, and prepares for the comprehensive exams. Candidates are required to take a teaching tutorial, a mentored practicum, and then to teach their own courses.

Students take three comprehensive exams, two written and one oral. One of the exams is on world history — for this exam, the student must address a significant portion of the literature summarized in the departmental bibliography on world history. A second exam focuses on the candidate's regional specialization and the third focuses on the candidate's methodological and thematic specialization. The dissertation proposal must be approved before the candidate takes comprehensive exams.

The dissertation is the crucial element of the program. It is commonly argued that students should begin with a localized study before taking on a broad study. In contrast, we argue that our students' formative book-length research should be with a global study, so that for the balance of their career they can advance their insights within that framework, rather than begin global work only after they have left graduate school. Dissertation projects in process indicate the range of topics and approaches of students in the program: comparative studies — women in bus boycotts in Montgomery and Johannesburg and the cultural revolution in China and the revolutionary offensive in Cuba; localized studies in global context — a letter-writing family in late eighteenth-century Massachusetts, communalism in nineteenth-century South India, and a French-Canadian parish in Massachusetts; broadly systemic studies — twentieth-century decolonization, Latin American migration in the twentieth century, and opinion management in the mid-twentieth century; intellectual biography — Owen Lattimore and his interpretation of world history; and curriculum development — creating thematic curricula for high school and college courses.

THE WORLD HISTORY CENTER

The World History Center is designed as a comprehensive center for research, curriculum development, and for strengthening the institutions of world history. The center has had significant success in gathering resources and assembling an active node of scholarly discourse, even now that hope is gone for gaining federal support for a world history equivalent to the area studies centers set up in the cold war era. The center's funding has come from multimedia projects, from professional development work for teachers of world history, and from research grants awarded to associates of the center.

The World History Seminar supports about fourteen presentations a year by visiting scholars, Northeastern faculty members, and graduate students. The multimedia work of the center has included the *Migration* CD-ROM, preparatory work on a CD-ROM on technology in world history, and a time line for *Encyclopaedia Britannica*. The web site of the center includes teaching resources, bibliography, papers and credentials of students and faculty, and working papers. Students are active in H-WORLD as coeditors and book review editors; they help maintain the H-WORLD web site; and participate as discussants. The World History Resource Center, linking the World History Center and the School of Education, conducts outreach and professional development for elementary and secondary teachers. It works cooperatively with school systems and with other outreach centers to provide teaching materials and to develop teaching skills and an awareness of issues in world history.

DIFFICULTIES FOR GRADUATE STUDY IN WORLD HISTORY

The greatest difficulty for graduate study in world history has been the first step: creating programs. For large departments in particular, the focus on specializations within world regions makes it organizationally difficult to find a space for world history. Historians of the United States and Europe have been preoccupied by their large literatures, so that ventures in world history have tended to remain in the hands of smaller factions of Third World historians. The lack of world history lines in these prestigious departments is itself a disincentive to training global historians. Nevertheless, several new programs have formed and others are under discussion.[4]

If the founding of programs has been difficult, enabling them to flourish has also had its problems. The World History Association (WHA) is an energetic organization, whose membership of 1,300 is now less than 10 percent of that of the AHA. But the WHA has low dues, no professional staff, and is not at the table of the American Council of Learned Societies along with the area studies organizations and the AHA. With the exception of Northeastern's World History Center, there are virtually no equivalents in world history to the research centers for national and area studies scholarship.

Locating fellowship funds for language study and dissertation research has not been easy. Fellowships for overseas study are generally tightly focused on regional study. Even the International Dissertation Research Fellowship of the Social Science Research Council, which includes comparative and global study within its purview, has in practice been awarded to students writing area students dissertations, and not to applicants with projects in global history.

Area studies scholars have been cautious about embracing world history, fearing that global studies are proposed as a substitute for area studies. It is true that the end of the cold war and the rising interest in globalization have brought cuts in area studies funding. There has not, however, been any equivalent rise in funding for global studies in history or other social sciences. Meanwhile, to address this potential conflict between world history and area studies, we have sought to form an alliance in New England among area studies specialists and those focusing on world history.

An analogous issue is the relationship between world history and the history of the United States and Europe. Roughly half the students in our program have a primary regional interest in the United States and Europe. This puts us in a position of learning how to articulate where the United States and Europe fit into global history. To pick two issues: studies of fascism in global context will necessarily focus heavily on Italy, but may elicit connections that would not come forth in a study in primarily European context; and studies of film history will naturally focus on Hollywood and on European film, but in global context may show unexpected parallels with Indian or Mexican film.

A Research Agenda

The theme of the WHA International Conference for 2000 (hosted by Northeastern in Boston, June 22–25, 2000) is "The Research Agenda for World History." This conference and the research agenda will address the analytical and empirical choices of world historians.

The analytical approaches among which world historians choose may be labeled as local, comparative, interactive, synthetic, and planetary. World history is more than a single field of study, and the world is more than an additional area to work into a crowded curriculum. Study of the world involves selecting among competing frameworks of analysis: Istanbul and Malacca are significant nodes in world history, but deforestation is a planetary issue. A major element of the debate on the research agenda should be the balance among these alternative approaches.

In empirical study, debate on the research agenda will focus on the allocation of research efforts among early and recent times and on the various themes, topics, and regions. For instance, political and economic studies have always been central in the literature on world history, and the current debate on the economic history of the modern world will surely be prominent at the conference. At the same time, issues in social and cultural history are open for important work — for instance on migration, on cultural connections among regions, and on the interplay of religious communalism and nationalism.

Developing global perspectives on history is already beginning to elicit a distinctive view of the past. The works of Alfred Crosby, Philip Curtin, William H. McNeill, Immanuel Wallerstein, and Andre Gunder Frank have had significant impact on historical studies generally. Yet with so vast a topic, we require organized and disciplined study. There is a great deal of work to be done, and over a long time, before the intellectual potential of global historical studies can be realized. It appears that, after false starts in earlier times, world history is now getting its grounding as a research field.

Notes

1. "Methodology and World History in a PhD Program," *Perspectives* 30 (April 1992), 22, 24. The present article was presented in an earlier form to the Southeast World History Association, Atlanta, on October 23, 1998.

2. The democratization movements of 1989–92 clearly reflect a global and interactive pattern of events. Yet even with the far simpler levels of technology and communications of the time, the events of 1789–93 present a remarkable parallel. The rise and decline of democratic fervor in those years linked such issues as the revolutions in France and Haiti, the antislavery movement in Britain and elsewhere, the U.S. Bill of Rights, the Polish constitution and then partition, and smaller movements in Brazil, Louisiana, and along the African coast.

3. Thanks are due to Colin Palmer, Eric Monkkonen, Philip Curtin, and Thomas Schlereth, external reviewers who assisted us in setting up the program. The program, formally proposed by the department in 1990, found its implementation delayed until 1994. In 1997–98 the department successfully reversed an administrative proposal to close the program, and as a result the program was changed to one granting degrees uniquely in world history. The department maintains its strong public history program at the M.A. level. Details on the department and the World History Center are on line at www.whc.neu.edu.

4. The University of California at Riverside has added an early modern world doctoral program to that of Minnesota; Rutgers offers world history as a second doctoral field; University of Pennsylvania has now established a graduate certificate in world history; the University of Texas at Arlington has established a doctoral program in Atlantic history; and the University of Texas at Austin is debating the creation of a doctoral program in world history.

SELECTED BIBLIOGRAPHY

Adams, Steven, Michael Adas, and Kevin Reilly, eds. *World History: Selected Course Outlines and Reading Lists from American Colleges and Universities.* New Enlarged and Updated Edition. Princeton, N.J.: Markus Wiener, 1998. An essential tool for teachers new to world history and a treasury of ideas for veterans. The book is organized in four sections: Graduate and Professional Courses, Surveys, Specialized Courses: Chronological, and Specialized Courses: Thematic.

Buell Frederick. "World Studies at Queens College." *Comparative Civilizations Review,* no. 26 (Spring 1992): 136–49. Reprinted in *World History Bulletin* 10 (Spring/Summer 1993): 8–14. This essay describes a series of four undergraduate interdisciplinary courses introduced at Queens College, the City University of New York. This interdisciplinary experiment is noteworthy particularly because the faculty from several departments who designed it took serious account of current methodological trends, including poststructural analysis.

Dunn, Ross E., and David Vigilante, eds. *Bring History Alive! A Sourcebook for Teaching World History.* Los Angeles: National Center for History in the Schools, University of California, Los Angeles, 1996. This volume of teaching ideas, which is correlated to the National Standards for World History, was produced mainly for K–12 teachers. College instructors, however, may find it surprisingly useful. It includes hundreds of sample teaching activities, fifteen essays on topics in world history, and a treasury of teaching resources from primary source texts to CD-ROM disks.

Hosgood, Chris. "Introductory World History as a Core Course: A Canadian Perspective." *Journal of World History* 1 (Fall 1990): 199–208. A professor at the University of Lethbridge, Hosgood makes a case for a modern world history program that embodies Canada's distinctive global commitment to multiculturalism, international peace-keeping, and mediation of dialogue between the industrial and less developed nations.

Kramer, Lloyd, Donald Reid, and William L. Barry, eds. *Learning History in America: Schools, Cultures, and Politics.* Minneapolis: University of Minnesota Press, 1994. This volume includes three essays pertinent to world history curriculum building: "Reports of Its Death Were Premature: Why

'Western Civ' Endures" by Lynn Hunt, "Teaching Western History at Stanford" by Daniel Gordon, and "Teaching Non-Western History at Stanford" by Richard Roberts. Hunt defends Western Civ but contends that it must be taught critically and with attention to interpretive debates. Gordon and Roberts offer insights on the famous "canon wars" that broke out at Stanford in the late 1980s and on the curricular changes that resulted from the struggle.

Miller, Montserrat Martí, and Peter N. Stearns. "Applying Cognitive Learning Approaches in History Teaching: An Experiment in a World History Course." *The History Teacher* 28 (February 1995): 183–204. This essay is one iteration of Peter Stearns's recommendation to world history teachers to take greater account of the "cognitive revolution," that is, investigations of how students learn, remember, and know the past and how they may develop analytical skills that lead to genuine understanding.

Roupp, Heidi, ed. *Teaching World History: A Resource Book.* Armonk, N.Y.: M. E. Sharpe, 1997. The author is a founder of the World History Association. Like that organization, this volume embodies the refreshing idea that K–12 and college teachers constitute a single intellectual community and face similar challenges. The book offers fifty gems for teachers, including essays, course outlines, strategies, and lessons.

Stearns, Peter N. "Teaching the United States in World History." *Perspectives* (American Historical Association) 27 (April 1989): 12–16. Also, "U.S. History Must Be Taught as Part of a Much Broader Historical Panorama." *Chronicle of Higher Education* 3 (January 1990): A44. Why is world history so often taught in a way that largely blanks out North America? Stearns challenges the notion that the human past should be understood as "divided into two parts, the United States and whatever else in the world is studied historically." On the contrary, students stand to gain a better understanding of U.S. history if they are given opportunities to make analytical comparisons and to relate events in North America to processes that spill across the world.

Vadney, T. E. "World History as an Advanced Academic Field." *Journal of World History* 1 (Fall 1990): 209–23. The author describes the University of Manitoba's world history program, which includes both undergraduate studies and a Ph.D. field. He also gives hard-headed advice to would-be innovators, warning then to show "political sensitivity" to the campus community and to strive "to assert the scholarly claims of global history, mainly by research and publication, and thereby to win the support of other professionals for expanding the field."

PART ELEVEN

THE FUTURE OF WORLD HISTORY

World history, like the history of the nation, is contested terrain: What should American youth know about the human past that is most likely to inspire them morally and intellectually to strive for a prosperous, less dangerous future? Two points of view have been conspicuous in the public debate over the proper relationship between world history education and the national purpose. One privileges the idea of a common Western heritage for all Americans. According to this model, the critical mission of history studies should be to transmit to the rising generation a shared legacy of values, institutions, and great ideas derived mainly from peoples of Europe and the ancient Mediterranean. The other point of view, whose blanket appellation is multiculturalism, argues that if mutual tolerance and respect are the keys to enduring democracy, students should explore and thus appreciate the differing histories of America's many distinct ethno-racial communities.

One side celebrates the social and cultural power of the West as the drive-shaft of progress. The other side emphasizes the inequalities in the balance of civilizational power and the consequences for social and economic justice. The first camp believes that if students concentrate on the history of the West, they will esteem its presumed core values and endeavor to perpetuate them. The second is convinced that such a focus will only make students culturally myopic and insensitive to world inequities. Students should explore a world history that is socially inclusive, attentive to the contributions and achievements of diverse cultures, and dedicated to the relativist precept that no culture is inherently better or worse than any other. Underlying both ideologies is the continuing quest for stable, enduring cultural identities and covenants in a turbulent world.

To its credit, the academic movement for a new world history has walked a reasonably straight line between these two positions. Generally speaking it has more affinity with multiculturalism than with the Western heritage model because multiculturalist educators are by definition internationally minded rather than culturally parochial.[1] On the other hand, world history advocates have often questioned multiculturalists for exhibiting a visceral anti-Western bias or for being too preoccupied with essential cultural differences, relativist arguments, and an approach to "contemporary problems" that discounts the value of historical analysis.

The world history movement, then, is multiculturalist in its inclusivism, but it also recognizes the importance of situating European history within the larger context. It has never advocated "dropping the West." Its singular contribution has been to describe a third way. Though the movement is still in the process of defining itself, its fundamental intellectual premise is that the history of the human species, to return to the words of R. L. Moore, is "the set of all sets."[2] Wherever and however human beings have come into contact with one another on this planet, relationships have been formed and conditions have arisen that are worthy of historical investigation. The social and spatial fields for such inquiry should be open and fluid, not predetermined by received cultural or geographical categories. Designing world history research and teaching is not a matter of deciding how to include all groups or of discovering the definitive grand narrative but of framing good questions unconstrained by preconceived ideas about which types of human association over time are properly open to study and which are not. This world history by no means invalidates the study of nations and civilizations as historical realities. It does, however, strive to connect their histories to larger world processes and to conceive of them not as opaque objects but as kaleidoscopes of human interaction whose identities and boundaries are perpetually in motion and often contested by their own members.

Moreover, the new world history is not inherently any more value-free than either multiculturalism or traditional Western Civ. World history scholars and teachers come to their subject from many ideological and confessional directions, but they seem to share at least a general set of moral convictions: that the history of the human species, not just one civilization or another, is worthy of respect and thoughtful inquiry; that the connections between human history and the condition of the biosphere must be taken seriously; that knowledge of economic, political, cultural, and environmental change *in the world*, not just group contributions and achievements, nourishes civil society and promotes international understanding; that attitudes of cultural arrogance toward the world-historical role of any particular nation or ethno-racial group are reprehensible and counterproductive to civil and global peace. The world's contemporary macro-trends, summed up in the term "globalization," have not on the whole converted world history teachers into moral advocates of some kind of centralized world order. On the contrary, these educators tend to have great empathy for people who seek firmer local communal bonds, which may include, to use William McNeill's term, ethnic or national "mythistories" that help legitimize those ties. Our yearnings for communal permanence, however, suggest that world historians have a great responsibility to try to explain and interpret large-scale developments, in some measure reducing the fear of change that ensues from ignorance.

Whether all world history teachers approve or not, the movement is implicated in the quest for a saner planet. Its moral usefulness, however, depends on the soundness and clarity of both its scholarship and its pedagogy. Looking over the past half-century, we can probably say, "So far, so good." But where do we go from here, acknowledging that as the world spins ever faster, new and contradictory ways of conceiving of the human past will confront us over and over again? As the pace of change accelerates, the social constructions that we once counted on to stay put — nation-states, races, geopolitical blocs, big institutions, national myths, class hierarchies, and received definitions of truth and beauty — seem to run between our fingers like sand. Since the world is not going to settle down in the new millennium, world history has little hope of settling down either. Certainly, there is no going back to Western Civ or the tidy categories of multicivilizationism. Rather, the dawning realization of our biospheric unity and the ecological, economic, and political restructuring that daily impresses itself upon us require that world history dedicate itself to fathoming the processes occurring *in the world* over long, intermediate, and short spans of time.

It also requires that we consider how human communities have *thought about* and *represented* what was happening in their world, including the arrival in their midst of strangers. World history teachers do not have to be disciples of Michel Foucault or Hayden White to recognize that postmodern sensibilities have exposed realms of inquiry pertinent to the discipline. These include investigation of the changing ways humans have represented culture, space, gender, and "the other." They also include research into the physical and cultural borderlands where groups of strangers meet and into the phenomena of social marginality, ethno-racial hybridity, and transnational citizenship. Indeed, the very idea of cultures as stable entities is thrown into question by the hypothesis that cultural communities *come into being* in the very process of interacting.

Postmodernist critique, including the historicizing of many of the discipline's categories and concepts, has undoubtedly caused anxiety among even committed world history practitioners, who may sometimes be heard pleading for a new but nonetheless sturdy set of narratives, themes, and categories they can employ to make sense of informational pandemonium. Surely part of the answer is to continue developing a suitable vocabulary and a conceptual tool kit for the field, a good deal of which may be drawn from postmodern discourse (or criticisms of it), to teach and write world history more effectively in terms of process, fluidity, representation, agency, and dynamic dialogue between the living and the departed. This program is preferable to searching for a new set of fixed metastructures to replace the old ones.

The ideological disputations of postmodernism, together with post-Soviet geopolitics, hair-raising swings in the world economy, electronic compression of time and space, the world wanderings of so many millions, and ominous signs that the planetary ecosystem is in transformation, have all conspired to rescue historians from becoming smug about what they know and understand. Rather, they are obliged to ask: "If the world has come to be like this, a world we could never have predicted, then isn't there much in human history that remains to be explained? What developments, over both the very long and very short term, could have produced such a world?" Questions like these push world history into new frontiers of inquiry.

One set of new trends is the bolder application of social scientific theory and ideas about "self" and "other" to world history research. Jerry Bentley, editor of the *Journal of World History* since its founding, has kept himself as well informed as anyone about methodological shifts and innovations. In the final section of *Shapes of World History in Twentieth-Century Scholarship*, the booklet he wrote in 1996 in the American Historical Association's "Essays on Global and Comparative History" series, he considers the field's new directions. In the first selection he describes three lines of scholarship that he finds especially promising. One is a new mode of macro-level sociology that is more systematically and rigorously comparative than earlier world-systems scholarship and not so closely married to either Weberian or Marxist structural categories. Another is the thrust of women's history and gender analysis into the cross-cultural and comparative spheres (see Part Nine).

The third, and in my view the most arresting of the three, is the use of anthropological and ethnohistorical methods to study encounters between peoples across cultural borders. Transcultural research is of course not new, but scholars have recently been focusing more precisely on the shatter zones of cultural consciousness and political action, the "middle ground" where new terms of communication, conflict, social interaction, and identity are negotiated.[3] These studies also represent something of a countercurrent to the macro-sociological trend, what Michael Adas refers to as "the impersonal and aggregate-oriented structural approaches that have thus far dominated" world history.[4] Scholars who explore the ways people have culturally represented or constructed ideologies about one another on the terrain of encounter aim in part to ensure that world history does not lose sight of human beings as creative agents, inventing and refashioning the cultural constructs they need to organize knowledge and make sense of the structural changes occurring in the world around them. Adas gives good advice when he urges world historians to undertake research that encompasses

> a variety of levels from the macroanalysis of the workings of global systems to the exploration, insofar as the sources permit, of the everyday, lived experience of individuals in societies drawn into cross-cultural exchanges. To do so, they must infuse the contextual analysis of world systems and structures and aggregate socioeconomic transformations with serious attention to ideas, human agency, and contingency.[5]

Accepting the importance of multilevel inquiry, we must consider just what the broadest possible level might be. For one group of scholars "global history" is not simply a synonym for world history but refers specifically to the study of contemporary processes of globalization. The exponents of global history in this sense contend that this subject is not only a new one but that it *must* be so because only in the past few decades has a full perception of the world as a single and unitary place in the universe dawned in human thought. As a particular approach to the past, global history begins with the present, that is, with our contemporary condition of relentless planetary integration coupled paradoxically with urgent localized quests for communal identity and security. The great puzzle of globalization is that integrative processes related to communications, migration, ecology, trade, finance, popular culture, transnational organization, and so on are not producing any form of "global civilization," let alone fulfilling the meganarrative of the West as synthesizer of all humankind. Integration, rather, is producing a world of endlessly multiplying communities, organizations, firms, professions, networks, religions, and ethno-racial groups, each proclaiming its distinctiveness.

In an excerpt from an essay in the *American Historical Review,* the globalists Michael Geyer and Charles Bright argue that world history must be thoroughly "reimagined." "We arrive at the end of the twentieth century in a global age," they write, "losing our capacity for narrating our histories in conventional ways, outward from one region, but gaining the ability to think world history, pragmatically and realistically, at the interstices of integrating circuits of globalizing networks of power and proliferating sites of localizing politics." Now that humankind has for the first time in history this capacity to "think the world," scholars have an obligation to try to explain how it came to its present state without recourse to the Western or any other culture-specific story line.

Most scholars of the globalization school, including Geyer and Bright, focus almost all their attention on the past one to two hundred years. A few of them, however, look for the beginnings of globalization far back in time, and they may make no rigorous distinction between their project and that of scholars who normally call themselves *world* historians.[6] All writers in this group appear to be united by commitments that distinguish them from, say, sociologically inspired world-systems scholars. One is their environmentalism and abiding sense of planetary holism, the "condition of globality" that they believe should inform all world-historical inquiry. Another is their moral thrust. Bruce Mazlish, one of the leaders of the school, writes with moral urgency about contemporary macrotrends: scholars must not only explain and interpret global processes but cultivate a new "global consciousness or perspective" in order to influence "the process of globalization itself."[7] Or, as Geyer and Bright declare, "For the first time, we as human beings collectively constitute ourselves and, hence, are responsible for ourselves."

Scholars of this persuasion believe that we must step well back from Earth to see globalization in its many manifestations but that we must also situate our inquiry squarely in contemporary times. A different group of writers agrees about the necessity of a planetary vision but aims to construct world history on the largest conceivable level of both time and space. These scholars, David Christian and Fred Spier, the best-known among them, are advocates of "big history." In the preface to his book *The Structure of Big History,* Spier explains this approach as an experiment in both scholarship and teaching:

At the University of Amsterdam, the sociologist Johan Goudsblom and myself, a biochemist, anthropologist and historical sociologist by training, are organizing an interdepartmental course in what Australian historian David Christian calls "Big History." That is: an overview of all known history from the beginning of the Universe until life on Earth today. . . .

In this book, I will advance one single, all-encompassing, theoretical framework for big history. The need for such a scheme arose while considering how to integrate into our course portions of scientific knowledge that are usually widely separated. As a result of this specialization, the various academic disciplines involved, ranging from astronomy to the social sciences, have all developed their own distinct theories, vocabularies and terminologies. And since very few people attempt to bring together all these forms of historical knowledge, the need for a single structuring scheme is rarely felt.

It is therefore not surprising that, as far as I know, no one before has suggested such an outline. However, we think we live in one single, undivided Universe, within one single Solar System, on one single planet, as one humankind, which, like all other living species, has descended from one single lifeform. In order to grasp this unity adequately, we need a type of unified knowledge that is not split along the fault lines of academic specializations, which developed as part of our social history. If we wish to reach a comprehensive understanding of our big past, we must devise one single synthetic scheme that allows us to combine all existing theoretical and factual knowledge.[8]

As Spier notes, David Christian pioneered big history at Macquarie University in Sydney. Christian argues, as have Hodgson and McNeill before him, that the detail required in addressing a historical question "depends purely on the nature of the question being asked." If big questions must be posed about interactions between humans and the changing natural environment within regions, then why not ask even bigger questions about the species as a denizen of the planetary biosphere, the solar system, the cosmos? To Christian, doing big history means exploring the past on all scales "up to the scale of the universe itself," a project that demands interdisciplinary approaches and collaboration far beyond what most world history teachers have thus far contemplated.

Indeed some teachers have protested that big history's empyrean approach to the past dismisses human agency. The record of deeds and events, they say, must not be allowed to drown in a sea of organic slime or vanish into a galactic cloud. On the contrary, says Christian, questions about human origins, evolution, and long-term interaction with the natural and cosmic environments are *historical* questions, and very important ones at that. Understanding creative human action over the very long term ultimately requires considering the largest conceivable context within which the species first appeared, then evolved, and finally transformed itself into a culture-making creature. Christian is surely a champion of environmental history, a branch of world history that is well established and growing. Other scholars in this subfield — Alfred Crosby, William McNeill, John McNeill, Philip Curtin, I. G. Simmons, and Clive Gamble among others — have already achieved in their work a remarkable integration of humanistic, scientific, and social scientific disciplines. As Crosby has written, "Environmental historians have discovered that the physical and life sciences can provide quantities of information and theory useful, even vital, to historical investigation and that scientists try and often succeed in expressing themselves clearly."[9] Christian aims to push interdisciplinary partnerships as far as possible, drawing on astronomy, cosmology, geology, meteorology, and evolutionary biology to fashion a world history that in Spier's words "allows us to combine all existing theoretical and factual knowledge."[10]

Christian argues that the walls between disciplines are "little more than conventions and that breaching them can only be healthy." But is world history on such a cosmic scale of interdisciplinarity likely to arouse interest among students and the reading public? If the huge success of Jared Diamond's Pulitzer Prize-winning book *Guns, Germs, and Steel: The Fates of Human Societies* is any indication, indeed it will. Several years ago when Diamond was in New Guinea, he took a walk one day with a local man named Yali. At one point Yali asked, "Why is it that you white people developed so much cargo and brought it to New Guinea, but we black people had little cargo of our own?"[11] In *Guns, Germs, and Steel* Diamond rephrases the question: "Why did wealth and power become distributed as they are now are, rather than the other way around? For instance, why weren't Native Americans, Africans, and Aboriginal Australians the ones who decimated, subjugated, or exterminated Europeans and Asians?"[12] These questions are hardly new to world history teachers, who for the past forty years or more have challenged students to grapple with the problem of "the rise of the West." Diamond, however, locates these questions in global space and in a time frame of thirteen thousand years of broad environmental and technological change. His big history is not quite so big as Christian's and Spier's, but like those historians he believes that if scholars are to pose giant questions, they should be prepared to draw on any discipline that might contribute to a holistic and persuasive answer. Also like Christian and Spier, he is convinced that even if the historical profession's early pretensions to qualify the discipline as a science are no longer convincing, history should collaborate with, not separate itself from, the other "historical sciences" such as cosmology and evolutionary biology. The final selection in this book is Diamond's reflection on "the future of human history as a science." Whether they agree with him or not, world history teachers should be encouraged by his success at reaching so many thinking people with his big vision of our growing field.

Notes

1. Critics of multiculturalism sometimes accuse its proponents of substituting for Eurocentrism other forms of cultural arrogance and exclusivism, such as Afrocentrism. I would not, however, regard Afrocentrism, especially its more extreme propositions, as expressing the multiculturalist tradition.

2. See Part Eight.

3. See Richard White, *The Middle Ground: Indians, Empires, and Republics in the Great Lakes Region, 1650–1815* (Cambridge: Cambridge University Press, 1991).

4. Michael Adas, "Bringing Ideas and Agency Back In," in *World History: Ideologies, Structures, and Identities,* ed. Philip Pomper, Richard H. Elphick, and Richard T. Vann, 81–104 (Malden, Mass.: Blackwell, 1998).

5. Adas, "Bringing Ideas and Agency Back In," 97.

6. One example is Robert P. Clark, *The Global Imperative: An Interpretive History of the Spread of Humankind,* which is annotated in the bibliography.

7. Bruce Mazlish, "An Introduction to Global History," in *Conceptualizing Global History,* ed. Bruce Mazlish and Ralph Buultjens (Boulder, Colo.: Westview Press, 1993).

8. Fred Spier, *The Structure of Big History: From the Big Bang to Today* (Amsterdam: Amsterdam University Press, 1996), vii–viii.

9. Alfred W. Crosby, "The Past and Present of Environmental History," *American Historical Review* 100 (October 1995): 1189.

10. For the syllabus of "Introduction to Global History," a "big history" course taught at the University of California, Santa Cruz, see <http://wwwcatsic.ucsc.edu/~hist80a>.

11. Jared Diamond, *Guns, Germs, and Steel: The Fates of Human Societies* (New York: W.W. Norton, 1997), 14.

12. Diamond, *Guns, Germs, and Steel,* 15.

JERRY H. BENTLEY

New Directions

In several ways, professional historians have addressed the challenge of world history and have generated substantial bodies of scholarly literature in the process. Their works do not always deal literally with the entire world, but they illuminate some of the most influential large-scale processes in world history. Analyses of technological development and diffusion; large-scale economic and social patterns; and environmental, ecological, and biological processes have enriched historians' understanding of the larger dynamics of world history even when they have concentrated attention on interactions between selected regions rather than the entire globe.

On the basis of recently published studies, indications are that scholarship in world history is branching out in several new directions. . . . Three emerging lines of study briefly discussed here include: efforts at the analysis of cross-cultural encounters informed by anthropological and ethnohistorical insights, a revival of comparative macrosociology, and the development of gender analysis in global perspective.

Anthropological and ethnohistorical inspiration has been most important for scholars examining the results of encounters between peoples of different civilizations or cultural regions. When peoples of different traditions became engaged in cross-cultural encounters, how did they establish communications and negotiate political, social, economic, and cultural relationships? How did they mediate differences and clashes between their respective sets of cultural values and expectations? How did differential political, military, or economic capacities affect the various parties engaged in cross-cultural encounter? How is it possible to account for the phenomenon of deculturation or for the process by which individuals abandoned their inherited traditions and adopted the cultural standards of other peoples? To what extent have embattled cultural traditions survived, or even undergone revival, after being overwhelmed by alien traditions often accompanied by advanced technologies, political support, and massive military might? Since anthropologists and ethnohistorians have long studied human cultural traditions in their broader political, social, and economic contexts, it comes as little surprise that historians have found their works suggestive

Jerry H. Bentley, *Shapes of World History in Twentieth-Century Scholarship* (Washington, D.C.: American Historical Association, 1996), 21–26.

in addressing these questions about the dynamics and the results of cross-cultural encounters.

Even when anthropologists and ethnohistorians have not specifically intended their works as contributions to world history, they have often thrown useful light on the dynamics of cross-cultural encounters. In *Islands and Beaches: Discourses on a Silent Land: Marquesas, 1774–1880*, for example, Greg Dening explored the early stages of the encounter between Europeans and Polynesians in the Marquesas. He found mostly cultural misunderstanding and alienation, ending ultimately in Marquesan deculturation. Both Europeans and Marquesan cultures presented a challenge to the other, but Europeans approached the islands in large numbers equipped with firearms, alcohol, and exotic diseases. Although Marquesans displayed considerable resilience, the avalanche of novelties that overwhelmed them had the effect of weakening traditional sanctions, undermining established roles, and dissolving the sinews of Marquesan culture. Ultimately, then, the encounter between Europeans and Marquesans resulted in the collapse of traditional Marquesan culture, without even the provision of a valid and thriving alternative.

Yet cultural survival, revival, and creation are also prominent themes in world history. Richard Price's fascinating studies of the Saramaka maroons — particularly *First-Time: The Historical Vision of an Afro-American People* and *Alabi's World* — chronicle the Saramakas' remarkable building and maintenance of a community in Surinam in the face of overwhelming odds. Similarly, David Hanlon's *Upon a Stone Altar: A History of the Island of Pohnpei to 1890* emphasizes the survival of embattled cultural traditions on a small island deluged by foreign influences.

Anthropological and ethnohistorical studies of cross-cultural interaction in the Americas suggest that deculturation was hardly uncommon when a people ravaged by devastating epidemic disease faced another people equipped with powerful weapons and technologies. Two works merit mention for their insightful examinations of the encounter between Spaniards and the Maya of the Yucatan peninsula: Nancy M. Farriss' *Maya Society under Colonial Rule: The Collective Enterprise of Survival* and Inga Clendinnen's *Ambivalent Conquests: Maya and Spaniard in Yucatan, 1517–1570*. Both works showed that the Maya nobility struggled to maintain the integrity of Maya traditions. Ultimately, however, as in the Marquesas, Maya culture largely succumbed to European numbers, weapons, and diseases. Some elements of Maya culture survived by adapting to Christian standards; thus, for example, the Maya readily embraced cults of the saints — particularly those whose feast days coincided with significant points in the traditional Maya calendar. By the nineteenth century, however, integration into an alien political, social, and economic system had largely devastated traditional Maya culture.

The encounter between Europeans and the indigenous peoples of North America followed a similar pattern. The works of James Axtell—most notably *The European and the Indian: Essays in the Ethnohistory of Colonial North America; After Columbus: Essays in the Ethnohistory of Colonial North America;*

The Invasion Within: The Contest of Cultures in Colonial North America; and *Beyond 1492: Encounters in Colonial North America* — concentrated on the early stages of this encounter, before Europeans overwhelmed the indigenous peoples. In *The Middle Ground: Indians, Empires, and Republics in the Great Lakes Region, 1650–1815,* Richard White offered a subtle analysis of the mechanisms by which Europeans and indigenous peoples established and maintained political, social, and commercial relations. In the visions of both Axtell and White, indigenous peoples played prominent roles in the making of North American history, often forcing Europeans to make adjustments in order to survive. Over the longer term, though, for indigenous peoples the European presence in North America brought demographic collapse, ecological imbalance, dependence on trade goods from abroad, heightened intertribal tensions, psychological despair, alcoholism, and deculturation. By the nineteenth century, waves of European and African immigrants had largely overwhelmed the indigenous peoples of North America.

By paying close attention to power relationships, several scholars have thrown new light on processes of cross-cultural encounter during the age of European imperialism. In *Between Worlds: Interpreters, Guides, and Survivors,* Frances Karttunen offered sixteen well-focused case studies of individuals who served as cross-cultural intermediaries — translators, interpreters, guides, and informants — mostly between indigenous peoples and representatives of Western imperial powers. Her analysis suggested that cross-cultural intermediaries have historically been individuals with unusual gifts, but that they have often become alienated by their own societies and marginalized by the foreign peoples whom they served. Two books by Michael P. Adas — *Prophets of Rebellion: Millenarian Protest Movements against the European Colonial Order* and *Machines as the Measure of Men: Science, Technology, and Ideologies of Western Dominance* — examined cultural clashes between Europeans and peoples of other societies during the imperial era. Both works explored the cultural dimensions of colonial encounters: the first by showing that European intrusion commonly provoked spirited reactions based on cultural and religious traditions of long standing; the second by showing that Europeans evaluated other peoples on the basis of their technological arsenals and formed ideologies of imperial dominance on the strength of their evaluations. European imperial ventures were the context also for Mary Louise Pratt's *Imperial Eyes: Travel Writing and Transculturation.* Concentrating on nineteenth-century travel accounts dealing with Africa and South America, Pratt argued that writers clearly reflected the interests of European imperial powers when they offered representations of the lands and peoples of Africa and South America.

Finally, two scholars have addressed the theme of cross-cultural encounter on a very large scale. Mary W. Helms examined the political and cultural effects of long-distance travel and the possession of foreign wisdom in *Ulysses' Sail: An Ethnographic Odyssey of Knowledge, Power, and Geographical Distance.* In both ancient and modern times, knowledge and recognition from afar often carried considerable cachet, and Helms's work explores some of the ways that peoples have made political and cultural uses of distant authority. In *Old World Encounters: Cross-Cultural Contacts and Exchanges in Pre-Modern Times*, Jerry H. Bentley undertook an analysis of cross-cultural encounters as global processes and identified patterns of cross-cultural conversion, conflict, and compromise that resulted from those encounters. He argued that cultural traditions did not readily cross boundary lines, that adoption of foreign values and cultural standards rarely took place except with the encouragement of powerful political, social, or economic influences. Even successful cases of cross-cultural conversion did not involve a process of exact cultural replication — the cloning, as it were, of a cultural tradition in new circumstances — but rather a merger of traditions by a process of syncretism. Again, then, the phenomenon of cross-cultural encounter emerges as a principal theme of world history. Given the significance of cross-cultural interactions in world history, it seems likely that anthropological and ethnohistorical studies will continue to work their influence in the literature of world history.

Alongside the increasing influence of anthropological and ethnohistorical approaches, recent years have also seen a revival of comparative macrosociology. Two recently published works fall in the tradition of Barrington Moore's famous study, *Social Origins of Dictatorship and Democracy: Lord and Peasant in the Making of the Modern World*, which explored the significance of social relations for the emergence of democratic and authoritarian polities in modern times. As represented in Theda Skocpol's *States and Social Revolutions* and Jack Goldstone's *Revolution and Rebellion in the Early Modern World*, this approach is more eclectic than earlier macrosociology, much of which fell rather clearly in either a Weberian or a Marxist camp. Moore, Skocpol, and Goldstone all drew inspiration from both Max Weber and Karl Marx, but without making irrevocable commitments to either, and also without ignoring alternative sources of inspiration. The result is a macrosociological perspective that is more analytically flexible and historically sensitive than those generally found in studies more firmly committed to Weber or Marx.

Skocpol's *States and Social Revolutions*, for example, not only analyzes the phenomenon of social revolution in France, Russia, and China with questions of class conflict in mind, but also represents part of a larger effort of macrosociologists to "bring the state back in" when dealing with large-scale social processes. Goldstone's *Revolution and Rebellion in the Early Modern World* seeks to explain revolution and rebellion not simply as expressions of class conflict, but also as a result of more fundamental population pressures that manifested themselves throughout early modern Eurasia. The works of Moore, Skocpol, and Goldstone all represent ambitious attempts to identify principles and dynamics that guide modern world history. Though it is too early to say whether or not comparative macrosociology will develop into a flourishing enterprise, the studies of Skocpol and Goldstone suggest that interest in the approach is growing. If it continues to develop, comparative macrosociology will certainly offer valuable perspectives for purposes of global historical analysis.

A third new direction in recent scholarship in world history involves the incorporation of methods and insights from the literature of women's history and gender analysis. Since women's history and gender analysis have emerged only recently as fields of study, most of the scholarly literature adopts national or regional rather than global frameworks of analysis. Even the most important large-scale interpretations — such as Gerda Lerner's two books, *The Creation of Patriarchy* and *The Creation of Feminist Consciousness: From the Middle Ages to Eighteen-Seventy*, or the two-volume study of Bonnie S. Anderson and Judith P. Zinsser, *A History of Their Own: Women in European History from Prehistory to the Present* — deal largely with a single civilization and do not undertake comparative or cross-cultural analyses beyond the Western experience.

Increasingly, however, scholars have begun to recognize possibilities for comparative and cross-cultural studies of women's history and gender analysis. In their edited volume, *Writing Women's History: International Perspectives*, Karen Offen, Ruth Roach Pierson, and Jane Rendall assembled a series of essays highlighting the global reverberations of women's history and gender analysis. Despite widely varying conditions in which scholars work in different lands — not to mention the even more varied historical experiences of women in different lands — *Writing Women's History* points toward cross-cultural studies and global analysis on themes of women and gender. Margaret Strobel's *European Women and the Second British Empire* illustrates the rich potential of such studies by examining the roles and experiences of European women in colonial societies. Though it focuses on European women, Strobel's work has deep cross-cultural implications, because in their capacities as missionaries, teachers, and organizers of women's associations, European women influenced the experiences of both women and men in colonized lands. The tightly focused essays in *Western Women and Imperialism: Complicity and Resistance*, edited by Nupur Chaudhuri and Margaret Strobel, also reveal the potential of cross-cultural studies that bring the perspectives of women's history and gender analysis to bear on colonial societies. Thus, like the other two new directions taken by the recent literature in world history mentioned above, the emergence of a school that draws on methods and insights from women's history and gender analysis holds unusual promises for purposes of global historical studies.

MICHAEL GEYER
CHARLES BRIGHT

World History in a Global Age

Th[e] reimagining of the world as history is under way. In the past decade or so, world history has become one of the fastest growing areas of teaching. More slowly and hesitantly, a body of scholarly writing has been emerging, branching out from the discontents of Western Civilization surveys and addressing world historical issues. While this turn, in part, may be explained by the economies of higher and secondary education (it is cheaper to hire one Third World generalist than five or six civilizations specialists) and, in part, may reflect the incandescence of the "world" on and for television, a nascent scholarship has set out to rethink the presence of all the world's pasts. It is still a hesitant and fledgling historiography, which remains mired in the old, unsure of its scholarly status, and with a tendency to service existing knowledge rather than create new knowledge. But a start has been made, and its impetus comes from many places, a great diversity of scholars, and a variety of disciplines. To present the world's pasts as history or, more likely, as a raid of intertwined histories is, once again, a shared concern; and, while not yet a viable academic program, it emerges, if only in the most general terms, as the agenda for world history today.

There are many ways to approach this agenda, including the most venerable and by all counts still-prevalent one, which imitates creation histories and proceeds "from the muck to the stars." The most interesting advances in historiographic knowledge, however, fall into roughly two camps. One of them has developed out of grand civilizational studies, with William H. McNeill and Marshall Hodgson as its godfathers. While McNeill had a strongly materialist and developmentalist bias and Hodgson leaned, in the manner of his time, toward an essentialist history of civilizations, recent initiatives are mainly concerned with the comparative history of ancient and medieval empires. The proponents of this approach aim, ultimately, at a comparative history of power, with the wider issue of "civilization" (what it is and what it does) lingering uneasily in the background. Perhaps, intellectually, the most intriguing venue of this research derives from the rarely acknowledged queries of Canadian scholar and theorist Harold Innis into the nature of empire. One effect of this kind of history

Michael Geyer and Charles Bright, "World History in a Global Age," *American Historical Review* 100 (October 1995): 1037–52, 1058–60.

is to position the West in the context of the world, especially Asia — both its un-exceptional history on a world historical scale and its truly exceptional late rise. The contemporary sequel of this history is the discussion of the rise and fall of great powers and the nature of large civilizational conflict in the manner of Friedrich Ratzel's and Karl Haushofer's geopolitics. The fact that this approach, as it focuses on the rise and fall of the American hegemon, promises also to his-toricize the United States, robbing this nation of its sublime presence as history entirely of and for itself, has made it a matter of political contention in historio-graphic debate but also a source of some fascination.

The other strand of world history is somewhat less well sorted out but has at-tracted an altogether more adventurous crowd of scholars from around the world. It has its origins in the histories of discovery, maritime empires, and no-madic formations — including, not least, the histories of forced and voluntary migration. It is a history of mobility and mobilization, of trade and merchants, of migrants and diasporas, of travelers and communication. It is a history, ulti-mately, of rootlessness with the more general issue of "nomadism" or its mar-itime equivalent, "piracy," shadowing it. Key words for this history are "dias-pora" and "borderlands," both as the "privileged site for the articulation of [national] distinction" and as the site for hybrid and mixed identities, created at the crossroads of many histories. This history comes in many contemporary (Hong-Kong Chinese, Indian, Jewish, Palestinian, Chicano, Asian-American, and Caribbean) as well as ancient (Hellenism, Inner Asia) or localist (Silesia, the Alsace, Michigan's Upper Peninsula) inflections. But in view of the cos-mopolitan airs of diaspora scholarship, it must be said that this approach is also the most recent version of an old American dream that cherishes, against all parochialism, the moments of a new beginning and the freedom of movement and expression necessary to that end. It comes as no surprise that this history flows easily into contemporary literary concerns with diasporic cultures and into anthropological studies of hybrid spaces, as these are championed by scholars such as Homi Bhabha and Arjun Appadurai, the present avatars of an old Chicago tradition.

A renewed interest in the histories of the world has thus found discrete sub-jects for study and teaching that can be expanded through time and space with-out — and, in fact, in deliberate and scholarly correction of — the biases of older world imaginings. It is a history that avoids the trap of setting one's own civiliza-tion against barbarisms everywhere else and deploys questions and frameworks in which "local" history can flourish while becoming more aware of its global historicity. As with any fledgling historiography, there are clumsy moments and unhelpful turns, but none of this should detract from the fact that a viable gen-eral history of the world's pasts is in the making, and we may hope that, at the next centenary, many more essays on world history will have been published in this journal.

To further that end, let the contention begin. The central challenge of a re-newed world history at the end of the twentieth century is to narrate the world's pasts in an age of globality. It is this condition of globality that facilitates the revival of world history and establishes its point of departure in the "actually existing" world of the late twentieth century. While this assertion may raise alarms about undue presentism, it will also dramatize the new situation historians face, which is neither the fulfillment of one particular history nor a compendium of all the world's histories. World history in the late twentieth century must be concerned with these conditions of its own existence.

Presentism only becomes a serious danger if the history of our world is constructed teleologically, as if all previous history leads to the present condition. But the grand meta-narratives of Western world history, grounded in an Enlightenment vision of universal humanity and a nineteenth-century practice of comparative civilizations, ceased to produce explanations at precisely the moment that a global history became possible and a history of our own age and of the condition of globality is necessary. The project of universal history that sought to narrate the grand civilizations comparatively was always an implicit meditation on Western exceptionalism and, as the West moved (comparatively) "ahead," a justification for Western domination. But it experienced increasing difficulty thinking beyond separate and "authentic" civilizations to the processes that were making a (new) world of sustained and deepening imbrication — that is, comprehending the kind of continuous and irreversible meshing of trajectories that dissolved autonomous civilizations and collapsed separate histories. World history, with Western history writ larger than others, did not turn out as the narrative prophesied, and historians, becoming perplexed by the present, turned away from the twentieth century and sought to make the early modern period look like the present ought to have looked if the teleologies of world history had worked out. This effort to get a running start on the present by going back in time amounted to a refusal to think about the world actually being made in the course of the twentieth century, and it has left us, at the end of that century, with no pivot of analysis and no way of narrating this century.

But, while the world as it is has been orphaned by the collapse of world historical narratives, this is not a loss that can be remedied by a more all-in, encyclopedic approach, as if equal time for all the world's histories will make history whole. Not only is a compendium of all histories likely to be bulky and unpresentable, something historians find distasteful and open to error and sloppiness, but it misses the nature of the break that constitutes world history in a global age. As such, it is compensatory history. World history in a global age proceeds differently. The recovery of the multiplicity of the world's pasts matters now more than ever, not for reasons of coverage but because, in a global age, the world's pasts are all simultaneously present, colliding, interacting, intermixing — producing a collage of present histories that is surely not the history of a homogeneous global civilization. Much hinges on the ability of historians to effect this recovery archivally, analytically, and intellectually. But, in bringing out this history, it is important to realize that the condition of globality that characterizes our age is no more the sum of all pasts than it is the fulfillment of a special (Western) past. Indeed, if every past were for itself, and every history leaked

over into its present, there would be no world history at all. It is precisely the
rupture between the present condition of globality and its many possible pasts
that gives the new world history its distinctive ground and poses the familiar historical questions, which do not, as yet, have clear answers: when and how was
the history of our world, with its characteristic condition of accelerating integration and proliferating difference, torn off from the many histories of the world's
pasts and set upon its separate course?

How and where to launch a specifically twentieth-century world history that is
neither an archaeology of comparative civilizations nor the history of one region's past writ large? Academic debate in international relations would suggest
that we begin with 1917 and make it a very short century of permanent crises and
contestations over world leadership, running through the two world wars and
the ups and downs of the Cold War, ending with the collapse of the Soviet empire and the reunification of Europe in 1989–1990 or with the break-up of the
USSR in 1991. This approach captures major aspects of twentieth-century development, to be sure, but it also presumes a world centered on a European-
Atlantic core (ignoring East Asian politics altogether) and ends on a triumphalist note that not only effaces continuing contestation over world politics but
reaffirms the notion that, at the end of the twentieth century, the "world revolution of westernization" is the only significant story. Thus advocates of a "short"
twentieth century converge with early modern specialists and world-systems theorists, who cannot start early enough and, turning their main attention to the
emergent empires and the world economy of the Atlantic, treat the integration
of the world as a culmination of the long rise of the West. Both these perspectives on the twentieth century end up writing world history in terms of a single
region, when in fact it is the imbrication of all regions into a world at once more
integrated and more fragmented that constitutes the specific problematic of
world history in a global age.
   An alternative view, pioneered by critics of Western imperialism and theorists of dependency, would anchor twentieth-century world history in world-
wide patterns of resistance against the imposition of Western rule. Nationalism
and communism were the confluent currents of this program, and the (re)con-
stitution of autonomy was its end. In linking the Soviet challenge (a "Second
World" break-out) with anti-colonial movements (a "Third World" renewal),
this approach sought to counter Eurocentric world history with the assertion of
subordinated peoples engaged in coordinated struggle. Yet this proved no more
secure as a framework of world history than did Western triumphalism, and not
simply because communism has collapsed and the nationalist project has
fizzled. The century ends with the world being drawn together as never before
but with peoples asserting difference and rejecting sameness on an unprecedented global scale. This is not a residuum of the past receding before a triumphant westernization, whatever the expectations that prevailed in the early
1980s, but it is not a renewal of autonomy either, whatever the promises
of the Iranian revolution. Rather, the recent waves of racism, nationalism,

fundamentalism, and communalism register, in the context of an accelerated global integration, the continuing irreducibility of the "local." Here lies a key to world history in the global age: for the progress of global integration and the attending struggles among would-be hegemons have persistently set loose contests over identity — or sovereignty, to use an old-fashioned but appropriate term — and for autonomy that, time and again, have renewed difference in the face of integration and thus continued to fragment the world even as it became one.

This history of world-wide contestations requires the perspectives of a "long" twentieth century. For as long as we continue to assume that the world is moving toward a homogeneous or westernized end, in which "traditional" and "other" societies take up modernizing paths toward a new global civilization, discrete regional histories are interesting only as a kind of "prehistory" specifying what went wrong with "others" and why the West won out. But once we acknowledge, reflecting on the conditions of the present world, that the processes of global integration have not homogenized the whole but produced continuing and ever-renewing contestations over the terms of global integration itself, then the histories of all regions (and their changing spatial, political, and cultural composition) become immediately relevant to world history — and not simply for reasons of equity or to establish the "essential" qualities of their civilizations but as actors and participants in the very processes being narrated. This history begins in the nineteenth century, more specifically in the grand transitions of the middle decades of that century.

Until that point, global development rested on a series of overlapping, interacting, but basically autonomous regions, each engaged in processes of self-organization and self-reproduction. This is a reality represented very successfully in the narrative and analytic conventions of comparative civilizations and empire studies. One would not want to discount the remarkable expansion of European-Atlantic maritime empires nor forget the deepening connections and interactions between regions, nor ultimately the growing role of European merchants, mariners, scholars, and especially soldiers in forging these interactions. But on a global scale and even within the maritime empires of the West, contacts between self-sustaining centers of power had more to do with keeping distance than with establishing relations. Contacts between regional centers extended *relationally* across space from one center to its margins and through physical (ocean and deserts) and social (nomadic and piratical) zones of transition to adjacent centers and distant others. Distance, hence space, remained crucial in governing the conduct of commerce and in the exercise of power. Moreover, on all sides, distance shaped global imaginings as regional *imaginaires* that went outward to envelop the world from distinct regional centers. Politically, economically, intellectually, and militarily, these patterns of regional autonomy, maintained by spatial distantiation and linked by specialized mediators and interlopers, organized the world at least until the middle of the nineteenth century.

A dramatic and rapid alteration took place during the course of that century, however. We cannot understand this transition if we focus exclusively on Europe or the surge of European and, for that matter, Japanese industrial and military power after mid-century, as undoubtedly important as these became. The crucial watershed inaugurating twentieth-century world history consisted in a series of parallel, simultaneous crises in the organization of power, production, and culture — that is, in the autonomous reproduction — of virtually every region of the world. A simple recitation of the wars and revolts that registered deeper systemic crises — the Taiping rebellion and civil war in China, which led to a revamping of imperial administration (and the regional breaking away of Japan toward industrialization), the Crimean War along the Eurasian seam, which provoked regime crises in both the Russian and Ottoman empires (with regional breakaways in Poland and Egypt), the multi-layered revolt against British rule in India, the war of extermination against Paraguay in Latin America, the Civil War in the United States, the white and black (re)settlement wars in southern Africa, the crisis of the post-Napoleonic concert, and the spate of wars for national unification (Italy, Germany, Spain, and Serbia) in Europe — may seem a random selection. They were, above all, crises of regional power and stability, reflecting autonomous trajectories of development. There was no single cause or prime mover at work, for they arose from indigenous causes and had their own chronologies. What made these violent crises transitional for world history was that, in every case, they were played out in the context of deeper and more competitive interactions among regions, the competitive driven largely (but not exclusively) by more vigorous European interventions. The result everywhere was that solutions to regional crises came to involve not simply efforts at restoration or conservation but strategies of self-renewal and self-improvement: the famous Chinese strategy of "adopting the ways of the barbarian in order to defeat the barbarian."

These interactions had "globalizing" effects. Solutions to regional crises involved a sustained recourse to interregional adaptations and appropriations. Regional development — that is, the self-preservation of imperial regimes — thus became predicated on quickly growing, interregional, and, quite literally, "globalizing" exchange, ending an era of self-sufficiency. Whether efforts at self-improvement succeeded or not, they began as proactive responses to specific regional crises, and they developed a competitive synchronicity that lifted regional interactions to a new global level, to a sustained, continuous, competitive, and often violent contact. The margins and peripheries that had assured distance evaporated, and the spaces between regions of once-autonomous development collapsed. Old ideas, expressed in the many ways of imagining the world, world space, and interregional relations across distance, gave way to new global imaginations. Again, the difference is tangible though rarely explored. For this imagination saw every part of the world (including one's own) in its relationships to others, and all engaged in a dangerous game of mutual imbrication; and, while this nascent "global" imagination saw the world as an interconnected whole, it saw these connections differently from every vantage point. In this way, processes of global integration were inaugurated, not simply by an expansionist Europe unilaterally superimposing itself on a passive world ripe for victimization but in a scramble of autonomous power centers, each struggling to mobilize its resources in the face of internal crisis and intensified interactions with other regions. This situation constitutes the rupture that marks the beginning of world history in a global age.

The process of globalization was not simply an acceleration along a continuum of European expansion but a new ordering of relations of domination and subordination among all regions of the world. This fact captures the revolutionizing quality of the European departure at mid-century. Unlike other regions in crisis at the mid-century passage, Europe alone resolved its regional crisis by turning outward, externalizing its quest for solutions in projections of power overseas, and it did so not by conquests in the old manner of empire building, through spatial expansion and occupation, but in a new effort, with new capabilities, to synchronize global time and coordinate interactions *within* the world. This development — the metaphors matter here: this was no longer quite a "thrust" or "projection" of force but an exercise in "webbing" or "enveloping" — was sustained by new technologies, especially the telegraph and, later on, radio and telephones, but it was fully articulated in transnational regimes of power made possible by the formation of communications-based systems of control (the gold standard, the global deployment of maritime force, or the futures markets) that began to envelop the world in global circuits of power by the end of the century. These systems of control, which proliferated throughout the long twentieth century, were the key that enabled a "new" European imperialism to exploit the self-improving strategies of all other regions, adapting the dynamics of competitive interaction among regions to move beyond mere extensions of power "over" others to the direct, sustained organization "of " others in global regimes of control. In this way, the European-Atlantic world became "the West" and gained its status as the centering axis of an integrating world.

As the dynamics of regional crisis drove Europe outward along externalizing paths, European initiatives collided, overlapped, and interacted with the dynamics of parallel crises in other regions and with strategies of competitive self-improvement that were devised to shore up regional power and to fend off or contain external pressures. Historiographic attention focuses on East Asia, but elements of these struggles can be observed in the Indian, Persian, Arab, African, and Latin American worlds as well. As regional power centers moved to defend autonomy, Europeans found in these self-improvement efforts the pathways and the allies for further and deeper intervention. This was a profoundly disruptive, extremely violent, and often callous process, but it was never simply the plunder of compradors. Instead, Western expansionism picked up and amplified regional and local processes of self-mobilization, permeating and transforming them in the course of using them. The projections of Western power were thus locally articulated as self-mobilizations and absorbed into the very fabric of local affairs — causing wider ramifications of change, much of it beyond the view, let alone the control, of European powers, but also beginning processes of utterly dependent integration that deepened as self-improvement strategies took hold.

Global integration was thus not a set of procedures devised in the West and superimposed on the rest as if a compliant world waited for its victimization, but, for this very reason, neither was global integration flatly or consistently rejected. Rather, intregration was carried forward, asymmetrically and unevenly, on a global scale. India and Egypt, as well as Argentina, China, Persia, and Africa, became victims of Western expansionism and of outright aggression. But imperialism was also able to exist because Indians, Egyptians, Argentines, Chinese, Persians, and Africans helped make it happen, and not simply as lackeys and dupes but pursuing strategies of renewal that synchronized in the web of European-dominated global regimes. Running at full tilt themselves, they engaged Western power in complex patterns of collaboration and resistance, accommodation and cooptation, as they tried (often against great odds but also, we may add, with remarkable success) to reproduce and renew local worlds, using imperialists to shore up or to create positions of power, using sites of indigenous power to make deals, using the European and American positions as interlopers in order to selectively appropriate the ways of the conquerors to local ends. In this way, *they* were the ones to produce the resources for global integration, creating in the process a more integrated world, albeit not exactly as Western imperialists had intended. Global integration was built with this kind of labor.

The surpluses of this labor forged an ever tighter (if always competitive and contested) concentration of power within the West. That is, military power was projected everywhere, but nowhere was it more concentrated and lethal than within the European region. State power was extended as colonial regimes throughout Asia and Africa, even as state power became concentrated and coordinated in Europe. Western communication and transportation systems reached into every corner of the world, yet nowhere were the linkages denser or their impact more far-reaching than in the European-Atlantic region. Industrial goods were available and traded everywhere, but both trade and production were most heavily concentrated and grew most rapidly in the core region. The intensification and concentration of capitalist production went hand in hand with its global extension, binding the world together in tighter, if always uneven and unequal, global circuits of power, capital, and culture.

Within this integrating world, Europeans and Americans increasingly drew the lines of demarcation that defined an emergent global center over and against the rest. Global integration entailed a spatial reorganization of human and capital mobility that came to the fore in a rush of imperial imaginings by travelers, expatriates, civil servants, and armchair enthusiasts. These were elaborated into universal knowledge in a set of new imperial sciences: geography, ethnology, and biology being pioneer disciplines of the day. It was also toward the end of the nineteenth century that barriers were erected to control the movements of non-European peoples and a more rigid racial segregation was devised to define white privilege and to ensure control over racial "others," not only in colonial and semi-colonial environments but very much at the centers of power as well. Racism became deeply entrenched in legal, social, and cultural practices. This division of people underwrote a new global division of labor that separated, world-wide, capital-intensive industrial production from handicrafts and extraction, agriculture from industry, and was further reinforced by new procedures for allocating and controlling the movement of wealth, grounded in the international acceptance of the gold standard and of financial rules enforced, primarily, by the Bank of England. Across an integrating world, new lines of segregation and distinction were thus drawn and powerfully imagined in racialist world views that set the white European-Atlantic region and its dispersed settlements around the world apart from the rest and ensured their privilege.

The deepening chasms that divided an increasingly integrated world, together with the proliferating distinctions between "us" and "them" that were handed down as social sciences (modern/traditional, advanced/backward) and constituted Western discourse about the rest, swallowed up the older, enlightened imagination of "humanity" that had previously informed world history narratives. As difference and distinction grew within an integrating world, the overarching simplicities of universal history were supplanted by naturalized histories of the "rest" — studied as the grand traditions of world civilizations in the humanities — and by a specialized and instrumental knowledge about progress — pursued as development and modernization theories in the social sciences. The West (in fact, a few core European states, subsequently enlarged to a European-North Atlantic world and only belatedly extended to the Pacific rim) *gained* in this process a new intellectual identity as a discrete region. Europe was constituted as the West in the context of forging a unified, scientific narrative for an integrating world. This was, one might add, a secular West that in the science of modernizing the world found a counter to and a strategy for surpassing its older religious identity as the site of (Latin) Christianity in juxtaposition, internally, to Judaism and, externally, to Islam. That Islam became a powerful and modernizing global imagination in its own right during the course of the long twentieth century (and not merely in the last two decades or so) is commonly forgotten.

The paradigm of global modernization was powerful knowledge with an unequivocal vision of the world to come. It underwrote a new narrative of world history, which left behind the pieties of Enlightenment thought. This history of a world being integrated predicted, first, that in dominating the world through its mastery of the technical and material means of global integration, the West would actually control the world and be able to shape the course of global development, and, second, that in shaping the world, the West held secure knowledge, positive empirical proof in its own development, of the direction and outcome of world history. The world would become more like the West in a protracted process of modernization, and, as the rest of the world moved toward uplift and progress, the division between "the West" and "the rest" would diminish.

It did not happen this way. First, efforts to establish global order proved notoriously unstable and short-lived. The two most powerful ventures, the *pax britannica* in the first half and the *pax americana* in the second half of the long twentieth century, came and went quickly as world-ordering efforts. Neither was able to transform a staggering superiority in force into lasting political order — that is, into a consensual global politics as opposed to domination and the threat of violence. This proved to be the single most abiding limitation on the West's ability to realize global control. Second, it did not happen this way because Western mastery of the powers of production and destruction (and of the scientific knowledge that underwrote it) never imparted a sure capacity to shape and mold the world into a homogeneous global civilization. What Western exertions produced instead was a disorderly world of proliferating difference, a world in which the very production of difference was lodged in the processes of globalization that the West had presumed to control. Even where difference was partially overcome by non-Western efforts to emulate and surpass Western productivity — a path taken by Japan and later, others in the northeast Asian region, for example — the power of the Western narrative, with its presumption of control and its racist exclusions, masked emergent dynamics of integration.

Thus not only did the destination remain cloudy but emergent realities in the global age ground powerfully against available images and expectations — creating a profound dissonance and proliferating fissures in the narration of the present. These are the signatures of accelerated times or, as Jacob Burckhardt called them, "world historical crises." This is, or should be, an exhilarating moment for historians, for it is now possible to set the *res gestae* of the origins of our actually existing world against the predictions and expectations of the past — no longer in order to announce the pending unification of the world or to criticize explanations and ideologies heretofore used but to account for the world as it is. Narrating world history in our global age means taking seriously (rather than fleeing from) the present. And it means recovering the spirit and intent of historical inquiry, as it is practiced in archival research, and adapting this to the task of writing contemporary history. For the basic operation of any modern *Historik* consists in teasing out the fissures and tensions between what happened (inasmuch as the sources allow us to tell) and what is said to have happened (in the lore, ideologies, imaginings, and general assumptions of contemporaries and memorialists). For modern historians, archival research is "investigative" practice. It is in applying these procedures to the present condition that we can begin to explore the question of endings.

"The infinite lies outside of experience, and experience is the sphere of history." At the end of the twentieth century, we encounter, not a universalizing and single modernity but an integrated world of multiple and multiplying modernities. As far as world history is concerned, there is no universalizing spirit, no *Weltgeist*, to be re/presented working its way out in history. There are, instead, many very specific, very material and pragmatic practices that await critical reflection and historical study. At the same time, there is no particular knowledge to be generalized or built up from these discrete practices into a general theory or global paradigm. Rather, there is general and global knowledge, actually in operation, that requires particularization to the local and human scale. Fundamentally, then, our basic strategies of historical narration have to be rethought in order to make sense of practices and processes of global integration and local differentiation that have come into play. Lacking an imagination capable of articulating an integrated world of multiple modernities, globality is enveloped in an eery silence, which, however, cannot mask its powerful effects; and contestations over the terms of globalization, lacking a language that can accommodate, even facilitate, difference, turn into implacably hostile rejections of otherness.

A reversal of this silence entrails, above all, thinking and narrating the history of *this* existing world and how it has come about. This project must proceed with an understanding that, unlike the systems builders of the European past, who visualized the world and thought world history long before they could possibly experience the world as a whole, we contemporaries of the late twentieth century experience the world long before we know how to think it. The aim of this world history becomes a dual one: to shatter the silence surrounding global practices, by tracking them, describing them, and presenting them historically and, at the same time — recognizing with George Simmel that, in an integrated world, we encounter only more strangers — to facilitate public cultures as the free and equal marketplace of communication among the many voices of different histories and memories. The practice of world history in this conception does not refuse or jettison the findings of world-systems theories or of a comparative history of civilizations, inasmuch as they survive a rigorous critique and shed their respective nostalgias for autonomous regions and essentialist civilizations. But the practice of world history in a global age does reconfigure the field in which these paradigms are deployed. It proceeds from the recognition that the trajectory of this world cannot be extrapolated from anyone's particular past, because globality is without precedent in any one specific society, religion, or civilization — although it is not without precedent in more syncretistic ages and spaces. In recognizing that global development in the twentieth century has broken through all historiographic conventions, historians must attempt to find a representation of the world as the field of human contestation in which the histories of the world are mixed together, but societies and peoples are not thereby transformed into one, or even made more alike.

But here we confront a startling new condition: humanity, which has been the subject of world history for many centuries and civilizations, has now come into the purview of all human beings. This humanity is extremely polarized into rich and poor, powerful and powerless, vociferous and speechless, believers and non-believers. There are clusters of dense interaction and clusters of loose and distant encounters. There are liminal zones and there are areas of devastation — wastelands both in the actuality of the present moment and in lingering memory. This humanity, in short, does not form a single homogeneous civilization. But in an age of globality, the humanity that inhabits this world is no longer a universalizing image or a normative construct of what some civilization or some intellectuals would want the people of this earth to be. Neither is this humanity any longer a mere species or a natural condition. For the first time, we as human beings collectively constitute ourselves and, hence, are responsible for ourselves.

This condition of globality can no longer be represented by notions of earth/nature or cosmos/world picture, as has been the case in the past. Instead, this condition of globality is the integrated global space of human practice. As a consequence, humanity no longer comes into being through "thought." Rather, humanity gains existence in a multiplicity of discrete economic, social, cultural, and political activities. In the past, such humanity has been the dream of sages and philosophers and, not to be forgotten, of gods, but now it has become the daily work of human beings. This daily work needs imagination. To this end, world history makes explicit and visible — it traces — both practices of global regimes and the imbrication of local communities. Its task is to make transparent the lineaments of power, underpinned by information, that compress humanity into a single humankind. And it is to make accessible to all human beings the diverse human labors, splintered into so many particularities, that go into creating and maintaining this global condition. This conclusion underscores both the promise and the challenge of the twentieth century as an age of world historical transition — that, in forging a world in which "humanity" has become a pragmatic reality with a common destiny, we do not arrive at the end of history. World history has just begun.

DAVID CHRISTIAN

The Case for "Big History"

What is the scale on which history should be studied? The establishment of the *Journal of World History* already implies a radical answer to that question: in geographical terms, the appropriate scale may be the whole of the world. In this paper, I will defend an equally radical answer to the temporal aspect of the same question: what is the time scale on which history should be studied? I will argue that the appropriate time scale for the study of history may be the whole of time. In other words, historians should be prepared to explore the past on many different time scales up to that of the universe itself — a scale of between 10 and 20 billion years.[1] This is what I mean by "big history." Readers of this journal will already be familiar with the case for world history. I will argue that a similar case can be made for teaching and writing about the past on these even larger time scales.

As I understand it, the case for world history turns to a large extent on the belief of many historians that the discipline of history has failed to find an adequate balance between the opposing demands of detail and generality. In the century since Ranke, historians have devoted themselves with great energy and

David Christian, "The Case for 'Big History,'" *Journal of World History* 2 (Fall 1991): 223–38.

great success to the task of documenting the past. And they have accumulated a vast amount of information about the history of a number of modern societies, in particular those with European or Mediterranean roots. But in history, as in any other academic discipline, you must look beyond the details if you are to understand their meaning, to see how they fit together. We need large-scale maps if we are to see each part of our subject in its context. Unfortunately, historians have become so absorbed in detailed research that they have tended to neglect the job of building these larger-scale maps of the past. Indeed, many historians deliberately neglect the task of generalization in the belief that the facts will eventually speak for themselves when enough of them have been accumulated, forgetting that it is we alone who can give the "facts" a voice. The result of this one-sided approach to historical research is a discipline that has plenty of information but a fragmented and parochial vision of its field of inquiry. Not surprisingly, it has become harder and harder to explain to those we teach and those we write for why they should bother to study history at all.

World history is, among other things, an attempt to redress this balance. The point is expressed well by David Sweet in a recent discussion of efforts to organize graduate study in world history:

> Perhaps the best argument for a program in world history is that it represents a long-overdue recognition by members of our profession that in the end history is all of one piece — that it is the whole story of humanity, seen in the context of humanity's changing relationship to nature. This includes an acknowledgment that all parts of that story are of importance to the whole, and that they have full meaning only when seen somehow in relation to the whole.[2]

Arguments of this kind will be familiar to readers of the *Journal of World History*. But the arguments that apply to world history are also true at larger scales. We cannot fully understand the past few millennia without understanding the far longer period of time in which all members of our own species lived as gatherers and hunters, and without understanding the changes that led to the emergence of the earliest agrarian communities and the first urban civilizations. Paleolithic society, in its turn, cannot be fully understood without some idea of the evolution of our own species over several million years. That however requires some grasp of the history of life on earth, and so on. Such arguments may seem to lead us to an endless regress, but it is now clear that they do not. According to modern Big Bang cosmology, the universe itself has a history, with a clear and identifiable beginning somewhere between 10 and 20 billion years ago. We can say nothing of what happened before this time; indeed time itself was created in the Big Bang. So this time scale is different from others. If there is an absolute framework for the study of the past, this is it. If the past can be studied whole, this is the scale within which to do it.

By "big history," then, I mean the exploration of the past on all these different scales, up to the scale of the universe itself. In what follows I will first discuss some possible objections to big history; then I will describe in general terms, and with some specific examples, some of its merits; and finally I will describe a university course in big history as an illustration of some of the practicalities of teaching history on this largest of all possible scales.

Some Objections to Big History

If the idea of big history seems strange at first sight, that is largely because it breaches in an even more spectacular way than world history a number of well-established conventions about the ways in which history is best taught and written. To explore the past on a very large scale means going beyond conventional ideas about the time scales on which history is best studied, and it means transgressing the traditional boundaries between the discipline of history and other disciplines, such as prehistory, biology, geology, and cosmology. Can these conventions about time scales and discipline boundaries be breached with impunity? For my own part, I am sure that they can; I believe that they are indeed little more than conventions and that breaching them can only be healthy.

To take first the issue of time scales. Although there are a number of outstanding exceptions (several of whom have played an active role in the establishment of the World History Association), the vast majority of professional historians continue to explore the past on the time scale of a human lifetime. Most courses tend to be taught, and most books tend to be written, on time scales from a decade or two to a century or so. Two similar, but opposite, objections are often raised against those who attempt to survey the past on larger scales. One is that large-scale history means sacrificing detail and retreating into empty generalities; the opposite objection is that at the large scale there is simply too much information for the historian to handle.

The same reply can be made to both objections: the very notion of detail is relative. What is central at one scale may be detail at another and may vanish entirely at the very largest scales. Some questions require the telephoto lens; others require the wide-angle lens. And as one shifts from smaller to larger scales, the loss of detail is, in any case, balanced by the fact that larger objects come into view, objects so large that they cannot be seen whole from close up. So there is no single appropriate level of "graininess" for the historian; nor is there any reason to regard the conventional time scales as sacrosanct. The amount of detail required depends purely on the nature of the question being asked.

This principle applies to all time scales. If the questions being asked concern the origins of human society or the human impact on the environment, then clearly we must be prepared to view the past on a scale of many millions of years.[3] If our questions concern the significance of intelligence or of life in the universe, they require an even larger scale. All that is required to pursue such questions is a willingness to shift lenses in a way that is familiar in principle to all historians, even if its application on so heroic a scale may induce a degree of vertigo the first time around. No difficulty of principle is involved, although the shaking of such well-established conventions does require a considerable effort both of the imagination and the intellect.

This leads to a second criticism of large-scale history, one that concerns expertise. In tackling questions on these huge scales, the historian is bound to breach conventional discipline boundaries as well as conventional time scales. Can historians legitimately stray like this beyond their patch? Clearly, no single scholar can acquire an expert's knowledge in all the different disciplines that have a bearing on history at the very large scale. But this does not mean that the historian should abandon such questions. If a question requires some knowledge of biology or geology, then so be it. All that is required is a willingness to exploit the division of intellectual labor that exists in all our universities. Far from being unusual, this is normal procedure in any science; indeed it is normal procedure within and among the many subdisciplines that make up history. Besides, such borrowing is more feasible today than it would have been even a decade ago; there exist now numerous fine works of popularization by specialists in many different academic disciplines, works that offer scholarly, up-to-date, and lucid summaries of the contemporary state of knowledge in different fields. So there is no fundamental objection to the crossing of discipline boundaries; the difficulties are purely practical.

The obvious objections to big history, then, reflect little more than the inertia of existing conventions about the way history should be taught and written. In principle, there is nothing to prevent the historian from considering the past at very large scales and using essentially the same skills of research, judgment, and analysis that would apply at more conventional scales.

THE CASE FOR BIG HISTORY

What are the positive arguments for big history? They follow from the negative arguments I have just discussed.

First, big history permits the asking of very large questions and therefore encourages the search for larger meanings in the past. If world history allows us to see the history of specific societies in a global context, history on even larger time scales allows us to consider the history of humanity as a whole in *its* context. It therefore invites us to ask questions about the relationship between the history of our own species and that of other living things. And it invites us to go back even further and try to place the history of life itself in a larger context. In this way, big history encourages us to ask questions about our place in the universe. It leads us back to the sort of questions that have been answered in many societies by creation myths. This suggests that history could play as significant a role in modern industrial society as traditional creation myths have played in nonindustrial societies; but it will do so only if it asks questions as large and profound as those posed in traditional creation myths.

In the second place, big history allows us to tackle these large questions with new approaches and new models because it encourages the drawing of new links between different academic disciplines. It can be seen, therefore, as an appropriate response to the intellectual apartheid between "the two cultures" of science and the humanities that C. P. Snow discussed in a famous lecture delivered in 1959.[4]

So far, the discussion has been at a very general level. In what follows, I would like to give some specific illustrations of each of these arguments. First I will discuss a specific historical issue that can be approached at several different scales, the issue of economic growth in human history. What is the scale on which such a question can best be discussed, and how do different time scales affect the way we view the question and its implications? I will argue that this is a question better debated at scales even larger than those conventional within the field of world history.

On the scale adopted in most histories of human society, growth of some kind, involving changed technology and increases in productivity, is palpably there. So it is easy to think of change, or even "progress," as a basic characteristic of human history, perhaps even a defining characteristic of our species. E. L. Jones has made these assumptions explicit in a series of recent studies that have done much to put large-scale historical questions on the agenda for professional historians. "Let us assume," he writes in a recent essay, "that a propensity for growth has been widely present in human society. This does not commit us to a neoclassical maximizing position. Not everyone need be engaged in maximizing on every margin at once. All that is needed is to accept that a desire to reduce material poverty is commonplace in our species, as well it might be considering that poverty exacts such a penalty in terms of dead babies, or at any rate of children without shoes."[5] On the scale of 5,000 years, this is all very plausible. And Jones himself has assembled the evidence for a long-term trend toward both extensive and intensive growth over this period.[6]

But is 5,000 years really the appropriate scale if our concern is with human beings and the societies they have created? If we are asking questions about the "propensities" or "desires" of the human species, surely the appropriate time scale is that of the species as a whole. How big is that? The earliest fossil evidence for Australopithecines, the first members of the hominid family, dates back about 4 million years.[7] The first evidence for *Homo habilis*, the earliest species that modern physical anthropologists are willing to classify within the genus *Homo*, dates back to almost 3 million years. The larger-brained species, *Homo erectus*, first appears in the record about 1.9 million years ago. The relationship between *Homo erectus* and our own species, *Homo sapiens*, is a subject of great controversy, but an age of between 50,000 and 400,000 years for *Homo sapiens* would cover most positions within this controversy, and a figure of 250,000 years is a reasonable compromise. So, on this evidence, when did human history begin? For my purposes, a precise answer is not important. One could argue that "humans" have existed for 5 million years. But even on the more modest scale of 250,000 years, a question posed on a scale of a mere 5,000 years is likely to produce aberrant answers.

What does the problem of growth look like on the larger scale? If we take world population as a measure of the capacity of human societies to support growth, then the story of human history over several hundreds of thousands of years is one of small populations and local fluctuations that have left little trace in the historical record, and then a sudden and spectacular burst of growth in recent times. Early hominid populations were probably of the same order of magnitude as those of other great apes in recent times: perhaps 1 million, all living in Africa.[8] We must presume that the migrations that led *Homo erectus* out of Africa and into the colder climates of Eurasia about 1 million years ago (migrations that might have been accompanied by the mastery of fire), led to a considerable increase in the world population of hominids, which suggests that 2 to 4 million may be a reasonable guess for the world population 250,000 years ago, By 10,000 years ago, when forms of agriculture and permanent settlements began to appear in several distinct parts of the world, the population of the world could hardly have been more than 10 million. On these very rough estimates, human populations increased from perhaps 2 million to 10 million over a period of some 250,000 years, and most evidence for intensification comes from the last 40,000 years of that huge range. This is a rate of growth so imperceptible that no modern economist would want to apply the word "growth" to it, and any "propensity for growth" one may claim to observe on this scale begins to look a pretty spectral thing.

In contrast, during the last 10,000 years, human populations have risen from 10 million to about 200 million (2,000 years ago), and then, in an even more spectacular acceleration, to nearly 5 billion today. On this reckoning, human history consists of about 250,000 years of relative stasis followed by a mere 10,000 years of growth, most of which has been concentrated into the last few hundred years. In other words, even on a rather restricted definition of our species, growth has occupied a mere 4% of its history; the really spectacular growth has occurred in the last 0.2% of that history.

The accompanying figure graphs no more than the last two and a half millennia of human population growth. To get a sense of human population growth over 250,000 years, one would have to add a further ninety-nine graphs to the left, and on most of those graphs, the line representing human population would merge into the graph's base line. Only in the last three or four graphs would it begin to rise above that line.

To the extent that population growth can serve as a surrogate for growth in average levels of productivity, we must conclude that growth, far from being the normal condition of humanity, is an aberration. The growth that E. L. Jones has documented over the past 5,000 years is evidence not for the normality of growth, but rather for a sudden breakdown in an ancient equilibrium between a large mammal species and the environment it inhabits. Carlo Cipolla comments: "A biologist, looking at the diagram showing the recent growth of world population in a long-range perspective, said that he had the impression of being in the presence of the growth curve of a microbe population in a body suddenly struck by some infectious disease. The 'bacillus' man is taking over the world."[9] Why did this particular large species of mammal suddenly begin to display the demographic behavior of a plague species? On the scale of human history as a whole, this is the really interesting question.

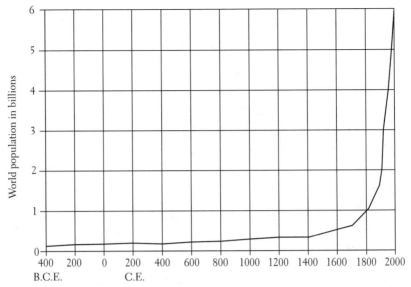

Figure 1. World Population, 400 B.C.E. to 2000 C.E. Adapted from C. McEvedy and R. Jones, *Atlas of World Population History* (Harmondsworth, 1978), 342.

A slightly different way of saying the same thing is to point out (what everyone knows, although few expend much intellectual effort on the fact) that the history of human beings has been above all a history of hunter-gatherer societies.[10] In an important sense, hunting and gathering are the "natural" activities of human beings, and what has occurred in the last 5,000 years is profoundly "unnatural." There is nothing "natural" about the state, or civilization, or economic growth. The entire history of agrarian and now industrial civilizations is from this point of view a curious and rather surprising coda tacked onto the end of human history.

The large perspective affects our approach to the problem of growth in other ways, too, for it raises a host of further issues, some of which are ethical, and some of which need to be discussed on a very large scale indeed. Should we admire the explosive growth of the past few millennia? Is it, perhaps, what distinguishes us from other living species? Or can we identify similar turning points in the history of other living species? Is human history governed, ultimately, by the rhythms of natural history as a whole? What is the likely impact of our own history on the history of the planet as a whole? Is the rapid growth of human society proof of a fertility in invention so astonishing (and so untypical of animal species as a whole) that it will continually outstrip the dangers it creates? Casual judgments about such questions lie behind much historical writing, so it is important that the questions be posed seriously and clearly. They should also be debated rigorously if history is to take itself seriously as a discussion of what it means to be human, a discussion that inevitably has ethical dimensions.

A discussion of "growth" highlights another advantage of thinking about the past on a very large scale. Thinking about the very long term means thinking about very large trends. This makes it possible to discuss the future in ways that are not possible if historians concentrate on the short term. Is accelerating economic growth a trend that can be projected forward identifiably into the future? Presumably not, simply because the mathematics of such a trend will soon lead us toward some embarrassing infinities: infinite population growth, infinite increase in consumption, and so on. So we can be certain, after exploring these very long trends, that they can not be projected indefinitely into the future. What, precisely, does that mean? What mechanisms will alter the accelerating trends we now observe? Will they be Malthusian in nature? Or climatic or ecological? Or will they involve rational human intervention? And when will the trend change? These questions, of vast significance for our view of the next few hundred years and for our understanding of political and economic decisions that have to be made today, can be tackled seriously by historians only if we look more seriously at very long trends. What drives the long-term trends? What drives the machinery of growth in the very long term?[11] How fast can that machine go, and at what point is it likely to stall? By raising questions of this sort, big history may make it possible to end the ancient historians' taboo on discussion of the future as well as the past. That taboo made sense, but only as long as historians refused to discuss trends large enough to yield significant hints about the future. These examples should indicate some of the ways in which large-scale history can make it easier to pose fundamental questions that cannot be tackled at smaller scales.

I also suggested earlier that one of the virtues of big history may be that it will encourage historians to become more familiar with the models, techniques, habits of thinking, and types of evidence used in other disciplines. This in turn may help historians view their own discipline in new ways.[12] I would like to give a brief illustration of what I mean. It concerns the problem of agriculture and its origins, and it draws on the work of David Rindos.[13] Rindos seeks the answer to a historical question (the reasons for the emergence of agriculture) using a Darwinian paradigm. He argues that the emergence of agriculture is a familiar process in natural history, where it can be described as a form of coevolution, the evolution of a symbiotic relationship between two very different species. Agriculture is not unique to humans, for many other species of animals, including several types of ants, can also be said to have developed forms of agriculture, or "domestication," in which the animal aids in the reproductive success of an edible plant. Within the Darwinian paradigm, coevolution, whether of ants and trees or of humans and grains, is a mutual process, one to which both partners contribute something. It is also an essentially blind process, one that involves no element of conscious intention. Here is Rindos's definition of "domestication":

> Domestication is a coevolutionary process in which any given taxon diverges from an original gene pool and establishes a symbiotic protection and dispersal relationship with the animal feeding upon it. This symbiosis is facilitated by

adaptations (changes in the morphology, physiology, or autoecology) within the plant population and by changes in behavior by the animal.[14]

In the case of human agriculture, coevolution was presumably encouraged by the fact that hunter-gatherers were likely to scatter the seeds of plants they favored around frequently used camp sites. Plants that offered the most attractive taste were the ones most likely to be selected in this way, so these plants were most likely to flourish near camp sites. This is what Rindos calls the "dump-heap model for agricultural origins."[15]

Is Rindos merely using a Darwinian analogy here, or is he claiming that the Darwinian arguments can be applied directly to human history? As I understand it, he claims (after preparing his ground with an elaborate exorcism of the ghost of Herbert Spencer) that the argument is more than analogy; however, the Darwinian argument needs to be modified in some important respects before it can be used as a tool for the interpretation of human history. As his definition of "domestication" suggests, in the natural world coevolution, although it requires behavioral changes, also involves genetic change in both partners to the relationship. In the case of the human domestication of grains, this is not necessarily true. It is certainly true that agriculture encouraged rapid genetic change on one side of the evolving relationship, that of the plants; but Rindos's argument does not require that this be true of both sides. Human groups evolved culturally. Their behaviors and cultures changed in ways that maximized the benefits they procured from domesticated plants, and simultaneously improved the reproductive chances of the plants. So in this case, coevolution involved genetic change on one side and behavioral change on the other. This line of argument leads Rindos to the notion of "cultural evolution": "Behavior, like any other phenotypic trait of an organism, is amenable to selection. Thus behaviors may influence the differential reproductive success of a lineage over time. If the presence of a new behavior increases the probability that a lineage will prosper (in numerical terms), the change in behavior has increased the fitness of that lineage."[16]

At issue here is not whether Rindos's account of agricultural origins is right or wrong. The crucial point is that historians can only gain by considering seriously the ways in which other disciplines solve problems. Drawing closer links between the traditional content and methodology of history and that of other disciplines can only enrich the theoretical and methodological toolbox available to historians.

A History of 15 Billion Years

But is big history manageable in practice? In particular, can history be taught at this scale? The best proof is in the doing. At Macquarie University in Sydney, we have been teaching since 1989 a first-year history course that does just what I have proposed. It discusses history on many different time scales, beginning with that of the universe itself.[17] Naturally, this course is only one of many possible ways of approaching big history, and the specific ways we approach it may or may not be palatable to other historians. But our experience suggests that there is nothing particularly difficult about teaching such a course once one has shifted mental gears. So I will end with a brief description of our approach to big history.

The Macquarie course is taught over thirteen weeks; it offers two lectures a week and one tutorial. Lecturers come from many different disciplines: astronomy, geology, biology, palaeontology, anthropology, prehistory, classical history, and modern history.

The course begins with lectures on time and creation myths. The lecture on time offers an introductory discussion of the medium within which historians operate (for the most part without questioning it); the lecture attempts to demonstrate the differences in conceptions of the nature of time in different societies and to help students begin to grasp large and unfamiliar time scales. The second lecture discusses creation myths from many different societies. Its aim is to suggest that history itself may best be regarded as a form of modern "creation myth," in the sense that it reflects the best attempts of our society to answer questions about origins, just as the Genesis account or the creation myths of Australian Aboriginal society reflect the attempts of very different societies to answer fundamental questions about the origins of the heavens, the planet, living things, human beings, and human society. The drawing of this parallel is also a way of suggesting that history, like traditional creation myths, can pose questions of the most fundamental kind. And this, it seems to me, is the first payoff for the teacher of a course on this scale; no special effort is required to explain why the subject matter being taught is important. Its importance is self-evident.

After these introductory lectures, the course starts at the beginning, offering a narrative that is unconventional only because of the scale on which it tells its story. Two lectures given by a professional astronomer discuss current theories on the origins of the universe itself and the clusters of galaxies and stars that are the largest structures the universe contains. Two lectures are given on the history of the solar system and the history of the earth and its atmosphere. These are followed by lectures summarizing current theories and evidence on the origins of life on earth, the main laws of biological evolution, and the main stages of the evolution of life. A lecture on the evolution of human beings from apelike ancestors follows. Our own species appears in the course only in the fifth week of the thirteen-week course.

Given the influence of conventional discipline boundaries, this appearance inevitably marks a crucial turning point in the course. This is the point at which disciplines conventionally classified as "sciences" are left behind in favor of disciplines conventionally classified as "social sciences" or "humanities." The transition requires some discussion of what is meant by the conventional distinction between scientific and nonscientific disciplines, which in turn requires some discussion of the nature of the "truths" offered by both scientists and historians. So at this point there is an introductory lecture on theories of science, which poses the question: is history less scientific than science? (The answer is a cautious but qualified "No.") This lecture is designed to highlight the way in which big history can pose issues not just of content, but also of methodology. Is history a science? In what sense can it claim to offer truths more certain than those of traditional creation myths? Should history aspire to its own "paradigms" (in the sense made familiar in the work of Thomas Kuhn)?[18] Is there any fundamental difference between the types of evidence offered by scientists and those offered by historians? (Is a written document fundamentally different from the red-shifted spectrum of a distant galaxy?) How useful are models? Problems of historical methodology do not vanish when history is viewed on a large scale; on the contrary, they can be posed more clearly when the methodologies and types of argument used by historians are contrasted with those of researchers in many other disciplines. To ensure that this is true, lecturers and tutors in the course concentrate at every point on the *evidence* for the theories they are discussing.

From this point, the content of the Macquarie course should be more familiar.[19] Lectures follow on the nature of paleolithic societies and the significance of hunter-gatherer technologies and life-styles in the past and present. Then come lectures on the emergence of agriculture, the earliest political and class structures, and the very earliest civilizations. Only at this point, in the ninth week of the course, do we begin to discuss problems that come within the domain of conventional history writing. Later lectures discuss early civilizations and the classical civilizations of Europe, Asia, and the Americas. Discussion of pre-Columban America is particularly fruitful as it poses fascinating questions about the parallel development of agrarian civilizations in parts of the globe that seem to have had no cultural contact for many thousands of years. Then there is a series of lectures on the emergence of a distinctively modern world and the nature of the world we inhabit at the end of the second millennium of the Christian calendar.

The final lecture, given jointly by myself (a historian) and a colleague who is a biologist, attempts an overview of the course as a whole. It asks a question that can only be asked in this kind of course: is there a discernible pattern to the past? It poses the question on three different scales — that of humanity, the planet, and the universe. Our answer? Yes, there are large patterns. In some sense history at all three levels is a fugue whose two major themes are entropy (which leads to imbalance, the decline of complex entities, and a sort of "running down" of the universe) and, as a sort of counterpoint, the creative forces that manage to form and sustain complex but temporary equilibria despite the pressure of entropy.[20] These fragile equilibrium systems include galaxies, stars, the earth, the biosphere (what James Lovelock has referred to as "Gaia"[21]), social structures of various kinds, living things, and human beings. These are all entities that achieve a temporary but always precarious balance, undergo periodic crises, reestablish new equilibria, but eventually succumb to the larger forces of imbalance represented by the principle of "entropy." They all share the rhythm of "punctuated equilibrium" that Stephen Jay Gould and Niles Eldredge have detected in the history of life on earth.[22] These are entities that live, develop, and then die. Such patterns can be found at all time scales, so in this sense history is, as the mathematicians of chaos would say, "self-similar." Seen in this perspective, human history is the story of one such equilibrium system, which exits on the scale of a million or so years. And the history of the last few thousand years deals with the experience of that system as a long period of equilibrium was punctuated by a period of turbulence and instability. In this perspective, the most profound question that can be asked by a member of the species *Homo sapiens* living in the modern era is this: will human society manage to establish a new equilibrium of some kind? Or will it succumb to the forces of entropy?

CODA

This paper has been concerned with presenting the case for big history. It may seem, therefore, that it constitutes an attack on "small history." So I will conclude by emphasizing that this is not so. My real complaint is not that historians have concentrated on the details; it is that the profession has tended in the century since Ranke to define its task almost exclusively in terms of detailed research. As a result, historians have neglected the larger questions of meaning, significance, and wholeness that can alone give some point to the details. If history is to reestablish its centrality as a discussion about what it means to be human, it must renew the interest in the large scale that was taken for granted by historians in the days before history became a "science."

Notes

1. This according to Big Bang cosmology, the dominant paradigm of modern astronomy and cosmology.
2. David Sweet, *World History Bulletin* 5 (1988): 7.
3. Which is presumably why the geological history of Pangaea, more than two hundred million years, rates a chapter in Alfred W. Crosby's marvelous *Ecological Imperialism: The Biological Expansion of Europe, 900–1900* (New York, 1986).
4. C. P. Snow, *The Two Cultures and the Scientific Revolution* (Cambridge, 1959).
5. Johan Goudsblom, E. L. Jones, and Stephen Mennell, *Human History and Social Process* (Exeter, 1989), 53.
6. E. L. Jones, "Recurrent Transitions to Intensive Growth" in *Human History and Social Process*, Goudsblom et al.
7. R. Lewin, *Human Evolution: An Illustrated Introduction*, 2d ed. (Oxford, 1989), offers a good introduction to hominid evolution.
8. The following is based on C. McEvedy and R. Jones, *Atlas of World Population History* (Harmondsworth, 1978).
9. Carlo M. Cipolla, *The Economic History of World Population*, 6th ed. (Harmondsworth, 1974), 114–15.
10. Marshall Sahlins's *Stone Age Economics* (London, 1972) was a pioneering attempt to construct an economics for such societies.
11. These questions lie at the heart of the recent work of E. L. Jones. See *The European Miracle: Environments, Economies and Geopolitics in the History of Europe and Asia* (Cambridge, 1981); *Growth Recurring: Economic Change in World History* (Oxford, 1988); and his essays in *Human History and Social Process*, Goudsblom et al.

12. One of the best recent discussions on the role of contingency in history can be found in a book by palaeontologist Stephen Jay Gould: *Wonderful Life: The Burgess Shale and the Nature of History* (New York, 1989).

13. David Rindos, *The Origins of Agriculture: An Evolutionary Perspective* (New York, 1984).

14. Ibid., 143.

15. Ibid., 134–35.

16. Rindos, *The Origins of Agriculture*, 255.

17. For a more detailed description see "The Longest Durée: A History of the Last 15 Billion Years," *Australian Historical Association Bulletin* 59–60 (1989): 27–36.

18. Thomas Kuhn's most influential work is *The Structure of Scientific Revolutions*, 2d ed. (Chicago, 1970).

19. To give some shape to the lectures that follow, we have adopted as a sort of provisional "paradigm" the model of social structure described in Eric Wolf's magnificent *Europe and the People without History* (Berkeley, 1982).

20. Some justification for these grand speculations can be found in Paul Davies, *The Cosmic Blueprint* (London, 1989).

21. James Lovelock, *Gaia: A New Look at Life on Earth* (Oxford, 1987) and its sequel, *The Ages of Gaia* (Oxford, 1988).

22. For a brief summary, see Stephen Jay Gould, "The Episodic Nature of Evolutionary Change," in *The Panda's Thumb* (Harmondsworth, 1980), 149–54.

JARED DIAMOND

The Future of Human History as a Science

The discipline of history is generally not considered to be a science, but something closer to the humanities. At best, history is classified among the social sciences, of which it rates as the least scientific. While the field of government is often termed "political science" and the Nobel Prize in economics refers to "economic science," history departments rarely if ever label themselves "Department of Historical Science." Most historians do not think of themselves as scientists and receive little training in acknowledged sciences and their methodologies. The sense that history is nothing more than a mass of details is captured in numerous aphorisms: "History is just one damn fact after another," "History is more or less bunk," "There is no law of history any more than of a kaleidoscope," and so on.

Jared Diamond, *Guns, Germs, and Steel: The Fates of Human Societies* (New York: W. W. Norton, 1997), 420–25.

One cannot deny that it is more difficult to extract general principles from studying history than from studying planetary orbits. However, the difficulties seem to me not fatal. Similar ones apply to other historical subjects whose place among the natural sciences is nevertheless secure, including astronomy, climatology, ecology, evolutionary biology, geology, and paleontology. People's image of science is unfortunately often based on physics and a few other fields with similar methodologies. Scientists in those fields tend to be ignorantly disdainful of fields to which those methodologies are inappropriate and which must therefore seek other methodologies — such as my own research areas of ecology and evolutionary biology. But recall that the word "science" means "knowledge" (from the Latin *scire*, "to know," and *scientia*, "knowledge"), to be obtained by whatever methods are most appropriate to the particular field. Hence I have much empathy with students of human history for the difficulties they face.

Historical sciences in the broad sense (including astronomy and the like) share many features that set them apart from nonhistorical sciences such as physics, chemistry, and molecular biology. I would single out four: methodology, causation, prediction, and complexity.

In physics the chief method for gaining knowledge is the laboratory experiment, by which one manipulates the parameter whose effect is in question, executes parallel control experiments with that parameter held constant, holds other parameters constant throughout, replicates both the experimental manipulation and the control experiment, and obtains quantitative data. This strategy, which also works well in chemistry and molecular biology, is so identified with science in the minds of many people that experimentation is often held to be the essence of the scientific method. But laboratory experimentation can obviously play little or no role in many of the historical sciences. One cannot interrupt galaxy formation, start and stop hurricanes and ice ages, experimentally exterminate grizzly bears in a few national parks, or rerun the course of dinosaur evolution. Instead, one must gain knowledge in these historical sciences by other means, such as observation, comparison, and so-called natural experiments (to which I shall return in a moment).

Historical sciences are concerned with chains of proximate and ultimate causes. In most of physics and chemistry the concepts of "ultimate cause," "purpose," and "function" are meaningless, yet they are essential to understanding living systems in general and human activities in particular. For instance, an evolutionary biologist studying Arctic hares whose fur color turns from brown in summer to white in winter is not satisfied with identifying the mundane proximate causes of fur color in terms of the fur pigments' molecular structures and biosynthetic pathways. The more important questions involve function (camouflage against predators?) and ultimate cause (natural selection starting with an ancestral hare population with seasonally unchanging fur color?). Similarly, a European historian is not satisfied with describing the condition of Europe in both 1815 and 1918 as having just achieved peace after a costly pan-European war. Understanding the contrasting chains of events leading up to the two peace treaties is essential to understanding why an even more costly pan-European war broke out again within a few decades of 1918 but not of 1815. But chemists do not assign a purpose or function to a collision of two gas molecules, nor do they seek an ultimate cause for the collision.

Still another difference between historical and nonhistorical sciences involves prediction. In chemistry and physics the acid test of one's understanding of a system is whether one can successfully predict its future behavior. Again, physicists tend to look down on evolutionary biology and history, because those fields appear to fail this test. In historical sciences, one can provide a posteriori explanations (e.g., why an asteroid impact on Earth 66 million years ago may have driven dinosaurs but not many other species to extinction), but a priori predictions are more difficult (we would be uncertain which species would be driven to extinction if we did not have the actual past event to guide us). However, historians and historical scientists do make and test predictions about what future discoveries of data will show us about past events.

The properties of historical systems that complicate attempts at prediction can be described in several alternative ways. One can point out that human societies and dinosaurs are extremely complex, being characterized by an enormous number of independent variables that feed back on each other. As a result, small changes at a lower level of organization can lead to emergent changes at a higher level. A typical example is the effect of that one truck driver's braking response, in Hitler's nearly fatal traffic accident of 1930, on the lives of a hundred million people who were killed or wounded in World War II. Although most biologists agree that biological systems are in the end wholly determined by their physical properties and obey the laws of quantum mechanics, the systems' complexity means, for practical purposes, that that deterministic causation does not translate into predictability. Knowledge of quantum mechanics does not help one understand why introduced placental predators have exterminated so many Australian marsupial species, or why the Allied Powers rather than the Central Powers won World War I.

Each glacier, nebula, hurricane, human society, and biological species, and even each individual and cell of a sexually reproducing species, is unique, because it is influenced by so many variables and made up of so many variable parts. In contrast, for any of the physicist's elementary particles and isotopes and of the chemist's molecules, all individuals of the entity are identical to each other. Hence physicists and chemists can formulate universal deterministic laws at the macroscopic level, but biologists and historians can formulate only statistical trends. With a very high probability of being correct, I can predict that, of the next 1,000 babies born at the University of California Medical Center, where I work, not fewer than 480 or more than 520 will be boys. But I had no means of knowing in advance that my own two children would be boys. Similarly, historians note that tribal societies may have been more likely to develop into chiefdoms if the local population was sufficiently large and dense and if there was potential for surplus food production than if that was not the case. But each such local population has its own unique features, with the result that chiefdoms did emerge in the highlands of Mexico, Guatemala, Peru, and Madagascar, but not in those of New Guinea or Guadalcanal.

Still another way of describing the complexity and unpredictability of historical systems, despite their ultimate determinacy, is to note that long chains of causation may separate final effects from ultimate causes lying outside the domain of that field of science. For example, the dinosaurs may have been exterminated by the impact of an asteroid whose orbit was completely determined by the laws of classical mechanics. But if there had been any paleontologists living 67 million years ago, they could not have predicted the dinosaurs' imminent demise, because asteroids belong to a field of science otherwise remote from dinosaur biology. Similarly, the Little Ice Age of A.D. 1300–1500 contributed to the extinction of the Greenland Norse, but no historian, and probably not even a modern climatologist, could have predicted the Little Ice Age.

Thus, the difficulties historians face in establishing cause-and-effect relations in the history of human societies are broadly similar to the difficulties facing astronomers, climatologists, ecologists, evolutionary biologists, geologists, and paleontologists. To varying degrees, each of these fields is plagued by the impossibility of performing replicated, controlled experimental interventions, the complexity arising from enormous numbers of variables, the resulting uniqueness of each system, the consequent impossibility of formulating universal laws, and the difficulties of predicting emergent properties and future behavior. Prediction in history, as in other historical sciences, is most feasible on large spatial scales and over long times, when the unique features of millions of small-scale brief events become averaged out. Just as I could predict the sex ratio of the next 1,000 newborns but not the sexes of my own two children, the historian can recognize factors that made inevitable the broad outcome of the collision between American and Eurasian societies after 13,000 years of separate developments, but not the outcome of the 1960 U.S. presidential election. The details of which candidate said what during a single televised debate in October 1960 could have given the electoral victory to Nixon instead of to Kennedy, but no details of who said what could have blocked the European conquest of Native Americans.

How can students of human history profit from the experience of scientists in other historical sciences? A methodology that has proved useful involves the comparative method and so-called natural experiments. While neither astronomers studying galaxy formation nor human historians can manipulate their systems in controlled laboratory experiments, they both can take advantage of natural experiments, by comparing systems differing in the presence or absence (or in the strong or weak effect) of some putative causative factor. For example, epidemiologists, forbidden to feed large amounts of salt to people experimentally, have still been able to identify effects of high salt intake by comparing groups of humans who already differ greatly in their salt intake; and cultural anthropologists, unable to provide human groups experimentally with varying resource abundances for many centuries, still study long-term effects of resource abundance on human societies by comparing recent Polynesian populations living on islands differing naturally in resource abundance. The student of human history can draw on many more natural experiments than just comparisons among the five inhabited continents. Comparisons can also utilize large islands that have developed complex societies in a considerable degree of isolation (such as Japan, Madagascar, Native American Hispaniola, New Guinea, Hawaii, and many others), as well as societies on hundreds of smaller islands and regional societies within each of the continents.

Natural experiments in any field, whether in ecology or human history, are inherently open to potential methodological criticisms. Those include confounding effects of natural variation in additional variables besides the one of interest, as well as problems in inferring chains of causation from observed correlations between variables. Such methodological problems have been discussed in great detail for some of the historical sciences. In particular, epidemiology, the science of drawing inferences about human diseases by comparing groups of people (often by retrospective historical studies), has for a long time successfully employed formalized procedures for dealing with problems similar to those facing historians of human societies. Ecologists have also devoted much attention to the problems of natural experiments, a methodology to which they must resort in many cases where direct experimental interventions to manipulate relevant ecological variables would be immoral, illegal, or impossible. Evolutionary biologists have recently been developing ever more sophisticated methods for drawing conclusions from comparisons of different plants and animals of known evolutionary histories.

In short, I acknowledge that it is much more difficult to understand human history than to understand problems in fields of science where history is unimportant and where fewer individual variables operate. Nevertheless, successful methodologies for analyzing historical problems have been worked out in several fields. As a result, the histories of dinosaurs, nebulas, and glaciers are generally acknowledged to belong to fields of science rather than to the humanities. But introspection gives us far more insight into the ways of other humans than into those of dinosaurs. I am thus optimistic that historical studies of human societies can be pursued as scientifically as studies of dinosaurs — and with profit to our own society today, by teaching us what shaped the modern world, and what might shape our future.

SELECTED BIBLIOGRAPHY

Clark, Robert P. *The Global Imperative: An Interpretative History of the Spread of Humankind.* Boulder, Colo.: Westview Press, 1997. Taking a long view of globalization, Clark focuses on seven "episodes" in the process, starting with the colonization of the world by *homo erectus* and *homo sapiens* and ending with the technological innovations and combinations that produced the "information age." Clark's explanation of globalization is based on the theory of entropy — the tendency of all systems to "energy loss, decay, and disorder" — and the resultant necessity for human systems to sustain and transform themselves by dissipating the effects of their own entropy outward to neighboring systems.

Crosby, Alfred W. *Ecological Imperialism: The Biological Expansion of Europe.* Cambridge: Cambridge University Press, 1986. Crosby poses the large question: How did Europeans and their descendants come to be "all over the place?" He finds the answer in the complex interplay of humans, plants, animals, and diseases since 1000 C.E. This book is widely used as a world history text (partly owing to Crosby's charmingly idiosyncratic writing style) and is responsible more than any other work for the recent environmental turn in world history.

Frank, Andre Gunder. *ReOrient: Global Economy in the Asian Age.* Berkeley and Los Angeles: University of California Press, 1998. This provocative book signals the beginning of what is almost certain to be a radical shift in the way we conceive of the emergence of modernity. According to Frank, a genuinely global perspective on the period 1400 to 1800 reveals that the economic center of gravity lay far to the east of Europe and that the idea of the "rise of the West" to global dominance any time before the nineteenth century is an illusion born of the presumptions of Eurocentric social theory. Several forthcoming books and essays that, in Frank's phrase, work "from the whole world inward" rather than Europe outward and that are more firmly grounded in primary source data than his sweeping treatment could be, lie just over the horizon.

Gamble, Clive. *Timewalkers: The Prehistory of Global Colonization.* Cambridge: Harvard University Press, 1993. Alfred Crosby asks why the progeny of Europeans are all over the place. Gamble moves back millions of years to ask the larger question: Why, when the European oceanic voyages began, were humans already just about everywhere? His answer repudiates the teleological notion that early human history was a complex series of progressive adaptations leading toward civilization.

Geyer, Michael, and Charles Bright. "For a Unified History of the World in the Twentieth Century," *Radical History Review* 39 (September 1987): 69–91. An earlier iteration of the authors' exploration of the tension between globalization and the assertion of communal identity and difference.

Mazlish, Bruce, and Ralph Buultjens, eds. *Conceptualizing Global History.* Boulder, Colo.: Westview Press, 1993. The seminal argument for a world-historical methodology founded on global consciousness. The eleven authors in this volume lack a clearly unified definition of their subject, but they all want to write world history that is fully attentive to "the lived reality of globalization."

Pomper, Philip, Richard H. Elphick, and Richard T. Vann, eds. *World History: Ideologies, Structures, and Identities.* Malden, Mass.: Blackwell, 1998. A collection of essays resulting from a conference sponsored by the journal *History and Theory.* Contributions from Janet Abu-Lughod, Michael Adas, William McNeill, Bruce Mazlish, Ashis Nandy, Theodore Von Laue, and others. One good reason to read this book is to learn about new approaches to world history informed by postmodernist theory and sensibility.

Schwartz, Stuart B., ed. *Implicit Understandings: Observing, Reporting, and Reflecting on the Encounters between Europeans and Other Peoples in the Early Modern Era.* Cambridge: Cambridge University Press, 1994. Twenty scholars from the disciplines of history, anthropology, sociology, and literature look at the "implicit ethnographies" that people brought to the worldwide cultural encounters of the early modern centuries. A rich contribution to the literature of world history demonstrating that change occurs not only in physical space but also in the mental realms where people new to one another give meaning to their encounters using the cultural materials they have at hand.

Simmons, I. G. *Changing the Face of the Earth: Culture, Environment, and History.* Oxford: Blackwell, 1989. A geographer's sweeping, multidisciplinary history of the human impact on the global ecosystem. A good starting point for teachers considering a world history course organized around the theme of environmental change.

Smil, Vaclav. *Energy in World History.* Boulder, Colo.: Westview Press, 1994. An environmentalist's sweeping history of the interplay between energy sources and energy-using technologies on the one hand and broad patterns of change in human society on the other. The numerous illustrations, graphs, and statistical tables are, quite apart from the text, an excellent resource for teachers who wish to probe this dimension of world history.

Spier, Fred. *The Structure of Big History: From the Big Bang until Today.* Amsterdam: Amsterdam University Press, 1996. Spier organizes his "single synthetic scheme" of human history on the scale of the universe around the analytical concept of the "regime," that is, "a more or less regular but ultimately unstable pattern that has a certain temporal permanence." Human cultural regimes and their transformations over time are thus set in a much larger context of ecological, biological, and astronomical regimes. This book will not serve as a survey textbook that "brings it altogether," but it is a thought-provoking world history in eighty-seven pages and worthy of much discussion.

(*Continued from copyright page*)

Gilbert Allardyce, "Toward World History: American Historians and the Coming of the World History Course" in *Journal of World History* 1 (1990): 23–76. Material reproduced by permission of the publisher.

Geoffrey Barraclough, *Main Trends in History*. From *Main Trends in History*, by Geoffrey Barraclough (New York: Holmes & Meier, 1991). Copyright © 1991 by Holmes & Meier Publishers, Inc. Reproduced with the permission of the publisher.

Jerry H. Bentley, "Cross-Cultural Interaction and Periodization in World History" in *American Historical Review* 101 (1996): 749–56. Reprinted by permission of the American Historical Association.

Jerry H. Bentley, "Graduate Education and Research in World History" in *World History Bulletin* 3 (1985–86): 3–7. Reprinted by permission of the author.

Jerry H. Bentley, *Shapes of World History in Twentieth-Century Scholarship*. Copyright © 1996 by the American Historical Association. Reprinted by permission of the publisher.

Ida Blom, "World History as Gender History: The Case of the Nation State" in *Between National Histories and Global History*. Reprinted by permission of the author.

Fernand Braudel, *Civilization and Capitalism*. Pages 21–44 from *Civilization and Capitalism 15ᵗʰ–18ᵗʰ Century, Vol. 3: The Perspective of the World* by Fernand Braudel. Copyright © 1979 by Librairie Armand Colin, Paris. English translation copyright © 1984 by William Collins Sons & Co. Ltd. and Harper & Row, Publishers, Inc. Reprinted by permission of HarperCollins Publishers, Inc.

George E. Brooks, "An Undergraduate World History Curriculum for the Twenty-First Century" in *Journal of World History* 2 (1991): 65–79. Material reproduced by permission of the publisher.

Edmund Burke III, "Marshall G. S. Hodgson and the Hemispheric Interregional Approach to World History" in *Journal of World History* 6 (1995): 237–50. Material reproduced by permission of the publisher.

Edmund Burke III and Ross E. Dunn, "Michael Doyle's Views on Western Civ: A Comment and Counterproposal" in *Perspectives* 36 (1998): 31–33. Reprinted by permission of the American Historical Association.

David Christian, "The Case for 'Big History'" in *Journal of World History* 2 (1991): 223–38. Material reproduced by permission of the publisher.

David Christian, "Inner Eurasia as a Unit of World History" in *Journal of World History* 5 (1994): 173–84. Material reproduced by permission of the publisher.

Julia Clancy-Smith, "The Middle East in World History" in *World History Bulletin* 9 (1992–93): 30–34. Reprinted by permission of the author.

Philip D. Curtin, "Depth, Span, and Relevance" in *American Historical Review* 89 (1984): 1–9. Reprinted by permission of the American Historical Association.

Philip D. Curtin, "Graduate Teaching in World History" in *Journal of World History* 2 (1991): 81–89. Material reproduced by permission of the publisher.

Philip D. Curtin, "What is an Attainable Global Perspective for Undergraduates in History?" in *The History Teacher* 18 (1985): 520–27. Reprinted with permission of The Society for History Education, Inc.

Thomas W. Davis, "Starting from Scratch: Shifting from Western Civ to World History" in *Perspectives* 34 (1996): 27–29, 38–39. Reprinted by permission of the American Historical Association.

Jared Diamond, *Guns, Germs, and Steel: The Fate of Human Societies*. From *Guns, Germs, and Steel: The Fates of Human Societies* by Jared Diamond. Copyright © 1997 by Jared Diamond. Reprinted by permission of W. W. Norton & Company, Inc.

Michael F. Doyle, "'Hisperanto': Western Civilization in the Global Curriculum" in *Perspectives* 36 (1998): 1, 24–28. Reprinted by permission of the American Historical Association.

Andre Gunder Frank, "A Plea for World System History" in *Journal of World History* 2 (1991): 1–28. Material reproduced by permission of the publisher.

Michael Geyer and Charles Bright, "World History in a Global Age" in *American Historical Review* 100 (1995): 1037–52, 1058–60. Reprinted by permission of the American Historical Association.

Steve Gosch, "Cross-Cultural Trade as a Framework for Teaching World History: Concepts and Applications" in *The History Teacher* 27 (1994): 425–31. Reprinted with permission of The Society for History Education, Inc.

William A. Green, "Periodizing World History" in *History and Theory* 34 (1995): 99–111. Reprinted by permission of the publisher.

J. H. Hexter, "Introductory College Course in Non-American History: An Ethnocentric View." Reprinted by permission of Ruth M. Hexter.

Marshall G. S. Hodgson, "The Interrelations of Societies in History" in *Cahiers d'Histoire Mondiale* 1 (1954): 715–23. Reproduced by permission of UNESCO.

Sarah S. Hughes, "Gender at the Base of World History" in *The History Teacher* 27 (1994): 417–23.

Donald Johnson, "The American Educational Tradition: Hostile to a Humanistic World History?" in *The History Teacher* 20 (1987): 519–44. Reprinted with permission of The Society for History Education, Inc.

Lawrence W. Levine, from *The Opening of the American Mind* by Lawrence W. Levine. © 1996 by Lawrence W. Levine. Reprinted by permission of Beacon Press, Boston.

Martin W. Lewis and Kären E. Wigen, *The Myth of Continents: A Critique of Metageography* by Martin W. Lewis and Kären E. Wigen. Copyright © 1997 by The Regents of the University of California. Reprinted by permission of the University of California Press.

Craig A. Lockard, "The Contributions of Philip Curtin and the 'Wisconsin School' to the Study and Promotion of Comparative World History" in *Journal of Third World Studies* 11 (1994): 180–223.

Craig A. Lockard, "Global History, Modernization and the World System Approach: A Critique" in *The History Teacher* 14 (1981): 489–515. Reprinted with permission of The Society for History Education, Inc.

Patrick Manning, "Doctoral Training in World History: The Northeastern University Experience" in *Perspectives* 37 (1999): 35–38. Reprinted by permission of the American Historical Association.

Patrick Manning, "Migrations of Africans to the Americas: The Impact on Africans, Africa, and the New World" in *The History Teacher* 26 (1993): 279–96. Reprinted with permission of The Society for History Education, Inc.

William H. McNeill, "Beyond Western Civilization: Rebuilding the Survey" in *The History Teacher* 10 (1977): 509–15. Reprinted with permission of The Society for History Education, Inc.

William H. McNeill, "The Changing Shape of World History" in *History and Theory* 34 (1995): 14–26. Reprinted by permission of the publisher.

The National Center for History in the Schools, "World History Standards for Grades 5–12." Copyright © National Center for History in the Schools, University of California, Los Angeles.

Jacob Neusner, "It Is Time to Stop Apologizing for Western Civilization and To Start Analyzing Why It Defines World Culture." Reprinted by permission of the author.

John F. Richards, "Early Modern India and World History" in *Journal of World History* 8 (1997): 197–209. Material reproduced by permission of the publisher.

John Rothney, "Developing the Twentieth Century World History Course: A Case-Study at Ohio State" in *The World History Teacher* 20 (1987): 465–85. Reprinted with permission of The Society for History Education, Inc.

William F. Sater, "Joining the Mainstream: Integrating Latin America into the Teaching of World History" in *Perspectives* 33 (1995): 19–22, 37. Reprinted by permission of the American Historical Association.

Tara Sethia, "Teaching India in a World History Survey" in *Perspectives* 34 (1996): 15–20. Reprinted by permission of the American Historical Association.

Lynda Shaffer, "Southernization" in *Journal of World History* 5 (1994): 1–21. Material reproduced by permission of the publisher.

David R. Smith, "Teaching Religions in the Medieval Period" in *World History Bulletin* 7 (1990–91): 23–26. Reprinted by permission of the author.

L. S. Stavrianos, "The Teaching of World History" in *Journal of Modern History* 31 (1959): 110–16. ©1959 by The University of Chicago. All rights reserved.

Peter N. Stearns, "Periodization in World History Teaching: Identifying the Big Changes" in *The History Teacher* 20 (1987): 561–74. Reprinted with permission of The Society for History Education, Inc.

John O. Voll, "Islam as a Special World-System" in *Journal of World History* 5 (1994): 213–36. Material reproduced by permission of the publisher.

John O. Voll, "'Southernization' as a Construct in Post-Civilization Narrative." Reprinted by permission of the author.

Marilyn Robinson Waldman, "The Meandering Mainstream: Reimagining World History." Reprinted by permission of Loren Waldman.

Immanuel Wallerstein, "World-Systems Analysis: Five Questions in Search of a New Consensus" in *The History Teacher* 18 (1985): 527–32. Reprinted with permission of The Society for History Education, Inc.

Helen Wheatley, "The World and the Northwest: The Fur Trade, Regional History, and World History." Reprinted by permission of the author.

Eric R. Wolf, from *Europe and the People without History* by Eric R. Wolf. Copyright © 1983 by The Regents of the University of California. Reprinted by permission of the University of California Press.

Judith P. Zinsser, "And Now for Something Completely Different: Gendering the World History Survey" in *Perspectives* 34 (1996): 11–12. Reprinted by permission of the American Historical Association.

Judith P. Zinsser, "Technology and History: The Women's Perspective: A Case Study in Gendered Definitions" in *World History Bulletin* 12 (1996): 2, 6–9. Reprinted by permission of the author.